Tourism in the New Europe

The Challenges and Opportunities of EU Enlargement

_____

Tourism in the New Europe

The Challenges and Opportunities of EU Enlargement

Edited by

Derek Hall, Melanie Smith and Barbara Marciszewska

www.cabi.org

CABI is a trading name of CAB International

CABI Head Office
Nosworthy Way
Wallingford
Oxfordshire OX10 8DE
UK

CABI North American Office
875 Massachusetts Avenue
7th Floor
Cambridge, MA 02139
USA

Tel: +44 (0)1491 832111
Fax: +44 (0)1491 833508
E-mail: cabi@cabi.org
Website: www.cabi.org

Tel: +1 617 395 4056
Fax: +1 617 354 6875
E-mail: cabi-nao@cabi.org

A catalogue record for this book is available from the British Library,
London, UK.

A catalogue record for this book is available from the Library of Congress,
Washington, DC.

ISBN-13: 978-1-84593-117-9
ISBN-10: 1-84593-117-3

Typeset by AMA DataSet, Preston, UK.
Printed and bound in the UK by Biddles Ltd, King's Lynn.

Contents

Contributors

Ilgvars Ābols, *Tourism Organization and Management Department, Vidzeme University College, Latvia; e-mail: ilgvars.abols@va.lv*

Habib Alipour, *School of Tourism & Hospitality Management, Eastern Mediterranean University, Famagusta, TRNC; e-mail: habib.alipour@emu.edu.tr*

Constantia Anastasiadou, *School of Marketing and Tourism, Napier University Business School, Edinburgh, UK; e-mail: c.anastasiadou@napier.ac.uk*

Aušrinė Armaitienė, *Department of Tourism and Recreation, Klaipėda University, Lithuania; e-mail: ausrine@gmf.ku.lt*

Irena Ateljevic, *Socio-Spatial Analysis, Wageningen University, The Netherlands; e-mail: Irena.Ateljevic@wur.nl*

Marin Bachvarov, *Department of Urban Geography and Tourism, University of Łódz, Poland (formerly Head of Tourism Department in Sofia St Kliment Ohridski University, Bulgaria; Member of the Tourism Commission of the IGU, 1980–1988 and 2000–2004); e-mail: bachvar@geo.uni.lodz.pl*

Vladimír Baláž, *Institute for Forecasting, Slovak Academy of Science Bratislava, Slovak Republic; e-mail: vbalaz@yahoo.com*

Sanda Čorak (ex Weber), *Institute for Tourism, Zagreb, Croatia; e-mail: sanda.corak@iztzg.hr*

Iveta Druva-Druvaskalne, *Tourism Organization and Management Department, Vidzeme University College, Latvia; e-mail: iveta_druva@va.lv*

John Fletcher, *International Centre for Tourism and Hospitality Research, Bournemouth University, Dorset, UK; e-mail: jefletch@bournemouth.ac.uk*

Alan Fyall, *International Centre for Tourism and Hospitality Research, Bournemouth University, Dorset, UK; e-mail: AFyall@bournemouth.ac.uk*

C. Michael Hall, *Department of Tourism, School of Business, University of Otago, Dunedin, New Zealand; e-mail: cmhall@business.otago.ac.nz*

Derek Hall, *Seabank Associates, Maidens, Scotland UK; e-mail: derekhall.seabank@virgin.net*

Jeff Jarvis, *National Centre for Australian Studies, Monash University, Australia; e-mail: Jeff.Jarvis@arts.monash.edu.au*

Eleri Jones, *Welsh School of Hospitality, Tourism and Leisure Management, University of Wales Institute, Cardiff, UK; e-mail: EJones@uwic.ac.uk*

Peter Jordan, *Austrian Institute of East and Southeast European Studies, Vienna, Austria; e-mail: peter.jordan@osi.ac.at*

Piret Kallas, *Estonian Tourist Board, Tallinn; e-mail: Piret.kallas@eas.ee*

Alžbeta Királ'ová, *International Relationships and Research, Institute of Hospitality and Management, Prague, Czech Republic; e-mail: cz530401@tiscali.cz*

Taneli Kokkila, *Liaison Manager, Finnish Tourist Board, Helsinki; e-mail: taneli.kokkila@mek.fi*

Raija Komppula, *Department of Business and Economics, University of Joensuu, Finland; e-mail: raija.komppula@joensuu.fi*

Maja Konečnik, *Marketing Department, Faculty of Economics, Ljubljana University, Slovenia; e-mail: maja.konecnik@ef.uni-lj.si*

Duncan Light, *Geography, Deanery of Sciences and Social Sciences, Liverpool Hope University, UK; e-mail: lightd@hope.ac.uk*

Barbara Marciszewska, *Academy of Physical Education and Sport Gdańsk, Poland; e-mail: marcisz@awf.gda.pl*

Arvo Peltonen, *Finnish University Network for Tourism Studies, University of Joensuu, Finland; e-mail: arvo.peltonen@joensuu.fi*

Ramūnas Povilanskas, *Department of Tourism and Recreation, Klaipeda University, Lithuania; e-mail: ramunas@service.lt*

László Puczkó, *Tourism Consultant, Xellum Ltd, Budapest, Hungary; e-mail: lpuczko@xellum.hu*

Tamara Rátz, *Professor of Tourism, Kodolányi János University College, Hungary; e-mail: tratz@uranus.kodolanyi.hu*

Greg Richards, *Tourism Research and Marketing, c/Gran de Gracia 183(4-1), 08012 Barcelona, Spain; e-mail: greg@tram-research.com*

Julie Scott, *International Institute of Culture, Tourism and Development, London Metropolitan University, UK; e-mail: j.scott@londonmet.ac.uk*

Agita Šļara, *Tourism Organization and Management Department, Vidzeme University College, Latvia; e-mail: agita.slara@va.lv*

Melanie Smith, *Business School, University of Greenwich, London, UK; e-mail: M.K.Smith@gre.ac.uk*

Nadia Theuma, *Tourism Unit, Faculty of Economics, Management and Accountancy, University of Malta, Msida, Malta; e-mail: nadia.theuma@um.edu.mt, nthe1@um.edu.mt*

Layik Topcan, *e-mail: layiktopcan@yahoo.com*

Cevat Tosun, *International Centre for Tourism and Hospitality Research, Bournemouth University, Dorset, UK; e-mail: ctosun@bournemouth.ac.uk, cevattosun@hotmail.com*

Tom Ylkänen, *Research Manager, Finnish Tourist Board, Helsinki; e-mail: tom.ylkänen@mek.fi*

The Editors

_____

Derek Hall is Visiting Professor at Häme Polytechnic, Mustiala and Forssa, Finland. He recently retired as Professor of Regional Development and Head of the Leisure and Tourism Management Department at the Scottish Agricultural College, Auchincruive. He has taught and published widely on tourism and development in Europe and the Mediterranean, the environment, transport, and development in socialist and post-socialist societies. With Darrick Danta he edited *Europe Goes East: EU Enlargement, Diversity and Uncertainty* (Stationery Office, 2000) and *Reconstructing the Balkans: a Geography of the New Southeast Europe* (Wiley, 1996), and with Tim Coles the special issue of *International Journal of Tourism Research* on Tourism and EU Enlargement (2005). He also edited *Tourism and Transition: Governance, Transformation and Development* (2004) and has jointly authored with Frances Brown *Tourism and Welfare: Ethics, Responsibility and Sustained Well-being* (2006) and with Lesley Roberts *Rural Tourism and Recreation: Principles to Practice* (2001), all three published by CABI.

Melanie Smith is a Senior Lecturer in Cultural Tourism Management at the University of Greenwich, London, where she has been running BA and MA Programmes in Tourism Management for the past 9 years. She is also a Visiting Lecturer in Budapest, Hungary. She is currently Chair of ATLAS (Association for Tourism and Leisure Education, http://www.atlas-euro.org), having been the Coordinator of ATLAS Europe for the past 3 years. She has extensive experience of teaching and researching European Tourism, and is author of the book *Issues in Cultural Tourism Studies* (Routledge, 2003). She has also edited two books entitled *Cultural Tourism in a Changing World* (for Channel View with Mike Robinson, 2006), and *Tourism, Culture and Regeneration* (for CABI, 2006). She has also edited a special edition of the journal *Tourism Recreation Research* with Catherine Kelly on *Wellness Tourism* (2006).

Professor **Barbara Marciszewska**, Director of the Institute of Tourism and Recreation, Academy of Physical Education and Sport, Gdańsk, Poland, long an active member of ATLAS, has substantial experience of teaching and researching tourism in Poland, and has wide experience of the other countries in the region.

Abbreviations

ABTA	Association of British Travel Agents
ACP	Africa, Caribbean and Pacific group of states
AICGS	American Institute for Contemporary German Studies
AWFiS	Akademia Wychowania Fizycznego i Sportu, Gdansk
BCU	Baltic Sea Tourism Commission
bn	billion
BSSSRC	Baltic Sea States Sub-Regional Cooperation
CAP	(The) Common Agricultural Policy
CARICOM	Caribbean Community and Common Market
CARIFORUM	Forum of Caribbean ACP states
CBC	cross-border cooperation
CBSS	Council of the Baltic Sea States
CEC	Commission of the European Communities
CEE	Central and Eastern Europe
CEE8	The eight 2004 EU accession countries from CEE
CEECs	Central and East European countries
CEI	Central European Initiative
CFSP	(a) common foreign and security policy
CIA	(US) Central Intelligence Agency
CIS	Confederation of Independent States (the post-Soviet association of former members of the Soviet Union minus the Baltic republics)
CMEA	The economic grouping of the former Soviet bloc, more commonly known as COMECON
CNS	Comisia Naţională pentru Statistică (Romania)
CNTO	Czech National Tourist Office
COMECON	The economic grouping of the former Soviet bloc, more formally known as the Council for Mutual Economic Achievement (or Advancement) (CMEA)
CTCA	Cyprus Turkish Construction/Contractors Association
CTO	Cyprus Tourism Organisation
CY£	Cyprus pound

€	euro
E	east
EAA	European Anglers Association
EBRD	European Bank for Reconstruction and Development
EC	European Commission; European Community
ECB	European Central Bank
ECAC	European Civil Aviation Conference
ECE	East Central Europe (Poland, Hungary, Czech Republic, Slovakia)
ECSC	European Coal and Steel Community
ECTAA	Group of National Travel Agents' and Tour Operators' Associations within the EU
ECU	European Currency Unit
EEA	European Economic Area
EEC	European Economic Community
EFCT	European Federation of Conference Towns
EFTA	European Free Trade Area
EIA	environmental impact assessment
EMU	European Monetary Union
ERDF	European Regional Development Fund
ESF	European Social Fund
ETAG	European Travel and Tourism Action Group
ETP	European Travel Policy
ETOA	European Tour Operators' Association
EU	European Union
EU15	European Union member states prior to the 2004 enlargement
EU25	European Union member states following the 2004 enlargement
EUCC	The [European] Coastal Union
Euratom	European Atomic Energy Community
FYR	Former Yugoslav Republic
GATS	General Agreement on Trade and Services
GDP	gross domestic product
GDR	German Democratic Republic (the East German state, 1949–1990)
GKM	Gazdasági és Közlekedési Minisztérium (Ministry of the Economy and Transport, Hungary)
GM	Gazdasági Minisztérium (Ministry of the Economy, Hungary)
GNP	gross national product
GNTO	Greek National Tourism Organization
ha	hectare
HCEB	Hotel and Catering Establishments Board (Malta)
HEI	higher education institution
HHA	Hungarian Hotel Association
HNTO	Hungarian National Tourist Office
HOTREC	Confederation of National Associations of Hotels, Restaurants, Cafés and Similar Establishments
HUF	Hungarian *forint*
ICZM	Integrated Coastal Zone Management
INS	Institutul Naţional de Statistică (Romania)
INTERREG	EU assistance programme to develop cross-border cooperation and help areas on the Union's internal and external borders to overcome specific problems arising from their comparatively isolated position

IQM	integrated quality management
IUCN	World Conservation Union (International Union for the Conservation of Nature)
kg	kilogram
KITREB	Turkish Cypriot Tour Guides Association
KITSOB	Turkish Cypriot Hoteliers' Association
km	kilometre
KSH	Központi Statisztikai Hivatal (National Central Statistics Office, Hungary)
LAC	limits of acceptable change
LGIB	Local Government Information Bureau
Lm	Maltese pound
LTDA	Latvian Tourism Development Agency
m	metre; million
MBE	Magyar Balnneológiai Egyesület
MEK	Finnish Tourist Board
MEP	Member of European Parliament
MEPA	Malta Environment and Planning Authority
MFA	Ministry of Foreign Affairs (Malta)
mg	milligram
MGIP	Ministry of Economy and Labour (Poland)
MHSR	Ministry of the Economy of the Slovak Republic
MICE	meetings, incentives, conferences and exhibitions (or events)
MNC	multinational company
MT	Ministry of Tourism (Romania)
MTA	Malta Tourism Authority
MVRRSR	Ministry of Construction and Regional Development of the Slovak Republic
MVSR	Ministry of the Interior of the Slovak Republic
MZSR	Ministry of Foreign Affairs of the Slovak Republic
N	north
na	not available; not appropriate
NATO	North Atlantic Treaty Organization
NBS	National Bank of Slovakia
NCHA	Northern Cyprus Hoteliers Association
nd	no date; no data
NFH	National Development Office (Hungary)
NGO	non-governmental organization
NIC	newly industrializing/industrialized country
NIT	Institut für Tourismus- und Bäderforschung in Nordeuropa GmBH
NSSDC	National Strategy for the Sustainable Development of Lithuania
NTA	National Tourism Authority (Romania)
NTOM	National Tourism Organization of Malta
ODDK	Ośrodek Doradztwa i Doskonalenia Kadr sp. z o.o.
OECD	Organization for Economic Co-operation and Development
OSCE	Organization for Security and Co-operation in Europe
PART	Polski Agencja Roznoju Turystyki S.A.
PHARE	EU assistance programme: Poland/Hungary Assistance for Economic Reconstruction (extended to much of the rest of Central and Eastern Europe)
PIT	Polish Institute of Tourism
PPP	purchasing power parity; public–private partnership
PT	Employers' Confederation of Service Industries (Finland)

PTO	Polish Tourism Organization
PWN	Polish Scientific Publishers
SEA	strategic environmental assessment
SFRJ	Socialist Federative Republic of Yugoslavia
SIA	sustainability impact assessment
sk	Slovak crowns
SLM	sustainable land management
SME	small- and/or medium-size enterprise
SMITEs	small units and micro-tourism enterprises
SMTE	small- and/or medium-size tourism enterprise
SPA	special protection area
ŠÚSR	Slovak Statistical Office
t	tonne
TACIS	EU assistance programme for the (ex-Soviet) 'newly independent states' and Mongolia
TDP	tourism development programme
TEU	Treaty on European Union
TNC	transnational company/corporation
TQM	total quality management
TRNC	Turkish Republic of North Cyprus
TTRI	Travel and Tourism Research Institute, University of Nottingham, UK
UBC	Union of Baltic Cities
UK	United Kingdom (of Great Britain and Northern Ireland)
UN	United Nations
UNCED	United Nations Conference on Environment and Development
UNDP	United Nations Development Programme
UNEP	United Nations Environment Programme
UNECE	United Nations Economic Commission for Europe
UNESCO	United Nations Education and Science Organization
UNHCR	United Nations High Commissioner for Refugees
UNSD	United Nations Statistical Division
US(A)	United States (of America)
USSR	Union of Soviet Socialist Republics (Soviet Union) (1921–1991)
VAT	value-added tax
WBI	World Bank Institute
WCED	World Conference on Environment and Development
WCS	World Conservation Strategy
WEU	Western European Union
WPDR	Working Party on Domestic Regulation
WSSD	World Summit on Sustainable Development
WTO	World Tourism Organization; World Trade Organization
WTTC	World Travel and Tourism Council
WWF	Worldwide Fund for Nature (formerly World Wildlife Fund)

Preface

_____

This book has been developed and coordinated by the ATLAS Association for Tourism and Leisure Education (http://www.atlas-euro.org). Although now a global organization, with more than 300 institutional members, the ATLAS network has its roots firmly established within Europe. It is therefore fitting that to complement the organization's first conference to be held in the 'New Europe' of Central and Eastern Europe – in Łódz, Poland September 2006 – this volume has been produced as the basis for generating a discussion on the relationship between tourism and EU enlargement. Structured to emphasize three types of chapters – contextual perspectives, sub-regional overviews, and country-specific discussions – the book pursues two overall aims:

- to address tourism-related issues of EU enlargement, both in general and specifically relating to the 2004 enlargement and prospects for subsequent expansions; and
- to set the tourism characteristics of individual accession and candidate countries within a wider European context.

To help meet the second of these aims, country-chapter authors were each set two objectives:

- to provide a background discussion of the country's basic tourism characteristics and trends; and
- to evaluate a specific tourism theme (as agreed with the editors) articulating the relationship between the county's tourism development and its EU accession processes.

We recognize that it was perhaps a little foolhardy to attempt to construct a text around an event that had so recently taken place. Yet the contributors to this volume have responded magnificently to the demands of the editors, as well as those of time, continuous change and perpetual uncertainty. We feel that this book is a worthy complement to the work of ATLAS and offers an important and timely baseline for the ongoing debate on tourism's relationship with, and role within, the European Union and its neighbours.

Acknowledgements are due to a wide range of people: to László Puczkó for his practical assistance in the production of this book (the logistics of which required the editors to coordinate, at various times, between England, Finland, Hungary, Poland and Scotland), as well to all the other (34 in total) contributors to the volume for their enthusiasm, cooperation and (mostly) punctual submissions. We are grateful to the cartographic unit of Exeter University who produced Fig. 1.1.

Many thanks are due to the commissioning, editorial and production team at CABI: Rebecca Stubbs, who left the organization before the manuscript was submitted (we were assured that there was no causal relationship between these two events), Nigel Farrar and Elaine Coverdale.

Part I

Introduction and Context

_____

1 Introduction

Derek Hall, Melanie Smith and Barbara Marciszewska

Aims, Objectives and Outline Structure of the Book

The enlargement of the European Union (EU) in May 2004, incorporating eight former communist states of Central and Eastern Europe and two major Mediterranean island states, has profound implications for structural and geographical patterns of European tourism development (Fig. 1.1). Both the presence of a new diversity of societies and environments within the European 'club', and the challenge of a significantly enlarged Union, require detailed examination and analysis from a tourism perspective.

This volume offers an informed and wide-ranging contribution to help meet that requirement. It draws on the expertise and experience of the ATLAS organization, especially that of researchers from the countries in question and those from further afield to provide a broader contextual perspective. This collection aims to explore beneath the rhetoric of EU politicians and tourism industry representatives about enlargement and its relationship with tourism. For example, the World Tourism Organization (WTO, 2004) predicted that expansion would foster the conditions for a 'more complete and coherent' European tourism industry, which should be recognized in the future European Constitution.

The book is divided into six parts. The first part of five chapters, written by the editors and invited researchers, establishes a number of key themes in the relationships between tourism and EU enlargement, thereby setting a framework for the country-specific chapters that follow in the next four parts. These examine each of the new member states as well as the next accession applicants, in terms of their current patterns and trends of tourism development, and the impacts that EU accession brings to them. Integrated with these analyses, each country chapter is framed within a particular theme that characterizes that country's tourism development processes.

Within this framework, the second and third parts of the book examine respectively those new EU entrants from Central and Eastern Europe that were outside of (East Central Europe), or within (the Baltics) the former Soviet Union. All country chapters comprising these parts are authored or co-authored by researchers from the specific countries concerned. Both parts are prefaced by a regional perspective chapter. These two chapters have been written by invited researchers from an adjacent pre-existing EU member that has strong historic ties with the region (Austria and Finland respectively). East Central Europe and the Baltics are two groups of countries that, both between and within their regional groupings, offer the experience of different trajectories and tourism development processes.

Part IV examines the new Mediterranean entrants and is again prefaced by an overview chapter setting their context. Malta and Cyprus

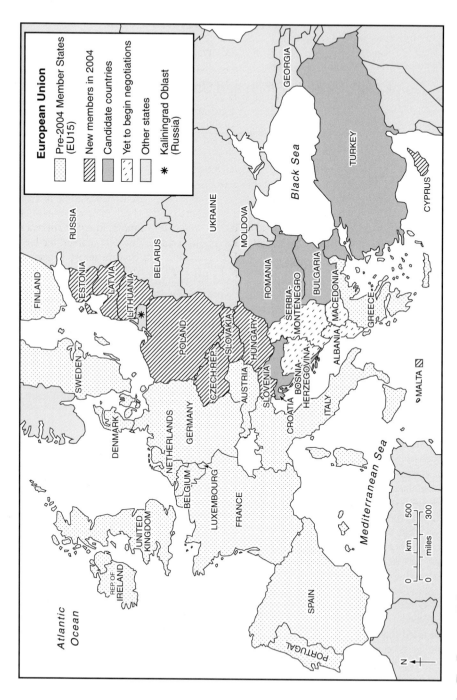

Fig. 1.1. The European Union.

are different from other member states, both old and new, in that they are characterized by an economically important, long-established mass tourism industry, largely based on the UK market, and both have had strong historic links with Britain. However, the complex issues of the division and recognition of Cyprus almost derailed the 2004 enlargement, and, at the time of writing, still act to complicate the potential accession of Turkey.

This leads directly into the fifth part of the book, which addresses those countries of South-eastern Europe seeking EU accession in the projected 2007 enlargement (or beyond). At the time of writing, it was beginning to look less likely that Bulgaria and Romania would be on track for likely 2007 entry, and obstacles still stood in the way of Croatia and Turkey. Further, as the chapters in this book suggest, the not always positive experience of EU preparation for, and the subsequent impacts of, the 2004 enlargement, could result in unforeseen consequences for future enlargement decisions.

In the light of the above issues, and within fluid circumstances, the editors' concluding chapter provides an overall summary of the book, synthesizes key themes, and offers a future agenda.

The Significance of 2004

The virtual implosion of state socialism in Central and Eastern Europe (CEE) in the late 1980s necessitated a redefinition of 'Europe' (Heffernan, 1998; Pinder, 1998, p. vii). Having thrown off the shackles that had bound them since the 1940s, the CEE countries – both governments and populace – were initially eager to re-join the Europe from which they had been estranged by the Iron Curtain and Cold War politics for almost half a century. Equally, the countries of Western Europe appeared all too happy to prepare to embrace them. In particular, several countries of CEE saw membership of the EU as their rightful due.

Although sufficient momentum was maintained to sustain the accession of ten new members in May 2004, earlier high levels of optimism had long subsided on both sides of the former divide. The countries of CEE had soon realized that the Europe they had left some 50 to 60 years before was quite different

now. In the clear light of day the Western countries for their part could see just how many obstacles their fellow Europeans would need to overcome to qualify for accession (Danta and Hall, 2000). Further, the EU had its own internal difficulties, not least concerning arguments over budget contributions and rebates and the restructuring or even elimination of the CAP. Euphoria had gradually turned to pessimism as these issues and the problems of transforming formerly centralized economies, replacing outmoded technology and management systems, and overcoming entrenched political mentalities became all too real. Additionally, there was the thorny issue of Cyprus.

That these issues were none the less overcome, if only in the short- to medium-term, rendered 1 May 2004 a major milestone in modern European history. This date marked the largest EU expansion yet, both in terms of area and population. The accession countries of Cyprus, the Czech Republic, Estonia, Hungary, Latvia, Lithuania, Malta, Poland, Slovakia and Slovenia transformed the EU15 member states into the EU25 with some 75 million new citizens, to increase the EU total population to more than 430 million, with an economy valued at €850 billion (Islam, 2004).

In retrospect, the 2004 enlargement can be viewed as having been driven by a number of key objectives (Islam, 2004):

- the enhancement of political stability in Europe almost a decade and a half after the end of the Cold War that had divided Europe since the Second World War (Woods, 2004a);
- the creation of a market and trade bloc to rival the United States, integrating the 'emerging' economies of Central and Eastern Europe and the Mediterranean, with their reserves of both skilled and low-cost labour; and
- the generation of a growth impetus in an otherwise largely stagnating European economy (Heath and Nelson, 2004).

EU Enlargement History and Process

The desire for closer European integration voiced at the end of the Cold War in 1990 echoed sentiments expressed following the end of the Second World War some 45 years earlier. Mikhail Gorbachev's 1989 speech to the Council of Europe, calling for a higher union in the 'Common European House' (Mayhew, 1998) was reminiscent of Winston Churchill's 1946 'United States of Europe' speech. This had helped to crystallize thinking towards a time when all Europeans would see themselves as part of a peaceful whole (Danta and Hall, 2000). Such ideas of a united Europe were the inspiration that led, via the setting up of the Benelux customs union in 1948, to Jean Monnet and Robert Schuman's 1950 plan for an alliance between France and Germany that established the first instruments of European integration:

- European Coal and Steel Community (ECSC), established in 1951;
- European Atomic Energy Community (Euratom), established in 1957;
- European Economic Community (EEC), also established in 1957 and which came into effect in January, 1958.

Alongside the EEC a number of complementary bodies were established to further its goals:

- European Commission, to handle the bureaucracy involved in running the institution;
- Council of Ministers, as the main decision-making body with responsibility for broad policy formation and implementation, with a Council Presidency rotating every 6 months;
- European Parliament, to provide a democratic forum for debate and to operate as a watchdog;
- European Court of Justice, to hear cases involving member states;
- European Council of heads of states meeting at least twice yearly to discuss issues before the Community (and later Union); and
- the Committee of the Regions, to bring local concerns to the attention of the Council.

Most functions are carried out in Brussels, but with Luxembourg and Strasbourg also as important centres of activity.

The Community set out to work closely with other European organizations, such as the Organization for European Co-operation (later the Organization for Economic Co-operation

and Development: OECD), the North Atlantic Treaty Organization (NATO, founded 1949), the Western European Union (WEU, founded 1954), and the Organization for Security and Co-operation in Europe (OSCE, founded 1973).

The main institution's name has changed over time, to some extent reflecting the evolving nature of its role and objectives. The EEC – also generally known as the 'Common Market' after a customs union came into effect in 1968 – Euratom, and the ECSC combined during the 1980s to form the 'European Community' (EC). In 1993 the Community underwent a major reorganization which subsumed, but did not replace, the EC; the new name became the 'European Union' (EU).

Two broad courses of action that have characterized the EEC, EC and EU have been those of 'deepening' and 'widening'. The first goal has involved mechanisms aimed at bringing member countries into closer economic, political, administrative, and security 'alignment'. Key dates and processes seeking this objective have included the following.

- 1951: Treaty of Paris established the European Coal and Steel Community (ECSC).
- 1957: Treaties of Rome established the EEC and Euratom.
- 1962: Common Agricultural Policy (CAP) launched.
- 1968: completion of Customs Union.
- 1975: European Council formed.
- 1979: European Monetary System begun.
- 1986: Single European Act, which set the goal of creating a single market by 1993.
- 1993: Treaty on European Union (TEU), also known as the Maastricht Treaty, set the goals of achieving monetary union by 1999; new common economic policies; European citizenship; common foreign and security policy; and common policy on internal security.
- 1997: Treaty of Amsterdam covering aspects of justice and home affairs.
- 1999: Launch of a common monetary policy and single currency, the euro.

The process of deepening was largely driven by an agenda which, although to some extent put on hold in the 1970s, was revived through the Single European Act and the

Maastricht Treaty. This latter treaty had three main pillars, each of which changed the 'architecture' of the Union to which the new applicants sought accession:

- Economic and Monetary Union (EMU);
- a commitment to a common foreign and security policy (CFSP); and
- internal security, including transborder mobility and crime.

Although the Single European Act had marked a decisive shift towards majority voting in the Council, and the Maastricht Treaty transferred some powers to the European Parliament, decision-making remained something of a compromise between inter-governmentalism and cooperative federalism (Williams and Baláž, 2000).

The second goal, 'widening', has been pursued from the organization's inception. The EEC consisted initially of the six members of the ECSC: Belgium, The Netherlands and Luxembourg (the former Benelux members), France, Germany and Italy. However, other countries sought membership and the Community underwent a series of enlargements.

- 1st. 1973: Denmark, Ireland and the United Kingdom.
- 2nd. 1981: Greece.
- 3rd. 1986: Spain and Portugal.
- Although not a formal enlargement, the former German Democratic Republic ('East Germany') was absorbed by virtue of German re-unification in 1990.
- 4th. 1995: Austria, Finland, and Sweden. This, the 'EFTA enlargement', was notable for all three entrants (as members of the European Free Trade Association) having higher GDP per capita levels than the EU average at the time (Edye and Lintner, 1996).
- 5th. 2004: Cyprus, Czech Republic, Estonia, Hungary, Latvia, Lithuania, Malta, Poland, Slovakia and Slovenia.

A major consideration for accession states has been the time taken for countries to gain membership. The United Kingdom first applied for membership in 1961, but was vetoed twice by the French president de Gaulle before gaining accession in 1973; the same 12-year period was also required for Denmark and Ireland

to join. Greece had shown an interest in joining the Community since the 1950s, was made an associate member in 1961, formally applied in 1975, negotiations began in 1976, and was admitted in 1981. Portugal and Spain both applied in 1977, but political issues prevented them from becoming members until 1986. Austria, Finland, and Sweden gained entry in 1995 after having applied in 1991.

Certain 'holdover' countries remain outside the Union. Norway applied for membership in 1962, negotiations were concluded 10 years later, but referenda held in the country in 1972 and again in 1994 failed to return the sufficient majority in favour of entry. The other notable West European country thus far remaining outside the EU is Switzerland, whose desire for neutrality (and financial secrecy) has outweighed any perceived advantages of membership. The country rejected membership of the European Economic Area (EEA) and thus the possibility of EU entry in 1995. Iceland has also shown no interest in membership. The one country to have actually withdrawn from the European Union is Greenland (Kalaallit Nunaat), which did so in 1985, having gained independence from Denmark in 1979 (Danta and Hall, 2000).

Turkey first applied for membership in 1987; Morocco has also sounded out the possibilities of accession from time to time.

While Bulgaria and Romania have been negotiating for possible accession in 2007, Croatia has been facing one of two political and administrative obstacles. Turkey's application has been reconfirmed by the EU, and the country is optimistic of future accession (Black et al., 2002; Woods, 2004b), although its position is complicated by the Cyprus situation (Hall, 2000b, 2004c). At the time of writing, the Balkan states of Albania, Bosnia, FYROM (Macedonia), Montenegro and Serbia had yet to begin formal negotiations towards possible entry, but had indicated their aspiration for membership.

The history of European integration has thus been marked by the dual forces of change and continuity (Danta and Hall, 2000). Periodic changes in the nature and constitution of the European Community or Union have preceded periods of relative stability as the organization of European economic, social and political systems both within and outside the new borders of the European supra-national body adjust to, and take shape from, new regulatory frameworks (Coles and Hall, 2004).

Accession

To be successful in their accession bids, EU applicant countries need to meet criteria as specified within three broad categories.

- political – institutions must be in place to guarantee democratic practice, rule of law, and respect for minorities;
- economic – a functioning market economy must exist and must be able to withstand the competitive pressure of the Union;
- administrative capacity – instruments must be in place to transpose and implement Community legislation.

These categories are usually referred to as the 'Copenhagen criteria' after the 1993 European Council meeting held there. They are supplemented by several other important considerations, such as: state of the environment; ability to achieve monetary union, fight corruption and assure human rights; provide for common defence; and generally assume other obligations of membership.

Despite superficial parallels with earlier enlargements, negotiations for the 2004 accessions took place under very different conditions:

- the economic challenge of transition was far greater in CEE than it had been for Portugal, Spain and Greece, which had functioning, if deformed, market economies;
- the recent history of democracy was arguably weaker in most of CEE than had been the case in Iberia and Greece;
- the deepening of integration in the 1980s and 1990s meant that greater adjustments were now required of new members, especially with respect to the single market and EMU;
- globalization, international competition and the growth of structural unemployment meant that the 2004 enlargement was approached ultimately by the existing member states in a less 'benevolent' way; and

- there were critical strategic defence and security issues in relation to the accession states' borders with the Balkans, Ukraine, Belarus, Moldova and Russia, being faced at a time when the relative equilibrium of the Cold War had given way to global strategic uncertainties and instabilities. Not least, during the 1990s, a wave of nationalism, especially in the Balkans, appeared to threaten the security of the continent (Williams and Baláž, 2000).

The accession procedure for an applicant country can be long and complicated, involving a sequence of several steps (Box 1.1).

Thus for the 2004 enlargement, ten CEE countries submitted applications to the EU during the period 1988–1997: Bulgaria, Czechoslovakia (which divided in 1991 into the

---

Box 1.1. The accession sequence.

1.   The applicant country opens diplomatic relations with the EU, signs certain trade and cooperation agreements, and develops a Europe Agreement.

2.   Once this Agreement has come into force, the country can formally apply for membership.

3.   This requires the submission of a lengthy document to be considered by the European Commission.

4.   On the basis of this the Commission prepares an Opinion, or acquis, on the suitability of the applicant's characteristics in relation to the stated criteria. This is then issued to the European Council.

5.   The Commission conducts regular meetings with the applicant country and regular reports on progress toward accession are published.

6.   When most of the criteria have been met or seem likely to be met in the near future, formal accession negotiations begin.

7.   At the successful conclusion of these the applicant country is invited to become a member state of the EU.

8.   The last step in the process is to hold a referendum in the country on the question of joining the European Union. If a majority of the voting population affirm, the country has met the full criteria for accession.

Sources: European Commission, 1998a, 1998b; Danta and Hall, 2000.

Czech Republic and Slovakia), Estonia, Hungary, Latvia, Lithuania, Poland, Romania and Slovenia. Cyprus, Malta, and Turkey were also regarded as viable candidates that had submitted applications. In 1997 the Council decided to treat the ten candidate countries of CEE in two groups. The so-called 'first wave' or 'fast-track' countries consisted of the Czech Republic, Hungary, Poland, Slovenia, and Estonia plus Cyprus; while the 'second wave' group included the other five CEECs plus Malta.

In late 1999 at its Helsinki meeting, however, and as an indication of the fluid nature of accession negotiations, the Council reversed its earlier position and elevated Latvia, Lithuania, Slovakia, Bulgaria, Romania, and Malta to fast track status, while Turkey was made a candidate country. Subsequently, Bulgaria and Romania were considered not to have made sufficient progress towards fulfilling the Copenhagen criteria, and their accession was deferred. The position of Turkey was less advanced and more complicated.

Each of the accession countries varies widely with respect to size, population, economic performance, political institutions, and environmental health (Table 1.1). At the time of accession they were generally much poorer than their West European counterparts, had less recent experience with democratic and administrative institutions, and their environmental quality was generally lower.

In addition to having to contend with difficult economic and political conditions, public attitudes toward the EU in most of the accession countries became less positive. In surveys carried out over the period 1900–1996 by the European Commission in the applicant countries of CEE, only four countries – Bulgaria and Romania (ironically), Poland and Hungary – exceeded a 50% rating for any of the years. Levels of popular support clearly declined during the decade (Grabbe and Hughes, 1999).

At the end of the 1990s, the development of an index of EU suitability based solely on economic criteria produced some interesting results (Anon, 1999). Using this index, all then current and applicant countries were ranked in terms of their suitability to be an EU member state. Belgium was found to be the most suitable, followed by Luxembourg, The Netherlands, Denmark, Portugal, Austria, Ireland, Sweden, France, Spain, Britain, Finland, and Germany

in 13th place. Surprisingly, the next highest ranked country was Slovenia, followed by the Czech Republic, Poland, Cyprus, and then EU founding member Italy. These were followed by Hungary, Malta, Latvia, Estonia, 1981 entrant Greece, Slovakia, Romania, Lithuania, and Turkey, with Bulgaria finishing in the position of least suitability. These findings pointed to the notable disparities that existed not only with and between the candidate countries, but also amongst the existing EU15 members. They raised questions that most in the EU appeared to prefer not to acknowledge.

Further considerations in the enlargement process that are as relevant today as they were prior to the 2004 enlargement concern the internal reforms required for EU structures and processes:

- remedial and equitable action is required in relation to the drain on EU resources, and in particular on the European Central Bank (ECB), that enlargement generates;
- continuing issues of political re-definition, especially in terms of voting regulations in the Council need to be resolved; and
- there has been general concern that the EU may grow so large that it collapses under its own weight, thus heralding a return to nationalism, tariffs, and trade wars (Danta and Hall, 2000). This expresses itself in terms of arguments over budget contributions and rebates, CAP reform and the cultural construction of Europe, not least in relation to the implications of Turkey's potential accession.

Development Background

The former Czechoslovakia had emerged from state socialism in 1989 with a relatively strong industrial sector, although in common with the rest of CEE, in terms of living standards, services and consumer choice – not least the ability to travel – it had lagged behind Western Europe since the 1960s. The country had been ruled by a rigid regime that remained hostile to economic and political reform to the end. The former East Germany (GDR) had a similar industrial character, and relatively high living standards. Its hardline government also had

Table 1.1. Accession states in perspective.

Country	Total population (millions)	Area ('000 km²)	Population density (per km²)	GDP PPP (US$bn)	GDP per capita PPP (US$)	Unemployment rate (%)	Life expectancy at birth Female	Male	Infant mortality rate (per 1000 live births)	Estimated internet users per 1000 pop.	Estimated Tourism receipts as % of GDP
2004 EU entrants											
Cyprus	0.8	9.3	82	9.1	11,567	4.0	80.4	75.3	5.6	176	34.4
Czech Republic	10.2	78.9	130	154.2	15,064	8.1	78.5	72.1	4.1	98	0.1
Estonia	1.4	45.2	30	13.7	10,049	12.6	76.1	65.2	8.4	272	0.6
Hungary	10.2	93.0	110	129.6	12,728	5.7	75.6	67.1	9.2	145	0.03
Latvia	2.3	64.6	37	18.5	7,809	13.1	76.0	64.9	10.4	62	3.0
Lithuania	3.5	65.3	53	29.1	8,359	17.0	77.9	67.6	8.6	61	0.9
Malta	0.4	0.3	1,239	3.6	9,255	5.0	80.3	76.0	6.0	130	39.4
Poland	38.6	312.7	124	380.5	9,844	17.4	78.0	69.7	8.1	72	0.9
Slovakia	5.4	49.0	110	66.2	12,314	19.2	77.2	69.1	8.6	120	0.05
Slovenia	2.0	20.3	98	35.4	17,762	5.9	79.1	71.9	4.9	151	*de*
The 2007 candidates											
Bulgaria	7.9	110.9	72	50.6	6,366	19.4	75.3	68.2	13.3	52	4.0
Croatia	4.4	56.5	78	36.0	8,118	15.8	76.7	69.1	7.4	56	1.8

Romania	22.4	238.4	94	156.3	6,976	7.3	74.2	67.0	18.6	172	< 0.01
Turkey	69.6	774.8	87	399.1	5,901	8.5	72.5	66.8	36.6	30	< 0.01
The neighbours											
Albania	3.2	28.8	119	12.8	3,743	14.5	78.0	72.0	11.6	1	0.1
Belarus	9.9	207.6	48	84.7	8,422	2.1	74.5	62.8	9.3	18	< 0.01
Bosnia and Hercegovina	4.1	51.2	84	11.7	2,626	39.9	74.7	68.7	15.0	na	0.2
Georgia	5.2	69.7	72	15.7	3,553	15.8	77.4	71.9	14.9	4	6.9
Macedonia, FYR	2.0	25.7	79	9.9	4,882	30.5	74.8	70.5	11.8	25	0.4
Moldova	4.3	33.9	108	8.4	2,307	7.3	71.2	63.9	18.4	12	0.3
Russia	144.1	17,075.4	8	1,229.0	8,490	8.9	72.3	59.0	14.6	7	0.1
Serbia/ Montenegro	10.7	102.2	104	18.1	3,532	21.2	76.7	70.6	13.0	na	na
Ukraine	48.7	603.7	81	204.1	4,155	11.1	73.6	62.3	12.0	6	1.2

Sources: Hall, 2004b and authors' additional calculations.

been staunchly opposed to political and economic reform.

By contrast, since 1968, the Hungarian party and government had implemented relatively liberal economic policies (while maintaining tight political control), and had one of the strongest private sectors in the region. The country's western border with Austria was one of the first physical elements of the Iron Curtain to be dismantled in 1989.

In Poland, the rise of the Solidarity free trade union movement, originating in the Lenin shipyard in Gdansk in 1980, was soon accompanied by both domestic and external political and economic crises that culminated in 1981 with a military 'coup', ostensibly to forestall a Soviet-led Warsaw Pact military intervention similar to that which had befallen Czechoslovakia in 1968 following the liberal political as well as economic reforms of Dubcek's 'Prague Spring'. Yet less than 8 years later, in the early summer of 1989, Poland held the Soviet bloc's first relatively free multi-party elections that heralded the beginning of the dismantling of the Soviet empire. In the 1980s Poland had experienced a sharp decline in GDP and shortages of consumer goods. However, relatively strong manufacturing and service sectors, coupled to a steady stream of remittances from the large Polish diaspora, helped to maintain living standards at levels similar to those in Hungary and Slovakia. The uniquely important role of the Roman Catholic church – it had helped to reverse the collectivization of agriculture in the 1950s – became critical with the heavily symbolic election of a Polish Pope.

At the end of the 1980s, Slovenia was the most developed republic in the former Yugoslav federation (which had been expelled from the Soviet bloc in 1948 for excessive 'nationalism'). Slovenia had strong historical ties to Austria and northern Italy, and large numbers of *Gastarbeiter* working within the EU (labour migration from Yugoslavia had been permitted since 1965) sent back valuable remittances. Indeed, for Yugoslavia as a whole, such remittances were of equal value to tourism as the most important source of foreign exchange. In both cases, Croatia, with its long Adriatic coastline and German-speaking Habsburg legacy, was the dominant generator of such income. None the less, Slovenia's relatively well-developed

manufacturing and service sectors together with geographical contiguity with Italy and Austria provided the highest living standards in Central and Eastern Europe. Small – with a population of less than two million yet blessed with a diversity of resources – the mountains, lakes and spas of this former Habsburg province had been popular with the Austrian upper classes. In the early 1990s, Slovenia's role in the break up of Yugoslavia was pivotal. Encouraged particularly by the German government, the Slovenes were the first to declare independence from Belgrade. The subsequent conflict with the largely Serb federal Yugoslav army was over in less than a week, and Ljubljana's success clearly acted as a role model for other Yugoslav republics whose exit strategies would prove to be far bloodier.

At the other end of the development spectrum, Bulgaria and Romania had been the least developed European CMEA members (Albania having effectively left the Soviet bloc in 1961 (and formally in 1967), ostensibly taking the side of China over the ideological differences which split world communism in the early 1960s). There had been attempts to build strong heavy industrial sectors in these two southeastern European states, and the austerity that characterized the later years of Ceausescu's rule in Romania was particularly brutal and corrupting. At the end of the state-socialist period, both countries still had distinctively rural characters. They were characterized by low living standards, poor infrastructures, substantial environmental problems, highly distorted economic structures and political cronyism that persisted as post-communist corruption; many former state and party functionaries made the apparently effortless transition to becoming 'good capitalists'.

The Baltic countries presented special challenges, having been forcibly incorporated into the Soviet Union during the Second World War to become something of a Russian milch cow within the USSR. But historically, there have been strong economic and cultural ties with Scandinavia, Poland and Germany. Despite Soviet pressures for cultural and economic assimilation, the Baltic republics were able to capitalize on their traditional advantages: favourable locations on the Baltic Sea, higher educational levels, developed infrastructures, and a degree of cultural autonomy. These helped to maintain the highest living standards and the least oppressive governments within the USSR. After regaining independence in 1991, they faced a double challenge: loss of traditional markets in the former Soviet Union, and difficult political relations with the Russian government, not least over the Baltic states' large Russian populations. These minorities, their use of the Russian language and the Cyrillic script, now present a distinctive cultural identity within the enlarged EU.

Although the CEE candidate countries were subject to relatively similar challenges in the 1990s – global competition, the loss of former markets and the re-orientation of trade to Western Europe, privatization, and the construction of democratic institutions and practices – their responses to these and the outcomes were different. In general, economic recession was experienced in the early 1990s, followed by strong economic growth from around 1993/4. Yet in most of these countries 1989 GDP levels were not attained until the late 1990s. Recovery was stronger in Poland and Slovenia, while Baltic and Balkan countries faced more severe difficulties in shaking off their economic and political legacies. In aggregate, by the late 1990s the average per capita GDP in the candidate countries represented only 37% of the EU average, but ranged from 68% in Slovenia to 23% in Bulgaria (Williams and Baláž, 2000).

Significance for Tourism

There are no specific chapters in the *acquis communautaire* (EU law) which specifically deal with the tourism industry. There are, however, a number of chapters that have a great influence on tourism, including those relating to the environment, transport, agriculture and consumer affairs. Closer integration clearly offers the opportunity to harmonize standards and practices throughout the growing 'European club', and for the first time to recognize the importance of tourism to economy, society, culture and environment across Europe. Enlargement, coupled with the liberalization of air transport operation, is encouraging significant new and modified tourist flows.

What emerges from an analysis of successive EU enlargements, is a need to learn from, and to share experiences of change, to better inform conceptualization of tourism and its relationship with macro-economic events (Coles and Hall, 2004). Cyclical models of tourism change may have been superseded by the application of chaos theory to tourism development (e.g. Faulkner and Russell, 1997; McKercher, 1999; Faulkner, 2001). Yet Farrell and Twining-Ward (2004, 2005) claim that most tourism researchers, and implicitly practitioners, have been schooled in a tradition of linear, specialized, predictable and deterministic cause-and-effect science. As such, they (we?) have not been conceptually equipped to appreciate that 'all natural and social systems are interdependent, nonlinear, complex adaptive systems' which are 'generally unpredictable, qualitative and characterized by causes giving rise to multiple outcomes' (Farrell and Twining-Ward, 2004). There is a need, they contend, for new collective thinking – an 'epistemic community' (Haas, 1992; Cinquegrani, 2002) – to respond to global challenges. Currently there is a propensity among tourism practitioners to react to events rather than to anticipate and plan for them (Coles, 2003), to search for understanding in steady state conceptions (WTO, 1998; Bierman, 2003), when economic, political, social and environmental disruptions are in fact more commonplace (Sönmez, 1998; Gössling, 2002; Hall and Brown, 2006).

European tourism needs to be managed with foresight, proactively rather than retrospectively responding to change. Its managers need to be more keenly sensitized to the regularity of enlargement events, adjustments in EU governance, economic and social reorganizations in existing and new member states, and the potential restructuring of markets (Coles and Hall, 2004; Hall et al., 2004).

This is particularly important given that preparations for each enlargement have been in train for several years prior to the event. In the case of the 2004 enlargement, pre-accession funding, especially since 2000 and through PHARE, ISPA and SAPARD (Hall and Danta, 2000), helped the accession states to meet their formal and legal membership requirements (Bradley Dunbar, 2003). Special interest groups and their members have also been active in contingency planning (e.g. HOTREC, 2003). The 2004 entrants are both destinations and tourism-generating markets, and their absolute levels of consumption and production have been predicted to grow dramatically (Coles and Hall, 2004; NIT, 2004).

Greater forecast wealth in the new member states, accompanied in some cases by greater freedom of movement, is likely to stimulate greater outbound travel, as well as changing patterns of domestic tourism, business and VFR travel, especially in the short term. Changes within their tourism sectors may have knock-on effects in adjacent states, those both within and outside the EU.

The accession states are, of course, as indicated above, far from representing a homogenous group. Although there are similarities among them, there are also important differences. Disparities exist not only at the inter-state level, but there are also notable intra-state variations, as detailed in subsequent chapters. Similarities and differences are of course evident in their tourism products and resources – natural and cultural, as well as the organization and structure of demand and supply. The 2004 accession states included both relatively long-established destinations such as Cyprus and Malta, and (re-)emergent ones such as Slovenia and the Baltic States. Among them are destinations primarily identified with mass tourism and the 'sun, sea, sand' formula, noticeably the Mediterranean entrants. There are largely unspoilt wildernesses in the Tatra mountains in Slovakia, the Julian Alps of Slovenia and the lakeland environments of the Baltic states, holding substantial appeal for the growth markets of nature and adventure tourism (Behr *et al.*, 2004). Other destinations offer high quality assemblages of cultural heritage, notably Prague, Budapest and Kraków, but with increasing competition. For more than a decade and a half Prague, Budapest and Warsaw have been important city-break destinations, and now Ljubljana, Tallinn, Riga, Vilnius and Bratislava are making concerted efforts to capture market share (Behr *et al.*, 2004; Hudson, 2004).

Key Themes

A major overarching issue concerns the relationship between tourism development and EU governance, the structural position of tourism within the EU, and the role of tourism within the Commission's large spending programmes. In a major paradox of EU policy, tourism is identified as one of the most significant and vibrant of economic activities, in terms of job, income and wealth creation in local communities in each member state, and also for the social benefits it offers and the potential it provides as a framework for the stewardship of distinctive cultures and environments (European Commission, 2002, 2003a, 2003b, 2003c).

Yet, despite such acknowledgement, there is no separate EC commissioner for tourism: it represents just one unit within the Enterprise Directorate-General in Brussels. Here it competes for resources and influence with demands from such diverse sectors as aerospace and automotives, cosmetics and defence, pharmaceuticals, and textiles and clothing (Coles and Hall, 2004; European Commission, 2004a).

However, this is little more than reflecting practice in a number of member states' national governments, where it often seems that tourism does not have a loud voice. If it is explicitly named at all, 'tourism' may be located within different state departments and ministries in different countries, and may even be moved from one to another, in some cases frequently. This perhaps reflects three realities:

- that governments and bureaucracies view the role of tourism in different ways and from different perspectives, reflecting tourism's multi-faceted nature – encompassing employment, regional development, trade, foreign policy, social welfare, leisure, culture, transport, environment;
- that, as a corollary, tourism does not present a coherent image or functional role within government, and as a consequence, it is seen as ancillary or even marginal; and
- that as a consequence of such marginality and ephemerality, the politicians finding themselves in the roles of handling tourism within government tend to be second rate functionaries and at best low level ministers, such that the voices of the tourism industry may not be best heard, interpreted and relayed through their offices (Hall and Brown, 2006).

In the case of the EC and EU, such apparent marginalization of tourism is compounded because there are no funding measures dedicated solely to it. Instead, those destinations looking for EU support for tourism projects must look to instruments designed primarily for other purposes. Project managers therefore need to think creatively and laterally about how tourism meets the aims and objectives of programmes such as the European Social Fund, the Framework Programmes, INTERREG, and eEurope (Coles and Hall, 2004; European Commission, 2004b). Formerly, the LEADER community development programme had been important for rural tourism development in such countries as Ireland (Roberts and Hall, 2001).

Clearly, in the shorter and longer term there will be winners and losers from EU enlargement:

- spatially, at a number of levels from community level to global relationships, and
- structurally, in terms of policy priorities and successful interdependencies, for example between culture and tourism policies – see Chapter 3.

The dynamics of capital and labour mobility and knowledge transfer will modify the conditions of tourism production and consumption across the new EU and beyond.

The 2004 accession countries enjoyed a high travel media profile as an immediate concomitant of EU entry. But just as in the wake of political change in the region in 1989, the novelty of a newly accessible 'playground' can soon wear off (Hall, 1991). One central tourism challenge for the new entrants is to communicate their products and attractions with greater visibility, to continue to invest in them and, where necessary, to reinvent them in order to anticipate and respond to the fickleness of dynamic tourist market demand (NIT, 2004).

Social costs of tourism may arise from the promotion of foreign investment opportunities. Media publicity highlighting low property values has led to an increased awareness among Western Europeans of attractively priced potential second homes in selected locations and regions, as emphasized by Marin Bachvarov in Chapter 19 in relation to Bulgaria. One consequence of this may be that, as elsewhere in Europe, local residents find themselves priced out of their own local housing markets, whether in desirable urban sectors, rural regions or coastal locations. Foreign direct investment in major infrastructure, accommodation and attraction projects may also leave new member states vulnerable to the power of transnational corporations and the vagaries of global market conditions, reinforcing trends experienced to varying extents in the previous decade and half (e.g. Behringer and Kiss, 2004).

The introduction and growth of flights operated by budget airlines from West European markets to regional airports in the accession states is a notable short-term impact. These are generating both advantages and disadvantages for destinations. The desire to attract the perceived benefits of such operations may lead to dependence and inappropriate markets for some destinations, while providing a useful market entry and image builder for others. Certainly there is no shortage of (ex-) military airfields that can be exploited as second or third tier airports with possible local benefits accruing from the diffusion effects of gateway development in hitherto marginal locations. The accumulated media imagery of clubbing and stag/hen weekends for youthful West Europeans has been instructive for the promoters of Dublin and Prague. Negative destination images can swiftly be generated to confound what may have been years of careful nurturing by national and regional authorities (Attard and Hall, 2004; Hall, 2004a). Profile and market positioning is a key consideration and requires careful, long-term management by all the 2004 entrants (Hall, 2000c).

Distinctions between tourism and other forms of temporary mobility, migration and cross-border activity have long been blurred, particularly in Central and Eastern Europe (Hall, 2000a; Williams and Hall, 2000; Hall and Williams, 2002; Coles et al., 2004). Use and meaning of the term 'tourist' will become increasingly ambiguous. Experience suggests that migration and temporary mobility will settle down to being relatively constrained in the longer term. Some commentators note that basic economic conditions are likely to generate more short-term than long-term stays. Until living standards are equalized, the costs of staying in a Western country may be too high for many citizens of accession countries pursuing legal employment. None the less, warnings of a 'brain drain' from the accession countries were

voiced as examples of well-educated professionals being attracted by higher remunerations
elsewhere. Reducing differentials between old
and new EU members may ameliorate this.
Early reports identified tourism labour markets
as the source and beneficiaries of short-term,
seasonal, but relatively highly-paid employment
(Woods, 2004a).

Evolving Europe

Smith (2000) argued that negotiation of EU
enlargement 'framework agreements' and
Balkan stability processes for a post-Cold War
European order exposed contradictions in the
EU's performance, and raised questions
about its capacity to shape the 'new Europe'.
None the less, for Dingsdale (1999), the
're-territorialization of Europe' has been
characterized by:

- the consolidation of the European Union
  project as the dominant idea of Europe;
- EU territory conceived as the economic,
  social, political and cultural core of the
  continent; and
- a peripheral status for post-socialist Europe
  within it.

Arguably, these factors have been expressed in:

- the terms defining which countries are fit to
  join the EU;
- the candidate countries' suppliant applications for membership;
- their compliance with EU rules for assistance; and
- their acceptance of disadvantageous terms
  of trade and the application of EU protocols.

Simplistic conceptions of an 'integrating'
west, a 'reforming' centre, and a 'struggling'
east within Europe ignore north-south disparities. For example, those in the eastern periphery
of the continent expose a relatively stable and
cooperative north-east – Poland and the Baltic
states, gaining EU membership in 2004, contrasting with a fractious and still unstable
south-east – Bulgaria and Romania being considered unready for 2004, the Balkan countries
not being in the frame, while the Cyprus situation almost derailed the whole enlargement
project.

Cyprus was politically divided in 1974
when a coup backed by military rulers in Athens
designed to annex the island to Greece triggered a Turkish military intervention. This
resulted in a long-term invasion and occupation
of 37% of Cyprus' territory – including some of
the most popular tourist areas – and expulsion
of 200,000 Greeks from that northern 'half'.
United Nations sanctions were subsequently
imposed against this Turkish 'occupation'. The
division has persisted (Kliot and Mansfeld,
1997), with the Republic of Cyprus government
representing the Greek Cypriot 'south', and the
Turkish Republic of North Cyprus, declared in
1983 but recognized only by Turkey, acting on
behalf of the 'north'.

The island's partition focused attention on
the role of tourism, which, in the 1970s and
1980s, took on a prime economic importance in
the south (see Gilmor, 1989; Kammas and
Salehiesfahani, 1992; Clements and Georgiou,
1998; Sharpley, 2001, 2003). With a UN economic boycott of Turkish Cyprus, however, pre-
cluding direct access except from Turkey,
tourism in the north has been severely constrained, receiving only around 10% of the
island's total (Lockhart, 1994; Scott, 1995;
Warner, 1999; Alipour and Kilic, 2004).
Reasons for this are discussed in Chapter 18.

In July 1997 the European Commission in
Agenda 2000, its communication to the European Parliament on the future development of
the Union, confirmed that accession negotiations would begin, and reiterated the EU's
determination to play a positive role in bringing
about a settlement in Cyprus. Greece repeatedly indicated that Athens would block enlargement if Cyprus was excluded, arguing that the
admission of other countries into the EU could
not proceed if the reason for not admitting
Cyprus was the island's political problem. The
Greek position was that Cyprus could not be
allowed to become a 'hostage' of Turkey, and
that the EU must not accept a Turkish veto
on the admission of Cyprus. Further, until the
Helsinki Summit of December 1999, Greece
had vetoed any move towards inaugurating
enlargement discussions with Turkey.

As 1 May 2004 rapidly approached, and
brokered by a number of interested parties,
referenda were held in both parts of Cyprus on
the question of re-unification as a precursor

to accession. The bitter irony of this exercise was that a majority in the Turkish North of the island voted for re-unification, while a majority in the Greek South voted against. The outcome was that in theory all of Cyprus acceded to the EU in 2004, but in practice only the Greek Republic of Cyprus actually did so. This was a poor compromise indeed, and continues to cast a shadow over both the 2004 enlargement and subsequent accession negotiations.

That in a globalized 21st century, a tourist island as small as Cyprus could potentially hold one of the major keys to the largest EU enlargement, to eastern Mediterranean stability, and to post-communist states' incorporation into mainstream Europe, was indeed a major irony and a portent for the future character, structure and enlargement plans of the EU (Hall, 2004c).

In the next chapter, Constantia Anastasiadou explores in greater depth the two-way relationship between tourism and the European Union. This is followed in Chapter 3 with an exploration of the relationships between tourism, citizenship and culture in Europe.

References

Alipour, H. and Kilic, H. (2004) Tourism development and planning in constrained circumstances: an institutional appraisal of the Turkish Republic of North Cyprus (TRNC). In: Hall, D. (ed.) *Tourism and Transition: Governance, Transformation and Development*. Wallingford, UK: CAB International, pp. 133–146.

Anon (1999) EU enlargement. *The Economist*, 18 December, p. 148.

Attard, M. and Hall, D. (2004) Transition for EU accession: the case of Malta's restructuring tourism and transport sectors. In: Hall, D. (ed.) *Tourism and Transition: Governance, Transformation and Development*. Wallingford, UK: CAB International, pp. 119–132.

Behr, R., Bird, L., Bowes, G., Eilers, R. and Wilkinson, C. (2004) Short breaks in the new EU: Europe's big playground. *The Observer*, 2 May.

Behringer, Z. and Kiss, K. (2004) The role of foreign direct investment in the development of tourism in post-communist Hungary. In: Hall, D. (ed.) *Tourism and Transition: Governance, Transformation and Development*. Wallingford, UK: CABI Publishing, pp. 73–81.

Beirman, D. (2003) *Restoring Tourism Destinations in Crisis. A Strategic Marketing Approach*. Wallingford, UK: CAB International.

Black, I., White, M. and Dymond, J. (2002) Dismayed Turks vow to meet the test. *The Guardian*, 14 December.

Bradley Dunbar Associates (2003) *Opportunities and Challenges of EU Enlargement*. Available at: http://www.scottish-enterprise.com/publications/contextpaper2.pdf

Cinquegrani, R. (2002) Futuristic networks: cases of epistemic community? *Futures* 34(8), 779–783.

Clements, M.A. and Georgiou, A. (1998) The impact of political instability on a fragile tourism product. *Tourism Management* 19(3), 283–288.

Coles, T.E. (2003) A local reading of a global disaster: some lessons on tourism management from an *Annus Horribilis* in Southwest England. *Journal of Travel and Tourism Marketing* 15(2/3), 173–197.

Coles, T.E., Duval, D.T. and Hall, C.M. (2004) Tourism, mobility and global communities: new approaches to theorising tourism and tourist spaces. In: Theobald, W. (ed.) *Global Tourism*, 3rd edn. Oxford: Butterworth-Heinemann.

Coles, T. and Hall, D. (2004) Tourism and European Union enlargement. Plus ça change? *International Journal of Tourism Research* 7, 51–61.

Danta, D. and Hall, D. (2000) Introduction. In: Hall, D. and Danta, D., (eds) *Europe Goes East: EU Enlargement, Diversity and Uncertainty*. London: The Stationery Office, pp. 3–14.

Dingsdale, A. (1999) New geographies of post-socialist Europe. *Geographical Journal* 165(2), 145–153.

Edye, D. and Lintner, V. (1996) Conclusion: prospects for the new Europe. In: Edye, D. and Lintner, V. (eds) *Contemporary Europe*. Hemel Hempstead, UK: Prentice Hall, pp. 393–411.

European Commission (1998a) The European Union's pre-accession strategy for the associated countries of Central Europe. In: Nicoll, W. and Schoenberg, R. (eds) *Europe Beyond 2000*. London: Whurr Publishers, pp. 9–28.

European Commission (1998b) The challenge of enlargement – the European Commission's opinion, July 1997. In: Nicoll, W. and Schoenberg, R. (eds) *Europe Beyond 2000*. London: Whurr Publishers, pp. 29–56.

European Commission (2002) *Early Warning System for Identifying Declining Tourist Destinations, and Preventive Best Practices.* Luxembourg: Office for Official Publications of the European Communities.

European Commission (2003a) *Towards Quality Coastal Tourism: Integrated Quality Management (IQM) of Coastal Tourist Destinations.* Luxembourg: Office for Official Publications of the European Communities.

European Commission (2003b) *Towards Quality Rural Tourism: Integrated Quality Management (IQM) of Rural Tourist Destinations.* Luxembourg: Office for Official Publications of the European Communities.

European Commission (2003c) *Towards Quality Urban Tourism: Integrated Quality Management (IQM) of Urban Tourist Destinations.* Luxembourg: Office for Official Publications of the European Communities.

European Commission (2004a) *Enterprise – Creating an Entrepreneurial Europe.* Available at: http://europa.eu.int/comm/enterprise/index_en.htm

European Commission (2004b) *EU Support for Tourism Enterprises and Tourist Destinations. An Internet Guide.* Available at: http://europa.eu.int/comm/enterprise/services/tourism/policy-areas/eu_schemes.htm

Farrell, B. and Twining-Ward, L. (2004) Reconceptualizing tourism. *Annals of Tourism Research* 31(2), 274–295.

Farrell, B. and Twining-Ward, L. (2005) Seven steps towards sustainability: tourism in the context of new knowledge. *Journal of Sustainable Tourism* 13(2), 109–122.

Faulkner, B. (2001) Towards a framework for tourism disaster management. *Tourism Management* 22, 135–147.

Faulkner, B. and Russell, R. (1997) Chaos and complexity in tourism. In search of a new perspective. *Pacific Tourism Review* 1, 93–102.

Gilmor, D.A. (1989) Recent tourism development in Cyprus. *Geography* 74(3), 262–265.

Gössling, S. (2002) Global environmental consequences of tourism. *Global Environmental Change* 12, 283–302.

Grabbe, H. and Hughes, K. (1999) Central and East European views on EU enlargement: political debates and public opinion. In: Henderson, K. (ed.) *Back to Europe: Central and Eastern Europe and the European Union.* London: UCL Press, pp. 185–202.

Haas, P. (1992) Introduction: epistemic communities and international policy co-ordination. *International Organizations* 46(1), 1–35.

Hall, C.M. and Williams, A.M. (eds) (2002) *Tourism and Migration: New Relationships Between Production and Consumption.* Dordrecht: Kluwer.

Hall, D. (ed.) (1991) *Tourism and Economic Development in Eastern Europe and the Soviet Union.* London: Belhaven Press.

Hall, C.M., Timothy, D.J. and Duval, D.T. (eds) (2004) *Safety and Security in Tourism. Relationships, Management and Marketing.* Binghamton New York: Haworth Press.

Hall, D. (2000a) Cross-border movement and the dynamics of 'transition' processes in South-eastern Europe. *GeoJournal* 50(2-3), 249–253.

Hall, D. (2000b) Cyprus. In: Hall, D. and Danta, D. (eds) *Europe Goes East: EU Enlargement, Diversity and Uncertainty.* London: The Stationery Office, pp. 155–167.

Hall, D. (2000c) Destination branding, niche marketing and national image projection in Central and East Europe. *Journal of Vacation Marketing* 6(2), 227–237.

Hall, D. (2004a) Branding and national identity: the case of Central and Eastern Europe. In: Morgan, N., Pritchard, A. and Pride, R. (eds) *Destination Branding: Creating the Unique Destination Proposition*, 2nd edn. Amsterdam: Elsevier, pp. 111–127.

Hall, D. (2004b) Introduction. In: Hall, D. (ed.) *Tourism and Transition: Governance, Transformation and Development.* Wallingford, UK: CABI Publishing, pp. 1–24.

Hall, D. (2004c) Key themes and frameworks. In: Hall, D. (ed.) *Tourism and Transition: Governance, Transformation and Development.* Wallingford, UK: CABI Publishing, pp. 25–51.

Hall, D. and Brown, F. (2006) *Tourism and Welfare: Ethics, Responsibility and Sustained Well-being.* Wallingford, UK: CABI Publishing.

Hall, D. and Danta, D. (2000) Enlargement. In: Hall, D. and Danta, D. (eds) *Europe Goes East: EU Enlargement, Diversity and Uncertainty.* London: The Stationery Office, pp. 377–393.

Heath, A. and Nelson, F. (2004) Economists pour cold water on Europe's party. *The Business*, 1 May.

Heffernan, M. (1998) *The Meaning of Europe: Geography and Geopolitics.* London and New York: Arnold.

HOTREC (Hotels, Restaurants and Cafes in Europe) (2003) *HOTREC EU Enlargement seminar & 47th General Assembly*. Catania, Italy: HOTREC, 10–12 April. Available at: http://www.hotrec.org/ D-0403-120-SC-Press%20Release%20Seminar+%20GA%20Catania.pdf

Hudson, M. (2004) Hot shots: if you want style in your city break, go Baltic. *The Sunday Times*, 2 May.

Islam, F. (2004) May Day or mayday for the EU? *The Observer*, 25 April.

Kammas, M. and Salehiesfahani, H. (1992) Tourism and export-led growth – the case of Cyprus, 1976–1988. *Journal of Developing Areas* 26(4), 489–506.

Kliot, N. and Mansfeld, Y. (1997) The political landscape of partition: the case of Cyprus. *Political Geography* 16(6), 495–521.

Lockhart, D. (1994) Tourism in Northern Cyprus – patterns, policies and prospects. *Tourism Management* 15(5), 370–379.

Mayhew, A. (1998) *Recreating Europe: the European Union's policy towards Central and Eastern Europe*. Cambridge: Cambridge University Press.

McKercher, B. (1999) A chaos approach to tourism. *Tourism Management* 20, 425–434.

NIT (Institut für Tourismus- und Bäderforschung in Nordeuropa GmBH) (2004) *Impacts of EU-enlargement on Tourism. Report from the International Conference 'A New Tourism for a New Europe'*. Available at: http://www.fiyto.org/Docs/home/Report_New_Europe.pdf

Pinder, D. (ed.) (1998) *The New Europe: Economy, Society and Environment*. Chichester, UK and New York: John Wiley & Sons.

Roberts, L. and Hall, D. (2001) *Rural Tourism and Recreation: Principles to Practice*. Wallingford, UK: CAB International.

Scott, J. (1995) Sexual and national boundaries in tourism. *Annals of Tourism Research* 22(2), 385–403.

Sharpley, R. (2001) The challenge of developing rural tourism in established coastal destinations: lessons from Cyprus. In: Mitchell, M. and Kirkpatrick, I. (eds) *New Directions in Managing Rural Tourism: Local Impacts, Global Trends*. Auchincruive, UK: Scottish Agricultural College, CD-ROM.

Sharpley, R. (2003) Tourism in Cyprus: challenges and opportunities. *Tourism Geographies* 3(1), 64–86.

Smith, M. (2000) Negotiating new Europes: the roles of the European Union. *Journal of European Public Policy* 17(5), 806–822.

Sönmez, S.F. (1998) Tourism, terrorism and political instability. *Annals of Tourism Research* 25(2), 416–456.

Warner, J. (1999) North Cyprus: tourism and the challenge of non-recognition. *Journal of Sustainable Tourism* 7(2), 128–145.

Williams, A.M. and Baláž, V. (2000) Western Europe and the Eastern enlargement. In: Hall, D. and Danta, D. (eds) *Europe Goes East: EU Enlargement, Diversity and Uncertainty*. London: The Stationery Office, pp. 15–29.

Williams, A.M. and Hall, C.M. (2000) Tourism and migration: new relationships between production and consumption. *Tourism Geographies* 2(1), 5–27.

Woods, R. (2004a) Our extended family comes knocking. *The Sunday Times*, 2 May.

Woods, R. (2004b) Europe cheers a brave new dawn. *The Sunday Times*, 2 May.

WTO (World Tourism Organization) (1998) *Guide for Local Authorities on Developing Sustainable Tourism*. Madrid: WTO.

2 Tourism and the European Union

Constantia Anastasiadou

Introduction

The EU is characterized by a complex web of institutional structures and multi-level relationships. Unlike other regional trading areas, economic and political integration has progressed in the EU far and wide (McCormick, 1999), covering an ever-growing number of policy areas and with a significant transfer of authority from the national to the supranational level. It would be very difficult, if not impossible, to think of an issue area in Europe that has remained untouched or uninfluenced by the EU.

Tourism is one of the areas that have influenced and have been influenced by the establishment of the EU. Its contribution to further European integration and the enhancement of the European identity has also been highlighted (Richards, 1996). In addition, tourism's role in urban and rural regeneration and its job creation ability have deemed it a preferred economic activity. Statistics show that approximately 9 million people are directly employed in tourism, which contributes close to 5.5% of the EU GDP (CEC, 2002).

According to the WTO (2002), the high level of economic development and integration in Europe means that international travel has become an integral part of the lifestyle of a substantial part of the population. In 2004, 414 million visitors were attracted to the area, a figure that corresponds to 54% of world international tourist arrivals (WTO, 2005a). More specifically the existence of the EU has had a profound impact on the growth of intra-regional travel with almost 85% of international arrivals to the region being intra-regional travellers (CEC, 2003).

However, Europe's world market share of international arrivals is still in steady decline, from 72% in 1960 to 58% in 2002 and 54% in 2004 (WTO, 2002, 2005a). In 2004, world tourism achieved its best growth rate for 20 years. Europe experienced the slowest rate of growth than all other regions, an increase of 4% when the world average increase was 10% (WTO, 2005a). Åkerhielm et al. (2003) argued that Europe would need to act as one group if it wishes to maintain its position as the world's most visited area and urged for the EU to undertake a more proactive role.

The Central and Eastern European (CEE) countries that joined the EU in May 2004 have the potential to become the new motor for European tourism by being primarily a receiving and potentially a generating area for the region (Mintel, 2004). According to the WTO (2005b) the rise in arrivals in 2004 for Europe was driven in part by the excellent performance of countries in Central and Eastern Europe (+8%). New and upcoming destinations in Eastern Europe are rivalling those of the more established southern destinations, as they offer novelty and a good value for money.

Tourism in the accession states has benefited from significant EU funding to improve their infrastructure and transport networks (DG Regio, 2003) and their accessibility has improved in psychological and pragmatic terms. Similar assistance has been offered to existing member states to develop new tourism products or improve the existing ones. Nevertheless, the involvement of the EU in tourism has been questioned for some time especially as there is little coordination of activity and no overarching tourism policy in place. Is the support provided for tourism through other policies adequate? Is the EU doing enough for tourism or should there be greater direct involvement?

The aim of this chapter is to provide examples of the EU's involvement in tourism and to discuss potential areas of involvement as these have been suggested in the tourism literature and were identified by institutional stakeholders at the supranational level.

EU Impact on Tourism

Due to the nature of the tourist activity, the impact of EU policies on tourism has been widespread and far-reaching (Lickorish, 1991; WTO, 2000). So wide-ranging is the impact of other policy areas on tourism that reports reviewed regularly (DG Enterprise, 2004) are put together to allow interested parties to keep track of funding mechanisms and initiatives relevant to tourism.

The EU's impact on tourism so far can be characterized as a mixed blessing. Tourism in the EU benefited from the establishment of the single market in 1993 and the abolition of all travel restrictions and visas for EU citizens (CEC, 1993). Subsequently the implementation of the Schengen agreement in 1995 conferred similar benefits on overseas visitors to the signatory members of the EU. At the same time the abolition of duty free sales for travellers within the EU area, taken on the premise that EU citizens should travel within the area as if it was a single country, has led to a loss of income for transport operators and an increase of prices for passengers (Davidson, 1998).

Tourism and tourism-related projects have received significant funding from EU regional development funds, which aim to assist with the development of Europe. In the period from 1994 to 1999 €4.4 billion were disbursed for tourism-related projects (DG Enterprise, 2004). However, there is little overview of where this support is going, there is no evidence of how the established tourism products fit within existing tourism demand (Hjalager, 1996), whether they generate new demand or are just detracting from an existing one (Anastasiadou, 2004a).

Finally, the introduction of the euro in January 2002 was seen as a great opportunity for tourism businesses as it would lead to greater transparency and the reduction of commission charges from currency exchange (Shackleford, 1998; WTO, 1998). However, the rise of the price indices that followed the conversion to the new currency has led to increased costs for tourism enterprises and a loss of price competitiveness over non-EU destinations. In 2004 the more mature destinations in the euro zone saw a decline in their market share and were particularly affected by the increased competition from non-euro destinations in Europe, North Africa (Morocco and Tunisia) and the Middle East (Egypt) (WTO, 2005a, 2005b).

It is clear from this discussion that it is difficult to aggregate whether the overall influence of the EU in tourism has been mostly positive or negative. It can be argued that tourism is so heavily influenced by EU policies, that the EU has acquired an implicit role in tourism dictated by its actions rather than the expression of priorities and objectives. The question then becomes whether this implicit role is adequate, and if not, what shape EU's involvement should take. These issues have been debated at some length in the tourism literature.

EU Tourism Policy, To Be or Not To Be?

The widespread influence of EU policies on tourism and the absence of a specific common policy or framework have put the sector at a disadvantage over other sectors (Lickorish, 1991, 1994) which have seen their priorities accounted for in the formulation of policy whereas tourism interests have not. For these reasons it was suggested that a more explicit role in tourism would be necessary.

A number of tourism studies in the early 1990s (e.g. Lickorish, 1991; Akehurst, 1992; Akehurst *et al.*, 1993) discussed the potential of tourism involvement at the supranational level. The need for more intra-regional cooperation in tourism (Sinclair and Page, 1993) and the necessity for an integrated, multi-year tourism development plan, formulated in the context of the overall regional policy which will coordinate the demand and supply of tourism across the space (Lickorish, 1991, 1994) have been stressed. The importance of tourism to the EU economy alone was considered an adequate justification of the necessity of a supranational tourism policy (European Parliament, 2002).

In addition, specific steps for the design of a successful supranational tourism policy were suggested in the early 1990s (Akehurst, 1992). A number of potential issue areas where the EU could be involved were also identified, but no notable progress has been made since then towards the establishment of a policy or a more coherent framework of action. Primarily, this has been attributed to a lack of interest (Åkerhielm *et al.*, 1990) and to the fact that tourism policy features in an area of weak common policy, the production and delivery of services (Williams and Shaw, 1989).

The main obstacles in formulating a more solid approach to tourism were identified as being the divergent views on tourism and in particular, what constitutes an EU and what a national issue (Davidson and Maitland, 1997). The sharing of competencies between the national and the supranational level is part of a wider issue for the EU. Some members are more willing than others to see greater EU involvement but there is a strong sentiment that a common approach to tourism may result in more regulation (Downes, 2000). In addition, the subsidiarity principle[1] has affected the transfer of a tourism competence to the EU level. In the past, suggested EU-wide initiatives such as the Philoxenia programme (CEC, 1996), were dismissed on the basis of the principle. Moreover, the existing reference to tourism in the Maastricht Treaty is inadequate and offers no basis for action. The implications are twofold: first, there is no clearly defined role for the EU, and second, any proposal made requires the unanimous agreement of all member states. Given the absence of a common vision for

European tourism among member states, the situation is very complex and the inclusion of ten new members in May 2004 has accentuated such differences (*see also* Chapter 1).

The lack of agreement concerning the need for a tourism policy has resulted in the adoption of only a limited number of concrete actions specifically aimed at tourism. Initiatives such as the European Year of Tourism (1990) (CEC, 1990) and the Action Plan to Assist Tourism (1993–1995) (CEC, 1991) are two such examples. Their priorities included: the improvement of the seasonal and geographical distribution of tourism; the improved use of financial instruments; better information for tourists; improved working conditions in the tourist industry, and finally, increasing the awareness of the problems of tourism (Davidson and Maitland, 1997). Overall, these initiatives were limited in scope and were criticized for their large number of priority areas and their overall insignificant impact (Davidson, 1998). Having failed to adopt the Philoxenia initiative, tourism now features under the Tourism and the Employment Process, the main priority of which is to create and improve employment in tourism (DG Enterprise, 2003).

Some criticisms have been expressed concerning the Tourism Unit in the European Commission, the administrative body of the EU. The Unit aims to ensure that tourism interests are fully taken into account in the preparation of legislation and in the operation of programmes and policies which are not directly related to tourism (DG Enterprise, 2003). It tries to ensure a proactive role where Commission activities do not embrace tourism. Its role is limited in scope yet of a significant breadth as coordinating responses to legislation proposed by the Commission is not straightforward in an area as wide-spanning as tourism. However, it has been argued that the Tourism Unit lacks influence and clout because of its small size and the range of functions it undertakes (Greenwood, 1993) and consequently tourism interests are not heard by the EU institutions. The absence of an explicit EU competence in tourism affects the ability of the Tourism Unit to perform its functions effectively.

The communication *Working Together for the Future of European Tourism* (CEC, 2001), which sets out the future direction and priorities for tourism, indicated a move away from establishing a common policy and towards a framework approach where the EU would be limited to a coordinating, complementary role. Furthermore, the communication discussed in detail the aspirations of the European Commission for the future, but failed to set up a specific course of action. Perhaps unsurprisingly, the feelings towards the communication and what it aimed to achieve were mixed (see European Parliament, 2002; HOTREC, 2002; Jeffries, 2002), another demonstration perhaps of the diversity of opinion that exists on what the EU should be doing about tourism.

The EU's involvement in tourism can thus be characterized as being fragmented, lacking in focus and direction, 'ad hoc and piecemeal' with no 'strategic direction, legal basis and underpinning' (Church et al., 2000, p. 324). However, the question of a role for the EU remains and its definition would be of benefit not only to tourism and the EU, but also to other regional trading blocs which aspire to become more integrated and may experience the same dilemmas.

Studies on this topic area have tended to focus on specific aspects of EU involvement (Richards, 1996; Wanhill, 1997) rather than addressing this issue in a holistic manner. In addition, those studies which have attempted a more holistic approach (Akehurst, 1992; Akehurst et al., 1993; Downes, 1997) have been of a prescriptive nature focusing on what the EU should be doing rather than what is actually being done and why. The literature has largely ignored the views of the stakeholders such as the European Commission, the European Parliament and tourism interest groups who are closely involved with decision-making at the supranational level and who are playing their own part in influencing and affecting the conditions created

for tourism. A detailed study of the EU environment undertaken by the author (Anastasiadou, 2004b, and unpublished PhD thesis, 'Tourism at the supranational level: The case of the European Union', University of Strathclyde.) sought to establish the views of the stakeholders on the issue of EU involvement. Interviewees included MEPs, Commission officials and representatives of interest groups who were asked to comment on the reasons why a specific policy had been evasive and the type of tourism competence they would like to see materialize.

EU Approach to Tourism: the Stakeholders' Perspective

Interviewees claimed that there is a division and a certain degree of polarization between member states in their perceptions of tourism and thus verified the notions expressed in the tourism literature (Downes, 1997). Certain member states (UK, Sweden, Germany and Austria in particular) appear more unwilling to see a greater involvement at this level and interviewees identified different causes of this apprehension. These can be divided into *financial, perceptual* and *pragmatic* reasons (Table 2.1).

The UK was presented as one of the more resistant states to the idea of an EU tourism competence. Interviewees argued that the UK's apprehension was part of its internal policy for no more expansion of the EU competencies and its fear that greater involvement at this level by the EU institutions would result in more regulation (*perceptual*). Sweden also did not wish to see the establishment of a new competence as that would have budgetary implications

Table 2.1. The EU: obstacles to a formal competence.

Financial	Perceptual	Pragmatic
Budgetary implications	Regulation	Apprehension towards new competencies
	Tourism sector may fare worse	Absence of state involvement
	Issue definition	Authority mismatch
		Subsidiarity

Source: Anastasiadou, 2004, 'Tourism and the supranational level: The case of the European Union' (unpublished PhD thesis, University of Strathclyde).

(*financial*) and they are also against the idea of a further expansion of the EU budget. Increasing scepticism of the effectiveness of the EU and the overall success of common policies has also fuelled these attitudes. Therefore, for some member states there is general apprehension towards the transfer of new competencies as a matter of political ideology rather than simply the reluctance towards a tourism competence (*pragmatic*).

In addition, in several member states there is already no central government involvement in tourism. In particular, in federal structures such as Austria, Belgium and Germany, federal governments tend to have limited powers over the regional governments, which often have exclusive competence in a number of policy areas. For instance, the German Länder are primarily responsible for tourism and the federal government does not have any authority or decision-making power for tourism. Strong regional governments such as the Länder want to ensure they maintain their powers over federal and supranational structures (Jeffery, 2000), so they object to the idea of an EU tourism competence, wishing to retain responsibility and control of tourism development in their areas.

However, it is not only federal states, but also countries with devolved authorities where tourism is only marginally handled at the national level. For instance, in the UK, Scotland, Wales, England and Northern Ireland each deal with tourism independently and in Spain each administrative region has its own tourism policy (Velanzuela, 1991). The style of political administration and the dominant political philosophy in the management of tourism at the national level ultimately condition expectations of involvement in tourism at the supranational level. In this way, the transfer of a competence to the EU level can be perceived as a step towards recentralization, as tourism policy issues in a number of member states are handled at the subnational levels – a step backwards rather than forwards.

Furthermore, these remarks highlight the importance of local and regional authorities in the design and delivery of tourism policy within member states. However, as decisions concerning tourism are made at ministerial level the authority mismatch in this institutional setting is evident. Despite their importance in tourism

management and development at the national level, regional authorities have no influence in the decision-making process at the EU level. By not including regional authorities as an equal partner in the equation, a dead-end situation is created, as some national ministers simply have no authority to make decisions on tourism matters.

Moreover, member states fear that under a common policy their respective tourism sectors might fare worse than now. In each policy area there are 'winner' and 'loser' member states because policy impacts are asymmetrical (McCormick, 1999). Intra-regional competition is fierce as the main market for European tourism are intra-regional tourists accounting for nearly 85% of all international tourist arrivals to Europe (WTO, 2000; Eurostat, 2002). An EU tourism policy could lead to potential imbalances with unexpected consequences to the tourism sector. It could affect the competitiveness of tourism enterprises and lead to a loss of control of the sector with member states unable to intervene. Member states, it was suggested, are simply very protective of their sectors and believe that they are better off on their own as they can sustain control.

Finally, because of the complex nature of tourism there is usually some degree of involvement at all levels of public administration: national, regional, local and destination. This in turn complicates how the EU would be involved as there is already so much being done within member states and at various administrative levels. An interviewee argued that a convincing case has not yet been made about what the EU can do that is not being done already at the national level. These comments raise the importance of *issue definition* and the apparent lack of it at the supranational level. The findings demonstrated that agreeing what needs to be done was the most problematic stage in deciding on an approach. In addition, member states were employing *subsidiarity* as the main argument against the transfer of a competence. Although the principle was established as a means of dividing power between the national and supranational level, it was being used largely as a constraint mechanism to any expansionist tendencies.

This situation was posing problems in institutional involvement in tourism. For instance,

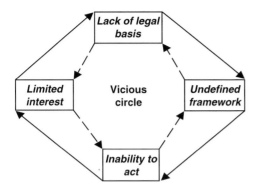

Fig. 2.1. The vicious circle of EU tourism policy.

the European Parliament is one of the institutions that encouraged dialogue with industry (Lickorish, 1991) and argued that tourism should constitute a common policy with a legal basis and a chapter of its own in the revised Treaty (European Parliament, 1997). Despite this positive outlook, it was suggested that only a relatively small number of Members of European Parliament (MEPs) are actively involved in tourism because it falls under the auspices of member states. MEPs were frugal in investing their time and resources in tourism because they knew that any recommendations they made were not binding for member states. Consequently, there were gradually fewer and fewer MEPs actively interested in tourism and in return, fewer voices in favour of tourism.

The lack of a framework at the EU level disables dialogue among interested parties whilst establishing conditions of a vicious circle. Figure 2.1 demonstrates how the vicious circle is created. The cause of all these complexities is the lack of a clear definition of what the involvement in tourism should be. Stakeholders are finding themselves handicapped in their decision-making process. Ultimately, involvement in tourism remains in a state of limbo; stakeholders are not involved because there is no legal basis and then there is no legal basis because there is not enough interest in tourism.

Preferences on Type of Involvement

Interviewees also commented on their preferred type of EU involvement in tourism. Diversity of

opinion was again apparent. Four types of involvement were suggested: no competence, sponsorship, framework-policy and common promotion.

No competence

Some interviewees mentioned that having an explicit reference in a treaty was not necessary, as there are already enough competencies in the European Union and tourism is handled efficiently at the national level. Tourism is regulated through existing measures from other policies such as consumer and environmental protection and, therefore, there is no need to have specific legislation. It was further suggested that establishing a formal competence would only make things worse for tourism as, generally, common policies had not been successful. This position argued very much in favour of the continuance of the current status quo.

Sponsorship

In this position, there is a clear preference to a *laissez faire* approach and against the bureaucratic interference a Treaty reference could create. The fear that a competence would lead to legislation is predominant. There are many items of legislation, it is argued, that are regulating the industry already so there is no need for further supranational legislation as it will only make things worse and affect tourism competitiveness. However, a sponsorship situation was welcome. This would bring people together to discuss the impact of legislative proposals on tourism, promote Europe as a destination and enable actions in favour of tourism. It was stressed that this would not constitute a policy as policy is more regimented and could lead to more legislation. This position did not object to a treaty reference outright, but stated that although it did not lead to additional legislation, it would be welcome.

Framework policy

According to this view, tourism should feature as a distinct Community policy. Europe's declining share of world arrivals, it was argued, necessitated collective action in order for it to remain the world's most visited region. The existence of distinctive policies across Europe without coordination and the absence of synergy worked against the competitiveness of the sector. A common tourism policy would not promote harmonization but rather establish the foundations for greater cooperation in areas of relevance to all member states. Harmonization of policy at the supranational level would work against tourism, as variety is its major element.

Rather than a single policy for the whole of Europe, this view argued in favour of a common or joint policy that will evolve in conjunction with member states' existing tourism policies and set out the parameters along which intra-EU cooperation can be developed. This idea of a competence is to work on measures that will develop tourism further within Europe where member states cooperate more actively. Measures that strengthen the image of Europe as a single destination, such as cross-border and transnational tourism projects, would be the focus of any joint attempts. In short, member states should be working towards the establishment of enabling strategies across Europe from which the various components of the sector could benefit.

Common promotion

Finally, almost all interviewees identified common promotion in overseas markets as a potential competence area. The basic premise of this view is that in the eyes of overseas visitors Europe is perceived as a single destination. Establishing a common visa for non-EU visitors and the introduction of the euro as legal tender have enhanced freedom of movement across the EU area and have further reinforced the image of Europe as one destination. Therefore, common promotion campaigns of Europe as a single destination were feasible, if not necessary, but member states' unwillingness and intraregional competition had ruled this out.

Establishing a brand Europe would work towards reversing the losses in world tourism arrivals and re-establishing Europe's competitive advantage (Åkerhielm et al., 2003). However, tourism marketing and promotion are jealously

protected by national tourism organizations (NTOs) who wish to control the projected image of the country and who believe that joint promotion efforts are irrelevant as their countries already possess a well-established image. Furthermore, competition is so intense between member states that it has been impossible to launch regional initiatives, for instance, the promotion of the Iberian Peninsula as one destination to third countries. Interviewees described this as a very myopic form of competition that failed to recognize the potential benefits of greater cooperation.

However, this type of involvement appears to be gaining ground as it is the least taxing in terms of a transfer of competence and appears to be popular among all stakeholders. A recent Council of Ministers meeting (European Council, 2002) gave the green light to the Commission to consider common promotion as a possible area for future action. This change of heart may be interpreted in light of the significant cut-back of promotion budgets in recent years by several member states (WTO, 1997), making joint efforts economically sound and of good value for money. It is, therefore, very likely that there will be common promotion campaigns in the near future.

Opting for this type of involvement would constitute a lowest common denomination approach as it will not address any of the challenges that the absence of a framework for tourism creates. As 85% of international arrivals to the EU area are intra-regional tourists (WTO, 2002), the significance and relevance of focusing resources and time on the minor part of the tourism market whilst ignoring the major part can be questioned. Given the increasing tendency of Europeans to travel further away for their holidays, sustaining the high levels of intra-regional tourist numbers might become a challenge earlier than might have been expected.

A number of observations can be made concerning the range of approaches discussed here. The common thing among all the approaches is the unwillingness to establish a common policy that will replace national policies and the preference for some additional actions that are taken in parallel to what is happening at the national level. The main difference between these positions is the degree of authority transfer that interviewees suggested would be necessary for tourism concerns to be handled adequately at the supranational level. A common ground approach that would probably satisfy both the skeptics and the enthusiasts would be the sponsorship approach as it suggests greater degrees of involvement and cooperation without increasing bureaucracy and legislation. There are good reasons to believe that this approach may already be gaining ground.

Tourism in the EU Constitution

The draft constitution was published by the Praesidium of the Convention on the Future of Europe on 18 July 2003. Its main aim is to replace the overlapping set of existing treaties and simplify procedures. Following long negotiations, the draft was agreed by the European Council on 18 June 2004 in Brussels with some modifications and now awaits ratification by all member states. Ratification is likely to take around two years and cannot begin until the text has been officially published in 21 languages (Nationmaster, 2004).

The main objectives of the Constitution are:

- to simplify the overlapping Treaties and Protocols providing the current legal constitution for Europe;
- to enhance and streamline decision-making in the Union now that it has 25 members.

The Constitution identifies areas of *exclusive*, *shared*, and *supporting*, *coordinating* and *complementary* action. Areas of exclusive competence are those in which member states have agreed that they should act exclusively through the EU and not legislate at the national level (i.e. customs union, Euro zone monetary policy, common commercial policy). Areas of shared competence are those in which member states act alone only where they have not acted through the EU, or where the EU has ceased to act. The areas of supporting, coordinating or complementary action are those where member states have not conferred any competencies on the Union and the Union may only act to support the work of the member states.

Tourism was one of the areas that had originally been dropped in the draft Treaty text submitted by the Praesidium of the Convention. During the Intergovernmental Conference in June 2004, it was finally agreed to add tourism to the Constitution (LGIB, 2004) after a lot of pressure from MEPs, member state officials and tourism interest groups to have tourism reinstated as an area of EU competence. According to European Travel Policy (ETP), tourism interest groups came to realize that 'the perennial complaints about EU neglect of tourism will stand even less chance of satisfaction if the last vestige of a formal EU role in tourism is swept away' (ETP, 2003). The omission of tourism from the draft Constitution was the much-needed incentive for the coming together of interested parties in tourism. It was also the proof of the claim that had been made during the conference on transport and tourism organized by the Greek Presidency that:

> there was a broad consensus at the ministerial meeting for the status quo of tourism to be reinstated in the text of the new Treaty, as one of the areas for supporting action, where the EU will have a complementary role alongside member states.
>
> (ETP, 2003; GNTO, 2003)

The move to include tourism as an area of shared competence was welcomed by some organizations (EAA, 2004; ECTAA, 2004) as it could lead to further funding of projects (ETOA) whereas others such as ABTA feared that it could lead to bureaucracy or further regulation (*Travel Weekly*, 2004). Overall though, it was suggested that it was better for tourism interests to be in rather than out of the constitution.

The relevant section of the EU constitution reads as follows (Article III–181a):

1. The Union shall complement the action of the Member States in the tourism sector in particular by promoting the competitiveness of Union undertakings in that sector.
2. To that end, Union action shall be aimed at:
(a) Encouraging the creation of a favourable environment for the development of undertakings in this sector;
(b) Promoting cooperation between the Member States, particularly by the exchange of good practice;
3. A European law or framework shall establish specific measures to complement actions within the Member States to achieve the objectives referred to in this Article, excluding any harmonisation of the laws and regulations of the Member States.

(ETOA, 2004)

It is unclear how this reference will be expressed in terms of policy or priority objectives but it serves the purpose of giving some indication of the type of action that will and will not be taken. It is vague yet specific enough to satisfy all members, noncommittal for the sceptics, yet promising enough for the enthusiasts. The main implication of the article is that for the first time there is legitimacy in the EU actions for tourism. The language and style that has been adopted in all documentation since the 2001 communication 'Working Together for the Future of European Tourism' (CEC, 2001) is also evident here. The emphasis on cooperation and good practice is common, as is the avoidance of talk of harmonization or substitution of member states' involvement. Arguably the reference also reflects the prevalence of the sponsorship/ framework-policy approach as a strategy for the future EU involvement in tourism.

The EU Constitution is an important milestone, as, at least in theory, it establishes how decision-making powers are going to be divided between the national and supranational levels for a significant length of time. Despite the fact that this reference is not unproblematic, it still constitutes the very first document where a specific course of action is implied and a clear division of power is attempted and is the first step towards the establishment of a framework or strategy for tourism. In addition, it is a reference that all heads of state have committed to regardless of how they have felt in the past about EU tourism involvement.

However, the EU Constitution will only become binding once it has been ratified by all member states. At the moment of writing only six of the 25 member states have ratified the Constitution (Greece, Spain, Italy, Lithuania, Hungary and Slovenia). Concerns have been expressed that a climate of negativity towards the Constitution is prevailing even in some of the more pro-European member states such as France (Anon, 2005). There is obviously still a long way to go and it is unclear what the future of the Constitution and the EU would be should several member states reject it. Whatever the future may hold, it would be a great irony if the one and only treaty document that expresses formally and for the first time a real commitment to tourism is the one that fails to be ratified.

Conclusions

The aim of this chapter was to provide examples of EU's involvement in tourism and to discuss potential areas of involvement as these have been suggested in the tourism literature and were identified by institutional stakeholders.

First of all, it was demonstrated that even in an institutional setting as evolved and sophisticated as the EU, member states retain their prominence as the key figures, which shape the integration process. This analysis indicated that an implicit policy created by the impact of other policy areas rather than an explicitly stated policy or strategy for tourism is in place. A type of 'creeping competence' has taken shape and form by the decisions and activities of other policy areas. This though, has happened with little or no consideration of tourism priorities and tourism interests are incapable of shaping this implicit policy (Anastasiadou, 2004a). By not assigning a competence and, thus, responsibility to the EU, the tourism agenda seems to be placed firmly on the backburner. Consequently, the impacts of regulation from other policy areas on tourism might always be an afterthought rather than a consideration at the onset of policy-making.

The literature had argued that a tourism policy at the EU level was necessary, as the existing support framework is inadequate. The institutional stakeholders also agreed that greater EU involvement was needed, but suggested that an approach based on complementary and subsidiary action to that undertaken at the national level would constitute a better approach. The difference in their views seemed to lie in how much more involvement would be necessary, ranging from establishing a joint policy to joint promotion campaigns with no policy implications.

The European Constitution has presented tourism interests with the opportunity to have tourism included on the EU agenda on equal terms as other policies and it constitutes a long anticipated expression of greater commitment to tourism. In attempting to establish a complementary competence, the EU has tried to carve for itself a little niche where it can develop its strategies in tandem with those of its member states and, on the face of it, it appears to have done so successfully. Having tourism reinstated in the final version of the Constitution is a victory in itself as it shows that tourism interests can be influential when they are better organized.

The implications should the Constitution be ratified are increased awareness, better positioning of tourism interests and acknowledgement of the implications of other policies on tourism. The EU could see joint promotion efforts, more cross-border cooperation and a degree of policy coordination which should help establish a truly European tourism sector. However, only time will tell how this reference will be translated into EU priorities and objectives and whether the full potential of this reference is achieved.

Note

1 According to the subsidiarity principle, action at the EU level should only take place if it is more effective than the action taken at the national, regional or local level.

References

Akehurst, G. (1992) European Community tourism policy. In: Johnson, P. and Thomas, B. (eds) *Perspectives on Tourism Policy*. London: Mansell, pp. 215–231.

Akehurst, G., Bland, N. and Nevin, M. (1993) Tourism policies in the European Community member states. *International Journal of Hospitality Management* 12(1), 33–66.

Åkerhielm, P., Dev, C.S. and Noden, M.A. (1990) Europe 1992: neglecting the tourism opportunity. *Cornell Hotel and Restaurant Administration Quarterly* 31(1), 104–111.

Åkerhielm, P., Dev, C.S. and Noden, M.A. (2003) Brand Europe: European Integration and tourism development. *Cornell Hotel and Restaurant Administration Quarterly* 44(5/6), 88–93.

Anastasiadou, C. (2004a) The characteristics of tourism interest representation at the European Union level. In: *Local Frameworks and Global Realities? Tourism, Politics and Democracy: Proceedings of 3rd International Symposium held at the University of Brighton*. Eastbourne, UK: University of Brighton.

Anastasiadou, C. (2004b) Stakeholder perceptions on tourism at the supranational level: the case of the European Union. In: R. MacLellan (ed.) *Tourism: State of the Art II*. Glasgow: University of Strathclyde, CD-Rom.

Anon (2005) Charlemagne: The great unravelling. *The Economist,* 23 April, p. 47.

CEC (Commission of the European Community) (1990) *European Tourism Year*. Brussels: CEC.

CEC (Commission of the European Community) (1991) *Community Action Plan to Assist Tourism*. Brussels: CEC.

CEC (Commission of the European Community) (1993) *Impact of the Completion of the Internal Market on the Tourism Sector*. Brussels: CEC.

CEC (Commission of the European Community) (1996) *Proposal for a Council Decision on a First Multiannual Programme to Assist European Tourism (1997–2000)*. Brussels: CEC.

CEC (Commission of the European Community) (2001) *Working Together for the Future of European Tourism*. Brussels: CEC.

CEC (Commission of the European Community) (2002) *Report on Community Measures Affecting Tourism*. Brussels: CEC.

CEC (Commission of the European Community) (2003) *Basic Orientations for the Sustainability of European Tourism*. Commission communication to the Council, the European Parliament, the Economic and Social Committee and the Committee of the Regions. Brussels: CEC.

Church, A., Ball, R., Bull, C. and Tyler, D. (2000) Public policy engagement with British tourism: the national, local and the European Union. *Tourism Geographies* 2(3), 312–336.

Davidson, R. (1998) *Travel and Tourism in Europe,* 2nd edn. Harlow, UK: Addison Wesley Longman.

Davidson, R. and Maitland, R. (1997) *Tourism Destinations*. London: Hodder & Stoughton.

DG Enterprise (2003) *Tourism and the European Union*. Brussels: DG Enterprise. Available at: http://www.europa.eu.int/comm/enterprise/services/tourism/tourismeu.htm#ec-involved

DG Enterprise (2004) *EU Support for Tourism Enterprises and Tourist Destinations: an Internet Guide.* Brussels: DG Enterprise. Available at: http://www.europa.eu.int/comm/enterprise/services/tourism/policy_areas/eu_schemes.htm

DG Regio (2003) *Regional Policy Inforegio.* Brussels: DG Regio. Available at: http://www.europa.eu.int/comm/regional_policy/intro/regions5_en.htm

Downes, J. (1996) The package travel directive – implications for organisers and suppliers. *Travel and Tourism Analyst* 1, 78–92.

Downes, J. (1997) European Union progress on a common tourism sector policy. *Travel and Tourism Analyst* 1, 74–87.

Downes, J. (2000) EU legislation and the travel industry. *Travel and Tourism Analyst* 5, 49–71.

EAA (European Anglers Association) (2004) New EU Constitution: EAA and EFTTA happy that tourism and sport brought in from the cold. Press release 24 June. Available at: http://www.eaa-europe.org/2003/PDF%20Files/Sport-Tourism-New-Constitution%20_EN.doc

ECTAA (Group of National Travel Agents' and Tour Operators' Associations within the EU) (2004) *Inclusion of Tourism in the New Treaty, Position of ECTAA.* Available at: http://www.ectaa.org.uk

ETOA (European Tour Operators' Association) (2004) *ETOA Welcomes the Qualified Inclusion of Tourism in the EU Constitution.* Available at: http://www.etoa.org/pdf/press_eu_constitution_july04.pdf

ETP (European Travel Policy) (2003) Treating tourism better in the Treaty? European Travel Policy [online], 5–6 May 2003. Available at: http://www.europeantravelpolicy.com/crete/tourism-treaty.html

European Council (2002) *Council Resolution of 21 May 2002 on the Future of European Tourism (2002/C 135/01).* Brussels: European Council.

European Parliament (1997) *Resolution on the Dublin European Council of 13 and 14 December 1996, B4-0021, 0024, 0026, 0027 and 0033/97.* Strasbourg: European Parliament.

European Parliament (2002) *European Parliament Resolution on the Commission Communication to the Council, the European Parliament, the Economic and Social Committee and the Committee of the Regions on Working Together for the Future of European Tourism.* Strasbourg: European Parliament.

Eurostat (2002) Stability of tourism flows in the European Union. *Statistics in Focus* Theme 4 – 28/2002. Available at: http://www.europa.eu.int/comm/eurostat/Public/datashop/printproduct/EN?catalogue=Eurostat&product=KS-NP-02-028_N EN&mode=download

Greenwood, J. (1993) Business interest groups in tourism governance. *Tourism Management* 14(5), 335–348.

GNTO (Greek National Tourism Organisation) (2003) *Informal Council of EU's Ministers about European Tourism.* Available at: http://www.gnto.gr/3/08/0802/ec80213.html

Hjalager, A.M. (1996) Agricultural diversification into tourism evidence of a European Community development programme. *Tourism Management* 17(2), 103–111.

HOTREC (Confederation of National Associations of Hotels, Restaurants, Cafés and Similar Establishments) (2002) *Live from Brussels* 22, 15 February. Brussels: HOTREC.

Jeffery, C. (2000) Subnational mobilisation and European integration: Does it make a difference? *Journal of Common Market Studies* 38(1), 1–23.

Jeffries, D. (2002) The European Union and European tourism: in search of a policy. *Travel and Tourism Analyst,* June, 1–23.

LGIB (Local Government Information Bureau) (2004) *EU Competence for Tourism.* London: LGIB. Available at: http://www.lgib.gov.uk/policy/tourism.htm

Lickorish, L.J. (1991) Developing a single European tourism policy. *Tourism Management* 12(3), 178–184.

Lickorish, L.J. (1994) *Developing Tourism Destinations: Policies and Perspectives.* London: Longman.

McCormick, J. (1999) *Understanding the European Union A Concise Introduction.* Basingstoke, UK: Macmillan.

Mintel (2004) New Europe: Markets and destinations. *Travel & Tourism Analyst* 10, June.

Nationmaster (2004) *Encyclopaedia: European Constitution.* Available at: http://www.nationmaster.com/encyclopedia/European-constitution

Richards, G. (1996) *Cultural Tourism in Europe.* Wallingford, UK: CAB International.

Sinclair, M. and Page, S. (1993) The Euroregion: a new framework for tourism and regional development. *Regional Studies* 27(5), 475–483.

Shackleford, P. (1998) Analysis by the WTO of the importance of the EURO area in European and world tourism. CEU/ETC Seminar on the Euro and Tourism. Conference speech: 11–14.

Travel Weekly (2004) Eye on EU. *Travel Weekly,* 15 July. Available at: http://www.travelweekly.co.uk/Articles/2004/07/15/19796/Eye+on+EU.html

Velanzuela, M. (1991) Spain: the phenomenon of mass tourism. In: Williams, A.M. and Shaw, G. (eds) *Tourism and Economic Development: Western European Experiences,* 2nd edn. London: Belhaven, pp. 40–60.

Wanhill, S. (1997) Peripheral area tourism: a European perspective. *Progress in Tourism and Hospitality Research* 3, 47–70.

Williams, A. and Shaw, G. (1989) *Tourism and Economic Development: Western European Experiences.* London: Pinter.

WTO (World Tourism Organization) (1997) *Towards New Forms of Public–Private Partnership. The Changing Role, Structure and Activities of National Tourism Administrations.* Madrid: WTO.

WTO (World Tourism Organization) (1998) *The Euro: Impact on Tourism.* Madrid: WTO.

WTO (World Tourism Organization) (2000) *WTO 2020 Vision Europe.* Madrid: WTO.

WTO (World Tourism Organization) (2002) *Tourism Market Trends: Europe.* Madrid: WTO.

WTO (World Tourism Organization) (2005a*) International Tourism Obtains its Best Results in 20 years.* Madrid: WTO. Available at: http://www.world-tourism.org/newsroom/Releases/2005/january/2004numbers.htm

WTO (World Tourism Organization) (2005b) *WTO World Tourism Barometer* 3(1). Madrid: WTO. Available at: http://www.world-tourism.org/facts/barometer/WTOBarom05_1_en_excp.pdf

3 Enlargement Implications for European Tourism

Melanie Smith and Derek Hall

Introduction

This chapter analyses the current situation of the EU from an economic, social and cultural perspective, focusing on the implications of enlargement for tourism and tourism education. Some emphasis is placed on the concepts of citizenship and identity, as these are hot issues in the field of contemporary European Studies. The dream of a united Europe has existed for many decades, but it has become recognized increasingly that it is only realistic to promote 'unity in diversity' – that is, celebrating a common European heritage at the same time as cultural diversity. Europe is far from being homogeneous, and the imposition of seemingly anodyne EU regulations and values can provoke some member countries and regions to seek protectionist directions (e.g. the French with their language, the British with their currency). At times, the European project seems to have been more about division than unification, especially for many of the regions struggling for autonomy from or within the nation state (e.g. Catalonia, the Basque provinces). In some cases, governments and electorates have rejected European initiatives, such as the euro and more recently, the Constitution. However, many relatively successful attempts have been made to unite Europe politically and economically, yet many readers will be familiar with Jean Monnet's declaration that if he had the chance to start the

European project all over again, he would have started with culture. One of the former French Ministers of Culture, Jacques Lang, also stated that the future development of Europeanism would be dependent on building a Europe of culture after having attempted to build an economic and political Europe (Council of Europe, 1994). This chapter therefore focuses to a great extent on this issue, starting with a discussion in relation to the East Central European accession countries (the Visegrad 5), for whom political, social and cultural changes in recent years have been significant.

From Transition to Accession

For some of the newer members of the EU, accession represents an extension of an already ongoing process of transition or political and social change. This process has particularly affected the accession countries of East Central Europe – the Czech Republic, Hungary, Poland, Slovakia, Slovenia. Having gained accession to the EU in May 2004, these countries have been adapting to their new circumstances after grappling with almost 15 years of post-communist transition. In the case of Slovenia, independence was gained from Yugoslavia in June 1991, and following a 10-day war, the country quickly gained recognition as an autonomous nation. Such a re-emergence to independence is not unique to these countries, of course, with the Baltic states of Estonia, Latvia and Lithuania (along with Finland and Poland) having once been part of the Tsarist Empire – the 'prison of nations', as Marxists called it – and more recently of the Soviet Union, a variant on the prison of nations metaphor. Cyprus and Malta have also at times grappled with the problems of British rule and the 'lingering colonial heritage' (as described in Chapter 16).

However, the most obvious recent commonality that East Central European countries share is their history of state socialism from the 1940s to 1989–1991 (it should, of course, be noted that the term 'communism' is more widely used, but it was effectively an unattainable political utopia for socialist governments). There were, of course, variations within this enforced structure. Apart from Yugoslavia, which left the Soviet sphere in 1948 to pursue 'Titoism' (see Chapter 1), Hungary was sometimes satirically referred to as 'the happiest barracks' within the Soviet bloc with its so-called 'goulasch communism', as, after 1968, following the introduction of reforms through the 'New economic mechanism', its citizens were deemed to have a greater degree of economic freedom and better stocked shops than most other Soviet bloc societies. However, state socialism was generally considered to be an oppressive and constraining force by political and social critics.

From 1989 onwards, Thomas (1998) suggests that all of the former communist states were faced with a similar problem of how to change their planning systems to meet the new circumstances of operating in a market economy. This has required new regulations and legislation, especially regarding Western investment and land use control. Uneven development has been a common characteristic of post-communist transition, intensifying the economic and social polarization that was re-emerging in the later years of state socialism. Through the initial 'shock therapy' period of the early and mid-1990s, often substantial price increases were not matched by employment creation and wage increases: often quite the reverse, with large-scale lay-offs from the inefficient and outdated white-elephant industrial plants, stagnating incomes in many other fields, and reduced social security provision, generating

the persistent urban poverty recognized in recent research (e.g. Tsenkova, 2004).

The new and sudden freedoms of unemployment, lack of guaranteed employment and consumer goods availability at prices virtually unaffordable was a quantum leap for many citizens, used as they were to extensive state support and relative continuity, albeit inertia. It is often forgotten in post-1989 writings, that the socialist aspiration towards a communist system had its merits, and for many people (especially older citizens) it afforded them a more stable life than recent capitalist upheavals. Of course, no training was received in how to exploit political and economic freedom, thus capitalist entrepreneurs have tended to emerge as an élite. There is still also considerable mistrust of politicians, and post-1989 governments have often tended towards political extremes (e.g. right-wing politics) to assert their anti-communist stance.

Thomas (1998) notes that transition pathways for former state socialist countries have been diverse, despite their previous shared experiences. Much has been written on the trajectories that Central and East European countries (CEECs) have followed. Here, it is perhaps sufficient to note that although rates of political and economic change have been varied, all of the aforementioned countries were eligible to join the EU in 2004 and are likely to join the euro by 2012 at the latest, indicating a similar level of fiscal preparedness, at least.

Almost half a century within an ideological 'bloc' left the CEECs with suppressed national and regional identities, to some extent replicating their experiences within the old empires prior to the First World War. Political freedom was not permitted and cultural expression was often censored. However, not least for the 'new' (Czech and Slovak republics, former Yugoslav republics) and newly independent CEECs of the 1990s, there was a clear desire to re-assert individuality and difference. Tourism, often employed as an emblem of this assertion of identity, has therefore an important role to play. As a consequence, most of the country chapters in this book discuss the issue of identity construction and promotion.

For example, East Central Europeans do not view themselves as being particularly similar. While it has been claimed that the Czech Republic is the most atheist country in Europe

(Cline, 2003), 92% of Poles are Roman Catholic (Encarta Encyclopaedia Online, 2005). The Hungarian language has nothing in common with those of its Slavic neighbours, belonging as it does to the Finno-Ugric group of languages, and although Central European food is often considered to be of a certain kind (e.g. heavy, hearty), there are considerable variations in the gastronomy, and more especially, wine production. Each country has its own distinctive approach to the arts, literature and entertainment.

All of these countries are now keen to join the euro, but analysts believe that this process may be delayed until 2012 in most cases, mainly because of budget deficits (Mehring, 2005). Whilst evidence has shown that there can be significant problems associated with adopting the euro, such as increasing unemployment, rising prices, insolvencies and a general stagnation of the economy (McNeill, 2005), these new accession countries remain undeterred. Indeed, Schadler *et al.* (2005) suggest that if certain conditions are met, then euro adoption is likely to bring substantial net gains in the long term, and will make these countries stronger, more self-reliant members of the EU.

Hungary, Slovenia and Slovakia have already ratified the controversial EU Constitution in Parliament, whereas the same Constitution has since been rejected by the French and the Dutch, who held a national vote instead. It is thought that many other nations (especially those from the 'old' EU), would also be likely to reject it. The reasons for this are not clear cut, but generally seem to stem from fears of central control from Brussels and subsidies being used to fund 'poorer' accession countries, who will become strong economic competitors in the future. For example:

> Nowadays the concept of a united Europe is increasingly synonymous with factories being moved to Hungary, cheap Polish laborers, and new guidelines for service industries that jeopardize jobs in better off countries like France and Germany.
>
> (Spiegel Online, 2005)

Such prejudices are largely unfounded, but on a positive note, it is has been argued that the productivity levels of accession countries would rise given greater EU support through a Constitution. Overall, it seems that a spirit of optimism regarding the advantages of EU accession prevails in many of the new member states, whilst many older members are apparently lapsing into increasing cynicism and mistrust. Nevertheless, Steele (2005) suggests that the election of a socially conservative, nationalist and Catholic president in Poland in 2005 symbolized the death of the 'New Europe'.

Politics and economics aside, it seems that the shift eastwards of the EU has also been a positive move in terms of tourism development and cultural integration, and many countries in Central Europe have seen a recent increase in tourist numbers. What is clear, however, is that there is more of a desire to promote national diversity than to sell a common Central European heritage. In recent years, many Central European countries have had similar problems creating adequate infrastructure for tourism after years of state neglect, as well as providing service levels suitable for Western tourists. The 'hangover' of state socialist mentalities often makes service appear to be more of a duty than a pleasure. However, tourism and hospitality education has become widespread and sophisticated (see Chapter 5), with both local and foreign expertise being offered in mixed curricula and in several languages. Many citizens in the region were already technically polyglot, with Russian as an enforced language and others being widely taught (e.g. German, English and some Scandinavian languages). However, many Central Europeans deny knowing any Russian as a protest against past enforcement, and Hungarians (along with the British) are currently said to be the worst linguists in Europe, with only 29% of the population speaking another language. When compared to Slovenians at 89%, this figure is low (EU Business, 2005). Nevertheless, it is worth re-emphasizing that Hungarian is only related to Finnish and Estonian, and even then, only in terms of structure rather than vocabulary. By contrast, the north and south Slavic languages of much of Central and Eastern Europe share a degree of commonality.

In terms of their economies, Central European countries still have quite a strong rural tradition, despite declining agriculture. Although emphasis in recent years has been placed on the development of cultural cities (e.g. Prague, Budapest, Kraków), diversification of the tourism product is now needed, as saturation point is often being reached. Natural and cultural resources also vary considerably. Despite being a small country, Slovenia is blessed with coast, mountains and lakes as well as cultural cities. Poland, the Czech Republic and Slovakia all have unique cultural and historic towns and villages, as well as mountain ranges suitable for skiing. Hungary has no mountains, but one of the largest lakes in Europe (Balaton). Different ethnic and folk cultures are also present in all of the countries, which are major assets for rural tourism development. Similarly, spa tourism has a significant history in the region and is once again being developed and promoted.

It is clear that Central Europe has become of considerable interest to international tourists. Although the post-communist fascination is perhaps wearing off, especially amongst repeat visitors, much of the region is still relatively under-visited and has great potential. EU accession has perhaps planted the idea in the minds of visitors that Central European countries have reached a certain level of economic and social development, and that infrastructure and service quality are improving. Budget airlines are offering new routes all the time, though it is worth noting the considerable price differentials between fares *to* Central Europe and fares *from* Central Europe. It is ironically much cheaper for tourists travelling from Western countries, even though incomes are still relatively much lower in Central European countries. There are also concerns that budget airline tourism is leading to the attraction of less desirable visitors (e.g. stag and hen parties), and multiplying visitor numbers in cities with limited capacity (e.g. Kraków, Prague).

Culture, Citizenship and Identity in the New EU

It is sometimes difficult to define exactly what 'Europe' represents, especially with regards to culture, citizenship and identity. Politically, Europe's current borders are limited, but cultural influences are pervasive, especially from Turkey, North Africa and the Middle East, not to mention the former colonies further afield. The extension of EU boundaries does not directly take account of such external influences, but it does potentially redress internal imbalances of political and economic power and influence. The social implications are perhaps less easily discernible, but are no less important for that. However, one of the biggest problems of the EU project is that its aims and objectives are rarely explained clearly enough to its citizens, thus referenda on key issues (e.g. the euro, the Constitution of Europe) tend to elicit minimal or negative responses.

In terms of citizenship, it is clear that the EU functions as a kind of constructivist actor, encouraging 'belonging', but complementing rather than replacing any sense of national allegiance. It is not only a legal or juridical body, but an inherently cultural one. Jean Monnet's notion that 'we have made Europe, now we have to make Europeans' must adapt to ever-changing political, economic and cultural frameworks, some of the most recent being the fall of Communism, the growing adoption of the euro, the accession of ten new countries, and the potential entry of several more. In addition, many aspects of globalization (often perceived as synonymous with 'Americanization' in more protectionist countries) are sometimes seen as being threatening to the protection of Europe's cultural and linguistic heritage. As elsewhere, Europeans are faced with the constant dialectic of re-affirming distinctiveness in the face of homogenization.

Citizenship is difficult to define, as it is based on the creation or emergence of communities with geographical and psychological attachment to place, culture and identity (all intangible and nebulous concepts to a large extent). There may be more attachment to regions than nations (e.g. in the case of Catalonia, the Basque country or Corsica). Many new nation states have emerged in the post-Communist era (e.g. the Czech Republic and Slovakia, and former Soviet states), as well as those in what was once Yugoslavia. Politicians and citizens of these new states often have the task of deciding how to redefine themselves, their culture and heritage, and presenting a new image to the outside world. This manifests itself in tourism marketing, heritage interpretation and cultural representation. It is sometimes difficult to know which aspects of culture should be presented, especially in countries where political systems suppressed cultural expression for many decades. Should countries clearly display aspects of their recent dissonant past (a tactic that is often open to political manipulation), or should they hark back to the heritage of previous centuries and civilizations, many of which might be common to other European citizens? (It should be noted that much of this heritage would also consist of colonial occupations and legacies.) Are they positioning themselves in relation to each other, thereby encouraging competition, or are they adhering to the common EU slogan of 'unity in diversity'? Arguably, political oppression and lack of economic and cultural freedom for decades (and for many regions, ongoing) do little to encourage allegiance to yet another 'bloc' with centralized political governance. Nevertheless, the voluntary decision made to join the EU is clearly based on a belief that the benefits outweigh the disadvantages (especially in political and economic terms).

Cultural theory seems to suggest that complex postmodern societies are less like 'melting pots' and more like 'salad bowls'. While integration or assimilation was previously seen as desirable, there is now more of a recognition that the coexistence of different cultures and the celebration of diversity are more appropriate. Individual or collective identities can be asserted independently within a national or regional political framework or ideology to which the individual or communities may or may not subscribe. This notion of democracy and freedom of expression is relatively new for many citizens in accession countries, thus this represents a period of exploration of both cultures and identities. The role of the EU within this process should surely be to promote and support cultural diversity, but this requires a complex understanding of both heritage and contemporary cultural developments within nation states. However, as elsewhere in the EU, general cultural or tourism strategies may clash with national priorities. Javrova (2005) states that European integration is hard work for many accession countries, who are still defining their own values and identities before they can even think about embarking on European projects relating to common policy. There may also be other barriers. The development of collaborative networks is common to EU cultural

development, especially in the arts, as the sharing of good practice and the enabling of cultural exchange is fundamental to the rationale behind European understanding and integration. However, certain ways of collaborative working may be treated with suspicion in some of the newer member states. For example, Farkas (2005) notes that in Hungary, many citizens spent their time devising ways to avoid political and social networks during the socialist era.

The Reconciliation of a Common European Heritage and Contemporary Cultural Diversity

There are clearly still dilemmas to be overcome in cultural terms within the EU. How does one reconcile, for example, the protection of a common European heritage whilst supporting contemporary cultural diversity? Much of the cultural diversity in Western Europe has its origins in post-colonial immigration and diasporic communities from outside Europe, which are not always easily reconciled with the imperial legacies of European history. Much of Central and Eastern Europe's common recent heritage is that of enforced socialist structures. Neither framework creates the kind of harmonious environment that lends itself simply to tourism product development and heritage interpretation. It is, instead, likely to be a contested battleground where political, economic, social and cultural priorities often become gridlocked.

At the same time that many countries in the new EU are redefining their heritage and adopting selective approaches to presentation and promotion, there are moves to develop a certain standardization in terms of conservation and preservation of Europe's common heritage. However, it could be argued that the European emphasis is still based too much on the built environment with less regard for more intangible aspects of heritage. These are, of course, difficult to measure and manage, but they are arguably the cornerstones of national, regional and European cultural continuity. Attempts are currently being made to redress the imbalance, for example, Mihailovic and Strachwitz (2004) from Europa Nostra focus on a sense of place, belonging and pride, and advocate qualitative changes in approaches to cultural development; but it is well known that the budget for culture in the EU is woefully deficient, therefore progress in this direction is likely to be slow. Much work is being done in the international arena on the links between creativity and quality of life in cities (Florida, 2003). There is seen to be an inextricable relationship between economic growth, creative clusters of people and businesses, science and new technologies. This research is proving interesting for European cities in the throes of regeneration, but the connections to heritage arguably need to be maintained if cultural development is to be protected from too much instrumentalism and homogenization.

In the modern world system, Wallerstein (2000) suggests that it is necessary to redefine who are 'we' and who are the 'others' both in our thoughts and in our politics. In recent times, the apparent conflicts between 'East' and 'West' have been taking place *within* as much as between societies. No longer can we reduce conflict management to a simple dialogue between political entities, trading blocs or geographical regions. It is much more subtle and complex, particularly in multi-cultural, multi-faith European societies, where extensive work is being done in both political and cultural arenas (particularly the arts) to promote cultural diversity, integration and social inclusion. Tourism also plays a key role therein, especially in some of the newer developments that focus on ethnic quarters or festivals. New mobilities, especially following the widening of the EU, are creating new relationships and negotiations within even more culturally diverse societies.

Education is a key issue for cultural understanding, along with mobility and cross-cultural exchange. The encouragement of multi-lingualism is important but sadly declining in some of the less EU-orientated countries (e.g. Britain). The way that the culture and history of Europe is taught in schools and universities is of paramount importance to the fostering of understanding and tolerance. This has traditionally been somewhat hegemonic and archaic, especially when confined by national boundaries. The 20th century in Europe was one of the most collectively tragic and violent in modern history, so there is much to come to

terms with, to interpret and to integrate into touristic development. Much has been written about the Nazi Holocaust and its legacy, which is commonly viewed as being almost beyond interpretation because of its enormity. Similar emotive (albeit smaller) debates are currently ensuing about the interpretation and representation of socialist or communist heritage and its legacy. Displaced symbols litter the landscape in the form of architecture or statues. Should they be removed or simply converted? Museums and galleries often have to rethink the presentation of their collections, and it is not uncommon for them to remain closed temporarily whilst curators consider reinterpretation. Who and what are heritage sites, museums and galleries for? Are they simply there as memorials or reminders of the past so that we can learn from them in the future, as sites of 'truth' and reconciliation? Or are they vehicles through which 'new' societies can explore and display their contemporary European, national or regional identities? Of course, one might argue that both approaches are necessary and complementary. As an oversimplification, heritage can feed one need (coming to terms with the past in the present and learning from it), and the arts can provide the means of celebrating contemporary cultures and creativity.

In the past, heritage and conservation tended to receive a larger slice of the budget in many EU countries, but there has been a noticeable shift in recent years towards supporting the cultural and creative industries, especially those involving young people and new technologies. However, there consequently appears to be a more instrumental approach to cultural development in many European countries, whereby it is used as a tool for something else rather than being valued for its intrinsic qualities (e.g. economic growth, regeneration, tourism development). Whilst this is perhaps inevitable given public funding restrictions and private business imperatives, care should be taken that societies and communities do not feel disinherited from their past or their contemporary modes of expression. Citizenship is as much about human rights as anything else, thus EU policy needs to focus on issues of ownership and empowerment in its cultural and tourism development strategies. This is particularly important in accession countries where non-local intervention and investment is omnipresent.

Furthering Tourism Education in the New EU

In the light of the previous paragraphs, it could be argued that tourism education should operate from a cultural base as well as an economic and business-orientated one. An understanding is needed of EU structures, policies and initiatives. At all levels, the relationship between tourism and cultural policy is relatively underdeveloped. If we accept that the unique selling point of the majority of European countries (especially those which have recently joined the EU) is culture, then this surely needs to be addressed. Some might argue more cynically, that many countries simply need better marketing and branding strategies to position themselves within an increasingly competitive marketplace. There is some truth in this statement, of course, but it is firstly necessary to identify one's unique features and resources. An understanding of history and heritage interpretation is needed for this, as well as an awareness of how best to promote and represent cultural diversity, especially the cultures of ethnic and minority groups.

An understanding of Europe's place in the world is also arguably essential, especially when marketing European attractions to non-European tourists. Globalization is a hotly debated term, though, of course, not a new concept for Europeans for whom history has always been a series of shifting hegemonic powers and occupations (internal and external). Europe has played a central role in global trading with its many empires and colonies scattered throughout the world. These are not always sources of dissonance, but can sometimes form the basis of tourist flows between the former 'core' and 'peripheral' countries. In addition, many diasporic groups who have had to leave their country of origin for political or economic reasons may be key markets for new developments, especially in liberalizing accession countries. The juxtaposition of a rich social and cultural heritage and a strong commercial and technological economy in Europe raises countless dilemmas, such as how do we reconcile economic growth, social welfare, and cultural conservation? Many governments are currently experimenting with what has been termed 'third way' politics, which aims to find a middle ground between capitalist growth and socialist democracy (Giddens, 1998). Thus, a knowledge of contemporary politics – both party politics and cultural politics – may also be needed for a true understanding of tourism and its related disciplines.

Many of the accession countries are grappling with issues relating to service quality following years of under-investment and government control. However, the dilemmas relating to an 'acceptable' level of foreign intervention and investment are by no means resolved. If a condition of entering the EU is based on economic status, how far can this be achieved without the inevitable standardization of development typical of the ubiquitous global brand? Often, the aspiration towards adequate service provision can be the very thing that undermines cultural character and uniqueness (e.g. the building of chain hotels and fast food restaurants in heritage quarters, and the displacement of local businesses or residents because of impossible rent increases). Nevertheless, global tourists apparently require certain levels of service quality and familiar brands, therefore this aspiration is by no means misplaced. The challenge surely then becomes to provide the service required by tourists, but within a localized cultural context. That is, drawing on aspects of hospitality that are familiar to that country rather than importing them from elsewhere, and ideally employing local people.

The buzzword for the 2000s in Europe has surely become 'regeneration', a term that seems to be synonymous with 'gentrification' (the aforementioned phenomenon whereby areas become upgraded through investment and prices soar). This is something of a double-edged sword. There is no doubt that regeneration contributes enormously to the economic and physical development of a city, encouraging the building of new 'flagship' architectural structures and attractions, the hosting of mega-events, the redevelopment of areas in decline (e.g. waterfronts), the reuse of old buildings (e.g. factories, warehouses, railway stations). However, the social and cultural implications are often ignored, and they are certainly under-researched. Tourism education definitely needs to take account of such developments, especially as many of the newly regenerated areas and attractions have a tourism focus, or at the very least, provide the baseline for future tourism development (e.g. infrastructure).

Of course, notwithstanding the need to understand the broader context in which tourism operates, students of tourism studies also need to find jobs within this growing and diversifying market. The standardization of qualifications and the loss of visa restrictions may facilitate employment mobility. In addition, there has been a certain standardization of the tourism curriculum thanks to the work of ATLAS and its members (for example, see Richards and Onderwater, 1998). It was generally accepted that the core body of knowledge should consist of the following elements:

- the meaning of tourism;
- the tourism industry;
- the dimensions and measurement of tourism;
- the significance and impact of tourism;
- marketing of tourism services;
- tourism planning and development; and
- management of the tourist experience.

Within this generic framework, the importance of more 'intangible' aspects of research have come to the fore in recent years, for example, the measurement of socio-cultural impacts, quality of life indicators, sensitive and ethical issues in interpretation and representation. New technology would be another prominent feature of most curricula. Potential areas for module development were also identified, many of which have since been implemented across European teaching institutions and have become the focus of numerous conferences. These were:

- globalization and localization;
- the single market and integration;
- the ethics of tourism;
- cross-cultural issues in tourism and leisure; and
- sustainable development of tourism and leisure.

The standardization of any curriculum is, of course, not always desirable as it may serve to stifle creativity or develop graduates with few distinguishing characteristics. Nevertheless, if it is delivered within a local context with attention to cultural specificities, such issues can be resolved. This is perhaps particularly important for accession countries, for whom the previous 'West is best' mantra is sometimes proving to be less than satisfactory.

Tourism Attractions Management and Development in the New EU

In terms of investment opportunities, attractions development in the accession countries has become something of a playground for external developers. The dilemma facing many countries has been between a rock and a hard place of becoming victims of economic imperialism and cultural standardization, versus stagnation, lack of development opportunities, and lagging behind competitors in the same market. Neither situation is entirely satisfactory, so a certain degree of political regulation is needed.

As stated by Rátz (2004) the main (initial) attraction of the former socialist countries in the new EU was 'an exciting experience on the other side of the Iron Curtain'. Of course, in recent years, this unique selling point has begun to wane as cities in particular become increasingly 'cosmopolitan' as a result of new developments and foreign investment and first-time 'curiosity' visitor numbers decreasing. However, the advent of low-budget airlines has had a significant effect on many such destinations, extending and transforming the market, if not always to the advantage of destinations' income and image, both in terms of short-stay, relatively low-per-capita spend and the social disruption of the weekend break 'stag and hen' party revellers. Rural areas and some of the less accessible accession countries, such as the Baltic States, have had to work a little bit harder at establishing a brand for attracting Western tourists. Conversely, others (e.g. Cyprus and Malta) have had to rethink their tourism strategies in the light of *over*-visitation. It is therefore difficult to generalize about the experience of new accession countries, though parallels can perhaps be drawn when comparing like with like (e.g. small islands, cultural cities, rural regions).

Richards' (2001) observation that cultural consumption had reached saturation point in the late 1990s, with cultural tourists suffering from 'monument fatigue' and museum overdose encourages one to question whether a *cultural tourism* strategy is actually the best way forward for many of the newer destinations in Europe. Nevertheless, the Commission of the European Communities (2001) noted that cultural and natural heritage tourism was expected to grow the most in terms of demand. Even former 'sun, sea, sand' destinations, such as Malta and Cyprus have begun to implement cultural tourism development plans. However, the consequences of this have not always been overwhelmingly positive in terms of social impacts, especially in small villages. Time is perhaps better spent on upgrading existing facilities and diversifying into more lucrative activities (e.g. business tourism, which is also a growth sector). Some of the cities in the new EU (e.g. Budapest, Prague, Kraków, Tallinn) are inherently cultural and historic, and therefore cannot easily avoid promoting their monuments, museums and galleries. Richards (2001) also notes that there has been a fall in the local consumption of 'high' culture in many Eastern countries since 1989, mainly due to a lack of state subsidy and declining incomes. Thus, foreign tourism may provide the boost that is needed for many flagging 'high' cultural attractions. Income levels are not yet such that residents from Central and Eastern Europe can always afford to travel far outside the region, so there is also a need to cater for domestic and regional markets that may be more favourably disposed to other forms of more affordable, popular or 'global' development (e.g. arts, festivals, creative tourism). Many of the accession countries are also now in a position whereby they are starting to encourage repeat visitation. Now that the post-Communist fascination has been satisfied, there may be a need to create new, contemporary attractions that provide unique selling points beyond heritage.

Pine and Gilmore's (1999) work on the 'experience economy' suggests the need for new approaches to both product and attractions development and marketing. A uniform approach to such processes is clearly not compatible with capitalist structures and changing consumer expectations. Tyrell and Mai (2001) also emphasize the need for innovative approaches to development, which satisfy the needs of 'money rich/time poor' consumers, who are highly individualistic and are increasingly seeking experiences rather than products. They note that even if visitors arrive together at a destination, they may be seeking individual experiences. Richards and Raymond (2000) analyse the importance of 'creative tourism' whereby visitors are more actively engaged in fulfilling their creative potential. This may include activities, such as painting, dancing, pottery, music, etc. It may involve direct interaction with a host community or attendance of a cultural event. Tourism is clearly becoming less prescriptive, more exploratory, and more experiential. This may explain the apparent growth in the number of festivals, events and spectacles that are being developed as part of the European tourism product. Despite their ephemerality, such events can be a celebration of both heritage and contemporary cultures. If they are repeated regularly, they contribute to cultural continuity and community pride, and if they are well managed, they can leave a permanent physical legacy too.

There has been an increasing interest in the cultures and activities of ethnic and minority groups in Europe. The development of cultural quarters or festivals that are based on the concentration of indigenous or diasporic communities are being marketed as tourist attractions (e.g. Chinatowns, Banglatowns (Indian districts), Jewish quarters). Caribbean Carnivals and Asian Mela Festivals are also growing in importance, as are events based on gastronomy, music or dance forms (e.g. gipsy violin). Although cultural political negotiations and tensions are still ongoing, this development demonstrates a shift away from the imperialism of so-called 'national heritage' towards the cultural diversity of 'minority' groups. Issues relating to interpretation and representation still need to be handled carefully and sensitively, but it is arguably a positive movement in terms of building a new Europe. However, there has also been a frightening resurgence of nationalism in Europe in recent years, often in some of the former socialist countries where right wing governments fight to kill off the last remnants of communist support. Sensitive interpretation is therefore only the icing on the cake of a process that requires a baseline of political and social support, tolerance and understanding.

As well as capitalizing on new, global developments in order to attract quality business tourism, many former Central and Eastern European countries are in the process of re-developing their health and wellness tourism products, namely in the form of spas. Many of these have traditionally had medical as well as 'aesthetic' properties (e.g. waters containing a variety of healing minerals). This is perhaps a unique selling point, as spas are becoming somewhat ubiquitous on an international scale. The landscapes and beautiful buildings in which some of the spas are located (especially in Hungary and the Czech Republic, for example) also provide a cultural specificity which is not typical of global hotel chain spas. A parallel development in much of Western Europe has been that of 'holistic tourism', whereby retreat centres cater for the psychological and spiritual needs of visitors. This may be achieved through alternative therapies and homeopathic treatments, many of which originated in the East (e.g. India, Asia). Spa culture may be more physical and less esoteric, but there is arguably potential for the development of combined products that take the spa concept beyond its traditional origins and attract new markets.

Many of the newer destinations may be in a position to capitalize on their rural tourism attractions, a strategy that was common for some less economically developed EU countries in the past (e.g. Ireland and Portugal). Arguably, the most distinctive aspects of national, regional and local cultures can be found outside major cosmopolitan and historic cities. Unique selling points abound in rural villages, where indigenous traditions are usually stronger, local 'authentic' products abound, and hospitality is often less standardized. For a certain kind of cultural or rural tourist, this form of attraction is strong, and affords considerable scope for development (e.g. eco-museums, festivals, gastronomy, handicrafts, nature trails, religious tourism). There are also numerous destinations offering relatively cheap and less crowded skiing opportunities (e.g. Poland, the Czech Republic and Slovakia, as well as Bulgaria and Romania).

Many of the new accession countries have arguably not yet reached their full potential for a number of reasons. Some of these are political and economic, some may be social or cultural, and others are partly commercial – i.e. the lack

of a distinctive enough brand image or the existence of a negative one. As stated thus far, there are decisions to be made about the features and resources that a destination wants to promote, and the way it wants to interpret its culture and heritage. This is a major challenge for all European destinations, especially those that have reached saturation point in terms of visitor capacity (e.g. mass seaside resorts and small historic towns). Competition is rife, not least from destinations outside Europe. Accession into the EU perhaps suggests that the countries in question have reached a level of development, management and service quality that can meet the needs of increasingly demanding international visitors. However, some of the countries with the most potential resources for tourism development (e.g. Romania, Bulgaria) did not meet the criteria to join the first round of entrants. Political and economic mismanagement (albeit under the auspices of 'protectionism') have been major barriers to tourism development in some cases. It can also be very damaging to a destination's external image, hindering both investment and visitation.

New Images for New Destinations?

Van Woudenberg (1999) concludes that European tourists overall are increasingly demanding a broader tourist product, which is based on 'multi-entertainment' rather than one sole activity (e.g. sunbathing, skiing). He also suggests that the inter-European market is declining in favour of external destinations. However, with an upgrade in the quality of services and accessibility, new destinations in CEE can expect a growth in their tourist numbers. So too, perhaps can islands like Cyprus and Malta, as there has been an upturn in Mediterranean tourism since the mid-1990s. However, the way in which they present themselves in a competitive marketplace may be a key factor in their future success.

In conclusion to this chapter, it is clear that there is an ongoing dilemma within the EU as to how far countries should promote their 'Europeanness' versus their national and regional identities, versus their international status as destinations of high quality. The shadows of imperialism and other forms of political and social oppression hang heavily over many countries, so they are forced to find ways of reconciling themselves to their past in the present. Many tourists are fascinated by the dissonant past and dark tourism (Lennon and Foley, 2000), therefore this is ironically a lucrative industry. However, no country wants to be associated purely with its legacy of brutality, therefore images of death or destruction need to be used sparingly and sensitively. On the other hand, a positive way forward may be to promote the cultures of diverse ethnic groups within a society, who may previously have been marginalized or persecuted (e.g. Jews, Roma), as well as those diasporic groups that form part of the legacy of Europe's colonial history. At a social level, this can help to raise political awareness and celebrate difference, and at a commercial level, it adds colour, vibrancy and uniqueness to a product. The out-migration of many populations from European countries (especially those from CEE) may represent an important external market in this respect, as many are interested in indigenous traditions.

Some destinations have a stronger brand image than others, especially those with major cultural and heritage cities. However, cynics might attribute the growth of tourism in such cases mainly to their location on budget airline routes. The short-break, weekend market is still growing, which is good news for destinations like Estonia, Latvia and Lithuania, countries that are perhaps less well-known outside the immediate region. Their potential for both cultural and rural tourism development is high, and they have the added bonus of being labelled 'relatively undiscovered'. Nevertheless, the establishment of a clear and distinctive brand image is still a challenge in a competitive market. Some cities are moving towards the model that has been established in many Western countries (e.g. London, Barcelona, Rotterdam) whereby extensive regeneration strategies are being implemented. These are increasingly taking into consideration the notion of the 'experience economy', the 'multi-entertainment' concept, and the economic potential of the creative industries. Emphasis is placed on a combination of activities, many of which are experiential, temporary, but with a lasting legacy for the city (e.g. festivals and mega-events). More permanent 'flagship' projects (e.g. art galleries, conference centres) are being developed as catalysts for the regeneration of whole areas of cities, eventually providing a boon to tourism.

Rather than putting themselves in the position of playing an endless game of 'catch-up' with the West, many new accession destinations are searching for their own innovative and creative approaches to tourism development. In many cases, they can promote what is unique to them (e.g. more traditional and 'authentic' forms of rural and indigenous cultural tourism). They can capitalize on their history and heritage, even if it is of a dissonant nature. Whether it is seaside or spa-based, the wellness tourism market is growing exponentially, and accession countries can revive and promote the facilities for which they have always been famous. In addition, they can identify what is new and vibrant within contemporary culture and the arts, providing unique experiences for visitors. With an upgraded infrastructure and an improvement to service quality, it will probably not be long before the declining destinations of Western Europe are looking eastwards for inspiration.

References

Cline, A. (2003) Czech Republic: most atheist country in Europe? *About*, 20 July. Available at: http:// atheism.about.com/b/a/009710.htm

Commission of the European Communities (2001) *Working Together for the Future of European Tourism.* Brussels: Commission Communication to the Council, the European Parliament, the Economic and Social Committee and the Committee of the Regions.

Council of Europe (1994) *Texts Concerning Culture at European Community Level.* Strasbourg: General Secretariat.

Encarta Encyclopaedia Online (2005) Poland. *Encarta Encyclopaedia Online.* Available at: http://encarta. msn.com/encyclopedia_761559758/Poland.html

EU Business (2005) Brits, Hungarians worst linguists in Europe. *EU Business*, 26 September. Available at: http://www.eubusiness.com/Living_in_EU/050926162418.tfu4we41

Farkas, B. (2005) Panel Debate. Session at The Readiness of Hungarian Society for European Unification Conference, Budapest, 6 April.

Florida, R. (2003) *The Rise of the Creative Class: and How it's Transforming Work, Leisure, Community and Everyday Life*. Washington, DC: Basic Books.

Giddens, A. (1998). *The Third Way: Renewal of Social Democracy*. Cambridge: Polity Press.

Javrova, Z. (2005) European integration is hard work. Presentation at Europe: Challenges, Examples and Opportunities: The European Union Approach to Culture, Euclid Seminar Series, London, 7 March.

Lennon, J. and Foley, M. (2000) *Dark Tourism: the Attraction of Death and Disaster*. London: Thomson.

MacNeill, S.K. (2005) *The Problems with the Euro: an Analysis from a Monetary and German Perspective*. London: The Monday Club. Available at: http://www.monies.cc/publications/euro.htm

Mehring, J. (2005) Central Europe: what's delaying the Euro? *BusinessWeek Online*. Available at: http://www.businessweek.com/magazine/content/05_39/b3952040.htm

Mihailovic, S.Q. and Strachwitz, R.G. (2004) *Heritage and the Building of Europe*. Berlin: Maecenata Verlag.

Pine, B.J. and Gilmore, J.H. (1999) *The Experience Economy*. Harvard, Massachusetts: Harvard University Press.

Rátz, T. (2004) *European Tourism*. Budapest: Kodolanyi Janos University College, p. 122.

Richards, G. (ed.) (2001) *Cultural Attractions and European Tourism*. Wallingford, UK: CAB International.

Richards, G. and Onderwater, L. (eds) (1998) *Towards a European Body of Knowledge for Tourism: Perspectives and Proposals*. Tilburg: ATLAS.

Richards, G. and Raymond, C. (2000) *Creative Tourism*. Tilburg: ATLAS News, No. 23.

Schadler, S., Drummond, P., Kuijs, L., Murgasova, Z. and van Elkan, R. (2005) *Adopting the Euro in Central Europe: Challenges of the Next Step in European Integration*. Washington, DC: International Monetary Fund Occasional Paper 234. Available at: http://www.imf.org/external/pubs/nft/op/234/op234.pdf

Spiegel Online (2005) Troubles for Europe: Who wants the EU? *Der Spiegel*, 9 May. Available at: http://service.spiegel.de/cache/international/spiegel/0,1518,355485,00.html

Steele, J. (2005) Poland's disenchanted killed off 'New Europe'. *The Guardian*, 28 October. Available at: http://www.guardian.co.uk/Columnists/Column/0,1602405,00.html

Thomas, M. (1998) A Transition Debate? *Aesop News Online*. Available at: http://www.brookes.ac.uk/other/aesop/features.htm

Tsenkova, S. (2004) Managing change in post-communist cities. Paper presented at conference *Winds of Societal Change: Remaking Post-Communist Cities*, University of Illinois, Chicago, 18–19 June 2004. Available at: http://www.reec.uiuc.edu/events/FisherForum/FisherForum2004/Tsenkova.pdf

Tyrell, B. and Mai, R. (2001) *Leisure 2010 – Experience Tomorrow*. Henley, UK: Jones Lang LaSalle.

van Woudenberg, G. (1999) *Outbound Travel and Tourism Patterns Among Europeans: Trends and Forecasts Until 2005*. The Hague: Royal Dutch Touring Club ANWB.

Wallerstein, I. (2000) Cultures in Conflict? Who are We? Who are the Others? Y.K. Pao Distinguished Chair Lecture, Center for Cultural Studies, University of Science and Technology, Hong Kong, 20 September 2000.

4 Tourism and the New Europe: Views from Beyond Europe

C. Michael Hall

The enlargement of the European Union through the accession of new member states is an event of global consequence for tourism, even though many of the impacts will likely be indirect and may also take many years to become apparent. From an external perspective, one of the most important points that can be made is that the latest accession of states to the EU follows a succession of 'New Europes'. Each time a country or group of countries has joined the EU or its predecessors there has been a shift in governance, policy settings and activities across a wide range of policy areas, many of which have directly and indirectly affected tourism not just in Europe but throughout the world.

One of the main areas, for example, in which bilateral and multilateral change has occurred in relation to EU expansion is with respect to international trade in products and services. Historically, international trade relations 'shift' for existing trading partners of accession countries upon joining the EU because of the priorities given to the members of the European Union or its predecessors and the creation of new bilateral and multilateral trading conditions. For example, the emergence of a 'crisis' in the agricultural economies of Australia and New Zealand is often traced back to the United Kingdom joining Europe in 1973 and the subsequent loss of preferential trade arrangements for those countries. Such shifts in trade often have far-reaching and

unexpected implications – in the case of the crisis in Australian and New Zealand agriculture, for example, the development of rural tourism opportunities as a response to problems of economic restructuring.

However, each 'new Europe' constitutes not just a shift in trade, but also a change in international relations, regulation and governance, although, clearly, trade is a significant component of such relations. Just as importantly, the latest EU enlargement was the largest in terms of population and created the world's largest market by economic output. This has been viewed as positive by international tourism bodies such as the World Travel and Tourism Council and the World Tourism Organization, although typically without any critical evaluation of the implications for non-EU countries. Indeed, within Europe itself there is arguably little interest outside of the tourism policy community as to the impacts of accession on tourism, and even less on the international community (e.g. Verheugen, 2003).

This chapter seeks to place the implications of the latest European enlargement into a wider international context. However, as the European Commission (2004) itself has observed, 'Any discussion of the EU's recent enlargement, as well as those still to come, risks "expanding to fill the available space"'. Nevertheless, some observations may perhaps be reasonably made, even if only to emphasize how little attention has been given in policy circles to the implications of EU enlargement. Focus is placed upon potential impacts with respect to changes in tourism flows, but, just as significantly, attention is given to broader policy implications of enlargement for cognate policy areas such as the environment and development. This approach is regarded as particularly important given the lack of a clear EU policy with respect to tourism although there exists a large number of policy areas that, though not tourism specific, nevertheless have a substantial affect on tourism (Hall, 2000).

Tourism and Enlargement: Trade

In terms of international trade much of the attention given to EU enlargement both inside and outside of the EU has been given to trade in commodities rather than trade in services. For example, in a speech to Doshisha University in Japan, the leader of the EU delegation to Japan, Bernhard Zepter argued that:

> Japanese companies will benefit in the enlarged EU from a single set of trade rules, a single tariff, and a single set of administrative procedures that will apply across the whole of the Single Market. This will simplify dealings for Japanese firms doing business with the EU. For trade in industrial goods, the new Member States will now adopt the Common Customs Tariff. This means on average a significant decrease in the tariffs applied. The average weighted industrial tariffs of the acceding countries decrease from around 9% on average to the 3.6% average applied by the EU. Japanese businesses will significantly benefit from extensively lower tariffs in their trade with new Member States as a result of enlargement.
> (Zepter, 2004)

In addition to trade in manufactured goods, in the United States and many other nations with substantial agricultural sectors considerable attention has also been given to implications for agricultural trade, particularly the Common Agricultural Policy (Kokubo, 2001; Crane, 2003). Although the CAP may have some implications for farm-based tourism because of the extent to which farm tourism subsidies and grants could be interpreted as a form of agricultural subsidy (Hall, 2000), the longer-term implications of the CAP for international tourism lie in the extent to which changes in international trade regimes influence economic growth in affected nations and therefore changes in personal consumption that may then be used to purchase tourism services. Similarly, EU accession may have further longer-term implications for tourism in terms of the growth of the Euro zone and therefore future exchange rates that are a major determinant in international travel flows, while an additional longer-term effect will be growth of the new EU members as potential source markets for both EU and non-EU destinations.

For students of tourism the unfortunate reality is that, in general assessments of economic, social and political implications of enlargement for the EU, tourism does not usually figure as a major, or even minor concern. This is even the situation with respect to government reports from existing EU members. For example, the UK Department of Trade and Industry (2004) failed to mention tourism or travel in terms of trade and investment potential of EU enlargement. Arguably, such a situation is somewhat surprising given the supposed importance of tourism for national and regional economies and for employment. Indeed, a survey conducted by the Economist Intelligence Unit (2003) on the business implications of EU enlargement, tourism was regarded as the biggest winner in terms of EU enlargement in the accession countries although the sector was not seen in such a favourable light for existing EU members. Nevertheless, the implications of enlargement for tourism remained the concern of the tourism policy community only and not other policy areas.

Consideration of changed patterns of economic development were central to the World Travel and Tourism Council's (WTTC) (2004) assessment of the implications of EU enlargement for tourism. According to the WTTC, the ten new member states, combined, stand to generate an additional €46bn of travel and tourism GDP and 3 million jobs by achieving average EU results. Nevertheless, forecasts of such growth will likely require shifts in both investment flows and tourism mobility in order to be achieved. Any such changes will occur both within the enlarged EU as well as in the transfer of tourists and capital from locations outside of the EU to within the new EU.

Some attention has been given to the potential implications in changes in tourism demand and corresponding effects at the macroeconomic and inter-sectoral levels (Blake *et al.*, 2003; Cochard, 2003; Lohmann, 2004). For example, the Executive Director of the European Tour Operators Association (ETOA), Tom Jenkins, warned that EU VAT laws will make accession countries a more expensive destination and that it may force tour operators who bring in tourists from outside the EU offshore as they were signing up for 'a taxation regime that will make their destinations less competitive', noting that, in general, travel to the EU accession countries will become more expensive to visitors from EU countries and to visitors from outside the EU who travel with a tour operator based within the EU (Enlargement Weekly, 2004). Unfortunately, there has been little such empirical examination of the implications of these transfers outside of the EU with the exception of highly tourism-dependent states, such as those of the Caribbean (Dunlop, 2003; Greenaway and Milner, 2004).

With respect to the Caribbean (CARICOM) Greenaway and Milner (2004, p. 75) suggest that 'The impact of longer term income effects on export opportunities is likely to be particularly important in the case of services exports. The relatively high income elasticity of demand for many services, including tourism, means that the indirect effects of EU enlargement are likely to increase tourism demand in the CARICOM from the new members of the EU.' However, it should be noted that the validity of these findings requires recognition of the need to solve broader trade issues, such as aviation access between the new EU members and the Caribbean, as well as substitutability of destinations as a potentially limiting factor in EU enlargement-induced tourism growth.

With respect to changes in travel flows, therefore, all one can accurately say is that there will certainly be changed patterns in travel flows and investment in tourism, including second homes, as a result of the EU accession, but that the extent of such changes is almost impossible to generalize outside of specific cases (e.g. see Coles, 2005). Nevertheless, the EU accession not only opens up potentially new destinations, but also opportunities for destination substitution and this, along with other contemporary

factors influencing international tourism flows such as the price of oil, is likely to lead to substantial turbulence in intra- and inter-European travel flows in coming years. However, although accession will have some direct affects on tourism, there are clearly also potentially significant indirect implications for international tourism trade as a result of new pressures being brought to bear on EU policy-making.

Changes in EU Policy-making

The accession of ten new members to the EU on 1 May 2004 is widely regarded as sealing the end of the division of the continent in the post-World War II period. Enlargement has been part of the EU success and has been a factor in further integration. However, with the latest accession the differences in per capita income between old and new members arguably make integration more difficult than ever before, not just in economic terms, but also in the policy settings that will be required with respect to closing economic and social divisions (Brimmer and Fröhlich, 2005). Indeed, difficulties with integration have already become apparent since accession, with substantial differences over the setting of the EU budget and discord over policy direction especially with respect to the relative emphasis given to knowledge-based economic development versus support for the Common Agricultural Policy (CAP) (Sciolino, 2005; The Age, 2005). Although such disputes have not yet impacted on tourism mobility, arguably they have had some implications for labour mobility. The prime ministers of both Sweden and the United Kingdom have raised concerns regarding the potential western movement of cheap labour from the accession countries and it is conceivable that such political comments may yet have impacts on European mobility, including tourism.

Although institutional adjustments following the progress of the Constitutional Treaty were still to be determined at the time of writing, as was the long-term fate of the Treaty (Sciolino, 2005), it was expected that substantial pressures would be placed upon EU policies by differences between members (Etzioni, 2005). Such divergencies cut across a number of policy axes and should not just be seen in terms of 'Old Europe' versus 'New Europe', as significant as such differences might be. Fröhlich (2005, p. 4), for example, identifies four potential sources of policy conflict:

- the economic disparity between members that provides pressure on regional policy and financial redistribution;
- the competition between old and new members regarding the implementation of reforms;
- the implications of the new geographic scope of the EU in terms of foreign and security policy, particularly with respect to its current and prospective European and Asian borders; and
- the effects of 'the structural diversity reinforcing the differences between "heavyweights" and "lightweights" in terms of population, society and economy impeding the development of a collective identity'.

After enlargement, all the problems have only become more difficult. More members with a veto power in certain policy fields will make a decision more difficult to reach and strengthen the tendency to reach minimalist decisions. And more members mean more possibilities for coalition building and pork barreling, further hindering reform.

(Fröhlich, 2005, p. 5)

Although the EU does not currently define tourism as a specific policy area, there are a number of policy areas that will affect international tourism in the short and long term. These include mobility, trade negotiations and development and the environment.

One of the most significant aspects of EU policy is that of encouraging the free mobility of people within the EU. This ease of travel is significant not only in terms of labour and educational mobility (see Chapter 5), but also has implications for leisure tourism. Concerns have been expressed in some old EU countries concerning the impacts of the provision allowing for the free movement of people within the EU in terms of the migration of cheap labour from the accession countries, and its potential impact on domestic employment. From an external perspective, the need to tighten the external borders of the Union is an inevitable counterpart to the removal of internal barriers to the flow of goods and people within the Union. With internal border controls dismantled, crossing the external borders of the Union to enter one member state means, in effect, legal entry into all member states of the Union (albeit with the internal differentiation between within and outside the Schengen zone). Governments in EU capitals are therefore insisting that their fellow EU members control their external borders (Jones, 2003; Brimmer and Fröhlich, 2005). As van Oudanaren (2003, p. 37) observes:

Fear of terrorism after September 11 has heightened these concerns, as have high-profile cases of human trafficking, illegal drug and weapons smuggling, and spillover from organized crime in the Newly Independent States (NIS) and the Balkans.

Such changes to cross-border movement, mobility and security measures can have an impact on tourism. For example, it has been suggested that tourists from the Arabian Gulf have been discouraged from visiting some new member states and candidate countries, such as Turkey, by enlargement-related rule changes. *Enlargement Weekly* (2004) reported that Turkey has been affected by new requirements for visas which visitors from the Gulf Cooperation Council countries could previously obtain on arrival, but which are now required prior to departure. Turkey has been pressured on this as part of the efforts to protect European borders. In the case of border control, it may be suggested that as a result of accession agreements the new members have had no real option but to adopt existing policy settings. It is likely that in the present policy environment in which security has such a high priority there will be little change in the foreseeable future. However, it seems likely that in other cognate policy areas the accession countries are likely to wield significant influence.

International trade negotiations will be substantially affected by EU enlargement. For example, with respect to the World Tourism Organization's proposed annexe on tourism to the General Agreement on Trade in Services (GATS). The European Communities (EC) (S/CSS/W/5 of 28 September 2000) was the only World Trade Organization member to formally submit a reaction to the proposed annexe. Although the EC stated its support for 'the main intentions' of the proposal, it did not explicitly endorse the establishment of a new Tourism

Annexe to the GATS. Instead, the EC proposed that the list of sectors proposed to be included in the annexe were too broad, as well as also noting that air transport services were currently excluded from the GATS negotiations, and that some of the issues raised by the sponsors could be better addressed in the World Trade Organization's Working Party on Domestic Regulation (WPDR) (Dunlop, 2003).

Interestingly, Dunlop (2003, p. 10) also noted that the EC (along with the United States) suggested that sustainable development needed to be considered within the annexe, with the EC stressing 'the importance of access to high-quality environmental services – a key offensive negotiating interest for the EC (and US) in the GATS negotiations' which would have significant impacts in a wide range of countries with respect to tourism trade with the EU. In addition, the EC sought to use any annexe to eliminate restrictions on foreign direct investment in tourism. Although such measures are likely to favour some of the wealthier countries in the EU it is also conceivable that if such measures were adopted they may also be utilized by accession countries in investing in other countries, particularly to their east, as well as attracting non-EU foreign investment in the accession countries themselves.

In addition to multilateral trade negotiations, an enlarged EU also has implications for bilateral relations with respect to tourism trade (Greenaway and Milner, 2004). For example, Caribbean (CARIFORUM) nations regard themselves as being at a disadvantage in gaining access to the distribution channels that place tourism products on the EU markets (e.g. tour operators, airlines, computer reservation systems) (Dunlop, 2003). In particular, the substantial costs of compliance with EU standards – in the form of national regulations implementing the EU Package Travel Directive 43 – are a major issue for CARIFORUM hoteliers. For example, some CARIFORUM properties have to introduce elaborate evacuation systems more suited to high-rise buildings when they have only two or three floors. Dunlop (2003, p. 34) also noted that under the Directive the interests of European consumers received special attention in contrast with the suppliers of tourism products and services such as CARIFORUM hoteliers – were not considered within the scope of the Directive. For example, there are no provisions to

mitigate the impact on tourism suppliers in the event that a European tour operator or travel agent becomes insolvent.

The extent to which accession countries may serve to influence bilateral relations in tourism is unknown, but previous history of EU trade negotiations including CAP would tend to suggest that the accession countries, as well as the EU as a whole, would not do anything to harm their own self-interest despite any rhetoric surrounding free trade or development.

Issues of trade also affect tourism flows between the EU and the United States. Although the transatlantic market is regarded as the 'leading edge of globalization', the service sector is regarded as demonstrating substantial potential for further growth following removal of internal barriers (Brimmer and Fröhlich, 2005; Hamilton and Quinland, 2005a). For example, although Hamilton and Quinland (2005b) fail to acknowledge the role of tourism as a service sector, Robyn et al. (2005) highlight the potential for growth in transatlantic tourist flows as a result of liberalization of transatlantic aviation, and argue that a single, open transatlantic market for air transport services could potentially increase annual passenger traffic by between 4.1m and 11.0m passengers on transatlantic routes, and between 13.6m and 35.7m on intra-EU routes. Such a situation would provide for a total increase of 17.7–46.7m passengers per year, an increase of 9–24% in total transatlantic travel, and 5–14% in intra-EU travel.

According to Robyn et al. (2005) 'consumer welfare' could increase by about €5.2bn annually, with transatlantic traffic accounting for just over half of that increase. They argue that the greatest share (up to €3.8bn annually) would come from gains to consumers that would not involve any reduction in airline profits and that the increased airline revenue would lead to additional economic output in 'directly related' industries ranging from €3.6bn to €8.1bn a year. However, these estimates of economic impact exclude the potential effects in the leisure and tourism industries and also exclude the ten new EU members, and are therefore regarded as conservative.

Nevertheless, potential changes in the transatlantic aviation market cannot be seen in isolation and are also likely to be related to other policy issues including European and

US conflict over the extent of subsidies to Airbus and Boeing (Aboulifia, 2005), as well as approaches towards the management of climate change (Egenhofer, 2005). Indeed, the development of an open transatlantic aviation market is often seen as a policy failure because of the extent to which authority for external aviation policy has been contested in the EU between the Commission and member states (European Commission, 2004). The DG External Relations of the European Commission itself observes that difficulties in developing a liberal aviation market

> highlights how liberalisation usually creates losers as well as winners and how likely losers will oppose it. Such opposition is particularly powerful when legislative changes are required to liberalise markets. . . intra-EU cooperation can be difficult and the Commission cannot always deliver the member states.
> (European Commission, 2004, p. 30)

Clearly, the situation is only likely to become more problematic given the accession of ten new members to the EU, each with their own series of intergovernmental aviation agreements.

The EU also has substantial international development programmes that affect tourism in a number of ways, indirectly through infrastructure development programmes (e.g. transport) and conservation assistance (Morgera and Durán, 2004) and directly through aid for tourism-specific projects (e.g. funding for the South Pacific Tourism Organization). EU development non-government organizations (NGOs) believe that enlargement of the EU is occurring simultaneously with the subordination of development to a narrow foreign policy agenda focused on security and migration issues (Press, 2003). As Press (p. 1) observes:

> Negotiations for membership to date have focused almost completely on trade and the compliance of the accession countries' political and public institutions with those of the EU. Until very recently there has been little attention to development co-operation yet this is a crucial activity of the EU in the context of its broader external relations agenda.

Implications for development policy may therefore be substantial given that the accession countries may be more interested in continuing to receive transfers of funds that had been available to them previously under aid programmes, while development aid and cooperation policies have historically also received a low priority. Indeed, Press (2003, p. 5) concludes: 'Enlargement in the short-term will have an adverse affect on the quantity and quality of EU aid programmes and funding opportunities'.

Conclusions

As noted at the outset, it is difficult to describe the potential wider implications of accession on tourism in the broader international sphere with any clarity. Arguably, the general difficulties in policy and budgetary decision-making that affected the EU in 2005 were likely to be a foretaste of some of the decision-making issues confronting the enlarged EU. Although such issues are not tourism-specific, they will affect tourism-related policies not only in the EU, but also internationally and particularly with respect to border controls, international trade agreements and aid programmes. Such a situation will not diminish the potential international role of the EU although it will make policy direction more confusing from an external perspective.

Indeed, a central theme of this chapter has been that specific EU policies for tourism are likely to be of far less significance for international tourism flows and tourism development than understanding the policies that affect tourism, arguably something that the small tourism policy community in either the EU or internationally often fails to recognize. Instead, the attitudes of the accession countries and of the EU itself towards trade in services, including aviation and transport, are likely to be as significant for international tourism trade and tourism policy as the CAP is for national agricultural policies. In addition, the EU attitude toward environmental agreements, including the Kyoto protocol, is also likely to have significant long-term impacts on international travel flows because of their potential affects on the cost of travel.

In both the immediate and longer term, therefore, EU enlargement will have implications for tourism beyond the EU borders in the same way that previous enlargements have also had implications in terms of changes in travel flows, investment patterns and inter-sectoral effects both inside and outside of tourism. The relative inertia of travel flows will mean that shifts in travel patterns will be relatively gradual though nevertheless significant for both new and substitutable destinations. Of far greater longer-term significance for tourism will be the role of the enlarged EU, with its new set of policy parameters, in the establishment of new regulatory regimes for human mobility and trade in services that will impact not only on those nations that trade in tourism with the EU, but also on global governance structures for tourism. And, although European colleagues may not wish to hear this conclusion, it is likely that, as noted above, the present self-serving policies of the EU which characterize its approach to issues such as agriculture, will continue to play a major part in the development of the governance architecture for international tourism.

References

Aboulifia, R. (2005) Commercial aerospace and the transatlantic economy. In: Hamilton, D. and Quinland, J. (eds) *Deep Integration: How Transatlantic Markets are Leading Globalization.* Washington, D.C./Brussels: Brookings Institutions and Centre for Transatlantic Relations/Centre for European Policy Studies, pp. 74–90.

Blake, A., Sinclair, M.T. and Sugiyarto, G. (2003) *Tourism and EU Accession in Malta and Cyprus.* Nottingham, UK: Nottingham University Business School, Christel De Haan Tourism and Travel Research Institute, Working Paper 2003/7.

Brimmer, E. and Fröhlich, S. (eds) (2005) *The Strategic Implications of European Union Enlargement.* Philadelphia, Pennsylvania: Center for Transatlantic Relations, Johns Hopkins University–SAIS.

Cochard, S. (2003) *Le Tourisme dans la Zone Élargissement.* Paris: Ministère de l'Economie, des Finances et de l'Industrie – Direction des Relations Economiques Extérieures.

Coles, T. (2005) *Telling tales of tourism: mobility, media and citizenship in the 2004 EU enlargement.* Paper presented at Mobilities and Tourism: The End of Tourism Conference, University of Brighton, Eastbourne, UK, 23–24, June 2005.

Crane, K. (2003) *EU Enlargement: Implications for US Trade and International Financial Policies.* American Institute for Contemporary German Studies (AICGS), Meeting Report 276, Washington, DC.

Department of Trade and Industry (2004) *The Trade and Investment Implications of EU Enlargement.* London: Department of Trade and Industry.

Dunlop, A. (2003) *Tourism Services Negotiation Issues: Implications for Cariform Countries.* Barbados: Caribbean Regional Negotiating Machinery.

Frölich, S. (2005) The EU after the big bang. In: Brimmer, E. and Fröhlich, S. (eds) *The Strategic Implications of European Union Enlargement.* Philadelphia, Pennsylvania: Center for Transatlantic Relations, Johns Hopkins University–SAIS, pp. 3–25.

Economist Intelligence Unit (2003) *The Business Implications of EU Enlargement: an Executive Survey in Co-operation with Accenture.* London: Economist Intelligence Unit.

Egenhofer, C. (2005) Climate change: could a transatlantic greenhouse gas emissions market work? In: Hamilton, D. and Quinland, J. (eds) *Deep Integration: How Transatlantic Markets are Leading Globalization.* Washington, D.C./Brussels: Brookings Institutions and Centre for Transatlantic Relations/Centre for European Policy Studies, pp. 204–220.

Enlargement Weekly (2004) Enlargement focus on tourism. *Enlargement Weekly* 2, June 2004. Available at: http://europa.eu.int/comm/enlargement/docs/newsletter/weekly_020604.htm

Etzioni, A. (2005) *How to Build a European Community.* Washington, DC.: The Brookings Institution, US–Europe Analysis Series.

European Commission (2004) *Review of the Framework for Relations Between the European Union and the United States.* Brussels: European Commission, Directorate General External Relations Relations Unit C1 – Relations with the United States and Canada, Final Report, Tender OJ 2004/S 83-070340, p. 59.

Greenaway, D. and Milner, C. (2004) *Implications of European Enlargement for CARICOM Countries.* Barbados: Caribbean Regional Negotiating Machinery: Report of a Policy Study under the Caribbean Regional Negotiating Machinery (RNM) and InterAmerican Development Bank (IDB) Regional Technical Cooperation Project [ATN/JF/SF-6158-RG].

Hall, C.M. (2000) *Tourism Planning.* Harlow: Prentice-Hall.

Hamilton, D. and Quinland, J. (eds) (2005a) *Deep Integration: How Transatlantic Markets are Leading Globalization*. Washington, DC/Brussels: Brookings Institutions and Centre for Transatlantic Relations/ Centre for European Policy Studies.

Hamilton, D. and Quinland, J. (2005b) Services in the transatlantic economy. In: Hamilton, D. and Quinland, J. (eds) *Deep Integration: How Transatlantic Markets are Leading Globalization*. Washington, DC/Brussels: Brookings Institutions and Centre for Transatlantic Relations / Centre for European Policy Studies, pp. 39–49.

Jones, S. (2003) EU enlargement: implications for EU and multilateral export controls. *The Nonproliferation Review*, Summer, 80–89.

Kokubo, Y. (2001) *The EU Enlargement: its Implications for Europe and Asia*. Shizuoka, Japan: University of Shizuoka, Graduate School of International Relations, Working Paper #01-02.

Lohmann, M. (2004) *New Demand Factors in Tourism*. Kiel: Institut für Tourismus- und Bäderforschung in Nordeuropa.

Morgera, E. and Durán, G.M. (2004) Enlargement and EU development policy: an environmental perspective. *Review of European Community and International Environmental Law* 13(2), 152–163.

Press, M. (2003) *EU Enlargement: Implications and Opportunities for EU Development Cooperation*. London: BOND Development Policy Briefing.

Robyn, D., Reitzes, J. and Moselle, B. (2005) The economic impact of a US–EU open aviation area. In: Hamilton, D. and Quinland, J. (eds) *Deep Integration: How Transatlantic Markets are Leading Globalization*. Washington, DC./Brussels: Brookings Institutions and Centre for Transatlantic Relations/ Centre for European Policy Studies, pp. 50–73.

Sciolino, E. (2005) EU constitution in 'too hard' basket. *The Age*, 18 June.

The Age (2005) EU summit collapses. *The Age* 18 June.

van Oudanaren, J. (2003) *The Changing Face of Europe: EU Enlargement and Implications for Trans-Atlantic Relations*. Washington, DC.: American Institute for Contemporary German Studies (AICGS) Policy Report No. 6.

Verheugen, G. (2003) *Keynote Speech: Symposium EU Enlargement: Prospects, Challenges and Implications*. Tokyo: Speech at Waseda University, Tokyo 23 September 2003. Available at: http://jpn.cec.eu.int/home/speech_en_speechobj158.php

World Travel and Tourism Council (WTTC) (2004) *Positions: Welcoming the New EU Member States with Jobs & Growth: a Practical Manifesto from the Travel & Tourism Private Sector*. London: WTTC.

Zepter, B. (2004) *EU Enlargement and its Economic and Business Implications*. Kyoto: Speech at Doshisha University, 8 May 2004. Available at: http://jpn.cec.eu.int/home/speech_en_speechobj294.php

5 Tourism Education in the New Europe

Greg Richards

Introduction

Since the ATLAS conference on 'Tourism Education in Central and Eastern Europe' was held in Poland in 1995, much has changed in the landscape of tourism education, both in the new European Union (EU) member states and the long established members. This chapter reviews some of these changes, and compares the situation today with that in 1995. The analysis is based on a review of tourism courses and educational data in the EU, as well as expert opinions from ATLAS members.

In spite of the significant changes that have taken place in the fields of tourism and tourism education in the 'New Europe' in recent years, there has been relatively little attention paid to tourism education in the region. The tourism education bibliography compiled by Tribe (2005) contains almost 300 references pertaining to tourism education in different areas of the world. Of these, only 22 cover the EU enlargement countries, and of these 12 come from one single publication – the proceedings of the ATLAS conference held in Poland in 1995 (Richards, 1996a). However, this also seems to reflect a broader decline in interest in Central and Eastern Europe as a focus of tourism research since the novelty value has worn off (Clarke *et al.*, 2001) and as funds for 'knowledge transfer' projects have dried up.

The majority of the previous research on tourism education in the region has been concerned with the content of the tourism curriculum. Such studies have also tended to be concentrated in a few countries, notably Poland (Golembski, 1991; Airey, 1994, 1999) and Croatia (Vukonic, 1995, 1996; Kivela 1997a, 1997b; Persic, 1998), which already had a well-developed system of tourism education during the Communist era.

This chapter attempts to bring the picture more up to date, with a review of tourism education in the former Communist states and Malta and Cyprus. It provides a review of some of the main trends in tourism education in the new Europe, concentrating particularly on the development of curricula, human resources and student exchange.

Significance and Implications of EU Enlargement for Tourism in Higher Education

The development of tourism education in Central Europe has been reflected in the growth in ATLAS membership in these regions. None of the European founder members of ATLAS in 1991 came from outside Western Europe, but membership in Central and Eastern Europe increased rapidly with the staging of the ATLAS conference in Poland in 1995. Today there are 22 ATLAS members in the new member states or in prospective accession countries.

There has been a significant expansion of tourism education in most of the countries in the New Europe. For example, in Romania there are now 15 universities (12 public and three private) offering tourism courses, compared with one before 1990 (Cristureanu, 1996). Up until 1994, Slovenia only had tourism education at vocational, post-secondary school level, in spite of tourism being one of the most important sectors of the economy. Today, there are three higher education institutions offering courses in tourism and hospitality.

The major driver for change in the former Communist states has of course been the transition to a market economy and increasing diversification and specialization of tourism products that this has stimulated. Specialization has also been stimulated by rising tourism demand and the growth in repeat visits to the region. However, more recently, as in the rest of the EU, curricula have had to be changed in line with EU guidelines, and the process of fitting courses into the Bologna Framework is now well under way in most of the new member states. Many of the former Communist states already started replacing their old higher education systems with the two-cycle Bachelor–Master system in the early 1990s. Today, most countries have adopted the European Credit Transfer System (ECTS) and are now introducing the diploma supplement as agreed under the Bologna Declaration of the EU (EURYDICE, 2005).

The extent of tourism education provision, just as in the rest of Europe, varies considerably from one country to another. Historic factors and the relative importance of tourism in the national economy still have a considerable influence. The following section considers some of the patterns of tourism curricula in the former Communist states and then in Cyprus and Malta.

Curricula

Former communist states

In the transition from Communism in the early 1990s, the countries of Central and Eastern Europe were mainly concerned with replacing education systems designed for a command economy with a market-based system. It was not surprising, therefore, that the main areas of discussion at the 1995 ATLAS conference revolved around the need for marketing and management education, and the transfer of 'know-how' from West to East.

As noted in the proceedings of the 1995 ATLAS conference:

> There is a pressing need to improve and extend the provision of tourism education and training in Central and Eastern Europe, in order to improve and upgrade the quality and effectiveness of tourism services. Although a well-developed system of tourism education existed in many countries during the Communist period, the focus of tourism education was often on spatial planning or economics, and did not have the management focus so common in tourism education elsewhere.
>
> (Richards, 1996a: 12)

In Poland, for example, Jung and Mierzejewska (1996, p. 67) noted the following weaknesses in Polish curricula:

> Higher tourism education in Poland still largely suffers from a clear lack of focus. In tradition, it was activity-orientated (preparation for 'animators' of social and qualified tourism), spatially-orientated (preparation of spatial planners specialised in tourism and recreation . . .) or functionally-orientated (administrators of state-owned hotels and travel agencies).

Thanks to an extensive process of educational development, however, these days basic curricula in the new member states do not differ much from those in the rest of the EU. By and large, management and marketing form important elements of tourism courses, which tend to be based on a business studies or management core. For example, in Slovenia, Turistica College in the resort town of Portoroz offers a BA in tourism with a business core and a strong language element. Students can take up to three languages and have units in management, finance, HRM and marketing, as well as tourism units in subjects such as tourism geography, tourism economics and event management (see Table 5.1).

However, some differences are observable. For example, there is a much stronger linkage

Table 5.1. University of Primorska,
Turistica – College of Tourism, Portoroz,
Turistica BA Tourism course.

Year One
Introduction to Tourism
Information Systems and Statistics
Geography of Tourism
Cultural Heritage
Sociology and Psychology of Leisure
Management
Foreign Language 1
Foreign Language 2
Foreign Language 3 (optional subject)
Professional Training

Year Two
Management Accounting and Business Finance
Human Resource Management
Business Operations of Tourism Enterprises
Hygiene and Sanitation
Sustainable Development Management
Tourism Law
Foreign Language 1
Foreign Language 2
Foreign Language 3 (optional subject)
Professional Training

Year Three
Tourism Economics
Marketing
Event Management
Selected Topics in Tourism
Gastronomy
Foreign Language 1
Practical Training
Options
Hotel Management and Operations
Food and Beverage Management
Travel Agency Management

Source: Lazanski, 2004, personal communication.

between tourism and hotel and catering and
tourism and sport than is usually found elsewhere. This is a legacy of a well-developed
system of hotel and catering schools and the
development of tourism courses in sports
academies. But as Rátz (1997) has pointed out,
many of the tourism courses in countries such
as Hungary have now been adapted to the
needs of the international tourism industry. In
general terms this has meant extending the
areas of management covered in the curriculum, adding marketing as a specific subject and

creating specialist modules such as ecotourism,
cultural tourism and leisure management.

Convergence with western European models
is also being encouraged by the Bologna Process. For example, in Hungary colleges have
been offering Bachelor programmes of 3–4 years,
and universities one-tier Masters programmes of
5 years. Now two-tier programmes are being
introduced of the 3+2 model (5 years, 300
credits) (Tauch and Rauhvargers, 2002).

The role of English is also becoming more
important in the tourism curriculum, partly as a
result of the needs of the tourism industry, and
partly because of the SOCRATES programme.
Swire (2003), for example, argues that English
courses are growing because many universities
have contracts with student-exchange schemes,
such as the SOCRATES-ERASMUS programme,
which brings a lot of money into the Czech
Republic from the European Union. Swire also
suggests that some students from non-English
speaking countries choose to take English
courses in the Czech Republic because they feel
their language skills are not good enough to
cope with courses in Britain or Ireland.

However, it seems that many of the students attracted to the 'New Europe' do not
always get the 'local' cultural experience they
bargained for. Zea Baca from Arizona lamented,
'I thought I would experience Czech culture
more, but I'm always speaking English. I wish
I could speak the language' (Swire, 2003).

This indicates that the exchange student
experience in countries such as the Czech
Republic is already fairly similar to that in
Western Europe, with a well-developed
'SOCRATES bubble' which isolates exchange
students from the local community and from
local students.

Malta and Cyprus

The situation in Malta and Cyprus is considerably different to those of the other recent
entrants. They already had fairly modern tourist
infrastructure and were more articulated with
international markets. Because of their relatively small size, however, systems of tourism
education were not particularly well developed.
Early school leaving is also a big problem, with
Malta having levels of continuing education

beyond 18 of only a third of that in the rest of Europe (Calleja, 2004).

The University of Malta runs a BA Tourism course, which has an intake of about 100 students. The University also assists the Malta Tourism Authority in providing courses for tourism staff, particularly tour guides and other 'front line' personnel. ITIS (International Tourism Institute) Malta is a branch of a Swiss institution which provides courses in tourism management. One of the current programmes of study (Higher Diploma in Hospitality Management) now enables graduates to join the degree course in tourism offered by the University of Malta. ITIS was recently benchmarked by the Department of Tourism against comparable institutions in the UK and Ireland.

In the Republic of Cyprus, the Higher Hotel Institute is the only public sector institution offering diploma courses in tourism. Bachelor and diploma degrees are offered by the private colleges on the island. In total, 23 private tertiary education institutions, colleges and institutes are registered with the Ministry of Education and Culture. The Frederick Institute of Technology offers a BA Travel, Tourism & Hotel Management course, and similar courses at other strong colleges on the island are now beginning to compete with the University of Cyprus, which recently incorporated the Higher Hotel Institute.

In general, the courses found in Malta and the Republic of Cyprus have a more vocational focus, which is perhaps not surprising given the relatively small size of the countries and the importance of tourism as an economic sector. There are also a large number of training courses run for the industry, often in collaboration between the tourist boards and educational institutions. For example, the Cyprus Tourism Organization is responsible for a Tourist Guides' School which offers a one-year course leading to the award of the Diploma of the Tourist Guide.

Educational Methodology

Educational methodologies are gradually changing to adjust to the new demands on tourism courses. For example, in Slovenia there are new teaching methods employed in vocational education, such as interactive lecture and small seminar discussion and assignments, selected guest speakers, selected videos and field trips. In Hungary, placements are also becoming an important part of tourism courses (Rátz, 1997).

Courses offered in English to cater for student exchanges are now becoming more common. For example, at Turistica, courses are offered in Current Topics in Tourism (9 ECTS); Event Management (5 ECTS); Travel Agency Management (9 ECTS) and Marketing (8 ECTS). It is interesting that the units offered in English are usually those with a more international flavour, which students could probably take in their home institutions as well. This echoes a fear expressed in the 1995 conference that 'Westernization' would reduce the amount of local content in the curriculum. The insistence of many institutions that exchange students take similar modules to those in their home programme in order to qualify for credits (or to avoid missing compulsory areas of the curriculum) probably adds to this trend.

The introduction of distance and open learning in most of the new member states has been slow, often due to difficulties in adapting to new learning methods.

Collaboration

The changing landscape of education in the new entrants is marked by a shift towards private sector provision and new models, particularly franchising. Many institutions in Western Europe and the US are taking advantage of the newly emerging educational markets in Central and Eastern Europe to spread their educational provision. Private institutions seem to be particularly important in such developments, as Dima (2003) notes:

> The emergence of private higher education in Central and Eastern Europe represented one of the most spectacular changes in the educational systems of the post-communist countries. These institutions came into being in the absence of a specific legal framework. After almost twelve years from its occurrence, the private sector reached almost 30% of the total level of student enrolments in countries like Romania, Poland or Estonia. The number of private education institutions surpasses in many countries the number of the public ones.

In the UK, almost 200 colleges of further education are involved in international programmes. Of these colleges, 133 are recruiting students to UK-based courses; 56 are delivering programmes in-country; 145 have non-commercial learning and quality improvement partnerships with overseas education institutions; and 72 are engaged in franchising abroad. Franchising is particularly important in Cyprus, where there are a number of private colleges that are now being turned into universities.

The Role of SOCRATES, ERASMUS and other Exchange Programmes

The ERASMUS programme, launched in 1987, is one of the most successful EU programmes in the field of education. In the past 18 years, a total of more than one million students have spent a period of study in another country under the ERASMUS scheme or its successor, SOCRATES.

As Fig. 5.1 shows, the growth in participation in the existing EU states was very steep

after the launch of the programme. Growth rates in participation by the new entrants have been slightly slower. The new and prospective entrants now account for 13% of student mobility, considerably less than their 18% share of the total population of the 30 SOCRATES participant countries. At the moment, students from the former communist bloc in particular face greater barriers to mobility, particularly in terms of low incomes.

Although individual students face barriers to mobility, there is a clear institutional desire to participate in exchange schemes. For example, while the 'take-up rate' or participation of eligible institutions participating in SOCRATES in the EU15 was 38% in 1999/2000, in the new participant countries this figure was 54%. The largest number of outbound students from the new member states going to Western Europe is generated by Poland (5400 in 2003) and the Czech Republic (3000), but even relatively small countries such as Lithuania (1000) are beginning to generate substantial outbound mobility. The lowest levels of participation are found in Malta (72) and Cyprus (91), probably reflecting their small population size.

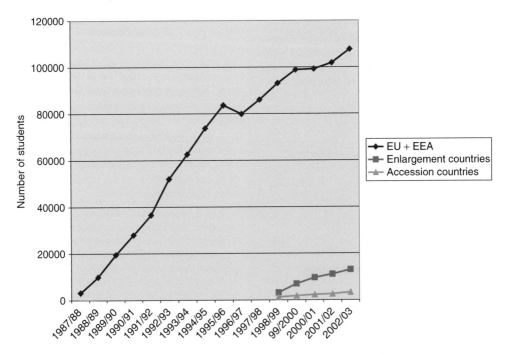

Fig. 5.1.   ERASMUS exchange student numbers 1987–2003. Source: EURYDICE, 2005.

However, there is a clear will to try and internationalize education in countries such as Malta, as the international orientation of study courses is also indispensable, especially for a small island like Malta. This includes foreign language segments as well as the widest possible integration of foreign teachers. Student mobility should be regarded as an integral part of study, and teacher mobility as a regular part of career development.

One of the impacts of the success of the SOCRATES programme has been a marked imbalance of incoming and outgoing flows in some countries. This is particularly marked in the UK, where the widespread knowledge of English among students in other countries makes it a popular destination. In 2001, for example, the UK sent out 8479 students, but received 17,632. Of the outbound UK students, only around 200 went to the new member states, whereas almost 1000 students came from these countries to the UK.

A large number of students from countries such as the Czech Republic, Poland and Hungary are also participating in working visa programmes. For example in 2003, the Czech student travel company GTS sent almost 1400 students abroad for work placements. The vast majority of these (over 1000) were to the USA and Canada, but the rest went to Western Europe, predominantly the UK. The distribution of these placements underlines the strong influence of English in the new member states.

Education and Human Resource Management

Many of the new member states already have significant high quality human resources. For example the 2002 European Commission report on Hungary states that:

> The quality of its labour force is an important asset in Hungarian competitiveness and growth. Hungary ranks high with regard to all major education indicators. The percentage of the 25–64-year-old population with university education, which indicates the share of highly-skilled human capital, is 14%. More importantly, the trend has been continuously rising since the start of transition. Enrolment in tertiary education at 72%, and the net entry

rate to university education at over 50%, point towards a continuation of this very favourable development.

(EC, 2005)

There are also signs that sectors such as tourism and other services are being targeted as particular growth prospects:

> Under its national development plan, the (Hungarian) government is trying to diversify further the pattern of specialisation towards services, and in particular tourism and business services, and also to attract foreign investors to underdeveloped regions.

(EC, 2005)

In spite of the overall high quality of human resources in general, however, the tourism industry remains problematic in terms of attracting high quality labour. For example, Szivas and Riley (1999) saw the Hungarian tourism industry as a sector which offered refuge to workers displaced from other sectors of the economy during economic transition. In contrast, in Bulgaria, Ghodsee (2001) found that

> . . . despite the seasonality of employment, jobs in the tourism sector are highly desirable and relatively well paid compared to other professions available to Bulgarians. This is particularly true for Bulgarian women who make up the vast majority of both the managers and operational staff. Additionally, tourism employs many educated and experienced women displaced from other shrinking sectors of the economy.

It is clear that the tourism labour market varies in each country. One of the main functions of tourism education and training, therefore, is to develop human resources that meet the needs of the tourism industry. In spite of many previous studies which show a poor level of coordination between tourism education and the human resource needs of the industry (e.g. Richards, 1996b; 2003), the development of tourism education is still generally related to the importance of tourism in the economy of the country concerned.

The importance of tourism as an employer varies considerably between the EU member states. In Western Europe, the proportion of the workforce employed in tourism is about 6% overall, but higher levels are found in countries such as Spain and Greece where there is relatively high dependence on tourism. Similar variations are found in the new member states, with a few countries recording relatively high levels of tourism employment (Estonia, 8%) and relatively low levels (Czech Republic 3%). However, the general indications are that demand for tourism employment is increasing. Direct employment in tourism grew by almost 9% in the Republic of Cyprus between 1999 and 2002, from 39,500 to 42,955.

In the Mediterranean countries there also appears to be better integration between tourism courses and the tourism industry. For example, a tracer study conducted by ITIS in Malta in 2000 indicated that 63% of their graduates ended up working in the tourism industry (Department of Tourism, 2001).

The need to develop tourism education is paralleled in many of the new member states by a need to improve human resource management. For example, in Bulgaria, Anastassova and Purcell (1995) noted the following pattern of human resource management practices in the hotel industry:

- selection often based solely on written applications;
- little evidence of job specification or predetermined selection criteria;
- most employees temporary full-time workers;
- little evidence of policies to promote numerical flexibility;
- little evidence of policies to promote functional flexibility;
- very little training;
- most supervisory recruitment internal;
- little evidence of employee appraisal or strategic staff development;
- little evidence of incentive pay;
- strong (but defensive and conservative) trade union representation;
- strong employment protection;
- poor communication between management and operatives; and
- enormous insecurity and confusion about probable future industry and wider socio-political trends.

This picture has changed considerably as market systems have introduced new management approaches, but there is still considerable work to be done in focusing on quality management and the development of appropriate skills in the labour force. As a recent report on Slovenia noted:

> (W)hereas natural and socio-cultural resources are Slovenia's major comparative advantages, the country is not as strong with respect to human resources. The service visitors receive appears to be a major issue of concern, with prices not always matching the quality of service provided. A recent survey revealed that around one-fifth of international visitors had expected lower prices. The service provision as well as the management and organisation of tourism are, generally speaking, a weaker element in the overall tourism product. There is a general need for the development and improvement of tourism education and training programmes.
>
> (Mintel, 2000)

There are, however, increasing signs that the need to develop service quality is now being acted upon by tourism organizations. For example, the *Cyprus Strategic Plan for Tourism 2010* emphasizes the development of quality and added value, which implies human resource development and the education and training of tourism professionals (CTO, 2003).

The need to develop human resources is being fuelled by rapidly developing tourism economies. For example, in Romania tourism has been one of the sectors of the economy with considerable growth rates, leading to an increase in its importance in educational policy and in demand for tourism oriented curricula from the private sector.

Of course, education and training play a major role in the development of human resources in tourism. However, many short-term human resource problems are being solved through the increased labour mobility offered by the expansion of the EU. Labour mobility is already relatively high in the tourism industry, with the proportion of foreign workers in the EU15 having been estimated at 12%, some three times the level of international mobility as in the economy as a whole (Richards, 2001). The relatively open labour market in tourism, where few jobs need formal qualifications, tends to stimulate mobility. The new member states are likely to add to overall labour mobility in the EU because of their widespread use of English, which is regarded as a vital skill in the EU tourism industry (Richards, 2003).

Labour Migration

In the run-up to the expansion of the EU, one of the major fears expressed in the existing member states related to a supposed flood of cheap labour from the east. Lengthy transition periods have been imposed on movement from countries such as Poland, Hungary and the Czech Republic into their nearest neighbours, Germany and Austria. However, the initial signs are that the 'flood' of immigrants from the new member states will be less than some had feared. In the UK, for example, immigration from the new member states began to tail off at the beginning of 2005, following an initial rush of work permit applications immediately following enlargement (EU Business, 2005). In fact, in some countries (notably Austria) a tightening of immigration regulations prior to enlargement actually had the effect of reducing immigrant numbers from the former Communist states in the last few years (Richards, 2001).

An EU study, *Migration Trends in an Enlarged Europe*, predicts an overall migration of some 1.1m people before 2010. The study also states that it is the candidate countries – Romania and Bulgaria – rather than the accession states that hold the greatest potential for migrant generation. It is clear that many of these migrants will find their way into the tourism and hotel and catering industries, given their role as gateways into the wider labour market (Hjalager, 2000; Richards, 2001).

With the rapid growth of tourism in the new member states, there is already evidence of a reverse flow of labour migration from west to east as unemployment rates fall and skill shortages become more acute. For example, significant skill shortages have been noted in the Maltese tourism industry (EC, 2001). In the case of the Czech Republic, Sorm and Terrell (2000) conclude that tourism is one of the major sectors of inbound labour migration as people seek employment in 'new' and 'dynamic' sectors of the economy.

There is still a mismatch between the human resources needs of the industry and educational provision both in the university and vocational sectors. In some senses this mirrors the experience in the West of a relatively weak labour market, in which formal qualifications are not needed to enter the industry. This in turn acts as a disincentive for students to follow specific courses in tourism, and a consequent lack of supply of courses. For example, in Hungary, Rátz and Puczkó (2005) show that over 85% of businesses in Budapest recruited staff by word of mouth, compared with only 22% who had built a relationship with a specific course or educational institution. The most highly valued skills in making recruitment decisions were foreign languages (65%) and practical experience (63%), while academic qualifications were only considered important by 48% of firms.

Challenges for the Future

The Bologna process has instituted widespread changes in the education system throughout the EU, and is also beginning to impact on non-member states as well. The move towards a Bachelor–Master system is producing a much more standardized educational landscape as institutions begin to compete internationally to attract students, particularly at Masters level.

Tourism courses in the former Communist states which were overhauled in the shift to a market economy a few years ago are again being revised to meet the new demands of a single market in higher education. In many cases this means developing a wider range of courses, with a much more important role for English-language teaching. The original idea of 'Europeanization' of the curriculum, in which individual countries or regions would develop their own specializations within an overarching European framework (Richards and Onderwater, 1998) seems to have been dropped in favour of a more international concept. This is now developing into the idea of 'virtual mobility', although the ability of students in Central and Eastern Europe taking advantage of such opportunities is likely to be restricted by the relative lack of access to information and communication technology (ICT) resources.

The single market in education will probably also mean that tourism courses will need to develop specialisms that can attract students from abroad. This may mean that the new member states may have to re-examine their past to discover those skills and areas of knowledge that they have a particular advantage in, rather than importing ideas.

The increasing mobility of students and workers in the tourism sector is also driving the development of a much more multicultural student body and tourism workforce across Europe. Dealing with issues of multicultural education and management of a multicultural workforce are likely to becoming increasingly important in future (Klidas, 2001).

There is a continuing gap between academic and vocational education in many of the new member states. This means there is a need for further development of vocational education, making it more oriented toward market needs. This includes the need to develop more specialized courses for areas of skilled labour shortage, such as qualified entertainers and guides (for sports tourism, cultural tourism, leisure tourism, eco-tourism, back-packing tourism). A recent report from the European Parliament emphasizes the need to improve the quality of professional training in tourism, and this is an issue that will concern all the member states.

However, at a very basic level, the development of tourism education that is relevant to the needs of the tourism industry also implies an improvement in the career structures available in the industry. Without these, the industry will remain at a disadvantage relative to many other career options for graduates.

Acknowledgements

The following ATLAS colleagues kindly submitted information regarding developments in tourism education in their countries, and their help is gratefully acknowledged: Chryso Panayidou (Cyprus); Tamara Rátz (Hungary); Cristiana Cristureanu (Romania) and Tadeja Jere Lazanski (Slovenia).

References

Airey, D. (1994) Education for tourism in Poland: the Phare programme. *Tourism Management* 15(6), 467–471.

Airey, D. (1999) Education for tourism – East meets West. *International Journal of Tourism and Hospitality Research* 1, 7–18.

Anastassova, L. and Purcell, K. (1995) Human resource management in the Bulgarian hotel industry: from command to empowerment? *International Journal of Hospitality Management* 14, 171–185.

Calleja, E. (2004) *Malta's industry aiming for global competitiveness through HR development.* Paper presented at the conference The Implications of the Bologna Process and the Lisbon Statement for Higher Education, Brussels, November 2004.

Clarke, J., Denman, R., Hickman, G. and Slovak, J. (2001) Rural tourism in Roznava Okres: a Slovak case study. *Tourism Management* 22, 193–202.

Cristureanu, C. (1996) The current state of tourism and tourism education in Romania. In: Richards, G. (ed.) *Tourism in Central and Eastern Europe: Educating for Quality.* Tilburg: Tilburg University Press, pp. 75–92.

CTO (Cyprus Tourism Organisation) (2003) *Strategic Plan for Tourism 2010.* Nicosia: CTO.

Department of Tourism (2001) *Annual Report.* Valletta: Department of Tourism, Malta. Available at: http://www.tourism.gov.mt/filebank/pdfs/annualreport2001.pdf

Dima, A.-M. (2003) *Privatisation and Organisational Evolution in Higher Education.* Available at: http://www.utwente.nl/cheps/research/current_projects/track_3/3cdima.doc/

EC (2001) *Joint Assessment of the Employment Policy Priorities of Malta.* Brussels: European Commission. Available at: http://europa.eu.int/comm/employment_social/employment_analysis/japs/malta_en.pdf

EC (2005) *Extract from Commission Report on Hungary, 2002.* Brussels: European Commission. Available at: http://www.fifoost.org/ungarn/EU_Hungary_2002/node31.php

EU Business (2005) *Influx of new EU work-seekers to Britain tapers off.* Brussels: EU Business. Available at: http://www.eubusiness.com/afp/050224165921.c2ynl0pa/view

EURYDICE (2005) *Focus on the Structure of Higher Education in Europe 2003/04. National Trends in the Bologna Process.* Brussels: EURYDICE.

Golembski, G. (1991) The needs of a higher level education in tourism in post-communist countries of Middle-Eastern Europe (as illustrated by Poland). *Tourist Review* 1, 3–5.

Ghodsee, K. (2001) Women, employment, and tourism in post-totalitarian Bulgaria. Paper presented at Black Sea Regional Policy Symposium March 29–April 1, Washington, DC. Available at: http://www.irex.org/programs/completed/black-sea/ghodsee.pdf

Hjalager, A.-M. (2000) Organisational ecology in the Danish restaurant sector. *Tourism Management* 21, 271–280.

Jere Lazanski, T. (2004) *Information Handbook for Erasmus Students.* Portorož, Croatia: Turistica.

Jung, B. and Mierzejewska, B. (1996) Tourism education in Poland: an overview. In: Richards, G. (ed.) *Tourism in Central and Eastern Europe: Educating for Quality.* Tilburg: Tilburg University Press, pp. 57–68.

Kivela, J. (1997a) Education and training of hotel and tourism managers in Croatia. *Turizam* 45(5/6), 107–124.

Kivela, J. (1997b) The globalization of hotel and tourism management education in Croatia: part 2. *Turizam* 45(7/8), 159–173.

Klidas, A.K. (2001) *Employee Empowerment in the European Hotel Industry: Meaning, Process and Cultural Relativity.* Amsterdam: Thela Thesis.

Mintel (2000) *Travel and Tourism Intelligence Country Report, Slovenia.* London: Mintel. Available at: http://www.mintel.com

Persic, M. (1998) Training of tourism professionals in Croatia. *World Leisure and Recreation* 40(3), 19–25.

Rátz, T. (1997) Transformation of Hungarian tourism education. Paper presented at the 2nd *International Conference on Education and Training in Tourism and Hospitality Studies*, Dahab, Egypt, April 1997.

Rátz, T. and Puczkó, L. (2005) *Employment Creation and Human Resource Issues in Tourism.* Budapest: University of Economic Sciences, Research Project Report (funded by the Hungarian National Scientific Research Fund, 1996–1998, F019731).

Richards, G. (1996a) The development of tourism in Central and Eastern Europe In: Richards, G. (ed.) *Tourism in Central and Eastern Europe: Educating for Quality.* Tilburg: Tilburg University Press, pp. 1–14.

Richards, G. (1996b) Developing tourism education in Central and Eastern Europe In: Richards, G. (ed.) *Tourism in Central and Eastern Europe: Educating for Quality.* Tilburg: Tilburg University Press, pp. 301–305.

Richards, G. (2001) *Mobility in the European Tourism Sector: The Role of Transparency and Recognition of Vocational Qualifications.* Thessaloniki, Greece: CEDEFOP.

Richards, G. (2003) Tourism and labour mobility in the European Union. *Tourism Recreation Research* 28, 77–86.

Richards, G. and Onderwater, L. (1998) *Towards a European Body of Knowledge for Tourism: Perspectives and Proposals.* Tilburg: ATLAS.

Sorm, V. and Terrell, K. (2000) *Sectoral Restructuring and Labor Mobility: A Comparative Look at the Czech Republic.* Institute for the Study of Labor. Bonn: Discussion Paper Series, IZA DP No. 111.

Swire, D. (2003) Foreign Students Flocking Here. *Prague Post.* Available at: http://www.asu.edu/educ/epsl/LPRU/newsarchive/Art1744.txt

Szivas, E. and Riley, M. (1999) Tourism employment during economic transition. *Annals of Tourism Research* 26, 747–771.

Tauch, C. and Rauhvargers, C. (2002) *Survey on Master Degrees and Joint Degrees in Europe.* Brussels: European Commission, Education Directorate.

Tribe, J. (2005) Tourism Education Bibliography. Available at: http://www.tourismeducation.org/bibliography.htm

Vukonić, B. (1995) Tourism as a field of research and education at the faculty of Economics in Zagreb. *Acta Turistica* 7(1), 3622.

Vukonić, B. (1996) Tourism education in Croatia. In: Richards, G. (ed.) *Tourism in Central and Eastern Europe: Educating for Quality.* Tilburg: Tilburg University Press, pp. 41–46.

Part II

East Central Europe

_____

6 Tourism and EU Enlargement: a Central European Perspective

Peter Jordan

Introduction

Since EU enlargement as of 1 May, 2004, Austria has shifted from the position of an EU eastern front state nearer to the centre, in the North, East and Southeast embedded into new fellow members, who up to the First World War had been part of the same country, the Austro-Hungarian Monarchy. However, 1 May, 2004 did not mean a sudden change. The enlargement and integration process had started practically immediately after the fall of the Iron Curtain and it is (even as the ten new members are concerned) not really completed. The new members still do not enjoy the full freedom of labour mobility, and are still not part of Schengen and Euro zones. So, 1 May, 2004 must be regarded as symbolic rather than as the great turning point in the socio-economic integration process.

This is also true for the field of tourism. The separated flow systems of tourism started to reintegrate immediately after the turn of politics, if not earlier – as in the cases of Hungary and former Yugoslavia; but the high expectations raised in the beginning were not really fulfilled. Integration in tourism and growth of mutual tourism flows proved to be slow and long-term processes. Nor is Western tourism to Central and Eastern Europe so far a strong engine of regional development and spatial disparity equalization. Rather it supports larger cities and regions that are any way in a favourable position.[1] Nor are guests from Central and Eastern Europe in Europe's West much more than a marginal phenomenon, not even in Austria, so close to the new member states.

The chapter first documents foreign tourism development in Central Europe with a focus on Austrian tourism relations with Central and Eastern Europe and then discusses perspectives of tourism development in Central and Eastern Europe from the receiving as well as from the generating angle.

The term 'Central and Eastern Europe' comprises in this chapter not only the new member states Poland, Czech Republic, Slovakia, Hungary and Slovenia, but also Croatia, not only because Croatia is a part of Central Europe, but also because it is the most important tourism destination in the whole region besides Austria.

Tourism Flows in Central Europe Before Communism: the Blueprint for Flows in a Reintegrated Central Europe?

Before World War I, when tourism was still very much an upper class phenomenon, cures in the winter season still had a major share in tourism. Railway and ship were the dominant means of transportation and the main generators of

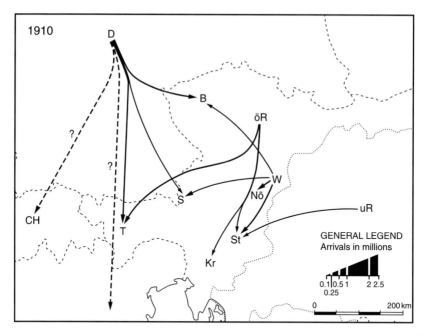

Fig. 6.1. Tourist flows, 1910.

tourism in Central Europe were the German Empire (D in Fig. 6.1) and the Austrian part of the dual Austro-Hungarian Monarchy (öR). Within these empires the large cities and the other urbanized and industrialized areas stood out: in the German Empire mainly Berlin and highly industrialized Saxony; in the Austrian part of the Habsburg Empire the capital Vienna (W) was the source of about half of the tourists. The second half came for the most part from the industrialized provinces of Bohemia (B) (mainly from Prague), Moravia and Silesia. The relatively small flow of tourists from the Hungarian part of the Monarchy (uR) originated mainly from Budapest.

One of the flows from the German Empire was directed to the Austrian Alpine provinces of Tyrol (T), Salzburg (S) and Vorarlberg; a second, somewhat smaller one, to Bohemia, above all to the Western Bohemian spas of Carlsbad (Karlovy Vary), Marienbad (Mariánské Lázne) and Franzensbad (Františkovy Lázně).

Among the flows originating from Vienna, only very weak ones were directed to regions outside the Austrian part of the Empire, and also to regions outside of present-day Austria. Just like the West Bohemian spas, the 'Austrian

Riviera' of Abazzia (Opatija), Istria (Istra) and Grado played a major role (see also Jordan, 1998). The Hungarian part of the Empire, for example, received only a few guests from Vienna.

Tourists from the Czech lands distributed themselves fairly equally over all Austrian provinces south of them. Germans from the Sudeten were numerous in the Alpine regions. For the rather small flow from the less urbanized Hungarian part of the dual Monarchy the numerous spas, the Tatra Mountains, Lake Balaton and the Croatian Coastland, all within the Hungarian part of the Monarchy, were preferred destinations. The few travels of Hungarians beyond their own part of the Monarchy were directed mainly to the eastern Alpine regions, to the Bohemian spas, to Vienna and also to the Austrian Riviera (Jordan, 1992a).

Tourist flows in the inter-war period

After participation in tourism had expanded to wider social strata, the summer season and bathing had gained importance and the automobile had become another important means

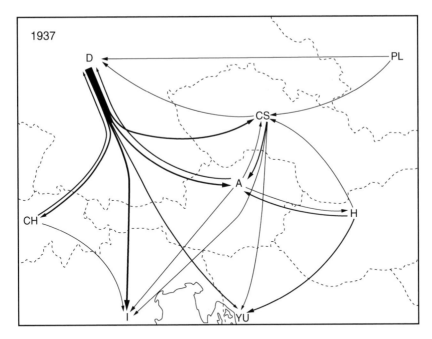

Fig. 6.2. Tourist flows, 1937.

of transportation, one of the most remarkable changes compared to the period before World War I is the flow of tourists from the German *Reich* (D) to the coast of the young Kingdom of Serbs, Croats and Slovenes (later Yugoslavia) (YU), where German tourists were hardly in evidence before the war (Fig. 6.2).

Also, the flow from the regions constituting the Republic of Austria (A) shifted during the interwar period from the former 'Austrian Riviera' and Istria, at that time belonging to Italy and to the Yugoslavian coast. Guests from post-Trianon Hungary (H) also played an important role all along the eastern Adriatic coast, and along the Italian section – a more important one than guests from Czechoslovakia. Hungary itself was not a much frequented destination for foreign tourists, the only great attraction being Budapest, registering two thirds of all foreign arrivals (mainly Germans, second Austrians). Lake Balaton had not yet been discovered by foreigners in spite of considerable popularity among Hungarians. As regards Austria, in the western part of the country German guests predominated until 1933,[2] whilst in the eastern part guests from Vienna mingled with guests from Czechoslovakia (CS) and Hungary.

In Czechoslovakia the West Bohemian spas remained the main attraction, attracting two thirds of foreign tourism. Germans and Austrians still accounted for the major proportion. The resorts in the Tatra Mountains were now frequented mainly by Czechs. Czechoslovakia was – in the same manner as the Czech lands before World War I – a main source of tourism in Central Europe. The tourist industries of Bavaria, Austria, Hungary and Yugoslavia were essentially adapted to Czechoslovakian guests.

The two situations may be regarded as a blueprint for flows in a Central Europe reunited by the enlargement process and hopefully completely reintegrated after all the restrictions have been removed. Offers, tourist motives, tourism trends, social participation in tourism, participation by age groups, means of transportation, economic relations, markets, economic situations in the markets and in the destinations are certainly too different today necessarily to assume anything of this kind. It is nevertheless true that (also under very different conditions) Germany is again the dominant market for all of Central Europe and it is remarkable that the Czech lands, with a population of enthusiastic travellers, were also a major source of Central European tourism when they were economically strong – as it was before World War I and in the interwar period.

Tourism Development in Central Europe after the Fall of the Iron Curtain: a Statistical Survey

Volume of tourism

The current intensity (Fig. 6.3) and volume (Fig. 6.4) of foreign tourism is in all former Communist countries now at a lower level than it was before the political change. This is mainly because of the collapse of social tourism, which was conducted on the basis of highly organized holiday recreation centres run by companies and trade unions and which played a dominant role in the tourism of all communist countries except for Yugoslavia (see Vukicević, 1971). The latter opened itself up early for commercial Western tourism (in the 1950s) while cutting back social tourism for its own population and those from other Communist countries. Hungary began to encourage large-scale Western tourism as part of the general liberalization of the services sector in the late 1970s (see Miczek, 1989) and Poland followed in the 1980s, but neither reduced their own welfare tourism.

Shortly after the fall of Communism in 1989/90, social tourism (which had hitherto cost the tourists themselves next to nothing) had to be curtailed, because it could no longer be financed by its former sponsors. The number of overnight stays fell accordingly with only the quota of commercial tourism remaining steady. The outbreak of war in Yugoslavia in 1991 added to the damage already done (see Jordan, 1995). Thus, 1991 and the following years represent a statistical nadir in the foreign tourism of all Central and Eastern European countries.

The levels shown in Figs 6.3–6.6 are the result of a slow recovery in commercial tourism that soon set in after this depression, but nevertheless failed to live up to the expectations it raised. Croatia was relatively the most successful, at some distance followed by the Czech Republic, Hungary, Poland and Slovenia.

Overnights of foreigners per inhabitant

0.5   1   2   3   4 9.2–10.7

Fig. 6.3. Tourism intensity, 2003.

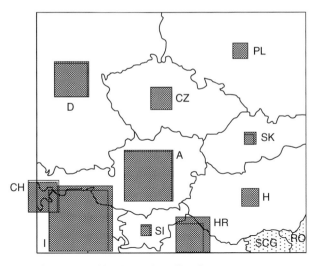

Overnights of foreigners (in millions)

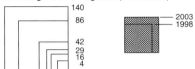

Fig. 6.4. Foreign overnights, 2003 and 1998. Source: Tourismus in Zahlen 2005, p. 80; national statistical yearbooks.

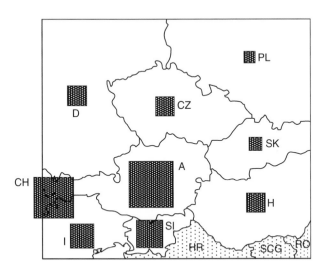

Tourism revenues per capita (in euros)

1,767
1,376
632
501
144

Fig. 6.5. Tourism revenues per capita, 2003. Source: Tourismus in Zahlen, 2005, p. 85.

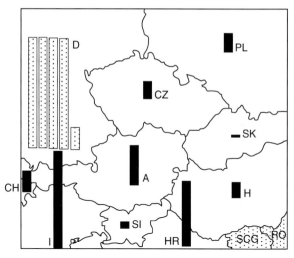

Balance of revenues and expenditures (in millions US$)

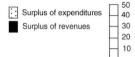 Surplus of expenditures
■ Surplus of revenues

50
40
30
20
10

Fig. 6.6. Balance of revenues and expenditures in international tourism, 2003. Source: Tourismus in Zahlen 2005, p. 84.

Travel Markets for Central and Eastern European Countries

As can be seen from the data presented in Fig. 6.7 representing the year 2003,[3] Germans enjoy a relative majority in the number of overnight stays amongst foreigners in all Central and Eastern European countries with the exception of Slovakia. This is most marked in Hungary, Poland and the Czech Republic where Germans make up 36%, 35% and 34%, respectively, of all foreign overnight stays. In Slovakia, German overnight stays are outnumbered by those of Czechs, whose share is one quarter. This emphasizes the traditional role Slovakia has played as a recreation area for Czechs since at least World War I (see Jordan, 1992b).

All other markets are far behind the Germans in playing a role as tourists in Central and Eastern European countries. The relatively most important are the Italians. Most markedly they are represented in Slovenia and Croatia, where they rank just below the Germans, in second place, followed by Hungary and the Czech Republic where they rank third and fourth, respectively. Britons are well-represented especially in the Czech Republic, where they rank second, but also in Poland, Slovenia and Hungary, where they hold ranks between four and six. Austrians play a major role in Hungary and Slovenia, where they rank second and third, respectively, while in Croatia and Slovakia they reach the fifth place in the order of tourist nations. Surprisingly enough they are rather weakly represented in the Czech Republic (2%, tenth place). Dutch tourists rank third in the Czech Republic, fourth in Hungary, sixth in Slovenia and seventh in Croatia.

Alongside these most important markets for Central and Eastern European tourism, the USA (particularly in the Czech Republic and Hungary) and France (mainly Poland) also have larger shares among Western nations, while the Czech Republic (particularly in Slovakia and Croatia), Poland (in Slovakia and the Czech Republic), Hungary (in Croatia, Slovenia and Slovakia), Russia (in Poland) and Slovenia (in Croatia) have the largest shares among Eastern nations.

In general, it can be stated that after more than a decade of transformation Central and Eastern European countries, with the minor exception of Slovakia, display a market structure typical for Central Europe and very near

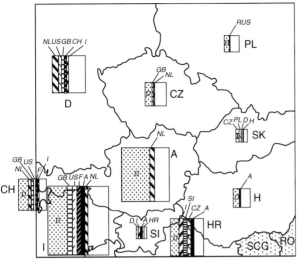

Overnights of foreigners (in millions) Country of origin (5% and more of all foreign overnights)

140	D Germany	GB United Kingdom	
86	I Italy	F France	H Hungary
42	NL Netherlands	CH Switzerland	PL Poland
29 16 4	A Austria	HR Croatia	CZ Czech Rep.
	US United States	SI Slovenia	RUS Russia

Fig. 6.7. Foreign overnights by countries of origin, 2003. Source: Tourismus in Zahlen 2005, p. 80; national statistical yearbooks.

to Western Central European countries like Austria, Switzerland and (as regards tourism also) Italy, showing a dominant impact second only to the huge German market. Central and Eastern European markets are in Central and Eastern Europe certainly better represented than in Western Central Europe, but they only exceptionally dominate.

Tourism Flows Between Central and Eastern Europe and Austria

Central and Eastern European tourists in Austria

Tourist flows from Central and Eastern European countries (Poland, Czech Republic, Slovakia, Hungary, Slovenia, Croatia) to Austria have increased in recent years, especially in the winter season. While for the calendar year 1999 2.753m overnight stays of Central and Eastern European citizens were registered in Austria (Wirtschaftskammer Österreich, 2004) and this meant 3.3% of all foreign overnight stays in

Austria in this year, their number increased to 3.439m or 4% in 2003. While Polish tourist nights were the most numerous among Central and Eastern Europeans in 1999 (0.795m or 1%), ranking them tenth among foreign nations (see Jordan, 2000),[4] in 2003 they ranked second to Hungarians, who with 1 million tourist nights (1.009m) made up 1.2% of all foreign overnight stays in Austria and ranked ninth among foreign tourism markets[5] (Wirtschaftskammer Österreich, 2004).

Still, these figures are not really impressive, although they have more than tripled compared to years before the fall of the Iron Curtain (e.g. 1987: 1.050m overnights from Central and Eastern European countries, 1.2% of all foreign overnights in Austria), although tourism from Central and Eastern Europe to Austria concentrates on the winter season with higher per capita expenditures and although by less concentration on top destinations it somehow contributes to the equalization of regional disparities in Austria.

In the calendar year 2003, 70.5% of all Central and Eastern European tourist nights

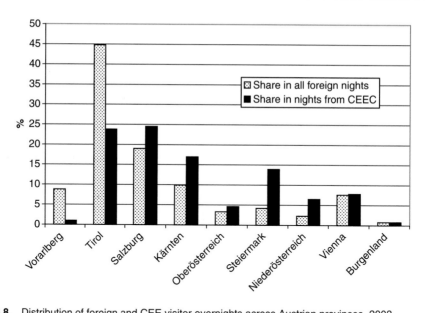

Fig. 6.8.   Distribution of foreign and CEE visitor overnights across Austrian provinces, 2003.

in Austria were spent in the winter season (November to April) (Statistik Austria, 2003). Tyrol (Tirol), Salzburg, Carinthia (Kärnten) and Styria (Steiermark) were the predominant winter destinations and Poles, Hungarians and Slovaks were, more than Czechs, Slovenians and Croats, inclined to spend winter holidays in Austria. It has, however, to be taken into account that for the latter it is easy to visit major Austrian skiing centres for a day trip.

The relatively strongest regional impact of Central and Eastern European tourists is noted in Styria, where Central and Eastern European (predominantly Hungarian) overnights amount to 13.2% of all foreign overnights (compared to 4% at the Austrian average). Second is Lower Austria [Niederösterreich] with 11.4% (also predominantly Hungarians); but also in the federal provinces of Carinthia (6.8%, also predominantly Hungarians), Upper Austria (Oberösterreich) (5.6%, relative majority of Czechs) and Salzburg (5.1%, relative majority of Czechs) the share of Central and Eastern Europeans is significantly above the Austrian average (Statistik Austria, 2004). This means that regions with a lower tourism intensity profit disproportionally from Central and Eastern European tourist flows. The spatial distribution of Central and Eastern European tourist nights

over Austria differs, however, not so significantly from the distribution of foreign tourist nights in total that it is justified to conclude that Central and Eastern Europeans avoid top destinations and form just overspill in cheaper tourism peripheries (see Fig. 6.8). It is, however, evident that the westernmost Austrian provinces (Tyrol, Vorarlberg), known for their elite tourism, receive relatively small tourist flows from Central and Eastern Europe.

Central and Eastern European countries as tourism destinations for Austrians

According to overnight stays in 2003 reported by the national statistical agencies, for Austrians Croatia is by far the most attractive destination (3.585m Austrian overnights) among Central and Eastern European countries, followed by Hungary (719,000) and Slovenia (691,000). This is supported by an Austrian statistical survey over holiday travels[6] of Austrians referring to the year 2001 (Statistik Austria, 2002). In this year, when Croatian tourism had again considerably recovered from the depression of the 1990s, Italy ranked first among Austrian holiday travels abroad (24.2%), followed by Croatia (13.1%). Hungary held the 8th (2.8%) and Slovenia the

14th (1.4%) position, while Poland attracted only 0.6%, the Czech Republic 0.5% and Slovakia 0.3% of all Austrian holiday travels to other countries (Statistik Austria, 2002). In 1996, shortly after the end of hostilities in Croatia, the share of Croatia was still only 5% while the shares of Hungary (4.2%), Poland, and the Czech Republic (0.8%) were higher than in 2001; 1.1% of all Austrian holiday travels were to Slovenia, 0.3% to Slovakia (Statistik Austria, 2002).

Taking into account that travels to Croatia and Slovenia are just approaching the level they had in the late 1980s before the Yugoslavian crisis, and that Austrian holiday travels to the other four countries (Poland, Czech Republic, Slovakia, Hungary) have even declined between 1993 and 2001 in absolute numbers, it becomes apparent that Austria is not a very prosperous tourism market for its northern and eastern neighbours.

In 2001, Austrians travelled to Croatia mainly for seaside recreation along the long and attractive coast, to Hungary for wellness and health treatment in the plentiful spas and for lakeside recreation at Lake Balaton, to Slovenia for wellness and health treatment in spas, to Poland for recreation, but also for theme and study tours, to the Czech Republic for theme and study tours and to Slovakia for theme and study tours and recreation (Statistik Austria, 2002).

With day trips, the situation is certainly different, although data are hardly available and statements must be based on accidental evidence. Most frequent are certainly shopping tours to western Hungarian border regions, but also to Budapest. Bratislava, the Slovakian capital at 70 km distance from Vienna, attracts a lot of Austrian shopping tourists, since large shopping centres are open at hours rather unusual in Austria. Also, the Slovenian border is frequently crossed by Austrian day-trippers, less so the Czech border.

Perspectives After Enlargement

Central and Eastern European countries as Austria's competitors at the international tourism market

Will Central and Eastern European countries successfully compete with Austria in the international tourism market, and which are the market segments in which competition will be successful?

Austria hosted in the early 2000s no more foreign overnights than in the late 1980s. This stagnation in quantitative terms and as regards the annual average (not in respect to revenues and to winter season) may lead to the conclusion that the fall of the Iron Curtain and the advancing political and economic integration of Central and Eastern Europe into European structures thereafter has absorbed Austria's potential growth in tourism. However, a closer glance at the development of foreign overnights in Austria from the late 1980s up to 2004 shows that Austria took advantage of the Yugoslavian crisis in the first half of the 1990s by receiving tourists (mainly Germans) who would otherwise have travelled to former Yugoslavia. Later, in the second half of the 1990s and the early 2000s, it was rather modernization problems in Austrian (summer) tourism, new trends in the European market not matched by the Austrian offer and the growing weakness of the German market than competition from the 'East' which caused stagnation (see Zimmermann, 1994, 1998, 2001). A very similar quantitative development in Switzerland, a country certainly less affected by competitors in Central and Eastern Europe and even unfavourably comparing to the Austrian case, may be taken as a proof of that.

The only two segments obviously affected by 'Eastern' competitors were wellness/health tourism as well as city tourism. In wellness/health tourism, the modernization of spas in western Hungary (Héviz, Bük, Balf, Zalakaros and some newcomers) and Slovenia (Rogaška Slatina, Laško, Atomske Toplice, Radenci, Dobrna) affected especially spas in eastern Austria (Burgenland, Styria) and brought some expansion plans to a halt. Further expansion, especially in western Hungary, may cause further damage on the Austrian side in a market that is already very tight. In city tourism, especially Prague (Praha) and Budapest compete with Vienna, but expanding the offer to three attractive destinations in close vicinity may also have contributed to the relative stability of Vienna's international tourism development (see Lohmann, 2004; Seitlinger, 2004).

Looking at future perspectives by market segments and comparing Central and Eastern European countries with Austria, a number of competitive advantages may be expected.

Lakeside tourism

Besides Lake Balaton in Hungary, the Masurian and Pomeranian lakes in Poland and mainly artificial lakes in the Czech Republic, the Central and Eastern European offer in this segment comprises only a few smaller attractions (like Blejsko jezero in Slovenia) which compare to the Austrian lake lands (Salzkammergut, Carinthia) and a lot of individual lakes in other parts of the country (e.g. Lake Constance (Bodensee), Lake Neusiedl (Neusiedlersee)). Lake Balaton is by no means a new competitor (see Miczek, 1989) for the Western (German, Austrian) market. It continued to be a destination of mass tourism even during the Communist period due to early liberalization in Hungary (late 1970s); but by quality improvements in tourism infrastructure and the offering of extra services and attractions (wellness, cultural attractions and events, conferences), partly under way, combined with the special Hungarian flair, it may succeed in detracting guests from Austrian lakes.

Compared to Lake Balaton, the Masurian and Pomeranian lakes are newcomers to the international tourism market. They impress by their natural beauty and by being embedded in a mild, unspoiled landscape and offer a variety of water sports as well as recreation near to nature (see Jordan, 1999; Österreichisches Ost- und Südosteuropa-Institut, 2003). Provided a qualitative tourism infrastructure will further be developed and the character of recreation near to nature can at the same time be preserved, these lake districts have certainly the potential to attract Western markets, especially the German and the Dutch. Nautical tourism is also advancing in these lake lands and on the inland waterways of northern Poland with considerable potential to grow. However, being so different in character from the Austrian lakes this will very likely not affect Austrian lakeside tourism. The many artificial lakes in the Czech Republic have so far attracted just a domestic clientele and will continue to do so.

Rural tourism

This includes summer vacations in the countryside and farm holidays (agrotourism). Summer vacations in the countryside used to be the classical form of summer tourism in Austria mainly frequented by German and domestic guests, but was subject to substantial erosion in recent decades mainly due to new tourism trends, the change in demographic structures and stagnation in the quality of the offer (see Zimmermann, 1994).

Rural tourism and farm holidays in the narrower sense can only succeed within a well-equipped tourist environment. A well-furbished individual establishment is insufficient; suitably developed activities and a pleasant environment in general must also exist to meet the expectations of guests. This includes a rural road network, walking paths, hiking trails, bicycle lanes, attractive inns, benches, shops and evening entertainment, as well as a cultivated rural landscape.

Central and Eastern European countries invest many hopes in the success of this segment and a lot of initiatives have been started aimed at the development of peripheral regions and the smoothing of spatial disparities by rural tourism (see Hall, 1991; Verhoeff, 1998). However, they meet several endogenous barriers:

- the poor infrastructure in rural areas in general (not only in tourism terms);
- an inadequate demographic structure in many regions (depopulation, an ageing structure, brain drain);
- the lasting impact of Communist collectivization (except in larger parts of Poland, in Slovenia and Croatia) which resulted in destroying traditional farm structures and the traditional cultural landscape; and
- the lack of care for the cultural landscape (partly a legacy of the Communist period).

In the near future, in Central and Eastern Europe the development of an environment adequate for rural tourism might only succeed very gradually. (A possible exception is Slovenia, which is affected by all the barriers mentioned to a much lesser extent.) Major public and private investment would be needed, certainly more than for most other tourism segments, if really larger areas should be affected. It might, however, be possible to develop some particularly suitable places and small regions for this type of tourism. First successful initiatives in this direction have been taken in the interior of the Istrian peninsula, where rural tourism partly succeeded in participating in the peninsula's intensive summer season.

Nature and adventure tourism

This does not represent a large market segment and by definition it needs to remain small as it would otherwise destroy its own sustainability. This includes 'soft tourism' over large areas for those seeking individual experiences often in conjunction with sporting activities such as walking, mountaineering, climbing, caving, bicycling, boating, canoeing, kite-flying, paragliding, horseback riding, hunting, fishing, etc. It needs an unspoiled and sparsely inhabited landscape and natural scenic beauty, not so much an elaborated tourism infrastructure.

This segment has some importance in many parts of the Austrian Alps. Central and Eastern Europe has, in principle, also very much to offer in this area. Apart from the Slovenian share in the Alps, there are the Dinaric mountain range and the extremely attractive eastern coast of the Adriatic with myriad islands, the Carpathians in Poland and Slovakia, outstanding individual natural attractions like the Plitvice Lakes (Plitvikča jezera) or caves (especially in Slovenia and Hungary) as well as many national parks and other protected areas (see Jordan, 1999; Österreichisches Ost- und Südosteuropa-Institut, 2003). Many of these attractions are well-known and already attract a substantial clientele, in this way not forming new competitors in the market. To generate or widen interest in less prominent attractions it would also partly be necessary to overcome the negative environmental image larger parts of Central and Eastern Europe still have. Another obstacle is also a legacy of the Communist period: heavy industrialization, dull uniformity in land utilization and weekend houses and second homes also in remote areas. Nevertheless, Central and Eastern Europe has a good opportunity to compete successfully in this market segment.

Winter (sports) tourism

This lucrative segment, with very high per capita expenditure, is well-developed in Austria as well as in the other Alpine countries west of it. In Austria it grows continuously, compensating losses in other segments (see Zimmermann, 1998; Wirtschaftskammer Österreich, 2005). Winter tourism infrastructure in Austria usually comprises not only accommodation and the technical means for winter sports like skiing, but also entertainment and alternative offers in a wider region. Even the largest and best-equipped skiing resorts in Central and Eastern Europe, like those around the Tatra Mountains (Tatry) in Poland and Slovakia, the Sudeten Mountains (Sudety) in Poland and the Czech Republic and the alpine part of Slovenia compare unfavourably even with the smaller ones in Austria and other Alpine countries. To compete against this capital-intensive and highly elaborate offer is practically impossible with a reasonable degree of effort, at least as far as Alpine skiing is concerned (which, because of its popularity is the only sector that really matters).

Thus, resorts in Central and Eastern Europe will depend, almost entirely, on low pricing to compete in the European market. However, for domestic tourists they will continue to play a significant role, as well as for international tourists from Eastern Europe, at least locations of exceptional appeal (e.g. the Tatra Mountains). Other winter sports, especially those needing little specific investment do, however, have a better chance as these sports become more popular (e.g. cross-country skiing, skating).

Health tourism

In the light of sharply curtailed government contributions to health-care costs, this part of the tourist industry grows if it can generate in healthy people the urge to indulge in luxury beauty services, for example, caring for their bodies, relaxing and acquiring a general sense of well-being such as was highly fashionable before World War I. At that time, it was customary to frequent health spas using one medical excuse or another and enjoy the entertainment and social life offered alongside health-related regimes (see Jordan, 1998).

Many of the existing health spas in Austria and Central and Eastern Europe date back to this era. They still possess some of the old, charming architectural features and ambience that satisfied the social need of the clientele of that time. In Central and Eastern Europe, under Communism, but to some extent also in Austria, many of these were operated as sanatoria and the buildings underwent structural changes. It is difficult to revert to former conditions where these changes were major, but where it is possible to re-establish health resort operations on a basis not dissimilar to pre-war conditions and installations, this is an up-market resource and the outlook is promising.

Many old spas in Austria underwent such a (re-)conversion, but a number of new wellness resorts have also been established, especially in Southeast Styria and Burgenland near to Slovenia and Hungary. In Central and Eastern Europe during transformation similar developments took place in Karlovy Vary and Mariánské Lázně (Czech Republic) or Opatija (Croatia), as the most prominent examples. Hungary and Slovenia were also extremely successful in this respect, affecting the market position of Southeast Austrian wellness resorts quite substantially. A lot of further potential rests with the old spas in the Polish and Czech Sudeten Mountains as well as the Polish and Slovakian Carpathians. Certainly, Central and Eastern Europe has the capacity to become a major European competitor in this field.

City and cultural tourism

City tourism, frequently combined with cultural tourism, is a segment that has grown considerably in recent decades. Its growth has been fed by a trend towards short vacations, entertainment and educational travel and low airfares. Fairs and conferences are an important component. It is highly profitable, but demands high quality standards as well as exceptional historic and cultural attractions. Vital factors include an excellent tourist infrastructure and easy accessibility (good air connections). It has so far proved to be relatively stable, provided that new attractions and events (e.g. new museums and galleries, commemorations of historical and cultural celebrities, sport championships) arouse periodical attention. Being predominantly longer-distance tourism, it is, however, also sensitive to political and other crises.

In this segment, in which Austria is represented mainly by Vienna (see Lohmann, 2004 and Seitlinger, 2004), but also by Salzburg and some other larger cities like Innsbruck, Central and Eastern Europe is a strong competitor, because it has on the one hand an extraordinary cultural heritage to offer (see Jordan, 1999; Österreichisches Ost- und Südosteuropa-Institut, 2003) and profits on the other from the fact that the large cities and metropolises were in the forefront of reform and innovation and acquired the necessary infrastructure quickly. Drawbacks such as the negative environmental and security image, important in other segments of the tourist market, do play a less significant role here.

Therefore, Western city tourism to Central and Eastern Europe is the type of tourism which has indeed met most expectations, although it is mostly limited to metropolises like Prague or Budapest and some extraordinary regional centres such as Cracow (Kraków), while others only slightly less attractive are rather neglected. This may be for reasons of publicity, accessibility or insufficiently developed tourist infrastructure. Smaller cities and places of interest still tend to lack the facilities that urban tourists have grown to expect.

The growth of city tourism in Central and Eastern Europe has so far not meant that Austrian competitors suffered from a decline in visitors. On the contrary, city tourism in Austria remains a flourishing segment (Lohmann, 2004; Seitlinger, 2004). Package tours for tourists from overseas including a couple of Central European cities may even have contributed to this phenomenon, but certainly, with the inclusion of further destinations in Central and Eastern Europe, competition will get tougher.

Study and theme travel

This segment has also grown rapidly since the fall of the Iron Curtain and has gained considerable stature in Central and Eastern Europe. It caters primarily to the growing number of educated, active retired people who, financially secure, well-spoken and flexible, are seeking intellectual stimulation, personal contacts and diversity rather than recreation. The quality of the tourist infrastructure is not a foremost criterion. This favours Central and Eastern Europe. Central and Eastern Europe is also especially attractive in this segment, since on the one hand it was practically inaccessible for decades and is therefore a relatively new, exciting, 'adventurous' and almost exotic offer for the market. On the other hand it is well-known to the older generation due to its close historic inter-linkages especially with Western Central Europe, due to personal and family relations and not least also to war experiences.

In spite of substantial growth it offers a multitude of possibilities which are still only partially utilized. The boom of study and theme travel to Central and Eastern Europe certainly detracts potential customers from Austria, but is not such a prominent segment in quantitative terms that this would have severe economic effects.

Central and Eastern Europe as a Tourism Market for Austria

Central and Eastern Europe is so far by no means a prominent tourism market for Austria (2003: 3.439m overnight stays or 4% of all foreign overnights), although it has been slowly growing during the transformation period. The question arises whether EU accession of five of the six Central and Eastern European countries in 2004 meant a change and what were the chances for a continued positive development or perhaps even an acceleration?

Similar to 'old' member states, Central and Eastern Europe undergoes a demographic change towards an aging society, but different from 'Old' Europe, the older and retired generation have smaller financial reserves, if any. Indeed, many of the retired are transformation losers with little hope that their situation will change. This does not nourish expectations that the older generation will even in the longer run play the role it plays in the tourism of Western societies right now.

Other, but perhaps much more ephemeral barriers for a more dynamic development of the Eastern tourism market are the still unfavourable currency parities, high unemployment rates as well as the still low level of income (Lohmann, 2004). An encouraging aspect is certainly economic growth, which is currently significantly stronger than in the 'old' member states and will more or less continue up to an equalization of East–West socio-economic disparities provided European integration proceeds and the chances of the new members to succeed in the European market are not reduced by continued or even new restrictions.

As noted already in the introduction, formal accession to the EU as of 1 May, 2004 is not much more than a symbolic date, since socio-economic integration is a long-term process which started earlier and is not yet completed. Formal membership meant neither the fall of all economic restrictions nor the end of border controls. Full mobility of labour, inclusion into the Schengen zone and the currency union will not be achieved much before 2010. It can therefore be expected that outbound tourism flows from Central and Eastern Europe will continue to grow slowly, more or less in line with economic growth.

A different question is whether Austria will be able to attract a larger portion of this potential. Traditions of travelling must not be neglected in this respect, but also not overestimated. A certain nostalgia to be found in many parts of the former Austro-Hungarian Monarchy for what is today Austria and especially for Vienna may also be favourable; but (in the first line) prices, a certain similarity of the offer (except winter sports), the usual drive of Central Europeans towards the Mediterranean, the change of tourism trends, cheap offers in overseas and low cost airlines are strong arguments speaking against a more prominent role of Austria in the Central and Eastern European tourism market.

However, an essential factor, which is fortunately completely under domestic control, is also a strategic vision and attitude in respect to the new markets in Central and Eastern Europe. If, first, guests from Central and Eastern Europe are treated personally as if they were major customers, if their specific interests are respected and their language is learnt, if they are granted special discounts and benefits although they play so far only a marginal role and are not the biggest spenders; if, second, specific marketing concepts streamlined to demands of the individual countries are developed, this may well help to establish a very specific relationship between Central and Eastern Europeans and Austria to the long-term benefit of the Austrian tourism industry, which is anyway over-dependent on the German market. While attitudes towards Central and Eastern Europeans at the personal and local level vary in practice between a very cultivated and personal treatment and contacts not very different from those with guest workers, the agencies responsible for federal as well as provincial tourism marketing – fully aware of the intrinsic importance of these new markets – have already developed a lot of specific marketing concepts. This may well contribute to expectations of doubling the share of Central and Eastern European guests in Austrian international tourism within 10 years, i.e. to 8–10% (Wolf, 2005).

Conclusion

For an 'old' member state, the Austrian perspective on Central and Eastern Europe is currently neither as a major competitor in the international tourism market[7] nor a major generating region. It has, however, potential to develop in both fields, however slowly, as a stronger, dynamic market.

As regards its role as a destination of international tourism, where Central and Eastern Europe meets the hard and professional competition of well-established destinations in other parts of Europe, success is estimated to depend mainly on the following factors:

- improving the quality of accommodation and catering by intensifying competition, for example, by the dissolution of large tourism enterprises and holdings, strengthening the position of small and medium-sized enterprises with the help of favourable credits and by establishing associations to represent their common interests, as well as by improving legal and economic conditions for domestic and foreign strategic investment;
- improving the quality of infrastructure in transportation and public services especially in the rural space and also on the micro-level to support regional and seasonal diversification in tourism;

- occupying a more prominent position on the tourists' mental map and getting rid of negative images (as regards politics, environment, security), e.g. by regional marketing and the development of regional brands to avoid being discredited by Communism and political crises and to emphasize the variety of the offer;
- spatial separation of tourism and environmentally harmful industry. It was characteristic for the Communist era to locate smoking, stinking and noisy factories, symbols of the 'working class', in a tourist resort, in order to take the aura of luxury from this activity, which was not in line with the ideology of Communism;
- reduction of state bureaucracy. A complicated, time- and money-consuming bureaucracy discourages and impedes private initiatives also in tourism; many a civil servant still displays a negative attitude to private entrepreneurship associating it with quick profit-making.

As regards Central and Eastern Europe's role as a market of international tourism, the development is supposed to be slow and dependent on economic growth and further European integration. For Austria it will not be 'natural' to receive the (relatively large) share of the cake it had in pre-Communist times, since tourism trends have changed.

Notes

[1] Except in Croatia. However, Croatia was a favourite destination of commercial tourism also in the Communist era and only recovered after the depression caused by the Yugoslav crisis.

[2] The decision of the German Reich in 1933 to levy 1000 German Marks from each German tourist crossing the Austrian frontier let Czechoslovakians account for the largest share among foreign tourists also in the provinces of western Austria.

[3] According to the statistical sources quoted in the appendix (mainly statistical yearbooks and websites of statistical agencies and tourist boards).

[4] After Germany (53.1m or 64.4%), The Netherlands (7.0m or 8.5%), the United Kingdom (2.8m or

3.4%), Switzerland (2.8m or 3.4%), Italy (2.7m or 3.2%), Belgium (2.1m or 2.5%), France (1.7m or 2.1%), the USA (1.6m or 1.9%) and Denmark (0.872m or 1.1%).

[5] After Germany (52.8m or 61.2%), The Netherlands (8.5m or 9.9%), Switzerland (3.5m or 4.1%), the United Kingdom (3.2m or 3.7%), Italy

(3.0m or 3.5%), Belgium (2.2m or 2.6%), France (1.6m or 1.9%) and the USA (1.2m or 1.4%).

[6] Travels with at least 4 overnights.

[7] Croatia, with its large tourism volume is, first, not a newcomer in the tourism market and, second, not a direct competitor of Austria, since the offer is clearly dominated by seaside tourism.

References

Hall, D.R. (ed.) (1991) *Tourism and Economic Development in Eastern Europe and the Soviet Union.* London: Belhaven Press.

Jordan, P. (1992a) The development of tourist flows within Central Europe (1910–1990). In: Terrazzi, M. (ed.) *Itinerari di Idee, Uomini e Cose fra Est ed Ovest Europeo.* Udine: Atti del Convegno Internazionale, pp. 589–601.

Jordan, P. (1992b) Slovakia in the scope of Central European tourism – present state and outlook. *Geografický Časopis* 44(2), 105–119.

Jordan, P. (1995) Auswirkungen der Kriege im ehemaligen Jugoslawien auf den Fremdenverkehr der kroatischen Küste. Eine regionale Untersuchung der Tourismusentwicklung. *Zeitschrift für den Erdkundeunterricht* 47(11), 438–445.

Jordan, P. (1998) Die Stellung Abbazias unter den Kurorten der Österreichisch-Ungarischen Monarchie. In: Jordan, P. and Peršić, M. (eds) *Österreich und der Tourismus von Opatija (Abbazia) vor dem Ersten Weltkrieg und zur Mitte der 1990er Jahre.* Frankfurt am Main: Peter Lang, pp. 169–194.

Jordan, P. (1999) International tourism attractions in Central and Southeastern Europe. In: Österreichisches Ost- und Südosteuropa-Institut (ed.) *Atlas of Eastern and Southeastern Europe.* Stuttgart and Berlin: Borntraeger, No. 3.4–G6.

Jordan, P. (2000) The growth of Polish winter tourism to Austria. In: Wyrzykowski, J. (ed.) *Conditions of the Foreign Tourism Development in Central and Eastern Europe.* Wrocław: Institute of Geography, University of Wrocław, pp. 133–146.

Lohmann, M. (2004) *Tourismus nach der EU-Erweiterung: was die Städte Erwartet.* Vienna: Paper presented at Wiener Tourismus Konferenz, 19 October, 2004.

Miczek, Gy. (1989) The Expansion of Tourism from Western Countries to Hungary in the Eighties. In: Österreichisches Ost- und Südosteuropa-Institut (ed.) *Atlas of Eastern and Southeastern Europe.* Stuttgart and Berlin: Borntraeger, No. 3.1–H1.

Österreichisches Ost- und Südosteuropa-Institut (ed.) (2003) *aos-web.* Available at: http://www.aos.ac.at

Seitlinger, K. (2004) *Das Projekt Wien 2010 im Fortschritt. Entwicklungen 2003–2004.* Vienna: Paper presented at Wiener Tourismus Konferenz, 19 October, 2004.

Statistik Austria (ed.) (2002) *Urlaubsreisen der Österreicher 2001.* Vienna: Statistik Austria.

Statistik Austria (ed.) (2004) *Tourismus in Österreich 2003.* Vienna: Statistik Austria.

Verhoeff, R. (1998) The transformation of international tourism in Central Europe – between state and market. In: Carter, F.W., Jordan, P. and Rey, V. (eds) *Central Europe after the Fall of the Iron Curtain. Geopolitical Perspectives, Spatial Patterns and Trends,* 2nd edn. Frankfurt am Main: Peter Lang, pp. 159–174.

Vukicević, M. (1971) Der Fremdenverkehr im Sozialismus als Objekt staatlicher Intervention. In: Ruppert, K. and Maier, J. (eds) *Der Tourismus und seine Perspektiven für Südosteuropa.* Regensburg: Verlag Michael Lassleben Kallmünz, pp. 121–127.

Wirtschaftskammer Österreich (ed.) (2004) *Tourismus in Zahlen: Österreichische und Internationale Tourismus- und Wirtschaftsdaten,* 40th edn. Vienna: Wirtschaftskammer Österreich.

Wirtschaftskammer Österreich (ed.) (2005) *Tourismus in Zahlen: Österreichische und Internationale Tourismus- und Wirtschaftsdaten,* 41st edn. Vienna: Wirtschaftskammer Österreich.

Wolf, G. (2005) Österreichs Fremdenverkehr verliert den Schwung der letzten Jahre. *GW-Unterricht* 97, 91–94.

Zimmermann, F. (1994) Tourismus in Österreich – Instabilität der Nachfrage und Innovationszwang des Angebotes. *Geographische Rundschau* 47(1), 30–37.

Zimmermann, F. (1998) Austria: contrasting tourist seasons and contrasting regions. In: Williams, A.M. and Shaw, G. (eds) *Tourism and Economic Development: European Experiences*, 3rd edn. Chichester, UK and New York: John Wiley & Sons, pp. 175–197.
Zimmermann, F. (2001) European Union cross-border cooperation: a new tourism dimension. In: Smith, V.L. and Brent, M. (eds) *Hosts and Guests Revisited: Tourism Issues of the 21st Century*. New York: Cognizant Communication, pp. 323–330.

Additional statistical sources drawn upon

Croatia

Croatian National Tourist Board: http://www.croatia.hr/home/Default.aspx
Državni Zavod za Statistiku (ed.) (2004) *Statistički Ljetopis Republike Hrvatske 2004*. Zagreb.
Republika Hrvatska, Državni Zavod za Statistiku: http://www.dzs.hr

Czech Republic

Český Statistický Úřad: http://www.czso.cz/eng/redakce.nsf/i/home
Český Statistický Úřad (ed.) (2004) *Statistická Ročenka Česke Republiky 2004*. Prague.

Hungary

Hungarian Central Statistical Office: http://portal.ksh.hu/portal/page?_pageid=38,119919&_dad=portal&_schema=PORTAL
Hungarian Tourism Office: http://www.hungary.com/servlet/page?_pageid=6176,6177,6181,6179&_dad=portal30&_schema=PORTAL30
Központi Statisztikai Hivatal (ed.) (2004) *Magyar Statisztikai Évkönyv 2003*. Budapest.

Poland

Central Statistical Office: http://www.stat.gov.pl/english/index.htm
Główny Urząd Statystyczny (ed.) (2004) *Rocznik Statystyczny Rzeczypospolitej Polskiej 2004*. Warsaw.

Slovakia

Slovak Tourist Board: http://www.slovakiatourism.sk/index.php
Štatistický Úrad Slovenkej Republiky (ed.) (2004) *Statistická Ročenka Slovenskej Republiky 2004*. Bratislava.
Štatistický Úrad Slovenkej Republiky: http://www.statistics.sk/

Slovenia

Statistični Urad Republike Slovenije (ed.) (2004) *Statistični Letopis Republike Slovenije 2004*. Ljubljana.
Statistical Office of the Republic of Slovenia: http://www.stat.si/eng/index.asp

General

Institute for Tourism (ed.) (1998) *Tourism in the CEI Countries. Key Figures 1994–1996*. Zagreb: Institute for Tourism.

7 Slovenia: New Challenges in Enhancing the Value of the Tourism Destination Brand

Maja Konečnik

Introduction

The Republic of Slovenia lies in the heart of Europe, where the Alps face the Pannonian plains and the Mediterranean meets the mysterious karst (Fig. 7.1). To the north lies Austria; Hungary is to the east; Croatia is to the south and Italy to the west. Its geographical area in Central Europe encompassing just 20,256 km² makes it one of the smallest countries in the world. It can also be similarly ranked according to the number of its inhabitants, which is somewhat less than 2 million. Slovenia is strengthening its international position and reputation as a democratic, stable and successful European state, but is also striving to preserve its national identity (Government Public Relations and Media Office, 2005).

Throughout its history Slovenia has always formed part of larger countries or even great empires. The country has seen many changes in its economic system – from the mainly agricultural and artisanal period of the Austro-Hungarian Monarchy, the slightly more industrialized Kingdom of Serbs, Croats and Slovenians, the socialist state-centred industrialization of the former SFR Yugoslavia, through to today's independent Slovenia directed towards development and a market economy. After gaining its independence, Slovenia managed to overcome the loss of the markets in former Yugoslavia within

a short time as its trade flows were redirected to the EU and associated partners (Government Public Relations and Media Office, 2005).

Slovenia is one of the most successful countries to transit from socialism to a market economy. It boasts stable GDP growth and is viewed as a safe country, ranked among the countries with the lowest degree of risk. Since its independence in 1991, Slovenia has privatized its economy, stabilized inflation and wage growth, halted the rising unemployment, strengthened its currency, relaxed the flow of capital and modernized its taxation system. On 1 May, 2004, Slovenia became a member of the European Union. In the economic sphere, Slovenia's development level is quickly catching up with that of the EU (Government Public Relations and Media Office, 2005).

Tourism is seen as an important, and one of the most promising, sectors in the Slovenian economy. In addition to its direct effect, the country also sees its indirect effect mainly through the enhancement of the country's brand value. The opportunity or challenge to enhance its value has even increased since Slovenia's accession to the EU. Therefore, this chapter presents the impacts which EU accession is bringing to the development of the tourism sector in Slovenia and especially to the development of Slovenia as a tourism destination brand.

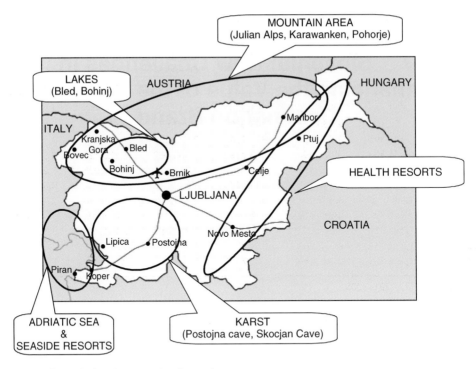

Fig. 7.1.   Slovenia: location map of major tourism resources.

The chapter is divided into two main parts describing the development of tourism in Slovenia. After the introductory part, which presents the main characteristics of the Republic of Slovenia, the chapter proceeds by reviewing tourism development in Slovenia since its independence. The focus is on presenting the main tourism indicators in Slovenia within the last two years. The latest changes in the tourism industry after Slovenia joined the EU are discussed. Contrary to this main part, which describes the direct effect of Slovenian tourism and presents it through statistics, the second part of the chapter stresses the development process of the tourism destination brand 'Slovenia'. Development of the 'Slovenia' brand is introduced through two views of a destination brand: the internal and external perspectives. This part concludes by describing the possible impacts of Slovenia's accession to the EU. In the author's opinion this could represent a new challenge for enhancing the value of the tourism destination brand 'Slovenia', which could lead to building up a strong country brand.

Review of Tourism in Slovenia

Tourism is one of the most promising sectors of the economy in Slovenia. Its important role was also recognized when Slovenia was part of former SFR Yugoslavia. In 1990, just a year before Slovenia's independence, 2.5m tourists were recorded, of which 1.8m were foreigners. The 10-day war in Slovenia that immediately followed its independence had a negative impact on Slovenian tourism. A considerable fall in foreign tourist numbers was recorded and, although the number of international tourists has been steadily rising since then, these figures have not equalled those from the beginning of 1991. In 2004, around 1.5m international tourists were recorded in Slovenia, who made almost 4.4m overnight stays. On the other hand, the opposite trend is recognized for domestic tourists because their numbers have increased significantly since Slovenia's independence. Further, in 2004 the country had 0.84m domestic tourists who made 3.2m overnight stays, representing a slight decline compared to 2003 (SORS, 1991–2005) (Table 7.1).

Table 7.1. Slovenia: number of arrivals and overnight stays, 1990–2004.

Year	Foreign		Domestic		Total	
	Arrivals	Overnight stays	Arrivals	Overnight stays	Arrivals	Overnight stays
1990	1,887,462	5,345,400	651,324	2,611,006	2,538,786	7,956,406
1995	732,103	2,435,467	844,569	3,447,579	1,576,672	5,883,046
1996	831,895	2,550,607	825,774	3,281,637	1,657,669	5,832,244
1997	974,350	3,078,400	848,779	3,305,662	1,823,129	6,384,062
1998	976,514	3,062,432	822,411	3,232,876	1,798,925	6,295,308
1999	884,048	2,741,218	865,484	3,315,345	1,749,532	6,056,563
2000	1,089,549	3,404,097	867,567	3,314,901	1,957,116	6,718,998
2001	1,218,721	3,813,477	867,001	3,316,125	2,085,722	7,129,602
2002	1,032,019	4,020,799	859,941	3,300,262	2,161,960	7,321,061
2003	1,373,137	4,175,385	872,931	3,327,184	2,246,068	7,502,569
2004	1,498,334	4,361,484	841,793	3,224,357	2,340,127	7,585,841

Sources: SORS, 1991–2005.

Table 7.2. Slovenia: international tourism receipts and expenditure, 2003 and 2004.

	2003 (in €000s)	2004 (in €000s)	Indices
International tourism receipts	1,186,270	1,310,693	110
International tourism expenditures	666,588	731,562	110
Balance	519,682	579,131	111

Source: Bank of Slovenia, 2005.

Since the number of international tourists and their overnight stays in Slovenia is increasing, a similar growth trend is also recognized in the measure of international tourism receipts (Table 7.2). However, international tourism receipts in 2004 compared to 2003 grew by 10%, representing an even higher growth rate than recorded for this period by either the number of foreign tourists (9%) or their overnight stays (4%) (Table 7.3). In addition, domestic tourists spent 10% more abroad in 2004 than in 2003 (Table 7.2) (Bank of Slovenia, 2005).

The majority of tourists in Slovenia came from European countries, a further five of which should be stressed: Germany, Italy, Austria, Croatia and Great Britain (Table 7.3). Although German tourists have made the highest number of overnight stays in the last few years, Italians exceeded this number in 2004 (0.78m compared to 0.77m). A similar situation is also recognized with British tourists, who made

0.27m overnights stays in 2004, representing a 32% growth rate in comparison to 2003. This growth rate was even higher when we consider the number of British arrivals (52%) (SORS, 2004, 2005).

Tourists who come to Slovenia can experience the destination's amazing contrasts. Because of the small land area, it is possible to enjoy many activities in totally different geographical areas on the same day. A morning swim in the Adriatic can be followed 2 hours later by skiing below the Alpine peaks, then an adventurous discovery of the karst's subterranean phenomena and an invigorating bath in a thermal spring. This can be followed by an encounter with history in a lively mediaeval city and, not far away, a more solitary stroll through primeval forests or undulating, wine-growing hills (Government Public Relations and Media Office, 2005). According to the official statistics, the diversity of the Slovenian

Table 7.3.   Slovenia: international tourist arrivals and overnight stays by country of origin, 2003 and 2004.

	2003		2004		Indices	
Country	Arrivals	Overnight stays	Arrivals	Overnight stays	Arrivals	Overnight stays
Germany	229,372	813,241	237,825	771,654	104	95
Italy	288,507	729,181	313,296	786,130	109	108
Austria	201,367	690,827	205,597	691,313	102	100
Croatia	93,639	264,827	92,018	260,782	98	98
Great Britain	50,220	202,181	76,267	266,970	152	132

Sources: SORS, 2004, 2005.

Table 7.4.   Slovenia: tourist arrivals and overnight stays by types of tourist resort, 2003 and 2004.

	2003			2004		
Type of tourist resort	Tourist arrivals	Overnight stays	Bed occupancy (%)	Tourist arrivals	Overnight stays	Bed occupancy (%)
Ljubljana	214,442	437,321	31	264,660	505,030	34
Health resorts	509,133	2,342,939	48	530,745	2,417,081	48
Seaside resorts	520,136	2,010,129	36	525,619	2,001,965	36
Mountain resorts	604,773	1,823,732	23	610,006	1,825,297	24
Other tourist resorts	372,131	797,776	28	376,713	765,995	27
Other places	33,249	74,426	13	33,538	73,369	14
Total	2,246,068	7,502,569	32	2,341,281	7,588,737	33

Source: SORS, 2004, 2005.

tourism offer is incorporated in the following types of tourism resort in Slovenia: Ljubljana as the capital city, health resorts, seaside resorts, mountain resorts, other tourist resorts and other places (Table 7.4).

The average bed occupancy in 2004 was 33%; however, the figure ranges from 14% in other places to 48% in health resorts. Excluding accommodation in health resorts, the other places remain seasonal. Most tourists arrive in the peak months of July and August. Besides July and August, the second highest occupancy period is the other two summer months of June and September. An average increase of 1% in overall bed occupancies was recorded in 2004 in comparison with 2003. The highest increase was seen in the capital city Ljubljana, where the average bed occupancy rate in 2004 was 34% (Table 7.4) (SORS, 2004 and 2005).

Review of Tourism in Slovenia after its Accession to the EU

Slovenia achieved a 9% annual change in international arrivals and a 5% annual change in overnight stays in 2004 compared to 2003 (SORS, 2005) and was, according to the research group of the European Travel Commission, recognized as one of the main winners in terms of tourism growth in 2004. Other winners were emerging destinations in Central and Eastern Europe like Estonia, Lithuania, Bulgaria and the Czech Republic (ETC, 2005). However, although a relatively huge growth rate in 2004 was identified, this rate was similar to the growth enjoyed in previous years (also see Table 7.1). Therefore, it is difficult to conclude that the high growth rate appeared due to accession to the European Union. However, the processes closely connected with

EU accession might partly help sustain this high rate.

One change in Slovenian tourism was recognized in the structure of foreign tourists in 2004. As we can see in Table 7.5, the ten fastest growing markets in 2004 were members of the EU (like Great Britain, Italy, France, The Netherlands, Ireland, and Spain) and some other non-European countries (like the USA and Australia). We could speculate that the awareness of Slovenia as a tourism destination has increased amongst European Union inhabitants. Further, by gaining the status of an EU member country Slovenia is also winning greater recognition in international markets. At the same time, Slovenia's accession to the EU could also be a signal of the more stable and improved security conditions in Slovenia. In the last group of tourists we can mainly stress American tourists.

The increasing price competition in the tourism market has already produced a remarkable effect on transport price policy. An obvious example influencing tourism development is the growing number of British tourists in Slovenia. The arrival of the low-cost carrier EasyJet at the end of April 2004 with its first route London–Ljubljana has boosted the numbers of Britons coming to Slovenia. The number of Britons has increased not only because of the new EasyJet line, but also due to the reduced flight ticket prices offered by the national airline Adria Airways along this route. A similar situation may be expected when other new lines are opened. In 2004 alone,

EasyJet opened several lines between Slovenia and other EU members.

Although the EU-related free movement across borders has been suspected as an important step for the development of tourism, so far this has not seen any major changes. On the contrary, the new visa requirements discourage non-EU visitors from visiting Slovenia. A sharp drop in demand in 2004 compared to 2003 was recognized for tourists from the Russian market (SORS, 2005).

Developing the Tourism Destination Brand 'Slovenia'

Despite earlier scepticism about transferring the brand concept to the destination area (O'Shaughnessy and O'Shaughnessy, 2000), branding has continued to attract interest in the destination area in the last few years (Anholt, 2000, 2002, 2003; Kotler and Gertner, 2002; Olins, 2002). In this categorization, destinations can be evaluated from different perspectives, mostly as tourism destinations (Gnoth, 1998, 2002; Curtis, 2001; Cai, 2002; Hall, 2002a, 2002b; Morgan and Pritchard, 2002; Morgan, Pritchard and Piggot, 2002; Morgan, Pritchard and Pride, 2002; Pride, 2002) or destinations that aim to attract foreign direct investment (Papadopoulus and Heslop, 2002).

Destinations as brands can enhance their own brand value (Ahholt, 2000). In order to enhance the value of the destination brand two main concepts should be considered. The first

Table 7.5. Slovenia: most important and fastest growing markets by number of overnight stays, 2004.

Top ten markets	Overnight stays	Ten fastest growing markets	Overnight stays
Italy	786,130	Great Britain	64,789
Germany	771,654	Italy	56,949
Austria	691,313	France	29,373
Great Britain	266,970	USA	23,020
Croatia	260,782	Netherlands	19,819
Netherlands	215,175	Ireland	11,248
France	105,264	Serbia and Montenegro	9,406
Hungary	105,217	Other non-European countries	8,276
Belgium	91,186	Spain	7,538
USA	90,749	Australia	6,590

Source: SORS, 2005.

concept – the concept of destination brand identity – describes it from the internal (mostly management) perspective (Cai, 2002; Konečnik, 2005, unpublished doctoral dissertation, Ljubljana University, Faculty of Economics). On the other hand, the concept of the customer-based brand equity of a tourism destination examines it from a tourist perspective (Konečnik, 2005, unpublished doctoral dissertation, Ljubljana University, Faculty of Economics). Although these concepts involve two opposing perspectives on brands (managers vs tourists), researchers suggest treating them as inter-related and connected approaches in modern brand analysis (de Chernatony and McDonald, 2001).

Because the destination of Slovenia involves some specifics, namely the value of its brand is currently not very high, it could eventually provide an example of how a systematically developed brand can enhance its own brand value. Not only this author, but also many other authors involved in research into brand destinations, believe Slovenia is one country that should work seriously towards building its destination brand (Hall, 2002a, 2002b; Olins, 2002) with the aim to build a modern and strong destination brand (Anholt, 2000). These views are also supported by the following factors (Konečnik, 2004). First, as a country newly established in 1991 Slovenia does not *per se* have centuries of history. Second, its geographical area in Central Europe encompassing just 20,256 km^2 makes it one of the smallest countries in the world. Third, although it is small, Slovenia features great variety within its regions (contrasting its mountains and lakes versus its coast and karst). Finally, as a former socialist country Slovenia has been associated with a similar image evaluating in competing quality indicators like the quality of infrastructure and suitable accommodation.

The opportunity to build a strong brand has also been recognized by Slovenia's practitioners, namely the various Slovenian stakeholder groups. As seen in the current activities, the main emphasis is on the tourism area. Because tourism is closely connected with other areas, the development of a tourism brand can also transfer its strength to economic, political, cultural and technological areas of the country. The first systematic approach following Slovenian independence came in 2004 with the Slovenian

Tourist Board (STB) working in cooperation with the Slovenian Ministry of the Economy. The main goal of their project was to boost the recognition and reputation of Slovenia upon it joining the EU in key European markets and to increase the value of the related trademarks that are communicated in the spheres of tourism, culture, the economy, and politics.

Indirectly, besides the goal of increasing tourist traffic from EU countries the campaign also had some other goals. These included:

- easier penetration and an improved position for Slovenian companies in the European Union market;
- the more noticeable role of Slovenia in international politics;
- greater possibilities to organize international events and conferences in Slovenia;
- simplified access to international connections and support for the penetration of Slovenian science and culture (STB, 2004).

The campaign was conducted in Germany, Italy and Austria in the first two months after Slovenia's accession to the EU. The marketing campaign with its slogan 'Slovenia Invigorates' sought to emphasize the opportunities Slovenia can offer. A similar campaign was repeated in 2005.

Related to the aim of projecting the desired image to foreigners through marketing activities, the STB is working hard on developing and building a brand identity of Slovenia as a tourism destination, which will reflect its unique competitive advantage compared to its main competitors. Although the process started in 2004, it is believed that it will take some time to develop a clear identity for Slovenia.

Compared to the unfinished process of building an identity, it is obvious that Slovenia's tourism stakeholders are themselves working hard on developing and offering quality tourism experiences. Consistent with the strategic (long-term) goals of Slovenian tourism, the STB is trying to encourage all participants in Slovenian tourism to improve the quality of their services or products (STB, 2002). The increase in tourism receipts in 2004 may provide a good signal that Slovenia's tourism is on the correct path.

Contrary to the tourism development process going on in Slovenia, like the internal perspective on brand development, the perception of Slovenia as a tourism destination from foreigners' points of view should definitely be considered. Slovenia was introduced to the global tourism market in 1991 (Brezovec, Brezovec and Jancic, 2004). However, some authors claim that for this introductory period the tourism product of Slovenia may have been influenced by the country's image (Brezovec, 2001; Brezovec, Brezovec and Jancic, 2004) which, according to Jancic, is weak (Jancic, 1998). Similar conclusions were drawn by the only available research in this period (Tavcar, 1997), which was carried out in Austria and France in 1997. Editors, politicians and tourism managers expressed a low level of awareness of the country Slovenia as well as some doubts about its democracy and product quality. Besides the previously mentioned findings, the lack of empirical results about foreigners' evaluations of Slovenia as a tourism destination is identifiable in the first decade after Slovenia's independence.

The first systematic analysis of the perception of Slovenia as a tourism destination was, to our knowledge, conducted in 2001 (Konečnik, 2001, unpublished Masters thesis, Ljubljana University, Faculty of Economics). Tourism representatives mostly from European countries expressed their opinions on Slovenia as a tourism destination. Of the 119 respondents, 4% were unaware of Slovenia as a tourism destination, 12% were aware of it but were unable to locate its geographical position, while 84% of respondents recognized it and were able to properly locate its geographical position in Central Europe. Those respondents who recognized Slovenia as part of Central Europe shared a relatively positive common image of Slovenia as a tourism destination. However, the worst evaluated attributes were some quality indicators in Slovenia such as the quality of its infrastructure. The investigation also indicates that the perception of Slovenia as a tourism destination differs between those respondents familiar with Slovenia (have visited Slovenia in the past or have personal contacts with Slovenians) in comparison to those respondents who were unfamiliar with Slovenia (Konečnik, 2002).

In 2003, another investigation about the customer-based brand equity of Slovenia as a tourism destination was conducted in the German and Croatian markets. In this research,

somewhat more than 400 potential tourists in each country expressed their opinions about Slovenia as a tourism destination. The research was carried out with a CATI (computer-assisted telephone interviewing) method and therefore representative samples were ensured. The results imply that German respondents are aware of Slovenia as a tourism destination, although they still have problems in their quick recall of some of Slovenia's characteristics. Further, they hold mostly neutral or even slightly positive opinions about Slovenia's image. On average, they perceive Slovenia as a country of friendly people and pleasant weather with beautiful nature, especially due to its beautiful mountains and lakes. In addition, they shared much worse opinions about Slovenia's quality dimensions (i.e. infrastructure, personal safety and its accommodation). The results also indicated only the slight attitudinal loyalty of Germans, mainly through their interest in visiting Slovenia in the future. Croatians are well aware of Slovenia as a tourism destination which can also be explained by their common historical connections as well as the geographical positions of both countries. On average, they had a positive opinion about Slovenia's image attributes, mostly its natural attractions. However, they shared a very positive opinion of Slovenia's health resorts. Further, they expressed a positive opinion about Slovenia's quality dimensions, especially its cleanliness, personal safety, unpolluted environment and quality of accommodation. They expressed an interest to visit Slovenia in the future and to recommend it to their friends and relatives (Konečnik, 2005, unpublished doctoral dissertation, Ljubljana University, Faculty of Economics).

The results of both investigations about the perception of Slovenia as a tourism destination imply a medium to strong level of awareness in the minds of the investigated group of respondents (tourism representatives from mostly European countries and potential tourists in the German and Croatian markets), as well as a positive image about Slovenia as a tourism destination and mostly neutral to even negative attributes in some quality evaluations. On the contrary, high quality was evaluated by the Croatian respondents. Although the presented results give us an important sign regarding the customer-based brand equity of Slovenia as a tourism destination, we cannot generalize it for other nations. It is possible that evaluations would differ totally were we to choose potential tourists or tourism representatives from other markets.

The Impacts of EU Accession on the Tourism Destination Brand 'Slovenia'

Drawing from the current situation of the tourism destination brand of Slovenia, we speculate on the possible impacts of EU accession on the brand's development. As in the previous chapter, we divide all the proposed impacts into the identity and equity destination concepts. Because of the interrelationship of both concepts we proceed to draw common conclusions about our view of the future position of the destination brand of Slovenia. The main impacts of EU accession on the tourism destination brand 'Slovenia' are also presented in Fig. 7.2.

The internal perspective on a brand is mostly represented in the processes of Slovenian tourism development. The development of the tourism sector is influenced by changes at micro and macro environmental levels. Because of EU accession, some other impacts can be identified:

- the larger common market resulted in more potential tourists;
- improved economic conditions meaning the faster growth of tourism demand;
- more demanding consumers who are willing to pay for higher-quality experiences;

- changes in socio-cultural attitudes (like taking several holidays through the year or spending more active holidays);
- increased competition between tourism suppliers with the effect of reduced prices;
- decrease in the regulation of some areas will boost competitiveness (as in the transport sector), which will lower prices; and
- the single common currency will increase price transparency and decrease exchange-rate risks.

In summary, the growing competition between companies will force or give the opportunity to raise the quality level of Slovenian tourism. At the same time, the well-situated larger common market with demanding tourists will provide enough potential tourists to visit Slovenia. Because the increase in competition will decrease prices for tourism products, it is important that companies are able to offer experiences that provide the highest added value. Therefore, they should be able to offer unique experiences. Although this situation will have a positive effect on the destination brand of Slovenia, the question arises of whether Slovenia's small- and medium-sized enterprises are already prepared and able to compete in an environment as competitive as the EU environment.

Slovenia's accession to the EU will mostly affect the tourist perspective of the brand 'Slovenia'. However, Slovenia as one of the new EU countries will be perceived better than in the past. Considering the elements of the

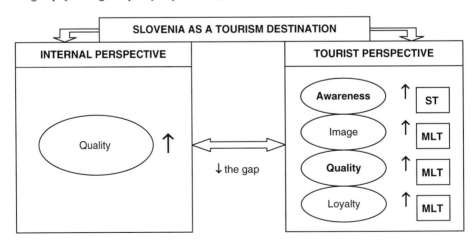

Fig. 7.2. Impacts of EU accession on the tourism destination brand 'Slovenia'. ST – short-term, MLT – medium- to long-term.

customer-based brand equity concept, some further predictions are made:

- an increase in the awareness of Slovenia – a short-term effect;
- an improvement in Slovenia's image as a tourism destination – a medium- to long-term effect;
- an increase in Slovenia's quality dimensions – a medium- to long-term effect; and
- a growth in Slovenia's attitudinal loyalty – a medium- to long-term effect.

Generally, we may assume that EU accession will mainly increase the awareness of Slovenia as a tourism destination. We suppose that the recognition of Slovenia has already improved and will also increase in the near future. This is extremely important especially in those markets where Slovenia has not been widely recognized. The second most evident effect will be shown in the perceptions of Slovenia's quality dimensions. However, previous investigations have shown that the biggest gap between what is perceived and what is given exists in quality evaluations. Accession to the EU will bring about an opportunity to close the existing gaps. We also speculate about some improvement in image evaluations from the foreigner's point of view, although this evaluation was already relatively positive in the past. The growing awareness of Slovenia as a tourism destination, positive evaluation of its image and quality dimensions could also boost the attitudinal loyalty dimension, meaning an increase in tourists' intentions to visit Slovenia as well as to recommend it to others.

Although EU accession will give some opportunity to improve the value of the destination brand of Slovenia, Slovenia's different stakeholder groups should undertake the most important activities. Here we have in mind all possible stakeholders who could add some value to the brand 'Slovenia' and, according to their abilities, ensure that Slovenia as a tourism destination will exist strongly in the minds of potential tourists. Apart from the STB as a national governmental organization, active roles in brand-building are expected from the tourism industry and the country's residents who should 'live the brand' and thereby take an active role in developing and building the strong tourism destination brand of Slovenia.

Conclusion

This chapter presents the Republic of Slovenia as a new country in the EU and summarizes its main economic characteristics. In this context, the importance of the tourism sector in Slovenia is emphasized. However, the steady growth rate of tourism indicators (such as the number of international tourist arrivals, international tourism receipts) since its independence imply it is also a promising sector for Slovenia's future.

Besides the encouraging results about tourism development in Slovenia from previous years, tourism could also represent a basis for the whole country's brand development. As far as tourism is closely connected with other activities of a country, the development of a tourism brand can also involve the transfer of its strength to other areas. Therefore, the chapter stresses the main idea of brand development and presents it through two main brand concepts: the brand identity concept and the concept of customer-based brand equity. The latest systematic approaches in tourism destination brand development in Slovenia regard the tourism destination brand as an important tool to enhance the value of the country.

Slovenia's accession to the EU in 2004 represents a challenge for further development of the tourism destination's brand. Although EU accession will bring some positive effects for Slovenia's brand development, mainly evident in its quality improvement, the biggest advantage of EU membership will, in the author's opinion, be reflected in tourists' perceptions of Slovenia as a tourism destination. Considering the elements of the customer-based brand equity of a tourism destination, the author predicts the main changes in Slovenia's awareness and its quality perception. First, we have assumed that EU accession will mostly increase awareness or recognition of Slovenia. Therefore, the destination Slovenia will be included in tourists' opportunity destination sets, giving the tourism destination of Slovenia equal chances for potential future visits as other known tourism destinations. Further, Slovenia's membership in the EU will improve foreigners' evaluations of its quality dimensions. However, previous investigations have shown that the biggest gap exists in the perception of the quality evaluation because many foreigners still connect Slovenia's quality with its previous socialist system.

Although EU membership will give an opportunity for a better evaluation of Slovenia from the foreigner's perspective and therefore the possibility to build a strong tourism destination brand 'Slovenia', the key role is still to be played by Slovenians. Therefore, the initial steps should be taken by different Slovenian stakeholders who should be prepared and able to take the proper action. Should foreigners receive positive signals from Slovenians about their country then the tourism destination brand of Slovenia is on the right track to becoming a strong brand.

References

Anholt, S. (2000) The nation as brand. *Across the Board* 37(10), 22–27.

Anholt, S. (2002) Foreword. *Journal of Brand Management* 9(4–5), 229–239.

Anholt, S. (2003) *Brand New Justice: The Upside of Global Branding*. Oxford: Butterworth-Heinemann.

Bank of Slovenia (2005) *Financial Data*. Ljubljana: Bank of Slovenia. Available at: http://www.bsi.si/html/financni_podatki/

Brezovec, A. (2001) Imidž države kot turistične destinacije. *Teorija in Praksa* 38(4), 739–754.

Brezovec, A., Brezovec, T. and Jancic, Z. (2004) The interdependence of country's general and tourism images. In: Weber, S. (ed.) *Reinventing a Tourism Destination: Facing the Challenge*. Zagreb: Institute for Tourism, pp. 115–129.

Cai, L.A. (2002) Cooperative branding for rural destination. *Annals of Tourism Research* 29(3), 720–742.

Curtis, J. (2001) Branding a state: the evolution of Brand Oregon. *Journal of Vacation Marketing* 7(1), 75–81.

de Chernatony, L. and McDonald, M. (2001) *Creating Powerful Brands in Consumer, Service and Industrial Markets*. Oxford: Butterworth-Heinemann.

ETC (European Travel Commission) (2005) *European Tourism Insights 2004*. Brussels: ETC.

Gnoth, J. (1998) Conference reports: Branding tourism destinations. *Annals of Tourism Research* 25(3), 758–760.

Gnoth, J. (2002) Leveraging export brands through a tourism destination brand. *Journal of Brand Management* 9(4–5), 262–280.

Government Public Relations and Media Office (2005) *Slovenia in Brief*. Ljubljana: Government Public Relations and Media Office. Available at: http://www.uvi.si/about-slovenia/in-brief/

Hall, D. (2002a) Brand development, tourism and national identity: the re-imaging of former Yugoslavia. *Journal of Brand Management* 9(4/5), 323–334.

Hall, D. (2002b) Branding and national identity: the case of Central and Eastern Europe. In: Morgan, N., Pritchard, A. and Pride, R. (eds) *Destination Branding: Creating the Unique Destination Proposition*. Oxford: Butterworth-Heinemann, pp. 87–105.

Jancic, Z. (1998) Nevidna povezava ugleda države in podjetij. *Teorija in Praksa* 35(6), 1028–1041.

Konečnik, M. (2002) The image as a possible source of competitive advantage of the destination – the case of Slovenia. *Tourism Review* 57(1/2), 6–12.

Konečnik, M. (2004) Evaluating Slovenia's image as a tourism destination: self-analysis process toward building a destination brand. *Journal of Brand Management* 11(4), 307–316.

Kotler, P. and Gertner, D. (2002) Country as brand, product, and beyond: a place marketing and brand management perspective. *Journal of Brand Management* 9(4–5), 249–261.

Morgan, N. and Pritchard, A. (2002) Contextualizing destination branding. In: Morgan, N., Pritchard, A. and Pride, R. (eds) *Destination Branding: Creating the Unique Destination Proposition*. Oxford: Butterworth-Heinemann, pp. 10–41.

Morgan, N., Pritchard, A. and Piggot, R. (2002) New Zealand, 100% pure. The creation of a powerful niche destination brand. *Journal of Brand Management* 9(4/5), 335–354.

Morgan, N., Pritchard, A. and Pride, R. (2002) Introduction. In: Morgan, N., Pritchard, A. and Pride, R. (eds) *Destination Branding: Creating the Unique Destination Proposition*. Oxford: Butterworth-Heinemann, pp. 3–10.

Olins, W. (2002) Branding the nation – the historical context. *Journal of Brand Management* 9(4–5), 241–248.

O'Shaughnessy, J. and O'Shaughnessy, N.J. (2000) Treating the nation as a brand: some neglected issues. *Journal of Macromarketing* 20(1), 56–64.

Papadopoulus, N. and Heslop, L. (2002) Country equity and country branding: problems and prospects. *Journal of Brand Management* 9(4–5), 294–314.

Pride, R. (2002) Brand Wales: 'natural revival'. In: Morgan, N., Pritchard, A. and Pride, R. (eds) *Destination Branding: Creating the Unique Destination Proposition*. Oxford: Butterworth-Heinemann, pp. 109–123.

SORS (Statistical Office of the Republic of Slovenia) (1991–2005) *Statistical Yearbook*. Ljubljana: SORS.

STB (Slovenian Tourism Board) (2002) *Strategija Trzenja Slovenskega Turizma 2003–2006*. Ljubljana: STB.

STB (Slovenian Tourism Board) (2004) *Slovenia invigorates – project*. Ljubljana: STB. Available at: http://www.slovenia-tourism.si

Tavcar, R. (1997) Drzava se je pogledala v ogledalo. *Marketing Magazin* 17(6), 12–13.

8 Slovakia: EU Accession and Cross-border Travel

Vladimír Baláž

Introduction

While the Czech and Slovak Republics, Hungary and Poland have accounted for fairly similar levels of social and economic development, this by no means applies to all regions within these countries. The shift from central planning to market mechanisms has been accompanied by sharp regional disparities, with border regions being particularly affected by the processes of convergence/divergence (see Smith, 1996). These disparities are expressed in different income and price levels between neighbouring border regions and generate specific types of cross-border exchange.

Cross-border visitor exchange is a distinctive part of international travel. While all international travel involves crossing borders, cross-border exchange is a much more local and/or regional affair. The volume and structure of cross-border travel are affected by a number of factors. These include:

- regulations related to international and trans-border travel, such as passport and visa regulations, rules on travel by local inhabitants in border areas, policies setting custom duties, VAT and excise tax rates;
- travel motives of the population in border areas. These depend on the structure of tourist destinations, ethnic composition of

population and structure of labour markets on both sides of the border;
- intensity of cross-border cooperation at state and regional levels, and the extent and quality of travel infrastructure such as numbers of border crossing points, quality of road and railway connections.

Some of these factors are subject to economic and political changes. These were particularly rapid and extensive in East Central Europe (ECE: Czechoslovakia, Hungary and Poland) after 1989 and were expressed in a thorough revamping of travel regulations and improvements in travel infrastructure. Travel motives, on the other hand, tend to result from demographic structures and tourist destinations on both sides of the border and do not change so quickly.

Slovakia has borders with five countries that range from a former constituent part of the Soviet Union to a pre-existing EU member state. Each border separates a unique combination of adjacent border regions:

- *Northern Slovakia*, a less-developed region adjoining a less-developed region in Poland;
- *Southern Slovakia*, a marginal region in Slovakia bordering a marginal region in Hungary;
- *Western Slovakia*, a developed industrial region, bordering a developed region in the Czech Republic;

Fig. 8.1. Slovakia: territorial structure – counties and borders.

- *Eastern Slovakia*, a peripheral region bordering a marginal region in the Ukraine; and
- *Bratislava City,* a developed region neighbouring Austria (Fig. 8.1).

Particular combinations of border regions provide for very diverse cross-border flows. In turn, diverse flows have very different impacts on economic and social developments in the border regions.

Within this context, this chapter, focusing on Slovakia, has three central themes:

- first, it looks at changes in volumes and structures of international travel in Slovakia in the period 1989–2004 and compares these with developments in other ECE countries. It examines particular factors underlying shifts in cross-border travel patterns before and after Slovakia's accession to the EU. This part of the chapter draws mostly on secondary statistical sources provided by the national statistical offices;
- second, it considers the importance of selected travel motives on the volume and structure of cross-border tourist exchange. Special attention is paid to understanding differential and selective integration of border regions into the global economy in terms of their position in a national economy subject to intense market reforms and internationalization, and also in relation to their trans-border international neighbours. Here the paper draws on tourist surveys by national tourist authorities and a survey with mayors of municipalities in Slovak border regions, conducted by the author (Williams *et al.*, 2001);
- third, it considers impacts of: (i) cross-border flows on the development of

adjoining border regions, and (ii) EU membership on the development of such flows. There were a number of EU-assisted programmes aimed at cross-border cooperation before its eastern enlargement in 2004. After 2004 Slovakia and other ECE countries developed a large number of initiatives in the field of transport infrastructure, cross-border cooperation and creation of Schengen-type borders (European Commission, 2001; MVSR, 2004a, 2004b, 2004c). Most of these initiatives were heavily subsidized from the EU Structural and Cohesion Funds (MVRRSR, 2004a, 2004b). This part of the chapter relies on the author's survey on border regions and information provided by Slovakia's central authorities and official documents.

Change and Stability

Transformation of international travel in ECE after 1989 was set by two groups of factors, with the first being of greater importance than the second:

1. Framework factors. These resulted in an overall change in the social and economic situation of the country. Changes in international travel were only a by-product of a wider transition, which included removal of passport and visa barriers; establishment of a market economy, and gradual incorporation of the ECE countries into EU structures.
2. Tourism industry-specific factors. These included state sponsorship of tourism marketing abroad and various financial aid schemes for the tourism sector. These initiatives lacked financial resources and had only a limited impact on tourism development, in the early phase of transition in particular.

The volume and structure of tourist flows to and from Slovakia before 1989 were mostly determined by political considerations (Johnson, 1995). Tourism flows with the EU were constrained by a number of passport and visa barriers. Visitors from Western countries accounted for only 5% of total movements. Tourism exchanges with three neighbouring state socialist countries (the German Democratic Republic, Poland and Hungary) were relatively free and accounted for 90% of all flows. The intra-eastern bloc exchanges were shaped by ideological priorities. These were to 'promote international friendship' and 'a better understanding of brother nations'. The real world was rather different. After the Solidarity movement had secured a position of political influence in Poland in 1980, the Czechoslovak authorities imposed complex barriers on travel to that country, and the need to develop a 'better understanding of a brother nation' was set aside. Instead, a system of special permissions was introduced for trips to Poland, so that after 1982, with martial law imposed in Poland, such tourism exchanges were severely reduced. Tourist flows with the former USSR were heavily restricted. While there was no problem buying a package trip, individual trips were restricted to strictly prescribed travel routes between borders and Black Sea coastal resorts. There were a number of areas closed to foreigners. Cross-border exchange between Slovakia and Ukraine was prohibited (MVSR, 2004b). Local inhabitants wishing to visit their relatives on the other side of the border (sometimes no more than a few hundred metres away), had to arrange visas in Prague and Moscow.

Hence, the most significant developments in international travel after 1989 were the removal of passport and visa formalities. In 1990 the former Czechoslovakia signed non-visa tourist exchange agreements with 18 countries, including Austria, Germany and Italy. Five other countries followed suit in 1991, and by 1992 agreements were in place with most European states. Restrictions on travel to Poland were also lifted and travel to Ukraine liberalized. In 1993 Slovakia signed the Association Agreement with the EU, which was another major impetus for liberalized travel.

Liberalization of travel was reflected in huge increases in the scale of international tourist flows (Figs 8.2 and 8.3). All four ECE countries (the Czech and Slovak Republics, Hungary and Poland) have experienced broadly similar trends in inbound tourism, with a period of rapid expansion after 1989 being followed by decline or static numbers. Whereas 29.6m foreign visitors came to Czechoslovakia in 1989, by 1996 this number had leapt to 109.4m visitors to the Czech Republic (CNTO, 2004) and 33.1mn to Slovakia (ŠÚSR, 1991–2005).

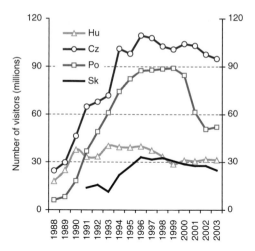

Fig. 8.2. Foreign visitors at frontiers in ECE, 1988–2003. Sources: ŠÚSR, 1991–2005; HNTO, 2003; CNTO, 2004; PIT, 2004.

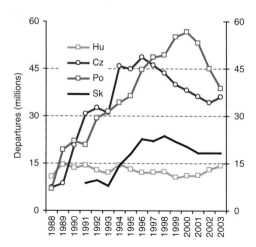

Fig. 8.3. Departures by residents in ECE, 1988–2003. Sources: ŠÚSR, 1991–2005; HNTO, 2003; CNTO, 2004; PIT, 2004.

There were a number of reasons for these increases, linked to the removal of the Iron Curtain, the growth of business tourism in newly opened economies, and the generation of trans-border shopping tourism from Germany and Austria. The period 1996–1997, however, was something of a watershed for the visitor inflows to all ECE countries. Slovakia experienced a similar trajectory to its neighbours, although its decline in numbers was less marked – there were still 26.3m foreign visitors in 2004 (ŠÚSR, 1991–2005). Arguably, this reflected lower levels of initial 'curiosity tourism' and a weak tourism image, as well as the late onset of economic reforms.

There were also marked changes in outbound tourism. In Slovakia, there are no reliable data for outbound travel prior to 1989. However, 9.6m Slovaks went abroad in 1991, rising to a peak of 32.7m in 1998, before falling to 21.2m by 2004 (ŠÚSR, 1991–2005). The decline in outbound travel, in part, reflected decay in the 'novelty factor', and in the initial exuberant 'curiosity tourism' which followed border liberalization; but it also reflected changes in neighbours' economic systems. Pre-1989 borders were reconstituted more as gateways than barriers, although they had different meanings depending on the economic and social complementarities of national territories. In the early stages of transition, the uneven pace of reform and the divergence between economic systems meant that the re-regulated borders provided opportunities for border *arbitrage* (Altvater, 1998). This was manifested in various forms of small-scale trading and shopping activities taking advantage of differences in the price and availability of goods in neighbouring economic systems. However, economic reforms subsequently eroded these differences as the ECE economies converged around western European models, particularly in the latter years of transition prior to EU membership.

In the Communist period, the ECE countries were heavily dependent on tourist demand from neighbouring countries. In Czechoslovakia in 1989, for example, 83% of inbound flows centred on just three countries: the German Democratic Republic, Poland and Hungary (see Hall, 1991 for comparisons with other Central and East European countries). These three countries were also the principal destinations for outward tourist flows, and accounted for 59% of outbound Czech and Slovak visitors. Surprisingly, at least at first glance, this 'nearest-neighbour' spatial pattern of tourist flows has changed very little since 1989 in all the ECE countries. Rather, there has been considerable stability, grounded in geographical, economic and cultural conditions. Most regions within Hungary, Poland, the Czech and Slovak Republics are easily accessible to each other and are pervaded by strong economic and social-cultural networks. There are formal and informal business relationships, and cross-border familial and friendship ties that generate international tourism amongst this group of countries. In addition, the geographical location of these countries has long given them a role in transit tourism (Williams and Baláž, 2002a).

If major changes in volume of international travel resulted from travel liberalization in the early 1990s, has EU membership had any impact on international travel to Slovakia? In 2004, there were some increases both in the inbound and outbound travel volumes on each of Slovakia's borders (Figs 8.4 and 8.5), but they may have been caused by high economic growth: Slovak GDP grew by 5.4% in that year. Simplification of travel regulations with the EU-members and increasing barriers in tourist exchange with Ukraine also became important for Slovakia after its accession to the EU (MVSR, 2004b).

The first of May, 2004 saw the single passport control introduced at borders with Austria, Hungary, Poland and the Czech Republic. Identity cards were recognized as official travel documents, in addition to passports. This change was little visible on the Czech and Hungarian borders. Travel between Slovakia on the one hand and Hungary and the Czech Republic on the other was little restricted and the local inhabitants, for example, enjoyed unhindered travel under the small cross-border regime before 2004. Simplification of travel regulation was most noticeable on the Austrian border, where the formerly long queues disappeared. It was, however, the Polish border which accounted (rather unexpectedly) for the most interesting development. The 1996 Slovak–Polish agreement enabled inhabitants of certain municipalities in border areas to cross frontiers under the small cross-border regime. They could, for example, use a much larger number of border crossing points than the rest of the population in both countries.

From 1 May, 2004 Polish and Slovak tourists (and other EU nationals) started to use the full range of border crossings, regardless of whether they were local inhabitants or not. Most of this exchange was related to informal shopping and business travel. This had not been envisaged by the Slovak and Polish authorities,

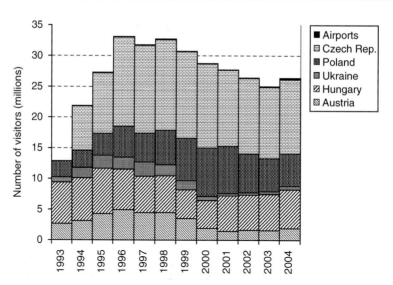

Fig. 8.4. Slovakia: foreign visitors by border of entry, 1993–2004. Sources: ŠÚSR 1991–2005.

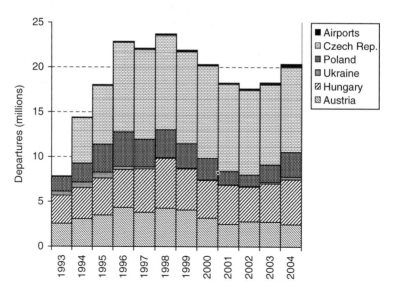

Fig. 8.5. Slovakia: Slovaks travelling abroad by exit border, 1993–2004. Sources: ŠÚSR 1991–2005.

as they were not able to check flows of travellers and goods. After a short period of toleration, in August 2004 Slovak and Polish authorities started to enforce the original travel regulations. The small cross-border regime was allowed only for inhabitants of border areas (MVSR, 2004a). Other travellers had to use the approved border crossings. The full liberalization of travel between Poland and Slovakia should take place with

their entry into the Schengen club in 2006/2007 (MVSR, 2004c).

As a European Union (EU) candidate, Slovakia needed to comply with the Schengen Treaty requirements before EU entry. These included securing the EU's external border, preventing illegal immigration and introducing a visa regime for non-member countries, including Ukraine (MVSR, 2004a, 2004b, 2004c).

In 2000, Slovakia (rather quickly) introduced visa requirements for Ukrainian nationals, and Ukraine responded in the same way. Introduction of visas had deeply negative consequences for cross-border travel. Numbers of Ukrainians travelling to Slovakia dropped from 1.5m in 1999 to 0.35m in 2001. Numbers of Slovak tourists going to Ukraine dropped from 62,000 to 54,000 in the same period. In the early 2000s Slovakia and Ukraine extended the number of their consulates in neighbouring countries and eased visa regulations. The cross-border exchange increased, but was far from its 1999 heyday.

Illegal immigration from Ukraine, extensive smuggling of alcohol and tobacco products and difficulties encountered by Slovak authorities when returning migrants back to Ukraine were regarded as major obstacles for the introduction of a more liberal regime for cross-border exchange. These issues were discussed during a visit by the Slovak Prime Minister Mr Dzurinda to Kiev in June 2004 (MZSR, 2004). The Ukrainian Government gave up the idea of free of charge visas for all Ukrainians travelling to Slovakia and no visa requirements for Slovaks travelling to Ukraine. The Slovak Government, on the other hand, was ready to follow recommendations by the Council of Europe from September 2003 on small cross-border exchange. These recommendations included free visas issued to inhabitants living in areas up to 50 km from each side of the border. The visa valid for a period of 1–5 years should enable both VFR and leisure travel and access to local labour markets. The Slovak government, however, pointed out that further liberalization of the visa regime depended on strict enforcement of the current readmission agreement.

Travel Motives and Composition of Cross-border Flows

There are no statistics covering structure and motives of cross-border travel and impacts of cross-border flows on local and regional economics in Slovakia. In the absence of reliable secondary statistics on cross-border personal mobility, surveys by tourist authorities and independent researchers can shed some light on this issue.

The 1998–2002 tourism surveys (MHSR, 1997–2003; also PIT, 2004) indicated that most foreign visitors came from neighbouring countries, such as Hungary, Poland, and the Czech Republic. They dominated the day visitor and the short-stay tourism markets. The average length of stay was about 3 days. In contrast, longer stay (4+ days) tourists were more likely to be from Germany, The Netherlands and Italy. Border crossing statistics reveal a remarkable stability in the cross-border travel patterns (Figs 8.4 and 8.5). There were no significant changes in travel motives in the period 1996–2002. Most visitors travelled for business, leisure and culture purposes, followed by visiting friends and relatives (VFR), shopping, and transit or one-day visits with undeclared objectives (Table 8.1).

Relatively stable underlying factors influenced these patterns. Most of the VFR travel, for example, had an ethnic dimension. The large Hungarian minority in Slovakia (some half a million people or 10% of the Slovak population), maintained strong contacts with their friends and relatives in Hungary. Adjacent border regions of Hungary provide them with plenty of opportunities for culture, shopping and small-time business, which are not always available in Slovakia. The same can be said for ethnic Slovaks and Hungarians living in Ukraine. A lot of Czech–Slovak travel originated in friendship and family ties established during the period of a common state (1918–1991). These ties were not broken after the 'Velvet Divorce' and establishment of the Czech and Slovak Republics. Ethnic and demographic composition in neighbouring countries has changed little in recent years. Similar stability can be found in the supply of culture and leisure destinations in Slovakia.

The above-mentioned tourist surveys characterize travel motives of foreign tourists coming to Slovak territory. Border areas, however, account for a rather different structure of travel motives. Williams, Baláž and Bodnárová (2001) undertook a key informant survey in September 1999. It was directed at all the municipal mayors in Slovakia's five border regions. The survey assumed that mayors of border municipalities were likely to possess the most complete information concerning impacts of cross-border

Table 8.1.   Slovakia: travel motives of foreign visitors, 1996–2002.

Motive	Year (%)						
	1996	1997	1998	1999	2000	2001	2002
Culture and incentive	7.6	7.4	7.5	8.0	8.2	6.7	9.9
Stay in spas	1.6	2.7	2.3	2.5	1.9	2.8	2.5
Skiing	–	2.8	2.7	3.5	4.6	3.2	–
Shopping	10.4	9.7	9.9	10.9	10.6	10.1	13.0
Visiting friends and relatives	16.4	17.8	18.5	17.4	14.4	15.0	13.7
Leisure	16.1	11.6	10.3	9.7	10.5	10.4	16.1
Transit	29.3	25.1	24.0	24.1	25.0	26.7	24.9
Business and other	18.6	22.9	24.8	23.9	24.8	25.1	19.9
Average length of stay, in days	–	–	3.1	2.3	3.2	2.6	2.9

Sources: MHSR, 1997–2003.

travel on local and regional economies, culture, trade and cross-border relations. Some 369 replies were received from 518 questionnaires dispatched, a response rate of 71%. The questionnaires addressed three major topics:

- impacts of the post-1989 border 'opening' on the districts' economies;
- employment issues; and
- the institutional framework of trans-border cooperation.

The first part of the analysis focused on the practices of the different forms of trans-border mobility, and especially on arbitrage or the circulation of commodities. The largest proportion of informants (42.1%) considered that leisure tourism was the main source of foreign visits to their area, followed by business and shopping visits (37.6%) and VFR (20.3%). Trans-border tourism generates different kinds of inbound and outbound spending, including shopping. Shopping has been an important element of expenditure by Slovak tourists abroad since the 1970s when Hungarian reforms increased the range of imported goods available in that country.

The removal of travel barriers after 1989 intensified shopping travel in both directions. Differences in the shopping practices of Slovak tourists abroad and of foreign tourists in Slovakia results from price differentials for particular goods, and these are expressed differently at each border. For example, food (63.6%) was considered to be the main objective of Ukrainian shopping, while cigarettes and alcohol were considered the most important foreign purchases by Poles (52.9%), reflecting higher sales taxes in Poland. For Slovaks' shopping abroad, food was the main objective in the Czech and Hungarian border regions (52.5% and 52.3%), while electronics were relatively important at the Austrian and Polish borders (28.6% and 23%). Clothing was also important for Slovaks shopping in the Polish (20.7%) and the Hungarian (19.9%) regions. These estimates indicate that trans-border shopping between neighbouring ECE countries with similar development levels (Hungary, Poland, Czech Republic and Slovakia) was mainly determined by price differences for particular items, while the range of goods on offer was more important for shopping trips between states with different development levels (Slovakia and Austria, Slovakia and Ukraine). Following substantial recent investment in shopping centres by international retail companies (e.g. Tesco and Billa), the cross-border shopping flows decreased in importance.

Slovakia's accession to the EU had no dramatic impacts on cross-border tourist and shopping flows between Slovakia and the Czech Republic, Hungary and Poland. There were few barriers for travel and shopping between these countries before May 2004. Most variations in cross-border flows were generated by changes in national regulations of the EU-candidate countries (such as sale taxes adjustments), rather than via applications of the EU regulations. The situation, however, has been different with Ukraine, where the range of goods has remained important, as expansion of international retail chains has been slow. Ukrainians, of course, can enjoy a better range of goods in Slovak, Czech and Polish hypermarkets, and purchase these goods for their own use or for resale. A major part of the cross-border shopping between Slovakia and Ukraine, however, has been related to trading and smuggling alcohol and tobacco products. After its accession to the EU, Slovakia had to increase sales taxes on these products, making trade in them even more lucrative. Slovak police, for example, have estimated that one-third of all cigarettes sold in eastern Slovakia are smuggled from Ukraine.

What were the economic implications of trans-border shopping? The mayors considered that the average Slovakian expenditure abroad exceeded that of foreign nationals in Slovakia. Most estimated that Slovak daily per capita expenditure was some Sk1000–5000 (US$25–125). If this is accurate, then given some 30m border crossings by Slovaks annually, total expenditure could be between $700m and $3500m (with the lower end of the range being more realistic). This has to be set against total Slovak imports in 1999 of approximately $10bn. Therefore, while not negligible, informal trans-border shopping of $0.7bn was of no more than moderate significance compared to formal trade.

Most shopping, however, was by local people living in the border regions, so the regional impacts of arbitrage may be more substantial. The situation varies according to the border under consideration and the time period. In the late 1990s, receipts from petrol sales to foreigners provided limited benefits for Slovakia's Hungarian border regions because the sales taxes were centrally accrued. The same applied to alcohol and cigarette sales to Polish tourists in northern Slovakia. After the introduction of a flat tax of 19% and substantial increases in sales taxes in Slovakia in 2004, the cross-border shopping flows changed. Slovak petrol became one of the most expensive in Europe and many Slovaks tried to buy it in the Czech Republic and Hungary. Many Slovaks living near the

Slovak–Polish border renewed their interest in shopping in Poland. Prices of selected food items (e.g. sugar, milk, poultry) in Poland were only 50% of those in Slovakia and became a major travel motive for hundreds of thousands of Slovaks travelling to Poland (Banačnský, 2004). These changes in cross-border flows illustrate how sensitive shopping tourism was to modifications in tax rates.

The foreign shopping expenditures by Slovaks resulted in income losses for border region businesses and in terms of direct and indirect taxes for the state. Customs barriers sought to protect the domestic food, textile and clothing industries, but high VAT rates in Slovakia and low production and circulation costs in the Polish and Hungarian shadow economies resulted in price differentials which could be as high as 30–50%. These were likely to have an important negative effect on local retailers in these sections, whilst benefiting individual consumers in the border regions.

The evidence from the survey suggested there was only limited cross-border labour migration, reflecting the reality of economic conditions in the Slovak–Hungarian, Slovak–Polish and Slovak–Ukrainian border regions. Instead, long-distance migration to Prague, Germany, and North America was of greater importance. The only exception was daily and weekly commuting (both of unskilled and professional workers) from Bratislava to Vienna, reinforcing the economic dynamism of what already constituted core economies. However, even this has to be kept in perspective for only a small proportion of the total Slovak labour force worked abroad (compared to say the Southern European countries in the 1960s). Most foreign workers in Slovakia also tended to gravitate to the more dynamic Bratislava, Central and Western regions, bypassing the Hungarian, Polish and Ukrainian border regions.

Role of the EU in Fostering Cross-border Cooperation and Travel Infrastructure

The isolation of border areas has been twofold. First, the presence of borders cuts off communities from each other economically, socially and culturally, and hinders the coherent management of ecosystems. Second, border areas have often been neglected within national policy, with the result that their economies have tended to become peripheral within national boundaries.

The fall of the Iron Curtain was followed by massive increases in cross-border exchange. But did it have positive impacts on development of the adjacent border regions? There certainly were positive gains by local tourism and leisure facilities on Austrian and Polish borders in particular. Cross-border shopping, and to a far lesser extent trading in response to price gradients for particular products did generate substantial tourist and other expenditures, but it is likely that a large proportion of the income generated was collected by agents located in core regions: either the state (through sales taxes on alcohol and petrol) or international companies. There is, then, no unequivocal evidence that cross-border mobility contributes to regional convergence.

The mayors in the above-mentioned survey themselves had ambiguous opinions with respect to the regional impacts of the liberalization of travel after 1989. On balance, a quarter to a third considered the changes had been positive for their local economies and for living standards and the development of local culture. More than one half of the mayors, however, related liberalized travel to increasing crime rates. Again, there were differences by border region. A positive balance was most likely in the Austrian (57.1%), followed by the Hungarian (45.8%) and the Polish (38.6%) border regions. The mayors in the Ukrainian border region were more likely to be negative. Those on the Czech border were more likely to consider there were 'no changes', reflecting the low barriers constituted by the border even after the 'Velvet Divorce'. In general, the more developed the neighbouring country, the more positive the opinions. The mayors in the region bordering Austria, for example, were strongly positive as to the impact on their economies, and of course this was the region where trans-border labour migration and trade opportunities were greatest.

There were also positive assessments of the impacts on cultural life in the regions bordering Austria, Poland and Hungary, probably related to increased tourism and intercultural contacts.

In contrast, the mayors of the regions bordering Ukraine complained mainly about the decline in living standards, increased crime and the impoverishment of local cultural life. Weak cross-border cooperation primarily was caused by the ongoing significance of the national state as a centre of regulation. Local and regional authorities were given few responsibilities in this area. The lack of effective regulation of national economic spaces, including a coherent regional policy, was another reason for the failure to facilitate cross-border cooperation. Despite these reservations, judging from the experience of Western Europe, cross-border cooperation is likely to become more prominent on the political agenda in future. The survey showed that most of the mayors did consider this to be an important issue for the future, and that 53% considered it could significantly boost the local economy, culture and tourism in their area.

Strengthening cooperation to the mutual advantage of border areas was an important task both for accession countries and the European Union. Enlargement has increased the number of EU internal borders and has progressively shifted its external borders eastwards. The EU programmes promoting the single market were strong catalysts for improvements in cross-border cooperation (European Commission, 1998). In Slovakia, these programmes developed in several stages.

- The Phare Cross-Border Co-operation (CBC) Programme started with a limited number of small projects aimed at improvement of local infrastructure in the 1990s (MVRRSR, 2004c). In 2004 Phare CBC was replaced by the Interreg III initiative.
- From May 2004 Slovakia was also able to access the Cohesion Fund, much of which funding has been allocated to building basic infrastructure (motorways and railways) (European Commission, 2001; MVRRSR, 2004a).
- Slovakia's planned membership of the Schengen area was reflected in the reconstitution of the Slovak–Ukrainian border as an external Schengen-type border. Here Slovakia has largely relied on means provided by the Schengen Transition Fund (MVSR, 2004c).

Conclusions

The year 1989 was a watershed in tourism for the ECE countries. Removal of passport and visa regulations facilitated a boom in inbound and outbound flows. Total numbers of inbound visitors in the four ECE countries increased from 97.6m in 1989 to 269.8m in 1996. With a population of 64.3m, the ECE Four accounted for some 4.2 international visitors per inhabitant. The later period saw decreases in visitor numbers to 203.5m in 2003; yet there remain few regions in the world with such a high density of international travel.

However, there was as much continuity as change in tourism after 1989. For Slovakia the main generating countries and destinations generally remained unchanged (Germany, Austria and the ECE countries themselves), as did the importance of transit tourism. Shopping, trading, VFR, leisure, and business are standard motives for crossing borders and happen simultaneously. Stability in structure of travel motives and tourist destinations is, hence, hardly surprising. Cross-border shopping and petty trading, for example, were not created during the transition period. Before 1989, there were similar economic tourism flows from ECE to Western Europe, or within ECE, generated by the way borders separated different economic systems, creating opportunities for what Altvater (1998) has termed *arbitrage*. Petty trading and shopping had also been features of tourism before 1989 and adapted to new opportunities as borders were reconstituted (Böröcz, 1996; Williams and Baláž, 2002b). However, while some flows were substantially shaped by the economic transition, notably petty trading and shopping (Czakó and Sik, 1999; Williams and Baláž, 2002b), others, such as those to visit friends and relatives, have been more enduring. Visiting friends and relatives has remained significant, given the complex territorial distribution of ethnic, linguistic and nationality groups across borders. As so many of these tourism flows are constructed around existing networks and deep-rooted social routines, post-1989 tourism necessarily 'was built on the ruins' (Stark, 1996) of pre-1989 tourism.

This discussion has focused on cross-border tourism flows, and it is true that international tourism in ECE does display 'nearest neighbour' characteristics (Williams and Baláž, 2002a). Most foreign visitors to Slovakia are from adjoining border regions and their visits are of short duration. Excursionists are the most frequent category of visitors. Business and shopping, leisure and VFR are identified as the main motives for visits to a neighbouring country. The structure of travel motives in cross-border travel is thus different from that in international travel. Tourists from non-neighbouring countries are likely to be more interested in culture and incentive travel, skiing and spa stays. They also stay longer, and spend more per capita than those from neighbouring countries.

The EU accession year of 2004 saw no dramatic changes in cross-border flows in Slovakia. Most of the fundamental changes had already taken place in the 1990s and were related to processes of economic and social transition and political integration into EU and NATO structures. Borders to the west have been opened and EU membership has no major implications for tourism in this respect. The processes of privatization of property rights were virtually complete in the tourism sector by 2004. EU regulation in this area has been limited to the package holiday directive.

The only significant change in cross-border flows resulting from the accession process was transformation of the Slovak–Ukrainian border to an external Schengen-type one. This transformation had rather ambiguous results. On one hand, it contributed to better filtering of cross-border flows and combating illegal migration. On the other hand, it significantly decreased the volume of cross-border exchange in the fields of tourism, VFR travel and labour migration.

Is EU membership likely to generate a significant transformation in cross-border travel in Slovakia? Assuming there are no fundamental shifts in other economic and political parameters (such as relationships with the CIS, or in the price of oil), no great and/or rapid changes in volumes and structure of cross-border flows are likely. EU membership is more likely to generate qualitative changes in cross-border travel, supported by transformation of the economic and social environment in ECE:

- Structural reforms undertaken in Slovakia since 1998 attracted a great volume of foreign investment. Stocks of direct foreign investment increased from 22.9% of GDP in 2000 to 37.2% in 2003 (NBS, 2004). Foreign investment may facilitate rising income levels, convergence with EU GDP per capita levels (at exchange rates), and increased outbound tourism oriented to business and leisure purposes. In contrast, shopping and petty trading continue to wane, following gradual price convergence and further integration of retail distribution systems through the foreign direct investment strategies of Western European transnational companies.

- Some inbound tourism may be facilitated by the EU structural aid which flows into transport infrastructure, farm tourism, and environmental and urban assistance programmes. The volume of this aid rose significantly, from several million euros in the early 1990s to billions after 2004. Some of the EU financial facilities were specifically aimed at fostering cross-border cooperation. Some, such as the Cohesion Fund, are oriented to improvements of basic infrastructure. Particular attention has been paid to the modernization of trans-European multi-modal corridors. Tourism has not been a main concern in these programmes. The Interreg IIIC programme stated cross-border cooperation in tourism a priority, but allocated only modest means to support it. The impact of EU financial assistance on the cross-border tourist exchange is likely to be indirect and reflected, for example, in better quality roads, higher speed and safety of travel, and increased numbers of border crossings.

However, any such change and growth are likely to be relatively modest in comparison with the shifts that occurred in the 1990s. The scale, spatiality and objectives of international travel have already been reshaped substantially in anticipation of EU membership.

References

Altvater, E. (1998) Theoretical deliberations on time and space in post-socialist transformation. *Regional Studies* 32, 591–606.

Böröcz, J. (1996) *Leisure Migration: a Sociological Study of Tourism*. Oxford: Pergamon.

Bančanský, A. (2004) Počet východniarov v poľských obchodoch sa zdvojnásobil [Numbers of easterners in Polish shops doubled]. *Národná Obroda*, 26 March.

CNTO (Czech National Tourist Office) (2004) *Compendium of Tourism Statistics in the Czech Republic 2003*. Prague: Czech National Tourist Office, Analytical Department. Available at: http://www.czechtourism.cz

Czakó, A. and Sik, E. (1999) Characteristics and origins of the Comecon open-air market in Hungary. *International Journal of Urban and Regional Research* 23(4), 715–737.

European Commission (1998) Commission Regulation (EC) No 2760/98 of 18 December 1998 concerning the implementation of a programme for cross-border cooperation in the framework of the PHARE programme. *Official Journal of the European Communities,* L 345/49.

European Commission (2001) *White Paper on European Transport Policy for 2010*. Brussels: European Commission, COM(2001)370.

Hall, D.R. (1991) Introduction. In: Hall, D. (ed.) *Tourism and Economic Development in Eastern Europe and the Soviet Union*. London: Belhaven Press, pp. 1–25.

HNTO (Hungarian National Tourist Office) (2003) *Tourism in Hungary 1990–2002*. Budapest: HNTO. Available at: http://www.hungarytourism.hu/

Johnson, M. (1995) Czech and Slovak tourism, patterns, problems and prospects. *Tourism Management* 16(1), 21–28.

MHSR (Ministerstvo Hospodárstva Slovenskej Republiky) (1997–2003) *Prieskum Cestovného Ruchu v Slovenskej Republike*. [*Tourism Survey in the Slovak Republic*] Bratislava: Ministry of the Economy of the Slovak Republic.

MVRRSR (Ministerstvo Výstavby a Regionálneho Rozvoja Slovenskej Republiky) (2004a) *Stratégia Slovenskej Republiky pre Kohézny Fond 2004–2006*. [*Strategy of the Slovak Republic for the Cohesion Fund*] Bratislava: Ministry of Construction and Regional Development of the Slovak Republic. Available at: http://www.telecom.gov.sk/top/sreu/kf_final.doc

MVRRSR (Ministerstvo Výstavby a Regionálneho Rozvoja Slovenskej Republiky) (2004b) Aby Štrukturálne Fondy slúžili Slovensku. [Structural Funds for Slovakia] Bratislava: Ministry of Construction and Regional Development of the Slovak Republic.

MVRRSR (Ministerstvo Výstavby a Regionálneho Rozvoja Slovenskej Republiky) (2004c) Zoznam Projektov Phare CBC. [List of the Phare CBC Projects] Bratislava: Ministry of Construction and Regional Development of the Slovak Republic.

MVSR (Ministerstvo Vnútra Slovenskej Republiky) (2004a) Na Hraniciach od 1. Mája 2004 po Novom. [New Border Regime Since 1 May 2004] Bratislava: Ministry of the Interior of the Slovak Republic. Available at: http://www.minv.sk/archiv

MVSR (Ministerstvo Vnútra Slovenskej Republiky) (2004b) Securing Slovak-Ukrainian Border. Bratislava: Ministry of the Interior of the Slovak Republic. Available at: http://www.minv.sk/

MVSR (Ministerstvo Vnútra Slovenskej Republiky) (2004c) Návrh Národnej Implementačnej Stratégie Schengenského Prechodného Fondu. [Proposal for the National Implementation Strategy of the Schengen Transitional Fund.] Bratislava: Ministry of the Interior of the Slovak Republic. Available at: http://www.minv.sk/pk/2004/ARCHIV/KM-79/vlastnymat_1.htm

MZSR (Ministerstvo Zahraničných vecí Slovenskej Republiky) (2004) Informácia o Priebehu a Výsledkoch Oficiálnej Návštevy Delegácie Vlády Slovenskej Republiky Vedenej Predsedom Vlády Slovenskej Republiky Mikulášom Dzurindom na Ukrajine v dňoch 21. a 22. Júna 2004. [Information on results of visit of the official delegation of the Slovak Government headed by the Prime Minister of the Slovak Republic Mr Mikuláš Dzurina in Ukraine on 21st and 22nd June 2004] Bratislava: Ministry of Foreign Affairs of the Slovak Republic. Available at: http://www.foreign.gov.sk/pk/mat/140-informacia.htm

NBS (National Bank of Slovakia) (2004) Balance of Payments Statistics. Bratislava: NBS.

PIT (Polish Institute of Tourism) (2004) Statistics. Warsaw: PIT. Available at: http://www.intur.com.pl

Smith, A. (1996) From convergence to fragmentation. Uneven regional development, industrial restructuring, and the transition to capitalism in Slovakia. Environment and Planning 28, 135–156.

Stark, D. (1996) Recombinant property in East European capitalism. American Journal of Sociology 101(4), 993–1027.

ŠÚSR (Štatistický úrad Slovenskej Republiky) (1991–2005) Ekonomický Monitor. Bratislava: ŠÚSR.

Williams, A.M., Baláž, V. and Bodnárová, B. (2001) Border regions and trans-border mobility: Slovakia in economic transition. Regional Studies 35(9), 831–846.

Williams, A.M. and Baláž, V. (2002a) The Czech and Slovak Republics: conceptual issues in the economic analysis of tourism in transition. Tourism Management 23(1), 37–45.

Williams, A.M. and Baláž, V. (2002b) International petty trading: changing practices in trans-Carpathian Ukraine. International Journal of Urban and Regional Research 26(2), 323–342.

9 Tourism in the Czech Republic

Alžbeta Királ'ová

Introduction

The nature and impacts of tourism activity in the Czech Republic have gained great significance. After 1989 tourism became an important social and economic force in several regions of the country. This chapter discusses tourism development in the Czech Republic within the context of the decade and a half of the state's existence, through post-Communist transition to EU accession, and beyond.

The Czech Republic is a land-locked country with a total area of 78,866 km² (land, 77,276 km²; water, 1590 km²), and boundaries totalling 1881 km (bordering Austria 362 km, Germany 646 km, Poland 658 km, and Slovakia 215 km). The country's climate is temperate, affected by the interaction of oceanic and continental effects.

The Czech Republic has a population of 10.23 million, with Czechs comprising the largest ethnic group (81.2%). Other groups present in the country include Moravians (13.2%), Slovaks (3.1%), Poles (0.6%), Germans (0.5%), Silesians (0.4%), Roma (0.3%) and Hungarians (0.2%). Since Czechoslovakia divided into two national components, the Czech and Slovak Republics on 1 January, 1993 (the 'Velvet Divorce'), the Czech Republic has become one of the most stable and prosperous of the post-Communist CEE states (CIA, 2005; see also Table 1.1). Per capita GDP reached US$15,700

in 2003, with unemployment around 8% (Czech Statistical Office, 2005). The Czech Republic joined NATO in 1999 and the European Union in 2004. Economic growth in 2000–2004 was supported by exports to the EU (87% of the total in 2004), primarily to Germany, and strong foreign and domestic investment.

The natural and cultural resources for tourism development are well developed:

- twelve historic monuments on the UNESCO World Heritage list: the historic centre of Prague, Český Krumlov, Telč, and Kutná Hora, the pilgrimage church of St John of Nepomuk on Zelená Hora at Žd'ár nad Sázavou, South Moravia's Lednice-Valtice Chateau and landscape area, the Archbishop Chateau in Kroměříž with Květná and Podzámecká gardens, South Bohemian village of Holašovice, Litomyšl Castle, the Baroque Holy Trinity Column in Olomouc, Villa Tugendhat in Brno, and the Jewish Quarter and cemetery and the St Prokop Basilica in Třebíč;
- over 2000 castles, chateaux and monuments;
- more than 40 protected historic towns and cities;
- four national parks (Krkonoše, Šumava, Dyje and České Švýcarsko), eight mountain ranges, and over 1200 protected landscape areas and nature reserves cover more than 10% of the country's territory;

- 38,500 km of walking trails, 19,024 km cycling routes, and 1240 km cross-country ski circuits;
- over 20,000 lakes and other water bodies; and
- more than 30 spas, some of them with a long tradition, such as Karlovy Vary (Karlsbad), Mariánske Lázně.

These are complemented by a wide range of accommodation facilities, including 8211 registered establishments, 19 five-star and 201 four-star hotels, and a total of 261 hotels with congress facilities, 478 tourist campsites, 1069 self-catering units and hostels (Czech Tourism, 2005).

Administration of Tourism

The state administration of tourism is undertaken by the Ministry for Regional Development, which has three major roles:

- proposing and implementing measures aimed at strengthening international cooperation in the field of tourism;
- preparing relevant legislation and analysis; and
- carrying out duties arising from membership of the World Tourism Organization and other organizations.

The country's Parliament is comprised of the Chamber of Deputies and the Senate. Within the committee structure of the former, there is a sub-committee for tourism and crisis regions overseen by the Committee for Economy, and a sub-committee for the promotion of the Czech Republic abroad falling within the Committee for Foreign Affairs. These sub-committees deal with legislative, promotional and developmental issues in an advisory capacity.

Since 1993, the Czech Tourism Authority has been the prime government agency responsible for the promotion of tourism. It has an office in Prague, and coordinates 29 international branch offices. Its mission is to develop travel to the Czech Republic from abroad as a stimulus to economic stability, growth of the Czech travel industry, and expanded foreign exchange earnings. To these ends, the Czech Tourism Authority conducts programmes of information, advertising, publicity and research, and is a member of international organizations engaged in tourism, such as the European Tourism Commission (ETC), European Federation of Conference Towns (EFCT), Association of German Coach Carriers, and German Association of Travel Agencies. It cooperates with regional authorities to provide a national tourism information system.

Regional offices, municipal authorities and communities perceive tourism as an important business activity and provide resources for its development. There are also several types of regional associations and destination management companies in the Czech Republic. These have been established by city councils, development funds, or as an initiative of tourism entrepreneurs. They aim to attract tourists to specific geographic regions, develop tourism marketing strategies, cooperate with partners, support and coordinate local businesses, develop tourism products, public relations and destination image, and provide crisis management. Most city councils have established visitor bureaux, some of which are operated by independent entrepreneurs. There are also a number of different special interest and professional organizations, associations, and unions acting to guarantee the quality of the services provided by their members. However, the administrative division of the country is not identical to that of tourism regions (Fig. 9.1). This geographical inconsistency, together with numerous administrative regulations, results in a low level of cooperation among regional administrative bodies in the field of tourism.

Impacts of EU Accession Processes on Tourism Development in the Czech Republic

The processes of EU accession compliance requirements, EU laws and norms have influenced and continue to impact upon tourism development in a number of both positive and negative ways:

- It can be argued that the harmonization of legislation, requiring the implementation of obligatory standards and norms can create familiar environments and quality criteria

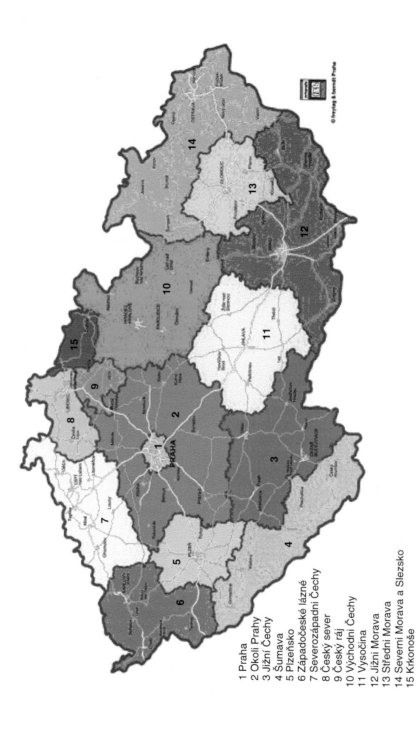

Fig. 9.1. The Czech Republic: tourism regions. Source: CzechTourism, 2005.

1 Praha
2 Okolí Prahy
3 Jižní Čechy
4 Šumava
5 Plzeňsko
6 Západočeské lázně
7 Severozápadní Čechy
8 Český sever
9 Český ráj
10 Východní Čechy
11 Vysočina
12 Jižní Morava
13 Střední Morava
14 Severní Morava a Slezsko
15 Krkonoše

encouraging European Union nationals to travel to other member states and particularly the new accession countries such as the Czech Republic.

- Free movement of services – the role of the internet, its visual presentation and ready availability of tourist information on destinations and products is resulting in the decreasing role of travel agents. More than a thousand travel agencies operated in the Czech Republic in 2003, but this number decreased to 800 in 2004 and this trend was continuing for 2005. By contrast, there has been a strong development of e-marketing and the availability of secure online reservations as well as a clear understanding of the importance of the role of destination management.
- Free circulation of people – one of the most important documents affecting tourism development in the European Union is the Schengen Agreement, which the Czech Republic has yet to implement. When the country has signed up to this agreement, it is likely to encourage stronger leisure interest in the arts, culture, history, and education of other European members, opening new opportunities for segmented tourism products. At the same time, it will enhance possibilities for Czech citizens to travel abroad for holidays, business and education.
- Transport policy – and the implementation of directives and regulations – has two major areas of impact: for land transport, concerning vehicle licensing, safety and roadworthiness; and air transport liberalization, opening up domestic routes to foreign competitors. Consequent increases in demand for transport access, safety and security, and price quality, can result in increased multiplier effects for the Czech economy: for example, with an increasing number of weekend trips especially to Prague, and in reviving small airports in the provinces.
- Health protection – the acceptance of European health insurance within the Union together with growing health-consciousness is increasing the demand for wellness and spa products. The environmental consciousness of European citizens is demanding sustainability in destinations. This requires an enhancement of destination management policies through more coherent and consistent planning, supported by the local population, and expressing cooperation between public and private sectors. Acceptance of health insurance also brings savings to Czech citizens when travelling abroad.

- Social and employment policy – this has wide-ranging importance, but the impact of regulations governing the use of work equipment is of particular relevance to restaurants and ski schools.
- Small and medium-sized enterprises – as a significant part of the tourism sector is created by small and medium-sized enterprises, EU support and funding mechanisms during the pre- and post-accession periods has assisted an increase in the number of businesses, providing new contacts, encouraging cooperation, facilitating the free movement of goods and capital.

Most EU policies influence or are influenced by tourism. These include social policy, consumer protection, environment policy and transport. As noted in Chapter 1, tourism is viewed by a number of bodies within the EU, as well as the WTO and WTTC, as the industry that will generate considerable employment in the next 10 years. Enterprises involved in the industry are perceived as potential contributors to a number of the EU's key objectives, such as those of sustainable development, social and economic cohesion, quality of life and European integration.

Most EU laws are resulting in higher standards and a better overall tourism product. Implementation of such standards, also deriving from Western tour operators and by the tourism market itself, are vital for the Czech tourism industry to remain competitive.

Foreign Exchange Receipts and Expenditure

As one of the largest international industries, tourism also has a noticeable impact on the balance of payments of the Czech Republic. Development of foreign exchange receipts and expenditure can be divided into two main periods – in the first, receipts increased and reached their peak in 1996 with US$4.1bn, then a decline was experienced, especially in 1999 and 2000. Table 9.1 shows a slight increase in 2001 but the international situation after September 2001 and the floods of 2002 resulted again in a decline for that year. However, the following years showed a resurgence in receipt levels.

The direct share of tourism in GDP, as shown in Table 9.2, again had a positive tendency up to 1996 when it reached its maximum (7.1%). This was followed by a decline to 2003. The estimated level for 2004 was between 3.0 and 3.5%; together with tourism-related activities, the estimated share grew to 12% of GDP. The share of tourism receipts in exports reached its maximum in 1997 and 1998. From 1999, a relative decline can be observed as a result of overall increasing export incomes.

Receipts from tourism as a proportion of all foreign exchange receipts from services reached its maximum in 1997 (Table 9.2). A significant decline set in from 1999, although a slight increase was experienced in 2003. The direct share of tourism in employment is estimated at

3.8%, but when tourism-related branches are also included, the estimated share grows to 12–13% (Mag Consulting, 2005).

Inbound and Outbound Travel

The Czech Statistical Office obtains information on tourism in two basic forms: (a) numbers of incoming visitors – each foreigner who crosses the border regardless of length of stay; and (b) number of incoming visitors who stay at least one night in registered accommodation. When compared to 2003, the number of arrivals to the Czech Republic in 2004 increased by 19.4%. From a total number of 7.9m arrivals, 6.06m visitors stayed in registered accommodation and 1.85m stayed with friends/relatives or in rented apartments.

Germany is the major visitor source, with 1.99m arrivals in 2004 (an increase of 9.1% on 2003), a share of 25.1% of the market, and an average length of stay of 4.8 days. Slovak visitors represent the second largest market, with

Table 9.1. The Czech Republic: foreign exchange receipts and expenditure, 1992–2004.

Indicator (bn US$)	1992	1993	1994	1995	1996	1997	1998	1999	2000	2001	2002	2003	2004
Receipts	1.1	1.6	2.2	2.9	4.1	3.6	3.9	3.2	3.0	3.1	2.9	3.6	4.2
Expenditure	0.5	0.5	1.6	1.6	3.0	2.4	1.9	1.5	1.3	1.4	1.6	1.9	2.3
Balance	0.6	1.1	0.6	1.3	1.1	1.2	2.0	1.7	1.7	1.7	1.4	1.6	1.9

Source: Czech National Bank, 2005.

Table 9.2. The Czech Republic: share of tourism in the national economy, 1993–2003.

Indicator	1993	1994	1995	1996	1997	1998	1999	2000	2001	2002	2003
Share of tourism receipts as % of GDP	5.0	5.6	5.5	7.1	6.9	6.8	5.8	5.9	5.5	4.2	4.2
Share of tourism receipts as % of exports	11.0	14.0	13.4	18.6	16.3	15.0	12.0	10.3	9.3	7.7	7.3
Share of tourism receipts as % of service receipts	33.0	43.2	42.8	49.8	50.9	50.6	44.8	43.5	43.8	41.7	45.8

Source: Czech National Bank, 2005.

0.78m arrivals in 2004 (an increase of 5.6% on 2003), a share of 9.9% and an average stay of 4 days. The 0.78m visitors from the United Kingdom, with a share of 9.9% and an average stay of 3.8 days, had a marked effect on the overall visitor statistics in 2004, as the numbers of Britons arriving represented an increase of 57.8% on 2003. The growth of budget airlines particularly contributed to this phenomenon (Šeligová, 2005a). Other markets that witnessed a significant growth in visitor numbers to the Czech Republic were Italy (5.1% share), the Netherlands (4.1%), Russia (3.0%), Spain (2.6%), and the USA (4.5%).

By contrast, there were large decreases in the numbers of visitors from Poland and Israel. Arrivals from Israel fell by 10.4% in 2004 (76,339 arrivals and a 1% share). Those from Poland had been falling since 2001 (0.37m arrivals in 2004, a 4.7% share).

From a total of 6.1m visitors who stayed in registered accommodation in the Czech Republic in 2004, Prague took by far the greatest share – 57% of all international arrivals. This was an increase of 31% on 2003. Prague's foreign visitors spent an average of 3.8 days there, less than the national average 4.1 days. None the less, the Czech capital was the sixth most visited city in Europe in 2004 after London, Paris, Rome, Madrid and Berlin. Particularly following budget airline route development, the largest market share for visitors to Prague is from the United Kingdom: a 17% share with 0.59m visitors and an average stay of 3.8 days. Germany is the second most important market (0.51m), with Italy third (0.31m).

Karlovy Vary is the second most visited region in the country, with 0.39m arrivals (6.4% of the national share, with an average stay of 7.6 days). The largest visitor flows in 2004 were from Germany (0.24m with average stay of 8 days) and Russia (0.04m, average 12.8 days). Third most visited region is South Moravia, with 0.35m arrivals (5.7% share), with major visitor flows from Germany (59,601) and Poland (55,481). By comparison, the Pardubice and Highlands regions were the least visited ones with just 53,018 (0.9% share) and 64,194 (1.1%) arrivals, respectively. The largest regional decreases in 2004 were registered in North Moravia (–9.3%), Olomouc (–8.9%) and Ústí nad Labem (–4.9%) (Šeligová, 2005d).

Table 9.3 shows the number of arrivals of visitors to the Czech Republic and the departures of Czech citizens abroad. Arrivals reached a record 8.5m in 2004, and average length of stay returned to the high 2001 level of 4.2 nights in 2004 (Šeligová, 2005b).

The number of foreign visitors in registered accommodation is indicated in Table 9.4. By far the most popular types of accommodation are three-star hotels (63.9%), with use of four- (17%) and five-star hotels (5.5%) being less significant. Earnings from tourism in 2004, at 107bn Czech Crowns (approximately €4bn or $4.2bn; Table 9.1), showed an increase of 6.8% on 2003 (Šeligová, 2005a, 2005b). The three highest spending groups are Japanese, Russian and Israeli visitors, each with an average daily expenditure of US$134.

Seasonality has a medium impact on visitor arrivals: the average annual share for November, December, January and February is 5–6% each, compared with the July and August share of 12.6% each. Travel agencies see a large part of their business in May, June and September. July and August are usually quieter, which could be due to more independent travellers arriving in the country with their own facilities such as tents and camper-vans (mobile homes). The quietest time for travel agencies is January. The most popular services provided by travel agencies are group outings to Prague (65.6%), the Central Bohemia region (8.2%), South Bohemia (8.1%), South Moravia (6.6%) and the Karlovy Vary region (5.1%). Some of the areas most visited in 2004 were Prague, Český Krumlov, the Krkonoše Mountains and the Šumava area (Šeligová, 2005c).

Method of Transport

The Czech Republic is easily accessible from much of Europe as the air transport network is being steadily expanded. The number of passengers carried by air exceeded 9.6m in 2004, an increase of 28% on 2003 (Johánek, 2004). However, as shown in Table 9.5, the most popular mode is still road transport. Trains are less used, although the railway system provides quality links with the European network.

The Czech Republic has one major international airport, Prague Ruzyne (Table 9.6),

Table 9.3. The Czech Republic: inbound and outbound travel, 2000–2004.

	Inbound						Outbound					
	Q I	Q II	VII	VIII	IX	I–IX	Q I	Q II	VII	VIII	IX	I–IX
2000	21,189	26,874	10,877	11,105	9,053	79,098	7,651	9,512	4,281	4,023	3,453	28,920
2001	21,393	26,283	10,851	11,187	8,821	78,535	7,352	9,153	4,042	3,973	3,259	27,779
2002	21,566	25,892	10,290	9,489	8,417	75,654	7,006	8,636	3,904	3,602	3,031	26,179
2003	19,873	23,651	9,508	10,111	8,751	71,894	6,933	8,789	4,012	3,926	3,356	27,015
2004	20,274	24,616	9,416	9,620	8,371	72,298	7,321	9,032	4,089	3,892	3,348	27,682
2004/2003	102.0%	104.1%	99.0%	95.1%	95.7%	100.6%	105.6%	102.8%	101.9%	99.1%	99.8%	102.5%
2004/2002	94.0%	95.1%	91.5%	101.4%	99.5%	95.6%	104.5%	104.6%	104.7%	108.1%	110.5%	105.7%
2004/2001	94.8%	93.7%	86.8%	86.0%	94.9%	92.1%	99.6%	98.7%	101.2%	98.0%	102.7%	99.7%
2004/2000	95.7%	91.6%	86.6%	86.6%	92.5%	91.4%	95.7%	95.0%	95.5%	96.7%	97.0%	95.7%

Source: Czech Statistical Office, 2005.

Table 9.4. The Czech Republic: foreign visitors in registered accommodation, 1992–2003 (in millions).

	1992	1993	1994	1995	1996	1997	1998	1999	2000	2001	2002	2003
Number of foreign visitors	2.61	2.67	3.04	3.38	4.56	4.98	5.48	5.61	4.67	5.19	4.74	5.08
Number of overnights	6.61	7.38	8.61	10.33	14.19	15.67	16.93	16.86	16.47	16.85	15.57	16.51

Source: Czech Statistical Office, 2005.

Table 9.5. The Czech Republic: mode of transport for inbound travel, 1996–2004.

% share of total inbound	1996	1997	1998	1999	2000	2001	2002	2003	I–IX 2004
Road	94.4	94.4	93.8	94.5	94.3	94.1	94.0	93.4	92.4
Rail	4.2	4.2	4.7	4.0	3.8	3.8	3.5	3.3	3.3
Air	1.4	1.4	1.4	1.4	1.8	2.1	2.5	3.3	4.3

Source: Czech Statistical Office, 2005.

Table 9.6. The Czech Republic: Prague Ruzyne Airport traffic statistics, 2000–2004.

	Passenger numbers (in millions)	Aircraft movements	Cargo (in tonnes)
2000	5.6	94,117	30,283
2001	6.1	97,542	29,570
2002	6.3	103,904	39,590
2003	7.5	115,756	41,439
2004	9.6	144,962	46,884

Source: Prague Airport, 2005.

and nine smaller international airports. The Czech Airport Authority was established in 1990 to manage and operate the country's four key international airports: Prague Ruzyne, Brno, Ostrava and Karlovy Vary. As a pilot project for private investment in state-run airport infrastructure, from July 2002 Brno-Turany airport was leased to a private corporation. Most of the remaining airports are owned and operated by local authorities.

Role of budget airlines

The most notable development in air transport is the growth of low-cost carriers to some 60 in number in little over 10 years. Almost 45% of the (then) EU population took a low-cost flight in 2003 (Welch, 2005). This growth, reflecting the EU's 'open skies' policy, has contributed to considerable interest in the Czech Republic from other EU member states.

Budget airlines' market share in European passenger traffic almost quadrupled from 5% in 2000 to 19% in the first quarter of 2005. Having to operate in a more sharply segmented customer market will require the airlines to consistently align their products, their network, their brand image, and their price policies with target customers in key market segments (Pollino, 2005).

While low-cost carriers today represent only around 8% of total civil aviation in Europe (ECAC member states), the figure is 35% in the United Kingdom and up to 60% in Ireland, largely the result of the consolidation of Europe's two major low-cost airlines, Ryanair (Ireland) and EasyJet (UK). The success of these carriers stems from their North American-inspired cost-efficient business model, often flying just one type of aircraft (Welch, 2005), which enables them to offer relatively low, but elastic fares based on yield management principles (Box 9.1). They have clearly opened new (down-)market customer segments and, despite a general increase in awareness of aviation's contribution to climate change, low-cost airlines appear to have stimulated further demand for air travel, particularly in Europe (Binggeli and Pompeo, 2002). A new and loyal customer base has been created at secondary airports (often former Soviet military bases), of which there are many across Central and Eastern Europe (Theunis, 2003).

One study estimated that 75% of the low-cost market share represents new customers, 70% of whom are leisure travellers: 20% are holiday-makers, 25% are on city breaks, weekend trips or visits to family/friends, and 25% are people travelling to their second homes. These new travellers generate additional tourism receipts in the

---

Box 9.1. Low-cost airlines' model characteristics.

The European Union's Committee on Economic Affairs and Development has noted the main operating characteristics of low-cost carriers:

- the creation of new routes, often at secondary airports;
- a broadening of the market to carry passengers who would not have previously travelled (by air);
- a concentration on short and mid-range distances;
- point-to-point flights between smaller airports allow more rotations (round-trips) in a single day, with no regard for connectivity at the place of arrival;
- flight timetables are flexible and ready to react to seasonal changes in demand;
- communication systems are standardized;
- pay levels are relatively lower;
- cabin crew are often used to clean the aircraft between flights thereby saving time and costs and helping rapid turn-round times (25 minutes for Ryanair), again permitting more flights to be undertaken within the same day;
- the aircraft used often have the maximum possible number of seats and thus less leg-room;
- low-cost carriers normally offer few or no frills: all food and drink on board is purchased at relatively high prices;
- landing fees at the airports used are low or non-existent;
- passengers may also pay indirectly due to longer and more costly land transport from remote secondary airports;
- point-to-point operation also means one-way fares are employed, no onward baggage facilities are provided, and no provision is made for missed connections;
- electronic, web-based reservation systems are employed, lowering costs for operators and obviating the need to issue paper tickets.

Source: after Masseret, 2003, pp. 6–7.

---

destinations, and since low-cost carriers operate primarily short and medium-haul flights, the tourism receipts are generated within European countries (Alderighi *et al.*, 2004).

Prague Ruzyne airport has developed a key position in relation to low-cost carriers for Central and Eastern Europe. The number of passengers passing through the airport using low-cost carriers increased by 116.5% in 2003, and movements increased by 84.6%. The share of low-cost passengers was 8% in that year, rising to 13% in 2004 (Prague Airport, 2005).

The first low-cost airline started to operate to the Czech Republic in 1999 (British Airways' spin-off GO, since sold to EasyJet), to Prague from London Stansted. At the time of writing 12 low-cost carriers operate into Prague Ruzyne airport – bmi baby, EasyJet, FlyBe, Germanwings, Jet2.com, SkyEurope Airlines, Snowflake, Smart Wings, WIZZ Air, Sterling European Al, Helvetic Airways, and Discovery Travel. These provide more than 20 routes, including nine UK destinations, Stuttgart, Cologne/Bonn, Stockholm, Paris, Zurich, Madrid, Amsterdam, Copenhagen, Budapest, Katowice and Košice.

The first Czech low-cost carrier, Smart Wings, launched regular flights to Paris, Zurich, Madrid, Amsterdam and Copenhagen in May 2004, and added flights to Vienna, Rome and London in October 2004. Smart Wings also operated flights to Palma de Mallorca, Heraklion, Larnaca, Milan and Solun in the summer season of 2005. Discovery Travel flew from Kunovice to Prague and Antwerp from 2004. Ryanair began operations between Brno and London Stansted in March 2005.

The increasing number of low-cost carriers in Prague is determined by a number of factors that include:

- the economic environment in the Czech Republic is very friendly, open and one of the most liberal to the low-cost carriers in Europe;
- Prague is an attractive destination both for leisure and business visitors;
- most low-cost carriers use the high quality passenger services available at the main Prague Ruzyne airport;

- the quality of services provided to low-cost carriers has a comparable standard to other, more expensive, European airports;
- low-cost carriers can take advantage of a 1 year 50% discount on landing fees when opening a new route to or from Prague (Kovaříková, 2003).

The availability of secondary airports such as Brno is likely to attract further services in the future, although the potential dangers of local dependence upon one (foreign) airline need to be monitored. Further, the structural role of the relatively down-market nature of budget airline customers – in relation to the equilibrium of the tourism economy and the destination image of Czech cities – needs to be carefully considered and managed in the future.

Conclusions

The Czech Government, recognizing the important role of tourism for economic growth and employment, has been increasingly involved in the sector since the early 1990s. A step forward was taken with the establishment of the Czech Tourism Authority in 1993. The enlargement of European Union has brought new dimensions to inbound as well as to outbound travel in the Czech Republic. The 20% increase in the EU population as a result of the 2004 enlargement has created new tourism demand supported by harmonized legislation, quality standards and norms, investments in infrastructure, and enhanced methods of transport and distribution.

It is expected that the growth of health and environmental consciousness among European Union citizens, together with the demand for education, history, adventure, eco- and agro-tourism, supported by low-cost carrier routes operated from Prague and other Czech centres, will further increase the demand for the Czech Republic's tourism products, with important economic, cultural and environmental implications for the country's future development.

References

Alderighi, M., Cento, A., Nijkamp, P. and Rietveld, P. (2004) *The Entry of Low-Cost Airlines: Price Competition in the European Airline Market.* Amsterdam: Tinbergen Institute, Universiteit van Amsterdam Discussion Paper 04–074/3.

Binggeli, U. and Pompeo, L. (2002) Hyped hopes for Europe's low-cost airlines. *The McKinsey Quarterly* 4. Available at: http://www.mckinseyquarterly.com

CIA (Central Intelligence Agency) (2005) *The World Fact Book – Czech Republic.* Washington DC: US Government Printing House. Available at: http://www.cia.gov

Czech National Bank (2005) *Czech National Bank.* Prague: Czech National Bank. Available at: http://www.cnb.cz

Czech Statistical Office (2005) *Czech Statistical Office.* Prague: Czech Statistical Office. Available at: http://www.czso.cz

CzechTourism (2005) *CzechTourism.* Prague: CzechTourism. Available at: http://www.czechtourism.cz

Johánek, T. (2004) Letecká přeprava zažívá v Česku boom. *Profit,* 25 October. Available at: http://www.profit.cz/clanek.php?iArt=9426&iSearch+Letecka

Kovaříková, A. (2003) *Pražské letiště se stalo největším uzlem low-cost dopravců v zemích střední a východní Evropy.* Prague: Czech Airports Authority. Available at: http://www.csl.cz (site changed from 30 October 2005 to Prague Airport: www.prg.aero).

Mag Consulting (2005) *The Tourism Share of GDP.* Prague: Mag Consulting. Available at: http://www.magconsulting.cz

Masseret, M. (2003) *European Air Transport Policy: Crucial Choices at a Critical Time.* Report. Available at: http://www.assembly.coe.int

Pollino, P. (2005) There's good news and bad news for Europe's low-cost airlines. *Mercer Briefs* 1. Available at: http://www.mercermc.com

Prague Airport (2005) *Traffic Statistics.* Prague: Prague Airport. Available at: www.prg.aero (formerly at http://www.csl.cz).

Šeligová, K. (2005a) *2004 was a record year for incoming tourism in the Czech Republic.* Prague: CzechTourism. Available at: http://www.czechtourism.cz

Šeligová, K. (2005b) *Foreign tourists spend more in the Czech Republic.* Prague: CzechTourism. Available at: http://www.czechtourism.cz

Šeligová, K. (2005c) *Survey on Czech travel agents' experience with the needs and wishes of foreign tourists.* Prague: CzechTourism. Available at: http//:www.czechtourism.cz

Šeligová, K. (2005d) *Which regions received the most visitors in 2004?* Prague: CzechTourism. Available at: http://www.czechtourism.cz

Theunis, G.T. (2003) *Hochgeschwindigkeitsverkehr zu Niedrigen Kosten Analogie und Unterschiede zu den Billigfliegern. Eisenbahntechnisches Kolloquium. Aktuelle Entwicklungen in Fernverkehr Realität und Visionen.* Darmstadt: Technische Universität Darmstadt, p. 1. Available at: http://www.tu-darmstadt.de

Welch, M. (2005) *Fly the Frugal Sky. How Low-cost Airlines Have Transformed Europe – And What it Means for America.* Los Angeles CA: Reason Online. Available at: http://www.reason.com

10 Product Development and Diversification in Hungary

László Puczkó and Tamara Rátz

Introduction

'The happiest barracks' is how Hungary was often referred to in the West before the political and economic changes of 1989–1990. Although, as the Hungarian National Tourist Office (HNTO, 2005) states, the country:

> is not fortunate enough to be endowed with spectacular features, either natural or man-made. However, this lack is compensated for by its geographical situation and the sheer number of its more modest attractions.

Hungary is situated in the centre of Europe and has always attracted visitors from other countries. This popularity has exhibited both stability and significant change over time. Because of the country's central location and its relatively developed status compared to most neighbouring countries, Hungary has been attracting high numbers of visitors for several decades. Although the data collection methods of tourist flows applied by the Hungarian National Central Statistics Office (KSH) have been modified since 1990, the main trends remain the same, and Hungary has been among the 15 most visited countries in the world with around 30 million international visitors per year (the highest position was 4th in 1994: HNTO, 2005).

During the 1990s, tourism in Hungary developed five major trends (Behringer *et al.*, 2001):

1. The number of foreign arrivals dropped by 15.7% between 1990 and 2000, alongside a fivefold increase in tourism income generation during the same period, whilst average spending per visitor and trip increased almost sixfold. The decline in numbers was attributable mostly to the reduction of cross-border shopping and petty-trading by visitors from CEE countries.

2. There was a clear shift towards higher quality services in the use of commercial accommodation establishments. The proportion of guest nights spent in hotels continued to rise and the rate of increase in the number of guests staying at 4- or 5-star hotels especially so. The turnover of guests at commercial accommodation sites shows strong geographical and seasonal concentration in Budapest and around Lake Balaton.

3. The purpose of visit was predominantly leisure, with business arrivals representing a secondary but growing proportion.

4. The growing role of domestic tourism since 1997: numbers of domestic guest-nights grew by 4.6% per annum between 1997 and 2002 in commercial accommodation.

5. Half of all international arrivals have been day-trippers or hikers, and the proportion of such visitors from Austria is close to 60%. Only about 12% of all international visitors stay in Hungary for more than a week.

Further, the late 1990s witnessed a new surge of interest from foreign investors fuelling a hotel construction boom (Behringer and Kiss, 2004).

Considerable imbalances can be observed when comparing visitor origins in terms of numbers of international arrivals and overnights spent by foreign visitors in Hungary (Figs 10.1 and 10.2).

Whereas arrivals figures are dominated by visitors from neighbouring countries, with the exception of Germany and Austria, the number of overnights spent in commercial accommodation establishments is led by Germany, with no neighbouring country source falling within the top ten.

There are specific reasons to explain this. Before 1990, Hungary, or more specifically,

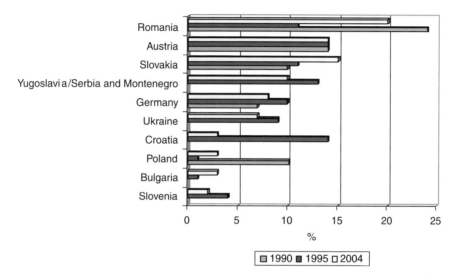

Fig. 10.1. Hungary: top 10 arrivals' source countries, 1990–2004. Source: KSH, 2005a.

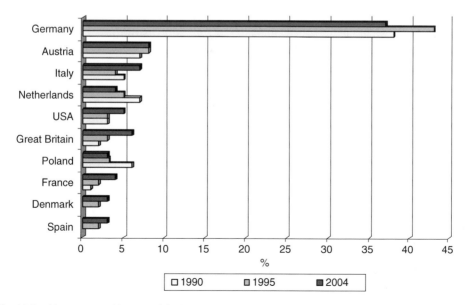

Fig. 10.2. Hungary: top 10 guest nights' source countries, 1990–2004. Source: KSH, 2005a.

Lake Balaton (the largest freshwater lake in Central Europe) was the meeting place for families and friends separated by the border between West and East Germany. Since travel within the Eastern bloc was relatively easy, while it was complicated or impossible to cross the border from East to West Germany, the lake became a destination that was close by and easy to visit for Germans from both sides of the border. The popularity of Hungary was further increased when, for the first time ever, the Hungarian government opened the border to allow East Germans to travel to Austria in 1989.

The image of Hungary became very positive in Germany and many people were grateful for this gesture. However, this popularity lasted for only 5 or 6 years. Since the mid-1990s, the share of German tourists to Hungary has been stagnating or (slightly) declining.

On the other hand, Hungary was a central location for many former Eastern bloc cross-border petty-traders. These generated the ironically-named 'Comecon-markets', which were often located in border towns and villages and were extremely popular in making available goods (and services) that were otherwise unavailable, had a long waiting list, or were available only at unattainable prices. Visitors to these markets, who did not want to know where the products came from and were happy to shop without warranty or guarantee, could buy (or sell) virtually anything at substantially discounted prices. Such markets and the petty-trading that supported them acted as a safety valve in response to the 'market failure' of central economic planning (see also Chapter 8). Post-Communist liberalization of the economy and foreign direct investment in commerce and trade caused these markets to vanish within a few years in the early 1990s, although the fact that part of Hungary's borders now act as the external EU border is likely to renew some degree of petty-trading activity with/from non-EU neighbours.

The imbalance of arrivals and dominance of German visitors have put incoming tourism and the suppliers of related services in a relatively vulnerable position. There were high hopes that EU accession would make Hungary a better known and more popular destination. Certainly, in the last few years, with EU (pre-)accession processes gaining pace, Hungary has been visited by a growing number of tourists from other EU-member countries. The increase in visitor numbers has been particularly significant from the UK, France, Spain and the Scandinavian countries (HNTO 2005).

In 2000, when the date of Hungary's EU accession was confirmed, the HNTO inaugurated a series of studies aimed at collecting information and data about the image of Hungary and perception of the country as a destination in the main tourist generating countries of Europe. It was confirmed by the results that, apart from Austria and Germany, the general image of, and knowledge about Hungary in other EU member countries were either based on false stereotypes or were rather limited. The Ministry of National Cultural Heritage together with the HNTO stimulated into action by the results of the studies, started to organize special events in selected countries (notably France, the UK, The Netherlands, Italy) under the title of 'Year of Hungarian Culture'. The rich cultural and arts programme of this series of events resulted in positive impacts, with incoming numbers increasing and a modification of national image appearing to have been generated. However, these events were not aimed primarily at attracting visitors with particular cultural interests.

The Main Impacts of EU Enlargement on Hungarian Tourism

Although a relatively short period has passed since Hungary's EU accession on 1 May, 2004, the country was an associate member for 10 years prior to that, so the EU integration process has influenced Hungarian tourism development for more than a decade. In preparation for Hungary's EU accession, the tourism industry underwent a step-by-step harmonization with the EU's legal framework. The country adopted the common body of EU law that governs areas such as foreign policy, movement of goods, persons and capital, transport and the environment. Although integration into the EU seemed to proceed smoothly during the first year of accession, the magnitude of future changes could not be fully anticipated.

According to recently published WTTC (2004) industry-supported research data, Hungary and Poland have the highest latent potential for tourism growth among the new EU member states. The prospective additional travel and tourism resulting from structural changes to Hungary's economy following EU accession is estimated at an additional US$22.8bn in GDP and 901,000 jobs. As a direct positive impact of EU accession, Hungary's image among EU members is expected to improve, leading to an increase in the number of visitors from both old and new member countries. This is particularly notable because EU nationals generally perceive other EU destinations as posing less risk, particularly in relation to laws, standards and access to health services (Blake, Sinclair and Sugiyarto, 2003).

During the preparation period for EU accession, Hungary received European aid within the framework of the Phare programme. Between 1995–2003, Phare CBC programmes contributed €135m to the establishment of cross-border cooperation projects in the fields of tourism, infrastructure and transport development, human resources and environmental protection (VÁTI, 2003). As a result of the latest regional development Phare programme for the period of 2002–2003, a total of €54.12m EU funds were allocated to projects that included: conference tourism development, rural tourism training, spa and health tourism development, transformation of heritage buildings into tourism facilities and urban rehabilitation (VÁTI, 2005).

By joining the EU, Hungary has obtained the right to benefit from the Community's Structural Funds which aim to support less developed regions in order to achieve economic and social cohesion between the different member states. Although the key objectives of the Structural Funds do not include the development of tourism explicitly, the tourism industry and tourism destinations may become direct or indirect beneficiaries of all the objectives (adjustment and development of regions where GDP per capita is less than 75% of EU average (European Commission, 2004); development of areas undergoing industrial conversion; economic diversification of rural areas; reduction of long-term unemployment and vocational training for young people). In addition to the Structural Funds, Hungary also receives aid from the EU's Cohesion Fund for infrastructural development in the fields of environment and transportation. The country's

participation in Community Initiatives such as INTERREG and Equal may also assist cross-border and inter-regional tourism cooperation, and the development of human resources in the tourism industry, respectively.

Altogether, as the whole territory of Hungary belongs to the Objective 1 area, during 2004–2006 the country will receive €3.21bn structural aid from the EU (European Commission, 2004). However, in this period, EU experts estimate that Hungary will only absorb 30% of funding at most. Specific programmes supported by the Structural Funds include the encouragement of a more diverse rural development and the growth of complementary activities such as rural tourism, as well as the exploitation of natural and cultural heritage resources in the least favoured regions through the development of tourism services.

The Immediate Consequences of EU Accession for Hungarian Tourism

Following EU enlargement, Hungary borders four non-EU nations and accounts for 15% of the EU's external land border. In order to comply with the far more stringent EU border control regulations, Hungary spent €40m to strengthen its eastern and southern borders over the decade prior to accession. Another €150m EU funding is expected in the following years to further improve border infrastructure, equipment and information technology and to organize training to enable Hungary to join the Schengen Treaty (NFH, 2005). However, the fact that Hungary's frontiers coincide with the external frontiers of the EU, at least until the next enlargement, unfavourably affects VFR tourism from the country's eastern and southern neighbours, as Hungarian minority members living in Ukraine, Romania, Croatia and Serbia are now subject to more stringent visa requirements.

One of the major direct impacts of EU accession is the growing number of budget airlines entering the Hungarian market. As the new member states are becoming more popular among European customers, accessibility to Central Europe is a key to international success, both for destinations and for airlines. Changes in the regulatory environment following EU accession, particularly the liberalization of air traffic, opened up the market for several European budget airlines that were ready to seize the opportunity. While in 2003 only two low-cost carriers operated from Budapest, the number of budget airlines grew to eight by the end of 2004, and by April 2005 the number serving Hungary had increased to ten, with new companies continuing to appear.

Low-cost airlines have contributed significantly to the growth of international passenger traffic at Budapest: in 2004, a record number of 6,456,983 travellers were registered at the capital's Ferihegy International Airport, a near 30% increase over 2003, which made Ferihegy the third busiest Central European airport after Vienna and Prague. Although this growth can also be attributed to the global rebound of air travel after the global depression following '9/11', the rising number of both incoming and outgoing budget airline passengers is a major factor of change in the overall increase of demand. While in 2004 every seventh customer travelled by budget airlines, in the first 3 months of 2005 already every third passenger was transported by low-cost carriers. Comparing the absolute volumes of budget demand, Budapest Airport registered 445,420 customers between January and March 2005, as opposed to 51,667 in the same period of 2004, representing a more than eightfold increase in the year following the country's EU accession (Budapest Airport, 2005).

Certainly the growth of budget airlines serving Hungary has helped to increase international tourism revenues. In 2004, low-cost airlines brought around 340,000 tourists to the country, increasing direct revenues from tourism by an estimated €90m and generating an additional €13m in tax receipts (Galla, 2004). In addition to attracting recognized budget airlines such as EasyJet or Air Berlin, the significant market demand for low-fare air travel from and to Central and Eastern Europe, together with the elimination of administrative boundaries with EU accession, have also led to the establishment of new low-cost carriers with a regional hub such as WizzAir and SkyEurope.

Further, as the EU accession is expected to result in growing incoming demand, the Hungarian government considers the development of regional airports as an economic priority. During 2004, €4.5m was spent to improve the infrastructure of six regional airports, including FlyBalaton Airport in Sármellék, the gateway to Lake Balaton and to the renowned spa destination Hévíz, and Airport Debrecen in the country's second largest city, which received €1.460m and €0.880m respectively (Galla, 2004). In 2005, the project continued on a similar scale as the development of regional airports was expected to reduce the spatial concentration of tourism demand and to extend the tourist season.

In the field of air transport, a potential negative consequence of enlargement is the likely future consolidation process that will particularly affect the Central Eastern European airlines, including the Hungarian national carrier Malév, because of their fragile financial situation.

Hungarian Tourism in the European Union

According to the marketing strategy of HNTO, there are four major tourism types that characterize the tourism supply of the country to foreign, predominantly EU visitors:

- health tourism: medical and wellness services that are provided in almost all parts of the country;
- MICE tourism: the supply of which is concentrated in some major cities, especially in Budapest, where high quality conference facilities have been available since the late communist period;
- cultural tourism: culture, heritage, historic cities, gastronomy, wine and village tourism are all important: there are nine World Heritage Sites within the country together with several cultural festivals, and, for example, the Tokaj wine region; and
- activity tourism: building on youth, sport, green and recreational tourism the facilities of which are available around major lakes (Balaton, Velence, Fertő) and along rivers (Danube, Tisza) and in the mountains.

Since 2003, in order to become more successful in the European tourism market, Hungary has developed stronger links in the field of marketing with the other members of the Visegrád Group: the Czech Republic, Slovakia and Poland. Experiences show that both intra-European and overseas tourists tend to see the Visegrád countries as one region (e.g. 'East-Central Europe'), such that, although all participants joined the EU in 2004, further tourism cooperation within the region is both a necessity and an opportunity. The lessons learnt from the Visegrád project may also help Hungary to become fully integrated into the enlarged EU's international tourism activities.

Obviously, in addition to being potential partners in regional tourism marketing, all Central and Eastern European countries are also Hungary's competitors in the European market. Throughout the region, one of the greatest challenges of EU accession is to meet the increased standards and expectations of European customers and to provide the same service quality that they are accustomed to in any other EU destination. Although the quality and the range of the Hungarian tourism supply have improved significantly in the past decade, the country's high 25% VAT rates levied on hotel and catering services may potentially prove a competitive disadvantage (HHA-KPMG, 2004). Since VAT rates are generally more favourable elsewhere within the EU (e.g. the Czech Republic boasts a 5% VAT rate on tourism, as does France at 5.5% and Spain at 7%, and even neighbouring Slovakia's 19% is lower), Hungary as a holiday destination may compare less positively among price-conscious leisure tourists. This therefore suggests a future strategy emphasizing higher quality, higher yielding tourism experiences.

Vienna and Prague have long been traditional competitors of the Hungarian capital, Budapest, and although they remain so following EU enlargement, the integration process has opened up further cooperation opportunities as well. With Vienna being the most successful of the three Central European capital cities, in international tourism Prague has been more popular than Budapest over the past decade. Although, in the short term, EU enlargement does not seem to threaten Prague's position as the leading CEE heritage city, Budapest has the geographical advantage of being closer to Vienna and Bratislava. Following Hungary's

and Slovakia's EU accession, visits to the three cities may easily be combined, which, in the medium term, may put geographically more separated Prague in a less competitive position. Cooperation between the national tourist offices of the Czech Republic, Austria and Hungary is aimed especially at the US and Japanese markets, particularly promoting the three capitals to likely visitors to Europe.

A significant future impact of EU accession is the introduction of the single European currency. To join the EMU, the country must meet the Maastricht convergence criteria in terms of price stability, long-term interest rate, budget deficit, government debt and exchange-rate stability. The past few years' economic policy has been characterized by considerable budget and current account deficits, rising inflation and exchange rate volatility. In the country's 2004 convergence programme, the target date for adopting the euro was set at 2010. Although this target seems to be relatively late after the country's EU accession, the euro is in fact already penetrating the Hungarian private sector. The country's service industry, particularly the hospitality sector, is taking its own steps towards euro integration, with many restaurants and retailers in tourist destinations accepting payment in euros. Hungarian tourists, on the other hand, seem to be relatively unaffected by the single currency: as the results of a recent survey suggested, adoption of the euro in member states does not seem to have influenced significantly the travel behaviour of Hungarian tourists, although there is a significant awareness as well as a favourable perception of the lower transaction costs brought about by the euro (Rátz and Hinek, 2005).

The Development of Spa Tourism in Hungary – a Past and Future Niche

Hungary as a tourist destination has been looking for a long time for a special product that can make the country appealing to its predominantly European visitors. Based on its rich resources, health tourism seemed to be a logical alternative, since health consciousness, more healthy living and use of natural healing resources are becoming more prevalent. Health tourism has been and can be the product that makes Hungary a favourite destination for European visitors, since thermal baths have a long history here.

The country's modern spa tourism supply is built on ubiquitous Roman, Turkish and Austro-Hungarian spa heritage, amongst others, and Hungary is the fifth richest country in thermal and healing waters after Japan, Iceland, France and Italy. According to the natural healing assets register (HNTO, 2002), Hungary has 1289 thermal wells, of which 148 are mineralized and 136 medicinal; five medicinal caves, four medicinal mud sources, one mofetta (a carbon dioxide bath); one natural healing lake (Lake Hévíz); 39 medicinal baths; 57 medical hotels; 41 wellness hotels; and 350 baths (with approximately 1200 pools). Additionally, Budapest has a special position among spa towns as being the only such capital in the world. This position was recognized in 1934 when it was awarded the title of international spa city and Budapest was chosen as a venue for the first International Bath Congress in 1937.

It was the Romans who first capitalized on Hungary's thermal waters in the 1st century, when they built baths on the banks of the river Danube. Although archaeologists have since uncovered 21 baths from the Roman era, these are only preserved as ruins today. The tradition of bathing continued during the 15th–17th centuries; the Turkish baths and the oriental spa culture that Hungarians adopted are among the positive legacies of the country's 150-year-long Turkish occupation. The historic baths of the capital city and the countryside are equally popular as leisure facilities for local residents and heritage attractions for tourists.

The third golden age of spa-going in Hungary started in the 19th century when balneology – the study of the art and science of bathing – became popular. The establishment of the 'Balneological Society of the Countries of the Hungarian Holy Crown' in 1891 (MBE, 2005) facilitated scientific cooperation in balneology, thus resulting in a more effective healing process and contributing to the development of medical spas around the country. The period's typically science-oriented focus on the medicinal values of natural waters significantly affected Hungarian spa tourism development during the 20th century.

By 1920, due to the Trianon Peace Treaty ending World War I, Hungary lost more than two-thirds of its territory, and the majority of the country's internationally established thermal and mineral spas (e.g. Pöstyén, Trencsénteplic, Bártfa, Szováta, Herkulesfürdő and Tusnád) were located beyond the newly-drawn borders. As a consequence, the focus of health tourism development shifted to the exploitation of the thermal resources of Budapest and other destinations within the country such as Hévíz and Balatonfüred at Lake Balaton. World War II interrupted the progress of Hungarian spa tourism development, and in the post-war decades tourism development in the newly established socialist political system was mostly limited to state-controlled social tourism, domestic trips subsidized by the state or by trade unions. Most of these domestic visitors chose a hotel or guest house that was either near to Lake Balaton or to a bath/spa. The number of guests showed a steady growth throughout the socialist period: while in 1949 only 250,000 state-supported domestic guests were registered, their number increased to 1,411,000 by 1986, a 560% increase (Lengyel, Puczkó and Rátz, 1996, unpublished research report, Budapest University of Economic Sciences, Tourism Research Centre). This reflected both a continuous increase in the state's financial support, and the expansion of the state-managed accommodation sector.

However, the state's financial contribution ceased to increase from 1982, so the National Council of Trade Unions, the coordinator of the system, was no longer able to operate it on the sole basis of social tourists' significantly discounted payments. Consequently, a certain proportion of the available beds were offered on the commercial market, resulting in a decrease in both bed capacity and guest numbers: while in 1984 social tourism offered 25,350 beds, by 1996 this figure had fallen to 11,286 beds, and commercial tourists accounted for 64% of all the registered guests (Lengyel, Puczkó and Rátz, 1996, unpublished research report, Budapest University of Economic Sciences, Tourism Research Centre).

The decline of social tourism demand in the 1980s may be attributed to various reasons. As state subsidies dwindled, operators were forced to either increase prices or find supplementary sources of income. However, due to the Hungarian population's decreasing real income and the generally rather mediocre quality of social tourism accommodation, price increases were only partly accepted by the market, which necessitated fundamental changes in the system (Lengyel, Puczkó and Rátz, 1996, unpublished report). Transformation of the trade union hotel resorts began in 1992, when, as part of the post-Communist privatization process of Hungarian tourism, the government established the Hungarian National Holiday Foundation as the owner of the former social tourism estates, and the Hunguest Company as the management body. Direct state subsidies through trade union membership were replaced by a holiday cheque system in 1998, providing organized holiday allowances to underprivileged social groups, and supplementing holiday bonuses offered by employers. As the system is now mainly aimed at those in the lowest income groups, participation is highly dependent on employers' attitudes towards this type of remuneration. In 2004, the total sum of HUF 5.4bn (€21.3m) was made available for social tourism purposes, but rising demand continues to exceed the availability of state subsidies (KSH, 2005a).

The Current State of Spa and Health Tourism in Hungary

The most important step to make this unique asset of the country competitive in the European and consequently in the world market, was the so called Széchenyi Plan. This development plan was aimed at the redevelopment of already existing baths and the erection of new ones, as the Ministry of Economy and Transport stated:

> As a medium-term economic development programme, the Széchenyi Plan aims at laying the foundations of permanent and sustainable economic growth, widen and deepen the basis of growth – according to sectors, branches and regions.
>
> (GM, 2001, p. 1)

The Tourism Development Programme (TDP) provided 33% of the total funds made available for this plan between 2000 and 2003.

The most important elements of the TDP related to health tourism, with state support provided for:

- development of health tourism attractions – medical, wellness and fitness services;
- increasing the capacity of accommodation facilities as well as extensions and quality improvements;
- infrastructure development in bath towns;
- cofinancing of feasibility studies;
- marketing of health tourism facilitated by the Health Tourism Department of the HNTO; and
- establishing bath clusters.

Altogether 74 baths and medical/thermal hotels received state support in the form of non-repayable subsidy amounting to HUF 29.2bn (€115m). It is estimated that state support generated additional investment €230m from the private sector and some 2700 permanent jobs were also created (GKM, 2003).

Since Budapest has been the most visited destination, its historical baths – which are in the top three attractions of the city (Budapest Tourism Office, 2005, unpublished research report) – attract large numbers of foreign visitors every year. Most visit for reasons other than health-related ones. They are more likely to be interested in the history and architecture of these establishments. The baths are strong and characteristic elements of the image and tourist attractions of Budapest. Since 1998, an approximately additional HUF 7.2bn (€28m) has been spent on reconstructions of baths in Budapest from funds provided by the local government, tenders and the baths themselves (GKM, 2003). Besides the investments in infrastructural developments, most of the resources were spent on the reconstruction of thermal pools, facades, installation of automated entrance systems and interior refurbishments.

It should be noted that baths and spas of Hungary can sometimes be different from what foreign visitors may expect by just looking at the names of places. In Western Europe baths, and especially spas, have been the cradle of a certain cultural tradition from Roman times to the mid-20th century (spa as a word probably comes from the Latin words *espa* (fountain) and *sparsa*, from *spargere* – to bubble up) (Trabel.com, 2005). These spas were places associated with elites and cultural events, not merely with curative stays. After World War II spas and baths in Hungary, now sponsored by the state or the trade unions (with, for example, trade-union rest houses, hotels and sanatoria), became 'healing combinats' for the working people, based on mineral waters, climate and other local natural resources. Accommodation facilities were typically large buildings with mineral water basins and healing devices, with a residential part, dining facilities and meeting halls. Other services were almost absent. In the last 5–10 years, however, these centres have experienced substantial change. For example, based on Western experience, standards for wellness hotels were established, baths and hotels started to create their own special character, and the wide adoption of water-based wellness services took place.

The EU, recognizing the rich history and heritage of baths and spas in many member and pre-accession countries (e.g. Austria, Italy, Greece, Hungary, Czech Republic, Slovakia, Slovenia, Romania and Bulgaria) has been providing financial support for the Itinerari Termali (ITER) project in recognition of this common cultural heritage that offers 'an extraordinary combination of archaeology, architecture, craft and landscape' (ITER-CADSES, 2005).

Although spa and health tourism is a key component of the Hungarian tourism supply, the education and training of spa tourism professionals has only recently become a priority. Because of the complex nature of the spa product, spa- and wellness-related education is currently provided within the framework of both tourism and physical education programmes, and the development of spa tourism management education as part of an undergraduate healthcare programme is under way. In addition, wellness training and education are provided by various short courses and post-secondary programmes around the country. Hungary's EU accession is affecting spa and health tourism education favourably, as wellness training in secondary education is supported by the Leonardo da Vinci programme, and spa tourism education may also be developed within the framework of employment creation and rural development projects.

Conclusions

Although tourism has been a major economic activity in Hungary since the 1970s, the industry's structure and characteristics have undergone significant changes in the last decades. Similar to the impacts of the political transition in 1989–1990, the country's EU accession has considerably influenced the Hungarian tourism industry.

During the pre-accession preparation period, the country received substantial EU funds that were allocated to development projects in such fields as conference tourism, spa and health tourism development. Wider access to EU funds as a member country may also contribute to the sector's development and growth. As part of the accession process, the Hungarian tourism industry gradually adopted the relevant body of European legislation to harmonize with the EU's legal framework.

In the relatively short period since EU accession, practical changes have proved to be the most important immediate impacts of EU membership, notably the expansion of the low cost airline market and the improvement of the border control system. Budget airlines have played a major role in stimulating both incoming and outgoing traffic, making Hungary a more accessible destination for foreign visitors and a more attractive market for investors. However, the low-income yielding end of the market that such visitors may represent, and potential issues of dependence on fickle, price-sensitive markets and operators, may require a reappraisal of the role of such airlines in the future.

There are high hopes that foreign health insurance companies operating in the EU will explore the country's rich healing assets and the favourable price/quality ratio that guests (patients) can enjoy in Hungary, and will pursue contracts with local service providers. A certain amount of uncertainty exists, since the state-financed health sector in almost all EU countries is facing a deficit and making attempts to limit its coverage to the patients' home country.

To facilitate health service developments the government has opened a special support scheme targeting spa and bath owners and operators. However, since most of these bathing establishments are managed by companies owned by local municipalities, they lack specialized services. International experience suggests that the operation of baths cannot easily be profitable without a well-balanced service portfolio (such as high quality accommodation and conference facilities), and such companies may face a high risk of financial imbalance in the near future. Several attempts by national, regional and local tourism and bathing organizations are being made to ensure that health tourism becomes the core product of the country. To make this happen, more specialized development and focused, well-segmented promotion are necessary.

References

Behringer, Z., Király, G., Kiss, K., Rátz, T. and Török, P. (2001) *Idegenforgalmi és Vendéglátói Ismeretek I, II*. Budapest: Szókratész Kiadó.

Behringer, Z. and Kiss, K. (2004) The role of foreign direct investment in the development of tourism in post-communist Hungary. In: Hall, D. (ed.) *Tourism and Transition: Governance, Transformation and Development*. Wallingford, UK: CABI Publishing, pp. 73–81.

Blake, A., Sinclair, M.T. and Sugiyarto, G. (2003) *Tourism and EU Accession in Malta and Cyprus*. Nottingham: University of Nottingham Tourism and Travel Research Institute (TTRI) Discussion Paper 2003/7. Available at: http://www.nottingham.ac.uk/ttri/pdf/2003_7.pdf

Budapest Airport (2005) *Duplázhatnak a Diszkontok Ferihegyen*. Budapest: Budapest Airport, 14 April. Available at: http://www.bud.hu/sajtoszoba/kozlemenyek/

European Commission (2004) *The European Structural Funds (2004–2006). Magyarország (Hungary)*. Brussels: European Commission. Available at: http://europa.eu.int/comm/regional_policy/atlas/hungary/factsheets/pdf/fact_hu_en.pdf

Galla, G. (2004) *Két év Alatt Másfélmilliárd Forint Regionális Repterekre*. Budapest: Magyarország.hu, 9 December. Available at: http://www.magyarorszag.hu/hirek/gazdasag/repterek20041209.html

GKM (Gazdasági és Kőzlekedési Minisztérium) (2003) *A Széchenyi Terv Hatásai*. Budapest: Gazdasági és Kőzlekedési Minisztérium (Ministry of the Economy and Transport).

GM (Gazdasági Minisztérium) (2001) *A Jövő Pillérei, A Széchenyi Terv*. Budapest: Gazdasági Minisztérium (Ministry of the Economy).

HHA-KPMG (2004) *A Szállodaipart Éintő Áfa-kulcs Emelésének Várható Gazdasági Hatásai Magyarországon*. Budapest: Hungarian Hotel Association and KPMG.

HNTO (Hungarian National Tourism Office) (2002) *The Marketing Concept of Health Tourism*. Budapest: HNTO.

HNTO (Hungarian National Tourism Office) (2005) *Tourism in Hungary 1990–2004*. Budapest: HNTO.

ITER-CADSES (2005) *Iter Spa Itinerary. Project Background*. Bologna: ITER-CADSES INTERREG IIIB. Available at: http://www.iter-cadses.it/en/main1.htm

KSH (Központi Statisztikai Hivatal) (2005a) *Turizmus Magyarországon 2004*. KSH, Budapest: Központi Statisztikai Hivatal (Hungarian National Statistics Office).

KSH (Központi Statisztikai Hivatal) (2005b) *A Fogyasztóiár-index Idősorai*. Budapest: Központi Statisztikai Hivatal (Hungarian National Statistics Office). Available at: http://portal.ksh.hu/pls/ksh/docs/hun/stadat/load2_01_06_21.html

MBE (Magyar Balneológiai Egyesület) (2005) *Az Egyesület Története*. Budapest: MBE. Available at: http://www.balneologia.hu – egyesulet_tortenet1.htm

NFH (National Development Office) (2005) *The National Institution System of the Schengen Fund and the Use of Funding*. Budapest: NFH. Available at: http://www.nfh.hu/angol/xindex2.htm?t=3&i=28&ci=61

Rátz, T. and Hinek, M. (2005) The implications of the single European currency for Hungarian tourism. In: *Proceedings of the First International Scientific Conference 'Theoretical Advances in Tourism Economics', Évora, Portugal, 18–19 March 2005. Évora, Portugal*: Urban and Regional Analysis and Research Laboratory, University of Évora, CD-ROM.

Trabel.com (2005) *Spa*. Brussels: Trabel Belgium Travel Network. Available at: http://www.trabel.com/spa/spa.htm

VÁTI (2005) *Phare 2002–2003. Promotion of Integrated Local Development Actions Programme. Granted Projects.* Budapest: VÁTI Kht, Hungarian Regional Development and Town Planning Non Profit Company.

VÁTI (2003) *Phare CBC Programok. Európai Uniós támogatások a határon átnyúló együttműködések elősegítésére 2003–2006.* Budapest: VÁTI Területfejlesztési Igazgatóság.

WTTC (2004) *Latent Potential of Travel and Tourism in New EU Accession Countries Totals an Additional US$54.6bn GDP and 2 Million Jobs.* London: WTTC. Available at: http://www.wttc.org/news50pdf.pdf

11 Tourism in Poland: Changes in Policy, Management and Education

Barbara Marciszewska

Introduction

The main purpose of this chapter is to discuss, within the context of Poland's EU accession, the importance of improvements in tourism education and in state/regional/local tourism policy for creating a competitive tourism strategy. Such a strategy, in its turn, should be implemented in order to exert a positive influence on the country's socio-economic development. Future directions for tourism education within the framework of current tourism policy are suggested as a contribution towards Polish socio-economic development.

The development of tourism in Poland faces a number of obstacles which have to be recognized and overcome by both national tourism administration and regional and local authorities. The process of globalization and Poland's accession to the EU have, to a certain extent, opened borders and lowered barriers for tourism exchange between nations, but it is also creating new directions for national policy due to the fact that globalization

> crosses the traditional borders of time, space, scope, geography, function, thought and cultural assumptions.
>
> (Knowles *et al.*, 2001, p. 176)

This, in turn, demands a new political approach to both small and medium-sized enterprises and tourism services which are shaped by

the market economy on one hand and social needs on the other. Hence tourism, due to its 'sensitive' and unpredictable nature, requires long-term policy at the national, regional and local level, taking into account the 'knowledge factor' (Marciszewska, 2004a, p. 29).

Tourist consumption in Poland is shifting from domestic tourism to international tourism, which calls for a new strategy for the tourism sector in order to stimulate the development of national tourist destinations. Religious sites, historical monuments, galleries, museums and theatres are fixed elements of the tourist package but they are particularly significant factors influencing demand among students and foreign tourists. These cultural attractions are partly being replaced by small cultural festivals, sporting events, popular culture events and the performing arts, which can bring tourists relaxation and a new experience (Marciszewska, 2001, p. 223).

Regional and local development strategies should therefore include building projects, such as new infrastructure, theme parks and leisure centres, and the adaptation of existing buildings to be used for cultural activities. While such projects can be supported by indirect investment, this means of funding is of little relevance in Poland at the present stage of its socio-economic development. Although the relationship between tourism and economy is discussed in the Polish literature (Marciszewska,

2000, 2002) little attention is paid to tourism impact on the national economy.

Many European countries regard tourism as a driving force for socio-economic development. Tourism itself is, at the same time, a local or community concern and a global phenomenon which reacts rapidly to changing circumstances at all levels of policy-making. In a world of dynamic change one constant is that tourism is an important human activity and an industry that will continue to grow.

Experience has shown that managers, academics and policy-makers must understand both the changes taking place in a region and the managerial reactions stemming from the changing socio-economic environment. This understanding must be reached both at national and global scales. Political and managerial lessons drawn from previous strategic and operational experience can be shared between various regions and enterprises. Private–public partnership can be seen as a specific testimony to the power of shared learning and regional development as a factor in competitiveness in the global tourism market. An innovative system of education for the tourism sector is crucial for this process.

Tourism Resources

Towards the late 1990s, after a spectacular increase in international arrivals numbers and receipts, Poland could be characterized by the World Travel Organization (WTO) as 'a tourist tiger' (Migdal, 1999). However, despite some fluctuations, the overall trend in recent years has been one of relative decline, and certainly when compared to neighbouring 2004 EU accession states. Factors appearing to constrain growth have been identified to include (Gołembski, 1996):

- insufficient political support for tourism development, especially for new construction and modernization of the existing infrastructure;
- insufficient encouragement for foreign capital investment in tourism, or the creation of equal investment opportunities for both home and foreign capital;

- poorly developed capacity to permit successful management of the tourist economy at local and regional levels; and
- the need to better develop provision of tourist information and marketing in tourism, at both national and regional levels.

As by far the largest 2004 EU accession state (see Table 1.1), Poland has a vast range of resources and attractions which are clearly too diverse to give justice to in this short piece. Dawson (1991) provides an excellent overview of Polish tourist sites and regions at the end of the communist period. Natural attractions are represented by five regions:

- the Baltic coast, an area of sandy beaches and coastal lagoons;
- the lowland lake districts of northern Poland; and
- the three upland regions of central Poland, and the Sudeten and Carpathian mountains of the south.

He noted that, representing what the authorities considered was of value for Polish children to learn in the 1980s, school text books brought together, almost unwittingly, an excellent introduction to the cultural and heritage underpinnings for the country's tourism development. These included historic cities such as Kraków, shrines to the Christian faith, notably the Black Madonna at Częstochowa, to national figures, most outstandingly Chopin's house at Żelazowa Wola, and to the victims of World War II, most depressingly the concentration camp at Oswięcim (Auschwitz). Alongside these were featured the spas of the Sudeten Mountains, skiing resorts of the Carpathians, castles (Malbork) and forest reserves (Białowieża) 'as well as such unlovely towns as Katowice and Łódz!' (Dawson, 1991). This was, of course, a long time ago.

Subsequently, Przezborska (2003; Hegarty and Przezborska, 2005) has written on the growing role of rural tourism within the country. During the 1990s, the Polish National Tourist Organization together with expertise from the European Union evaluated the potential of developing unique Polish tourism products. Five segments were identified that were considered sufficiently competitive in European tourism markets:

- city and cultural tourism;
- active tourism;

- rural tourism and agri-tourism;
- transit tourism; and
- border-zone weekend tourism (Legienis, 2000; Ziolkowski, 2003).

Rural tourism, agri-tourism and active tourism in particular were seen to be important in assisting rural restructuring through the consolidation of economic back-linkages and stimulating value-added quality produce. Although tourism had existed in Polish rural areas since the nineteenth century, its development was considerably accelerated during the 1990s as a result of the introduction of a market economy and the restructuring of the Polish agricultural sector.

The Polish Tourist Organization and the Institute for Tourism have acknowledged an increased interest in Poland since EU accession, and especially from young people, schools and students (Ziolkowski, 2003). There are implications here for developing educationally oriented rural tourism packages targeted towards younger markets with group travellers. Rural tourism entrepreneurs may not, however, wish to attract such low budget visitors on relatively short stays (Hegarty and Przezborska, 2005).

State Tourism Policy: the Changing Role of Tourism

Any tourism body, whether public or private, national or regional, has to base its activities on policy, at least to some extent. Many factors should be taken into account in order to properly design policies and to adopt effective measures facilitating the implementation of such policies and strategies which should provide both consumer satisfaction and sustainable development of the country or region. Such a purpose leads to the choice and design of tourism policy which has to be built on existing tourism resources, including comparative and competitive advantages in the actual and potential tourist destinations (Handszuch, 2005, p. 223). Tourism policy should therefore identify resources to be used and developed for expected economic and social benefits. Policy should describe goals and tools (Gaworecki, 1997, pp. 110–111) while strategy defines ways

and means by which policy can be implemented (Handszuch, 2005, p. 224).

State tourism policy in Poland is created by the Ministry of the Economy (Department of Tourism) and the Polish Tourism Organization (Polska Organizacja Turystyczna) established in 2000. The main players at regional level are the regional authorities and regional tourism organizations. The aim of this part of the chapter is to analyse the perceived changing role of tourism in the new economic system in Poland in the context of state and regional tourism policy in relation to a new approach to this branch of the economy adopted in the process of Poland's accession to the European Union.

The process of post-Communist change in tourism policy began in the early 1990s, when Poland was engaged in implementing three stages of the PHARE Programme: Tourin I, II and III, which were aimed at developing human resources and tourism products. The work of Tourin identified four paths for tourism development in Poland: cultural, business, activity (adventure) and agri-tourism. These four were seen as the driving force of both the tourism sector and the economy as a whole. Their identification was based on the tourism potential of the country and their promotion and enhancement was taken into account in most subsequent official documents relating to international tourism development. However, these forms of tourism activity did not establish themselves in the real world. The tourism sector was more interested in working in conjunction with foreign tour operators than in creating its own products. Even newly qualified personnel were unable to carry through the reorientation when collaboration with tour operators appeared to be a more efficient strategy. This short-term view ignored the value of the country's tourist attractions and their potential role in socio-economic development. At the time the tourism policy at state level was weak and unable to facilitate progress in the tourism sector.

During the late 1990s and the onset of the new millennium, the situation changed. Researchers began to focus in their publications on the attractiveness of Poland and analysed the role of this asset in the context of the dynamic economic development of the country and its component regions. The first regional tourism strategies were accepted for implementation at the beginning of the new millennium, but lack of appropriate mechanisms for such implementation proved to be the main obstacle to effective development. Much has been said by the authorities about the need to give priority to tourism and so it is somewhat surprising that rarely have effective political instruments been employed to motivate tourism enterprises to develop national and regional tourism products.

In the face of adverse macro-economic factors such as a high rate of unemployment, a slowing down of economic growth, and a decreasing demand (in common with many other branches of the economy) as a result of low salaries and the instability of the Polish currency (złoty), politicians have remained unconvinced that tourism should become a priority. However, the approach to the management of the sector has changed with the setting up of a new institution to oversee tourism. The Polish Tourism Organization (PTO) was established in 2000 to create, with the Ministry of Economy and Labour, a responsible tourism policy and to promote it at both national and international scales. This move was a matter of some urgency, as ongoing globalization of competition and the failure of central planning in the decades leading up to 1990 had led to the collapse of the centrally planned economy and tourism; it was clear that a market-oriented approach was the right one to adopt. Despite some questioning of the role of the government in industrial and service policy early in the transition period, the PTO has been seen to fulfil an important informational and promotional function (MGIP, 2005). The focus of its activities has been on cooperation with regional and local tourism organizations, acting as a 'bridge' between these and the tourism private sector.

Mechanisms are thus in place to facilitate tourism organizations at all levels actively participating in the creation of tourism policy. Although the market itself dictates decisions concerning the production and allocation of goods and services, the government and regional/local authorities have the task of providing the framework for the institutional collaboration necessary to obtain economically and socially desirable effects from tourism. Cooperation and various types of partnership are thus prerequisites for the success of the tourism sector.

The strategy for tourism development in the years 2001–2006 (the governmental programme of tourism development support) pointed out that:

> In the Polish Government's policy presented in the most important strategic documents concerning the economic policy of Poland, tourism is considered as a sector that is able in an essential way to support the implementation of important governmental programmes, in particular a programme of the fight against unemployment. Also in several governmental documents and strategies of voivodships development, tourism is regarded as one of the sectors that could ensure dynamic economic development, and at the same time diminish the negative effects of necessary transformations.
>
> (MGIP, 2005)

The document was formulated with the broad participation of economic development agencies and voivodships (local government), and

> formulates a strategy of tourism development as a part of the strategy of social–economic development of the country. It assumes an increase in tourism's role in the realisation of social–economic objectives of the state policy, as well as in complementary activities of other sectors.
>
> (MGIP, 2005)

However, the social and economic objectives for tourism development indicated in the strategy do not refer directly to Poland's accession to the European Union and the new economic and political environment arising from that. These objectives include:

- an increase in incomes of inhabitants of regions requiring a deep reconstruction of the economy;
- a decrease of unemployment in areas located on the borders, of high tourist values, suffering from structural unemployment;
- activization of inhabitants of rural areas;
- transformation in the sector of health resorts and recreation centres owned by enterprises;
- support for cultural heritage, civil society, and the natural environment's role in education; and
- an improvement of the image of Poland and its inhabitants on the international scene (MGIP, 2005).

Tourism enterprises, as main actors in the 'new' market had to consider their own economic goals in a wider context. Traditional and modern demand-management policies have run alongside each other. Satisfying the demand for holidays abroad has met the needs of Polish tourists, but it has not contributed much to the national or regional economies. The need for national tourist products and socio-economic development has called for a new approach to tourism policy aiming at improvement of the quality of services and utilization of the national and regional potential for innovation in tourism. On the basis of regional and tourism development strategies, many regions are now seeking new tourism products in order to provide meaningful incentives for Polish and foreign tourists to visit these areas.

Selected Features of the Tourism Sector in Poland

The institutional structure of the tourism sector in Poland is intended to complement the macro-scale market economy. The Department of Tourism is an integral part of the Ministry of the Economy and undertakes many initiatives on behalf of government, that foster partnership in tourism, including common market research, seminars, restructuring and educational reform in the tourism sector.

Tourism policy-making in Poland is framed in terms of *guardianship of the resource base.* The concept of sustainable development is a major plank of the Polish tourism strategy as developed by the Ministry of the Economy. This indicates that the government is both concerned about safeguarding the future of tourism and of future generations of the Polish nation. Tourism policy is thus intended to be socially compatible and economically rational.

Unfortunately, little attention is paid to *tourism market control* in Poland. Tourism demand is therefore generated by those who wish to go abroad for their holidays, while regional and local tourism products suffer due to the small number of visitors out of season. Currently, the Polish regions look to more profitable foreign rather than domestic visitors. Intervention by the regional authorities can be a means of encouraging greater mobility of

Poles to visit the regions of their country and to generate more income for them.

The complexity of tourism products is indicated in some tourism strategies in Poland but there are many obstacles to be overcome in implementing development. Tourism businesses prefer to sell flexible products which can be cheaper than complex ones and can find clients relatively quickly, usually without considering the fact that foreign tourists prefer complexity. It has to be pointed out, therefore, that market success for Polish tourism depends on a change of attitude on the part of tourism managers (and tourists themselves, perhaps).

Public–private partnership: a means of tourism development?

Public–private partnership (PPP) in tourism has received little attention from Polish writers (Oszoro, 2000; Marciszewska and Miecznikowski, 2003; Zysnarski, 2003; Marciszewska, 2004b; SDTPV, 2004), and the discussion has been largely based on foreign literature. According to Linder (2002, p. 26) there are at least six distinctive uses of the term, each invoking certain premises about the relevant problems to be solved and how best to solve them.

Taking into account that:

> partnership as power sharing can alter business–government relations in fundamental ways [and] . . . as a management reform, partnerships are promoted as an innovative tool that will change the way government functions, largely by tapping into the discipline of the market.
>
> (Linder, 2002, pp. 31, 26)

PPP applied to the tourism sector in Poland has the potential to bring the following social and economic benefits:

- improve quality of services for tourists;
- integrate tourism promotion abroad;
- develop new tourist products based on the attractiveness of the country;
- improve managerial skills of employees in the sector; and
- improve the quality of education for the sector.

Membership of the EU has required a new service quality which tourism enterprises have established incrementally. This has involved some improving information and promotion systems and personnel skills. However, such processes need additional financial resources, and these are limited in both the national budget and the tourism enterprises.

A Shift in Education for the Tourism Sector Toward Quality and Innovation

In order to maintain or increase market share in the intensified competition, customer orientation and non-price factors have taken on strategic significance in the management of product development (Faché and Marciszewska, 2004) and distribution. Competition through quality has had a demonstrably beneficial effect on market retention and return on investment, as well as supporting and improving competitiveness and contributing to cost reduction, increased efficiency and improvements in productivity. Having recognized the role of customer-perceived quality and satisfaction in generating repeat business and increased hospitality, tourism organizations elsewhere have adopted quality strategies and evaluation techniques (Augustyn and Pheby, 2000; Gyimóthy, 2000). As a consequence of this, quality management is becoming a crucial subject of study for students of tourism; but national perspective on service quality in tourism is not enough: cross-cultural aspects of service in tourism require cross-cultural understanding. The service demand expectations of tourists are dependent on their national/cultural background. Therefore, an analysis of cultural differences is important, considering that internationalization is fundamental to the industry, and cultural diversity is vital to the attractiveness of the product itself (Pizam, 2000, p. 396).

Further, those who supply the service, such as hotels, also have different concepts of service quality, depending on their national and cultural background. Polish tourism enterprises have to compete with foreign tour operators, and thus it is important for Polish tourism personnel and students that they acquire a cross-cultural understanding by experiential learning, not least because 'national cultures have a moderating effect on tourist behaviour' (Pizam, 2000, p. 406). This requires a different pedagogical approach from that usually adopted

in tourism education and training (Faché, 1998, 2000).

New Features of Tourism Education in Poland

The necessity for change in tourism education standards has been created by the two major transformations in the political and economic situation in Poland: the implementation of a market economy after 1989, and EU accession in 2004. These two factors placed the national tourism sector in a more competitive environment, demanding that tourism enterprises seek highly skilled personnel. Therefore, both education curricula and training are being revised both by the Ministry of Education and higher education institutions (HEIs). Some aspects of the development of tourism education and training in Poland are now discussed.

The development of a curriculum in tourism higher education which focuses on business-oriented or management-oriented subjects

A decade ago, Jung and Mierzejewska (1996, p. 67) could point out that

> higher education in Poland still largely suffers from a clear lack of focus. It has traditionally been activity-oriented (preparing 'animators' of social and qualified tourism), spatially-oriented (preparing spatial planners specialised in tourism and recreation, destined to work in planning commissions and local government) or functionally-oriented (preparing administrators of state-owned hotels and travel agencies).

This approach has been changing due to triangular cooperation between the Ministry of Education, HEIs and the Ministry of the Economy. This is initiating changes in the curriculum to make it more skills-oriented and appropriate to the requirements of the job market. The current curriculum for tourism and recreation has been under discussion in terms of how to adapt it to meet new national and global requirements. One move is to replace some of the sport recreation activities with economic and managerial subjects such as tourism markets, tourism environments, sustainable development and customer service. Such a replacement could lead to an improvement of students' skills but it does not change the old activity-oriented approach. New teaching methods have to be implemented to create wider opportunities for students to learn more about real-world problems.

Focus on practical training and fieldwork as problem-based action learning: future direction of tourism education?

The concept of problem-based action learning was originally modelled on the lines of problem-based education in some progressive medical schools in North America, where students work in clinics and see *real* patients with *real* feelings and *real* problems (Barrows and Tamblyn, 1980) and of engineering education at the Harvey Mudd College (Claremont, California) where students work on campus on *real* projects for *real* clients with *real* budgets and *real* deadlines (Remer, 1992).

In professional education relating to leisure, culture and tourism, student teams can solve real problems for real clients in problem-based fieldwork projects. As a consequence, the fieldwork project is not only related to the content of students' academic subjects, but also allows students to make positive contributions to organizations in the community. Problem-solving fieldwork can therefore best be carried out with the collaboration of businesses, such as hotels, boat trip operators and tour-operators, and governmental organizations, such as tourist information centres and museums. Such an approach is implemented by many higher education institutions, mainly at the bachelor (first degree) level. Efforts to educate skilled people who will both meet tourists' needs and attain economic benefits, is important for effective, practical business. Real-world problems, project selection and team work – new components of the educational process in Poland – are essential for preparing students for effective employment in the tourism sector.

Fieldwork with students and professors on one hand and with professionals on the other is an appropriate and innovative methodological approach to learning how to improve quality in tourism. This approach has already been partially adopted in a number of situations (Faché, 1996), but it is still unpopular in tourism education in Poland.

International student and teacher exchange

Undertaken mainly within the framework of the SOCRATES-ERASMUS scheme and via bilateral cooperation between universities and schools, this provides an opportunity to transfer knowledge and skills and adapt them to a national socio-economic context, thereby assisting benchmarking. Polish students are interested in the Erasmus programme, but it is difficult to assess if this is a temporary, transient interest arising from the initial enthusiasm for Poland's EU accession.

An increase in the role of the private sector in higher education

The private sector is usually more flexible than the state sector and is quicker to react to market changes. Private higher education institutions fill many niches in the labour market including hospitality management, tourism management, and small enterprise management.

A focus on the teaching of foreign languages and information technologies

Foreign languages and ICT are of course essential tools for effective work in the sector, and have become a specific feature of every educational tourism programme. Such a focus provides an opportunity to improve communication between tourism companies and clients and builds a competitive environment for tourism in a global market.

On the whole, the process of reforming tourism education in Poland is well on its way and it is expected that graduates will possess skills linked to the development of both Polish and international tourism markets. However, both private and public institutions of higher education in Poland engaged in educating for the tourism sector need to work together to

establish a competitive position for their graduates in a global job market that requires
managers well trained in proactive behaviour
(Marciszewska and Faché, 2004, p. 242).

Conclusions

The fluctuations of government interest in
tourism as a branch of the national economy
and an important area of public policy over the
past 15 years can be summarized as:

- an initial interest (in the early-1990s) in
  tourism as an access to the free market service economy, with the social and political
  reforms as a result of 'shock therapy';
- an increased interest in the mid-1990s
  when foreign tour operators entered the
  Polish tourism market; and
- active tourism policy created by the Ministry
  of Economy and the Polish Tourist Organization at the central level at the beginning
  of this century when tourism was recognized as a significant contributor to the
  national economy.

Tourism development is considered as an
essential factor of enterprise support and contributor to the national economy, mainly as a
job-creating activity (Dziedzic, 2005, p. 202).
Tourism has been gaining support in Poland as
a legitimate branch of the economy, partly associated with the fact that it is perceived as a
dynamically developing sector in many regions
of the country. Poland's accession to the EU
opened a new door not only to the demand, but
also to a new quality of tourism activities and
education for this sector. However, economic
benefits from tourism perceived as a direct
effect of Poland's accession to the EU cannot be
easily assessed. Social changes are expressed
by knowledge exchange, the influence of fashion, changes in life-style and culture, and they
too shape the tourist activities of Polish society.

A lack of integrated tourism information for
Poland as a whole and unified promotion of the
country's regions, particularly abroad, constitute a barrier for international tourism development at all levels. This task is beyond the
means of individual sub-regions and has to be
included in the national tourism promotion
policy. Domestic tourism suffers due to poor
cooperation between the regional authorities
and the local administrative units in the field of
information distribution and tourism product
development. The macro-economic situation
characterized by a high rate of unemployment
and, as a consequence, low purchasing power,
reduces demand from domestic tourists. Relatively low levels of investment in tourism and
limited financial resources for the restoration of
historical buildings are the reason for looking to
horizontal collaboration between local authorities and the private sector or between administrative units in the public sector itself.

A low awareness that information and
knowledge are the major prerequisites for any
development in the contemporary world, push
many small tourism enterprises to focus on outbound tourism because they can sell ready
made products which are prepared by tour
operators. In this context it seems to be obvious
that the rich experience of tourism enterprises
and owners has to be supported by knowledge
exchange between different actors of the
tourism sector. Such a philosophy can put the
Polish tourism sector in a competitive position
utilizing a number of institutional measures and
changes in managers' attitudes to tourism
products such as:

- the use of regional identity as a strong
  factor in outbound tourism development;
- the organization of new cultural and sports
  events;
- cooperation with the cultural sector; and
- the engagement of students in new tourism
  projects.

References

Augustyn, M. and Pheby, J.D. (2000) ISO 9000 and performance of small tourism enterprises: a focus on
    Weston Cider Company. *Managing Service Quality* 10(6), 374–388.
Barrows, H. and Tamblyn, R. (1980) *Problem-based Learning: an Approach to Medical Education.*
    New York: Springer.

Dawson, A.H. (1991) Poland. In: Hall, D.R. (ed.) *Tourism and Economic Development in Eastern Europe and the Soviet Union*. London: Belhaven, pp. 190–202.

Dziedzic, E. (2005) Measurement of tourism's economic effects in the light of tourism policy – theoretical and practical aspects. In: Alejziak, W. and Winiarski, R. (eds) *Tourism in Scientific Research*. Krakow and Rzeszów: Academy of Physical Education and Krakow University of Information Technology and Management in Rzeszów, pp. 201–209.

Faché, W. (1996). Europeanisation of leisure and tourism education at the University. *Spectrum Freizeit* 18(2/3), 166–183.

Faché, W. (1998) Consultation on the tourism body of knowledge with tour operators and travel agents. In: Richards, G. and Onderwater, L. (eds) *Towards a European Body of Knowledge for Tourism*. Tilburg: Atlas, pp. 46–47.

Faché, W. (2000) Methodologies for innovation and improvement of services in tourism. *Managing Service Quality* 10(6), 356–366.

Faché, W. and Marciszewska, B. (2004) A taxonomy of leisure education goals. In: Steinbach, D., Petry, K. and Tokarski, W. (eds) *International Conference on Leisure, Tourism & Sport – Education, Integration, Innovation, LEDU 2004*. Köln: F&B Offset Druckerei Fischer und Bronowski GmbH, pp. 46–47.

Gaworecki, W.W. (1997) *Turystyka*. Warsaw: PWN.

Gołembski, G. (1996) Factors which block the development of tourism in Poland. In: *Current Issues of the Tourism Economy*. Academy of Economics, Poznań, pp. 87–99.

Gyimóthy, S. (2000) *The Quality of Visitor Experience*. Nexø, Denmark: Bornholms Forskningscenter.

Handszuch, H. (2005) Between theory and practice: research as an input to tourism policies from the point of view of the World Tourism Organization. In: Alejziak, W. and Winiarski, R. (eds) *Tourism in Scientific Research*. Krakow-Rzeszów: Academy of Physical Education and Krakow University of Information Technology and Management in Rzeszów, pp. 223–233.

Hegarty, C. and Przezborska, L. (2005) Rural and agri-tourism as a tool for reorganising rural areas in old and new member states – a comparison study of Ireland and Poland. *International Journal of Tourism Research* 7(2), 63–77.

Jung, B. and Mierzejewska, B. (1996) Tourism education in Poland: an overview. In: Richards, G. (ed.) *Tourism in Central and Eastern Europe: Educating for Quality*. Tilburg: Tilburg University Press, pp. 57–68.

Knowles, T., Diamantis, D. and El-Mourhabi, J.B. (2001) *The Globalisation of Tourism and Hospitality: a Strategic Perspective*. London: Continuum.

Legienis, H. (2000) *Atrakcyjnosc Turystyczno-wypoczynkowa Terenow Polski*. Warsaw: Institute of Tourism. Available at: http://www.intur.com.pl

Linder, S.H. (2002) Coming to terms with the public–private partnership. In: Vaillancourt, P. (ed.) *Public–Private Policy Partnership* Cambridge Mass: MIT Press, pp. 19–35.

Marciszewska, B. (2000) Turystyka kulturowa a rozwój społeczno-gospodarczy. In: *Prace i Materialy. Teoria Ekonomii*. Gdańsk: Wydawnictwo Uniwersytetu Gdasńkiego, pp. 75–87.

Marciszewska, B. (2001) Consumption of cultural tourism in Poland. In: Richards, G. (ed.) *Cultural Attractions and European Tourism*. Wallingford, UK: CABI Publishing, pp. 215–226.

Marciszewska, B. (2002) Społeczno-ekonomiczne uwarunkowania rozwoju turystyki kulturowej w Polsce. *Problemy Turystyki i Hotelarstwa* 3, 5–9.

Marciszewska, B. (2004a) Kreowanie wiedzy warunkiem racjonalnego wykorzystania potencjału turystycznego Pomorza. In: B. Marciszewska and S. Miecznikowski (eds) *Usługi a Rozwój Gospodarczo-społeczny*. Gdańsk: GTN-AWFiS, pp. 24–31.

Marciszewska, B. (2004b) Partnership in tourism: experience gained from public debates on tourism strategy in the Pomerania Region (Poland). In: Petrillo, C. and Swarbrooke, J. (eds) *Networking and Partnerships in Destination Development and Management. Proceedings of the ATLAS Annual Conference 2004*. Naples: ATLAS, pp. 293–298.

Marciszewska, B. and Faché, W. (2004) Europejskie trendy wpływające na funkcjonowanie sektora kultury. In: Marciszewska, B. and Odziński, J. (eds) *Rekreacja, Turystyka, Kultura. Współczesne Problemy i Perspektywy Wykorzystania Czasu Wolnego*. Gdańsk: AWFiS, pp. 239–249.

Marciszewska, B. and Miecznikowski, S. (2003) Partnerstwo publiczno-prywatne a rozwój turystyki w regionie. In: *Unia Europejska a Przysżłość Polskiej Turystyki*. Warsaw: Szkoła Główna Handlowa, pp. 75–88.

MGIP (Ministry of Economy and Labour) (2005) *Tourism: Tasks of Minister as 'in charge of tourism'*. Warsaw: Republic of Poland Ministry of Economy, Ministry of Regional Development. Available at: http://www.mgip.gov.pl/English/TOURISM

Migdal, M. (1999) Perspectives of the development of tourism on the Western Pomerania. *Firm and Market*, 13, 54–60.

Oszoro, M. (ed.) (2000) *Partnerstwo Publiczno-prywatne w Dziedzinie Usług Komunalnych.* Warsaw: Municipium.

Pizam, A. (2000) Cross-cultural tourist behavior. In: Pizam, A. and Mansfeld, Y. (eds) *Consumer Behavior in Travel and Tourism.* New York: The Haworth Hospitality Press, pp. 393–411.

Przezborska, L. (2003) Relationships between rural tourism and agrarian restructuring in a transitional economy: the case of Poland. In: Hall, D., Roberts, L. and Mitchell, M. (eds) *New Directions in Rural Tourism.* Aldershot, UK: Ashgate, pp. 205–222.

Remer, D.S. (1992) *Experiential Education for College Students: the Clinic.* Claremont, CA: Harvey Mudd College.

SDTPV (2004) *Strategy for Development of Tourism in Pomorskie Voivodship in the period of 2004–2013.* Gdańsk: Office of the Marshal of Pomorskie Voivodship, Pomeranian Regional Studies.

Ziolkowski, P. (2003) Tourism: finding a niche. *The Warsaw Voice,* 4 April. Available at: http://www.balticdata.info/poland

Zysnarski, J. (2003) *Partnerstwo Publiczno-prywatne. Teoria i Praktyka.* Gdańsk: ODDK.

Part III

The Baltics

_____

12 The Baltics' Accession: Finnish Perspectives

Raija Komppula, Arvo Peltonen, Tom Ylkänen and Taneli Kokkila

Introduction

The purpose of this chapter is to briefly examine the implications for the Finnish tourism industry of the Baltic countries' accession to the European Union. First of all, the relationships between Finland and Estonia, and between Finland and Russia, are briefly introduced. In the second section, reflections on transformations and EU enlargement in the Baltic Sea rim are offered at a general level. This is followed by a brief introduction to multi-level, cross-border cooperation in the area, focusing on tourism development. Development of tourism flows in the Baltics and Finland are then compared, and a short introduction to the Baltics and Finland as tourist destinations is presented. We then look at some of the most interesting trans-national projects in the field of infrastructural development. Finally, the results of a Finnish tourism practitioners' interview on the implications of the Baltics' accession are presented (Fig. 12.1).

The Relationship Between Finland and Estonia

The eastern enlargement of the EU from a Finnish perspective has important implications for the economic, cultural and political relationships of the countries around the Gulf of Finland. Along the course of history, the relative permeability of borders in the region has changed, reproducing and reflecting the historical processes of power divisions in the region. The 2004 EU enlargement has had substantial impact on the relationships between the neighbouring countries around the Gulf.

Economic and cultural cooperation between Finland and Estonia has always been strong, partly because of the nations' similar ethnic backgrounds: both are Finno-Ugric, speaking languages that are closely related to each other; but there are some differences reflected in divergences of cultural heritage as well. The cultural and political roots of Finland have linked it more closely to Scandinavian countries, especially Sweden, with independent peasants' political and cultural sentiments. Estonian cultural and political heritage has been orientated more to Central Europe, especially Germany, with more Hanseatic and feudal features.

Both countries have been influenced also by the past political dominance of Imperial Russia: for Finland from 1809 to 1917, and for Estonia for about three centuries up to 1918. The proximity of the imperial capital, St Petersburg had strong economic and cultural impacts on both countries. During the collapse of the Russian Empire and the Bolshevik revolution both nations gained their independence, Finland in 1917 and Estonia in 1918.

Although the economic-political history of the nations has been slightly different, their mental and cultural ability to communicate and change ideas has been extensive and versatile.

Fig. 12.1.   Location map of the Baltic region.

The mutual communication, for example, of writers, scholars, and architects, was intense during the period of independence and even earlier under the Russian Empire, when scholars of both nations could exploit the wide-ranging imperial cultural and economic resources and international networks. A prominent feature of collaboration among ordinary people was *söber* trade: barter trade between Finnish and Estonian peasant families during the Imperial period and the later decades of independence (Sepra, 2005). Fish and agricultural products were exchanged (and, unlawfully, spirit from Estonia to Finland in the 1930s).

Finland succeeded in preserving her independence after the Second World War, but Estonia and the other two Baltic states lost theirs in 1941, and became socialist republics within the Soviet Union until regaining their independence after the collapse of the USSR in 1990. The Soviets closed the border, and economic and cultural cooperation between the nations was minimal and strictly controlled by the coercive Soviet policy and measures. However, tourism started to develop in spite of these circumstances, organized by the Soviet state tourism operators (e.g. Intourist, Sputnik) from the late 1950s. Official political, cultural and labour delegations were characteristic for 'tourism' between Finland and Soviet Estonia, and indeed with the whole Soviet Union during the following three decades (Kostiainen, 1998). The situation was normalized after the collapse of the Soviet Union. From the moment that the three Baltic states regained their independence, preparations were begun for EU accession.

The Post-war Finnish–Soviet/Russian Relationship

World War II was a painful process for Finland, and its outcome required a revised attitude to foreign relations, especially with the Soviet Union. In the Paris peace treaty, Finland lost about 10% of her surface area, more than 10% of her industrial and agricultural resources, the country's second biggest city, Viipuri (Vyborg), the Petsamo corridor to the Arctic Ocean, and the tourist islands in the eastern Gulf of Finland. Further, besides the financial and material reparations paid to the Soviet Union, Finland had to resettle more than 400,000 inhabitants from the lost region into a 'mutilated' Finland.

Former Finnish villages, towns (mostly destroyed), cultural monuments and cemeteries were left beyond the new border. All these remnants have become tourism attractions for the generation that left the region and their offspring. Nowadays one of the more important types of tourism to Russia from Finland is comprised of 'nostalgia tours' to the lost region of Karelia. The battlefields of the war have become resources for military tourism, where especially war veterans and military historians like to visit (e.g. the Mannerheim line).

An agreement for mutual cooperation was concluded with the Soviet Union in 1947, and it flavoured Finnish–Soviet policy for the next 40 years, a situation that produced the pejorative term 'Finlandisation'. Bilateral trade was based on annual barter agreements. Soviet exports to Finland consisted especially of raw materials, such as fossil energy resources (oil and natural gas), timber and chemicals. Finland provided manufactured goods, particularly machinery products and consumption goods. A special feature of the barter trade was huge construction projects.

Tourism was, as in Estonia, strictly controlled, consisting of official delegation visits, cultural exchanges, and ordinary Finns visiting St Petersburg as cultural tourist groups – often motivated by cheap vodka. After the collapse of the Soviet Union, tourism from Finland slowed down quite a lot, partly because of uncertainty and lack of organization. The biggest former Soviet tour operators owned by the government or labour unions were split and privatized, and some 10,000 SMTEs were created in Russia, in an initially wholly unregulated environment.

Finland's accession to the EU in 1995 changed the instruments of tourism development on both sides of the border. Russian subjects received TACIS funding for joint development projects. Finland, beside her own 'neighbourhood' development funding for adjacent Russian regions, now also had at her disposal EU initiatives such as INTERREG for cross-border cooperation. In the EU, Finland started to advocate a Northern Dimension programme with a strong emphasis on European Russian policy in the sectors of energy, security, environment, legislation and health care. Finnish direct investment in Russia had begun immediately after the collapse of the Soviet Union.

Mobility across the Finnish–Russian border has intensified during the last decade. Tourism from Russia has become more important in Finnish international tourism than the country's neighbours. Finns are slowly returning to St Petersburg, not so much for vodka anymore, but for cultural and architectural attractions, and to Russian Karelia as a destination for nostalgia and military tourists.

Beside tourism, there is emigration from Russia to Finland. One group of these emigrants are the 'returnees', the offspring of Finnish Russian orthodox families who had to move to Russia from Finland under Swedish rule in the 17th century. Among the emigrants there are also members of 'original' Finno-Ugrian tribes living in Russia. A third group consists of offspring of the Finns who moved to the Soviet Union after the 1917 revolution. Ethnic Russians are also among the newcomers to Finland for family or employment reasons.

Reflection on Transformations and EU Enlargement in the Baltic Sea Rim

There are five major implications of the fall of communism and successive EU enlargement to be addressed here.

First, the Baltic Sea has become almost an 'inland sea' of the EU. With the break-up of the Soviet Union and empire, Russia lost the majority of its most effective international harbours and, consequently, the Gulf of Finland has become an important logistical corridor for Russian oil, gas and other bulk exports (Peltonen, 2004, pp. 101–102). The growing importance of this Gulf and the whole of the Baltic Sea in Russian international logistics also has repercussions for environmental considerations and, for example, on the ways in which marine tourism can be developed in the region.

Second, the Russian enclave of Kaliningrad Oblast remains in the middle of the Baltic rim, with its need to maintain access to Russia proper and thus to sustain appropriate relations with its Baltic neighbours and Poland. The Kaliningrad question is a challenging test for the European Union's Russian policy and especially its neighbourhood policy for bordering countries, which has implications for international tourism incentives in the southern part of the Baltic Sea rim. This situation is significant when considering the plan to upgrade the road connection from Finland to Berlin, the Via Baltica Nordica. This route will be a part of a pan-European north–south corridor development from Finland to the Balkans and Greece.

Third, the effectiveness of international mobility and tourism is dependent on border formalities and border-crossing facilities. Ways of crossing borders have also become easier with accession. However, the three Baltic States are not yet Schengen countries, so a passport, but no visa, is needed for crossing their borders from other EU states. Some prejudices or exaggerated security measures that may prevail in the borders hindering flexible crossing date back to Soviet times, but these are changing.

After the Soviet collapse, a passport and visa barrier was formed. The citizens of the Baltic Republics encountered similar formalities for crossing the Russian border as all other visitors from abroad. This led also to the fourth implication, an aggravated situation for the Russian-speaking minorities, especially in Estonia (28% of the total population of 1.4m inhabitants) and Latvia (30% Russian plus 10% other minority groups out of 2.4m inhabitants). In Lithuania (3.6m inhabitants), the minority groups consist of 8.7% Russian and 7% Polish. The unclear citizenship situation of minorities still obstructs, for example, VFR mobility from reaching the 'expected' level. The political strain is also reflected in discussions about visa-free access between the EU and Russia. Tension in this matter is echoed in the media every now and then, expressing the sentiment of reluctance towards deepening cooperation on both sides of the EU–Russian border, with consequences for trans-national tourism.

Last, the deep gap in living standards and income levels between the EU15 countries and the Baltic accession countries and Russia is narrowing only slowly. The salary and price differences between Finland and Estonia were enormous during the years of pre-accession and were still so in the first year of the enlargement, 2004. GDP for Finland was US$23,000 and $25,000 for Sweden in 2002; for Estonia $4200, Latvia $3500, and Lithuania $3700. The difference for Finland was thus 5–6 times higher than in the Baltic States. However, figures of GDP, adjusted for purchasing power parity reveal that the gap is not that impressive: Finland and Sweden $25,000, Estonia $11,000, Latvia $8940, and Lithuania $9900 (Statistics Finland 2004, p. 657).

The unadjusted GDP figures show us the relative salary differences between Finland and the Baltic States, but the adjusted figures reveal that living costs and prices have been much lower in the Baltic States. The higher salary level is luring Estonian experts to work in Finland (e.g. as doctors), indicating a higher risk of brain drain in Estonia. However, for more than a decade the neo-liberal economic policy, well-educated labour force and lower price levels in the years of pre-accession, and especially after accession, have created a very attractive environment for Finnish direct investment in all the Baltic States. Finnish companies are especially investing in the Estonian retail trade and hotel business. When, for example, Ireland, Portugal and Spain entered the EU, the level of foreign direct investment increased exponentially (e.g. Karismo, 2002). In the Baltic countries this trajectory occurred prior to accession.

Regionalization of the Baltic Sea Rim Linked to the EU Eastern Enlargement

One of the most important effects of the EU has been the multi-level regionalization of the European economic space. The cohesion and structural instruments of the EU have contributed to a deepening cooperation between the regions at the provincial level through the realization of the multi-provincial projects. These instruments have been of great importance especially in deepening cross-border cooperation, and in the Baltic Sea rim trans-national tourism projects have been significant.

The inter-governmental Council of the Baltic Sea States (CBSS) is, among other issues, advocating and coordinating the EU's Russian policy in the Baltic Sea region (CBSS, 2002). Partly in order to gain these objectives, Finland launched the Northern Dimension initiative of the EU in the late 1990s. The joint European strategy for cooperation between the EU and Russia has been delineated in the Northern Dimension Action Plan 2004–2006.

Although in the Action Plan tourism is only implicit at present, it emerges as an important tool for regional development in the contributions of various regional and thematic organizations contributing to the Action Plan, e.g. in the initiatives of the Union of the Baltic Cities (UBC), and the Baltic Sea States Sub-Regional Cooperation (BSSSRC). These organizations are also promoting trans-regional projects serving tourism, for example, the above-mentioned Via Baltica, South Baltic Arch, and Via Hanseatica (CBSS, 2002, pp. 11, 16).

Just to mention some other examples, the Baltic Sea Tourism Commission (BCU) is a supra-national apparatus of the national tourism boards and respective ministries. One of its important contributions has been *Agenda 21 for Baltic Sea Region Tourism*, which offers guidelines for sustainable tourism development in the Baltic Sea region. Tourism also has its own working group among the other industrial clusters in the Baltic Rim Competitiveness Council showing that tourism is seen as a promising sector in multinational economic development, thus enhancing the overall competitiveness of the Baltic rim (Porter, 2001, p. 36).

Besides cooperation between states and governments, regionalization at the NUTS III (Nomenclature of Territorial Statistical Units) level is creating practical forums for most of the trans-regional and cross-border cooperation (CBC) projects on regional development, cultural and environmental collaboration and tourism. A new phenomenon created through the EU measures for activating cross-border cooperation is the formation of a process of 'Euroregions' that link the border areas of Finland and the Baltic EU countries and their adjacent areas in Northwest Russia and Belarus. There are 12 Euro-regions being consolidated in the Baltic rim (e.g. Radvilavicius, 2004).

The Euro-region of the Gulf of Finland wil provide neighbouring countries with an opportunity to develop the Gulf rim as an international, marine-based tourism destination. Here, three metropolises (Helsinki, Tallinn and St Petersburg), with their cultural heritage, tourism facilities and attractive natural surroundings could create a strong single market area of international tourism at the global level. Also, Hoghland Island in the middle of the Gulf of Finland may possess promising potential for international tourism, although its political status in the Russian vision is still uncertain. In some of the schemes the rim has been referred to as the 'growth triangle of the Gulf of Finland' (Council of General Affairs and External Relations 2003, p. 38). The eastern enlargement of the EU and the 'regionalization' of the Northern Dimension initiative and programme have created a mental and material base for the realization of this tourism vision.

Euro regions have already launched cross-border cooperation projects with infrastructural emphases, supporting means for privatization and small and medium entrepreneurship, marketing, environmental protection, land-use planning and upgrading governance. The majority of the projects are directly or indirectly linked with the tourism sector. From the viewpoint of Finland, it will be crucial that border crossings throughout the Baltic region along the Via Baltica start operating properly without any unexpected obstruction.

Tourism in the Baltic Countries and in Finland

2004, when the EU was enlarged from the previously 15 member states to 25, was a very good year for international tourism. International tourism grew by 10% and incoming tourism to and within Europe grew by 4% measured by the number of international arrivals (WTO, 2005). The best results in Europe were achieved by the 'emerging' destinations of Central and Eastern Europe (ETC, 2004, pp. 13–15).

The number of accommodation overnights increased by 21.1% in Estonia and 30.4% in Lithuania (Table 12.1). Data on the number of overnights in Latvia were not available to the authors for 2004, but measured with the number of foreign departures (including day visits)

Table 12.1. Foreign overnight stays in all accommodation facilities in Finland, Estonia and Lithuania, 2001–2004.

Year	Finland			Estonia			Lithuania			Total foreign over-nights in Finland, Estonia and Lithuania	% change from previous year	Total %
	No. of stays	% share	% change from previous year	No. of stays	% share	% change from previous year	No. of stays	% share	% change from previous year			
2001	4,183,206	58.3		1,911,000	26.7		1,072,548	15.0		7,166,754		100
2002	4,290,288	57.7	2.6	1,998,000	26.9	4.6	1,144,557	15.4	6.7	7,432,845	3.7	100
2003	4,441,829	56.4	3.5	2,268,000	28.8	13.5	1,170,369	14.9	2.3	7,880,198	6.0	100
2004	4,407,158	50.7	−0.8	2,747,000	31.6	21.1	1,526,282	17.6	30.4	8,680,440	10.2	100
% change 2001–2004	5.4			43.7			42.3			21.1		

Sources: Enterprise Estonia/Estonian Tourist Board, 2004; Finnish Tourist Board 2005; State Department of Tourism, 2004; Statistics Finland, 2002, 2003, 2004.

from Latvia, the number of foreign visitors grew by more than 20% (i.e. from 2.47m in 2003 to 3.033m in 2004), a remarkable growth of more than half a million visitors (Latvijai Statistika, 2005) (see also Chapter 14).

In order to examine to what extent the EU accession of the Baltic States has influenced tourism flows, a comparison of the development in Finland and the Baltic countries is presented in Table 12.1. As comparable data for Latvia were not available to the authors, the comparison is limited to Finland, Estonia and Lithuania for 2001–2004.

Finland's share of all foreign overnights among these three countries has diminished from 58.4% in 2001 to 50.8% in 2004. Of all these countries, Estonia has had the best growth of 43.7% from 2001 to 2004, while the overall growth for these countries was 21.1%, which was the result of very positive development in the Baltic countries.

Foreign tourism in Estonia is more or less dependent on Finnish guests, which are in a very dominant role, as they represent over 60% of all foreign overnights. Of the total growth of approximately 480,000 overnights in 2004, the majority still come from Finland. The biggest absolute growth after Finland comes from Sweden and Germany. The most important foreign markets for Lithuania are Germany (18.7%), Poland (13.7%), Belarus (12%) and Russia (8.8%).

To obtain a more precise comparison between Finland and the two Baltic countries, the development of foreign overnights are compared according to the most important foreign markets (Sweden, Russia, Germany, the UK, France, Italy, Denmark and the USA), which are common for all these countries (Table 12.2).

For the markets described above, Finland showed an overall decrease of 1.2% in 2004. By contrast, Estonia experienced 37% growth and Lithuania 42.8%. Estonia and Lithuania combined had about 700,000 overnights from the above-mentioned countries, whilst the corresponding figure for Finland was about 2.8m.

Although Finland is still the market leader in relation to the Baltics for the Russian market, the Baltic countries can now be seen as competitors. In the Swedish market, Estonia improved its overnight figures by 37.8% and Lithuania by 19.6%, while in Finland there was a decline

of 4.2%. Finland had a decrease of 0.8% in German overnights, while at the same time in Estonia the growth was 34.1% and in Lithuania 45.8%. Finland has strong winter attractions for French and Italian tourists, and these should help to maintain Finland's competitive advantage against the Baltic countries in the future.

Finland and the Baltic Countries as Tourist Destinations

In order to better understand the competitive position of Finland as a tourism destination in relation to the Baltic countries, a short summary of research undertaken on the induced images of Finland and the Baltic countries is now presented. An induced image is derived from a conscious effort towards tourism promotion directed by tourism organizations (see e.g. Gunn, 1972). A content analysis conducted on travel brochures of Estonian, Latvian, Lithuanian and Finnish national tourist boards showed some differences and similarities in the images of these countries (the brochures from Latvia and Lithuania concerned only summer tourism).

In the Estonian brochures, nature was emphasized. In the winter brochure (*Nordic with a Twist*), most illustrations were of natural scenery and forests. This brochure seemed to be targeted at people looking for peace and quiet. In addition, both summer (*Explore Estonia*) and winter activities described in Estonian brochures were outdoor ones taking place in nature. Further, the summer brochure emphasized experiences of unspoilt beaches, the countryside, small villages on the islands and forests. Both brochures also strongly promoted the history and architecture of Estonia. Especially in the summer brochure, mansions and castles, medieval churches, ruins of castles, museums and even cemeteries were illustrated. The nightlife in Tallinn and Tartu was advertised as being sophisticated and versatile. In the winter brochure, the focus was on the advantages of Estonia as a tourist destination, and notably accessibility (see Chapter 13).

The emphasis in the Latvian brochure (*Latvia Discover*) was on the history, culture and traditions of Latvia. Latvian history was promoted in pictures from castles and palaces, as well as in stories of Latvian royalty. The cultural side of Latvia was pointed out by the presentations

Table 12.2. Number of overnights from residents of selected countries in all accommodation facilities in Finland, Estonia and Lithuania, 2003 and 2004.

Country of residence	Finland			Estonia			Lithuania		
	2003	2004	% change	2003	2004	% change	2003	2004	% change
Russia	489,486	447,982	-8.5	81,321	101,546	24.9	108,277	134,746	24.4
Sweden	637,141	610,184	-4.2	134,189	184,871	37.8	29,674	35,493	19.6
Germany	551,636	547,410	-0.8	122,189	163,842	34.1	196,121	285,958	45.8
UK	420,237	409,150	-2.6	73,060	94,843	29.8	46,564	64,575	38.7
France	201,070	219,200	9.0	15,350	28,962	88.7	18,760	34,607	84.5
Italy	153,948	162,859	5.8	28,200	52,507	86.2	22,957	45,158	96.7
Denmark	99,328	105,600	6.3	26,008	28,510	9.6	24,088	37,381	55.2
EU-countries above total	2,063,360	2,054,403	-0.4	398,996	553,535	38.7	338,164	503,172	48.8
USA	193,532	211,930	9.5	30,254	44,492	47.1	36,108	51,090	41.5
Total for countries above	2,746,378	2,714,315	-1.2	510,571	699,573	37.0	482,549	689,008	42.8

Sources: Enterprise Estonia/Estonian Tourist Board, 2004; Finnish Tourist Board, 2005; State Department of Tourism, 2004; Statistics Finland 2004.

of different cultural events including music and ballet, as well as by highlighting museums and galleries. The traditions of the country were shown in the stories celebrating Christmas and midsummer. The capital city of Latvia, Riga, was especially promoted in the brochure. The nightlife in Riga was described as intensive and sophisticated. The city was also mentioned to be the fashion centre of the Baltic countries. Nature was also highlighted: long beaches and rare animals were emphasized. An orientation towards children was also evident: the country was presented as a safe and natural holiday resort for families.

The national tourist board of Lithuania provided only brochures of Vilnius for our survey. A brochure for walking tours emphasized buildings: churches, mansions, castles and the town hall.

Finland's winter brochures tend to focus on Lapland and its attractions: Santa Claus, Lapps, reindeers, northern lights, constructions of snow (snow castles and igloos, ice hotel) and eating by the fire. Brochures promise 'the ultimate snow adventure'. Summer promotions emphasize nature and the activities that can be carried out in it, with an emphasis on water. Culture is a second emphasis.

In all the brochures from the Baltic countries and those from Finland, nature was a central focus. However, there were some differences in emphasis. In Latvia, sandy beaches were promoted. In Finland, the focus was also on water and the beautiful scenery of the inland lakes. In Estonia, the emphasis was more on forests and nature trails. Nevertheless, in the Baltic countries, the induced image communicated in the brochures placed stress on cultural and historical aspects. The medieval architecture was especially portrayed. In Finnish brochures, culture was more in a supporting role to nature. In Finland, the versatility of services and activities was emphasized and the information concerning these activities was much more detailed than in the brochures of the Baltic countries.

During the ITB fair in Berlin in 2004 and 2005, it appeared that Baltic and Central European countries (especially Poland, and also the Czech Republic and Slovakia) now offer similar travel experiences as Finland and other Nordic countries. For example, Estonian spas, the Polish lake district, hiking and snow holidays in the Tatras, are serious competitors for Finnish travel products.

Most new member countries have several benefits compared to Finland. The accessibility of these countries, not only due to their location, but also due to their tourist attractions will develop further in the near future. Already today, several low-cost airlines fly to the new member countries (Davidson, 2004). In addition, the quality of road and railway networks is improving at a brisk pace.

The new member countries will tempt tourists with their exoticness, moderate price levels and easy accessibility (Lohmann, 2004). The European Tourism Forum in Budapest in October 2004 found that the new member countries had become more attractive in the eyes of international chains and investors. It is to be expected that their tourist infrastructure will improve at a fast pace (Davidson, 2004). EU subsidies will also enable more intensive investments in product development and marketing. In addition, EU membership itself will promote positive publicity for the countries concerned.

Improving Consistency Through Infrastructure Developments

The World Tourism Organization (WTO, 2001, p. 44) has envisioned that Central and Eastern Europe, accession countries of the Baltic rim included, will be the fastest growing tourism area in Europe by 2020. The Baltic rim might be one of the Northern European cultural and economic 'hot spots' (Ellerman-Jensen, 2002). From the viewpoint of Finland, an important dimension will be the substantial upgrading of the infrastructure of the eastern side of the Baltic Sea and the activation of the measures of the sub-regions (administrative provinces) towards reaching deeper and wider cooperation.

There are three trans-national routes, which have been on the Finnish agenda as to the infrastructural development of the northeastern Baltic Rim. The Middle Nordic Corridor will link the provinces of the middle parts of Norway, Sweden and Finland and will increase their mutual cooperation partly by INTERREG funding. Also, the Mid-Scandinavian link to St Petersburg has been added to the scheme, and funded partly by TACIS CBC. The concept implicitly includes tourism as an industry to be jointly developed.

The King's Road links the Nordic capitals, Oslo, Stockholm and Helsinki to St Petersburg. This concept emphasizes provincial and local tourism developments along the road. The touristic purpose of the King's Road was further strengthened, when a cruise line started operations along the northern shore of the Gulf of Finland in 2000. Improving Estonian access to the EU, her northern provinces also joined this project. New financial instruments will be used to extend the project to the south, and thus also link Latvian and Lithuanian cities to the extension of the King's Road.

The third trans-national route is Via Baltica Nordica, for which the provincial authorities of southern Finland have argued for more than a decade. It has been highly prioritized in the Finnish international traffic policy. Now the concept links Mo-i-Rana (Norway) with mid-Swedish and Finnish provinces through Helsinki to the Baltic capitals, Tallinn, Riga and Vilnius, continuing to Warsaw and Berlin, or through Kaliningrad directly through northern Poland to Berlin. The main objective of the route is to develop a chain of national economic development zones in order to link the 'smart regions' of the respective countries together (Hämeen Liitto, 2002).

None of the bigger infrastructural developments has been very successful at the transnational level yet, and, for example, they do not serve Finnish international ground traffic as effectively as had been expected. In all the transnational projects, besides basic construction and reconstruction of roads and railways, border-crossing facilities, traffic services, safety systems and information facilities for serving international tourism have been on the supra-national agenda, but international coordination is still scant and the border crossings are especially weakly organized.

Impacts of Baltic Countries' EU Accession on the Finnish Tourism Industry

The Finnish tourism industry

Although tourism is increasingly being recognized as an export industry in Finland, over 80% of tourism income currently comes from domestic sources. The sub-sectors that benefit from tourism income are:

- personal and public transport and related activities (44%);
- accommodation, restaurants and catering (17%);
- travel agents, operators and tourism supporting services (16%);
- retail trade (13%);
- petrol stations and car repairers (6%);
- cultural, recreation, sports and activity services (3%); and
- other tourism-related industries (1%).

Across most of these sub-sectors the ownership structure is based on small units and micro-tourism enterprises (SMITEs), with only few large or medium-sized firms. For example, 85% of the country's 10,100 hotels, restaurant and catering enterprises employ fewer than five people, and only 0.5% have more than 100 employees. The ten largest firms employ approximately 20% of all the labour force (72,000) in this sector. Approximately 28% of all the tourism-related enterprises are located in the Finnish countryside, and almost all of these can be classified as SMITEs. Tourism is the main source of income for only 25% of SMITEs, with around 40% being part-time entrepreneurs (Peltonen, Komppula and Ryhänen, 2004).

About three-quarters of all foreign travellers visiting Finland are on a leisure trip. July is the busiest month in general, but in Lapland Christmas and the ski season are the busiest times of the year. More than one-third of foreign travellers regard Helsinki as their main destination in Finland. About 5% of all the foreign visitors go to Lapland (Finnish Tourist Board, 2004). According to research on organic images of Finland in European markets, nature is a strong although not overwhelming element of the image held by continental Europeans, both for those who have visited Finland and those who have not. As a whole, winter elements are associated with Finland more often than summer elements (e.g. the midnight sun) (Komppula and Saraniemi, 2004).

General impacts and perspectives

The impacts of Baltic enlargement on the Finnish tourism industry were investigated by interviewing Finnish tourism specialists representing transport operators, the Finnish Ski Area Association, spas, the Association of the Finnish Tourism Industry and persons responsible for tourism marketing in the cities of Helsinki and Turku.

One important impact relates to changes in air traffic and the EU 'open skies' policy. After the Baltic countries' accession, air traffic increased considerably. The price level for the national airlines in the Baltic countries is now generally lower than in other EU countries as a response to the arrival of budget airlines. Favourable air fares have clearly increased travelling in general, not merely shifting passengers from other modes of transport or from other airlines.

It is believed that the Baltic countries attract mid-European tourists for their history with the Soviet Union. Moreover, accessibility from mid-Europe to the Baltic countries is easier than, for example, to Helsinki. Mid-European tourists travelling to the Baltic countries by car do not have to cross the sea, while by plane they are an hour earlier at their destination. It is believed that travel will increase considerably when the Baltic countries join the Schengen Treaty and the Euro zone, and as infrastructure improves further. The accession of the Baltic countries into the EU has strengthened Western Europeans' feeling of security towards travelling to the Baltic region.

Today, Finland, as well as Helsinki, is positioned as a part of Scandinavia, and the image is Scandinavian. It will be interesting to see in the future if, and how, the tour operator sector will combine Helsinki with Baltic countries. Already today one can find several tour operators which have at least included Helsinki as a destination in their Baltic brochure (e.g. Dertour, Mare Balticum Reisen).

Opportunities for the Finnish tourism industry following EU accession of the Baltic countries

It is thought that integration into the EU will not enhance travel from the Baltic countries to Finland significantly. Considering the small population and its weak economic situation, it is unlikely that leisure travel will increase greatly

in the Baltic countries for many years. Initially, the possible increase in the number of tourists will be caused by business travel. Nevertheless, the image of Finland in the Baltic States is positive and Finland has received a lot of media publicity. Finland is still the nearest destination, or at least the most easily accessible European destination, especially for the Estonians, and, for example, Finnish amusement parks offer very attractive family tourism destinations.

The Baltic countries' accession is believed to have the biggest impact on Estonian tourists, but the majority of these new tourists are likely only to visit Helsinki and the surrounding area. The tourist office of Helsinki estimated that even in the longer-term the maximum growth in tourist numbers would only be about 4%. Yet EU membership has made it easier to travel from Estonia to Finland and the demand for tourism products has clearly diversified. In addition to Helsinki, now more tourists are interested, for example, in ski centres in southern Finland. Due to high prices of fuel in Finland, typical Estonian tourists travelling by car drive only as far as they can get with the fuel they have bought in their home country. Consequently, in winter the ski centres in southern, and perhaps some in southern mid-Finland benefit most. For example, the ski centre of Himos is marketing heavily in Estonia. Currently, the driving distance is too long and plane tickets are far too expensive for a typical Estonian tourist to travel to Lapland.

Because of easy travel between Tallinn and Helsinki, Helsinki could serve as a starting and return point for American and Japanese tourists making a tour in the Baltic countries. This could, however, also create a threat. At present, Tallinn offers added value to Helsinki as a day-trip destination. In the future, the situation could reverse: Tallinn might be the main destination, from where tourists will visit Helsinki for a day-trip. This can result from lower price levels and developing air connections. In the international markets Helsinki has until now promoted Tallinn at its own expense. In the future, it will be important to have a common marketing plan, as Tallinn puts more effort into marketing.

Impacts of EU integration on the protection of the Baltic Sea may be significant. With the Baltic countries within the sphere of the EU's environmental laws, there are better possibilities for cooperation in the protection and improvement of the condition of the Baltic. The Baltic countries are already collaborating in attracting large cruise liners, and if pollution is reduced, it will influence the attractiveness of the Baltic as a cruise destination (notwithstanding that some cruise liners can produce considerable marine pollution). Although St Petersburg is not involved in this cooperation, it is still the prime Baltic attraction for American cruise lines, for example.

Recently, both Turku and Helsinki have started novel forms of collaboration with the cities of Estonia. If Finland and other countries in the Baltic Sea region are going to place the archipelago and the sea as main attractions in their international marketing, the quality of the water will be a key factor. Direct flights from Finland to certain Baltic cities and especially low cost airlines offer new possibilities, such as city breaks for new markets. Volumes will not be big, however, because of the poor economic situation of the countries concerned. The representatives of the cities believe, however, that with the help of different events and other major attractions the new EU member travellers could be persuaded to travel north instead of to mid-Europe.

Threats

The lively spa culture in Estonia forms a threat to the Finnish spa industry. Rehabilitation that is meant for working people to maintain their ability to work is a growing business. Moreover, more and more Finnish senior citizens are using these wellness services. Estonia and other Baltic countries have a long history of rehabilitation, well-being and relaxation services. Their price level is considerably lower than in Finland and their service quality levels have risen noticeably in recent years. Many completely new spas have been built in Estonia and old ones have been renovated to meet the requirements of Western customers.

It is predicted that in the near future the social insurance institution of Finland will fund rehabilitation provided to Finnish citizens in other EU countries such as Estonia, if it is more economical than in Finland. Most of the spas in Finland have not segmented their markets and they simultaneously try, for example to serve noisy families with children and the over-55s who want peace and quiet.

In the short term, the lower level of wages in the Baltic will influence the competition in passenger ship traffic. Consequently, the market shares of the shipping companies in Estonia, Finland and Sweden will be reallocated. The Baltic countries' accession eliminated the market for tax-free trade, so the shipping companies have been forced to rethink their strategies. This has brought about versatile product supply and increased programme offerings. In the long run, the increased supply is expected to show in increased demand. Subsequently, the weakest companies will be eliminated from the market and the good ones will survive. This is considered to be a positive development.

The Baltics' accession has also brought some distinct drawbacks to the Finnish national airline. Previously, the main part of the air traffic between Tallinn and Helsinki consisted of connecting flights, but now direct flights from Tallinn are also possible, so there is no longer a need to fly through Helsinki.

Although Finland reduced alcohol taxes as Estonia was about to enter the EU, the high prices and monopoly position of the Finnish government in the alcohol market presents problems for the hospitality, travel and tourism industry. It is now much cheaper to spend weekends, have business parties, birthdays and other family celebrations in the restaurants of Tallinn than in those of Helsinki. In addition, there is now a possibility to import alcohol and other purchases much more advantageously and without restrictions. Consequently, many Finnish customers, private or business, prefer Tallinn to Helsinki.

Other Baltic countries are also predicted to become competitors in MICE markets. New destinations, like Riga, have always been interesting for conference organizers, but both Latvia and Lithuania have a lot to learn before they can achieve important positions in MICE markets. Especially in Estonia, old mansions and castles have been renovated for the use of tourists, and for Finnish conference visitors these are exotic and therefore attractive alternatives. Moreover, in the future when interesting programmes are developed to suit these historic surroundings, this area will also become a competitor in incentive travel markets.

Summary and Conclusions from a Finnish Perspective

Tourism development in the Baltic countries has been very positive in recent years. Although 2004 was an exceptionally good year in international tourism generally, the growth figures in Estonia and Lithuania are much higher than the average of 4% in Europe. This indicates that interest in these 'new' destinations with their rich cultural heritage, improving services, seaside resorts and beautiful countryside, competitive price levels, and the extra publicity given by the EU accession have increased incoming tourism significantly.

Although Finland is still a more considerable destination for incoming tourism than the individual Baltic countries, Finland cannot neglect the competition emanating from these countries. In 2004 Estonia and Lithuania combined had nearly as many foreign overnights in commercial tourist accommodation as Finland. If the figures of Latvia were also taken into account, the Baltic countries as an entity would be a bigger incoming destination than Finland. When the very competitive price level, proximity to, for example, the German market, and the availability of low cost flights is added to the attractions mentioned above, the Baltic countries can be seen as serious competitors to Finland for the immediate future.

Lower prices for alcohol and other consumer goods and services have made Estonia a shoppers' paradise for the Finns and Swedes, although the earlier trans-national tax-free shopping on the ferries ceased after EU accession. Daily shopping trips, short breaks, 'mini cruises', and spa and wellness tourism have been the impetus for substantial growth in Estonian tourism development. The Finnish consumption of tourism services acted as a trigger for the upgrading of the Estonian tourism industry to replace the Soviet monolithic structures. Although there have been many unacceptable side-effects linked with the Finnish (and Swedish) 'booze tourism', the rapidly growing tourism industry as a whole has pushed the Estonian economy forward and nowadays tourism accounts for over 8% of Estonia's GDP (e.g. Huang, 2000).

On the other hand, there are also factors that hold back the growth of tourism for some of the new member countries, such as safety and the hygiene conditions, underdeveloped infrastructure, weak service levels and, to some extent, also a relatively high level of criminal activity (Employers' Confederation of Service Industries, 2003). Moreover, the countries are not known very well. However, all these drawbacks can be remedied in the course of time.

The EU programmes and financial instruments and initiatives have also helped Finland to upgrade her tourism industry, especially in the more peripheral areas and border regions through tourism projects funded by ESF, ERDF and INTERREG. Also, the profile of foreign tourist markets became more diverse (Statistics Finland 2004, pp. 31–32). Cohesion and structural instruments have assisted Finland to activate her cross-border cooperation (CBC) tourism development especially with Estonia and Russia, which implemented their programmes for CBC development, PHARE and TACIS respectively, in the mid-1990s.

It is clear that Finland will become one of the net payers in the EU budget and the amount of agricultural, structural and regional subsidies received will be reduced. Thus, one of the effects of the new member countries on the structure of present funding is, for example, the reduction of subsidy areas and levels for Finland. It is clear that the tourism industry in Finland will also be supported in the future, but the conditions for funding will tighten and competition for public funding will become even tougher. Tourism must compete for 'subsidy euros' with other sectors. Tourism will not be supported as such, unless it is competitive. Thus, in the future, the Finnish tourism industry must be prepared for less EU funding for development projects.

The Finnish tourism industry needs to become more customer-oriented, to have a clearer focus on markets and to strengthen the structure of the industry in order to sustain a competitive advantage in European markets. This means that business unit sizes should grow and the efficiency as well as the flexibility of distribution channels should be developed. The industry also needs to pay more attention to product design.

Finland is nearer to the Baltic countries than, for example, Sweden or Norway, so there are good preconditions for cooperation in this new situation, in which the centre-point of the

Baltic Sea countries has moved more to the east. Winter tourism will be even more important for Finland, while that time of the year will be very challenging for the Baltic neighbours, especially in leisure travel.

Acknowledgements

The authors wish to express their warmest thanks to the following people, whose help and assistance has been crucial in the process of this work: Ms Helen Reijonen M.Sc. and Ms Hanna Varis M.Sc. (the University of Joensuu), who assisted with the data on induced images, and Rein Luuse M.Sc. (University of Tartu, Pärnu College, Estonia), who revised the text dealing with Estonia and her cooperation with neighbouring countries. The authors would also like to thank all the interviewed experts and cooperative partners who contributed to this study.

References

CBSS (Council of the Baltic Sea States) (2002) *Contributions Towards a Northern Dimension Action Plan 2004–2006. Compilation of Written Contributions from CBSS Working Bodies and Partner Organisations.* Stockholm: The Secretariat of the Baltic Sea States. Available at: http://www.cbss.st

Council of General Affairs and External Relations (2003) *Northern Dimension – Second Northern Dimension Action Plan, 2004–2006.* Brussels: Council of the European Union Note 13112/03.

Davidson, R. (2004) *Economic Trends Report September 2004.* London: EIBTM. Available at: http://www.eibtm.ch/images/100278/Docs/EIBTMEconomicTrendsReport.pdf

Ellerman-Jensen, U. (2002) *Opening of the 11th CBSS Ministerial Meeting. Baltic Development Forum, March 2002.* Copenhagen: Baltic Development Forum. Available at: http://bdforum.org/sideindhold.asp?sideid=506&sprog=1

Employers' Confederation of Service Industries (PT) (2003) *EU Enlargement and Private Service Branches.* Helsinki: PT. Available at: http://www.ek.fi/ek_suomeksi/ajankohtaista/arkisto_tiedostot/eunlaajentuminen2003.pdf

Enterprise Estonia/Estonian Tourist Board (2004) *Tourism in Estonia in 2004. Preliminary Results by Enterprise Estonia/Estonian Tourist Board as of 31 March 2004.* Tallinn: Enterprise Estonia/Estonian Tourist Board. Available at: http://www.visitestonia.com/index.php?page=360

ETC (European Tourism Commission) (2004) *Tourism Insights – Outlook for 2005.* Brussels: ETC Research Report No 2005/2.

Finnish Tourist Board (2004) *Border Interview Survey 2003. Foreign Visitors in Finland in 2003.* Helsinki: Finnish Tourist Board (MEK) A:136.

Finnish Tourist Board (2005) *Monthly Data on the Number of Nights in Accommodation Facilities in Finland for the Biggest Origin Markets from January 1993 Onwards.* Helsinki: Finnish Tourist Board. Available at: http://www.mek.fi/web/stats/index.nsf

Gunn, C.A. (1972) *Vacationscapes: Designing Tourist Regions.* New York: Van Nostrand.

Hämeen Liitto (2002) *Via Baltica Nordica – Vyöhykeen Kehittäminen Jatkuu.* Hämeenlinna: Hämeen Liitto. Available at: http://www.viabalticanordica.com

Huang, M. (2000) Estonia: beyond alcohol tourism. *Central Europe Review* 2(14), 10 April. Available at: http://www.ce-review.org/00/14/amber14.html

Karismo, A. (2002) Sijoitukset Itä-Eurooppaan kasvavat. *Helsingin Sanomat*, 24 May, p. D5.

Komppula, R. and Saraniemi, S. (2004) Organic images of Finland in European markets. *Tourism Today* 4, Autumn, pp. 37–51.

Kostiainen, A. (1998) Mass tourists, groups, delegates: travel from Finland to the Soviet Union from 1950 to 1980. In: Peltonen, A. and Heikkinen-Rummukainen, M. (eds) *Trends in Russian Research on Tourism. International Forum for Tourism Research.* Savonlinna: University of Joensuu, the Finnish University Network for Tourism Studies No. 3.

Latvijai Statistika (2005) *Basic Socio-Economic Indicators: Number of Latvia's Border Crossings.* Riga: Central Statistical Bureau of Latvia. Available at: http://www.csb.lv

Lohmann, M. (2004) *New Demand Factors in Tourism.* Budapest: Presentation at the European Tourism Forum, October 15.

Peltonen, A. (2004) Matkailu ja logistiikka Itä-Suomen lähialueyhteistyössä [The role of tourism and logistics in the neighbourhood cooperation in eastern Finland]. *Muuttuva Matkailu [Tourism in Transition]* 2–4, 100–109.

Peltonen, A., Komppula, R. and Ryhänen, H. (2004) Overview of SMEs in Tourism: Finland. In: Morrison, A. and Thomas, R. (eds) *SMEs in Tourism: an International Review*. Tilburg: ATLAS, pp. 25–33.

Porter, M.E. (2001) *The Baltic Rim Regional Agenda*. Stockholm: Baltic Development Forum, Institute of International Business, Stockholm School of Economics, September 25.

Radvilavicius, S. (2004) *Cross-border Cooperation in the Baltic Countries and North-West Russia*. Copenhagen: Norden, Nordic Council of Ministers.

Sepra (2005) *Summary*. Hamina, Finland: Sepra. Available at: www.seprat.net/kansainv/?kieli=englanti

State Department of Tourism (2004) *Lithuanian Tourism Statistics 2003–2004*. Vilnius: State Department of Tourism. Available at: www.tourism.lt

Statistics Finland (2002) *Tourism Statistics 2002*. Helsinki: Statistics Finland.

Statistics Finland (2003) *Tourism Statistics 2003*. Helsinki: Statistics Finland.

Statistics Finland (2004) *Statistical Yearbook of Finland 2004*. Helsinki: Statistics Finland.

WTO (World Tourism Organization) (2001) *Tourism 2020 Vision. Global Forecasts and Profiles of Market Segments*. Madrid: WTO.

WTO (World Tourism Organization) (2005) *World Tourism Barometer, Volume 3, No.1*. Madrid: WTO.

13 Estonia – Switching Unions: Impacts of EU Membership on Tourism Development

Jeff Jarvis and Piret Kallas

Introduction

It wasn't that long ago that the Baltics in general, and Tallinn in particular, were regarded as a fringe destination, an exotic stopping place for cruise ships and a pin on the map for the more adventurous backpackers. Rest assured that those times are no more.

(In Your Pocket, 2005)

The above guidebook quote highlights the fact that the Estonian tourism industry is booming with investment and tourists flocking to the country. In 2004, overnight visitors were estimated to have increased by 20%, receipts from tourism by 21%, the supply of bed spaces throughout the country by over 33% (Enterprise Estonia/ Estonian Tourist Board, 2005) and passenger numbers at Tallinn airport grew by 40% (Tallinn Airport, 2005). Indeed, Eurostat (2005) indicated that in terms of total number of overnights compared to the same period in the previous year, Estonia was the fastest growing tourism destination in the EU25 for the first 9 months of 2004. Tallinn's strategic location in the Baltic Sea is also leading to its growth in popularity as a cruise destination, with 331 ships due to dock in 2005, an increase of more than 100 on the previous year (Baltic Stand-by News, 2005). CNN World Business Report even broadcast on 9 November, 2004 that the former Soviet socialist republic was one of their tourism 'hot spots' to visit for the following year.

Economically, it can be seen that Estonia has benefited greatly from the tourism industry, with over €5.8bn in receipts being generated between 1993 and 2003 (Enterprise Estonia/ Estonian Tourist Board, 2004a). The economic impact of the industry, as highlighted in Fig. 13.1, has grown dramatically from €91.8m in 1993 to over €900m in 2004, with a substantial increase occurring in the year Estonia acceded to the EU (Enterprise Estonia/Estonian Tourist Board, 2005). In terms of total exports, the industry in 2003 accounted for 40% of all service exports and 13% of total exports, a rise from 32% and 9% in 1993. Additionally, the Statistical Office of Estonia estimated in 2000 that the industry accounted for 8.2% of GDP and over 45,000 full-time jobs (Enterprise Estonia/Estonian Tourist Board, 2004b). With demand forecast to grow annually by 6.4% to 2015 and capital investment by 7.7% (WTTC, 2005), the long-term outlook for the Estonian industry is positive.

Estonia has responded proactively to the opportunities presented to it in the tourism industry, launching the 'Brand Estonia' campaign in 2002 to act as a point of focus for their marketing strategy as they moved towards EU membership. Since 1995 the industry has moved away from being over-reliant on same-day visitors and the Finnish market, and has seen investment in and the development of product sectors such as the convention industry,

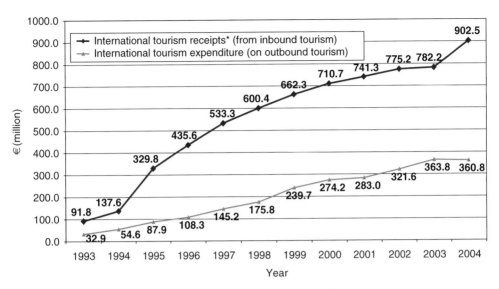

*Since 1995, the figure has been based on the Foreign Visitor Border Survey

Fig. 13.1. Estonia: international tourism receipts and expenditure, 1993–2004 (€m). Source: Enterprise Estonia/Estonian Tourist Board 2005.

health spa tourism and off-season city breaks. Overall it can be argued that the road to EU accession has impacted positively on the tourism industry in Estonia, accelerating its development, although most of the impact has been indirect. This can be divided into three categories:

1. EU accession, in association with NATO membership, has assisted in creating a perception of safety and security in the country. This in turn with the economic management of the country has created the foundation for a positive business environment and increased the flow of both foreign and local direct investment to the industry as well as international visitors.

2. EU membership has facilitated increased access to the country by making it easier to visit, with the removal of cross-border bureaucracy and increased transport access to the country, most notably stimulating the arrival of budget airlines into the industry.

3. The imminent arrival of a 'new' country into the EU also led to unprecedented quantities of free publicity for Estonia in the media, both within the EU and internationally. This in turn raised awareness of the destination in the international marketplace and provided a platform on which to promote 'Brand Estonia'.

Evolution of the Tourism Industry in Estonia

Tallinn, the walled medieval capital city is currently the chief attraction for the majority of tourists visiting the country. It has fulfilled this role over the centuries as it was one of the initial destinations where tourism developed in Estonia. However, mirroring the contemporary trend for spa tourism (Enterprise Estonia/Estonian Tourist Board, 2004b), the primary attraction for visitors to Estonia was the discovery that the sea mud from the Baltic coast town of Haapsalu could be of therapeutic benefit. Subsequently, the first health resort built by the town doctor, Carl Abraham Hunnius, opened in 1825 and immediately became popular with the Russian aristocracy (including Tsar Nikolai II), intellectuals and artists, as well as the local Baltic Germans. This led to the growth of similar health spas throughout the 1800s in Parnu (1838), on Saaremaa (1840) and Narva-Joesuu (1872) (Kallas, 2002).

The first geopolitical shift to affect the region was World War I and, not unexpectedly, it had a major impact on the tourism industry. The lifeline of the Russian inbound market was cut off after the revolution of 1917 and the

Table 13.1.   Estonia: international visitors by citizenship, 1926–1939.

Country of residence	1926	1928	1930	1932	1934	1936	1939
Latvia	52,738	8,211	74,809	66,277	61,761	127,056	53,643
Finland	4,528	7,834	13,899	5,587	6,559	12,221	13,286
Germany	3,523	4,299	5,686	3,852	5,072	5,566	5,008
Sweden	861	1,261	1,361	1,024	1,903	5,432	7,074
Russia	2,172	2,373	1,247	1,091	1,074	1,032	778
UK	875	1,774	2,799	3,068	1,070	1,414	1,108
USA	596	885	1,102	772	514	801	712
Lithuania	877	693	688	563	539	927	1,409
Other countries	3,689	4,146	5,157	3,382	3,862	5,661	5,310
Total	69,859	105,375	106,748	85,616	82,354	160,111	88,328

Source: Kallas, 2002.

majority of tourism infrastructure lay in a state of decay. Inbound tourism in the newly independent Estonia of the 1920s focused on rebuilding the industry. This led to a reorientation that saw the country being marketed to her near neighbours, the Finns, Swedes and Latvians, many of whom were attracted to her coastal resorts (Unwin, 1996). Table 13.1 shows that by 1936 over 160,000 international visitors were travelling to Estonia, an increase from 1926 of 129% (with a heavy reliance on Latvia and Finland); but by the end of the 1930s, World War II led to the destruction of much of the tourism infrastructure and saw the country occupied by both the Nazis and the Soviets.

The Soviet Tourism Era in Estonia

The structure of leisure tourism that existed pre-World War II in Estonia was regarded as a 'non productive' industry by the Soviet occupiers and its major benefit was redefined either as a propaganda tool or as a means to recuperate the workforce (Hall, 1991). After the death of Stalin in 1953 international travel to the USSR became easier, but the tourism industry in Estonia had become primarily associated with internal or inter-republic domestic travel. International tourism to Soviet Estonia increased substantially when the sea link to Finland was re-established in July 1965, with the ferry *Vanemuine* (named after an Estonian folk hero)

operating up to twice per week between Tallinn and Helsinki. In its first year of operation some 10,000 foreigners came to Estonia on a quota system related to available bed spaces, through the Soviet travel agent *Intourist* and selected travel agents in Finland (Kallas, 2002). 'Capitalist' tourists were only permitted to stay in approved accommodation for international guests and were expected to purchase a pre-packaged tour of Tallinn where they would be shown the Old Town (Fig. 13.2) as well as the 'new and improved' 1960s housing projects, such as the suburb of Mustamae (a 1960s high-density, high-rise 'village').

The opening of the 829-bed Hotel Viru in 1972 altered the landscape of international tourism and by the end of the 1970s it alone was accommodating between 40,000 and 50,000 visitors (Jaakson, 1996). Estonia still remained a mainly closed country with the majority of visitors only permitted to go to Tallinn and even the historic university town of Tartu was off limits due to the proximity of a military airport (Unwin, 1996). The Moscow Olympics came to Tallinn in 1980 in the form of the yachting regatta. This further stimulated Soviet hotel construction, which led to the Hotel Olympia and the Pirita Sport Hotel. The freedoms gained under Gorbachev and Perestroika in the late-1980s stimulated a boom in tourism as restrictions were eased. This importantly encouraged an 'independent' tourism industry to emerge to fill the gaps left by Intourist,

Fig. 13.2.   1960s tourist guide to Tallinn.

including the servicing of the ferry traffic by the provision of guided tours, excursions, folk entertainment and meals (Worthington, 2001). This also encouraged the establishment of tourism organizations such as the Estonian Association of Travel Agents in April 1990 (Estonian Association of Travel Agents, 2005).

The Transition Era 1991–1994

The importance of tourism as a stimulation agent in the transition process has been proposed by a number of researchers. Hall (2001) argues that theoretically tourism as an industry was integral to post-Communist regional economic restructuring and the transition process as a whole. Worthington (2001) builds on these arguments by adding that tourism in common with the rest of the entrepreneurial service sector is not capital intensive, employs large numbers of workers, attracts foreign investment and produces results within a remarkably short time frame. Additionally, in the case of Estonia, it would provide the model for the transformation of an industry exposed to market forces and

reflect the region's reintegration into Europe (Worthington, 2001, 2004).

The ferry link to Tallinn from Helsinki had been the lifeline of Estonian tourism since the 1960s and in the period post-1991 it almost threatened to overwhelm Tallinn with Finns. This led some guidebooks to describe the capital as a 'virtual suburb' of Helsinki (Williams *et al.*, 2000). The number of Finnish visitors increased from an estimated 120,000 in 1985 (personal communication from O. Sööt, Director of *Intourist*, Estonia (1966–1991)) to 1.52m in 1995 when they accounted for 72% of all foreign arrivals to Estonia. Most of this increase can be attributed to same-day visitors and can be explained by the close proximity of Helsinki, the linguistic and cultural links, and by the economic incentive of cross-border trade (Unwin, 1996).

Tallinn quickly became an established shopping destination for Finns where, after taking a short ferry ride, they could purchase Western goods at a heavily discounted rate in comparison to Helsinki. This led to the fact that by 1994 up to 40% of all retail purchases in the Estonian capital were attributed to them (Worthington, 2001).

Most importantly, the arrival of large numbers of foreigners acted as a stimulant in the early years of independence for entrepreneurs to generate employment and foreign exchange earnings either independently or with the assistance of a Western partner (primarily Scandinavians and Finns). Additional benefits with Finnish partner involvement in tourism included adoption of Western business ethics and managerial knowledge, such as in the spa industry in Estonia. As Worthington (2001) argues, this in turn acted as a stimulant in the overall transition process, and possibly even the catalyst. His thesis here is based on the premise that those economies with a larger service sector directed at the international market attracted higher levels of foreign investment and thus achieved a greater rate of progress in the transition process.

The Road to the European Union: Estonian Tourism 1995–2003

In November 1995, Estonia submitted its application to accede to the European Union and since then a steady market reorientation has occurred, as can be clearly seen from Table 13.2.

Table 13.2. Estonia: international visitor arrivals, 1996–2003.

Country of residence	1996	1997	1998	1999	2000	2001	2002	2003
Finland	1,689,416	1,761,019	1,813,380	1,912,157	1,913,622	1,809,617	1,824,728	1,787,576
Finnish share	69%	67%	62%	60%	58%	56%	56%	53%
Sweden	74,921	100,763	108,790	132,818	158,159	109,756	134,232	149,822
Norway	12,195	15,338	17,692	20,091	24,418	27,940	36,025	43,457
Denmark	12,244	17,542	18,476	15,933	16,269	16,190	16,694	17,800
Germany	38,084	33,384	45,071	48,124	57,784	70,491	85,850	104,957
UK	18,582	23,059	33,263	35,417	44,297	57,050	59,324	71,097
Italy	8,381	9,092	15,100	17,181	15,226	18,537	21,103	33,053
France	8,487	6,798	9,750	10,579	10,703	12,157	14,852	20,293
The Netherlands	8,382	6,971	7,700	7,748	9,383	10,536	11,916	16,422
Spain	3,631	3,794	5,106	9,362	9,748	12,907	17,358	22,276
Latvia	230,000	249,000	325,000	437,000	419,000	450,246	401,536	414,447
Russia	142,000	188,000	232,000[a]	299,100[a]	332,000[a]	280,751	281,041	295,620
Lithuania	72,597	80,168	82,593	80,330	92,544	112,981	129,493	127,275
Ukraine	7,685	8,806	14,300	13,376	14,842	15,319	15,810	16,806
Belarus	3,370	3,493	4,000	4,832	5,669	6,877	7,457	
Poland	10,902	14,529	17,164	12,746	16,122	22,390	29,250	38,055
Czech Rep.	3,394	3,160	4,767	6,743	7,648	9,236	10,965	12,457
Hungary	2,803	3,812	4,666	4,787	7,033	8,253	7,928	9,084
USA	45,925	35,372	67,442	58,248	88,286	98,672	70,958	83,144
Canada	6,243	6,047	7,148	4,438	6,679	8,097	6,974	
Japan	4,228	4,536	5,900	7,594	9,562	9,595	8,765	9,488
All foreign arrivals	2,434,621	2,618,484	2,908,819	3,180,530	3,310,300	3,230,323	3,253,012	3,377,837
Same-day visitors	1,769,621	1,888,484	2,083,819	2,230,530	2,090,300	1,910,323	1,891,012	1,915,837
Overnight visitors[b]	665,000	730,000	825,000	950,000	1,220,000	1,320,000	1,362,000	1,462,000

[a]Russian arrivals in 1998–2000 include a number of Estonian residents with Russian passports.
[b]Includes visitors staying at paid and unpaid accommodation.
Source: Enterprise Estonia/Estonian Tourist Board, 2004.

Although Finnish visitors still dominate the market for total visitor arrivals, the reliance the Estonian tourism industry has on the market is diminishing. In 2003, visitors from Finland accounted for 53% of all arrivals compared with 72% in 1995 (Enterprise Estonia/Estonian Tourist Board, 2004b). Over the same time period, a reorientation towards the more distant EU markets has occurred, in particular Germany, the UK, Italy, France, The Netherlands and Spain. As a group, these countries grew by over 213% in contrast with total visitor arrivals to Estonia, which only grew by 39% over the same time period. Market share has also been gained by the near Eastern markets of Russia, Latvia, Lithuania and Ukraine, up from 19% to 25% in 2003, a numerical increase of 95%, and the nearby Scandinavian markets of Sweden, Denmark and Norway significantly growing by 112%.

The earlier lifeblood of the industry, same-day visitors, only grew by 8% between 1996 and 2003, while overnight visitors increased by 120% and from 27% to 43% of all international arrivals. Clearly the market was reorientating towards overnight visitors and away from cross-border shopping, or 'vodka tourists', as some early Finnish visitors were described (Worthington, 2001).

Given the high percentages of same-day visitors it is worthwhile to consider the data for those who stayed overnight. Figures shown in Tables 13.3 and 13.4 demonstrate that these

Table 13.3. Estonia: number of foreign tourists staying in registered accommodation, 1995–2003 (excluding health spas).

Country of residence	Year				
	1995	1997	1999	2001	2003
Finland	185,040	341,407	467,082	611,895	610,182
Sweden	22,748	34,546	51,226	55,943	60,513
Germany	23,006	25,592	28,369	43,617	66,615
Latvia	10,239	16,046	21,527	25,219	28,333
UK, Ireland	7,739	14,608	16,537	23,513	31,557
Russia	12,914	12,190	14,953	24,989	35,340
Norway	4,542	7,556	10,731	16,298	29,213
Lithuania	8,615	11,981	11,536	12,267	14,092
Denmark	6,540	9,368	11,725	11,107	14,527
Benelux countries	4,002	4,624	6,132	6,981	10,815
Italy	3,233	3,773	5,622	7,180	13,003
France	2,119	3,193	5,281	4,958	8,233
Poland	1,661	2,031	2,443	5,343	11,424
Spain, Portugal	865	1,804	2,208	5,107	9,033
Switzerland	1,481	1,452	2,049	2,945	3,745
Austria	1,277	2,341	2,271	2,309	3,450
Czech Republic, Slovakia	1,003	963	1,608	1,202	2,586
Hungary	691	624	877	986	1,477
Other Europe	12,644	19,478	12,178	10,719	15,462
USA	13,516	13,830	14,398	14,687	12,513
Canada	1,681	1,937	2,175	2,191	1,517
Japan	–	–	5,405	6,907	6,893
Other countries	5,297[a]	11,070[a]	7,337	11,709	9,843
Total foreign visitors	330,853	540,414	703,670	908,072	1,000,366

[a]Includes Japan.
Source: Enterprise Estonia/Estonian Tourist Board, 2004.

Table 13.4.   Estonia: number of tourist overnights in registered accommodation, 1995–2003 (excluding health spas).

Country of residence	Year				
	1995	1997	1999	2001	2003
Finland	305,663	469,081	616,068	877,623	896,978
Sweden	45,443	60,012	81,224	93,936	100,201
Germany	47,913	46,818	53,859	80,392	117,386
UK, Ireland	16,452	29,937	36,458	56,291	75,315
Russia	23,939	21,897	27,306	52,401	71,305
Latvia	16,539	25,438	29,968	37,504	40,739
Norway	9,942	14,316	20,642	33,642	59,062
Lithuania	15,305	17,899	17,359	20,468	22,446
Denmark	13,248	20,413	22,480	21,769	24,937
Benelux countries	7,925	8,910	12,598	15,195	22,805
Italy	6,939	8,010	11,870	15,708	27,993
France	4,431	5,949	9,191	9,895	15,169
Poland	3,285	3,968	4,608	11,200	38,168
Spain, Portugal	1,563	2,617	4,562	8,363	16,048
Hungary	1,362	1,175	2,771	2,792	3,859
Switzerland	3,298	3,074	3,542	5,859	6,973
Austria	2,089	4,308	3,841	4,673	6,333
Czech Republic, Slovakia	2,314	2,033	2,846	3,089	4,937
Other European countries	29,611	36,565	23,920	23,460	34,966
USA	31,475	29,150	31,808	34,975	29,264
Canada	4,192	4,783	4,908	5,097	4,110
Japan	–	–	8,780	11,379	12,637
Other countries	14,688[a]	18,407[a]	13,994	20,011	18,644
Total foreign visitors	607,616	834,760	1,044,603	1,445,722	1,650,275

[a]Includes Japan.
Source: Enterprise Estonia/Estonian Tourist Board, 2004.

visitors increased significantly between 1995 and 2003, breaking the one million visitor mark for the first time. Importantly, more Finns were encouraged to stay in overnight accommodation with an increase of 230% from 1995 to 2003 accounting for 61% of the market (Table 13.4).

The Estonian National Tourism Development Plan 2002–2005 and 'Brand Estonia'

In order to manage the development of the industry, the Estonian government published a strategy to chart a course for the future direction of the industry to 2005. The stated objectives listed were:

- maintaining the on-going growth trend of tourism receipts and domestic tourism;
- increasing the average length of stay in accommodation establishments;
- increasing the relative share of overnight visitors;
- increasing expenditures made by overnight visitors;
- diversifying into a wider range of markets;
- widening the product range; and
- achieving a better regional distribution of tourism (Enterprise Estonia/Estonian Tourist Board, 2004b).

The strategy identified that the key target markets for Estonia were Finland, Sweden, Russia, and the more distant markets of Germany and the United Kingdom. Additionally, the plan highlighted the development of four priority products in Estonian tourism: conference tourism, historical and cultural heritage tourism, nature tourism and national parks and activity holidays (Enterprise Estonia/Estonian Tourist Board, 2004b).

During 2001, and timed to take advantage of the media coverage associated with the hosting of the 2002 Eurovision song contest, Estonia commenced the marketing initiative 'Brand Estonia'. Branding is increasingly gaining recognition in tourism marketing as an essential step in the international marketing of destinations. Van Ham discusses the development of the branding of states in the political context and defines the 'brand state' as the outside world's ideas about a particular country that can have an impact on a country's economic and political attention. This he defines as a state's strategic equity (Van Ham, 2001). Tourism destination brands are also increasingly beginning to reach beyond the tourism industry (Morgan *et al.*, 2002). Estonia's stated multiple objectives of the branding campaign were:

- to enable the country to achieve greater success in attaining foreign direct investment;
- to expand the tourist base beyond Sweden and Finland; and
- to increase exports to European markets (Enterprise Estonia, 2002).

These objectives are similar to those followed by other post-Communist states as noted by Hall (2002). In branding a destination, establishing a differentiation from other competitors is essential, as is developing a brand identity. Brand identity involves the development of a vision of how that brand should be perceived by its target market (Aaker and Joachimsthaler, 2000; Grönroos, 2000). This then helps establish a relationship between the brand and the customer by generating a value proposition potentially involving functional, emotional or self-expressive benefits (Aaker and Joachimsthaler, 2000).

The Estonian brand essence emphasized the essential character of the country and people and was described as 'positively transforming'. This was primarily based on the successful transition the country had just experienced and the positive nature of the changes

Fig. 13.3. 'Estonia: Nordic with a twist'. An example of a marketing brochure to promote Estonia in winter (2004). Note the 'Brand Estonia' logo, launched in 2002, in the top right corner.

that were taking place (Enterprise Estonia, 2002). Additionally, the country was identified as 'a Nordic country with a twist' (Fig. 13.3), and the Estonian people as radical and reforming, resourceful and environmentally minded, calm and peaceful (Gardner and Standaert, 2003). Importantly, this shifted the perception of Estonia to the Nordic/Scandinavian region, differentiating it from the other Baltic States and Russia. The logo for the brand was the words 'Welcome to Estonia' in the shape of the country. Although hotly debated internally amongst Estonians, the branding campaign provided a marketing focus in the prelude to EU accession in May 2004.

Inbound Tourism to Estonia in 2004

Tourism to Estonia boomed in the EU membership year of 2004. Additional visitors staying in paid accommodation numbered 261,000, a substantial percentage increase of 24%, while visitor nights increased by 21% (Tables 13.5 and 13.6) (Enterprise Estonia/Estonian Tourist Board, 2005). This growth trend was not merely a reflection of the summer peak season as each month of 2004 demonstrated high growth rates in comparison to the respective month of 2003 (Enterprise Estonia/Estonian Tourist Board, 2005). Among the 1.37m overnight tourists, 200,000 stayed at health spas, an increase of 66,000. In total, this rapidly growing segment accounted for 32% of foreign visitor overnight stays in accommodation establishments (Enterprise Estonia/Estonian Tourist Board, 2005).

Reviewing the market by type of holiday, the main growth sectors have been: (i) city breaks to Tallinn, (ii) tours combining Estonia and its neighbouring countries, popular with tourists from Western and Southern Europe, and (iii) spa holidays, popular with tourists from Finland and Sweden. To a lesser extent, conference tourism has also increased by 20%, although from a smaller base. According to the

preliminary data of 2004, holiday tourists account for 66% of foreign tourists at accommodation establishments, with 5% being conference delegates, 18% other business tourists and 12% travelling for other purposes (Enterprise Estonia/Estonian Tourist Board, 2005).

In terms of the major source markets, the substantial growth rates in the number of Finnish, German, Swedish, Italian, Latvian and British tourists mainly contributed to the overall increase, although tourist arrivals from almost all other markets have increased substantially as well (Enterprise Estonia/Estonian Tourist Board, 2005). While between 2001 and 2003 tourism flows from Finland to Estonia had been stabilizing, the number of Finnish tourists started to increase again in the fourth quarter of 2003. This was related to additional ferry capacity being available on the Tallinn–Helsinki route and the opening of several new hotels and spas. Tourists staying at the hotels of Tallinn account for almost 66% of the increase in Finns, while

Table 13.5.   Estonia: visitor arrivals, 2004 (staying in paid accommodation including health spas).

	Arrival numbers		Change 2004/2003 growth	
Country of residence	2003	2004[a]	Nos	%
Finland	706,473	843,871	137,398	19
Sweden	66,751	89,042	22,291	33
Germany	68,151	85,643	17,492	26
Russia	37,320	42,348	5,028	13
Latvia	29,230	40,956	11,726	40
UK	30,151	38,903	8,752	29
Norway	29,842	35,798	5,956	20
Italy	13,127	25,642	12,515	95
Lithuania	14,320	20,555	6,235	44
USA	12,761	19,411	6,650	52
France	8,326	15,086	6,760	81
Denmark	14,894	13,915	−979	−7
Spain	7,921	12,177	4,256	54
The Netherlands	7,826	10,490	2,664	34
Japan	6,901	7,362	461	7
Austria	3,487	5,757	2,270	65
Switzerland	3,791	4,694	903	24
Czech Republic, Slovakia	2,624	4,997	2,373	90
Hungary	1,489	2,267	778	52
Canada	1,567	2,981	1,414	90
Foreign tourists	1,112,746	1,374,414	261,668	24

[a]Estimated.
Source: Enterprise Estonia/Estonian Tourist Board, 2005.

Table 13.6.   Estonia: number of overnights for visitor arrivals, 2004 (staying in paid accommodation including health spas).

Country of residence	Overnights by country of residence		Growth 2004/2003	
	2003	2004	Nos	%
Finland	1,411,623	1,664,799	253,176	18
Sweden	134,189	184,871	50,682	38
Germany	122,189	163,842	41,653	34
Russia	81,321	101,546	20,225	25
Latvia	42,682	59,532	16,850	39
UK	73,060	94,843	21,783	30
Norway	61,381	81,288	19,907	32
Italy	28,200	52,507	24,307	86
Lithuania	22,977	32,068	9,091	40
USA	30,254	44,492	14,238	47
France	15,350	28,962	13,612	89
Denmark	26,008	28,510	2,502	10
Spain	13,631	21,878	8,247	61
The Netherlands	16,094	21,698	5,604	35
Japan	12,648	14,174	1,526	12
Austria	6,420	10,620	4,200	65
Switzerland	7,059	8,905	1,846	26
Czech Republic, Slovakia	5,025	10,255	5,230	104
Hungary	3,877	4,844	967	25
Canada	4,254	7,245	2,991	70
Total foreign visitors	2,267,873	2,746,806	478,933	21

Source: Enterprise Estonia/Estonian Tourist Board, 2005.

spa tourists (mainly in Pärnu and near Tallinn) account for a quarter of the increase. In total, spas accounted for 19% of Finnish tourists and 44% of Finnish overnights at all accommodation establishments in 2004 (Enterprise Estonia/Estonian Tourist Board, 2005).

The number of Swedish tourists in 2004 showed a substantially larger increase of 33%, in comparison to the average growth rate of around 8% in previous years. The growth in Swedish visitors occurred mainly in Tallinn and the resort town Pärnu (in the latter due to increasing popularity of spa holidays). In 2004, spas accounted for 35% of Swedish overnights at Estonian accommodation establishments (compared with 26% in the respective period of 2003) (Enterprise Estonia/Estonian Tourist Board, 2005).

Tourist arrivals from Germany continued to increase at a similar rate as they had done in the past few years (20% in 2002; 30% in 2003 and 2004). In addition to the increasingly popular touring holidays in the Baltics (in the summer season), also the number of Germans' off-season city breaks to Tallinn increased substantially, apparently thanks to additional flights from Germany to Tallinn and the lower prices offered by airlines (Enterprise Estonia/Estonian Tourist Board, 2005). After a decline in 2003, tourist arrivals from Latvia soared in 2004, exceeding considerably also the 2002 result. This was mainly brought about by simplified border crossing regulations after joining the EU, which stimulated touring in Estonia by car and led to an increase in Latvian overnights especially outside Tallinn (Enterprise Estonia/Estonian Tourist Board, 2005).

Impacts of European Union Membership

From examining the statistical evidence it is clear that the Estonian tourism industry is in a positive growth phase and undergoing a market reorientation away from same-day visitors and an over-reliance on the Finnish market. As a replacement, Tallinn appears to be developing as a year-round city break destination for more distant EU markets. In addition, market niches are developing in segments such as spa tourism, cruise tourism, conference tourism (Enterprise Estonia/Estonian Tourist Board, 2004b) and backpackers (Clark and Jarvis, 2005). Membership of the EU has had a significant role in this growth and the development of the industry. There are three broad arguments that can be proposed on how membership has impacted upon the industry.

EU membership fostered a positive business climate and stimulated investment in infrastructure: increased supply

The move towards the EU, in association with Estonia joining NATO in March 2004, generated a favourable business climate that increased the perception of security for both investors and tourists. This in turn led to increased investment in accommodation and the marketing of Estonia (including the launch of the 'Welcome to Estonia' brand), which in turn contributed to the stimulation of increased visitor flows. In terms of tourist perceptions of the destination, the linking of Estonia to the EU

conveyed some of the attributes associated with the union to 'Brand Estonia', most notably in regard to issues of perceived safety and security (Managing Director of the Estonian Association of Travel Agents, personal communication).

In expectation of a considerable increase in visitor flows (especially overnight visitors) after EU accession, the accommodation and spa sectors attracted substantial investments (D. Visnapuu, Managing Director of Estonian Hotel and Restaurant Association, personal communication). This investment flow has resulted in a 33% increase of bed places between January 2003 and July 2004. During the same period, the number of bed places in Tallinn increased by 37% (Enterprise Estonia/Estonian Tourist Board, 2005). Figure 13.4 shows an investment peak in 2003 as membership of the EU drew nearer. Additionally, in order to further develop the industry, tourism infrastructure development and marketing funds were also available for strategic projects under the EU's PHARE project prior to May 2004 (Enterprise Estonia, 2005).

Regulatory changes associated with EU membership stimulated increased transport access and removal of border controls: ease of access facilitated increases in demand

The structural changes associated with moving toward EU membership facilitated streamlined

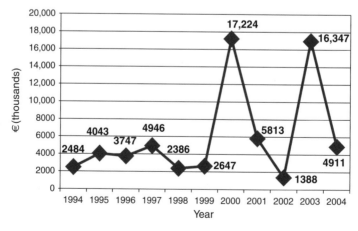

Fig. 13.4. Estonia: foreign direct investment in hotels and restaurants, 1994–2004 (€000s). Source: Enterprise Estonia/Estonian Tourist Board, 2005.

border-crossing procedures and increased transport access to Estonia by road, air and sea. The Enterprise Estonia/Estonian Tourist Board also believe that faster border-crossing procedures and simplified requirements for car insurance after EU enlargement contributed to an increasing number of Finnish, Latvian, Lithuanian and Polish car travellers, as well as continuing growth in the number of German tourists travelling via Baltic countries by car, coach or caravan (Enterprise Estonia/Estonian Tourist Board, 2005).

On the Stockholm–Tallinn sea route, new ships entered service. One ferry with the capacity to carry 2500 passengers added a stopover on the Åland Islands so as to maintain duty-free sales, whilst another offered cruises from Stockholm to Tallinn three times a week targeted at Swedes (Fig. 13.5). Another route also opened up between Tallinn and St Petersburg and a high-speed catamaran entered service on the Tallinn–Helsinki route.

The fifth freedom 'open skies' policy of the EU and the competitive threats posed by budget airlines influenced Estonian Air to alter its structure prior to EU membership to shore up its competitive position. This is a strategy that has been followed by other incumbent airlines in response to the arrival of low-cost carriers (Pender and Baum, 2000). This restructure involved the national carrier introducing substantially lower one-way airfares that were available to be purchased over the internet starting from October 2003 (Enterprise Estonia/ Estonian Tourist Board, 2005). Additionally, Estonian Air launched new routes to Amsterdam, Berlin, Oslo, Munich, Brussels and Dublin and increased frequency to Copenhagen, London and Hamburg.

Once EU membership was attained, the Italian budget carrier, Volare (May 2004), and easyJet (November 2004) started flying between Tallinn and the UK, Germany and Italy (Fig. 13.6). The arrival of easyJet on the London–Tallinn route stimulated a 185% increase in the number of British visitors in November and December 2004 (Enterprise Estonia/Estonian Tourist Board, 2005). During the first 4 months of these flights to Tallinn, 10,000 additional British tourists stayed at accommodation establishments in Estonia compared to the same months in the previous year (Enterprise Estonia/ Estonian Tourist Board, 2005). This correlates with the findings of Pender and Baum (2000) that low-cost carriers can create new markets. However, there is some

Fig. 13.5. Brochure from the Nordic Company Silja Line promoting the commencement of a thrice weekly 'day trip' cruise to Tallinn from Stockholm (October, 2004). The caption reads 'Now in Autumn you can travel with the West Indian cruise ship *Silja Opera* to Tallinn'.

Fig. 13.6. A poster in central Tallinn advertising the launch of budget airline easyJet's London and Berlin services.

concern about the type of segments that can be attracted initially, with adverse comment being passed on the number of British stag/hen weekends being attracted to Tallinn (Anon, 2004), raising the issue of the impact of these on the image of Estonia. Overall, however, only a small percentage of total visitors to Estonia are on such weekends and many bars in 2004 had started to publicize that such groups were not welcome in their establishments (as broadcast on the TV series *Fast Track*, November 2004 (BBC World Television)). Coles and Hall (2005), however, warn of the potential long-term impact that such segments may have on the branding and positioning of destinations.

Imminent EU membership led to increased media coverage of Estonia both within and outside the EU: stimulated demand

As the 2004 accession countries moved closer to the EU, this stimulated substantial media coverage (Coles and Hall, 2005). Media coverage is widely sought after in tourism marketing as it is essentially free and is regarded by consumers as far more believable than paid advertising. Many countries, such as Australia, have sponsored visiting journalist programmes to encourage publicity of the destination (Tourism Australia, 2005). An effective story in a targeted magazine can be highly powerful, especially if it can convey the desired brand attributes. In Estonia's case, the latent or dormant brand image may have in fact been non-existent or at least extremely limited, thus providing a unique opportunity for positioning the brand. This fact was identified in the background on the development of 'Brand Estonia' by the government in 2002.

> Our re-emergence on the European stage has given us a critical and rare opportunity to make a first impression on millions of European business people and potential tourists. For most of them the name Estonia will be unfamiliar, or, if they have any impressions at all they will more likely than not be vague or even negative regarding Estonia's occupied past or perceived poor weather.
> (Enterprise Estonia, 2002, p. 46)

The advantage for Estonia was that the EU accession was a big enough story to encourage a regular stream of reporters and feature writers directly to the country. This pre-EU coverage further built on the increased exposure Estonia secured in the European media during the hosting of the Eurovision Song Contest in 2002. In 2004 alone, newspapers and magazines, such as *Le Figaro, The Times, Newsweek, Wall Street Journal, Elle, Time, The Economist, Le Monde, Marie France, The Daily Telegraph, Cote Est* published articles promoting a positive image of Tallinn as a tourist destination (Estonian Foreign Ministry, 2005). Importantly, a positive image makes people more perceptive to favourable word of mouth and it also helps them screen information, making it easier for the firm (or tourism board) to communicate effectively (Grönroos, 2000). This positive publicity can be equated to hundreds of thousands of euros worth of promotion.

Future Implications

It can be seen that a number of factors associated with Estonia's accession to the EU have positively impacted on the tourism industry and further accelerated its development. Dr Reinhard Klein, Head of the European Commission's tourism unit, was correct in March 2004 when he predicted that due to the low levels of existing demand all new EU countries would experience remarkable growth (Coles and Hall, 2005). The challenge for the future of the industry is to manage the growth to ensure that the industry is sustainable. This was already identified in the tourism development strategy 2002–2005 (Estonian Ministry of Economic Affairs and Communications, 2005). Strategically, the Estonian industry needs to focus on a number of points.

Initially, the focus must be placed on attracting high-yield visitors and dispersing tourists outside the capital. This can occur in a couple of ways, initially by encouraging existing visitors to stay longer. Generally, this can be achieved by product development, and the response of Finns and Swedes to spa holidays in Estonia is a case in point. Additionally, Estonia can also target high-yielding niche markets such as convention delegates and segments with high dispersal and greater length of stay, such as spa tourists, special interest visitors, backpackers and international students. Although backpackers and international students may not spend a lot of money per day, their extended length of stay and lower levels of economic leakage increases their strategic importance and makes them high-yield visitors (Jarvis, 1994). Efficient research is the key to identifying these high-yield segments, however, as an indirect impact of EU accession the industry lost access to border-guard statistics of total visitors and the government is yet to commission a fully funded replacement international visitor survey.

Second, the industry needs to effectively manage the marketing of the destination and 'Brand Estonia'. Managing the brand involves trying to sustain and leverage the media coverage the country is now gaining as a new EU member, and ensuring the desired brand attributes are conveyed. Third, the continued diversification of their source market needs to be maintained by targeted marketing and associated product development to suit the desired segments. Fourth, seasonality needs to be addressed by targeting the segments that are likely to visit between November and March to ensure consistent returns for investors. A case in point is the success of marketing Tallinn as a winter city break, especially to the more distant EU markets. Fifth, if the growth potential of the industry is to be realized, further investment in education is necessary, with in 2004 only one tertiary institution offering tourism education. Finally, the growth in tourism the country is currently experiencing, particularly in the Old Town of Tallinn, must be managed effectively to ensure that the city doesn't develop into a medieval theme park to the exclusion of the locals.

Conclusion

The evolution of the tourism industry in Estonia presents a case study in major market reorientation due to associated shifts in the geopolitical environment of the country. The most recent shift of 'switching unions' from the Soviet to the European has had a substantial impact on the industry. The country initially sought a replacement market for internal USSR visitors, first turning to the Finns who flocked to the country primarily as same-day visitors motivated by cross-border shopping in the early years of transition (see also Chapter 12). Over time, and as EU membership was placed on the agenda and then slowly grew closer, the market started to reorientate away from the reliance on Finland and same-day visitors towards overnight stays and more distant EU markets.

It is clear that the EU accession process has had a positive, albeit indirect impact on accelerating the development of the tourism industry in Estonia. First, it has assisted in facilitating the increase in investment in the industry by, along with NATO membership, increasing the security associated with foreign direct investment. This has led to an increase in accommodation and the supply of tourism products. This has also affected demand where the increasingly secure image of Estonia within Europe directly countered the lawlessness perceived in the initial break-up of the Soviet Union. In effect, some of the positive attributes associated with the European Union were transferred to 'Brand Estonia'.

Second, the policy shifts associated with joining the EU, namely the removal of border controls and the 'open skies' policy has increased access to the country from the other EU member states. Within months of Estonia joining the EU the first budget carriers began touching down at Tallinn airport. Additionally, in response to EU membership the national carrier, Estonian Air, was restructured into a low cost carrier with an increased number of routes.

Finally, membership of the EU generated a deluge of foreign media coverage of Estonia, primarily within the EU, but also globally. This media coverage then acted as free promotion of the country in key markets and can be associated with stimulating demand and acting as a platform for communicating the elements of the 'Brand Estonia' strategy that was devised in 2002. The EU accession process has firmly put Estonia on the road to being recognized as a small but significant player in the Northern European tourism industry: it has helped to upgrade tourism infrastructure, facilitated increased access to and from the country, and stimulated demand for visitors, primarily from other EU countries, to be 'welcomed to Estonia'. The primary challenges for the industry are to address some of the structural anomalies and focus on high-yield international visitors who will spread the economic benefits throughout the whole country and to manage 'Brand Estonia' effectively in the global marketplace.

References

Aaker, D. and Joachimsthaler, E. (2000) *Brand Leadership*. New York: The Free Press.

Anon (2004) A Baltic hot spot for boozy Brits. *The Economist*, 13 May.

Baltic Stand-By News (2005) *Tourism and Travel Trade Magazine*. Riga: Baltic Stand-By News. Available at: http://www.standbynews.info/

Clark, G. and Jarvis, J. (2005) *Backpackers in Estonia: Pilot Study*. Melbourne: National Centre for Australian Studies, Monash University.

Coles, T. and Hall, D. (2005) Tourism and European Union enlargement. Plus ça change? *International Journal of Tourism Research* 7, 51–61.

Enterprise Estonia (2002) *Brand Estonia Guide*. Tallinn: Enterprise Estonia. Available at: http://www.eas.ee/?id=12

Enterprise Estonia (2005) *Phare ESC 2003 Tourism Infrastructure Development Programme*. Tallinn: Enterprise Estonia. Available at: http://www.eas.ee/?id=1198

Enterprise Estonia/Estonian Tourist Board (2004a) *Tourism in Estonia 1993–2003: Key Indicators*. Tallinn: Enterprise Estonia/Estonian Tourist Board. Available at: http://public.visitestonia.com/files/statistika/040703_4.pdf

Enterprise Estonia/Estonian Tourist Board (2004b) *Overview of Tourism in Estonia as of June 2004*. Tallinn: Enterprise Estonia/Estonian Tourist Board.

Enterprise Estonia/Estonian Tourist Board (2005) *Tourism in Estonia in 2004: Preliminary Figures*. Tallinn: Enterprise Estonia/Estonian Tourist Board. Available at: http://public.visitestonia.com/files/statistika/Tourism_in_Estonia2004.pdf

Estonian Association of Travel Agents (2005) *Estonian Association of Travel Agents*. Tallinn: Estonian Association of Travel Agents. Available at: http://www.etfl.ee/etfl/ajalugu/tegevus1990_1996en.shtml

Estonian Foreign Ministry (2005) *Discovering Estonia*. Tallinn: Estonian Foreign Ministry. Available at: http://web-static.vm.ee/static/failid/098/avastades_eestimaad.pdf

Estonian Ministry of Economic Affairs and Communications (2005) *Tourism*. Tallinn: Estonian Ministry of Economic Affairs and Communications. Available at: http://www.mkm.ee/index.php?id=3436&&langchange=1

ETC (European Tourism Commission) (2005) *Tourism Insights 2004 – Outlook for 2005*. Brussels: ETC Research Report No 2.

Eurostat (2005) *Tourism in the enlarged European union* [sic]. Luxembourg: Eurostat. Available at: http://epp.eurostat.cec.eu.int/portal/page?_pageid=2053,47527283&_dad=portal&_schema=PORTAL

Gardner, S. and Standaert, M. (2003) *Estonia and Belarus: Branding the Old Block*. Tallinn: Brandchanel. Available at: http://www.brandchanel.com

Grönroos, C. (2000) *Service Management and Marketing – a Customer Relationship Management Approach*, 2nd edn. Chichester, UK: John Wiley & Sons.

Hall, D. (ed.) (1991) *Tourism and Economic Development in Eastern Europe and the Soviet Union*. London: Belhaven Press.

Hall, D. (2001) Tourism and development in communist and post-communist societies. In: Harrison, D. (ed.) *Tourism and the Less Developed World*. Wallingford, UK: CABI Publishing, pp. 91–107.

Hall, D. (2002) Branding and national identity: the case of Central and Eastern Europe. In: Morgan, N., Pritchard, A. and Pride, R. (eds) *Destination Branding: Creating the Unique Destination Proposition*. Amsterdam: Elsevier, pp. 87–105.

In Your Pocket (2005) *Tallinn*. Vilnius: In Your Pocket. Available at: http://www.inyourpocket.com/estonia/tallinn/en/feature?id=55676

Jaakson, R. (1996) Tourism in post Soviet Estonia. *Annals of Tourism Research* 23(3), 617–634.

Jarvis, J. (1994) *The Billion Dollar Backpackers*. Melbourne: National Centre for Australian Studies, Monash University.

Kallas, P. (2002) *Tourism and Holiday Business*. Tallinn: Estonian Encyclopedia.

Morgan, N., Pritchard, A. and Pride, R. (2002) *Destination Branding: Creating a Unique Destination Proposition*. Amsterdam: Elsevier.

Pender, L. and Baum, T. (2000) Have the frills really left the European airline industry? *International Journal of Tourism Research* 2, 423–436.

Tallinn Airport (2005) *Tallinn Airport Traffic Statistics*. Tallinn: Tallinn Airport. Available at: http://www.tallinn-airport.ee

Tourism Australia (2005) *Tourism Australia*. Sydney: Tourism Australia. Available at: http://www.tourism.australia.com

Unwin, T. (1996) Tourist development in Estonia. *Tourism Management* 17(4), 265–276.

Van Ham, P. (2001) The rise of the brand state: the postmodern politics of image and reputation. *Foreign Affairs* 80(5), 2–6.

Williams, N., Kokker, S. and Galbraith, K. (2000) *Estonia, Latvia and Lithuania*, 2nd edn. Melbourne: Lonely Planet Publishing.

Worthington, B. (2001) Riding the 'J' curve – tourism and successful transition in Estonia. *Post Communist Economies* 13(3), 389–400.

Worthington, B. (2003) Change in an Estonian resort: contrasting development contexts. *Annals of Tourism Research* 30(2), 369–385.

Worthington, B. (2004) Estonian national heritage, tourism and paradoxes of transformation. In: Hall, D. (ed.) *Tourism and Transition: Governance, Transformation and Development*. Wallingford, UK: CABI Publishing, pp. 83–94.

WTO (World Tourism Organization) (2005) *Facts and Figures: Information, Analysis and Know-how*. Madrid: WTO. Available at: http://www.world-tourism.org/facts/menu.html

WTTC (World Travel and Tourism Council) (2005) *Country Report Estonia 2005*. Available at: http://www.wttc.org/2004tsa/frameset2a.htm

14 Latvia Tourism: Decisive Factors and Tourism Development

Iveta Druva-Druvaskalne, Ilgvars Ābols and Agita Šļara

Introduction

Latvia is located on the eastern coast of the Baltic Sea, bordering Estonia in the north, Lithuania in the south, Russia and Belarus in the east, the latter acting as an EU external eastern border. The territory of Latvia (64.589 km²) is only a little smaller than that of The Netherlands and Belgium together; it is larger than Switzerland or Denmark, but its population is one of the smallest among EU member countries at just 2.3m, with a low population density averaging 36 people per km² (Central Statistical Bureau of Latvia, 2004a, p. 32).

An ethnic demographic mix is largely the result of massive post-war immigration, which resulted in a decline in the proportion of ethnic Latvians from 77% in 1935 to 52% in 1989. In the post-Soviet period the proportion of Latvians has grown, reaching 58% in 2004. Russians and other Baltic groups make up most of the remaining population. Nearly one third of Latvia's population (739,000) lives in the capital city, Rīga, founded in 1201. The value of Rīga's cultural and historical significance has been recognized by the fact that the city's historic centre has been included in UNESCO's list of the world's most important cultural and natural sites.

Latvia is a land of diverse terrain where plains alternate with hillocks and river valleys; 57% of the territory lies above 100 metres although the highest land is just 311 metres above the sea level. The country has more than 2,250 lakes, most of which are found in eastern Latvia. Nearly all inland waters are pollution-free and ideally suited for swimming and fishing. The sea coast stretches 497 km along the Baltic Sea and the Gulf of Rīga. At present, 8.5% of Latvian territory is protected by law. There are four state reserves, three national parks, 22 nature parks, 211 nature reserves, six protected landscape areas, and one biosphere reserve. They offer important environments for ecotourism (Central Statistical Bureau of Latvia, 2004a, pp. 6–8; Pilāts, 2004).

Latvia is divided into four historical cultural regions: Kurzeme, Zemgale, Latgale and Vidzeme, named after ancient tribes who used to live in each area. They present a diversity of cultural landscapes. These include distinctive farmhouses and a range of wooden buildings in traditional architectural styles, castles from medieval times, manor houses and churches.

In 1991 Latvia declared the restoration of its independence, and in 2004 the country's most important foreign policy goals – membership of both the European Union and NATO – were fulfilled.

©CAB International 2006. *Tourism in the New Europe: the Challenges and Opportunities of EU Enlargement* (eds D. Hall, M. Smith and B. Marciszewska)

Factors Influencing Tourism Development of Latvia

Global tourism tendencies are favourable to tourism development in Latvia

Various global events have affected travel to a certain extent; therefore, due to security reasons travellers prefer destinations closer to their place of residence (Hall, 2005, p. 283) and Latvia is located near the tourism generating regions of Europe and Russia.

One of the most significant factors that will affect world tourism in future is the ageing demographic structure in industrialized countries (UN, 1998; Hall and Page, 2002, p. 341). By 2050 one in five people will be aged 60 or older (UN, 1998). Along with the improvement of living conditions the average life expectancy will increase, although in Latvia the average life expectancy is 8 years less than the average in Europe: 71.4 years in 2003, compared to 66.7 in 1995 (Tīsiņa, 2004). This factor will present challenges for the development of tourism product and infrastructure in future. Considering its tourism resource potential, Latvia is ready for these challenges. The country is also well positioned in relation to the globalizing driving forces of IT, telecommunications and international trade.

Political and geographical position

Germans, Swedes, Poles and Russians have recognized the advantages of Latvia's geographical position. However, Latvia should better position itself as the centre of the Baltic States, promoting the development of Rīga as the capital of the Baltic region. Within a 1-hour flight of Rīga live 100m people. The Baltic States should collaborate to develop common tourism products for the international tourism market, with Latvia at the heart of such cooperation (Latvian Institute, 2005).

Natural and cultural heritage tourism resources

Latvia is characterized by a variety of natural and cultural landscapes, ancient folklore and folk-art traditions and traditional cuisine. UNESCO declared the Latvian Song and Dance festival together with the Lithuanian and Estonia Song festivals 'masterpieces of intangible culture heritage' in 2003 (Ministry of Culture of the Republic of Latvia, 2003).

The presence of a number of religions within the country helps to promote tolerance in society. Aglona Basilica in the south-east is a major Catholic pilgrimage destination, which annually celebrates the Assumption of Blessed Virgin Mary, attracting more than 420,000 people (District Council of Preiļi, 2004). Soviet heritage provides new tourism products, such as the employment of military objects in Liepāja Military port and Ventspils International Radio Astronomy Centre (former USSR military cosmic communication centre).

Latvia as a new tourism destination

As a member of the EU, Latvia is now better positioned in the international tourism market. Many EU citizens mainly travel around the territory of the EU. Over a period of 2 years it was found that three-quarters of all EU citizens did not travel outside of the Union's borders (European Commission, 2003). Latvia is a comparatively cheap, relatively high quality, comfortable and not overcrowded destination. In 2004, border-crossing data indicated that 37% of foreign visitors were arriving in Latvia for the first time (Briksne, 2005b). Indeed, arrivals have increased every year since 1995, rising by 2004 to 3m (0.7% of all European travellers), a 22% increase on the previous year (Table 14.1).

A majority of foreign visitors are still from neighbouring countries, notably Estonia and Lithuania (in 2004, 28% and 30% of the total, respectively). The number of foreign travellers from the CIS countries has diminished (Briksne, 2005b). German arrivals in 2004 occupied third place (7%). More than 50% of all foreign tourist overnights in provincial areas were by German tourists (Seilis, 2005).

Tourism management and administration: institutional capacity strengthening

In the period 1993–2003, tourism was the responsibility of the Ministry of Environment and

Table 14.1.   Latvia: inbound tourism, 1997–2004.

	1997	1998	1999	2000	2001	2002	2003	2004
Non-residents entering Latvia ('000)	1824	1801	1718	1914	2039	2273	2470	3033
% change against the previous year	6.5	−1.3	−4.6	11.4	6.5	11.5	8.7	22

Source: Briksne, 2005a.

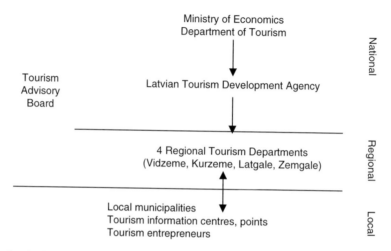

Fig. 14.1.   Latvia: institutional structure of tourism administration.

Regional Development and was not considered a priority requiring serious investment. One of the arguments for making tourism the responsibility of the Ministry of Economics was commonality with other EU countries. This ministry established a Department of Tourism (www.em.gov.lv) employing eight professionals (see Fig. 14.1). The main task of this department is the creation of tourism policy, elaboration of legislative documents, and promotion of international cooperation. The Latvian Tourism Development Agency (LTDA), responsible to the Ministry of Economics (with 20 employees) is responsible for implementation of tourism policy and marketing. However, a high turnover of employees provides a major problem for continuity, morale and long-term development. None the less, in 2004 tourism received more than a doubling of its budget (Fig. 14.2) to a figure of LVL1.1m, or €1.45m. This compares with Estonia's budget of €1.7m and that of Lithuania of €669,000 (Lithuanian State Tourism Department, 2005).

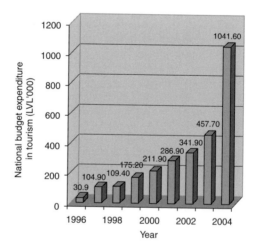

Fig. 14.2.   National budget expenditure in tourism in Latvia, 1996–2004. 1 LVL = €0.72 (April 2005). The currency rate has rapidly changed from 1996 to 2005 due to pegging of Latvian Lats to the SDR currency basket. Source: Ministry of Economics, 2004b.

Most of the tourism budget growth in 2004 was assigned to international and domestic tourism marketing, including participation in international tourism fairs and the opening of new tourism information offices abroad. In order to promote the development of religious tourism, an additional €1.6m was assigned to the maintenance of churches in autumn 2004. In 2003, the VAT rate for tourist accommodation was changed from 18% to 5%.

Domestic tourism information is provided by tourism information centres (TICs: 55 in 2004) and points (TIPs) financed and maintained by local municipalities (Ministry of Economics of the Republic of Latvia, 2004b). In 2004, a state-financed TIC was opened in Rīga, providing visitors to the capital with information about tourism attractions and services across the country. Organization improvements required include a decentralization of tourism services, effective local tourism advertising and an extension of the tourism season. The Latvian Tourism Development Agency maintains tourism information offices in Helsinki, London and Berlin (the last being shared by all three Baltic States). In 2005, tourism information offices were opened in Stockholm and Moscow.

In 2004, the government adopted tourism development basic guidelines, whose main purpose is to increase the value of tourism during the period 2004–2008, at the end of which GDP contribution is planned to increase by 5–7%, and tourism export earnings to average 10–15% per annum (Ministry of Economics of the Republic of Latvia, 2004a). It is planned to achieve these targets by positioning and promoting Latvia in the international market as a different, safe and recognizable international tourism destination while also promoting the development of domestic tourism (NTDP, 2001). Latvia is a member of the European Travel Commission, the Baltic Sea Tourism Commission and, from 2005, a full member country of the World Tourism Organization. Participation in these organizations opens wide cooperation possibilities in a number of sectors.

According to CSB information, 112 tourism companies operated in Latvia in 2004, servicing 370,000 travellers, 80% of whom were Latvians who travelled abroad. The majority of Latvian tourism enterprises are small family companies. Most are concentrated in Rīga.

There is a tendency of relatively small foreign tourism companies to enter the market, which currently appears too small to attract the larger international groups.

One must emphasize also investment of EU pre-structural and structural funds in tourism. These have been especially important in the renovation of accommodation and development of new products, as well as enhancing the involvement of local government and NGOs in the provision of tourism information. Compared to other new EU member countries, indicators of tourism activity in Latvia were low in 2002 (Table 14.2). For example, tourism income in that year was €170m, the lowest level among the new EU member countries and 28 times smaller than that of Poland. This reflected the limited horizons (focus on nature and rural tourism), restricted budgets (Fig. 14.2) and dominance of domestic tourism prior to the administrative changes of 2003.

In terms of accommodation capacity in 2002, Latvia had the second lowest provision after Lithuania among the new EU member countries. Compared to the Czech Republic, Latvia had 13 times fewer rooms. This reflects the relatively slow construction of new accommodation and refurbishment of Soviet-era hotels and resorts.

Tourism development still requires greater investment. Overseas promotion is still inadequate, and an integrated state tourism development strategy is required, which should include the development of infrastructure, quality improvement, service diversification, and improved availability of information provision. These dimensions are receiving attention, as tourism is now recognized as one of the priority branches of the national economy (Lujāns, 2004).

General improvement in the economic situation

The recent economic development of Latvia is reflected in annual GDP growth rates of 8% (2001), 6.4% (2002), 7.5% (2003), 8.5% (2004), and 7.4% (forecast for 2005). For all the quarters of 2004 and the first two quarters of 2005 Latvia had the strongest growth rate in GDP among all EU countries compared to the same

Table 14.2. Latvia: comparative indicators of tourism in the new EU member countries, 2002.

Country	Area ('000 sq km)	Tourist arrivals ('000)	Tourism receipts (€mn)	Accommodation capacity (no. of rooms)
Poland	323	13,980 (TF)	4,759	65,658
Hungary	93	15,870 (VF/2)	3,461	73,000[b]
Czech Republic	79	4,579 (TCE)	3,110	91,490[a]
Cyprus	9.3	2,418 (TF)	1,970	45,058[a]
Slovenia	20	1,302 (TCE)	1,145	15,056
Slovakia	49	1,399 (TCE)	766	34,619
Malta	0.3	1,134 (TF)	601	20,346[a,b]
Estonia	45	1,360 (TF)	587	10,845
Lithuania	65	1,433 (TF)	543	5,649[a]
Latvia	65	848 (TF)	170	7,034[a]

[a]2001.
[b]number of bed-places × 0.5. TF, tourist arrivals at frontiers; TCE, tourist arrivals at all accommodation establishments; VF/2, visitor arrivals × 0.5.
Source: Cabrini, 2004.

quarter of the previous year. During the second quarter of 2005 Latvia's GDP growth rate reached 11.6% (Eurostat, 2005). The general economic situation has positively affected domestic tourism development, is promoting outbound tourism, and is a prerequisite for business travel destination development.

Similar growth rates in the other two Baltic States (2004 GDP growth of 6.1% for Estonia and 6.6% for Lithuania) have been a regional driving force for domestic demand, service industry and construction growth. The share of transport and communication in GDP was about 2% (Mārtiņa, 2005), and passenger numbers increased by nearly 50%, largely due to the rapid growth of air transport.

Changes in air transportation market in Latvia

The international airport at Rīga is the busiest air transport junction in the Baltic States. Since 1993 the number of air passengers has doubled (1.1m in 2004). In 2004, six new airlines began flying to Rīga, doubling the number of companies serving the city. The airport now serves more than 30 destinations in Europe, Asia and America, and current capacity is 2m passengers per year (Rīga Airport, 2005).

The national airline, Air Baltic, was established in 1995. Major shareholders include the Latvian state, with a 52.6% share, and SAS AB, with a 47.2% share. In 2004, Air Baltic carried almost 590,000 passengers, an increase of 75% compared to 2003. In 2005, Air Baltic offered direct flights to 27 destinations (Air Baltic, 2005).

In autumn 2004, the competition increased with the two leading European low-cost airlines, Ryanair and easyJet, inaugurating services. In the autumn of 2005 another two European airlines – Aer Lingus and Norwegian Air Shuttle – started operations into Rīga Airport. As a consequence, Air Baltic has been forced to reduce flight costs and the range of services included in the ticket price (food and beverages are now offered for additional payment). At the same time, Uzbekistan Airways opened a twice-weekly Tashkent–Rīga–New York service.

Increase of travellers from Latvia abroad – increase of leisure and business trips

After the restoration of independence the number of Latvians travelling across the border rapidly increased. The peak year was 1993 when 2.45m did so – the last year that it was possible to travel to CIS countries without a visa. In 1994, after such visa requirements were introduced, the number of Latvian resident travellers diminished to 1.78m, although gradual growth has taken place since then, with a notable speeding up in 1999 and 2000. Main destinations are Lithuania, Estonia and Russia; the main purpose of travel is shopping, which is explained by cheaper prices in neighbouring countries. In 2000, 41.1% of those stating a reason for travelling indicated shopping. With a subsequent equalization of prices in neighbouring countries, this motive has become less significant, accounting for just 16% of the number of travellers going abroad in 2004 (Central Statistical Bureau of Latvia, 1998, p. 11, 2001, pp. 18–19).

Visiting friends and relatives (29% in 2004) has been consistently the most popular stated reason for travelling out of the country since independence. It can be explained by the multinational ethnic composition of Latvia, as well as the development of new links and networks with EU countries. The number of travellers going on holiday is increasing every year. In 1996 it was only 6% of travellers, but in 2004 it was 20%. The number of business travellers is also increasing, rising to 19% by 2004 (Briksne, 2005b).

Development of domestic tourism

Only in 2004, implementing the EU Directive 95/57/EC of 1995 on the collection of statistical information in the field of tourism, did the Central Statistical Bureau of Latvia begin regular surveying of inhabitants of Latvia about their travel. In that year it was found that just over 54% of inhabitants travelled for holiday purposes across an internal administrative boundary. The most popular destination was Rīga. Day trips without accommodation comprised 44% of all such recorded travel. About 23% took short holiday trips with overnights of 1–3 days. Only 6.4% of travellers chose domestic holiday trips of 4 days or more. Of all domestic holiday travellers, 54% were women and the most typical age group was 15–24 years. Private accommodation accounted for 91% of overnights, and 62.2% travelled by car (Briksne, 2005b).

Persisting negative balance of Latvian tourism payments

From a state economic perspective, inbound tourism needs to be developed because of the negative tourism balance of payments (Table 14.3), even though since 2002 the number of inbound travellers has exceeded those outbound.

In Latvia, balance of payments data indicated the share of tourism to be 2.2% of GDP in 2003, compared to an EU average of 4.8%. However, there is steady growth in Latvia, at about 7%, with plans to reach 2.5% of GDP in 2007 (WTO, 2003, p. 233). Further, inbound traveller expenditure is increasing by an average of 10% per annum, even though the average length of stay between 1997 and 2004

Table 14.3. Latvia: tourism balance of payments, 1996–2004.

Year	Income from foreign tourists (million LVL)	Latvian tourists' expenditures abroad (million LVL)	Tourism balance of payments (million LVL)
1996	108.7	201.8	−93.1
1997	118.4	167.2	−48.8
1998	98.2	171.1	−72.9
1999	66.0	157.1	−91.1
2000	74.4	147.9	−73.5
2001	70.8	137.0	−66.2
2002	96.0	137.4	−41.4
2003	124.4	182.5	−58.1
2004	141.9	197.5	−56.6

Sources: Central Statistical Bureau of Latvia, 1999, 2004b; Briksne, 2005a.

diminished by 2.4 days to 1.77 days (Briksne, 2005a).

Increase in tourism accommodation occupancy rate

Since 1991 the occupancy rate of tourist accommodation has been steadily growing. The year 2004 was exceptionally successful for the hospitality industry, stimulated by EU entry, new air services from Western European markets and the growing significance of Rīga as a business centre. Summer occupancy in Rīga increased by 15–20% (rising to an occupancy rate of 90%), and over the whole year by an average of 10%. Indeed, some inbound tourism service companies complained about a constraining shortage of tourist accommodation. For 2005 there were plans to begin construction of 20 new hotels, when Rīga could accommodate 8000 people and Jūrmala 2000 (23 km from Rīga). Consequently, accommodation for the 2006 World Ice Hockey Championship in Rīga is supposed to

include hotels up to 50 km from the capital (Fig. 14.3).

There were 326 tourist accommodation establishments in 2003, a 9% increase on 2002. In 2003 the number of serviced visitors increased by 13% to 759,500. Hotel, guest house and motel service quality assessment is undertaken by the Hotel and Restaurant Centre. It is a voluntary procedure and frequently tourism accommodation owners themselves decide on their qualification category. Some 118 establishments had passed the voluntary certification at the time of writing (Central Statistical Bureau of Latvia, 2004b; Association of Hotels and Restaurants of Latvia, 2005).

The rural tourism accommodation sector has seen considerable recent growth (a 770% increase in 9 years) (Table 14.4). Perhaps because they have been driven out of the cities, and especially Rīga, by an influx of foreign tourists, domestic tourists actually accounted for 75% of rural tourism customers in 2004, compared to 61% in 2003. By far the most important overseas market for rural tourism is

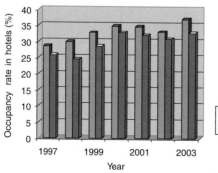

Fig. 14.3. Occupancy rates in Latvian hotels, 1997–2003. Source: Central Statistical Bureau of Latvia, 2004b.

Table 14.4. Latvia: rural tourism accommodation provision, 1993–2004.

	1993	1995	1997	1999	2001	2003	2004
Hotels and other accommodation establishments[a]	170	180	200	210	274	326	343
Accommodation in rural areas[b]	Association founded	38	70	116	210	275	294

[a]Excluding state special sanatoria and centres of rehabilitation which render state orders in the field of health care.
[b]Members of professional association, Lauku Ceļotājs.
Sources: Central Statistical Bureau of Latvia, 2004b, 2005; Lauku Ceļotājs, 2005.

Germany with 44% of the total in 2004. Next come Finland and France with 9%, Sweden 6%, USA 5%, Britain and Estonia 4%, Denmark 2% and other countries 17%. The duration of foreign travellers' stays in rural tourist accommodation establishments is longer than that of local travellers, in 2004 averaging 2.73 days compared to 1.28 days (Central Statistical Bureau of Latvia, 2004b).

Many rural tourism accommodation establishments have been improving the quality of their services in order to meet the necessary requirements for a 'green certificate' (environmentally friendly housekeeping). This is promoted by the rural tourism association Lauku Celotājs ('Countryside Traveller'), the Environment Protection Fund of Latvia and by rural tourism enterprises within the EU Life programme project. The work of Lauku Celotājs includes educational and marketing activities and the creation of a collective booking system for the rural tourism accommodation establishments in the Baltic States (Lauku Celotājs, 2004).

Growth of tourism marketing activities

The marketing activities of Latvian tourism are stated in the annual Latvian Tourism Development Agency (LTDA) action plan, but a long-term marketing strategy has not been elaborated as it has been, for example, in Lithuania. A Latvia tourism basic development guideline 2004–2008 identifies the main problems:

- lack of tourism marketing strategy, insufficient promotion in domestic and international markets, and insufficient coordination of joint marketing activities;
- a poorly defined tourism product;
- frequent changes of leaders and employees, often determined by political factors, constraining longer-term views; a change of government is often followed by a change of LTDA management.

The main marketing tools are:

- participation in international fairs (15 fairs in 10 countries in 2003, 17 exhibitions in 12 countries in 2004, 23 exhibitions in 14 countries were planned for 2005);

Fig. 14.4.   Latvia tourism logo and motto.

- production of informative material about tourism possibilities in Latvia in different foreign languages;
- information about tourism possibilities in the mass media and an internet portal;
- the organization of workshops for (potential) entrepreneurs;
- the organization of tour operator and journalist visits;
- 2005 marketing campaigns for the international television channel CNN, in four cities in France (Paris, Bordeaux, Lyon, Strasbourg) during the festival *Etonnante Lettonie* ('Surprising Latvia') (Latvian Tourism Development Agency, 2005; Reinberga, 2005; Urpena, 2005).

From a 2002 competition, the logo and strapline for promoting Latvia, 'The land that sings', was adopted to characterize the country's mentality and traditions, manifesting themselves in song and dances (Fig. 14.4). However, it was not effectively employed in such special events as the 2003 Eurovision Song Contest, XXII Latvian Song Festival and XII Dance Festival in 2003. This emphasized the need for Latvia to work on strengthening its tourism image and raising its visibility.

A future challenge in this respect is to compete for the status of European Culture Heritage Capital, which the ten 2004 EU entrants can apply for from 2009–2019.

Tourism Product Development

The origins of tourism development began in the 19th century when Latvia was part of the Russian Empire. As in many other places in Europe, this was based on curative tourism, especially emphasizing sea baths and air, mineral water spas and mud baths. The number of holidaymakers increased each year until

World War I. After the restoration of independence following the collapse of Czarist Russia, domestic tourism was developed, based on familiarizing citizens with their native land. Rural tourism and activity tourism became popular, alongside curative tourism, and after the world economy crisis of the 1920s and early 1930s the number of foreign tourists every year increased. The Soviet period brought a curtailment of natural ties with much of Europe and tourism became subordinate to Soviet ideology. None the less, activity tourism (re-)developed, while leisure and curative tourism flourished.

Post-socialist change

After disruption of the planned economy in 1991, the structure of employment rapidly changed, especially in rural areas. Along with the land and building privatization process, many inhabitants regained their former land and properties, including those with considerable cultural and historical value (manors, castles – the Association of Latvian Castles, Palaces and Manors has 80 members, 30 of whom provide tourism services: www.castles. lv), and land in nature-protected areas. In the following years this restructuring of ownership influenced the provision of attractions and facilities, development and competition among the local enterprises, as well as with Baltic and European tourism entrepreneurs.

Until 1991, a limited number of destinations in Latvia were available to local and especially foreign tourists, such as Sigulda, Jūrmala, Rundāle Palace, Cēsis and Ērgļi. Holiday and tourism opportunities were directly influenced by the availability of public transport, as the level of access to motor cars was low for many people. Between 1997 and 2005 the number of registered cars in the country rose from almost 380,000 to more than 686,000 (CSDD, 2005), an increase of some 80%. This growth, while bringing various problems of pollution and congestion, has facilitated the wider availability of tourism products and services outside the major cities, thereby stimulating greater competition between destinations and attractions.

Yet tourism opportunities have been offered in a chaotic way, and products need to be systematically assessed, developed and promoted.

In particular, with regard to global trends, demographic change in Europe, and the renewal of Rīga as a Baltic business centre, tourism product development should be viewed in terms of two large product groups: leisure and business tourism.

Leisure tourism products

Leisure tourism products need to relate to target groups according to age, social status or interests. Latvia can offer senior tourists culture and curative tourism. Germans, Russians, Swedes and Poles have all left their footprints in the culture landscape from ancient times, and the country's rich cultural heritage, supported by well-established tourism infrastructure, should witness an increased demand for this type of product.

Latvian folk traditions and events, such as the Līgo Festival (Midsummer) and song and dance festival, could be offered to cruise tourists whose numbers are likely to increase in the coming decade. Latvia must employ its geographical position and three port cities Rīga, Liepāja and Ventspils to advantage in this respect. At present, Tallinn (Estonia) is the Baltic leader in sea passenger transport, but Rīga has considerable growth capacity. The city municipality must therefore promote accessibility by sea, while small ports in the Rīga Gulf (Roja, Skulte) and on the Baltic Sea coast (Pāvilosta) have the potential to attract yachting tourists.

The ageing of Europe and the variety of health problems require curative and medical leisure products. Latvia possesses top-class medical professionals, but they often choose to work abroad. It is important to encourage cooperation between medicine and tourism, creating tourism products related to dentistry, planned surgery or plastic surgery. Prices of various beauty, relaxation and related medical services in Latvia can be two to ten times lower than in other EU countries. Jūrmala could become a significant centre of curative tourism: during Soviet times it was one of the most popular resorts in the USSR, and attracted 6m tourists every year (Slava, 2004).

Since the turn of the century, several water amusement parks have been built in Latvia, the largest being in Jūrmala. Currently the biggest water amusement park in Northern Europe, it was opened in December 2003, and in 2004 received 435,000 visitors (Līvu Akvaparks, 2005). It offers a new experience for families with children, and complements other family-oriented recreational attractions such as Rīga Zoo and Līgatne nature paths.

Ecotourism was started in the 1990s, while rural cultural tourism has been reinvigorated. Growth has been particularly marked in the northwest part of Latvia. Slītere National Park, for example, is the home of the Liv (Latvia's Finno-Ugrian minority) community, whose maintenance could be supported by the income from ecotourism; but compared to Estonia, Latvia lacks an understanding about these types of activities – for example, there are difficulties in accommodating bicycles on buses or trains. However, several projects have been initiated for the development of infrastructure – creation of cycling paths, cycle rentals, ease of transportation – within the framework of the international cycling path Eurovelo 11 (Leitis, 2005).

There are more than 1200 organic farms in Latvia, but marketing organic food is complicated by different certification systems. Yet food freshness, originality and difference are major tourism attractions in both rural and urban areas. For example, Germany and Denmark have adopted home-producer friendly legislation, and tourists can easily purchase typical local food directly from producers, supported at both the state and municipal levels. However, in Latvia there have been bureaucratic delays in the development of this tourism product.

Latvia may possibly experience the same wave of entertainment seekers as has been previously experienced in Dublin, Amsterdam and Prague. There are several dozen tour operators specializing in 'stag' and 'hen' weekend packages. Rīga is now targeted as a possible 'hot spot' that offers 'amazing nightlife, fantastic cheap local beer – and the most stunning-looking women on the Continent' (Naish, 2004). The relationship between the flow of such tourist groups and the growth of budget airline connections is strong. The privately published *Rīga Visitor's Guide*, which is available for free at Rīga airport and in the hotels, advertises Rīga as an entertainment city and the last page devoted to nightlife offers clear sex tourism. The government of Latvia and Rīga municipality should improve legislation and its implementation in entertainment entrepreneurship to avoid Rīga becoming a European sex tourism capital. During 2005, action was taken by the state and city authorities to reduce advertising of sex-related tourism products in Rīga and across Latvia.

Business tourism products

The territory of Latvia has interested merchants and leaders of many states since ancient times. It has been known as the road from the East to the West since the 6th century. In the 10th–12th centuries the Daugava river was the most important trade route. Via the Daugava and then the Dnepr, one could reach the Black Sea and the rich Constantinople. Ancient trade routes are well marked by discoveries of imported articles, coins and silver in former trade centres. These include Arabian 8th–11th century, Byzantium 10th–11th century and 10th–13th century European coins.

Rīga joined the Hanseatic Union in 1282, and acted as a trade centre between East and West. At the beginning of the 20th century Rīga was one of the most developed industrial cities and trade centres in the Russian Empire. Currently, Rīga is again establishing itself as the Baltic business centre, with the location of many international enterprises' Baltic central offices in the city.

Rīga tourism operators, hotels, Air Baltic and Rīga airport have created an organization – Inspiration Rīga (www.inspirationriga.com) – promoting Rīga and Latvia as attractive congress, meeting, incentive and business travel destinations within the context of EU and NATO membership. In May 2000, for example, Rīga hosted the 9th EBRD (European Bank of Reconstruction and Development) annual meeting, involving 4000 delegates.

Conclusions

In summary, we can conclude that tourism development in Latvia is taking place slowly but surely, exhibiting both positive and not so positive tendencies:

• Latvia is located at a geographical 'crossroad', which can be employed to promote tourism development;

- global change, notably the expansion of the EU, can be favourable for Latvia if opportunities are recognized and taken;
- the number of inbound tourists in Latvia is gradually increasing;
- tourism infrastructure is improving, as tourism is now recognized as one of the priority branches of the national economy;
- the number of direct flights to Rīga is increasing, and an intensification of regional airport operation in Liepāja, Ventspils and Daugavpils is planned;
- budget airlines may not generate the best markets for a positive image for Rīga and Latvia;
- both the quantity and occupancy rate of tourist accommodation are growing;
- Latvia has a negative balance of tourism income;
- the country lacks a comprehensive tourism marketing strategy, although the financial provision for marketing activities from the state budget has been increased;
- Latvia can promote business tourism products, emphasizing Rīga as the Baltic business centre;
- the quality of leisure tourism products – cultural, curative and natural – is high.

After 1991, tourism development in Latvia was greatly influenced by necessary changes in national economic planning. The influences on tourism change since EU accession in May 2004 include the following:

- a new demand for Rīga as a destination, especially from the EU15 countries;
- the experience of having a European Union external border – this has a dual impact of acting as a sightseeing attraction but also constraining movement and socio-economic development;
- significant tourism markets – Russia (Saint Petersburg, Moscow, Pskov) and Belarus (Minsk) – are located beyond EU external borders, and to optimize their potential better cooperation in border-crossing formalities is desirable. This would also help to promote the development of Jurmala as a resort and the country's border regions;
- the three Baltic states are often perceived together and visits may encompass all three, thereby shortening the length of stay

in each. Within Latvia, many foreign travellers only see Rīga, and at best cross the rest of the country in transit. This suggests the need for greater collaboration and rationalization of products between the three neighbours;
- the reduction of VAT from 9% to 5% for tourism accommodation enterprises has improved the sector's competitiveness within the EU;
- budget airlines flying into Rīga have increased the flow of foreign tourists and accommodation occupancy rates;
- visa requirements have been abolished for a number of countries since 1991;
- Latvia is becoming an important destination for higher education mobility, both for networks within the EU and as an attractive environment for non-EU neighbours. This, in its turn, can promote the development of business and conference tourism.

Future Activities and Proposals

It is clear that a number of measures are necessary to take better advantage of Latvia's tourism opportunities. First, cooperation among the Baltic and Nordic countries must be developed, creating complementary tourism product and promotion opportunities. Latvia should cooperate in Asian markets with the Nordic countries, in the North American market with Poland, and in Western and Southern European markets with Lithuania and Estonia. Further, there should be a strengthening of collaboration between the three Baltic States through the Baltic Cabinet of Ministers Tourism Committee. At a different level, emphasis should be placed upon the development of cooperation among EU tourism enterprises, local municipality and NGO sectors, in pursuit of European Commission initiatives.

Second, tourism marketing research is needed in order to identify priority goals and markets for each available product. This needs to be undertaken in tandem with tourism product development in the country's different regions, helping to promote the development of micro- and small enterprises. This needs to be allied to an emphasis on quality of the tourism product, with trained and qualified employees, high-quality marketing, employment of environmentally friendly technologies and sustainable use of resources.

Finally, a fundamental requirement is the development and elaboration of necessary infrastructure (water, gas, sewage, electricity, waste, telecommunications). This should complement both domestic and international objectives, such as assisting the development of international transport corridors with EU and other neighbours – for example, the Via Baltica highway, RailBaltic and Eurovelo 11.

References

Air Baltic (2005) *Statistics*. Riga: Air Baltic. Available at: http://www.airbaltic.com

Association of Hotels and Restaurants of Latvia (2005) *Atbilstības novērtēšana un sertifikācija*. Riga: Association of Hotels and Restaurants of Latvia. Available at: http://www.lvra.lv/lvra/sertification.do

Briksne, I. (2005a) *Latvijas Iedzīvotāju Aptaujas Rezultāti par 2004.gada Trešajā Ceturksnī Veiktajiem Ceļojumiem*. Press release 17 January, 2005. Rīga: Central Statistical Bureau of Latvia. Available at: http://www.csb.lv/lteksts.cfm?tem_kods=cel&datums=%7Bts%20%272005%2D01%2D17%2013%3 A00%3A00%27%7D

Briksne, I. (2005b) *Survey: Traveler in Latvia*. Press release 17 February, 2005. Rīga: Central Statistical Bureau of Latvia. Available at: http://www.csb.lv/ateksts.cfm?tem_kods=rob&datums=%7Bts%20% 272005%2D02%2D17%2012%3A50%3A00%27%7D

Cabrini, L. (2004) *International and European Tourism 2003 and Beyond*. Rīga: Paper presented at International Rural Tourism Workshop, 3 June, 2004. Rīga: Lauku Ceļotājs.

Central Statistical Bureau of Latvia (1998) *Tourism in Latvia Statistical Bulletin*. Rīga: Central Statistical Bureau of Latvia.

Central Statistical Bureau of Latvia (1999) *Tourism in Latvia Statistical Bulletin*. Rīga: Central Statistical Bureau of Latvia.

Central Statistical Bureau of Latvia (2001) *Tourism in Latvia Statistical Bulletin*. Rīga: Central Statistical Bureau of Latvia.

Central Statistical Bureau of Latvia (2004a) *Statistical Yearbook of Latvia*. Rīga: Central Statistical Bureau of Latvia.

Central Statistical Bureau of Latvia (2004b) *Tourism in Latvia Statistical Bulletin*. Rīga: Central Statistical Bureau of Latvia.

Central Statistical Bureau of Latvia (2005) *Tourism in Latvia Statistical Bulletin*. Rīga: Central Statistical Bureau of Latvia.

CSDD (Road Traffic Safety Department) (2005) *Statistics*. Rīga: CSDD. Available at: http://www.csdd.lv/ default.php?pageID=1098883151

District Council of Preiļi (2004). *Preiļi Rajona Padome. Tourism*. Preiļi: District Council of Preiļi. Available at: www.preilirp.lv/informacija/turisms.pdf

European Commission (2003) *Tourism and the European Union*. Brussels: European Commission. Available at: http://europa.eu.int/comm/enterprise/services/tourism/tourismeu.htm#future

Eurostat (2005) *Euro Zone GDP up by 0.3% and EU25 up by 0.4%*. Euro-Indicators News Release 128/2005, 13 October 2005. Brussels: Eurostat. Available at: http://epp.eurostat.cec.eu.int/pls/portal/ docs/PAGE/PGP_PRD_CAT_PREREL/PGE_CAT_PREREL_YEAR_2005/PGE_CAT_PREREL_ YEAR_2005_MONTH_10/2-13102005-EN-AP.PDF

Hall, C.M. (2005) *Tourism: Rethinking the Social Science of Mobility*. Harlow, UK: Pearson Education Limited.

Hall, C.M. and Page, S.J. (2002) *The Geography of Tourism and Recreation*. London: Routledge.

Latvian Institute (2005) *Latvijas Institūts Turpina Sadarbību ar Zīmola Ekspertu Voliju Olinsu*. Press release 1 March 2005. Rīga: Latvian Institute. Available at: http://www.li.lv/lv/?id=3&news=2

Latvian Tourism Development Agency (2005) *Press release 21 February*. Rīga: Latvian Tourism Development Agency. Available at: http://www.tava.gov.lv/

Lauku Ceļotājs (2004) *Latvian Rural Tourism Association: Statistics*. Rīga: Lauku Ceļotājs. Available at: http://www.celotajs.lv/cont/prof/market/statistics.html

Leitis, Ē.(2005) Neizpostītas dabas nestā peļņa. *Latvijas Vēstnesis*, 1 March.

Lithuania State Tourism Department (2005) *Medium Term Marketing Strategy 2005 to 2009.* Vilnius: Lithuania State Tourism Department. Available at: http://64.233.183.104/search?q=cache:yeS9JTn60 H0J:www.tourism.lt/nsv/engl/LMS.doc+&hl=lv

Līvu Akvaparks (2005) *Līvu Akvaparks Welcomes its 500,000th Visitor.* Press release, 7 April 2005. Jūrmala: Līvu Akvaparks. Available at: http://www.akvaparks.lv/en/news/article.php?id=15476

Lujāns, J. (2004) *Tourism in Latvia – Priority Industry of National Economics.* Rīga: Paper presented at International Rural Tourism Workshop, 3 June. Rīga: Lauku Ceļotājs.

Mārtiņa, I. (2005) SEB ekonomisti optimistiski par Baltijas attīstību. *Dienas Bizness,* 16 March. Available at: http://www.db.lv/online/news.php?aid=43725

Ministry of Culture of the Republic of Latvia (2003) *LR Kultūras Ministrija, Dziesmusvetki, Vesture.* Available at: http://www.dziesmusvetki2003.lv

Ministry of Economics of the Republic of Latvia (2004a) *Guidelines for Tourism Development in Latvia.* Rīga: Ministry of Economics of the Republic of Latvia. Available at: http://www.em.gov.lv/em/2nd/?cat=373

Ministry of Economics of the Republic of Latvia (2004b) *Main Legal Acts and Policy Planning Documents in the Field of Tourism.* Rīga: Ministry of Economics of the Republic of Latvia. Available at: http://www.em.gov.lv/em/2nd/?cat=5002

Naish, J. (2004) Baltics braced for new kids on the Bloc. *Times Online,* 1 May. Available at: http://www.timesonline.co.uk/article/0,160-1092380,00.html

NTDP (2001) *National Tourism Development Programme for Latvia, 2001–2010* (in Latvian). Ministry of Environmental Protection and Regional Development. Available at: http://www.em.gov.lv/em/2nd/?cat=373

Pilāts, V. (2004) *Nature and Ecotourism in Latvia.* Rīga: Latvian Institute. Available at: http://www.li.lv/en/?id=27

Reinberga, E. (2005) Viesu skaits un aktivitātes kļūst ievērojamas. *Industry Reports nozare.lv.* Available at: htpp://www.nozare.lv

Rīga Airport (2005) *Statistics.* Rīga: Rīga Airport. Available at: http://www.riga-airport.com/index.php?view=statistics&lang=lat

Seilis, G. (2005) Atbilde uz jautājumu par vācu tūristu piesaistīšanu. *Ventspils Dome,* 29 March. Available at: http://www.ventspils.lv/NR/exeres/00001646yujsowjewozkdhxn/Jaunumu+ievade.asp?NRORIGINA LURL=%2fNR%2fexeres%2f2C86B3F6-EC91-495D-B3D5-6B0BDB50777D&FRAMELESS=false&NRNODEGUID=%7b2C86B3F6-EC91-495D-B3D5-6B0BDB50777D%7d&Lang=lv

Slava, L. (ed.) (2004) *Jūrmala: Daba un Kultūras Mantojums.* Rīga: Neptūns.

Tīsiņa, V. (2004) *Latvijas Sievietes Demogrāfiskā Skatījumā.* Press release, 27 April 2004. Rīga: Central Statistical Bureau of Latvia. Available at: http://www.csb.lv/lteksts.cfm?tem_kods=dem&datums=%7Bts%20%272004%2D09%2D27%2013%3A00%3A00%27%7 D

UN Division for Social Policy and Development (1998) *The Ageing of the World's Population.* New York: United Nations. Available at: http://www.un.org/esa/socdev/ageing/ageing/agewpop.htm

Urpena, E. (2005) *Pārsteidzošā Latvija.* Press release, 1 April 2005. Rīga: Ministry of Economics of Republic of Latvia. Available at: http://www.em.gov.lv/em/2nd/?id=5291&

WTO (World Tourism Organization) (2003) *Tourism Highlights.* Madrid: WTO.

15 Lithuania: Sustainable Rural Tourism Development in the Baltic Coastal Region

Aušrinė Armaitienė, Ramūnas Povilanskas and Eleri Jones

Introduction

Following 50 years of Communist rule, Lithuania had the distinction of being the first Soviet republic to declare independence in 1990, joining the United Nations in 1991, applying for NATO membership in 1994 and getting full NATO membership in 2004. In 1998, Lithuania became an associate member of the European Union (EU) and in 2003 signed the EU Accession Treaty, becoming a full member of the EU on 1 May, 2004. Increasingly close ties with the West have been extremely important in Lithuania's economic development and, for example, have widened opportunities to participate in international trade and tourism fairs, such as the World Travel Market in London and fairs in Berlin, Milan, Göteborg, Moscow and St Petersburg, through which the Lithuanian State Tourism Department and Lithuanian tourism companies have been able to significantly broaden their sphere of influence. Participation has been supported mainly from EU pre-accession PHARE funds. The importance of EU funding and its judicious deployment in supporting much of the tourism development in Lithuania today cannot be underestimated. EU support has enabled Lithuania to build on strong tourism development traditions to exploit an abundance of tourism resources.

Lithuania enjoys a rich diversity of landscape – forests, lakes, rivers and notably about 100 km of sandy coastline along the Baltic Sea and in the Curonian lagoon offering the best locations for coastal tourism in the whole of the Baltic Sea region. Lithuania has five national parks and 30 regional parks together with an abundance of cultural heritage reflecting a rich cultural history. Over 10,000 objects enjoy the official status of a monument although only about 350 are under the protection of the state with a still smaller number developed as tourist attractions. Perhaps of particular interest in relation to this chapter is Lithuania's centrality as a European tourist destination with Vilnius (Lithuania's capital) only 26 km south of Europe's current geographic centre at 54°54'N and 25°19'E, as commemorated by a 9 tonne boulder in Europas Park, Bernotai in eastern Lithuania.

Lithuania's traditional markets have been its neighbouring countries: Russia, Belarus, Latvia, and Poland. As a consequence of German being taught in Lithuanian schools, German-speaking markets – Germany, Austria and Switzerland – have also become important. Increasingly close links with the West, and particularly associate and later full EU membership, are seen as being the key to an upturn in the number of incoming tourists from other EU countries, particularly Spain, France and Italy. Whilst the number of foreign visitors to Lithuania decreased through the late-1980s and in the first half of the 1990s, since 1996 the opposite trend has developed with tourist flows increasing each year by 12–19% (National Tourism Development Programme, 2003).

Lithuania's *Medium Term Marketing Strategy 2005 to 2009* (European Commission, 2004) identifies six broad product categories: coastal holidays, city breaks, coach tours, health spas, countryside/rural tourism, meetings and incentive travel. Strengthening of the image and identity of Lithuania and the creation of a Lithuanian brand are seen as being issues extending across all product categories and markets. Each product category has its specific and different priority markets. Coastal holidays, for example, prioritize Germany, Russia, Latvia, Belarus and the domestic market, with each market having its preferred resorts (Neringa or Palanga). City breaks are linked to cultural interest or sporting events and the importance of developments in the transport infrastructure are noted. For example, strategic partnerships with 'no frills' airlines are seen as critical to the competitiveness of Vilnius, the Lithuanian capital, in the European city-break market; the opening of the new ferry terminal in Klaipeda in 2006 is key to the Scandinavian market; while railways are important for domestic, Polish, Latvian and Belarus markets. Coach tours are perceived as a straightforward product, especially for more distant markets – the UK, the USA, Sweden and other original EU member countries, particularly Italy. Lithuania recognizes four health resorts: Neringa, Palanga, Druskininkai, Birštonas, each with very different specializations. Meetings and incentive travel is identified as having the advantage of a higher per capita spend and the disadvantage of a long lead time (at least 3–5 years). The establishment of a Lithuanian Convention Bureau is seen as being key to the development of the meetings and incentive travel market.

Countryside/rural tourism in Lithuania is a product category that is of particular interest. Bicycle tourism is particularly important as a rural tourism activity. There are opportunities to promote countryside accommodation in association with nature reserves and cultural sites in rural locations and walking, canoeing, bird watching, hunting and fishing are seen as having potential in the longer term (European Commission, 2004). Rural tourism is seen as having the potential to generate 30–40% of total income and being particularly important in areas where agricultural land is less fertile

(National Tourism Development Plan, 2003). The demand for rural and farmhouse accommodation outstrips supply, and the quality of accommodation is identified by the Marketing Strategy (European Commission, 2004) as being of sub-standard quality and requiring further investment. The majority of rural tourism visitors come from neighbouring countries and, more recently, German-speaking countries. People living in rural areas are generally not prepared for tourists from further afield due to communication and language barriers and lack of business skills. However, an increasing number of Lithuanian city dwellers are travelling to rural areas for short breaks resulting in several benefits: Lithuanians become acquainted with their homeland, which helps build Lithuanian identity and encourages the cherishing of natural and cultural values. In an economic development sense, increased domestic demand for rural tourism products is important in developing a quality platform for incoming tourism. Ritchie and Crouch (2003, p. 24) identify that:

> generally the supply of tourism product is driven by domestic or local demand that is typically more stable and reliable and less fickle than demand from distant markets. Hence, solid domestic demand provides a healthy competitive environment and the critical mass of demand necessary to support a thriving tourism and hospitality industry. Strong domestic demand therefore helps to provide a climate that also encourages inbound tourism and discourages outbound tourism.

Ritchie and Crouch (2003, p. 102) further assert that:

> Strong local demand creates an environment that fosters the development of a rich variety and range of tourism amenities, facilities, attractions and services. Indeed, without substantial local demand, many of these facilities and services, particularly those provided by governments and funded through taxation, would not exist to the same extent. Governments provide public services which the private sector cannot or will not provide. While foreign tourists may be able to enjoy the benefits of these public services and facilities, where they exist, it is domestic demand that provides the real basis for their need and funding.

So rural tourism can be seen as a distinct phenomenon in Lithuania's rapidly growing tourism industry and is particularly relevant to the concept of sustainable development. The National Tourism Development Plan (2003) identifies the integration of tourism development into the wider economic development strategy and the need for the public sector to be active participants in the dissemination of information and training of providers of rural tourism services. As in many developed and developing countries, rural tourism has been recognized as a vehicle for economic and social development (Sharpley, 2002), providing opportunities for revenue generation as well as employment. Rural tourism development has become an issue of major significance in Lithuania, a country in which 20% of the inhabitants live in rural areas, and where, as the agricultural industry becomes selectively industrialized, there are few alternative opportunities to enhance the economy. As emphasized by Wanhill (2005, p. 251):

> the spillover benefits of tourism in terms of income and employment creation are well known and, more than any other industry, tourism deals with the use of natural and cultural resources, which in outlying regions are often their major asset.

Rural tourism offers important opportunities for the diversification of rural activities in Lithuania and has the added advantage of providing a vehicle to ensure the ongoing conservation of Lithuania's globally significant, but fragile ecosystems. Appropriately managed rural tourism development offers the potential for triple bottom line sustainability, i.e. a way of balancing the economic, social and environmental agendas. Rural tourism has experienced rapid growth in Lithuania, as evidenced by the number of officially registered rural tourism service providers. However, demand still outstrips supply. Such rapid growth raises questions about the sustainability of Lithuania's rural tourism development activities and in answering these questions it is important that 'both positive and negative impacts are evaluated' (Ap and Crompton, 1998, p. 120). Whilst 'triple-bottom-line' sustainability is undeniably an appropriate goal for tourism development the question of whether such sustainable development is anything more than a 'guiding fiction' (McCool and Moisey, 2001, p. 3) is a more debatable point.

This chapter presents three case studies of sustainable coastal rural tourism development in Lithuania which are contributing to the diversification of rural activities in Lithuanian coastal areas: Rusnė Island in the Nemunas river delta adjacent to the Curonian lagoon, Minija village in the Minija river delta – the 'Venice of Lithuania' – and Karklė, a seaside village situated north of Klaipėda on the Baltic Sea coast. All three case studies were developed through the first-hand experiences of staff from the Department of Tourism and Recreation at Klaipėda University investigating social and economic changes since 1997 in the Lithuanian coastal rural areas following the collapse of the Soviet Union and its centrally planned economic system. Through interviews with key stakeholders, including relevant officials and local interest groups, and interrogating Lithuanian government tourism statistics and a range of reports and policy documents, the chapter explores the policy context for rural tourism development in Lithuania, the 'triple-bottom-line' sustainability of rural and water tourism developments in Lithuania at a local community level, and the conflict between social and economic development on the one hand and environmental issues on the other.

Governance and Sustainable Rural Tourism Development

Amongst tourism's potential contribution to rural development, Hall et al. (2003) include: regenerating local economies and improving the quality of life; supplementing income generation for the farming, craft and service sectors; countering isolation of social groups and remote areas; re-evaluating heritage and other resources and rural identity; assisting environmental, economic and social sustainability policies and helping to realize the economic value of key elements of rural life – quality foods, scenery, spaces and culture. However, Hall et al. (2003) go on to caution the fragile nature of rural tourism development, which may result in limited inward investment, business start-ups and employment generation because of its small scale, dispersed nature and low return on investment, requires skills for success, is often controlled by people without specific tourism training, may be constrained by shortage of capital and has a short time-scale for success. Rural tourism is generally dominated by micro-businesses, which perform an important role economically and socially in stabilizing fragile areas (Middleton, 2001) but emphasize the fragmentation of the tourism industry across different economic sectors.

The modern countryside has become an arena where a multitude of tensions and competing ideologies are played out (Sharpley, 2003). Sharpley (2003, citing P. Stone's unpublished MSc Thesis, University of Northumbria, 2000) contrasts two ideological perspectives. First is the resource-oriented 'conservation ideology' in which the environmental agenda dominates and the countryside is maintained as a rural idyll to support appropriate recreational pursuits. Second is the profit-oriented 'commercial ideology', which adopts a rational approach to the countryside focusing on the profitable development of tourism and where the economic agenda triumphs. However, as Wanhill (2005, p. 251) points out, 'the short-term gains sought by capital markets are often at odds with the long-term sustainability of tourist environments'.

Sharpley (2003) develops a model of governance which recognizes these two orientations and identifies a middle ground which he labels 'authority' adopting a power-orientation through appropriate planning and control asserting that successful governance must 'recognise, satisfy and balance the opposing needs of the conservation and commercial groups of actors within broader development objectives' (Sharpley, 2003, pp. 42–43). Sharpley stresses the importance of partnerships of relevant stakeholders in the planning and control of rural tourism development at a local level and the close alignment of tourism policy with the wider economic development policy. This will become increasingly important as tourism movements increase:

> there will be a need for more regulation, direction and improved management of tourism resources to prevent environmental degradation and implement tourism development plans in a sustainable manner.
> (Wanhill, 2005, p. 251)

This balancing of internal and external agendas for rural tourism development come together in the European-led initiative of integrated quality management (IQM), which offers the benefits of:

- more local awareness and support for tourism generally in the destination, amongst local people and across all rural sectors;
- better coordination between local tourism enterprises themselves, and greater support for, and involvement with, the management and marketing of the destination;
- an improved image of the destination which is real and not based on false expectations;
- a set of rural products which can be promoted with confidence;
- increased customer satisfaction, with more repeat business and recommendations; and
- better knowledge of the economic, social and environmental impacts of tourism and ability to adjust for them (European Commission, 2000, p. 8).

Through IQM, a consensus on appropriate development for a particular rural area can be negotiated with private and public sectors working in partnership using whatever mechanisms are available to be able to facilitate the achievement of goals. Wanhill (2005, p. 251) highlights the role of investment incentives in proactively ensuring appropriate development:

> investment incentives are policy instruments that can be used to correct for market failure and ensure a development partnership between the public and private sectors. The partnership approach has a particular significance for regional development, particularly in peripheral areas due to the existence of many small communities, lack of resources, areas in decline and the fragmented nature of the supply being a range of small and micro-tourist establishments. The disparate character of the industry at this level requires a proactive role from public bodies in the form of a coordinated tourism strategy and business support, in order to give a sense of direction and engender confidence through local community involvement.

Thus, to have any potential for the achievement of sustainable rural tourism there must be a consensus on development goals, an appropriate policy framework which recognizes the agendas of different stakeholders and the use of investment support to proactively orchestrate rural tourism developments. Thus, of particular interest is the policy framework for sustainable rural tourism development in Lithuania, particularly the way that local and regional tourism planning is vertically integrated with national development objectives, and the way that financial incentivization is used to coordinate rural tourism development in the three case studies presented in this chapter.

Rural Tourism Development in Lithuania

The 'flagships' for sustainable rural tourism development in Lithuania are its five national and 30 regional parks and these territories were the first to be involved in the implementation of Agenda 21 in Lithuania. Lithuania has a mild climate and a diverse and beautiful landscape with enormous potential for a wide variety of recreational activities. It has a rich history and cultural heritage through the broad ethnic mix of its population that creates favourable preconditions for tourism development and can lead to enhanced employment opportunities and income generation. Tourism has been recognized in the post-Communist transition of Lithuania to a market economy and the economic restructuring therein as a vehicle for balancing the economic, social and environmental agendas, especially in rural areas. Tourism development in rural areas enables not only social and economic development through exploitation of Lithuania's rich natural and cultural resources, but also ensures their ongoing conservation which can be under threat at times of economic downturn. Rural tourism development is seen as

involving elderly people, reducing depopulation in rural regions and minimizing the unemployment rate and antisocial phenomena. Rural leisure and tourism activities are recognized as encouraging understanding of Lithuanian culture and traditions, encouraging mobility and impacting positively on human health. However, there has been conflict between protection of the natural territories and the private interests of land owners.

Rural tourism is growing rapidly in Lithuania with the number of visitors increasing from 18% to 49% between 1999 and 2004. The number of officially registered rural tourism service providers has grown fourfold from 89 registered providers in 2000 to 361 in 2004 and growth in demand for tourism is constrained by the rate of growth in supply, especially of accommodation (see Fig. 15.1). However, despite raised awareness of sustainability issues in Lithuania at a policy level, sustainability terms are not used to market Lithuania at a national, regional, local or individual tourism business level, and terms such as 'undamaged nature', 'natural spaces', 'ecological farm', 'natural vegetables and food' prevail. However, this is probably more a reflection of the market than of attitudes towards sustainable rural tourism development in Lithuania.

The Lithuanian Policy Framework for Sustainable Rural Tourism Development

As widely documented, the concept of sustainability and Agenda 21 dates back to 1992 and

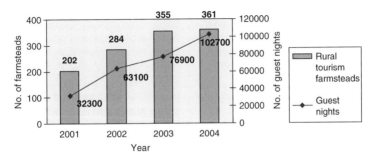

Fig. 15.1. Lithuania: rapid growth of rural tourism, 2001–2004. Source: compiled by A. Armaitienė, 2005, using statistics from the Lithuanian State Tourism Department website at http://www.tourism.lt/en/default.htm.

the Johannesburg Summit. Lithuania's initial response to the sustainability agenda, as for many other countries, fell short of that outlined in the Johannesburg Summit. Discussions in Lithuania about Agenda 21 were very often narrowly focused on environmental issues and maintained by the Environment Ministry rather than being implemented in a more holistic and integrated manner. There were several mitigating factors for this:

- the period 1992–1993 coincided with economic transition in Lithuania which posed serious economic challenges, with questions of economical survival and avoidance of poverty higher on the agenda than those of sustainability;
- Lithuania had one of the strongest and best organized environmental protection policies amongst the ex-Soviet states and is still amongst the best in the European Union; and
- the focus for tourism was for the creation of system, structure, markets and readjustment to different European standards and in this arena the concept of sustainability simply did not resonate.

Lithuania's strategy for tourism development is outlined in the National Tourism Development Programme (2003). It emphasizes sustainable development and integrates tourism into the wider strategy for economic development providing vertical integration between national and regional policy through the provision of recommendations for the planning of sustainable development of tourism at the level of municipalities. The strategy for sustainable tourism development is a significant, but separate, aspect of the wider sustainable development strategy for Lithuania and nests within the National Strategy for the Sustainable Development of Lithuania (NSSDL) which was approved in 2003 and presents sustainable development as a 'classical' balanced 'triple-bottom-line' approach, based on a vision of 'three pillars of equal importance – environmental protection, economic development and social development' establishing a set of sustainable development indicators (NSSDL, 2003, p. 2). Thus, sustainability is perceived as a key policy and planning tool and guiding principle of the administration of territory and a major consideration in the master plans for Lithuanian regions,

counties and districts. Tourism is explicitly recognized as being of significant importance to the Lithuanian economy and to the diversification of activities in rural areas and the resolution of associated social problems. The National Tourism Development Programme (2003) aims to use tourism resources sustainably to maintain the growth of income from the tourism sector.

Integration of environmental concerns into sectoral development strategies is a key priority for sustainable development in Lithuania. The NSSDL (2003) builds on the national priorities and objectives formulated in three documents approved by Seimas (the Parliament of the Republic of Lithuania) during 2002, namely: the 'National Long-term Development Strategy'; the 'National Long-term Economic Development Strategy' and the 'Master Plan of the Republic of Lithuania'. The NSSDL (2003) was developed to align with the European Union's strategic provisions for sustainable development in anticipation of Lithuania's membership of the European Union in 2005 and integrates the work of the ministries of environment, social security and labour, transport, health, education and science, economy, foreign affairs, interior and agriculture, emphasizing the complexity of a holistic response to the sustainable development agenda. The strategy emphasizes the importance of minimizing environmental impacts from the main industrial sectors (transport, industry, energy, agriculture and tourism) whilst increasing their eco-efficiency, and stresses the need for reduction in the consumption of energy and water per GDP unit whilst highlighting the benefits of tourism and its relatively lower impact on the environment in comparison with other economic sectors. The priorities for the exploitation of European Union structural funding, which plays a key role in the implementation of the National Strategy, are outlined in the 'Lithuanian Single Programming Document for 2004–2006' (Government of the Republic of Lithuania, 2004). Measure 3.4, for example, covers 'public tourism infrastructure and services' and emphasizes a sustainable approach to the environment. Cross-cutting – horizontal – themes relating to sustainable development include specific consideration of the information society, equal opportunities and regional development.

Rural tourism in Lithuania is defined in the 'Requirements of Rural Tourism Service

Provision' (Lithuanian State Tourism Department, 2003) as the provision of accommodation, catering, attractions, amusement and related services to tourists in farmsteads or individual living houses by persons with rural tourism business licences in the rural areas or towns with less than 3000 inhabitants and is based on previous legislation, building on experience in response to the metamorphosis of the economic context and business conditions. Interestingly this document is the only one that does not explicitly consider sustainability issues – it focuses instead on the regulation of practical issues arising from rural tourism activity.

There are a number of opportunities to further develop Lithuania's response to the sustainability agenda: eco-labelling, for example, is underdeveloped. In place are the Blue Flag programme, which provides municipality awards for beach quality, and the Green Key programme, which focuses on the accommodation sector. Blue Flag has been achieved by two municipalities, Neringa and Palanga. Large hotels in Vilnius and Klaipėda – the Reval and Baltpark hotels – have participated in the Green Key programme. No labelling schemes have been implemented for rural tourism products despite evidence of high awareness of the importance of environmental protection and the balancing of economy and social questions (Armaitienė et al., 2004).

The Case Studies

Figure 15.2 shows the location of the three case studies: Rusnė Island, Minija village and Karklė, on the Baltic Sea coast.

Rusnė Island

Rusnė Island is the largest island in the Nemunas river delta adjacent to the Curonian lagoon with a total area of 45.2 km^2. It is isolated from the mainland by the two main branches of the river: Atmata in the north and Skirvytė in the south, which also serves as the state border separating Rusnė Island from the Kaliningrad enclave of Russia. A few minor river branches cut the island into separate parts. The township of Rusnė

(2500 inhabitants), six villages and over 20 manors are located on the island and administrated by the Šilutė district municipality. The island is a flat and open alluvial plain and parts are protected from flooding by dykes. The unsealed floodplains of the island make a critically important ecozone between the aquatic and terrestrial habitats (Breber et al., in press) and in the spring provide a nursery for Curonian lagoon fish and a foraging place for migratory birds. Both of these offer important resources for the development of sustainable rural tourism products.

Since 1993, the entire Nemunas delta has been listed under the Ramsar Convention as a wetland of international importance. Rusnė Island is also protected as a managed landscape reserve within the Nemunas Delta regional park. Sandy islets and reedbeds of the lagoon foreshore in front of the island are protected as a strict nature reserve with no activities or access allowed. The regulations of the managed reserve relevant to sustainable rural tourism development constrain expansion of arable land acreage at the expense of meadows and establish the basis for interpretation of the resources of the area for tourists and residents which should stimulate interest and tourism activity (Deinoravičius et al., 1999).

Traditionally, fishing has been an important part of the economy. Before the changes of the 1990s, the Rusnė fishing cooperative shared fishing in the Lithuanian part of the Curonian lagoon with three other cooperatives. Besides fishing, people were employed in dairy and duck farming. Fishing quotas, milk and poultry production plans were determined centrally, and the local economy was dependent on cheap fuel and low-cost manual labour (Roepstorff and Povilanskas, 1995). The economic reforms of the 1990s caused a decline of fishing in the Curonian lagoon and dissolution of the cooperatives. On Rusnė Island, large-scale husbandry and duck-farming was economically unviable and collapsed. Unemployment and emigration from the island soared as the remaining locals, mostly people in their 40s and 50s, had to meet new survival challenges without possessing proper knowledge and skills.

In this situation, rural tourism development was perceived as a cure-all by many local people. In 2000, the first steps to facilitate the provision of rural tourism services on selected pilot

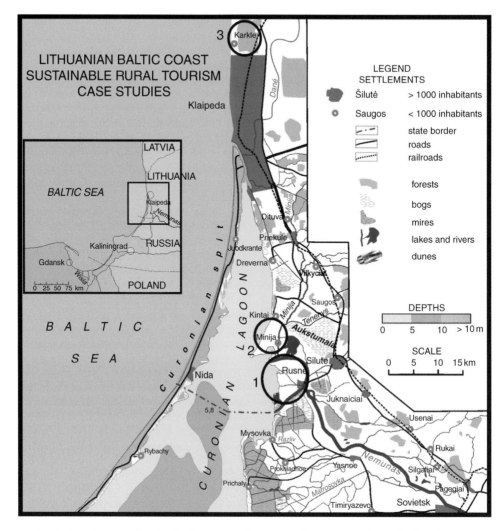

Fig. 15.2. Location map showing the three case study areas. Source: drawn by R. Povilanskas, 2005.

farmsteads of the island were taken by the Department of Tourism and Recreation at Klaipėda University. These efforts proved to be a real success, and the number of farmsteads providing rural tourism services doubled each year from just two in 2000 to 28 in 2004, catering for the growing visitor demand from the large cities of Lithuania attracted mainly by the excellent all-year-round angling on the island (Vaitekūnas *et al.*, 2001). The Šilutė district municipality encourages environmentally friendly rural tourism development on Rusnė Island through the provision of a range of financial incentives, including tax relief for rural tourism

service providers for the first 5 years, provision of capital for public tourism facilities on the island (e.g. bird observation towers and bike paths), education and training of local tourism service providers.

Thus, rural tourism development on Rusnė Island is resulting from the growing interest of the island's community and tourism service providers in turning local conservation values and rich traditions into an asset for sustainable development. Such interest has manifested itself in restoring and cherishing the environment-friendly traditional approaches of deltaic farming and fishing combined with the provision of rural and nature tourism services. An ancient fishing boat, *Kurenas*, has become a potential icon for local cultural traditions and ecological thinking and has been recommissioned by locals to carry tourists around the island (Armaitienė *et al.*, 2004).

Minija

Minija village is a tiny village located in the Minija river delta, adjacent to the Nemunas delta and is unique – the 'Venice of Lithuania'. It is part of the Šilutė district municipality and features narrow parcels of land with houses protected by dykes and stretching along both banks of the river (Povilanskas *et al.*, 2002a). Movement around the village is possible only by boat. Minija has 45 permanent inhabitants living in 15 farmsteads with ten more farmsteads made into second homes. The area around Minija has a series of valuable habitats, including floodplains, shallow lakes and coastal wet forests and boasts the greatest biodiversity in Lithuania in terms of fish and waterfowl species (Povilanskas *et al.*, 2002b), of which several are considered as threatened species in Europe.

Before the economic reform of the 1990s, fishermen from Minija belonged to the fishing cooperative of Kintai and fished in the northern part of the Curonian lagoon (Povilanskas *et al.*, 2002a). Besides fishing, farmers of Minija were employed in dairy farming and the production of grass pellets on the floodplains. The early 1990s saw the dissolution of the fishing cooperatives and collapse of grass pellet production as they lost viability in the new economic environment. Whilst a few locals became involved in private fishery or husbandry, many were forced to leave the village. Those who remain are generally socially deprived, retired persons surviving on subsistence farming and poaching. Remarkably, the area's attractive scenery and unique cultural heritage caused a rush to purchase property for conversion into second homes by the residents of Klaipėda, Lithuania's third-largest city. Since 1997, one Minija household has started to provide bed and breakfast and leisure boating services. The main focus for promoting Minija as a rural and coastal tourism destination has been the construction of a marina for small-scale sailing boats in 2003, which was supported by co-funding from European Union and Šilutė municipality. In 2004, the village had 200 water-borne daily visitors during the peak summer season and accrues a total of about 11,000 visitors per year. The potential conflict between conservation and commercial imperatives arising out of this will be interesting to follow.

Minija village is protected as a managed ethno-cultural reserve within the Nemunas Delta regional park. The prevailing regulations impose restrictions on the construction of new buildings and the reconstruction of existing ones, including expansion of tourist facilities and forbid the entry of motor boats to the Minija river delta. Comprehensive education campaigns are provided for local people to raise awareness of the environmental significance of the area. As on Rusnė Island, the key incentives to promote environmentally friendly rural tourism development in Minija village include tax advantages for the providers of rural tourism services for the first 5 years.

Sustainability in rural tourism development in Minija is reliant upon further promotion of Minija as an important rural and water tourism destination catering for the increasing demand of the visitors for a unique ('wild') environment. The marina of Minija, which is managed by the Kintai Sailing Club, has become an important promoter of advanced ideas about sustainable rural and water tourism development to the local community. Thus, in 2003 ecological wastewater treatment was introduced in the marina in cooperation with the Zvejone environmental club from Klaipėda and Coalition Clean Baltic.

Karklė

Karklė is a seaside village with 100 inhabitants situated north of Klaipėda. It belongs to the Klaipėda rural district municipality and stretches along the coast of the Baltic Sea. Its landscape includes the highest coastal cliffs in Lithuania and mature mixed forests, making this small village a popular year-round destination for weekend visitors from Klaipėda. The area around Karklė hosts several valuable coastal and marine habitats forming a series of Lithuanian coastal and marine NATURA 2000 sites (Olenin and Klovaite, 1998). These include parabolic dunes and, particularly, 'hard bottoms' of pebbles and boulders with the highest biodiversity in the southeast Baltic proper (Olenin and Labanauskas, 1995).

Before the changes of the 1990s, Karklė village was part of the heavily militarized seaside frontier zone of the Soviet Union with restricted access for tourists and devoid of any tourist facilities. The Soviet authorities did not allow local inhabitants to fish in the Baltic Sea fearing their escape to the West. Hence, everyone was forced into farming at local *kolkhoz*. (Kolkhoz was a form of farming in the former Soviet Union that existed along with state farms. The word is a contraction of 'collective household', usually translated as 'collective farm'. Members of kolkhoz were paid a share of the farm's product and profit according to the number of workdays.)

After the collapse of the 'Iron Curtain', Karklė opened to the outer world and became immediately popular among the inhabitants of Klaipėda, both as a destination for seaside recreation and as a residential suburb. Such rapid development of leisure facilities and housing led to dramatic changes in the village and its environs, which had been left intact for 50 years. Since the beginning of the 21st century, active efforts have been undertaken by the seaside regional park administration to reverse negative developments and to promote local sustainability through facilitation of the provision of small-scale rural tourism services in Karklė. During 2002/2003, a comprehensive public awareness and capacity building campaign was launched by the staff of the seaside regional park and the Department of Tourism and Recreation at Klaipėda University. This campaign, however, has not resulted in an increase in the number of farmsteads providing rural tourism services in Karklė beyond the three extant farmsteads. According to the results of a visitor survey, current demand for tourism services outstrips supply (Spiriajevas, 2003).

Karklė village is protected as a managed ethno-cultural reserve within the Pajurio (seaside) regional park. The management regulations of this reserve are some of the strictest in Europe regarding construction and reconstruction, including expansion of tourist facilities (Povilanskas and Urbis, 2004). So, according to the Law of the Coastal Zone of the Republic of Lithuania

(2002), any new buildings in the 300 m seaside zone must be approved by the Prime Minister's cabinet [sic]. The adjacent nearshore of the 'hard-bottom' is protected as a managed marine reserve with restricted fishing and navigation. Under such a restrictive management regime, sustainable tourism incentives are critically important. The regional park administration controls the development of tourism facilities (e.g. stairways leading to the beach, bird observation hides and nature trails), and provides training and capacity building to local people. Unfortunately, the inhabitants of Karklė do not enjoy any tax relief in relation to rural tourism service provision.

The policy for sustainable tourism development in Karklė is in keeping with the policy to diversify the Lithuanian tourism product following membership of the European Union and is primarily linked to the promotion of specific local rural tourism services based on local traditions, e.g. amber fishing in the Baltic Sea as part of an international 'Amber Trail' and riding traditional, locally raised Samogitian horses, which contributes to their preservation as well as maintaining habitat diversity in the dunes. The capacity of Karklė as a sustainable rural and coastal tourism will be enhanced by the anticipated integration of the seaside regional park into the Baltic network of sustainable coastal dune tourism (Povilanskas, 2004).

Discussion

Recent years have seen a significant global shift in land use and rural employment towards more emphasis on the non-farm sector (Bouma *et al.*, 1998; Bryden and Bollman, 2000; Lanjouw and Lanjouw, 2001). The sustainability of coastal habitats and landscapes depends to a significant degree on the sustainability of the patterns of human activities. To date, the maintenance of wildlife sanctuaries in the Lithuanian coastal areas has fallen mainly on the shoulders of the taxpayer, albeit supplemented with voluntary donations. Whereas this may work in affluent societies, if serious economic difficulties arise such contributions are the first to suffer. A better guarantee for the continued existence of these valuable coastal habitats would be to consider them not only for their ecological value, but also for their economic and social potential. To achieve this requires the application of biodiversity protection policies through top-down regulation and voluntary incentive-based ones (Breber, 1995; Hurni, 2000; Doremus, 2003; Shogren et al., 2003). Without a determined local collaborative network, which involves all relevant stakeholders, including owners of recreational amenities, hunters and anglers, any top-down conservation system fails to prevent poaching and misuse of the resources. To achieve environmental, economic and social sustainability of rural tourism requires the empowerment of local communities to effectively exploit the natural resources whilst also conserving them (Deinoravičius et al., 1999; Bridgewater, 2002).

The emerging trend of urban-to-rural in-migration in both developed and transition countries (Stockdale et al., 2000; Brown and Schafft, 2002; Paquette and Domon, 2003) and the strong emotional attachment of Lithuanians to the coast provides an opportunity to foster a robust local identity based on the sustainable use of diverse natural resources and conservation of valuable habitats. The three case studies presented in this chapter illustrate that Lithuania has a strong policy framework to support sustainable rural tourism development, which is vertically and horizontally integrated. Financial incentives are used variably between districts to orchestrate tourism product development in line with policy objectives. The continued balancing of the environmental, economic and social agendas will require the ongoing resolution of conflict between the conservation and commercial agendas. The key to resolving such conflict might lie in anticipated shifts in the European Union's Common Agricultural Policy towards increasing support for environmentally friendly farming, sustainable rural tourism development and maintenance of biological diversity (Donald et al., 2002). Certainly the National Tourism Development Plan (2003) emphasizes the importance of opening up the eligibility of investment support for tourism-related activity from wider funding posts, e.g. the Rural Support Fund. Such changes would enhance the horizontal integration of tourism development with wider

economic development strategies at a local, regional and national level. There is good vertical integration from country to regional to local level. It is clear that tourism is firmly on the economic development agenda in Lithuania and is recognized as an industry sector with important implications for Lithuanian prosperity. Lithuania has warmly embraced the sustainability agenda and has strongly integrated sustainability into the wider development strategies.

The three case studies evidence the importance of tourism in providing sustainable development opportunities in Lithuanian rural/coastal areas. Each case study provides evidence of the understanding of the opportunities afforded to rural coastal areas of repackaging traditional industries and cultures into a new range of leisure and tourism products. Income streams for rural inhabitants can be derived from servicing leisure and tourism opportunities for city dwellers using traditional skills. Each of the case studies has a strong regulatory framework to minimize environmental impact, with the most fragile ecosystems having the strictest regulations. However, the importance of a high quality environment in sustaining tourism activity and the increasing environmental pressure resulting from increased tourism activity has led to a search for national and international funding to enhance the environmental quality. The case studies exemplify the importance of partnerships of key stakeholders in protecting these fragile ecosystems whilst providing development opportunities for local people, thus balancing the conservation and commercial agendas.

Lithuania has made very effective use of EU funding to support marketing and promotion activities, which has enabled a major shift from declining ex-Soviet markets to improving European markets. This has required a paradigm shift in terms of the quality of provision and in this context rural tourism is an important issue providing an effective platform for incoming tourism building on domestic tourism demand. The domestic market is important in contributing to the critical mass of demand that will encourage public-sector response to the tourism product quality issue and develop the infrastructure to meet the needs of incoming tourism markets.

References

Ap, J. and Crompton, C. (1998) Developing and testing a tourism impact scale. *Journal of Travel Research* 39, 317–318.

Armaitienė, A., Raišutienė, J., Popa, L. and Poruncia, A. (2004) Comparative aspects of cultural sustainability for tourism development in European coastal wetlands. In: Green, D. (ed.) *Delivering Sustainable Coasts: Connecting Science and Policy – 7th International Multi-Disciplinary Symposium on Coastal Zone Research, Management and Planning, Aberdeen, September 2004*, Volume 2. Cambridge: Cambridge Publications Ltd., pp. 678–679.

Bouma, J., Varallyay, G. and Batjes, N.H. (1998) Principal land use changes anticipated in Europe. *Agriculture, Ecosystems and Environment* 67(2–3), 103–119.

Breber, P. (1995) The situation of lagoons in Italy today. *Journal of Coastal Conservation* 1, 173–175.

Breber, P., Povilanskas, R. and Armaitienė, A. (2006) Modern biogeographical evolution patterns of European lagoon ecosystems. *Hydrobiology*, in press.

Bridgewater, P.B. (2002) Biosphere reserves: special places for people and nature. *Environmental Science and Policy* 5(1), 9–12.

Brown, L.D. and Schafft, K.A. (2002) Population deconcentration in Hungary during the post-socialist transformation. *Journal of Rural Studies* 18(3), 233–244.

Bryden, J. and Bollman, R. (2000) Rural employment in industrialised countries. *Agricultural Economics* 22(2), 185–197.

Deinoravičius, E., Gjoel Soerensen, U. and Stoškus, A. (1999) *Management Plan for Nemunas Delta Regional Park*. Copenhagen: WWF.

Donald, P.F., Pisano, G., Rayment, M.D. and Pain, D.J. (2002) The Common Agricultural Policy, EU enlargement and the conservation of Europe's farmland birds. *Agriculture, Ecosystems and Environment* 89(3), 167–182.

Doremus, H. (2003) A policy portfolio approach to biodiversity protection on private lands. *Environmental Science and Policy* 6(3), 217–232.

European Commission (EC) (2000) *Towards Quality Rural Tourism: Integrated Quality Management (IQM) of Rural Destinations*. Brussels: EC.

European Commission (EC) (2004) *Lithuania: Preparation of the Lithuanian Marketing Strategy and Tactical Plans and Marketing of the National Tourism Information System: Medium Term Marketing Strategy 2005 to 2009*. Brussels: EC.

Government of the Republic of Lithuania (2004) Lithuanian Single Programming Document for 2004–2006. Government of the Republic of Lithuania, Resolution No. 935, 8 February, Valstybės žinios 2004, No. 123-4486. Vilnius: Government of the Republic of Lithuania.

Hall, D., Mitchell, M. and Roberts, L. (2003) Tourism and the countryside: dynamic relationships. In: Hall, D., Roberts, L. and Mitchell, M. (eds) *New Directions in Rural Tourism*. Aldershot, UK: Ashgate, pp. 3–15.

Hurni, H. (2000) Assessing sustainable land management (SLM). *Agriculture, Ecosystems and Environment* 81(2), 83–92.

Lanjouw, J.O. and Lanjouw, P. (2001) The rural non-farm sector: issues and evidence from developing countries. *Agricultural Economics* 26(1), 1–23.

Law of the Coastal Zone of the Republic of Lithuania (2002) Vilnius: Seimas of the Republic of Lithuania Law IX-1016,7 February, Valstybės žinios 2002, No. 73-3091.

Lithuanian State Tourism Department (2003) *Requirements of Rural Tourism Service Provision*. Resolution of the Lithuanian State Department Nr. 26-V, March 27. Vilnius: Lithuanian State Tourism Department.

McCool, S.F. and Moisey, R.N. (2001) *Tourism, Recreation and Sustainability: Linking Culture and the Environment*. Wallingford, UK: CAB International.

Middleton, T.C.V. (2001) The importance of micro-businesses in European tourism. In: Roberts, L. and Hall, D. (eds) *Rural Tourism and Recreation. Principles to Practice*. Wallingford, UK: CAB International, pp. 197–214.

National Tourism Development Programme (2003) Vilnius: Government of the Republic of Lithuania, Resolution No. 1637, 18 December.

NSSDL (National Strategy for the Sustainable Development of Lithuania) (2003) Vilnius: Government of the Republic of Lithuania, Resolution No. 1160, 11 September.

Olenin, S. and Klovaite, K. (1998) Introduction to the marine and coastal environment of Lithuania. In: von Nordheim, H. and Boedeker, D. (eds) *Red List of Marine and Coastal Biotopes and Biotope Complexes* of the Baltic Sea, Belt Sea and Kattegat. Baltic Sea Environment Proceedings, No. 75. Helsinki: Helsinki Commission, pp. 39–43.

Olenin, S. and Labanauskas, V. (1995) Stony bottom communities near the Lithuanian Coast: the conservation value. In: Gudelis, V., Povilanskas, R. and Roepstorff, A. (eds) Coastal Conservation and Management in the Baltic Region. Proceedings of the EUCC-WWF Conference, 3–7 May, 1994, Rīga – Klaipėda – Kaliningrad. Klaipėda: University Publishers, pp. 81–84.

Paquette, S. and Domon, S. (2003) Changing ruralities, changing landscapes: exploring social recomposition using a multi-scale approach. Journal of Rural Studies 19(4), 425–444.

Povilanskas, R. (2004) Landscape Management on the Curonian Spit: a Cross-border Perspective. Leiden–Klaipėda–Barcelona: EUCC (The Coastal Unon).

Povilanskas, R. and Urbis, A. (2004) National ICZM strategy and initiatives in Lithuania. In: Schernewski, G. and Loeser, N. (eds) Managing the Baltic Sea. Leiden: EUCC Coastline Reports 2, pp. 9–15.

Povilanskas, R., Purvinas, M. and Urbis, A. (2002a) Minija ir Karklė: Pamario Paveldo Kaimai ir jų Aplinka. Leiden–Klaipėda: EUCC.

Povilanskas, R., Purvinas, M. and Urbis, A. (2002b) River villages of Mysovka and Minija and their environment. In: Veloso Gomes, F. and Taveira Pinto, F. (eds) The Changing Coast: Proceedings of LITTORAL 2002 – 6th International Multi-Disciplinary Symposium on Coastal Zone Research, Management and Planning, Porto, September 2002. Porto: EUROCOAST–EUCC, Volume 3, pp. 153–157.

Ritchie, J.R.B. and Crouch, G.I. (2003) The Competitive Tourism Destination: a Sustainable Tourism Perspective. Wallingford, UK: CAB International.

Roepstorff, A. and Povilanskas, R. (1995) On the concepts of nature protection and sustainable use of natural resources: a case study from the Curonian Lagoon. In: Gudelis, V., Povilanskas, R. and Roepstorff, A. (eds) Coastal Conservation and Management in the Baltic Region. Proceedings of the EUCC–WWF Conference 2–8 May, 1994, Rīga–Klaipėda–Kaliningrad. Klaipėda: University Publishers, pp. 223–232.

Sharpley, R. (2002) The challenges of economic diversification through tourism: the case of Abu Dhabi. International Journal of Tourism Research 4, 221–235.

Sharpley, R. (2003) Rural tourism and sustainability – a critique. In: Hall, D., Roberts, L. and Mitchell, M. (eds) New Directions in Rural Tourism. Aldershot, UK: Ashgate, pp. 38–53.

Shogren, J.F., Parkhurst, G.M. and Settle, C. (2003) Integrating economics and ecology to protect nature on private lands: models, methods and mindsets. Environmental Science and Policy 6(3), 233–242.

Spiriajevas, E. (2003) Pasiūla, Paklausa, Galimybės Pajūrio Regioniniame Parke. Klaipėda: Pajūrio Regioninis Parkas.

Stockdale, A., Findlay, A. and Short, D. (2000) The repopulation of rural Scotland: opportunity and threat. Journal of Rural Studies 16(2), 243–257.

Vaitekūnas, S., Armaitienė, A. and Povilanskas, R. (2001) Social and geographical strengths and weaknesses of tourism development in the Curonian Lagoon region. Tiltai 1(14), 51–58.

Wanhill, S. (2005) Investment support for tourism SMEs: a review of theory and practice. In: Jones, E. and Haven-Tang, C. (eds) Tourism SMEs, Service Quality and Destination Competitiveness. Wallingford, UK: CAB International, pp. 227–253.

Part IV

The Mediterranean Enlargement

_____

16 The Mediterranean Enlargement: an Overview

Habib Alipour and Derek Hall

Introduction

This Mediterranean overview chapter has a number of objectives in supporting its overall aim of contextualizing the following two chapters on Malta and Cyprus:

- to briefly highlight common and contrasting elements between the Mediterranean and CEE accession states;
- to highlight common and contrasting elements between Malta and Cyprus themselves;
- to exemplify this through aspects of tourism–environment relationships; and
- to consider the wider Mediterranean implications of the EU accession of Malta and Cyprus.

Contrasts Among the Accession States

It might seem simplistic, but none the less largely true, to argue that few points of comparison exist between the Mediterranean and Central and Eastern European (CEE) 2004 accession states. Of the CEE entrants, Estonia, Latvia and Lithuania had been incorporated within the Soviet Union, had distinctive non-Slav majority cultures, a largely Baltic maritime tradition, and a history embracing the waxing and waning Northern European imperial

powers of Germany, Sweden, Poland, Lithuania and Russia. Of the other five CEE accession states, all but Slovenia had been part of the Soviet bloc since World War II, all but Hungary have Slav cultures, and all, with the partial exception of Poland, had been part of the Hapsburg Austro-Hungarian empire up to World War I. Climatically Central or Northern European, with distinctly cold winter continental components, many of the basic characteristics of the CEE entrants are thus far removed from those of Cyprus and Malta.

Indeed, although a maritime heritage is an element that the Mediterranean entrants may be said to share with the Baltic States, Poland and perhaps Slovenia, that is certainly not the case with the other three, land-locked CEE members (Hungary, Czech Republic and Slovakia). The characteristic of a small population figure (see Table 1.1) is certainly an element Cyprus and Malta share with Slovenia (a nation state only since 1991), Estonia and Latvia, although all three CEECs are much larger in terms of land area. Notably, Malta's population density is far greater than any other EU or Mediterranean country (Table 16.1; see also Table 1.1 and Chapter 17).

Three key and interrelated characteristics link the two Mediterranean entrants while acting to contrast them with the CEE8: a history of British colonial occupation, and the linguistic and tourism heritage flowing from that.

©CAB International 2006. *Tourism in the New Europe: the Challenges and Opportunities of EU Enlargement* (eds D. Hall, M. Smith and B. Marciszewska)

Table 16.1. Selected Mediterranean and European countries in comparison.

Country	Area (in km²)	Population density (per km²)	Motorways (in km)	No. of passenger cars per 1,000 population	Hotels and similar accommodation No. of establishments	No. of beds ('000s)
Malta	316	1,239	0	508	188	39
Cyprus	9,251	82	268	405	803	92
Greece	132,000	80	742	333	8,899	668
Italy	301,000	192	6,478	590	33,840	1,969
Spain	505,000	78	9,910	460	17,402	1,512
France	544,000	108	10,223	490	18,217	1,207
Turkey	814,578	77	1,851	66	1,862	NA

Source: Eurostat, 2005.

A history of British colonial occupation

North African Arabs occupied the Maltese islands from the 9th to the 13th century and left behind notable imprints of their culture, particularly on the Maltese language. Ruled by the throne of Aragon from the early 14th century, in 1530 the islands were granted to the International Order of the Knights of St John of Jerusalem by Charles V of Spain. The Knights administered the islands for the next 268 years until Napoleon occupied the country in 1798 in the name of the French Republic. Within two years the French were forced to surrender following a land and sea blockade by combined Maltese and British forces, and in 1800 Malta became part of the British empire.

Independence was gained in 1964 and Malta was declared a republic within the British Commonwealth in 1974. Until the 1960s the economy had been dependent upon require- ments of the British armed services and the naval dockyard (Mizzi, 1994). On independ- ence, the country's small internal markets, insu- larity, and limited range of natural resources, appeared to severely limit development options (Bramwell, 2003). Subsequently, light industry (textiles, electronic components) and tourism were developed as major sources of employ- ment (Lockhart and Mason, 1989; MTA, 1999).

Greeks have inhabited Cyprus – 800 km from the mainland of Greece and less than 100 km from Turkey – since ancient times. The island was absorbed by the Ottoman Turks in 1571 and remained in their hands until 1878, when it was ceded to Britain for administrative purposes. At the outbreak of World War I the British formally annexed Cyprus. Civil violence began in 1955 with Greek demands for *enosis* – union with Greece. This was resisted strongly by the Turkish population, who, as a counter, pressed for a partition of Cyprus into Turkish and Greek sectors. Britain had two military bases on the island, reflecting Cyprus' role as a last remaining British defence garrison in the eastern Mediterranean. In 1959 preparations for independence began, and the Republic of Cyprus was constituted in 1960, being admitted to the British Commonwealth the following year. Independence was guaranteed by Britain, Greece and Turkey, under agreements signed in Zurich and London. This status prohibited union with another state, or partition of the island into two or more parts. The president would be Greek and the vice-president Turkish. British sovereignty was retained over the two areas used as military bases. Despite throwing off the colonial yoke, there developed little concept of a Cypriot nationhood. Citizens con- tinued to think of themselves either as Greek or Turkish Cypriots (Hall, 2000a), and at the time of independence, the island's demographic (im)balance was 80% Greek Cypriot and 20% Turkish Cypriot.

The use of the English language as *lingua franca*

The contemporary common use of English on both islands is of course a heritage of their colonial past. The Maltese language is Arabic-derived, while employing the Roman script – the only Semitic language to do so. Greek or Turkish, of course, represents the first language for most Cypriots, with English often employed as a mediating vehicle for communication.

A mass 3Ss tourism industry based to a large extent on the demands of the UK market

As English-speaking with a colonial heritage coupled to a warm and sunny Mediterranean climate, tourism development aimed at the UK market was an obvious economic option for both countries which gained independence just as the inclusive holiday industry was taking off. In both islands the tourism industry's evolution has also resulted in patterns of uneven regional development, albeit not untypical for the Mediterranean (Hadjimichalis, 1987; Dunford, 1997).

That both Malta and Cyprus have sought subsequently to diversify away from mass-market dependence – a lingering colonial heritage whose erosion EU membership could either encourage or constrain – is emphasized in the following two chapters (17 and 18). What this overview chapter wishes to suggest is that there are comparable underlying structural issues influencing the effectiveness and implications of such policies. In Malta, for example, in the process of trying to change that mass image, as discussed in Chapter 17, a number of environmental conflicts have arisen (e.g. Markwick, 2000, 2001; Bramwell, 2003).

Political Division and the Accession Process

Political division has characterized the recent history of Malta and Cyprus and has notably interacted with processes of accession.

However, the nature of such division differs markedly between the two, spatially, structurally and culturally.

Three years after independence, Malta indicated that it wished to establish formal contractual relations with the EEC. Subsequent negotiations led to the signing of the EC–Malta Association Agreement which came into force in April 1971, and covered trade-related issues, legal approximation and other areas of cooperation, including industry, environment, transport and customs (EC, 2000). It formalized close links between the Community and Malta, with a gradual removal of trade barriers to allow unhindered access to each other's markets by the end of the 20th century. This resulted in the EU accounting for more than half of Malta's exports and over two-thirds of total imports by the late 1990s (EC, 1999a).

Malta's essentially two-party post-independence political system has generated fierce political debate within the islands, and on certain issues – not least EU membership – this has proved to be severely divisive. Although a small and relatively ethnically homogenous state, Malta has been viewed as having one of the purest two-party political systems in the developed world (Cini, 2002). Intense political rivalry, and its polarization of Maltese society, have been complemented by a culture of patronage, exacerbated by the fact that elections have often been won by small margins of votes, often leading to inaction due to an inability to pass and enforce laws. As a result, government policies 'may end up as a tattered patchwork of conflicting client demands' (Mallia, 1994, p. 700). Within this context, political polarization has also been viewed in terms of 'traditionalists' and 'modernizers' (Mitchell, 2002).

This division complicated Malta's path to EU accession, rendering an ambivalence to the concept of the country's 'Europeanization' (e.g. Cini, 2000). Baldacchino (2002) contended that this was partly the result of Malta's status as a 'nation-less state', characterized by post-colonial, small island nationalism, but with a history of attempted integration with France, Italy, Britain and Libya. Yet the country's small size has also allowed the Maltese to win concessions from the EU (e.g. Pace, 2002). This is exemplified later in the chapter.

The Nationalist Party government formally applied for European Community membership in 1990. Three years later, publication of a favourable *Opinion* by the European Commission saw EU-Malta relations oriented towards the goal of accession. However, the coming to power of a nationalist, anti-Europe Labour government in October 1996 saw Malta's application for EU membership placed in abeyance, only for accession negotiations to recommence in September 1998 with a return to government of the Nationalist Party. Five months later the European Commission recommended that accession negotiations should commence by the end of 1999; but reports in the Maltese press suggested that Brussels was concerned about the country's anti-EU membership lobby. Led by the opposition Labour Party, this movement appeared to be better organized and more vocal than pro-accession supporters. The message was clear that the Maltese government urgently needed to crystallize a distinctive policy framework favouring EU membership as other applicant countries had done (Manduca, 1999).

Despite a deeply divisive internal party political structure, the European Commission's 1999 *Regular Report* (EC, 1999b) concluded that Malta was a functioning market economy and should be able to cope with competitive pressures and market forces within the EU, although it needed to continue with industrial restructuring (Hall, 2000b). The EU leaders' meeting in Helsinki in December 1999 formally invited Malta, along with five other applicants, to start accession talks, and negotiations with the EU were brought to a successful conclusion in December 2002. In Malta's subsequent referendum of March 2003, a 53.65% majority vote in favour of membership led the government to call a general election in the following month. The governing Nationalist Party won 51.7% of the vote based on a 96% turnout, reinforcing the government's confidence to confirm acceptance of the package presented to Malta by the European Union for accession in May 2004.

In 1971, the Government of Cyprus entered into negotiations with the EEC and in December 1972 an association agreement was signed between the two parties. This was one of the EEC's first such treaties, aiming to establish a customs union within a period of 10 years. The agreement came into force the following

year with arrangements intended to benefit the population of the whole island. As noted in Chapter 1, Cyprus was politically divided in 1974 when a coup backed by Athens to annex the island to Greece triggered a Turkish military occupation of the north (Fig. 16.1). The political and economic consequences of these actions delayed full implementation, such that a second stage of the Association Agreement was only signed in Luxembourg in 1987, with provisions for a customs union between 'Cyprus' and the EU to be completed by 2003 at the latest.

In 1990 the (South) Republic of Cyprus applied to join the European Community. The European Commission's 1993 *Opinion* considered Cyprus to be eligible for membership, and 'in expectation of progress on the political problem' (i.e. reunification) confirmed that the EC was ready to start the process with Cyprus that should lead to its eventual accession (EC, 1997).

Substantive accession negotiations began in November 1998. Prior to the important December 1999 Helsinki summit, the European Commission's report on (the Republic of) Cyprus' progress towards EU accession concluded that it had fulfilled the Copenhagen political criteria, was a functioning market economy able to cope with the competitive pressures and market forces within the EU, but should accelerate progress towards privatization (EC, 1999c). This was a similar response to that for Malta. However, there was a caveat: Cyprus needed to adopt several pieces of sectoral legislation to permit alignment with the environment *acquis*, and needed to reinforce administrative capacity in the maritime transport and environment sectors (EC, 1999c).

The EU position on political division was that the status quo imposed by the Turkish invasion of 1974 and the continued occupation by Turkish troops of 37% of the island's territory, was unacceptable. The EU supported the efforts of the United Nations to reach a negotiated and comprehensive settlement that would respect the sovereignty, independence, territorial integrity and unity of the country within a bi-communal and bi-zonal federation. These principles – the Ghali 'set of ideas' established by the UN Secretary General Boutros Boutros-Ghali in 1992 and endorsed by the UN Security Council – stipulated that EU membership should be decided upon only

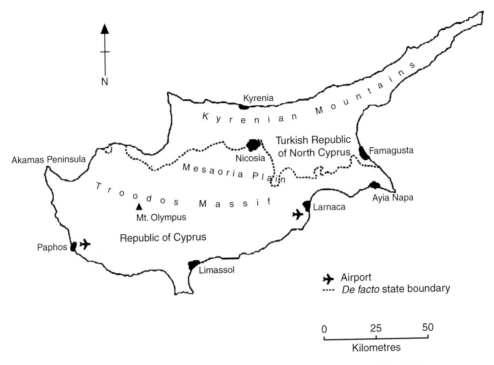

Fig. 16.1. Cyprus: location map with the demarcation line. Source: Alipour and Kilic, 2004.

after the Cyprus problem had been settled, and through separate referendums of the two peoples (Bolukbasi, 1995, 1998).

The Commission's *Agenda 2000* (EC, 1997) confirmed that accession negotiations would begin as planned and reiterated the EU's determination to play a positive role in bringing about a just and lasting settlement in accordance with UN resolutions. Yet, almost paradoxically, the timetable agreed for accession negotiations meant that they could start before a political settlement was reached, with the EU arguing that negotiations could stimulate the search for a political settlement. If sufficient progress was made between the parties to allow representatives of the Turkish Cypriot community to be involved in the accession process, this would permit a faster conclusion to the accession negotiations. However, *Agenda 2000* indicated that if progress towards a settlement was not reached before the negotiations were due to begin, they should be opened with the government of the Republic of Cyprus as the only authority recognized by international law.

For its part, the Greek government indicated that Athens would veto the process of wider enlargement if Cyprus was omitted. It argued that Cyprus could not be allowed to become a 'hostage' of Turkey. Further, until the December 1999 Helsinki Summit, Greece had blocked moves towards inaugurating accession discussions with Turkey (Anon, 1998).

Since the end of the Cold War, Turkey's relationship with Europe had been changing. Having been a loyal eastern NATO bastion and crucial listening post, its strategic importance for the West had declined just at a time when the EU was forging ahead for economic and political integration with some of the states against whom Turkey's NATO role had been employed. Turkey had also been experiencing domestic instability concerning the role of Islam in its society and the rights of its Kurdish minority population. Until the 1999 Helsinki Summit there had been growing recrimination between the EU and Turkey as the latter had watched former Cold War 'enemy' countries from CEE leapfrog its own long-standing application for membership.

The Turkish Cypriot view of the 1990 application for EC membership was that it was a unilateral action on the part of the Greek Cypriot administration and not on behalf of Cyprus as a whole. The North's position was that the bi-communal Republic of Cyprus established in accordance with the 1959–60 Zurich and London Agreements was still in force. Turkish Cypriots viewed the Greek Cypriot objective to be the destruction of these fundamental rights and status by the accession application, and by so doing to shift the equilibrium between Turkey and Greece over Cyprus substantially in favour of Greece. Once 'Cyprus' was accepted as a member of the EU, the Treaty of Guarantee would be inapplicable against an EU member state and, by virtue of EU laws, all the basic principles enshrined in the Ghali proposals regarding a bi-zonal, bi-communal settlement would be of no effect (Richmond, 1999).

In talks with NATO counterparts, Turkey threatened to proceed with a 'partial integration' of the Turkish-controlled north of the island if the EU started membership negotiations with the Greek Cypriot government in the spring of 1998. Some Turkish politicians argued that Ankara should block entry of the Czech Republic, Hungary and Poland to NATO by refusing to ratify that organization's expansion. For their part, the Greek Cypriot government's ordering of S-300 missile systems from Russia further heightened tension in the region (Mather and Krushelnycky, 1998).

It was therefore with some relief that, at the December 1999 EU leaders' summit in Helsinki, Greece lifted the veto it had wielded for the past decade on accession talks with Ankara. Turkey was now assigned the status of a candidate country, although a timetable for accession discussions was not established. Greece had not accepted the principle of eventual Turkish EU membership without imposing conditions. In addition to the normal EU requirements for improving human rights, democratic structures and economic reform, Turkey would have to agree to take any territorial disputes with Greece in the Aegean to the International Court of Justice in The Hague. Further, Turkey had to face the subsequent prospect of 'Cyprus' becoming an EU member in May 2004 before any internal political settlement had been reached (Müftüler-Bac, 1999).

Environmental Issues

The path of accession has acted as a catalyst for change in many aspects of national policy for all new member states. It was during this process that increasing attention was paid to Malta's environmental questions, and not least issues related to growing traffic and pollution problems. This was reinforced by the fact that the EC's *Regular Report* for 2002 (CEC, 2002, pp. 60–62, 84–88) highlighted the need for administrative capacity strengthening in the fields of both transport and environment. These problems held clear implications for the vitality of the tourism industry (Attard and Hall, 2004).

Malta has one of the highest per capita levels of car ownership in the Mediterranean and Europe, with over 500 cars per 1000 inhabitants (Malta Transport Authority, 2003). The number of motor vehicles on the islands grew by 116% in the last 15 years of the 20th century. By 1998 there were four times as many work-related trips being made by car than by public transport (MEPA, 2002). Further, all major international rental companies are represented in Malta, together with a larger number of small local businesses that run rental vehicle services in tourist areas, such that by 2000 there were almost 340,000 annual tourist hire car contracts being issued. The growth of this mode of transport has heightened pressure on infrastructure and the need for road space. Demand for such space has been skewed by the high population densities concentrated in just under 22% of the land area, exacerbated by a large tourist population concentrated in many of the same areas, and increasing dependence on the motor car (albeit with no motorway-grade highway), there being no heavy or light rail systems surviving (Attard and Hall, 2003, 2004). Table 16.1 presents a comparative overview of different European and Mediterranean countries.

Malta has attracted more than a million tourists every year since the early 1990s. Marked seasonality has heightened pressures on the country's infrastructure, especially energy supply, water quality, waste disposal and transport provision (Lockhart, 1997). The physical impact of tourism is complicated and to some extent obscured by a number of dynamic processes. Most notable of these are:

- the increasing incidence of retirement immigration, particularly from the UK, with migrants being both participants in, and recipients of, visiting friends and relatives tourism (Williams *et al.*, 2000); and
- new housing appears to have contributed much more to land-take than has new tourism development (Ministry of Tourism, 1999; Planning Authority, 2001), but an unknown number of new apartments and houses are used by Maltese as second homes, by returning émigrés, by international tourists, and by retirement immigrants.

Certainly, as tourism has grown, it is clear that resulting increased physical congestion both on the country's roads and on its beaches has become less acceptable (Boissevain and Theuma, 1998) (Fig. 16.2). The country's 1989 tourism master plan called for the development of higher quality tourism and for the encouragement of winter and spring attractions to reduce the high level of seasonality of international arrivals. As a result, sports such as diving and golf, alongside cultural and rural tourism, were given a higher level of development

encouragement and promotion (Markwick, 1999, 2000, 2001). Such a policy has, however, led to environmental conflicts involving both the natural resources and residents of the islands, exacerbating social and environmental pressures, in terms of:

- traffic congestion pinch-points;
- tourist congestion and intrusion at cultural sites;
- excessive land-take at key locations for luxury hotels;
- land and water demands for golf courses; and
- the space demands and marine pollution impacts of marina development.

Critically, such continued encroachment on the Maltese people's own leisure space has been seen to echo colonial times when the British administration prevented public access to large areas of rural Malta (Boissevain and Theuma, 1998, p. 114–115). Notably, the promotion of golf tourism requires the diversion of scarce water resources and valuable land-take (Planning Authority, 1997; Markwick, 2000). On the other hand, logistical and moral conflicts have arisen as a consequence of foreign tourists visiting the countryside and

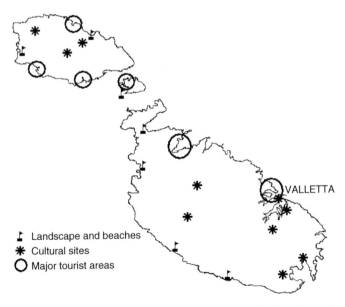

Fig. 16.2. The Maltese islands: distribution of tourist areas and cultural sites. Source: Attard and Hall, 2004 (compiled by Maria Attard).

being intimidated by local hunters and trappers, of whom there are an estimated 20,000 (Fenech, 1992), especially where the latter have carried out their pursuits in 'protected' areas (Markwick, 2001).

Attempts to align Malta's environmental legislation with EU requirements precipitated strong reaction from the politically articulate hunting lobby on a number of occasions (Borg, 1996). These issues entered party politics and have contributed to the often sharp tensions on questions of EU accession. As a consequence, and to the dismay of many environmentalists and nature lovers, Malta gained a number of concessions from the EU during its accession negotiations relating to environmental issues. In particular, the hunting and trapping of wild birds was allowed to continue. While Malta accepted that it should adopt EU law (EC, 1979) on the protection of birds, it argued that hunting and trapping wild birds was a traditional pursuit. As a central element of Maltese culture it reflected Malta's particular biogeographical circumstances, and as such, should be maintained (Box 16.1).

In Cyprus, challenges to the tourism sector have been exacerbated in the short term by the unsatisfactory process and outcome of accession (Warner, 1999), although tourism's prime developmental characteristics – boosterism (Hall, 1999) in the south, and institutional fragility in the north – remain. In summary, the challenges facing the sector include:

- the overall sustainability of tourism activity and growth;
- lack of policy or policy clarity, and the low level of priority for resolving problems and lack of authority vested in tourism bodies to overcome them, with consequently poor monitoring and feedback;
- lack of environmental education and community information, and thus absence of a culture of environmental awareness and informed participation;
- lack of economic diversification and thus dependency on tourism, with only limited success in diversifying away from the 3Ss markets;
- inability to curb over-development and coastal degradation resulting from the intensity of construction, with the coastal

---

Box 16.1. Hunting and trapping in Malta.

The two main species hunted are turtle dove and quail. Under EU law (EC, 1979), hunting in spring is normally prohibited to protect migrating birds. Yet the EC acceded to Malta's derogation from this part of EU law so that the Maltese could continue to hunt in spring for these birds. Hunting was also permitted to continue to take place between September and the end of January each year. Bird hunting at sea was also allowed to continue from 3 km off the coast: the argument for this is that Malta has no wetlands to attract wildfowl onto land.

Trapping is a traditional method of capturing birds through the use of personally operated nets. Birds that are trapped are not killed but are kept in captivity. Trapping was allowed to continue, conditionally, for a number of songbird species, including goldfinch, greenfinch, chaffinch, linnet, hawfinch and siskin. The conditions relate to a number of measures that need to be implemented by 2008:

- a study conducted to assess the sustainability of trapping finches by establishing how many birds may be captured from the wild to maintain the genetic diversity of the birds in captivity;
- a full captive breeding system established with trappers trained in avian breeding;
- the registration of all trapping sites; and
- no new licences issued during the period of study.

Sources: Attard and Cordina, 2002; FKNK, 2003; IAR, 2003.

---

concentration of physical development and urbanization constraining opportunities for establishing strong back-linkages with rural hinterlands; and
- unsatisfactory implementation of planning approaches (e.g. Ioannides, 1995; Saveriades, 2000; Sharpley, 2001; Alipour and Kilic, 2004; CTO, 2005).

These raise issues of 'policy credibility' (Grabel, 2000), whereby the political economy of partition in both South and North Cyprus has exacerbated the environmental consequences of tourism (Fig. 16.3). The 'policy credibility' model emphasizes that endogenously determined factors are crucial (Box 16.2), challenging the approach of the

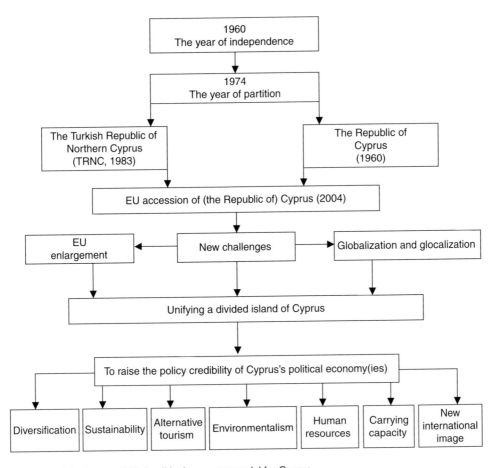

Fig. 16.3. A 'policy credibility' political economy model for Cyprus.

Box 16.2. Endogenous factors constraining environmental policy in Cyprus.

- Under-utilization of the island's resources.
- Spatial and organizational discontinuities and fragmentation of development and infrastructure.
- Disrupted mobility.
- Land market, planning and development uncertainties.
- The psychological impact of the North's lack of recognition by the UN and other international bodies, and the lack of recognition of the South by Turkey.
- Militarization.
- Ethnic tension.
- Regional imbalances.
- High transaction costs.
- Environmental apathy and neglect in respect of sustainability.

Sources: Zetter, 1994; Kliot and Mansfeld, 1997; Ioannides and Apostolopoulos, 1999; Milne, 2003.

island's authorities who argue that exoge-
nous forces are paramount in determining
continuing division and its manifold consequences (e.g. see Jayasuriya, 2001; WBI,
2003; Alipour and Kilic, 2004).

The 'environment' has remained a neglected area both in terms of institutional capacity and policy implementation, as emphasized
in the Republic of Cyprus *Strategic Plan for
Tourism 2000–2010* (CTO, 2005). This is
in stark contrast to the perceived importance
of the environment within EU policy-making
and the fact that environmentally related policies have become one of the fastest growing
areas of policy implementation elsewhere
(Ruzza, 2000). The EU 1992 framework document *Towards Sustainability*, expressly targeted the environmental impact of tourism.
The influential Fifth EC Environmental Action
Programme, approved by the Council in
1993, made explicit the intention to incorpo-
rate environmental awareness into a wide
number of sectors, including tourism (Ruzza,
2000, p. 292).

> The EU has transformed environmental
> policymaking for the states of Europe. There
> are now close to 300 environmental regulations
> and directives governing environmental policy
> throughout the member states. In many
> environmental policy areas the EU now plays
> an international leadership role.
>   (Schreurs, 2004, p. 27)

This is important, for example, because
coastal over-development and urban visual
pollution (e.g. Anon, 1999, 2001) have hitherto not been constrained, because of weak
environmental bureaucracies in both the South
and North. However, the twin forces of EU
environmental requirements and apparent
market pressures for tourism 'sustainability'
now require a better understanding and holistic approach to ecological issues by tourism
managers.

The issue of 'sustainability' as a conceptual paradigm has become a significant policy
issue within the international development
community. It has evolved beyond being just a
fashionable buzzword, but has become a policy dimension emphasizing 'values associated
with cultural and community diversity, concern
for social issues of justice and fairness, and a
strong orientation toward stability. The evolution

of the term "sustainable development" refers
to all development paths that are environmentally beneficial and lasting' (Ahn *et al.*, 2002,
p. 2). With the EU accession of (South)
Cyprus in 2004, the opening of the borders
between two Greek and Turkish enclaves on
the island, and the acceptance of Turkey to
start negotiations in October 2005 towards
full membership, a euphoric wave of investment and development, especially in tourism,
swept the North, raising numerous questions
concerning the credibility of 'sustainability'
policies.

In the South's strategic plan for tourism
2000–2010, a great deal of environmental
concern is elaborated, its practical expression
having been contingent upon alignment with
EU environmental practices and norms (CTO,
2005). In the North, while institutional short-
comings and their consequences are similar in
degree, more than three decades of sanctions
and embargoes have had an environmental
dividend in terms of the limited nature of new
capital development, not least in mass tourism. Indeed, an intriguing question faces the
North, caught between the struggle for recognition on one hand and the possibility of unification on the other: assuming the island's
political situation improves, will EU norms
and practices be adopted and implemented
before the rush of (re-)development takes
place in response to a reopening to mass
markets?

With the inauguration of accession negotiations with Turkey, and enhanced hopes for
North Cyprus to become a *de facto* functioning
part of the EU, it is time to institutionalize
the issue of tourism sustainability beyond *ad
hoc* mechanisms of integrating environmental
elements into tourism plans. At present,
there appears not to be an appropriate and
well- thought-out model available, especially in
the areas of strategic environmental assessment
(SEA), environmental impact assessment (EIA),
and sustainability impact assessment (SIA)
(Basiago, 1999; Boulanger and Bréchet, 2005).
This is at a time when the EU has adopted such
models as a fundamental policy element of its
development agenda, and across Europe a
great deal of effort is being put into
operationalizing these models in the tourism
sector as well as in regional planning strategies

(Ahn *et al.*, 2002; Masters, 2004; Boulanger and Bréchet, 2005).

Irreversible damage can be inflicted upon the fragile and small-scale nature of North Cyprus if policies are not in place, especially in newly developing tourist zones in the coastal areas (e.g. Bafra), and in the form of intense urbanization around Kyrenia. In both cases, 'sustainability' remains uncertain as there is no sign of any policy or measure to assess limits of acceptable change (LAC) as an essential mechanism for sustainability management (Ahn *et al.*, 2002). For example, the daily Turkish language newspaper *Kibris* has pointed to both the impact caused by mining companies in the current construction boom and the apathy of the government in response to it (Kibris, 2005, pp. 1–4). Over 211 registered construction firms are busy building without environmental impact assessment or a master plan in place. This situation is exacerbated by an unknown number of construction firms who are not registered with the Cyprus Turkish Construction/Contractors Association (CTCA). This most likely will have irreversible consequences upon the environment and the sustainability of this fragile destination (personal interview with the CTCA, 2005).

An environmental strategic partnership between at least the appropriate bodies from the South, the North, the EU and the UNDP (which is highly active in a number of developmental and cultural areas including small ecotourism projects), is required.

Certainly, one area of concern for Cyprus as a whole is actual or potential unfettered coastal development, since the island lacks an integrated coastal management plan (ICMP). This fundamental priority for managing coastal areas (Tagliani, 2003) requires integration with resource and structure planning at local and regional levels (Gunn and Var, 2002). Clearly, the two communities of Cyprus share the same ecosystems, and (inter-) community level tourism and other development planning processes need to be implemented within a collaborative framework (e.g. Murphy and Murphy, 2004). Indeed, public participation has become a fundamental aspect of planning and environment within the EU, and this needs to be acknowledged and implemented within Cyprus as a whole.

Conclusions

Cyprus and Malta are no longer small, peripheral entities in the Mediterranean, but are integral elements of a larger and globally important socio-economic and political structure. Being a part of this structure calls for modified or new policy behaviour while confronting existing and new challenges. In their pre-accession economic model, Blake *et al.* (2003) suggested that accession would be beneficial to both countries, although as a percentage of GDP, Malta would benefit considerably more than Cyprus. However, the effects of accession on tourism would be negative for Malta because greater impacts from trade and EU funding allocations would lead to a higher demand for labour that would increase wage rates and divert manpower away from tourism.

Malta and Cyprus constitute important crossroads and cultural links between Europe and the lands of the south and east Mediterranean Basin. Both need to address issues of capacity building, and, specifically within tourism, the generation of credible diversification policies that express sustainability objectives. Being linking agents comes at a price: while Malta's Valletta harbour has been restructured to accommodate increasing numbers of cruise liners, so the country's security institutions are having to confront the political and moral dilemmas of a rapid increase in numbers of economic migrants and asylum seekers from Africa (116 in 2001, rising to 1227 in 2004) (Campbell, 2005). For Cyprus, the interrelated issues of overcoming division and establishing a working relationship with the rest of the eastern Mediterranean have profound implications for the development of tourism in the region.

Ensuring good prospects for European tourism requires the preservation of its regional diversity as an asset for competitiveness, ensuring quality and considering community well-being in tourist destinations, conserving or protecting the environment and heritage resources and using them wisely, and promoting sustainable inter- and intra-destination mobility. It also depends on equitable access and remuneration for local providers (EU, 2003, pp. 6–7). These requirements present serious challenges to all stakeholders in Cyprus and Malta.

References

Ahn, B.Y., Lee, B.K. and Shafer, C.S. (2002) Operationalizing sustainability in regional tourism planning: an application of the limits of acceptable change framework. *Tourism Management* 23(1), 1–15.

Alipour, H. and Kilic, H. (2004) Tourism development and planning in constrained circumstances: an institutional appraisal of the Turkish Republic of North Cyprus (TRNC). In: Hall, D. (ed.) *Tourism and Transition: Governance, Transformation and Development*. Wallingford, UK: CAB International, pp. 133–146.

Anon (1998) Cyprus problem could threaten EU expansion. *Cyprus Mail*, 11 November, p. 3.

Anon (1999) Kotu Turizm. *Cyprus Daily*, 22 January, p. 4.

Anon (2001) Turizmde Husran. *Cyprus Daily*, 17 July, p. 14.

Attard, C. and Cordina, E. (2002) Hunting and trapping. *Aġġornat* 13, 1–2.

Attard, M. and Hall, D. (2003) Public transport modernisation and adjustment to EU accession requirements: the case of Malta's buses. *Journal of Transport Geography* 11(1), 13–24.

Attard, M. and Hall, D. (2004) Transition for EU accession: the case of Malta's restructuring tourism and transport sectors. In: Hall, D. (ed.) *Tourism and Transition: Governance, Transformation and Development*. Wallingford, UK: CAB International, pp. 119–132.

Baldacchino, G. (2002) A nationless state? Malta, national identity and the EU. *West European Politics* 25(4), 191–206.

Basiago, A.D. (1999) Economic, social, and environmental sustainability in development theory and urban planning practice. *The Environmentalist* 19(1), 145–161.

Blake, A., Sinclair, M.T. and Sugiyarto, G. (2003) *Tourism and EU Accession in Malta and Cyprus*. Nottingham: University of Nottingham, Tourism and Travel Research Institute (TTRI) Discussion Paper 2003/7. Available at: http://www.nottingham.ac.uk/ttri/pdf/2003_7.pdf

Boissevain, J. and Theuma, N. (1998) Contested space: planners, tourists, developers and environmentalists in Malta. In: Abram, S. and Waldren, J. (eds) *Anthropological Perspectives on Local Development*. London: Routledge, pp. 96–119.

Bolukbasi, S. (1995) Boutros-Ghali Cyprus initiative in 1992 – why did it fail? *Middle Eastern Studies* 31(3), 460–482.

Bolukbasi, S. (1998) The Cyprus dispute and the United Nations: peaceful non-settlement between 1954 and 1996. *International Journal of Middle East Studies* 30(3), 411–434.

Borg, A. (1996) Rural versus urban: environmental perceptions in Malta. In: Fladmark, J. (ed.) *Sharing the Earth: Local Identity and Global Culture*. Wimbledon, UK: Donhead, pp. 111–125.

Boulanger, P.-M. and Bréchet, T. (2005) Models for policy-making in sustainable development: the state of the art and perspectives for research. *Ecological Economics* 55(3), 337–350.

Bramwell, B. (2003) Maltese responses to tourism. *Annals of Tourism Research* 30(3), 581–605.

Campbell, D. (2005) Saved from the sea. Stuck in limbo. *The Guardian*, 5 October, p. 17.

CEC (Commission of the European Communities) (2002) *2002 Regular Report on Malta's Progress Towards Accession*. Brussels: CEC. Available at: http://europe.eu.int/comm/enlargement/report2002/ml_en.pdf

Cini, M. (2000) The Europeanization of Malta: adaptation, identity and party politics. *South European Society and Politics* 5(2), 261–276.

Cini, M. (2002) A divided nation: polarization and the two-party system in Malta. *South European Society and Politics* 7(1), 6–23.

CTO (2005) *Strategic Plan for Tourism 2000–2010*. Nicosia: Cyprus Tourism Organization.

Dunford, M. (1997) Mediterranean economies: the dynamics of uneven development. In: King, R., Proudfoot, L. and Smith, B. (eds) *The Mediterranean Environment and Society*. London: Arnold, pp. 126–154.

EC (European Commission) (1979) *Council Directive 79/409/EEC of 2 April 1979 on the Conservation of Wild Birds*. Brussels: EC. Available at: http://europa.eu.int/comm/environment/nature/bird-dir.htm

EC (European Commission) (1997) *Agenda 2000*. Brussels: EC.

EC (European Commission) (1999a) *Economic Developments and Structural Reform in the Candidate Countries. Country Notes: Malta*. Brussels: EC Economic Reform Monitor No. 3.

EC (European Commission) (1999b) *Regular Report from the Commission on Progress Towards Accession: Malta – October 13, 1999*. Brussels: EC.

EC (European Commission) (1999c) *Regular Report from the Commission on the Progress Towards EU Accession. Cyprus – October 13, 1999*. Brussels: EC.

EC (European Commission) (2000) *Enlargement. Pre-Accession Strategy. Pre-Accession Instruments.* Brussels: EC.

EU (European Union) (2003) *Basic Orientations for the Sustainability of European Tourism.* Brussels: Commission of the European Communities.

Eurostat (2005) *Eurostat.* Luxembourg: Eurostat. Available at: http://epp.eurostat.cec.eu.int/portal

Fenech, N. (1992) *Fatal Flight: the Maltese Obsession with Killing Birds.* London: Quiller Press.

FKNK (The Federation for Hunting and Conservation, Malta) (2003) *The Federation for Hunting and Conservation, Malta.* Valletta: FKNK. Available at: http://www.huntinginmalta.org.mt

Grabel, I. (2000) The political economy of 'policy credibility': the new-classical macroeconomics and the remaking of emerging economies. *Cambridge Journal of Economics* 24(1), 1–19.

Gunn, C.A. and Var, T. (2002) *Tourism Planning.* New York: Routledge, 4th edn.

Hadjimichalis, C. (1987) *Uneven Development and Regionalism: State, Territory and Class in Southern Europe.* Beckenham, UK: Croom Helm.

Hall, C.M. (1999) *Tourism Planning: Policies, Processes and Relationships.* Harlow, UK: Longman.

Hall, D. (2000a) Cyprus. In: Hall, D. and Danta, D. (eds) *Europe Goes East: EU Enlargement, Diversity and Uncertainty.* London: The Stationery Office, pp. 155–167.

Hall, D. (2000b) Malta. In: Hall, D. and Danta, D. (eds) *Europe Goes East: EU Enlargement, Diversity and Uncertainty.* London: The Stationery Office, pp. 245–253.

IAR (International Animal Rescue) (2003) *Report on the EU-Malta Agreement.* Valletta: IAR (Malta). Available at: http://www.iar.org/malta/articles/aug03.shtml

Ioannides, D. (1995) A flawed implementation of sustainable tourism: the experience of Akamas, Cyprus. *Tourism Management* 16(8), 583–592.

Ioannides, D. and Apostolopoulos, Y. (1999) Political instability, war, and tourism in Cyprus: effects, management, and prospects for recovery. *Journal of Travel Research* 38(1), 51–56.

Jayasuriya, K. (2001) Globalization and the changing architecture of the state: the regulatory state and the politics of negative co-ordination. *Journal of European Public Policy* 8(1), 101–123.

Kibris (2005) Doga yok oluyor ['Murdering the environment'] *Kibris,* 16 September, pp. 1–4.

Kliot, N. and Mansfeld, Y. (1997) The political landscape of partition: the case of Cyprus. *Political Geography* 16(6), 495–521.

Lockhart, D. (1997) Tourism to Malta and Cyprus. In: Lockhart, D. and Drakakis-Smith, D. (eds) *Island Tourism: Trends and Prospects.* London: Pinter, pp. 152–178.

Lockhart, D. and Mason, K. (1989) *A Social and Economic Atlas of Malta and Gozo.* Keele, UK: Department of Geography, University of Keele.

Mallia, E. (1994) Land use: an account of environmental stewardship. In: Sultana, R. and Baldacchino, G. (eds) *Maltese Society: a Sociological Enquiry.* Msida: Mireva, pp. 685–705.

Malta Transport Authority (2003) Country Profile: Malta. Cagliari, Sardinia: Paper presented at the conference *Public Transport Laws and Operating Systems,* 28 March.

Manduca, A. (1999) Brussels wants pro-EU lobby to be better orgnised. *The Malta Business Weekly,* 26 August.

Markwick, M. (1999) Malta's tourism industry since 1985: diversification, cultural tourism and issues of sustainability. *Scottish Geographical Journal* 115(1), 53–72.

Markwick, M. (2000) Golf tourism development, stakeholders, differing discourses and alternative agendas: the case of Malta. *Tourism Management* 21, 515–524.

Markwick, M. (2001) Alternative tourism: change, commodification and contestation of Malta's landscapes. *Geography* 86(3), 250–255.

Masters, M. (2004) Basis and tools for a sustainable development of estuaries and coastal areas: a case study from Cullera Bay. *Management of Environmental Quality* 15(1), 25–32.

Mather, I. and Krushelnycky, A. (1998) Moscow's missile meddling raises spectre of war. *The European,* 6 April, pp. 14–16.

MEPA (Malta Environment and Planning Authority) (2002) *Transport Topic Paper.* Floriana: MEPA.

Milne, D. (2003) One state or two? Political realism on the Cyprus question. *The Round Table* 368, 145–162.

Ministry of Tourism (1999) *Carrying Capacity Assessment for Tourism in the Maltese Islands: Survey Draft.* Valletta: Ministry of Tourism.

Mitchell, J.P. (2002) Corruption and clientelism in a 'systemless system': the Europeanization of Maltese political culture. *European Society and Politics* 7(1), 43–62.

Mizzi, L. (1994) *Socio-economic Development and the Environment in Malta.* Bristol, UK: Centre for Mediterranean Studies, University of Bristol.

MTA (Malta Tourism Authority) (1999) *A New Brand Image for Malta.* Valletta: MTA.

Müftüler-Bac, M. (1999) The Cyprus debacle: what the future holds. *Futures* 31(6), 559–575.

Murphy, P.E. and Murphy, A.E. (2004*) Strategic Management for Tourism Communities.* Clevedon, UK: Channel View Publications.

Pace, R. (2002) A small state and the European Union: Malta's EU accession experience. *South European Society and Politics* 7(1), 24–42.

Planning Authority (1997) *Golf Course Development in Malta: a Policy Paper.* Floriana: Malta Planning Authority.

Planning Authority (2001) *Structure Plan for the Maltese Islands: Tourism Topic Paper Draft for Public Consultation: Response to Comments.* Floriana: Malta Planning Authority.

Richmond, O.P. (1999) Ethno-nationalism, sovereignty and negotiating positions in the Cyprus conflict: obstacles to a settlement. *Middle Eastern Studies* 35(3), 42–63.

Ruzza, C. (2000) Environmental sustainability and tourism in European policy-making. *Innovation* 13(3), 291–310.

Saveriades, A. (2000) Establishing the social tourism carrying capacity for the tourist resorts of the east coast of the Republic of Cyprus. *Tourism Management* 21(2), 147–156.

Schreurs, M. (2004) Environmental protection in an expanding European Community: lessons from past accessions. *Environmental Politics* 13(1), 27–51.

Sharpley, R. (2001) Tourism in Cyprus: challenges and opportunities. *Tourism Geographies* 3(1), 64–86.

Tagliani, P.R.A. (2003) Integrated coastal zone management in the Patos Lagoon estuary: perspectives in the context of a developing country. *Ocean and Coastal Management* 46(9–10), 807–822.

Warner, J. (1999) North Cyprus: tourism and the challenge of non-recognition. *Journal of Sustainable Tourism* 7(2), 128–145.

WBI (World Bank Institute) (2003) *Glocalization.* Rome: World Bank Institute.

Williams, A.M., King, R., Warnes, T. and Patterson, G. (2000) Tourism and international retirement migration: new forms of an old relationship in southern Europe. *Tourism Geographies* 2(1), 28–49.

Zetter, R. (1994) The Greek-Cypriot refugees: perceptions of return under conditions of protracted exile. *International Migration Review* 28(2), 307–322.

17 Malta: Re-imaging the Mediterranean Destination

Nadia Theuma

Introduction

Situated at the centre of the Mediterranean, the Maltese islands are very often seen as a sun-and-sea destination attracting mainly summer tourism and mass tourists. The islands are also endowed with rich cultural and historical assets, that until recently were seen as an 'add-on' rather than a main feature of the tourism product. Tourism in Malta is based on tour-operator business, with about 76% of the business being tour-operator generated.

Malta's tourism development pattern follows closely the classic model of a tourism development cycle (Butler, 1980) where, after very modest beginnings, tourism in Malta went through a phase of rapid growth in volume, followed by stagnation and rejuvenation. Throughout the years there has been an emphasis on Malta's image as a destination. This chapter will analyse changes in tourism in Malta over the past three decades and the actions adopted by Maltese tourism authorities to reposition the islands. In doing so, it will highlight the difficulties encountered when operating in an environment of increased competition, limited financial resources common to small scale economies and a new political and strategic alliance brought about by the accession to the European Union.

Tourism Development in the Maltese Islands 1950s–1990s

Although present since the beginning of the 20th century, tourism in Malta was officially launched in 1958, when Malta was still a British colony (Pollacco, 2003). Since then, tourism has experienced a rapid growth with the number of visitors increasing from 12,583 in 1959 to 1.13m in 2003 (Table 17.1). Today, tourism is considered the backbone of the Maltese economy, with gross tourism earnings for 2000 reaching LM260.7m (€600m) (MTA 2001).

Early beginnings (1960s–1970s)

Malta's natural resources of abundant sunshine and mild climate, a rich cultural heritage (Pearce, 1955) and its status as a British colony, were crucial in establishing Malta as a tourism destination. During the early 1960s, tourism enjoyed a positive but gradual growth; yet it was not perceived as an important economic activity and was not actively encouraged by the government. However, by the mid-1960s, as the termination of the British presence in Malta drew nearer, the Maltese authorities saw tourism as the ideal replacement for the economic activities generated by the naval base.

©CAB International 2006. *Tourism in the New Europe: the Challenges and Opportunities of EU Enlargement* (eds D. Hall, M. Smith and B. Marciszewska)

Table 17.1. Malta: growth in visitor numbers, 1959–2005.

Year	Total number of visitors (including excursionists) (000s)
1959	12.6
1965	47.8
1970	170.9
1975	334.5
1980	728.7
1985	517.9
1990	871.8
1995	1116.0
2000	1215.7
2001	1180.1
2002	1133.8
2003	1126.6
2004	1157.7
2005 (Jan–Sept)	931.9

Sources: Theuma, 2004; MTA, 2005.

Mass tourism (1970s–1989)

During the 1970s high numbers of tourists were sought (Lockhart, 1997; Pollacco, 2003), with the numbers of visitors often far exceeding the targets outlined in government development plans. The type of tourism sought was mainly mass summer tourism. The Maltese government gave incentives for the building of a new tourism infrastructure (Commonwealth Secretariat, 1972), which transformed tourism activity and stimulated the development of summer resorts in the coastal areas of St Paul's Bay, Mellieha and Bugibba. Unfortunately, very little planning was carried out; tourism grew unbridled, fuelled by speculation and with the supply of accommodation being demand-led. The growth of tourist numbers and increase in tourist accommodation placed enormous pressures on local infrastructure, leading to water and electricity shortages and sewage overflow problems. This, in turn, exerted a negative impact on the islands' tourist image. Further, Malta was highly dependent on the British market, which in 1980 contributed 77% of the total number of visitors (Lockhart, 1997). Malta felt the adverse impacts of over-reliance on this single market when, as a result of the European economic recession of the early 1980s, tourist

arrivals declined by 40% between 1981 and 1984 (MTA, 2000a).

Remedial action and counter-reactions

These fluctuations in visitor numbers and their impact on the Maltese economy encouraged the Maltese tourism authorities to take action. Initially, rather than pursuing market diversification, Maltese authorities introduced a preferential currency exchange value (a forward buying rate) for UK-based tour operators. This led to an increase in visitor numbers, but it also continued to create over-dependence on the British market. A more strategic approach was adopted in the late 1980s, when the Maltese government commissioned a Malta tourism development plan, referred to as the *Tourism Master Plan* (Horwath and Horwath, 1989). This outlined seven marketing actions, including market diversification, an upgrading of products, tourist segmentation and season extension.

In the early 1990s the National Tourism Organization of Malta (NTOM), the body responsible for the marketing of the Maltese islands, embarked on a series of initiatives to implement the objectives of the Master Plan. New markets within continental Europe and beyond were targeted. The authorities also tried to improve visitor quality by diversifying away from the '3Ss' product and by improving the quality of accommodation available. Following this strategy, numbers of tourists started to grow incrementally until 1994, when a record of 1.2m visited the islands. This success, however, was short-lived as numbers started to decrease leading to debates as to whether the action taken was indeed justified. Newspaper correspondents argued that poor infrastructure, low service quality and lack of emphasis on heritage were to blame for the decline (Borg, 1996; Grech, 1995; *Times of Malta*, 1996). They also advised that Malta should seek an alternative type of tourism such as culture and heritage (Cacciottolo, 1996). However, the notion of shifting the focus from a '3Ss' destination to a greater cultural orientation was questioned by others. Amid this debate, more hotels were built, further compounding the issue since the supply of bed stock exceeded demand, stimulating the bigger hotels to intensify a price war on smaller ones.

The mid-1990s proved to be turbulent years for tourism. The quest for quality tourism accommodation led to tensions between the Maltese population and entrepreneurs (Boissevain and Theuma, 1998; Ioannides and Holcomb, 2001). This was compounded by Malta's continuing dependence on tour operator business, whereby in the late 1990s, 85% of Malta's tourism business was generated by large multinationals. In an attempt to encourage operators to sell Malta, Maltese tourism authorities had provided UK tour operators with advertising assistance and a preferential rate of exchange for 15 years (1985–2000). Although this support sustained visitor numbers it was counter-productive in terms of market and product since Malta's image still remained predominantly that of a '3Ss' Mediterranean destination (N. Theuma, 2002, unpublished PhD thesis).

In addition, Malta was facing competition from other newly established destinations within the Mediterranean region such as Tunisia, leading to further price competition among Maltese hoteliers. In an attempt to retain economic viability, local entrepreneurs undercut one another to the extent that five-star hotels sold three-star priced holidays, in turn jeopardizing service quality, leading to many 'consumer complaints about the facility and service standards' (Cleverdon, 2000, p. 85).

In summary, tourism during the 1990s in Malta was characterized by an over-reliance on price factors, large hotel developments and a tourism service that lacked quality. The application of Malta to join the EU had forced the Maltese government to cease its preferential treatment under EU competition law.

Malta Tourism Authority: a New Approach

A more strategic approach to tourism management had to be found. A government paper (Ministry of Tourism, 1997) led to the production of two studies – on economic impact (Vella and Mangion, 1999) and carrying capacity assessment (Ministry of Tourism 2001). These three documents resulted in the formation of the Malta Tourism Authority (MTA) in September 1999.

The MTA took over the responsibilities of the NTOM, the Hotel and Catering Establishments Board (HCEB) and also became involved in human resources. The new tourism authority was empowered to address the key challenges facing the industry, namely:

- visibility, competitiveness and attractiveness of the Malta brand in source markets;
- product upgrading, presentation and interpretation;
- development of core service skills to enhance visitor experience;
- the establishment of standards and regulation of the industry; and
- the provision of relevant information to enable critical decision-making by the MTA itself, by government and by the industry (MTA, 2000a, p. 15).

Strategies adopted by MTA

The approach adopted by the MTA addressed the main stakeholders in Malta (local population, tourism providers) and abroad (tour operators and prospective visitors). For many years, Malta's competitive advantage as a tourism destination was price (Brigulio and Vella 1995). Despite the fact that price remains an important element in determining the choice of holiday destinations, the MTA's main objective is to move away from this position through new marketing activities. Malta had to become a destination of choice (MTA, 2000a, p. 40) by emphasizing non-price factors of quality, service and product.

In analysing the work conducted by the MTA since the inception, one could argue that its strategic focus was based on three main areas: product development, re-imaging of the Maltese Islands, and, a redefined marketing campaign. These three factors are discussed below.

The Malta product

As part of the author's survey (N. Theuma, 2002, unpublished PhD thesis), informants from the public and private tourism sectors opined that the Malta product was 'very fragmented' since Maltese tourism authorities sell Malta as a sun-and-sea destination, a cultural destination as well as an activity destination. One informant described these different perceptions as a spectrum ranging from the perception of 'a cheap mass market to a cultural destination with shades of other perceptions in between'. This overall fragmentation of the product is a cause of concern for the industry, since Malta has not been associated with a clearly defined characteristic, leading to a confused image of what the Maltese Islands stand for.

This fragmented approach is further reinforced by the practice that each overseas MTA representative office has its own separate marketing and advertising campaigns, thus imparting a mixed image of the islands (N. Theuma, 2002, unpublished PhD thesis). According to informants, this approach leads to the creation of conflicting signals – Malta stands for beach tourism (UK), culture (France and Italy), English language teaching institutions (continental Europe), and a destination that attracts elderly visitors (UK). A clearer and more recognizable image and one that truly represents Malta is required. This would imply a stronger advantage, when trying to get the message across on the international arena. This observation is based on the argument that as a small island Malta has a limited advertising budget and thus it is imperative that the available space is used effectively:

> The windows of opportunity at our disposal are very, very, limited. We have a number of competitors, and a lot of 'noise'. Thus, we have to use the space at our disposal very effectively by mentioning the more salient points of our destination. Our promotion has to be concise but effective. [Tourism public sector informant]

In order to create a more coherent image, one of the first assignments adopted by MTA was the creation of a logo and a brand image. The chosen logos, the eye of Osiris and 'Malta: More than meets the eye', are aimed at encouraging the visitor to look beyond – an invitation to experience the diversity and depth offered by Malta and its people. These are mandatory in all adverts or literature published by MTA and its associated partners, such as the national airline. However, the creation of this logo meant that the name of the sister island of Gozo was completely removed from the marketing literature

produced by the national tourism entity. Not surprisingly, this led to a negative reaction from the Gozitan operators.

The Maltese product was another area that was addressed. For the first time, Maltese tourism authorities had a directorate that could focus entirely on the quality of product. The MTA strategic plan defines product as 'the environment, national and tourism infrastructure and cultural heritage' (MTA 2000a, p. 11). Through its Product Planning and Development Directorate, the MTA has addressed the various elements of the product in terms of accommodation, activities and events, beach development, and the creation of country walks. This directorate also linked up with a number of local communities and NGOs in sponsoring tourism-related projects.

The process of accession to the EU also provided Malta with structural and cohesion funds. The Ministry for Tourism and Culture and the Malta Tourism Authority accessed LM90m (€210.6m) between 2004 and 2006, covering four major areas of intervention concerning tourism, namely:

- projects of assistance to tourism enterprises;
- projects leading to the upgrading of Malta's cultural heritage;
- projects for the upgrading of tourism infrastructure at key tourism areas; and
- human resources development programmes aimed at tourism and support services enterprises, employers and employees.

Imagery

An issue related to the challenges faced by the future development of tourism in Malta is the current prevalent image of the Maltese islands locally and abroad. The MTA is determined in its quest to transform the prevalent image to one that is more competitive and culture-oriented (Grech, 2003). Informants perceive this to be a major challenge.

This aspect is being tackled at two levels:

- a destination image shift from multiple images to a coherent image of what the islands represent; and
- clarifying and promoting the actual product on offer.

One theme that keeps emerging in debates is the extent to which the images presented abroad actually reflect the product on offer. The following section will explore the changes that have been implemented in the creation of a new image for Malta.

'Malta: More than meets the eye' – a new destination image

To complement its new image, the MTA launched a new set of brochures in 2000: one each on Malta and Gozo, and five smaller brochures focusing on the segments/themes of diving, prehistory, history (including monuments and high culture), leisure and sports, and learning English. The strap lines of the Malta and Gozo brochures – 'Malta: The Island at the Heart of the Mediterranean' and 'Gozo: The Island of Love and Honey' – were carefully chosen:

- 'island' denotes the underlying geographical characteristic of Malta;
- 'heart' signifies the warmth and hospitality of its people;
- 'honey' is closely associated with one of Gozo's agricultural products (although in fact this is not entirely correct, as it is the name of Malta and not Gozo that originates from the word *melith* meaning honey); and
- 'love' refers to the myth of Calypso who is believed to have kept Ulysses prisoner for 7 years in a cave overlooking Ramla Bay in Gozo.

Both strap lines were designed 'to capture the imagination of the potential traveller' (tourism public sector informant, personal communication). The images used on the brochures are well-known tourist landmarks. The Malta brochure depicts the lower parts of Valletta, Malta's capital city, the bastions and St Paul's Anglican Cathedral overlooking the Grand Harbour, while in the foreground is a girl and her mother preparing fishing tackle. The Gozo brochure depicts the Azure Window in Dwejra Bay and a small *luzzu* (traditional fishing boat). In contrast to the tourist literature published in the previous years by NTOM (NTOM, 1989), the MTA literature is more image-based. Tourism personnel argued that the new approach would have a

wider (popular) appeal and would reach a bigger audience.

The two major brochures have a central image spread with much smaller pictures aligned along the perimeter of the pages. Each set of pages describes a theme relevant to the Maltese islands: two themes are based on the natural and physical environment of water and climate, and four are related to heritage and culture – history, buildings, hospitality, and feasts.

The islands are depicted as idyllic settings with honey-coloured stone buildings, sunrises, harbours and fishing villages: as a 'tranquil celebration of sea and sun' inhabited by a population that is 'lively, warm-hearted, typically Mediterranean'. The Maltese are described as having 'a unique sense of welcome' extending back to mythological times, with figures such as St Paul and the Knights of St John being depicted as having benefited from Maltese hospitality. For the first time, Malta's historical past is referred to as '7000 years of history', a strap line adopted with repetitive use. For example:

> Widely known as a sun-drenched land of mystery, Malta is much more than a bridge between sea and sky. It is an image of its past: **7000 years of history** which, from the megalithic temples built at the dawn of humanity to the grandiose saga of the Knights of St John, have endowed Malta with extraordinary heritage [emphasis in the original].
>
> (MTA, 2000b, p. 7)

Finally, the MTA makes it a point to remind the visitor that although the islands are historical they offer the visitor a number of modern activities, such as water and land sports and entertainment. For example, the visitor is invited to 'live to the rhythm of your dreams' and then, after dancing the night away, to head for a well-known local tea-shop to eat *pastizzi* (a local savoury) in the early hours of the morning. Parts of the text accompanying each theme are written in bold, with highlighted text referring to, for example, megalithic temples ('heritage') and St Paul ('historic figures'). In this manner, the bold text acts as a 'marker' (MacCannell, 1976) for history, thus identifying those attractions and characteristics that, according to the MTA, are worthy of tourist consumption. The MTA is acting as a mentor indicating to the visitor 'this is what you should look out for'. This approach permeates the literature.

The language used gives the islands a mythological image with a hint of mystery. This is elicited from references made to the painted eye of Osiris on local fishing boats (*il-luzzu*), and the myth of Calypso's cave reputed to be located on the island of Gozo. The historical and the mythological are intertwined in the brochure dedicated to prehistory. However, even amid myth and prehistory the modern visitor is not that far away since there is a continual juxtaposition of old and new, history and modernity.

Images of Malta – the MTA's perspective

The images used by the MTA in its brochures emphasize heritage (22.9%), water sports and activities (22.3%) and art and architecture (13.4%). They depict local characteristics to a lesser extent, with 8.3% of the images of local crafts, the local 'pub', *hanut tat-te*, and the *luzzu*, towns and villages including Valletta (7%), and cultural expressions through the depiction of *festas*, invented and religious pageantry (5.7%). These images do not pay much attention to people, giving the impression of a sparsely populated island. The image transmitted is one of tranquillity hiding the fact the islands are some of the most densely populated territories in Europe. Such images can mislead the visitor and can have a negative impact on visitors who arrive to find that the Maltese islands are heavily built up, with road congestion and busy local people. Thus, in the author's survey (N. Theuma, 2002, unpublished PhD thesis) one German tourist commented 'I never knew Malta was so built-up'.

In the brochures just 12.7% of the images depict the local people. The largest proportion of these (35%), show the Maltese during festive celebrations. The remaining images depict people at leisure or appearing relaxed in traditional work (children at play, people talking, fishermen mending nets or engaging in fishing or lace-making). Tourists, on the other hand, are represented mostly as young couples, without children. Such imagery indicates that the MTA has moved away from depicting the country as a family destination, so popular with the UK market hitherto (M.L. Callus and S. Bajada, 1994, unpublished report for National Tourism Organization of Malta).

In assessing the sites singled out for tourist attention, one immediately sees that MTA's imagery does not focus on the actual sites (i.e. localities) but focuses more on the 'object' – a palace, or a building, which could be anywhere on the islands. This approach dissociates the object from its context but highlights the actual attraction. An analysis of the localities depicted show that there are no images of the major tourist resorts; again reinforcing the idea that Malta is a quiet and tranquil destination.

Apart from these brochures, the MTA uses coloured posters for campaigns in particular countries. These are employed in newspapers and hoardings. As mentioned earlier, each destination has its own imagery and character. For instance, Dutch MTA promotions combine history or culture with activities such as sailing, diving and walking. The composite image of each advertisement is based on two pictures – one is an activity-based image and the other is a heritage-related image. Each has a caption that highlights the two activities represented in the image, for example 'Sail into 7000 years of history and culture' (Verkeerbureau Malta, 2001). The emphasis of the UK campaigns focuses more on the water element, tranquillity and quietness, where the visitor can get away from it all. Images used by the MTA office in London are less coherent in their message. The images used include the water element – an empty pool with the exception of the visitor, a couple standing in front of an empty beach and diving. These images do not fit in with the 'cultural image' but emphasize relaxation.

One promotion that did have a 'cultural' theme was of an old Malta bus driving along a country road with two farmers and some goats blocking the way. Using bus times (19.57 and 20.00), this image gives the impression that Malta has stopped in time (1957) at a gentler age, yet it is also modern (2000) since a number of amenities (bars and restaurants) are available for the visitor. The themes explored by these images are contrasted in the text, which indicates to the visitor that they can engage in a range of activities – history, culture, *festa* (described as 'party') or even join the locals in their evening walk (N. Theuma, 2002, unpublished PhD thesis). In Italy, Malta's image presents leisure – sea, casino, dining – and appeals to the fashion-conscious market with captions, such as 'Malta . . . profumo di mare' (Malta . . .

a hint of sea) pouring out of a perfume bottle (A.M. Caruana, 2003, unpublished BA(Hons) Tourism dissertation). This mix of images brings forth the third element of the MTA's new role – its revaluation of the marketing process.

The Marketing Process and the Art of Negotiation

Marketing campaigns are mainly carried out by the Marketing and Promotion Directorate of the MTA. They have been conducted through an international network, providing tactical and strategic support to tour operators, developing new and niche markets (MTA 2000b, p. 24). In 2004, MTA changed its marketing practices and began to withdraw from a number of overseas offices. Rather than focusing on individual markets, the MTA is now focusing on specific segments within its target countries. These segments include the MICE market, culture, sports, religion and food. To complement participation in an average of 70 fairs per year, the mechanisms used to market Malta overseas include consumer advertising, public relations, newsletters, regular press releases, publications for the local trade in Malta as well as foreign markets, and the internet. In the latter case, the MTA started to complement the above activities through its website, www.visitmalta.com; subsequently the corporate site www.mta.com.mt was launched. These sites have direct links to activities, events, specific and general information about the Maltese Islands. For a country like Malta whose marketing budget is limited by its economies of scale, they are an important asset, although the traditional forms of marketing (advertising and public relations) are still considered important.

Much importance is placed on advertising campaigns and familiarization trips for around 600 journalists and travel writers. Journal and newspaper articles are aimed to target a relatively affluent market and have so far included features on diving, farmhouses, history, interior design, food and wine. These also serve as a bridge between stakeholders, since all articles include the name of the operators selling the type of activity/holiday described, hotels in Malta and the contact address of the MTA office. The changes within the marketing policy of the MTA will in the future focus on direct marketing

through the web and meetings with specific sector leaders in the target markets. Thus, it is envisaged that Malta will at last start targeting those characteristics that are unique to it.

Further fine-tuning of current operations will result in more effective marketing. The concept of destination marketing in Malta, until recently, has been rather traditional in focusing on the importance of getting people to Malta first and then introducing them to activities once they have been 'captured'. This approach is now changing so that there is more emphasis on the true value of the Malta destination.

'Building trust': the tour operator

MTA is also seeking to redeem its relationship with tour operators. This role is based on re-establishing dialogue within the tourism sector and rebuilding trust with tour operators. This is sought through consultation with, and the involvement of, various stakeholders in strategic meetings. Joint advertising campaigns with tour operators and other partners such as Air Malta, Malta's national airline, are also being employed.

The discourse used by informants in describing the process adopted by the MTA to reach its target audience is one based on interaction. Yet, at the same time the MTA adopts the role of the instructor who *educates, reaches out* and *convinces* the target audience and the operator to perceive Malta differently. This approach is aimed at counteracting the pressures brought about by large tour operators that often dictate the manner in which particular countries are marketed and sold (Sastre and Benito, 2001). Informants from the tour operator sector have indicated that the approach adopted by the MTA was welcomed (N. Theuma, 2002, unpublished PhD thesis). This role of educator has been extended subsequently to include formal teaching through e-learning programmes offered to travel agencies and tour operator personnel. A total of 1752 employees within 500 tour operator companies had benefited from this programme between 2002 and 2005.

In its newly acquired role, as summarized in Fig. 17.1, the MTA is trying to redress some of the past practices adopted by the NTOM. This approach is more proactive and focuses directly on the consumer while still targeting the operator.

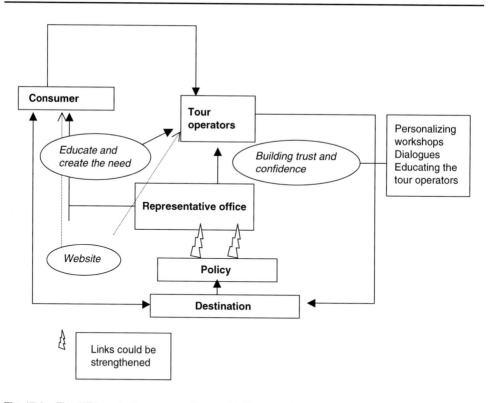

Fig. 17.1. The MTA marketing process. Source: N. Theuma, 2002, unpublished PhD thesis.

In addition, tour operators and other stakeholders such as the airline industry are seen as partners with whom joint business is conducted. Stakeholders have welcomed this initiative, acknowledging the need for cooperation and partnership. However, the MTA still needs to review its functioning at the local level. In particular, there should be more coordination between the head office and overseas branches to ensure that a consistent policy is adopted. Further, the application of research needs to be more widespread and made more accessible to overseas offices.

Malta's status as an EU country also means that it will have exposure in more European countries than before. However, a major factor inhibiting equal competition remains accessibility to the Maltese Islands. Most international visitors have to arrive by air, and the Maltese Islands have been served in the past mainly by the national air carrier, Air Malta, which was set up in 1974. The airline's near-monopoly position in the market is now diminishing with EU 'open skies' and competition regulations. With the threat of budget airlines as well as the more traditional chartered sector, Air Malta has had to restructure and rethink its strategies in terms of:

- introducing budget-level fares (Fare 4 U), initially to London (2003) and Köln (2005);
- consolidating its package holidays arm Flyaway Tours;
- extending its charter activities;
- securing code-sharing agreements with global airlines such as Qantas and Emirates;
- publicizing the development of a corporate environmental policy; and
- undertaking a restructuring both of operations logistics, commensurate with the above developments, and of senior management (Air Malta, 2005).

Discussion

This chapter has suggested that reviewing a destination's products and image and managing the course of tourism development is a far from simple task (Selänniemi, 2001). Research shows that some stakeholders still perceive tourism to be composed of bed-nights and arrivals numbers rather than the holistic vision suggested by the MTA. There is also an element of frustration since, while operators have started to shift towards including more elements of Maltese culture, visitor numbers have remained static, with the resulting perception that no momentum has been gained. Tour operators still emphasize resorts and hotels, and Malta's image in the tour operator brochures has remained rather standardized and dated, depicting concrete hotels, sea and swimming pools.

In his opening speech at the 2003 MTA annual conference, the organization's chairman admitted that:

> We have not yet managed to sufficiently impress the strategic repositioning of the islands on the way tour operators sell Malta. . . . Another major challenge we are facing lies in the mismatch between the brand promise and the delivery of our own product.
> (Grech, 2003, p. 1)

So what is missing? What needs to be done? Primarily, Malta has needed to identify the product and the image it would like to project. Since July 2005, when a re-branding exercise was launched by the MTA, this has been under way. Major stakeholders were invited to participate in a 2-day workshop in which the re-branding exercise was initiated. Local stakeholders identified the main aspects that they, and not outsiders, would like to project.

Indeed, this chapter has emphasized that destination images may be created and promoted both by tour operators and tourism authorities, but they may not correspond or be complementary. Recent changes within MTA's operations have highlighted the pivotal role that local actors need to establish in directing tourism development (Selwyn, 2001). Looking at the recent changes that have occurred in tourism throughout the Mediterranean, it is becoming increasingly evident that local players – whether tourism authorities or providers – have been gaining a more active role in tourism management and development. Clearly the policy adopted by the MTA is a step in this direction: towards creating a type of tourism activity that fits within the constraints of a small island that is rich

in cultural assets, yet poor in the availability of space. This approach is not easy to digest especially for individuals who feel that there is safety in numbers (Arrigo, 2004). Taking an active role in the way tourism is developed is perhaps the only answer to developing a competitive tourism product. Education and awareness campaigns by the MTA highlight the need for the Maltese people to better appreciate the importance of tourism quality. Moreover, the increase in the number of students attending the degree programme in tourism at the University of Malta is helping towards creating a greater consciousness that tourism is an activity that needs to be harnessed and directed rather than allowing it to take its own course of action and be directed by outsiders. The challenge is for all stakeholders involved to create sufficient interest in what has to be offered. Malta's assets lie in its high value product; but while clearly culture, history, climate and landscape are all valuable, Malta's strongest asset is its people.

Conclusions

This chapter has highlighted the major challenges facing the Malta Tourism Authority (MTA) in trying to find a new course of direction for tourism in Malta in the context of EU accession, increasing competition, and continuing pressures, both internal and external, to pursue low-value mass tourism. By adopting a more proactive marketing approach and by determining its own image overseas, the MTA aims to shift Malta's competitive advantage from one based on price to high quality non-price factors. This chapter has identified the need for improved consistency within MTA for better coordination between stakeholders. This reinforces that it is prerequisite for local participation to be at the core of tourism development in an economy where the industry touches so many local people's lives.

Note

An earlier draft of this chapter was presented at the 2004 'Tourism: State of the Art II' conference at Strathclyde University, Glasgow (Theuma, 2004). The material has been subsequently updated, supplemented and substantially edited.

References

Air Malta (2005) *Welcome to Air Malta. News.* Valletta: Air Malta. Available at: http://www.airmalta.com/page.jsp?id=74&siteid=1

Arrigo, R. (2004) It's all a question of strategy. *Times of Malta.*

Boissevain, J. and Theuma, N. (1998) Contested space: planners, tourists, developers and environmentalists in Malta. In: Abram, S. and Waldren, J. (eds) *Anthropological Perspectives on Local Development.* London: Routledge, pp. 96–119.

Borg, V.P. (1996) Renewing the country's tourist bait. *Times of Malta,* 9 August, pp. 9, 11.

Brigulio, L. and Vella, L. (1995) The competitiveness of the Maltese islands in Mediterranean international tourism. In: Conlin, M.V. and Baum, T. (eds) *Island Tourism: Management, Principles and Practice.* Chichester, UK: John Wiley & Sons, pp. 133–147.

Butler, R.W. (1980) The concept of a tourism resort area cycle of evolution: implications for management of resources. *Canadian Geographer* 24(1), 5–12.

Caciottolo, A. (1996) Call for tour-operators in promoting Malta's heritage. *The Times of Malta,* 6 September, p. 20.

Cleverdon, R. (2000) Malta. *Travel and Tourism Intelligence* 2, 85–101.

Cockerell, N. (1996) Malta. *Travel and Tourism Intelligence International Tourism Reports* 4, 71–91.

Commonwealth Secretariat (1972) Malta. In: *Organisation of the Tourist Industry in Commonwealth Countries.* London: Commonwealth Secretariat, pp. 156–159.

Grech, E. (1995) Mass movement. *The Malta Business Weekly,* 9 February, p. 25.

Grech, J. (2003) Are we equipped to compete? Paper presented at the MTA Annual Conference, 10 December. St Julian's, Malta.

Horwath and Horwath (1989) *The Maltese Islands Tourism Development Plan.* London: Horwath and Horwath (UK) Ltd.

Ioannides, D. and Holcomb, B. (2001) Upmarket tourism in Malta and Cyprus. In: Ioannides, D., Apostolopoulos, Y. and Sönmez, S. (eds) *Mediterranean Islands and Sustainable Development: Practices, Management and Policies.* London: Continuum, pp. 23–44.

Lockhart, D.G. (1997) 'We promise you a warm welcome': tourism to Malta since the 1960s. *GeoJournal* 41(2), 145–152.

MacCannell, D. (1976) *The Tourist: a New Theory of the Leisure Class.* Stanford CA: University of California Press.

Ministry of Tourism (1997) *Strategic Development Framework.* Valletta: Ministry of Tourism.

Ministry of Tourism (2001) *Carrying Capacity Assessment for Tourism in the Maltese Islands.* St Julian's, Malta: Ministry of Tourism.

MTA (Malta Tourism Authority) (2000a) *Malta Tourism Authority Strategic Plan 2000–2002.* Valletta: MTA.

MTA (Malta Tourism Authority) (2000b) *Malta: the Island at the Heart of the Mediterranean.* Valletta: MTA.

MTA (Malta Tourism Authority) (2001) *Malta Tourism Authority Annual Report and Financial Statements 2000.* Valletta: MTA, Communications and Business Development Division.

MTA (Malta Tourism Authority) (2005) *Malta Tourism Digest: Statistics.* Valletta: MTA. Available at: http://www.mta.com.mt/index.pl/statistics

NTOM (National Tourism Organisation of Malta) (1989) *Malta: Where the Sun shines from the Heart.* Valletta: NTOM.

Pearce, F.R.G. (1955) *Illustrated Guide to Historic Malta,* 2nd edn. Valletta: Giov. Muscat.

Pollacco, J. (2003) *In the Interest of the Nation.* Valletta: Fenech Foundation.

Sastre, F. and Benito, I. (2001) The role of transnational tour operators in the development of Mediterranean tourism. In: Ioannides, D., Apostolopous, Y. and Sönmez, S. (eds) *Mediterranean Islands and Sustainable Tourism Development.* London: Continuum.

Selänniemi, T. (2001) Trapped by the image: the implications of cultural tourism in insular Mediterranean. In: Ioannides, D., Apostolopous, Y. and Sönmez, S. (eds) *Mediterranean Islands and Sustainable Tourism Development.* London: Continuum.

Selwyn, T. (2001) Searching for sustainable tourism development in the insular Mediterranean. In: Ioannides, D., Apostolopoulos, Y. and Sönmez, S. (eds) *Mediterranean Islands and Sustainable Development: Practices, Management and Policies.* London: Continuum.

Theuma, N. (2004) Malta: more than meets the eye – Destination marketing challenges of a small island state. Paper presented at *Tourism: State of the Art II Conference*, Strathclyde University, 27–30 June.

Times of Malta (1996) Editorial. Tourism: cleaning up our act. *Times of Malta,* 3 December, p. 8.

Vella, L. and Mangion, M.L. (1999) *The Economic Impact of Tourism in Malta*. Valletta: NTOM, Research and Planning Division.

Verkeerbureau Malta (2001) MTA Advertisements. Amsterdam: MTA.

18 Cyprus: Building Bridges in the Borderlands of the New Europe

Julie Scott and Layik Topcan

Introduction

After years of division in Cyprus, a referendum held in April, 2004, on the United Nations-brokered peace plan (the Annan Plan), followed one week later by the accession of the Republic of Cyprus to the European Union, produced dramatic but ambiguous changes on the island. The failure, after 30 years of negotiation, to reach a political settlement between the Greek Cypriot south and the Turkish Cypriot north before the scheduled accession date of 1 May, meant that the southern two-thirds of the island, constituting the *de facto* territory of the internationally recognized Republic of Cyprus, entered the European Union unaccompanied by the Turkish Republic of North Cyprus (TRNC: declared unilaterally in 1983). The Green Line – the militarized border marking the cessation of hostilities in 1974, which runs across the island and continues to divide its capital, Nicosia – now defined the outer edge of the European Union, and the limits of the *acquis communautaire*.

Nevertheless, this latest European border remains highly contested, creating a fluid and uncertain borderland which has become the focus for on-going attempts to construct both the new Cyprus and the new Europe. Indeed, as the Commissioner for European Enlargement, Olli Rehn, made clear in a speech marking the first anniversary of Cyprus's accession to the EU, Cyprus in many ways embodies the

meaning and mission of the European Union, which was born out of conflict and the need to '[eliminate] . . . the age-old opposition of France and Germany'. The first year of enlargement saw considerable efforts within the Commission to promote cooperation and rapprochement between the two sides in the Cyprus conflict, to create favourable conditions for settlement, and to prepare the ground for the eventual entry of the north into the European Union as part of a united federal Cyprus.

Tourism has a central, yet contradictory role to play in these processes. With the natural tourism assets of the north largely undeveloped due to the political and economic embargoes of the past three decades, tourism offers an avenue for stimulating economic activity and raising income levels which lag a long way behind those of the more prosperous south. This need is generally regarded as a prerequisite to obtaining a workable settlement on the island.

Moreover, the opening up of the north presents an opportunity to develop complementary tourism products to the south that could widen the appeal of the island as a whole and promote collaborative marketing and business ventures between Greek and Turkish Cypriots (see Sönmez and Apostolopoulos, 2000). On the other hand, achieving these aims requires that Cyprus' most controversial and politically charged issues be confronted head-on. Control of movement over and within borders, access to the physical and economic assets of land, landscape and property, the packaging and representation of cultural heritage for tourist consumption, environmental protection and the regulation of construction – all problematic areas in any tourism development context – remain the hot topics of the Cyprus dispute, to which the Annan Plan was unable to provide a satisfactory resolution. Tourism development in Cyprus thus has enormous symbolic, as well as economic, social and political significance.

In this chapter we explore the place of tourism in the current arrangements for Cyprus' membership of the EU, looking at the impact of enlargement on tourism, but also on the part tourism is playing in both helping and hindering progress towards agreement and the process of 'Europeanization'. We start with a brief survey of tourism development on the island and a comparison of the tourism industry north and south. Following sections summarize the provisions of the 'Green Line Regulation' and its impact on cross-border traffic and cooperation. In subsequent sections we consider the current legal impasse over ownership and investment in land and property in the north, and attempts to achieve EU standards of environmental protection in the teeth of a construction boom driven by a strategy of confronting uncertainty by creating 'facts on the ground'. Information was gathered by interviewing individuals and representatives of professional associations in the tourism industry, a survey of secondary sources such as newspapers and statistics gathered by government bodies, and participation in urban and environmental planning processes in Northern Cyprus. The data presented here represents the most recent information available in July 2005.

Tourism in a Divided Island: 1974–2004

After the division of the island in 1974, following a coup engineered by the junta in Greece and decisive military intervention by Turkey, the north of Cyprus became relatively isolated from the rest of the world as a result of comprehensive diplomatic, economic and cultural boycotts. Attempts to develop its tourism languished

(Scott, 2000). Tourist arrivals to the north are low compared to those for the south, and the north remains heavily dependent on the Turkish market, which makes up approximately 80% of total arrivals.[1] The Greek Cypriot tourism industry, by contrast, has been subject to the full force of globalization, and has derived substantial economic benefit from it. Tourism revenues generated by the stays of 2.1m tourists in 1995 amounted to CY£810m (US$1.62bn) or 40.1% of total export receipts, with more than 10% of employment provided by the hotel and restaurant sector, making tourism the 'chief earner of foreign exchange and the economy's driving force' (Ioannides and Apostolopoulos, 1999, p. 52; Sönmez and Apostolopoulos, 2000). More recently, however, attention has also been drawn to some of the problems and costs of tourism's rapid growth in the south. Whilst research in the mid-1990s suggested that local residents (both north and south of the Green Line dividing the island) were on the whole prepared to pay a social and environmental price for tourism-led prosperity (Akiş, Peristianis and Warner, 1996), uncontrolled coastal strip development, pressure on scarce water resources, congestion and noise pollution arguably made Southern Cyprus less attractive to tourists (Ioannides and Apostolopoulos, 1999; Ioannides and Holcomb, 2001). Further, by the year 2000, 20–30% of all tourism in the south was controlled by a single tour operator, Thomson-Preussag (Bianchi, 2001), and the traditional sun, sea and sand product was facing problems of over-capacity and declining per capita spending by tourists. Tourist arrivals in 2003 were 4.76% down on the previous year, with average expenditure per tourist at €750.[2] Meanwhile, the proportion of the labour force directly employed in tourism has risen to 13%.

The north's dependence on the Turkish market is paralleled in the south by the dominance of the UK market, which has formed a growing proportion of the total number of tourist arrivals for more than a decade. The popularity of Cyprus as a British holiday destination builds on the long-standing relations between the UK and its former colony. From driving on the left, to the style of post boxes, colonial buildings, and stone drinking troughs dedicated to Elizabeth II and dating from her coronation year of 1953, there is much about the landscape of

Cyprus to render it familiar and 'safe' to the British visitor. Constituting 49% of arrivals in 1998, rising to 61% in 2003, UK tourists to southern Cyprus outnumber by several-fold the German tourists who form the next largest category.[3] In the north, the UK forms the second largest tourist market after Turkey, at around 10% of total arrivals, with Germany in third place at 4–5% (Devlet Planlama Örgütü, 2001). The age profile of tourists to the north tends to be higher than the south, and includes a good number of retired British servicemen and their families revisiting the scene of their military service from the 1950s. The international club scene centred on the resort of Ayia Napa, in contrast, attracts many younger, single tourists to the south.

The north of Cyprus has attempted to develop its tourism under substantially different conditions from the south, closed off from the major global tourism players, but with its border wide open to Turkey (Scott, 2000). Of the 351,000 visitors to Northern Cyprus in 1994, 73% were short-stay visitors from Turkey (Sönmez and Apostolopoulos, 2000). This trend has been deepened by the development in the north of a casino tourism sector, directed primarily at gambling tourists from Turkey and Israel (Bicak and Altinay, 1996; Scott and Aşikoğlu, 2001).[4] Despite this, the north has not been able to emulate the south's prosperity, and its annual per capita income of $3538 lags far behind the $10,591 per capita of the south. However, it is the north's very exclusion from mainstream tourism which now makes it potentially a particularly attractive 'nature/culture' tourism product for the European market.

Opening up the North: the Green Line Regulation

The north's seclusion was largely the result of the cutting of direct transport and communication links following the war of 1974. Nicosia International Airport, which had previously served the island as a whole, remained stranded and out of use in the buffer zone between the two sectors. The construction of Larnaca and subsequently Paphos airports filled this gap in the south. In the north, by contrast, the international civil aviation boycott on direct flights meant that only planes from Turkey could land at Ercan Airport, just northeast of Nicosia, with passengers from non-Turkish sources such as London and Frankfurt being required to change planes or, in some cases, simply touch down en route at Istanbul, Izmir or Antalya. Like Ercan airport, the north's seaports of Famagusta and Kyrenia were deemed illegal points of entry, and all transport and communication links to the north were diverted through Turkey.

Internally, traffic across the Green Line was also closely regulated and liable to be terminated abruptly at times of dispute or political tension. Limited transit was permitted to enable a number of Turkish Cypriots to work in the south, largely in construction and labouring, and the British sovereign bases, straddling the buffer zone and occupying roughly 2% of the land area of Cyprus, also provided employment for both Greek and Turkish Cypriots. Foreign nationals entering via a port of entry in the south were allowed limited entry into the north during daylight hours, but were not permitted to bring goods purchased in the north back with them. Foreigners entering via the north were not admitted into the south, either across the Green Line or subsequently, if they carried a TRNC stamp in their passport.

In April 2004 the Council of Europe called on the European Commission to bring forward comprehensive proposals to put an end to the isolation of the Turkish Cypriot community. A high priority for the north in this regard has been to lobby for the authorization of direct flights, although there seemed little likelihood that this would be granted in the immediate future.[5] Nevertheless, there was a steady increase in the number of arrivals through Ercan in the 3 years from 2002 (Table 18.1), and there are plans to expand the existing terminal and even to build a new runway. The number of non-Turkish visitors staying in hotels in the north has also risen over the same period (Table 18.2).

At the beginning of May 2004, following a period of uncertainty and some disagreement among government ministries in the south, foreign nationals with EU passports who had entered Cyprus via the north were permitted to cross into the south for the first time. These first steps inaugurated the free movement of EU citizens around Cyprus, as provided for by the Green Line Regulation which had been adopted

Table 18.1. Arrivals through the Northern Cyprus airports (Ercan and Geçitkale[a]), 2000–2004.

Year	Number of arrivals	% annual change
2000	416,596	NA
2001	345,601	−17.0
2002	386,097	11.7
2003	410,142	6.2
2004	509,501	24.2

[a]Geçitkale is a small airport north of Ercan used for short periods when the latter is undergoing maintenance or renovation.
Source: unpublished data, General Directorate of Police/Ministry of Tourism and Economy, TRNC.

Table 18.2. Non-Turkish foreign visitors staying in Northern Cyprus hotel accommodation, 2000–2004.

Year	Number of foreign tourists	% of total tourist numbers
2000	65,321	25.6
2001	65,455	28.6
2002	89,139	31.2
2003	82,465	30.2
2004	112,921	36.8

Source: Ministry of Tourism and Economy, TRNC, 2005.

on 29 April, 2 days before the south's entry into the EU, and became fully operational the following August.[6] A special protocol which recognizes the north's anomalous status as existing both inside and outside the EU,[7] the Green Line Regulation controls the passage of goods and people across the line, offers special conditions for trade between Northern Cyprus and the EU, and aims to foster trust and cooperation between the two communities through opportunities for joint commerce.[8]

In the words of the DG Enlargement Commissioner, Olli Rehn, 'the Green Line Regulation has been a great success in the crossing of persons'. Many of the people crossing the Green Line are tourists visiting the north, with monthly arrivals of non-Cypriots showing an average increase of 57% for the first 5 months of 2005 compared with 2004, and figures for

May 2005 (the latest month for which figures were available) up 67% on the previous year (Table 18.3). Thus, whilst the value of goods traded across the Green Line so far remains low, at around €100,000 per month, and the ban on direct flights to Northern Cyprus remains in place, nevertheless, the operation of the Green Line Regulation has had a considerable economic impact by enabling tourists from the EU – as many as 10% of all the tourists staying at some of the larger hotels[9] – to enter the north after flying direct to Larnaca.

Tourists may be aware only of a quicker and cheaper journey to the north of Cyprus, but in effect their journey requires the negotiation of multiple spaces characterized by the political conditions regulating the mobility of different classes of people and objects in transit. In the next section we consider the nature of these spaces and the types of collaborative relationship that are being established across them.

Crossing the Border

At the time of writing, there are four points at which the Green Line may be crossed: Akyer and Beyarmuda, through the British base area near Famagusta, and Metahan in Nicosia, are all open to vehicular traffic, whilst the Ledra Palace crossing, close to the walled centre of old Nicosia, is for pedestrian use only.[10] From being a no-man's land populated by UN soldiers stationed at the Ledra Palace, the large and formerly grand hotel that dominates the buffer zone, the crossing has reassumed some of the appearance of a normal street, with crowds of Cypriots and tourists using the checkpoint every day to cross for shopping, sightseeing, work and leisure. For the tourist, the experience of crossing the border encapsulates the contradictory nature of Cyprus. Passing by the cafes located conveniently close to the barricades, where jokes and conversation are swapped in Greek and Turkish, the tourist is confronted by the uncompromising political slogans and notice board displays documenting the atrocities committed by the 'other side', which mirror each other from either end of the buffer zone, and finally reaches a cluster of booths where Greek and Turkish Cypriots sell car insurance.

Table 18.3. Southern Cyprus: arrivals and departures, 2004 and 2005.

| | 2004 | | | | 2005 | | | |
| | Total | | Foreign[a] | | Total | | Foreign[a] | |
Months	Arrivals	Departures	Arrivals	Departures	Arrivals	Departures	Arrivals	Departures
January	242,180	238,918	23,487	22,251	278,051	275,547	36,933	36,138
February	281,425	279,527	25,860	24,460	270,082	266,873	35,426	33,589
March	294,095	290,034	30,745	29,332	323,984	314,944	51,086	47,134
April	277,105	272,458	37,512	35,172	325,743	317,570	57,977	52,863
May	291,177	286,741	39,644	37,248	326,484	323,828	66,248	62,757
June	300,098	296,860	42,645	40,627	na	na	na	na
July	330,229	324,360	51,201	47,093				
August	343,693	333,582	61,958	58,197				
September	322,343	319,140	52,757	49,358				
October	323,082	319,433	60,613	56,841				
November	279,151	281,099	42,669	40,908				
December	313,238	312,770	40,025	38,538				

[a]Non-Cypriot.
Source: unpublished data, General Directorate of Police/Ministry of Tourism and Economy, TRNC.

The arrangements for bringing vehicles over the Green Line were not, at the time of writing, yet entirely reciprocal. Private cars registered either in the north or the south are allowed to cross, provided that additional insurance is taken out to provide cover on the 'other side'. Taxis, buses and rental cars registered in the south may cross to the north, but their northern equivalents are not allowed into the south. Whilst it is not clear whether the immediate reason for this concerns the recognition of Turkish Cypriot commercial driving licences, as recently suggested by Leopold Maurer of the European Commission,[11] or the testing arrangements for commercial vehicles, what is evident is that the nub of the matter is the contest for legitimacy between the apparatus of state organization north and south, linked, in turn, to the contested sovereignty of the island.[12]

The responses to the current status quo are illuminating, and range from the pragmatic to the partisan. Domestic tourism on the island, including Greek Cypriots heading north and Turkish Cypriots south, has grown, despite the fact that numbers of Greek Cypriots, offended by the requirement to show their passport, prefer not to make the crossing, whilst Turkish Cypriot tour parties have to change on to Greek Cypriot buses at the checkpoint.[13] The transfer of international tourists, however, requires forms of collaboration which frequently cut across the formal positions of the respective communities. The gradual opening up of the north of the island, with its reputation as an unspoilt and undeveloped corner of the Mediterranean, is attracting overseas tour operators working either through Turkish Cypriot agencies or directly with hotels in the north, to bring tour groups to the TRNC via direct flights to Larnaca. According to the current operation of the Green Line Regulation, the logistics of bringing the tourists from Larnaca into the north require a division of labour in which the transfer is done by a Greek Cypriot operator whilst the Turkish Cypriot agent does the handling.

So far the data available on this type of business arrangement are anecdotal at best, but, clearly, involvement in such relationships is politically sensitive. Greek Cypriot public opinion condemns any activity promoting the use of hotels in the north which were in Greek Cypriot ownership until 1974 or were subsequently built on Greek Cypriot owned land, and in fact the Green Line Regulations specifically exclude trade in goods and services of which expropriated property is a component. Twenty thousand cases are currently pending in the European Court of Human Rights, brought by Greek Cypriot owners for restitution of land and property in the north, including hotels being operated by Turkish and Turkish Cypriot companies and individuals.[14] Amongst many Turkish Cypriots, on the other hand, there is a suspicion that the business contacts entered into with partners in the south echo Turkish Cypriot dependence on the mediation of Greek Cypriot gatekeepers, which had been characteristic of the 1960s and early 1970s. There is also criticism that bringing in tourists via Larnaca is undermining Ercan Airport and taking business away from Turkish and Turkish Cypriot carriers. Tourism activity in the North, it is argued, needs to be built on the development of the Turkish Cypriot tourism infrastructure if it is not to lead to dependent development. This conviction is reinforced by the fact that the benefits of the increased traffic are by no means evenly spread. Whilst three-quarters of hotel accommodation in the north is in small, family-run businesses, it is the larger four- and five-star establishments that are now reporting occupancy rates of 90–100% in the summer months, whilst the occupancy rates for the smaller hotels remain low at under 40% over the year (Table 18.4).[15]

Table 18.4. Northern Cyprus: occupancy rates by hotel classification, 2004.

Classificaton	% occupancy rate			
	2004	2003	2002	2001
*	29.8	–	–	–
**	35.1	–	–	–
***	39.6	–	–	–
****	45.2	–	–	–
*****	51.2	–	–	–
Average overall	41.2	37.5	38.6	31.5

Source: Ministry of Tourism and Economy, TRNC, 2005.

Tours and Tour Guides

Another sensitive area connected with the transit of tourists over the Green Line concerns the role of tour guides accompanying daily coach tours. Trips to the empty beaches of the Karpas Peninsula and the northern towns of Kyrenia and Famagusta, taking in famous sites such as the mountain-top crusader castles of St Hilarion and Kantara, the ancient ruins of Salamis, and the monastery of Bellapais, are widely advertised in southern resorts such as Ayia Napa at prices from CY£20 upwards, and during 2005 seven tourist buses a day or more were crossing the Green Line into the north. This was a situation which had been envisaged under the Boutros-Ghali 'confidence building measures', a series of proposals by the then UN General Secretary for cooperation in tourism and other economic activities designed to encourage rapprochement between the two sides in the mid-1990s (see Chapter 16). At public meetings held in the north to discuss the proposals at that time, much concern was raised about who would accompany and guide coach tours over the Green Line, and the opportunities they offered for positive and negative propaganda. The same concerns are being raised again in the context of an arrangement that does not permit Turkish Cypriot guides to lead the tours emanating from the south.

The current situation provides an illuminating example of the merging of the political and the instrumental in relation to particular issues. As with the licensing of Turkish Cypriot buses and drivers, the Cyprus Tourism Organisation recognizes only CTO-registered tour guides, whom tour operators working in the south are contractually obliged to use. At one level this concerns the quality and training of tour guides, and the protection of local jobs. At the same time, the history of ethno-national conflict in Cyprus makes the interpretation of the heritage and landscape, and who has the right to represent and 'perform' it for an external audience, politically extremely sensitive (see, for example, Bowman, 1992).

Responses to the situation pit diverse interests against each other in the north. The daily tours from the south have injected new life into the shops and restaurant businesses, and have increased visitation, and consequently, income, to the sites administered by the cash-starved Turkish Cypriot Department of Antiquities. The Turkish Cypriot Tour Guides Association (KITREB), on the other hand, is opposed to the exclusion of Turkish Cypriot tour guides. Whilst acknowledging that low levels of training and language skills is a problem, KITREB is attempting to raise the professional standards of an occupation which has been in low demand in the north for three decades. The training requirement has been raised from 1-month ad hoc courses organized by the Ministry of Tourism, to 6-month university diploma courses, and language training in German, Swedish and Italian is now being offered to Turkish Cypriot tour guides, with funding from the United Nations Development Programme (UNDP). A compromise with the tours from the south has been reached, whereby unregistered Turkish Cypriot guides accompany the tours as silent escorts. The dilemma can again be viewed in terms of the trade-off between the need for the immediate economic boost of increased tourism activity, and the longer term development of the tourism infrastructure in the north; deeper still is the problem of the legacy of division concerning notions of cultural 'property', which urgently needs to be addressed (see Scott, 2002).

What Kind of Tourism, What Kind of Cyprus?

The accommodations and compromises being reached by individuals and groups within the tourism industry, north and south, suggest partial and halting progress towards treating the island as a single destination within the limitations of the current division, and at least one German tour operator has started offering dual destination holiday packages in both parts of the island. At the government level, in contrast, policy and planning remain strictly separate, and there is no arena for collaborating on a tourism strategy for the island as a whole. One outstanding exception to this general rule is the Nicosia Master Plan, which, under the auspices first of the UNHCR, and subsequently the UNDP, has for two decades provided an umbrella for cooperation on the strategic planning of the divided city and for the regeneration of the historic walled city in which culture-based tourism is expected to play an increasingly significant role.

In response to the downward trend in tourist arrivals currently being experienced in the south, the Cyprus Tourism Organisation (CTO) has instituted a *Strategic Plan for Tourism 2010* which it started to implement in 2003. The plan aims at sustainable tourism development for Cyprus by repositioning the product as a high quality destination centred on culture and the environment. The Plan has the goal of doubling total tourism revenue to reach CY£1.8bn by 2010, by increasing the number of boutique hotels, tourist villages, villas and traditional houses. Tourist arrivals are expected to increase by 3.5% per annum to reach 3.5m by 2010.[16]

The CTO's sustainable tourism strategy comes after a long period in which the Republic of Cyprus has benefited from the 'critical mass' of large-scale tourism development, which was simply not available to the TRNC. With the prospect of mass tourism development opportunities opening up in the north, the dilemma now is how to 'catch up' with the south by achieving that critical mass of tourism development in a way which does not jeopardize the environment nor threaten existing tourism stakeholders.

Over the years of the north's isolation, a number of specialist companies have developed successful niche tourism products which are increasingly being taken up and developed by larger companies. One such company is Jewels of the World, which is linked to the charter flight company TWI. Their 2005 catalogue offered a variety of specialist holidays ranging from walking tours and sea diving to weddings, blessings and honeymoons and a tailored 'connoisseur programme'. As the second largest incoming operator for Northern Cyprus, Jewels of the World brings in 15,000 package tours per year, and is optimistic about expanding and developing its markets, but its plans for growth require the availability of larger units of accommodation in order to meet the requirements of the major European tour operators for economies of scale. However, the question of the extent to which Northern Cyprus should aim to attract the large operators is one which divides the industry. Representatives of the Turkish Cypriot Hoteliers' Association, KITSOB – the majority of whose members own small family-run hotels with fewer than 200 beds (Table 18.5) – argue that Northern Cyprus needs to keep out mass tourism, continuing instead to develop small-scale niche tourism, and focus on maintaining Northern Cyprus' reputation as a quiet and relatively undeveloped location that offers an alternative to the tourism of the south. For the owners and operators of the larger hotels, on the other hand, the south offers a model of a different kind. As the head of Net Holding, an important tourism company in Turkey which, under the trading name of 'Merit', has major investments in hotels in the north of Cyprus, observed: 'We need to decide on our priorities and ask ourselves why we attract only 300,000 tourists

Table 18.5. Northern Cyprus: hotels and holiday village accommodation by number of beds.

No. of beds	2004		Under construction 2005–2006		Combined total	
	No. of hotels	As % of total hotels	No. of hotels	As % of total under construction	No. of hotels	As % of total hotels
< 50	59	50.0	22	38.6	80	45.7
50–100	26	22.0	11	19.3	37	21.1
100–200	22	18.6	8	14.0	29	16.6
200–300	5	4.2	8	14.0	13	7.4
300–400	2	1.7	2	3.5	3	1.7
400–500	1	0.8	2	3.5	4	2.3
500 >	3	2.5	4	7.0	9	5.1
Total	118	100	57	100	175	100

Note: these totals reflect the construction of additional bed capacity in some of the existing establishments.
Source: Extrapolated by the authors from unpublished figures supplied by the Ministry of Tourism and Economy, TRNC.

when our neighbours in the south manage 3 million' (NCHA, 2005).

The current pattern of tourism investment in the north suggests that the profile of the accommodation sector there is about to change dramatically. Bed capacity was scheduled to double in little over 2 years to about 24,000 by the end of 2006. Whilst hotels with over 500 beds would still form only a small proportion (5.1%) of the total number of establishments, these would contribute 51.6% of the total bed capacity, with four out of the nine largest establishments offering more than 900 beds each, and three of these, totalling around 3000 beds, concentrated in one small village location (Table 18.5). Such developments have raised questions not only about the desirability of the mass tourism route, but also about its environmental impact, and the ability of the north to meet the infrastructure requirements implied by this increase in capacity.

The Annan Plan, the Referendum and the Construction Boom

The referendum on the Annan Plan on 24 April, 2004, was swiftly followed by a massive boom in the construction sector in Northern Cyprus, closely related to the failure of the referendum to resolve the property issue. This opened the door to widespread speculation in land and property in anticipation of a likely settlement in the future. The current situation regarding property in the north dates back to a law enacted in Northern Cyprus in 1977, and subsequently subject to several amendments, which distributed Greek Cypriot owned properties in the north to displaced Turkish Cypriot refugees from the south (see Morvaridi, 1993; Scott, 1998). The intention of the Annan Plan was to introduce a new property regime in compliance with international law, recognizing the needs and sensitivities of the two communities and the basic requirements for bi-zonality and bi-communality.

According to the property provisions of the Annan Plan, current users of affected properties who are themselves dispossessed owners or persons who own significant improvements to affected properties may apply to receive title to such properties. This has been widely interpreted as meaning that a current user who carries out

substantial development on Greek Cypriot land would be entitled to receive the title deed, on payment to its original owner of the value of the land alone. This provision in the Annan Plan provides a strong motivation for Turkish Cypriots, as the current users, to secure the right to keep the property allocated to them in place of their property in the south, either by erecting a building on the land, or by selling Greek Cypriot owned land to developers as soon as possible. The suggestion that a future settlement would safeguard such investments has also stimulated a keen foreign interest in property ownership and speculation in the north.[17] Real estate values have seen a steady steep increase, with investors principally from Britain and Israel establishing new estate agencies in partnership with Turkish Cypriots living in Cyprus or abroad, and offering current users prices of from £5000 to £50,000 sterling per donum (1338 m^2). Many European purchasers have been convinced by the promise of a continuing rise in property prices in the north in the coming years.

These recent developments have introduced a new and complicated dimension to the problems of the property issue in Cyprus. Whereas, in the past, this took the form of Turkish Cypriots and Turkish settlers living in former Greek Cypriot property, with Greek Cypriots living in Turkish Cypriot property left in the south, now, not only are foreigners being issued 'unrecognized' titles to land in an 'unrecognized state', but Greek Cypriots are seeing their dreams of return destroyed by bulldozers and housing complexes. Events have taken a further turn with the issuing of lawsuits against foreign investors for the use or development of Greek Cypriot owned property. The 'Orams' case[18] and the 'Hurma Restaurant'[19] are two landmark cases which have made Greek properties less favourable for development, and have diverted the attention of developers to Turkish Cypriot or publicly owned land, regardless of their location, environmental or cultural sensitivity.

Environmental Consequences of the Construction Boom

After the referendum, the number of planning or building applications tripled. The number of applications for new construction in the Kyrenia region (the north's main tourist resort) in the first year exceeded the number of total applications made in the previous 30 years for the entire north of Cyprus. Again, political calculations, and the prospective future implementation of the Annan Plan, or something like it, play their part in shaping development. It is interesting to observe, for example, that the total number of applications for building permission is very low in the Güzelyurt area, which is subject to territorial readjustment under the terms of the Annan Plan. Turkish Cypriots living here are prepared to move to other places, despite having been refugees both in 1963 and 1974, and do not invest in the Güzelyurt area, nor even bury their dead there, preferring to invest instead in Nicosia, Kyrenia or elsewhere, which would remain under Turkish Cypriot control under a future settlement.

The current intense building activity in Northern Cyprus has stimulated ribbon development at the edge of the cities and along highways, and the spread of scattered development. Tourism and second home developments are the major construction activities placing pressure on the coastline and other environmentally sensitive or fragile areas, including forestry areas, agricultural lands, aquifers, riverbeds, mountain ranges and dune systems. Numerous natural resources and sensitive sites are already being exploited, polluted or destroyed by rapid development and sprawl, and many other areas are in danger of being taken into tourism use without proper planning or impact analysis. The regions between Lapitos/Karavas-Kyrenia, the northern coastal line between Kyrenia and Karpasia, and the eastern coastal line between Famagusta and Karpasia, have all undergone particularly rapid development, with buyers or sellers in some places clearing acres of citrus, olive and carob groves to open up land for construction.

The construction free-for-all is exacerbated by the lack of a comprehensive spatial development plan for the entire territory of the northern part of the island covering spatial development strategies and delineating and designating areas for various types of economic sectors such as tourism, industrial transportation, waste management, and protected areas. Planning legislation is in force in an *ad hoc* way, in areas where a development plan exists, or where a development ordinance has been prepared under the

planning law. There is no overall development policy grounded on sustainable development.

Current levels of construction are placing an immense strain on certain areas, such as the popular tourist resort of Kyrenia, in terms of the carrying capacity of natural resources and present public service infrastructure, and severely compromising the sustainable future of the island for coming generations. The expansion of stone quarries is a case in point, with the use of dynamite in the excavation process severely compromising water resources and irrevocably changing the topography of a region which enjoys natural heritage status under the constitution. Besides the capacity increase in stone quarries, the general import of iron, cement and similar materials had increased by well over 200% in just 1 year.

Planning authorities and local municipalities in the north are unable to keep pace with the scale of illegal construction and lack of compliance with the environmental, planning and building legislation. The Union of Chambers of Cyprus Turkish Engineers and Architects, environmental groups and NGOs criticize the speed and poor quality of construction, as well as the failure to enforce the existing legislation. The municipalities, who are responsible for the inspection of construction sites within their territories, face the dilemma of trying to achieve a trade-off between their need for the cash generated by the building activity, and the environmental damage it causes. In general, tourism and the construction sector are considered the driving sectors for boosting the economy, and the main source for local budget revenues to enable Northern Cyprus to become less dependent on Turkey. Whilst Turkish Cypriots complain about the effects of construction on the environment, they also argue that, as long as they are under embargo and cannot export goods, they do not have many choices. The dominance of these perceptions and arguments in the public arena acts as a disincentive for the government to create alternative development policies.

Planning and Interim Measures for the Protection of the Environment

Although the government regards the construction boom as an opportunity for increasing local revenues, there is also awareness that this trend would have significant negative impact on the environment. The government in the north has enacted two development ordinances in 2004, one for the Karpas peninsula and the other for the Tatlisu area, in order to minimize the damage to environmentally sensitive areas which are habitats for turtles, historical and cultural heritage sites, dunes, forests and maquis landscapes under pressure from tourism development. The main aim of these development ordinances is to take precautionary measures and prohibit development in special protection areas (SPAs) until a comprehensive development plan for these areas can be prepared, approved and enforced under the planning legislation. However, it is unclear whether these ordinances will be effective in controlling haphazard development and securing environmentally sound and culturally aware sustainable development, given the economic pressures for development and the problems of enforcement.

failure to secure a settlement has sparked off a frenzy of unplanned development and speculation, driven by the expectations of the Annan Plan and the apparent opportunity to second-guess the conditions of a future agreement, which will no doubt cause long-term damage both to the environment and to the quality of bi-communal relations.

There is no immediate prospect of a solution at the official level to the political problems that are inseparable from the very ingredients of tourism in Cyprus. The political landscape is constantly shifting, in response both to initiatives from the political centre of Brussels, and to new developments in the periphery, particularly in relation to the process of Turkey's accession to the European Union. The question of how strategic alliances are made in these conditions of uncertainty, who is able to make them, and what benefits they bring, will be critical in shaping the contours of Cyprus' emerging tourism landscape.

Conclusion and Future Prospects

The current state of tourism in the Cyprus of the new, enlarged Europe presents a complex and contradictory picture. Despite the lack of a political settlement, there are signs that Cyprus is moving towards a single tourism economy, as business interests find common cause across the Green Line, and, to a limited extent, recruit from a common labour market. At the same time, the restructuring of the tourism industry – as the north scales up for an element of mass tourism, and the south seeks to reposition its product in the face of declining numbers and per capita spend – is creating new winners and losers, contributing to a sense of insecurity amongst some tourism stakeholders, exacerbating the political tensions surrounding tourism development on the island.

On one level, the continued separation of the two parts of the island and the maintenance of 'no-go areas' of various types could be viewed as forcing the creation of relationships to negotiate the divide and assuring a role for both Greek and Turkish Cypriot actors as gatekeepers to 'their' part of the island. On the other hand, the

Notes

1 In 1999 and 2000, Northern Cyprus received 414,000 and 433,000 tourists respectively, of which 334,400 and 347,700 were from Turkey. In the same years, arrivals to the south numbered 2.4 million and 2.6 million respectively.

2 www.cyprus.gov.cy. Recent reports suggest that the decline in foreign tourist arrivals is being offset to some extent by an increase in domestic tourism (see Christou, 2005).

3 German tourists made up 10% of total arrivals in 1998, declining to 6% in 2003 (Statistical Service of the Government of Cyprus).

4 In Southern Cyprus the issue of casinos has long been a matter of debate. Despite a vociferous lobby in favour, pressures to allow casinos to operate have so far been opposed and resisted, both out of traditional moral concerns, and also on cultural and political grounds (*Sunday Mail*, 17 September, 2000). However, this policy is being reconsidered, in view of the steady stream of Greek Cypriots who, since the relaxation of border restrictions between north and south in April 2003, have been heading northwards to gamble in the casinos (*Cyprus Mail*, 23 June, 2004).

5 'Direk uçuşta kararliyiz ama' *Londra Gazete* 3/2/05. The then European Minister of the UK

Government, Denis MacShane, emphasizes in the article the legal complexities of the issue, explaining: 'Ercan airport in north Cyprus has not been designated as an approved international airport, so under the existing UK Cyprus air services agreement, no regular direct flight could operate to it from the UK'.

6 Cypriot citizens had already been crossing using their passports/ID cards.

7 North Cyprus could be said to have slipped into the gap between model and reality of the political map of Cyprus, hence its current state of limbo. The Cypriot territory established under the 1960 Constitution, and still upheld by the government of the Republic of Cyprus based in the south, extends to the whole of the island, with rights to citizenship of the Republic of Cyprus similarly available to Turkish Cypriot citizens of the TRNC. Thus, the *acquis communautaire* is described as being merely *suspended* in the north, whilst individual Turkish Cypriots, as citizens of the Republic of Cyprus, may enjoy the rights of individual EU citizenship both in Cyprus and throughout the territory of the EU.

8 Council Regulation (EC) No 866/2004 of 29 April, 2004, on a regime under Article 2 of Protocol No. 10 of the Act of Accession as amended by Council Resolution (EC) No.293/2005 of 17 February 2005.

9 See Baceli 'This will be our best summer yet', *Cyprus Mail,* 21 June, 2005.

10 With exceptions for UN and other diplomatic/governmental vehicles and the odd cyclist.

11 European Commission and European Parliament Conference, 'Facilitating Commercial Activity Across the Green Line' Tuesday 2nd November 2004, Ledra Palace, Nicosia. Content Report by the Management Centre and Highway Communications www.highway communications.com.

12 In fact, some Turkish Cypriot drivers register their taxis in the south and change their number plates at the border in order to take passengers to and from Larnaca airport. The duplication of registration and insurance requirements increases their operating costs significantly.

13 Restaurant menu boards written in Greek around the harbour in Kyrenia, and large roadside billboards advertising the casinos of the north in Greek, are visible signs of the presence of Greek Cypriots in northern Cyprus, although there is anecdotal evidence that these numbers may be tailing off in the face of the current polarization of political positions. Turkish Cypriot tour parties to the south are often informally arranged by private and family groups who club together for the coach hire. In a recent incident, seven coaches taking a party of Turkish Cypriots for a day out to visit the shrine of Hala Sultan near Larnaca were allowed to cross, after a stand-off of some three hours waiting at the checkpoint. Despite the claims by the head of the Turkish Cypriot coach operators' association, it is not yet clear whether this will form a precedent. See 'Otobüslerimizle Hala Sultan'da', *Kibris,* 19 June 2005.

14 See further the Orams (note 18) and Hurma Restaurant (note 19) case, below.

15 Baceli, 'This will be our best summer yet', *Cyprus Mail,* 21 June, 2005. According to the head of the Turkish Cypriot Hoteliers Association, on the other hand, 12 of the smaller Turkish Cypriot hotels closed in the past year (Beydarli, personal communication).

16 www.cyprus.gov.cy

17 According to existing legislation, foreigners may buy and sell properties in the north on the approval of the Turkish Cypriot Council of Ministers, but risk losing their investment in properties with anything other than original Turkish Cypriot title deeds in the event of a settlement (see Scott 1998). Since the floating of the Annan Plan, there has been substantial foreign interest in properties in the north, since the plan suggests that foreigners too would be compensated for their investments in the event of a settlement.

18 A British couple, David and Linda Orams, who built a villa on land owned by a Greek Cypriot displaced person in the north, have been sued in the Nicosia District Court and ordered to demolish the house and pay court costs and damages of CY£7654 (€13,166) and CY£294.41 (€506.95) a month until the property is returned to the original Greek Cypriot owner. Since the entry of the Republic of Cyprus into the EU, the court in Cyprus can request that the judgement be enforced by the courts in the UK, leading to the possibility of arrest and the confiscation of the Orams' property assets in Britain. See *Warning by the Cyprus Embassy:* www.cyprusembassy.fi

19 The original Greek Cypriot owner of the Hurma Restaurant in Famagusta is suing the Turkish Cypriot currently operating the restaurant through the court in Larnaca and claiming compensation of between CY£100,000 and CY£250,000 for the loss of the property. See 'Rum Mahkemesi'ne Itiraz': www.netbul.com 13/05/05

References

Akiş, S., Peristianis, N., and Warner, J. (1996) Residents' attitudes to tourism development: the case of Cyprus. *Tourism Management* 17(7), 481–494.

Bianchi, R. (2001) Beyond the periphery: exploring the "new" regional dynamics of tourism in Southern Europe. In: Toivonen, T. and Honkanen, A. (eds) *North–South: Contrasts and Connections in Global Tourism.* Tilburg: ATLAS, pp. 249–265.

Bicak, H.A. and Altinay, M. (1996) Economic impact of Israeli tourists on North Cyprus. *Annals of Tourism Research* 23(4), 928–931.

Bowman, G. (1992) The politics of tour guiding: Israeli and Palestinian guides in Israel and the Occupied Territories. In: Harrison, D. (ed.) *Tourism and the Less Developed Countries.* London: Belhaven, pp. 121–134.

Christou, J. (2005) Domestic tourism hits all time high. *Cyprus Mail,* 10 July.

Devlet Planlama Örgütü (2001) *2002 Geçiş Yili Programi.* Lefkoşa (Nicosia): Devlet Planlama Örgütü.

Ioannides, D. and Apostolopoulos, Y. (1999) Political instability, war, and tourism in Cyprus: effects, management, and prospects for recovery. *Journal of Travel Research* 38(1), 51–56.

Ioannides, D. and Holcomb, B. (2001) Raising the stakes: implications of upmarket tourism policies in Cyprus and Malta. In: Ioannides, D. Apostolopoulos, Y. and Sönmez, S. (eds) *Mediterranean Islands and Sustainable Tourism Development.* London: Continuum, pp. 23–44.

Ministry of Tourism and Economy, TRNC (2005) *Tourism Statistics.* Lefkoşa (Nicosia): Ministry of Tourism and Economy.

Morvaridi, B. (1993) Demographic change, resettlement and resource use. In: Dodd, C.H. (ed.) *The Political, Social and Economic Development of Northern Cyprus.* Huntingdon, UK: Eothen, pp. 219–268.

NCHA (Northern Cyprus Hoteliers Association) (2005) Cyprus Passion of 'Net Group'. *Tourism Monthly,* 10 May.

Scott, J. (1998) Property values: ownership, legitimacy and land markets in northern Cyprus. In: Hann, C.M. (ed.) *Property Relations: Renewing the Anthropological Tradition.* Cambridge: Cambridge University Press, pp. 142–159.

Scott, J. (2000) Peripheries, artificial peripheries and centres. In: Brown, F. and Hall, D. (eds) *Tourism in Peripheral Regions.* Clevedon, UK: Channel View, pp. 58–73.

Scott, J. (2002) World heritage as a model for citizenship: the case of Cyprus. *International Journal of World Heritage Studies* 8(2), 99–116.

Scott, J. and Aşikoğlu, Ş. (2001) Gambling with paradise? Casino tourism development in northern Cyprus. *Journal of Tourism and Travel Research* 26(3), 47–57.

Sönmez, S.F. and Apostolopoulos, Y. (2000) Conflict resolution through tourism cooperation? The case of the partitioned island-state of Cyprus. *Journal of Travel and Tourism Marketing* 9(3), 35–48.

Part V

The Next Enlargement

In this penultimate section of four chapters, the candidates for EU membership – Bulgaria, Romania, Turkey and Croatia – are examined. While the first two had entered membership negotiations in the 1990s and had been included within the group of 12 candidates for possible accession in 2004, they were found not to be able to meet fully the Copenhagen criteria, but were encouraged to continue pursuing their full implementation. Despite Ankara's considerable history of seeking a closer relationship with the EU, not until October 2005 did the EU member states agree that both Turkey and Croatia could now enter into accession negotiations. That this took place on the same day represents one of the many important symbolic elements of the EU trajectory. For it was in the 1520s, as Ottoman armies were overwhelming the Kingdom of Croatia, that the Pope sent a message to the Croatian parliament, urging it to continue to resist, and extolling Croats as the 'ramparts of Christendom' (Tanner, 1997; Hall, 2000).

Just as a founding objective of the EEC in the 1950s was to bring France and Germany into a core partnership within a wider community that would remove the possibility of conflict within Western Europe, so successive enlargements have acted to wipe away past – and often ancient – animosities, rivalries and conflicts, whether cultural, ideological or territorial (or indeed all three). In this respect alone, the EU member states' attitude towards the speed and nature of the Union's enlargement has taken on a global significance, not least in terms of the signals it conveys to non-European as well as to domestic audiences. The EU is not a white, Christian, European club, and tourism is one of the contexts in which the richness and importance of (multi-)cultural heritage and its relationship with European citizenship and identity can be expressed (Chapter 3). Debates on the accession of Turkey to the EU thus appear fundamental to an evolving conception of 'Europe' and the appropriateness of this conception in a globalizing world that confronts man-made and natural potential disaster.

As a brief introductory overview of the candidates, this short piece aims to address their commonalities and contrasts, and to reflect on the significance for tourism of their likely accession to the EU.

Commonalities

There are two, perhaps interrelated, obvious commonalities that the candidates share. Geographically, all four are located in south-eastern Europe, although this needs qualification. First, of course,

is the fact that less than 10% of Turkey actually falls within geographical Europe, although this territory does include the country's, and arguably Europe's, largest city, Istanbul. The rest of the country
extends across the Dardanelles and Bosphorus into Asia, as the geographical entity of Anatolia
(historically 'Asia Minor'), extending to borders with Georgia, Armenia, Iran, Iraq and Syria. Kemal
Ataturk's capital for a modern secular Turkish state, Ankara, was established in the centre of
Anatolia in 1923.

The second qualification is that the geographical description south-eastern Europe does not
equate with 'the Balkans' or Balkan, an essentially geographical term, but one which has acquired, at
least in the West, pejorative connotations of instability, division, under-development and a certain
mentality (e.g. Todorova, 1994, 1997; Hall and Danta, 1996). While Bulgaria and Turkey would
accept that they are Balkan countries, if only in the geographical sense, Romanians argue that the
Balkans begin south of the Danube, and Croatians might suggest that while Serbia and Bosnia fall
within the Balkans, Croatia most certainly does not, being a Central European and/or Mediterranean
country. Some might argue that Balkanism is historically associated with Ottoman rule, and one
related commonality is the fact that present-day Bulgaria, Romania and Croatia were, to varying geographical extents and historical periods, occupied by the Ottoman Turks. The mythic imagery of
Transylvania, for example, is based on the fact that this upland element of present-day Romania
acted as a Habsburg bastion against the Ottomans. The latter had incorporated what are now
Romania's other two major regional components, the lowland Moldavia and Wallachia, which,
extending over fertile Danubian plains, became known as the 'breadbasket' of the Ottoman empire.

The second commonality is that all four candidates' tourism has tended to be (perceived
as being) dominated by the '3Ss' market, historically associated with such all-inclusive brands as
Balkan Holidays and Yugotours. Within Yugoslavia, Croatia held a dominant role in international
tourism, embracing a large proportion of the country's Adriatic coastline, leaving relatively short
coastal stretches within Slovenia to the north (e.g. Izola, Piran) and Montenegro to the south (e.g.
Sveti Stefan, Budva and the Neretva Delta). Major economic reforms and construction of the
Adriatic Highway in the 1960s opened up the Yugoslav coast to Western markets. By the end of
the 1980s the hard currency generated by tourism in Yugoslavia, and largely within Croatia, was
greater than the total for the rest of Communist Central and Eastern Europe (Hall, 1991). As
Chapter 22 suggests, despite a wide range of cultural and natural assets, only in recent years,
following independence, and especially after the devastating wars of Yugoslav succession in the first
half of the 1990s, has the Croatian tourism industry pursued substantive efforts to diversify its
markets, products and regional distribution (e.g. see Jordan, 2000).

In the 1970s and 1980s the Black Sea beaches of Bulgaria were far more popular for Western
tourists than those of Romania, although both also attracted the lower end of the market, such as
school groups and novices, to their mountain winter sports centres. Spas and other natural and cultural attractions, while present in abundance, were poorly promoted in the West and lacked good
infrastructure and information services. In particular, Romania had a deservedly poor image in the
1980s, not least because of food and power shortages, although bad publicity in the Western popular press also afflicted the image of Bulgarian resorts. Until 1989, both countries were members of
the Soviet bloc, with currency exchange and potential visa complications. Further, acting as an
attraction for some Western tourists and a disincentive for others, most Romanian and Bulgarian
coastal and inland resorts tended to be dominated by domestic tourists whose own international
travel opportunities were severely limited.

As Chapter 21 relates, almost unrestricted tourism and related urban development along
stretches of Turkey's Aegean and Mediterranean coasts from the 1970s saw that country exhibiting
some of the fastest growth rates in international tourist numbers during the 1980s and 1990s. This
process saw Turkey taking over the momentum of Mediterranean coastal tourism from the more
mature and diversifying tourism economies further west, and almost replicating scenes characteristic of the Spanish *costas* in the 1960s and 1970s. The experience of Turkey is instructive in suggest-
ing that far from declining, mass tourism is continually being rejuvenated as new markets – notably
former Soviet bloc citizens in the 1990s – are drawn into the consumption activity.

Contrasts

Perhaps the most obvious contrasts between the four candidates are cultural. Turkey, as a predominantly (Sunni) Islamic country, with relatively high birth rates, a rapidly growing population and a consequently relative young demographic structure, contrasts markedly with most other European countries. Yet, with a classical heritage reflected in numerous archaeological sites, it shares a great deal with much of Europe. The Turkish language is related only to Hungarian, Finnish and Estonian in Europe, and is not part of the Indo-European linguistic group. The dominant religion of both Romania and Bulgaria is Eastern Orthodoxy, the churches and monasteries of both countries representing an important cultural legacy; but whereas Bulgarian is a Slavic language using the Cyrillic alphabet, Romanian is essentially a Latin-based romance tongue using the Roman alphabet. Croatia is mostly Roman Catholic, particularly since the migrations and other consequences of conflict in the 1990s saw many Orthodox Serbs and Muslim Bosnians no longer living within the country.

Recent political and military histories certainly represent a contrasting legacy. Turkey was a stalwart member of NATO throughout the Cold War and an important base for eavesdropping across the Soviet bloc. Bulgaria and Romania, as members of that bloc, belonged both to its economic grouping CMEA (COMECON: viewed somewhat optimistically by some in its time as the Communist equivalent of the EEC), and its military umbrella, the Warsaw Pact, and were thereby part of 'the enemy'. Croatia, meanwhile, was the second most important component of the Yugoslav Socialist Federation, a country whose leader, Josip Broz Tito (along with India), tried to steer the non-aligned movement as a third way between the capitalist and communist worlds.

Romania had been put together as a sovereign state with the loss of Wallachia and Moldavia by the Ottomans in 1859, and then in the aftermath of World War I, following the collapse and dismemberment of the Austro-Hungarian empire, with the addition of Transylvania. Bulgaria gained independence from the Turks in 1878 following intervention from Russia. Croatia, like Transylvania, had also been a Hungarian part of Austria-Hungary, and became a major component of the post-First World War Kingdom of Serbs, Croats and Slovenes, the forerunner of Yugoslavia. Although south Slavs, and thus regarded as an inferior race by the Nazis, Croatians gained a degree of independence during World War II following German occupation. The Turkish Ottoman empire, just as Austria-Hungary, was largely dismembered as an outcome of World War I. What had been an enormous multi-ethnic Islamicized empire, the western arm of which had stretched across south-eastern and central Europe, was reduced, in Europe, to a small territory barely representing the western hinterland of Istanbul.

Tourism Significance

The accession of these four candidates would mean that the EU would embrace the whole of the north Mediterranean coast except for the relatively short strip between Dubrovnik and Greece, through Montenegro and Albania. Further, the western and southern shores of the Black Sea would also be within 'Europe'. This has at least two implications:

- virtually all of the summer sun mass tourism locations in Europe and Asia Minor would be subject to EU directives and laws relating to tourism, environmental and employment issues; and
- it would act as an incentive for at least some of the other Black Sea and Mediterranean coastal states, both north and south, to forge closer relations with the EU.

Further, Turkey's accession to the EU could help to draw closer both fellow Islamic and Turkic states of Western and Central Asia, whose cultural and natural resources appear to have been little developed for tourism purposes. None the less, as Chapter 21 indicates, at the time of writing there exist a number of obstacles particularly for Turkey to overcome on its path to accession, a process that may continue until 2020, by which time the world is likely to look a very different place. Despite the goodwill of most of the EU 25 member states for Turkish accession, the issue of the Union's 'absorption capacity' for further enlargement was raised at the start of negotiations in October 2005 (e.g. Watt and Smith, 2005). One suspects that this concept will take on a dynamic of its own in the months and years ahead.

References

Hall, D. (ed.) (1991) *Tourism and Economic Development in Eastern Europe and the Soviet Union*. London: Belhaven Press.

Hall, D. (2000) Croatia. In: Hall, D. and Danta, D. (eds) *Europe Goes East: EU Enlargement, Diversity and Uncertainty*. London: The Stationery Office, pp. 275–288.

Hall, D. and Danta, D. (1996) The Balkans: perceptions and realities. In: Hall, D. and Danta, D. (eds) *Reconstructing the Balkans: a Geography of the New Southeast Europe*. Chichester, UK: John Wiley & Sons, pp. 1–13.

Jordan, P. (2000) Restructuring Croatia's coastal resorts: change, sustainable development and the incorporation of rural hinterlands. *Journal of Sustainable Tourism* 8(6), 525–539.

Tanner, M. (1997) *Croatia: a Nation Forged in War*. New Haven, CT: Yale University Press.

Todorova, M. (1994) The Balkans: from discovery to invention. *Slavic Review* 53, 453–482.

Todorova, M. (1997) *Imagining the Balkans*. Oxford: Oxford University Press.

Watt, N. and Smith, H. (2005) Sweet and sour climax to Turkey's long march. *The Guardian*, 4 October, p. 14.

19 Tourism in Bulgaria

Marin Bachvarov

Introduction

Bulgaria emerged onto the international tourism market in the 1960s as a 'sun, sea and sand' destination and was the most successful among COMECON countries in attracting foreign tourists, particularly for summer holidays on the Black Sea coast. Throughout the 1970s and 1980s the Bulgarian international tourism industry was one of the most competitive in Central and Eastern Europe (Koulov and Marinov, 1997).

The downfall of the Communist system after 1989 led to a deep crisis in Bulgarian tourism and it fell behind developments elsewhere, particularly those in Central Europe (Hall, 1995). Along with other destinations on the European periphery, Bulgaria suffered from an absence of good and rapid transport links with the more developed parts of the continent. This was, and still is, a serious obstacle for the development of tourism in the country. On the other hand, the removal of the Iron Curtain and subsequent integration into European economic and infrastructure networks has made the country more easily accessible for tourists from Western Europe. In the new conditions Bulgaria could make better use of its location between Europe, Turkey and the Eastern Mediterranean.

Bulgaria is accessible by air, including charter flights, but is not within driving distance of Western Europe and especially from Northern Europe including the British Isles. The upgrading of the motorways in Serbia and Romania and in the country itself, as well as the building of a second bridge over the Danube at Vidin and the EU financed E-8 corridor to link Bulgaria with Italy via FYR Macedonia and Albania, will enhance Bulgaria's accessibility. Sofia airport is currently being enlarged and similar projects will soon start in the other three international airports: Varna, Bourgas and Plovdiv.

The country has a number of strengths that favour its tourist development:

- rapid economic growth and 4.5–5.5% GNP annual growth;
- lower (though rising rapidly) prices of property, services and goods;
- currency (the *lev*) pegged to the euro;
- expected accession to the EU in 2007;
- full NATO membership;
- regular and seasonal flights to the larger European cities from the country's four international airports (see the house page of Worldwidepropertyinvestment.com (www. worldwidepropertyinvestment.com)).

Resource Base, Types and Spatial Structure of Tourism

About 35–40% of Bulgarian territory offers good conditions for recreation and tourism

©CAB International 2006. *Tourism in the New Europe: the Challenges and Opportunities of EU Enlargement* (eds D. Hall, M. Smith and B. Marciszewska)

(Evrev, 1988). The changes during the post-Communist transition did not result in serious shifts in the spatial structure of the tourism industry, which is still characterized by an over-concentration on the Black Sea coast accounting for 63% of beds and 67% of over-nights (Marinov, 2004). Traditionally, tourism in Bulgaria has been associated with coastal resorts and to a much lesser degree with cultural tours, spas and ski resorts. The areas with differing tourism specializations (tourism regions) are presented below (see Fig. 19.1) (Bachvarov, 1997b).

Black Sea coast

The Bulgarian Black Sea coast between Romania in the north and Turkey to the south is 378 km long. Fine sandy beaches cover about 30% of the coast, while there are 9 million m^2 of beach (16 million m^2 including dunes) (Vodenska, 1992). This capacity allows simultaneous recreation for up to one million tourists. In the peak months of July and August the number of tourists is close to 70% of this capacity, but some popular beaches are over-crowded. Here the problem of congestion is serious and demands concerted management efforts to reduce it. The Black Sea region is the most developed tourism area in the country, leading in terms of international tourism with about 75% of overseas tourist overnight stays and about 50% of domestic overnights. A peak of its development was reached at the end of the 1980s, but recently a new cycle of rapid development has been inaugurated under changed geopolitical and economic conditions.

The region includes two major urban centres and ports (Varna and Bourgas), ten smaller towns and 20 villages. There exist about 2000 separate tourism establishments; many of these are clustered in two areas north of Varna and Bourgas (Fig. 19.2) as parts of these conurbations.

Tourist visits are highly concentrated in the summer (June–September) and 60% of the overnights take place in July and August. Around 60–65% of the country's total accommodation capacity is located in the Black Sea region (Bachvarov, 1999).

Secondary zones

Besides the Black Sea region there are several secondary tourist zones.

- The south-west interior of the country is the second largest recreational and tourism zone. It has a composite character and serves both shorter and longer domestic holidays, and in a number of places (cities, monasteries, winter resorts and spas) it also attracts foreign visitors. The interior tourism areas are at a different stage of development and those better known, and better prepared to cater for tourism, include those listed below (see Fig. 19.1);
- the Sofia conurbation with the high mountains to the south-west (Vitosha, Rila and Pirin). Here the cultural and business importance of the capital is diversified with skiing resorts, spas, national parks and Orthodox monasteries including the famous Rila monastery;
- the Plovdiv conurbation and the adjacent West Rhodope skiing and spa resorts, with cultural and natural attractions, and wine and folklore tours; and
- Central Stara Planina – the Balkan range and sub-Balkan valleys including the Valley of Roses – with many historic, spa and rural tourism opportunities.

Northern Bulgaria and the Thracian Plain

Much of northern Bulgaria and the Thracian Plain has less tourism and recreational potential and consequently are not included in the specialized tourism regions. Actually, behind the Black Sea region lays a hinterland which is a vacuum rarely attracting tourists based in the seaside resorts. On the other hand, the fact that the most appealing tourism areas lie in the eastern and western peripheries of Bulgaria can potentially activate the central parts of the country along communication corridors. At present only about 5% of coastal package tourists take organized trips inside the country.

Winter tourism

Bulgaria is among the most southern of European winter tourism destinations. Typical winter

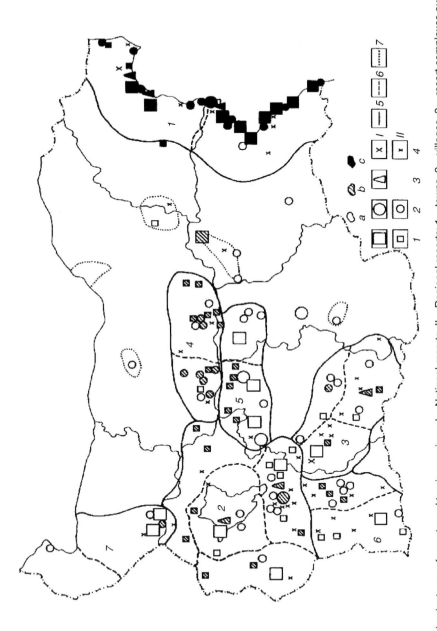

Fig. 19.1. Bulgaria: types of resorts and tourism regions. I – National resorts; II – Regional resorts; 1 – towns, 2 – villages, 3 – resort complexes outside permanent settlements, 4 – designated resorts outside permanent settlements; a – spa resort, b – mountain resort, c – seaside resort; 5 – boundary of a region, 6 – boundary of sub-region, 7 – boundary of micro-region. Regions marked with numbers in the map: 1 – Black Sea coast, 2 – Sofia region, 3 – West Rhodope, 4 – Central Stara Planina (Central Balkan range and mountain valleys), 5 – Sredna Gora (Anti-Balkan range and Valley of Roses), 6 – Pirin, 7 – North-West. Source: Bachvarov, 1997b.

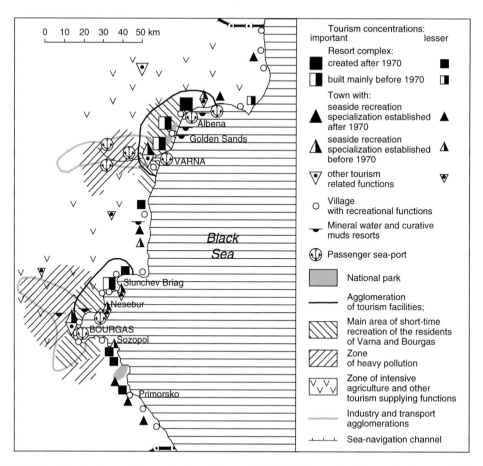

Fig. 19.2. Bulgaria: the spatial organization of the country's Black Sea region. Source: Bachvarov, 1999.

weather is sunny in the five high mountain ranges above 2000m altitude: Rila, Pirin, Vitosha, Balkan and Rhodope. Despite the proximity of warmer regions, snow cover is stable and lasts 4–6 months. This explains Sofia's joint bid with Borovets to host the 2014 Winter Olympic games. At present there are four international mountain resorts:

- Vitosha – at 2285 m with good snow conditions on its northern slopes yet within Sofia municipality. Vitosha is a national park with good tourism and skiing infrastructure visited by over three million skiers and hikers annually. A crucial factor is the excellent road and lift connections and the 1.2m population capital city next-door.
- The oldest and largest Bulgarian mountain resort is Borovets on the northern

slopes of Rila the highest mountain in the Balkans (2925 m). Borovets is only 65 km from Sofia and since the 1980s has been promoted as an inexpensive downhill skiing venue in the UK, Holland, Finland and Greece.

- Frequently visited by foreigners, Pamporovo is 80 km south of Plovdiv in the central part of the Rhodope mountains. Nearby is Chepelare another developing ski centre, as well as the Bachkovo monastery and several picturesque towns and villages offering cultural heritage, rural tourism and folklore attractions.
- The newest and most rapidly expanding ski centre is Bansko in the Pirin mountains, including the nearby resort of Dobrinishte, which has a skiing area linked with the Bansko region. Bansko, a small heritage

town on the piedmont attracted US$40m investments in tourism in 2004. A new gondola cableway, eight other lifts and 50 snow-guns have been installed.

Hiking and trekking

Hiking and trekking has a long tradition in Bulgaria: the Bulgarian Union of Hikers was founded in 1895. A network of over 200 mountain hostels (huts) is located mostly in high and medium mountain areas. A few of them have been modernized and upgraded to accommodate more demanding guests.

Spa resorts

Spa resorts used to play a very important part in the Bulgarian health system, but now have a minor role. Only 20% of the rest homes run by the Association of Trade Unions up to 1991 still function as a recreational network. The remainder were privatized, some changed functions, others turned into hotels or were simply abandoned. The Bulgarian sanatoria network was reduced between 1990 and 2000 from 184 to 30 establishments (NSI, 2001). Many of the former sanatoria were transformed into rehabilitation hospitals and private clinics. The main spa centres of Velingrad, Hisarya, Varshets, Sandanski, Kostenets, Pomorie, Bankya are situated in attractive environments and in combination with water sports, mountain hiking, rural tourism and retirement migration, are well patronized by a domestic market. None the less, because of ongoing changes in function, the average length of stay has decreased.

Rural tourism

Rural tourism is deeply rooted in tradition as the majority of the Bulgarian population are of rural origin. There are 480,000 second homes throughout the country. As a participant in the foreign tourism market, however, Bulgaria is a newcomer. In spite of the fact that the country is not within driving distance of Western Europe, there is considerable potential for rural tourism on the basis of the rich natural and cultural

heritage and the numerous second homes available for renting to tourists (see the website www.netinfo.bg). So far the most successful rural tourism areas are near the mountain resorts and the cultural heritage towns (e.g. Veliko Turnovo). However, the poor state of infrastructure and depopulation of large areas of the countryside are barriers to rural tourism development.

Cultural and business tourism

Cultural tourism and business visits in Bulgaria are largely restricted to the cities and some small towns with Bulgarian Orthodox Revival sites in the mountain foothills or at the seaside, such as Nesebur, Sozopol, Triavna, Melnik, Zheravna, Bozhentsi, Samokov, Koprivshtitsa, Elena, Etropole. Other important urban tourism centres are Plovdiv and Veliko Turnovo, which have the appeal of what Hall (1991) has termed 'cultural capitals' in Central and Eastern Europe.

The Orthodox churches, and especially the 160 monasteries, among them Rila, Bachkovo, Troyan, Preobrazhenski and Rozhen, are one of the strengths of Bulgarian cultural tourism. Together with the country's rich folklore tradition, they should play a much bigger role in the country's range of tourist attractions. At present, few foreigners on holiday at the Black Sea, or in the mountain resorts, travel inside the country in order to visit cultural heritage sites. This is often a result of the poor promotion of the latter, although there is a considerable potential for tempting these groups away from their bases for a short time, as well as developing exclusively cultural tours.

During the post-Communist transition the political importance of the cultural tourism has been acknowledged, although dominance of the prevailing perception of 'heritage' within the country rather than market-oriented development (Hughes and Allen, 2005) has been hindering the expansion of cultural tourism despite its considerable potential.

Ecotourism and adventure tourism

Ecotourist and adventure itineraries and other activities organized by specialized tour operators have attracted limited numbers of foreign tourists. They are functioning in the mountain areas and national parks and more specifically in the Rhodope, Stara Planina and Pirin. These should not be developed as mass tourism destinations as this would be contrary to the very appeal of the discovery of little known places.

Gastronomic tourism

Bulgarian traditional food and drink can be one of the strengths in the tourism attraction mix of the country. Bulgaria is alleged to be the homeland of wine, as Homer writes that Thracians (the ancient inhabitants of the eastern Balkans) learnt to prepare wine from grapes. Bulgarian wines, especially the dry red varieties, are of good quality and good value. Visits to vineyards and wine cellars (and the development of wine trails) should be promoted and combined with folklore events, archaeological tours and other special interest visits. There is also a variety of other drinks based on the Bulgarian yoghurt and different types of brandies.

Bulgarian Tourism During the Post-Communist Transition

Institutional change

After establishing the necessary legal framework, privatization in the Bulgarian tourism sector was carried out during the period 1997–2002. Employees in tourism enterprises were allowed to buy up to 20% of the shares, the rest were sold on competitive terms to Bulgarian and foreign financial groups.

The new owners immediately started reconstructing old premises and building new facilities. In a short time the Bulgarian coastal and mountain resorts were modernized although some serious problems emerged. The rapid transformation, and particularly the construction and upgrading of premises and the marketing of the new Bulgarian tourism product, could not have been possible without the financial and logistic support of European tour operators, especially the German and British.

Until February 2005 the tourism sector was the responsibility of the Ministry of the Economy, which implemented public policy for tourism and coordinated tourism development with other sectors. This entailed:

- initiating regulations for tourism activities;
- supervising international relations in the field of tourism;
- supporting the activities of regional and local organizations, and with those in specific sectors;
- developing information technology resources;
- undertaking marketing research, analysis and forecasts; and
- developing the tourism product and training.

On 18 February 2005 the government transferred tourism to a combined Ministry of Culture, Tourism and Sport. The first reaction of the business community to this was not enthusiastic.

The National Tourism Board has been established as a body to consult with the Ministry. As a national tourism organization its role is to assist the implementation of national policy in the field of tourism. The members of the National Board are representatives of tourism-related ministries, national airlines and of sector and regional tourism organizations. According to the Tourism Act, municipal administrations have statutory rights and obligations to implement tourism policy in their areas.

By September 2004, 1876 companies had a state licence to operate in the tourism sector (NSI, 2005) with the majority (1112) registered as tour operating companies, and 764 as travel agents. A serious concern is the lack of experience of many smaller firms operating in marketing: their service quality is low and long-term plans are rarely implemented or are absent. A new law referring to the management of the Black Sea coast is being prepared in order to regulate: building licences against interference from other interests, access to public spaces and the use of beaches, the location of shops and other commercial activities, and ecological requirements.

From January 2007, any difference in accommodation price for foreigners and Bulgarians will become illegal as one of the requirements of EU entry (see www.netinfo.bg). Currently some hoteliers offer lower prices to Bulgarians, justifying a dual pricing policy by arguing that domestic tourists have a lower purchasing power.

Transformation Trends

Since 1990, Bulgarian tourism has faced a radical transformation (Vodenska, 1992; Harrison, 1993; Bachvarov, 1997a; Kasatschka and Marinov, 2003), and a number of trends can be distinguished. First, as might have been expected, there has been a significant change in markets, with the share of EU countries in foreign tourism overnights increasing from 36% in 1990 to 72% in 2002. Such a trend might be expected to continue.

Second, there has been a substantial reduction in the domestic tourism market. A major reason for this is changes that have taken place in subsidized welfare and recreation due to the withdrawal of financial support from the state. The majority of trade union and spa facilities have been privatized, and have often changed their function, while some have been abandoned. At the same time, better-off domestic tourists have more frequently used commercial accommodation in the mountains and at the seaside. By contrast, many former domestic tourists will have been adversely affected by short- to medium-term rising prices and relatively lower incomes.

Third, tourists from former COMECON countries, so numerous in the 1970s and 1980s, have almost entirely disappeared, with the notable exception of wealthier Russians and Ukrainians, who, in the 1990s, represented a large share of tourists and were preferred as customers by the local population. In 2001, Bulgaria introduced a visa requirement for CIS visitors and the result was a considerable reduction in arrivals from former Soviet countries.

Fourth, the rapid privatization of state property – hotels, catering, shops and many services – has taken place, while outdated infrastructure in the resorts is still run by the state or local government. This causes constant problems with hotel and restaurant owners. In many cases tourism facilities were built on land now claimed by its former owners or their heirs. Koulov and Marinov (1997) assessed that 80% of land in the coastal resorts of Slunchev Briag and Albena is liable to re-privatization.

Fifth, there have been notable policy changes to respond to a market environment, and appropriate administrative structures have been set up. The role of the state is now mainly limited to legal and administrative regulation and destination marketing.

As noted earlier, attempts, albeit still insufficient, are being made to change the structure of the country's tourism product from a sole emphasis on summer seaside holidays to a wider range of activities and locations including mountain and cultural tourism. This is related to attempts to establish a new image to better position Bulgaria in the international market. This is particularly required to counteract mass media generalizations concerning 'war in the Balkans' that had a strongly deflecting effect on potential tourists during the 1990s. International promotion of the country as a tourist destination was almost totally abandoned during this time, and between 1990 and 1997 official tourism offices abroad were reduced from 27 to just four. Recently their number has increased to 12, but all are within EU countries, except those in Moscow and New York.

Arguably, a major reason for the recent successful development of tourism in Bulgaria is the country's political stability since 1997, along with the privatization of the tourism infrastructure and catering facilities. A further reason is the considerable foreign investment in Bulgarian resorts. As a result, in just a few years the Bulgarian Black Sea region has been thoroughly modernized and is now better prepared to accommodate the requirements of Western tourists. Generally, the Bulgarian tourist product has been found attractive to those of lower or average income. An investigation in 1998 disclosed that only 2% of foreign tourists belonged to the affluent segment of the market. A recent survey in Poland of 540 internet users found that low-spending tourists from Central and Eastern Europe remain a problem, with 61% of those planning to spend their holidays in Bulgaria having a budget of less than €360 (from the website www.bulgaricus.com, 2005). As might be expected, the largest revenue contribution is provided by visitors from Germany, the UK, Greece, Russia, Benelux and Scandinavia who stay for longer periods. By contrast, visitors from neighbouring countries tend to stay for a short time and often for non-leisure purposes.

Tourism Infrastructure

Most tourism infrastructure in Bulgaria relates to 102 resorts (seaside, spa and mountain) and 66 settlements with cultural attractions (Bachvarov, 1999). The large seaside and mountain resorts were centrally planned and financed exclusively for tourism. In 2004, the capacity of hotels and similar establishments was 86,000 rooms, or 190,000 beds, out of a total 450,000 beds in all forms of commercial and subsidized accommodation. Between 2002 and 2004 the country's hotel capacity increased by up to 50%. In the official statistical sources for 2002, the capacity for hotel and similar establishments was only 170,000 (Marinov, 2004), but there is a considerable undeclared capacity. For example, in 2004 the mayor of Bansko declared that there were 1000 'hidden' beds in his town (from www.netinfo.bg, 2005). Private lodgings, formerly very popular, have declined as well as trade union 'rest houses' and other subsidized 'welfare' accommodation.

The overwhelming trend in the years since the start of privatization in 1997 has been the rapid reconstruction of older hotels and restaurants and the building of many new hotels, catering and entertainment establishments. It is estimated that in 2004 about 70% of tourists from the EU stayed in the Black Sea resorts, 10% in the mountain resorts and 20% in urban (business trips and cultural tours) and rural areas (ecological and rural tourism, game hunting).

A characteristic feature of Bulgarian accommodation in the past was its low quality and limited variety of services. The dominant category was 2-star with small rooms and poor sanitation, often in noisy places and without sports facilities. This was appropriate for simple 'sun, sea and sand' tourism when the majority of tourists came from other Communist countries. The proportion of luxury hotels in the 1980s was only 3–4%. This situation is gradually changing as new private hotels offer a higher quality and the proportion of 4- and 5-star hotels in 2004 was 27% (of which 5.4% were 5-star – see Table 19.1).

Sofia's proportion of the number of overnights spent within the country is 10.1% (for foreign visitors, 15.6%), but due to a higher standard, prices and occupancy rates, the capital city's share of revenue was actually 30% (Marinov, 2000, 2004).

A similar trend can be observed in catering and entertainment establishments that have also expanded in capacity, standard and variety of services (Table 19.2). The price : quality ratio of food and other services is among the

Table 19.1. Bulgarian accommodation and 'lodging' establishments, September 2004.

Category	1-star	2-star	3-star	4-star	5-star	Total
Number	0	266	276	100	20	662
Rooms	0	20,238	29,662	14,715	3,646	68,061
% of total rooms	0	29.44	43.58	21.62	5.36	100

Accommodation establishments include hotels, motels, holiday clubs and villages. Lodging facilities include specially built second residences (villas).
Source: Republic of Bulgaria Ministry of the Economy, 2005.

Table 19.2. Bulgaria: catering and entertainment establishments, September 2004.

Category	1-star	2-star	3-star	4-star	5-star	Total
Number	31	578	869	222	51	1,751
Seats	2,399	48,005	84,488	23,696	5,002	16,590
% of total seats	3.06	14.48	51.65	29.34	1.47	100

Catering and entertainment establishments include restaurants, fast-food restaurants, pubs, cafes and bars.
Source: Republic of Bulgaria Ministry of the Economy, 2005.

most attractive in Europe, reflecting the impact of privatization.

The expansion of good quality private hotels, usually small and family run, is one of the strengths of Bulgarian tourism, although it has meant a growth of room capacity greater than the increase in tourists. As a result, the average occupancy rate fell from 56% in 1990 to 32% in 2000 (Marinov, 2004). Even more troublesome is the fact that this accommodation growth has not been matched by infrastructural development in the resorts. The condition of the infrastructure in some seaside (Slunchev Briag is the obvious example) and mountain resorts (Bansko) is extremely poor. The inflow of tourists to many areas is far greater than the capacity of the infrastructure to support them. Such a situation can hardly be regarded as sustainable (Bachvarov, 1999).

What is the reason for this unfortunate situation that could in the near future endanger the overall development of the Bulgarian tourism industry? Taking into account that hotels and other tourism facilities are no longer state-run, the state cannot subsidize the infrastructure any longer. Local authorities earn considerable income from resorts, but appear to fail to maintain the infrastructure sufficiently. Re-privatization of land in the resorts has also created a maze of legal problems and contradictions regarding management responsibilities.

In order to cope with this situation, in December 2004 the government granted municipality status to nine resorts – seven on the coast (Albena, Zlatni Piasatsi, St Konstanin, Eleni, Slunchev Briag, Primorsko 'Youth Centre' and Duni) and two in the mountains (Borovers in Rila and Pamporovo in the Rhodope). They are defined as settlements of national significance. The construction and urbanization plans in these resorts will have to be approved by the Minister of Regional Development, unlike previous practice when municipal councils could decide on local spatial development policy (Sofia News Agency, 2005).

Another threat is the illegal building of hotels and restaurants on the coastal strip, often on the beaches themselves. This has disturbed the physical planning of the resorts producing unplanned development. Thus, the incompatibility of the 'get rich quick' attitude with an orderly, ecological and sustainable development lies behind these problems. Often, violations of the 50m zone above the water line, which is legally protected from development, are in favour of local politicians and businessmen who have often exerted pressure on local officials.

One problem facing both the functioning of the infrastructure and employment in tourism is the question of seasonality. Over 90% of the coastal facilities are operational only between June and the end of September, although seasonality is less important in urban hotels and in spas. In the mountain resorts there are two peaks of occupancy, with domestic tourists in summer and both foreign and Bulgarian visitors in winter. In terms of overnight stays and revenue, the winter season from the end of December until mid-April is the more important.

Tourism Markets

Since 1989 a dramatic change has occurred in foreign tourist arrivals by region of origin. Central and East European tourists, who represented 80% of overnights until 1990, practically disappeared. Visitors from adjacent countries (Turkey, Greece) increased dramatically, although their stays were usually short or in transit, thus having a weak economic effect. The Western European share remained relatively stable, Germany and UK being the major inbound tourism markets, but in terms of overnight stays and revenue this sector also seriously declined.

The assumption that tourism could become a priority sector did not prove correct in the early stages (1990–1996) of transition to a market economy (Bachvarov, 1997a), but in 1997 the ineffective socialist government was overthrown and the country embarked on a large-scale market transformation. The tourism sector developed dynamically, and since 1998 tourism indicators have constantly risen. In 2001–2004, in spite of the crisis in global tourism after '9/11', inbound tourism to Bulgaria exhibited one of the steepest increases in Europe. In 2004, when the country was visited by 7 million foreigners, including 4 million for tourism purposes (and a further 2.3m in transit), revenue of €1.8bn was generated. Yet, this is only 0.3% of the global and 0.5% of the European income directly generated by tourism. The revenue was earned mainly in summer (June–September), while during the winter season (January–April) it reached only €263m.

Within the EU market, Bulgaria is viewed as a typical package tourism destination, while visitors from neighbouring countries arrive almost exclusively on individually arranged trips.

In 2004, arrivals of foreign tourists grew by 13.6% (see Table 19.1), and accommodation capacity expanded by almost 30%. Such dynamic tourism growth places Bulgaria among European growth leaders together with Turkey and Croatia.

Foreign visitors registered nearly 10m overnight stays, while Bulgarians contributed 5m, making a total of 15m overnight stays in commercial accommodation. The leading source country continues to be Germany, followed by rapid growth from the UK and Greece. Smaller source markets that are also growing quickly are the Scandinavian countries, The Netherlands, the USA, Israel, Austria, Switzerland and new EU members: the Czech Republic, Hungary, Slovakia, Poland and Slovenia, as well as neighbouring Romania and Turkey (see Table 19.3).

Table 19.3. Bulgaria: international arrivals in Bulgaria for leisure and recreation, 2004.

Top 30 countries	No. of leisure and recreation visits	2004/2003 % change
Greece	707,453	+29.17
FYR Macedonia[a]	655,974	−2.44
Serbia and Montenegro[a]	576,965	−2.50
Germany	565,337	+5.75
United Kingdom	259,092	+62.60
Russian Federation	120,523	−0.67
Czech Republic	102,045	+30.17
Poland	99,684	+61.25
Sweden	96,131	+36.43
Romania[a]	91,539	+19.43
Israel	79,172	+14.65
Slovakia	75,253	+17.74
Finland	58,463	+19.72
Denmark	52,594	+23.15
France	48,634	+35.98
USA	39,276	+26.18
Turkey	37,600	+13.92
Hungary	33,028	+51.17
Austria	32,219	+38.79
Belgium	30,022	−6.69
Ukraine	29,793	−29.71
Italy	28,337	+15.28
The Netherlands	25,874	+19.09
Norway	21,403	+37.15
Switzerland	20,085	+39.43
Cyprus	13,400	+52.93
Belarus	12,037	−1.38
Slovenia	11,824	+73.40
Rep. of Ireland	11,460	+83.39
Spain	9,638	+40.27
Total	4,010,326	+13.56

[a]Including cross-border petty traders.
Source: NSI, 2005.

In 1989, 80% of foreign tourists were from former Communist countries, while in 2003 about 60% of arrivals and 75% of overnights were from EU countries. The German share is especially large, and the British and Greek proportion substantial too, while Russia and some of the new EU members such as Poland are far below their 1989 level.

There are strong seasonal variations in the different markets. For the majority, summer holidays dominate, while among Greek and UK tourists the January–April period is favoured (Greeks representing 25% of tourists in this period, while the UK proportion grew by 43% in 2004 compared to 2003) (Devnik, 2005). During the 2002–2004 period the rate of winter tourism arrivals has grown faster than summer.

Bulgarian outbound tourism increased in the first years of transition, but after 2000 it stabilized at around 3–4 million trips, mainly to neighbouring Turkey, Greece and FYR Macedonia. Bulgarian expenditure abroad reached US$800m in 2004. About one million Bulgarians travel abroad primarily for tourism, but most trips are not recreational in character; however, the number of recreational holidays to Turkey and Greece is rising. According to Turkish frontier statistics in 2003, Bulgarians represented the second largest group after Germans. Bulgarians are the biggest group of visitors to FYR Macedonia, while Romania, and Serbia and Montenegro also attract a considerable number of trips. Visits to neighbouring Balkan countries are usually short and spread throughout the year. The main reason for such a pattern is the dramatic increase in transport costs, especially airfares, causing a reduction in more distant trips.

The majority of foreign arrivals are by car and coach, though the proportion by air is increasing dynamically and now supplies about 25% of all tourism visits. Proportions by train and ship are not significant.

In general, the financial performance of Bulgarian tourism has improved since 1997 and more specifically in the years 2001–2004 when a considerable rejuvenation in the international tourism market occurred. There was a positive balance of payments in tourism reaching €1bn in 2004; but the impressive results of Bulgarian inbound tourism would be considerably better if the country was promoted abroad more consistently. In 2004, Bulgaria had a national stand at only five tourism fairs and had smaller stands at 36 other events (30 in EU countries, the rest in the CIS, Israel and the Middle East) (from www.netinfo.bg, 2005).

Quality Issues

The growth of Bulgarian tourism in the last few years should not hide existing serious problems which could impede the development of the country as a sustainable tourism destination. Tourism quality is still judged according to service providers' perceptions rather than an evaluation of clients' preferences. The supply side dominates, partly based on real demand, partly on long-standing myths of what foreign tourists are interested in. This is particularly the case in gastronomy; many tourists now seek local produce, yet there persists the belief that foreign tourists would consume Western food and drinks such as hamburgers and whisky.

Such quality issues are at least in part a legacy of the Communist period when services were perceived as mass, non-personalized and inflexible. Considering the image of the country as a seaside holiday destination and the less developed resources of its interior, tourism at the Black Sea coast will continue to be crucial for Bulgarian tourism. Pursuing diversification and flexibility within the basic seaside product is probably a more realistic proposition than introducing alternative forms of tourism. Such a diversification should be based on an extension of the season and the continued operation of more hotels throughout the year adapted to hosting such activities as conferences, training sessions and group therapy. The main trend should be away from mere sunbathing and include more water sports and outdoor activities.

The diversification and upgrading of the level of services should be one of the strategic objectives of Bulgarian tourism. This cannot be achieved without upgrading the infrastructure and improving training for those in the industry. Both tourists and entrepreneurs complain about the poor roads and infrastructure, continued construction activity in the resorts producing noise and refuse, the poor hygiene of some beaches and public toilets, and the outdated purification of water and waste treatment. They blame the local authorities and the withdrawal of the state from investment in local infrastructure. At the same time, however, the owners of hotels and restaurants and tour operators also lack the will to enter into joint efforts in an attempt to resolve such issues (Holiday-Truth.com, 2005). One recent response has seen the Minister of Culture and Tourism banning all construction works in the largest coastal resorts for the duration of the 2005 summer season. Further, an additional investment of about €35m was allocated from the national budget in 2005 to improve the road infrastructure. Access to historic sites will be a priority and signs in English will be updated.

The existing system of professional education for the needs of tourism is outdated. Higher educational institutions offer theoretical teaching but little practical implementation: a particularly weak element is work experience in companies. The high percentage of seasonal workers in the industry tends to reduce commitment and the quality of service. This is aggravated by the shortage of qualified and experienced middle management, especially in 4- and 5-star hotels. High rates of emigration of young skilled labour appear to exacerbate the situation. In spite of the unemployment rate of 12–13% of the population in all economic branches, there are a large number of job vacancies requiring specific skills and qualifications. One requirement is for a radical upgrading of work productivity levels that can consequently raise employee earning levels.

Security in the resorts has improved, but prostitution is still a major problem along the motorway from Sofia, between Slunchev Briag and Varna, and near the busier frontier check-points. A niggling problem is the cheating of tourists by some smaller currency exchange offices in the resorts. The overall impression in the larger coastal resorts is of congestion of the resort centres with dense and noisy commercial areas with restaurants, fast-food outlets and shops having little to do with tourism and the recreational activities in the resorts.

Bulgarian Tourism in the Context of EU Enlargement

Patterns of flows

The number of foreign tourists in Bulgaria in the first eight months of 2004 rose by 18.39% in comparison with the same period in the previous year. At the same time the EU15 share of international arrivals grew by 28% (Republic of Bulgaria Ministry of Economy, 2005). This suggests that the European Union is the principal and most promising market for Bulgarian tourism. It remains to be seen if, in the shorter term, the ten new accession states will be preferred as tourism destinations for EU tourists at the expense of candidates Bulgaria, Romania, Croatia and Turkey.

Much may depend on the border regime and regional cooperation. If the EU visa obligation is waived for Russians and Ukrainians, as has been promised to President Putin, this will change the geography of the tourism flows in the whole continent. Certainly, the Bulgarian government has withdrawn the visa requirement for package tourists from Russia and other post-Soviet countries and Bosnia at least for an interim (from the website www.tourist.ru, 2005). It can be expected that tourists from Poland and Hungary will return to Bulgarian resorts as has already happened with Czechs and Slovaks.

The 2004 EU enlargement is resulting in both higher salaries in the new member states, but also higher prices of consumer goods and services. For several years at least, prices in Bulgaria will remain significantly lower and this will attract more tourists and investment, provided the geopolitical situation does not change. The seaside hotels in Bulgaria, for example, offer 30–40% lower prices in comparison with Spain and Greece, and 20–25% lower than Turkey, while service quality in establishments of the same category is now comparable.

Inward investment

A further important issue is the mutual interaction between tourism and other socioeconomic sectors. A crucial question is whether tourism development will boost the local economy, or will rely upon EU assistance, or, more likely, will result in a combination of both of these characteristics.

In December 1999, Bulgaria started the process of conforming to EU membership requirements. This was a clear signal to European business communities about investment opportunities in Bulgaria and in its tourism industry. The volume of foreign investment for construction and the upgrading of tourism facilities promptly increased. Foreign banks, tour operators and hotel chains have shown interest and started various projects and ventures jointly with local partners. In the context of economic growth and the creation of jobs, foreign investment plays a crucial role in the country's coastal region, the larger cities and mountain resorts. In the 1970s Bulgaria came to rely on Western expertise in coastal and mountain resorts and later in the urban hotels constructed or managed jointly with Western hotel chains.

In the ski resorts most technical equipment is imported from France and Austria, while in the coastal resorts the know-how and ideas reflect German, Greek and British experience. Accession to the EU will provide more opportunities for such investment.

Second homes and foreign ownership

Bulgaria has liberalized its property law and amendments are being prepared to allow direct purchase of land by citizens of EU states, as well as the building and reconstruction of existing premises. Foreigners will be able to buy land from the moment of accession. At present the direct purchase of land by foreigners is not allowed, but in practice many own land and other property through intermediary companies set up jointly with a Bulgarian citizen, or contract the use of land through specialized agencies. As a result, many foreigners already have access to land and property as prices and costs are much lower than in the country of origin. In order to meet the demand, British banks have included Bulgaria on the list of countries where a loan is available for buying property. In fact, in many places Britons, Greeks, Russians, and smaller numbers of Scandinavians, Dutch and Germans have bought or rented property.

Bulgarian property attracts buyers who acquire property in city centre areas and coastal resorts to let for profit, and in some cases rural property is bought with the aim of modernizing and selling at a profit. Apart from representatives of the banks, large tour operators and hotel chains, smaller speculators include all ages and income groups. Although land and property in Bulgaria is much cheaper than in EU member states, prices are rising rapidly due to both external and internal pressures. Even in remote villages prices have risen considerably. The appearance of foreign speculators has contributed substantially to this rise and its geographical differentiation.

Many foreigners have already purchased property (factories, houses, hotels, restaurants) and the number of transactions has risen dramatically since 2000. For instance, many Greek and British nationals have bought houses as well as land on the Black Sea coast and in some mountain areas in the interior – Rhodope, Pirin and Central Stara Planina (Balkan). For example, the author was told in the village Galata near Varna that during 2004, foreign buyers caused an increase in the price of property from €7 to €20 per m², while in the ski resort of Bansko the price rose from €40 to €70 in the same year (Dnevnik, 2005). Overall, during 2004 prices in the second home property market in Bulgaria have risen by 35%, and a growth of 25% was expected for 2005 and 2006. In 2004, the price of building lots at coastal resorts started at €35,000 (from www.netinfo.bg, 2005). In rural areas, prices of plots with old houses differ substantially, but normally do not exceed €30,000. Here the highest prices reported are associated with the mountain resorts.

Bulgaria is still in the initial stage of its host–guest relationship cycle of behaviour, and local populations appear to be on good terms with foreigners. It is not premature to say that tourism has benefited host communities in terms of improved infrastructures and higher service standards. A political dividend has also been recognized: during the first free elections in the 1990s, voters living in the tourist regions massively supported pro-Western and market-oriented political parties. Anecdotal evidence suggests that foreign home owners appreciate the friendly attitude of local populations and their Bulgarian neighbours, although at the same time they often complain about service and infrastructure quality, bureaucratic practices and poor information provision (Holiday-Truth.com, 2005).

Conclusion

Bulgaria had been expected to accede to the EU at the beginning of 2007, and this objective had already brought a profound and positive impact on the country as a whole, and especially on the nature and extent of its international tourism both inbound and outbound. However, by the time this chapter was being submitted, doubts were beginning to be raised concerning the realism of the 2007 date. This was constraining foreign interest in property purchase and also possibly the rate of foreign investment. None the less, the EU share of Bulgarian tourism will grow, and after accession the pace could accelerate further. Bulgaria is already firmly in the EU tourism market and this trend will intensify. It is perceived as a hospitable and calm country with a Mediterranean style of living and is not associated with terrorist threats, although after becoming a NATO member in 2003 and having sent a detachment to Iraq, this could change.

In Western Europe, Bulgaria is associated with all-inclusive summer package tours to the Black Sea coast, but also increasingly cheap packages to ski resorts. There is considerable potential for various types of tourism inside the country which are little promoted and practically unknown to the wider European public. One of the strengths of Bulgaria on the tourism market is that it offers holidays in less congested resorts, but the recent building boom in the resorts that are becoming too urbanized and lacking in coherent planning is a major challenge to Bulgaria's sustainability as a tourism destination.

For Bulgaria there is no alternative to development, further restructuring and the rejuvenation of its tourism industry to adapt to the EU market environment and to provide a greater variety and higher quality of tourism services. Priority should be given to the training and retraining of those professionally involved in a sector that expects 20,000 new jobs to be created annually.

Such expectations will become reality only if the existing serious problems are adequately addressed and alleviated. Particular attention should be given to the promotion of the country, which at the moment is practically non-existent. Ecological issues, for example, the grave problem of pollution in the Black Sea (practically a closed basin), can be solved only in the framework of broad international cooperation led by the European Union.

References

Bachvarov, M. (1997a) End of the model? Tourism in post-communist Bulgaria. *Tourism Management* 18(1), 43–50.

Bachvarov, M. (1997b) Recreational and tourism functions of the settlements. In: *Annuaire de l'Université de Sofia 'St. Kliment Ohridski' Vol. 2 – Geography*. Sofia: Sofia University Press, pp. 7–28 (in Bulgarian).

Bachvarov, M. (1999) Troubled sustainability: Bulgarian seaside resorts. *Tourism Geographies* 1(2), 192–203.

Dnevnik (2005) *Dnevnik: the News*. Available at: http://www.dnevnik.bg

Evrev, P. (1988) *Territorial Planning of Recreation and Tourism*. Sofia: Sofia University Press (in Bulgarian).

Hall, D.R. (1991) *Tourism and Economic Development in Eastern Europe and the Soviet Union*. London: Belhaven.

Hall, D.R. (1995) Tourism change in Central and Eastern Europe. In: Montanari, A. and Williams, A.M. (eds) *European Tourism: Regions, Spaces and Restructuring*. Chichester, UK: John Wiley & Sons, pp. 221–244.

Harrison, D. (1993) Bulgarian tourism: a state of uncertainty. *Annals of Tourism Research* 20, 519–534.

Holiday-Truth.com (2005) *Bulgaria Discussion Forum*. Manchester: Holiday-Truth.com. Available at: www.holidaytruths.co.uk

Hughes, H. and Allen, D. (2005) Cultural tourism in Central and Eastern Europe: the views of 'induced image formation agents'. *Tourism Management* 26(2), 173–183.

Kasatschka, D. and Marinov, V. (2003) Der Tourismus in Bulgarien während der Übergangsperiode. In: Becker, C., Hopfinger, H. and Stainecke, A. (eds) *Geographie der Freizeit und des Tourismus: Bilanz und Ausblick.* Oldenburg: Oldenburg Verlag.

Koulov, B. and Marinov, V. (1997) Post-socialist change: Bulgaria's international tourism. *Journal of American Geographers* 4, 23.

Marinov, V. (2000) Tourism accommodation facilities in Bulgaria during the transition: main quantitative and structural changes. In: *Annuaire de l'Université de Sofia 'St. Kliment Ochridski', Facultie de Geologie et Geographie, Livre 2 – Geographie, Vol. 94*, pp. 112–130 (in Bulgarian).

Marinov, V. (2004) Situation and dynamics of tourism development in Bulgaria by planning regions and districts. In: Petrov, P. (ed.) *Geography Yesterday, Today and Tomorrow.* Sofia: 'St. Kliment Ohridski' Publishing House, pp. 218–232.

NSI (Republic of Bulgaria National Statistical Institute) (2001) *Tourism: Annual Bulletin.* Sofia: NSI.

NSI (Republic of Bulgaria National Statistical Institute) (2005) National Statistics. Sofia: NSI. Available at: http://www.nsi.bg

Republic of Bulgaria Ministry of Economy (2005) *Analyses and Overviews.* Sofia: Republic of Bulgaria Ministry of Economy. Available at: http://www.mi.government.bg/eng/tur/stat.html

Sofia News Agency (2005) *The yearly performance of our tourism.* Sofia: Sofia News Agency, 5 February. Available at: http://www.novinite.com/view_news.php?id=43778

Vodenska, M. (1992) International tourism in Bulgaria: problems and perspectives. *Tijdschrift voor Economische en Sociale Geografie* 83(5), 409–534.

20 Romania: National Identity, Tourism Promotion and European Integration

Duncan Light

Introduction

This chapter examines the role of tourism promotion in Romania in presenting and affirming a post-socialist identity as one component of the country's protracted process of Euro-Atlantic integration. At first sight tourism promotion may seem unrelated to questions of identity, particularly given the long tendency to regard it as essentially a marketing activity underpinned by particular economic imperatives. However, in recent years there has been increasing attention within tourism studies to the political and ideological dimensions of tourism promotion (Morgan and Pritchard, 1998; Hall, 1999; Pritchard, 2000; Pritchard and Morgan, 2001; Ateljevic and Doorne, 2002; Hall, 2002a). As Morgan and Pritchard (1998, p. 148) argue:

> decisions which shape tourism policy, the extent and nature of government intervention and the kind of tourism development which is encouraged are *political* acts which result from *political processes*. Equally, the images used in the promotion of destinations are similarly ideological.

The ideological dimension of tourism promotion is most apparent in the officially sponsored promotion undertaken by National Tourist Offices. The agenda of such promotion is, of course, economic and is intended to contribute to economic development through attracting increased numbers of tourists to the country. However, it is also underpinned by political imperatives: the role of a National Tourist Office is to project and affirm a particular identity for the respective country. It is one means through which that country can seek to present and legitimize itself to 'others'. The language and imagery of state-sponsored tourist promotion is underpinned by messages such as 'this is who *we* are' and 'this is how *we* want *you* to see *us*' (Light, 2001).

Nowhere is this relationship between tourism promotion and the projection of national identity more important than in the formerly socialist countries of Central and Eastern Europe (Morgan and Pritchard, 1998). During the socialist period the use of tourism promotion to project an overtly ideological message about the nature and achievements of state socialism was a well-established practice. Since 1989, as the countries of this region have sought to redefine national identities, their state-sponsored tourism promotion has been equally ideological in nature. Although different countries have adopted different strategies, a common characteristic has been the requirement to project an image of 'European-ness' that demonstrates and legitimizes their claims as aspirant members of the EU (Hall, 1999, 2002a, 2002b; Hughes and Allen, 2005).

This chapter considers the role of officially sponsored tourism promotion, produced during the mid- and late-1990s, in presenting a new

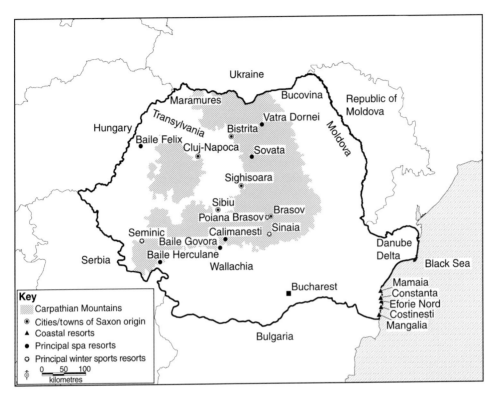

Fig. 20.1. Romania: location map of major tourist resources and regions. This map includes data provided by the MapInfo Corporation from the National Imagery and Mapping Agency (NIMA).

identity for Romania (Fig. 20.1). In particular, it examines the efforts to draw a line under the tyranny of Nicolae Ceauşescu's regime (and the political and economic instability that followed his downfall) and to reposition Romania in the Western popular imagination as a potential future member of the EU. The chapter begins with an overview of tourism development in Romania in recent decades. It then considers Romania's often ambivalent relationship with Europe. The final section presents an analysis of tourist promotional materials produced by the Romanian Ministry of Tourism in the 1990s. It considers what these materials tell us, both about the kind of country Romania imagines itself to be, and the way in which it wants to be understood by the West.

Romanian Tourism in Context

Romania started to promote itself for international tourism during the 1960s and 1970s

and, like many of the other socialist countries of Central and Eastern Europe, the need to generate hard currency to fund imports was paramount (see Hall, 1991). However, in Romania, the enthusiasm for international tourism was also a component of the country's efforts to assert its independence from the Soviet Union (a policy developed during the early 1960s and pursued with vigour by Nicolae Ceauşescu after 1965). Considerable investment in tourism was undertaken, particularly during the periods of the 1966–1970 and 1971–1975 Five Year Plans (see Turnock, 1977). These efforts were initially successful: the number of foreign visitors rose from 676,000 in 1965 to 2.2m in 1970 and to 7m in 1981 (Gavrilescu, 1973; CNS, 1995). The majority of international tourists visiting Romania were from the other socialist countries of Central/Eastern Europe (particularly Poland and Czechoslovakia) or the Soviet Union, but nevertheless, in 1975 Romania received over 630,000 visitors from non-socialist countries.[1]

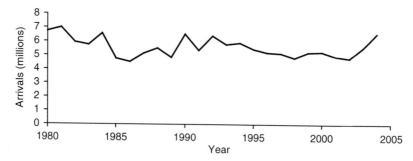

Fig. 20.2. Romania: arrivals of foreign visitors, 1980–2004. Sources: CNS, 1995; INS, 2003a, 2004a, 2005a.

However, international tourism declined during the 1980s due to the austerity and repression of Ceauşescu's regime: by 1985 the number of foreign tourists had fallen to 4.7m (CNS, 1995).

Following Ceauşescu's overthrow in December 1989, Romania experienced a brief tourism boom (see Fig. 20.2). Visitor arrivals in 1990 were 35% higher than the previous year (due largely to visits by journalists, charity workers, 'revolution tourists', returning Romanian émigrés and cross-border traders from neighbouring countries). Thereafter the trend in arrivals has been more erratic and after 1992 international tourism entered a long period of decline. Over the 1990–2002 period visitor arrivals fell by 27% and by 2002 Romania attracted fewer foreign visitors than in 1989 (INS, 2003a). In 2001, tourism contributed just 2.5% of Romania's GDP (Andrei, 2004).

The origins of foreign visitors to Romania have also changed significantly since 1989. Romania rapidly lost its former Central European market, although during the early 1990s there was a large increase in visitors from neighbouring states, who accounted for 61% of visitors in 1995 (CNS, 1997). Many such visitors arrived in Romania for the purpose of business or cross-border trading, while others were in transit through Romania (at a time when conflict in the former Yugoslavia had closed the main transit routes through this region). Others (particular from Hungary and the Republic of Moldova) travelled to Romania for the purpose of visiting friends and relatives. However, Romania was unable to attract large numbers of visitors from Western Europe and has failed to enjoy the post-socialist tourism boom experienced elsewhere in Central Europe

(Hall, 1995). In 1995, citizens of EU countries and America accounted for just 13% of foreign visitors (CNS, 1997).

Romania's poor performance as a tourist destination after 1989 can be attributed to both internal and external factors. Within Romania itself tourism has enjoyed little governmental support, since successive post-socialist administrations have, understandably, been pre-occupied with the challenges of reforming and restructuring the hyper-centralized economy created by Ceauşescu. Yet, the process of macro-economic restructuring has been a protracted process. Between 1990 and 1996 the Romanian government (dominated by former Communist Party members) pursued a 'gradualist' course of reform, reflecting both its suspicion of Western models and its need to retain popular support. This policy brought about the first 'transformation recession' in the early 1990s whilst delaying major economic structural reorganization (Smith, 2001). A centre-right coalition government elected in 1996 attempted to implement a form of 'shock therapy' that produced a second recession but failed to bring about major economic restructuring (Smith, 2001). As a result, successive reports by the European Commission noted that Romania was making little progress towards creating a functioning market economy (Phinnemore, 2001). In 2000, the former socialists (now renamed as Social Democrats) returned to power and in the following years succeeded in bringing about a degree of economic stability.

In this context, Romania's post-socialist administrations have not regarded tourism (and tourism reform) as a priority. This is reflected in the changing fortunes of the country's Ministry of Tourism itself (originally established in 1971). In 1990, the Ministry was combined with the Ministry of Commerce. A separate tourism ministry was re-established in November 1992, but was replaced during a governmental reorganization in 1998 by a National Authority for Tourism. A tourism ministry was re-established in November 2000 only to be combined with the Ministry of Transport and Construction in 2003. Each administrative reorganization has been accompanied by changes in personnel and leadership so that there has been little consistency or continuity in the development and implementation of tourism policy and little long-term tourism planning.

Perhaps the most significant problem that has faced the tourism sector has been continual delays with the privatization of the accommodation sector (see Dumbrăveanu, 2001). These delays have meant that much of Romania's tourist accommodation has deteriorated in quality (due both to neglect in the later socialist era and the lack of investment after 1989). Although tourism privatization was launched in 1993, only 15% of hotels were in private ownership by 1997 (CNS, 1998). Some hotels were successfully privatized through management/employee buyouts, while others (particularly in larger cities) were purchased by international hotel chains. However, there were many others (particularly those in need of considerable refurbishment) that were not regarded as attractive prospects by either Romanians (during the 1995 Mass Privatisation Programme) or by foreign investors. In addition, the state's privatization agency pursued a policy of privatizing hotels (particularly those at the Black Sea) as part of large complexes (sometimes comprising several hotels, along with restaurants and other associated facilities) rather than individually, but such an offer failed to attract the interest of Western investors or tour operators.

The repeated delays in privatization of the tourist accommodation sector has meant that many hotels have experienced sustained under-investment and are unable to offer services which meet the expectations of Western tourists. Moreover, the persistence of so many hotels in state ownership hindered the development of a commercially orientated and customer-centred style of management. The situation was most acute at the Black Sea coast, Romania's major

offer for mass tourism (Fig. 20.1). It was not until after 2000 that progress was made in pushing forward the privatization of the tourism accommodation sector: by 2004, 81.3% of tourist accommodation was in majority private ownership (INS, 2005a). However, by this time Romania had largely lost its competitive position as a destination, particularly in comparison with neighbouring Bulgaria (where, due to much earlier tourism privatization, Black Sea resorts have successfully retained their position as destinations for Western tour operators).

While the internal situation (particularly the dilatory pace of economic reform) accounts in large part for the under-performance of Romanian tourism since 1989, external factors (over which Romania has less control) are of equal importance. Perhaps the most important is Romania's image among Western tourists as a potential destination (Light and Dumbrăveanu, 1999). Romania's reputation as a destination had deteriorated during the 1980s so that the country entered the post-socialist period from an already disadvantaged position. Subsequent events further tarnished Romania's international image. These included violent civil unrest in Bucharest in the 1990s; much-publicized ethnic tension between Romanians and Hungarians in Transylvania; and the rise of extreme nationalist political formations (some of which formed part of a coalition government between 1992 and 1995, causing considerable concern in the West about Romania's commitment to minority rights). The presence of a neo-communist élite (which was frequently linked with high-level corruption) in government between 1990 and 1996 also raised doubts regarding the extent to which real change had taken place in Romania.

However, in the Western popular imagination perhaps one issue – orphans – has dominated the image of Romania. In the early 1990s the state of Romania's under-funded orphanages was widely reported in the Western mass media and the West acted with incredulity and horror. Many Westerners subsequently arrived in Romania to assist the Romanians who were represented as being unable or unwilling to deal with the problem themselves and who were in need of Western compassion and expertise (Light, 2001). In the process, Romania came to be viewed by the West as somewhere marginal and not 'fully' European. In fact, this was just one manifestation of a long-established discourse about South-East Europe that Todorova (1997) has labelled 'Balkanism'. Todorova argues that the Balkanist discourse in the West has constructed South-East Europe as somewhere ambiguous, 'in between' and only partly European. It is a region that is Europe's 'other', but at the same time it is the 'other within' (Todorova, 1997, p. 188). The West has long viewed Romania in such terms. As one Romanian historian notes, while 'the West defines itself as an ordered and predictable world, Romania belongs, on the contrary, to a vague and unpredictable space' (Boia, 2001, p. 185). Events in Romania after 1989 – of which the orphans issue is just the best-publicized – have contributed to keeping Balkanist 'ways of seeing' Romania alive.

Nevertheless, in recent years Romania's international reputation has ameliorated considerably. Civil unrest has largely disappeared and ethnic tension between Romanians and Hungarians decreased significantly after 1996 from which time Romania's governments have stressed partnership rather than conflict with Hungary. The nationalist Right, while still active in Romanian politics, is a much diminished force. Romania's orphan 'problem' has received concerted attention by both Romanian and Western NGOs, with EU support. Since 2000, the country has achieved political and economic stability, and this was recognized by both the EU (which invited Romania to begin accession negotiations) and by NATO (which Romania joined in 2004).

Indeed, in recent years there is evidence that Romanian tourism has started to enter a period of recovery (see Fig. 20.2). In 2004, Romania attracted 6.6m foreign visitors, a 38% increase on 2002 (INS, 2005b). Although citizens of neighbouring states still accounted for the majority of visitors in 2004, the proportion arriving from EU countries (which now included Hungary) had risen to 39% (INS, 2005b), much arising from business tourism generated by Romania's increasingly close ties with the EU. In 2003, the contribution of tourism to Romania's GDP had risen slightly to 3.5% (Andrei, 2004) although this figure was much lower than in neighbouring Bulgaria. Nevertheless, tourism remains a low priority for the Romanian government: in 2005 the budget for tourism promotion was just €3.7m, less than a quarter of that of neighbouring Hungary (Anon, 2005).

Romania's tourism planners continue to prioritize mass tourism (particularly at coastal, winter and spa resorts) as playing a central role in the relaunch of Romanian tourism (Fig. 20.1). Yet, while mass tourism has not recovered from the decline of the late socialist period, Romania has emerged during the late 20th and early 21st century as a destination for both independent travellers and for various forms of niche (or post-mass) tourism (Hall, 1998; Hughes and Allen, 2005). This includes cultural and heritage tourism (particularly in Transylvania) and rural tourism (in Maramureş and Bucovina). The development of such tourism is due more to promotion by Romanian NGOs or independent Western travel agencies than to initiatives by the Romanian tourism authorities. Although Romania has considerable potential for ecotourism (particularly in the Carpathian Mountains and Danube Delta) the country has been slow to promote this potential and it was not until 2004 that the National Tourism Authority prepared a national ecotourism strategy (Dumbrăveanu, 2004), something that was itself stimulated by the imperative of EU accession.

The enlargement of the European Union in May 2004 had an unexpected (if highly localized) impact on tourism in Romania. The accession of neighbouring Hungary meant that for the first time Romania shared a border with an EU state. There was subsequently a significant increase in the number of Hungarians visiting the western region of Romania for the purposes of cross-border shopping, since the prices of basic foodstuffs (such as sugar, flour, rice and oil), petrol and building materials were lower in Romania. The total number of Hungarian visitors to Romania in the first 6 months of 2004 was 51% higher than in the same period in 2003, while between April and May 2004 the number of Hungarian visitors increased by 71% (INS, 2003b, 2004b).

Tourism Promotion and European Integration

Romania and Europe: a brief history

For much of the past three centuries Romania has had an ambivalent relationship with Europe.

In particular, since the 18th century two discourses of national identity have emerged within Romania (Verdery, 1991). One emphasizes historical and cultural ties with 'Europe' and seeks to assert that Romania is part of the European mainstream; the other stresses indigenous and autochthonous values and is more hostile to European influences. Each representation of national identity has enjoyed different periods of influence at different stages in Romania's recent history.

Romania's location in South-east Europe meant that the country was long subject to 'Eastern' (Ottoman and Russian) influences. However, after achieving political independence in the second half of the 19th century Romania's rulers looked to Western Europe for models. During the period 1860–1870 the political elite adopted almost everything it could (including a constitution, parliament, legislative system, universities and even an alphabet) from Western Europe, with France representing a particular model (Boia, 2001). However, during the 1880s there was a counter-reaction and many Romanian intellectuals sought to stress native (rather than 'imported') values. By the end of the 19th century the struggle between 'indigenism' and 'Westernism' was firmly rooted in discourse about Romania's identity (Verdery, 1991).

Nevertheless, by the inter-war period Romania was at its most integrated ever into the European economy and therefore most exposed to Western influences. However, a nationalist emphasis on native values remained dominant for much of this period and during the 1930s found expression in the rise of the extreme Right in Romanian politics. After the Communist Party take-over of power in late 1947, all emphasis on national values was firmly suppressed in favour of socialist internationalism. Moreover, under Soviet influence, priority was given to 'Eastern' (i.e. Russian) influences on Romanian history and cultural life (Deletant, 1991; Verdery, 1991). Once again, there was a reaction in favour of national values and during the 1960s Romania pursued a course of asserting its national independence from the Soviet Union. This found its most extreme expression under Nicolae Ceauşescu who, from the 1970s onwards, promoted a version of Romanian-ness that was hostile to external (i.e. Western) influences and which instead championed indigenous and distinctly Romanian national values.

The 1989 revolution did not bring about a dramatic change in Romania's relations with Europe. Instead, the ruling élite that came to power in December 1989 recognized that an appeal to national sentiment was one way of retaining popular support. Romania's first president, Ion Iliescu, was openly sceptical of Western influences and famously argued for 'original democracy' (a distinctly Romanian form of democracy rather than an adoption of the Western European model). Similarly, early post-socialist administrations were suspicious of foreign investment (and for much of the early 1990s foreign investors were not permitted to own land in Romania). Romania showed little inclination to embrace the agenda of the European Union with regard to issues such as economic reform, respect for the principles of democracy and human and minority rights: on the other hand, the EU's position with regard to Romania during this period was distinctly cool (Phinnemore, 2001).

However, during the mid-1990s the 'neo-communist' administration looked to escape from its increasing international isolation and recognized that its main hope for economic recovery lay in closer ties with Europe (Gallagher, 2001). Romania was also concerned to distance itself from the turmoil in the former Yugoslavia. Consequently, Romania's leaders gradually moved towards embracing the agenda of the EU. Romania signed an association agreement with the Union in February 1993 and submitted a formal application for membership in 1995 (Phinnemore, 2001). The prospect of EU membership led both Romania and Hungary to sign a historic treaty of friendship in 1996 that involved recognition of the existing borders and guaranteed rights for the Hungarians of Transylvania.

The increasing reconciliation between Romanians and Hungarians was demonstrated after 1996 when the ethnic Hungarian political party joined a centre-right coalition government. This collaboration was continued (either in the form of parliamentary alliances or formal coalitions) following the elections of 2000 and 2004. Romania's progress in achieving political stability was recognized in 1998 when the

European Commission accepted that Romania fulfilled the political criteria of the 1992 Copenhagen conference for EU membership (Phinnemore, 2001). The 1999 Helsinki meeting of the European Council agreed to begin accession negotiations with Romania and, in December 2002, the European Council suggested 2007 as a possible accession date. In October 2004, Romania finally achieved the full conditions for membership when the European Commission's annual report declared Romania to be a functioning market economy. The country was scheduled to join the EU on 1 January 2007.

Tourism promotion and the re-branding of Romania

During the mid-1990s, as Romania sought to engage with the European Union, tourism promotion was one component of a strategy to present and legitimize the country as a potential future member. The use of tourism promotion in this way to project the country's national identity was nothing new. Throughout the socialist period Romania's external tourist promotion – particularly the monthly magazine *Holidays in Romania*, published in various foreign languages – had stressed the achievements of socialist Romania, exalting the contribution of Nicolae Ceaușescu and presenting overtly nationalist accounts of Romania's history. After 1989, *Holidays in Romania* sought to present Romania's new face to the West (for example, the first issue in 1990 included a lengthy account of the Revolution). However, tourism promotion was hit by lack of funding and the magazine was published less frequently (and in some years seems not to have appeared at all). Along with a reduced budget was a lack of expertise in marketing and promotion among a team trained for 'external propaganda' during the socialist period. As a result, Romania's tourism promotion was ill-equipped for the role of presenting a post-socialist identity to the wider world.

In this context, a PHARE project (worth 4.5m ECU) was launched in 1993 to address the problems of restructuring the tourism industry in Romania (Florian, 1994). One component was the production (in 1994) of a new set of high-quality promotional materials by the Ministry of Tourism with the assistance of Western consultants. A new brand for Romanian tourism was also launched under the slogan 'Come as a tourist, leave as a friend'. A second PHARE project in May 1995 allocated a further 300,000 ECU for the production of brochures and other promotional materials (Anon, 1995). These materials, produced within a context where Romania was seeking to engage with the EU, were intended to ameliorate Romania's image in the Western imagination and ultimately to ease progress towards accession by presenting Romania as a plausible candidate for membership. The following section presents an analysis of these promotional materials, produced during the mid- and late 1990s for the Western European market. The discussion is not concerned so much with the nature of the brand that Romania was seeking to develop, but instead examines the ideological agenda that underpinned tourist promotional materials during this period.

Romania as a 'new' country

While after 1989 the exact nature of Romania's post-socialist identity and orientation was contested within the country, there was almost unanimous rejection of Ceaușescu's extreme form of Stalinism. As such, the 1989 revolution has come to represent the 'foundation myth' for a new Romania (Boia, 2001) and the country has been eager to present itself as 'reborn' after more than four decades of totalitarian rule. As Morgan and Pritchard (1998) observe, such themes of new beginnings and rebirth have underpinned the redefining of national identities throughout the former socialist countries of Central and Eastern Europe. Yet for all the efforts to present itself as a new country, Romania remained inextricably linked with Ceaușescu in the Western popular imagination (Gallagher, 1995). The presence of the former *nomenklatura* in government, the reluctance to embrace economic reform and the persistence of nationalist rhetoric directed against Romania's minorities further reinforced the belief in the West that Romania had not fully broken with the Ceaușescu era.

Consequently, Romania's tourist promotion sought to assert that Romania was a new and emphatically post-Ceauşescu country. For example, one brochure (Ministry of Tourism, undated a, p. 3) from the mid-1990s proclaimed the 'rebirth of a nation'. It continued:

> In December 1989 Romania was reborn as a free nation. Now this multi-faceted country is welcoming tourists to enjoy a wonderfully varied heritage of traditional culture, scenic splendours and leisure opportunities. A resurgence of endeavour and enthusiasm is re-invigorating the country's tourist facilities to create a unique holiday destination.

The narrative of a new beginning is underlined by stressing that, now freed from the enervation of socialism, the 'new' Romania is an energetic and reinvigorated country. Another brochure describes Romania as 'heading for a new future' (Ministry of Tourism, undated b, p. 2). Similarly: 'Romania is on the move. Come and see for yourself' (Ministry of Tourism, undated a, p. 3). Romania's new start is best illustrated in Bucharest where 'the capital's restaurants are regaining their vigour' (Ministry of Tourism, undated a, p. 9). The process of reform in Romania has been so protracted that, well over a decade after Ceauşescu's fall, a website established by the Ministry of Tourism continues to talk of 'a new Romania' (www.turism.ro).

There are other attempts to present 'reborn' Romania as an explicitly European country. For example: 'Now that Romania has rejoined mainstream Europe, it is welcoming visitors to share and enjoy a civilized heritage, spiced with touches of Byzantine influence' (Ministry of Tourism, undated c, p. 2). Presenting Romania in such a way is intended to demonstrate that the country adheres to European norms and values from which it was only temporarily detached during the period of state socialism. It also represents a rejection of the emphasis on indigenous over European values that characterized Ceauşescu's reign and the early years after his overthrow.

In addition to presenting itself as a new country, Romania has been eager to assert itself as a state that adheres to Western political and economic values after four decades during which it was, in political terms, 'other' to the West. For example: 'The revolution of 1989 brought Romania firmly back into democratic Europe' (Ministry of Tourism, undated a, p. 7). Similarly: 'Today Romania is a fully democratic

state with a free economy' (National Tourism Authority, undated a, p. 3). One brochure also emphasizes the 'new' Romania's respect for minority rights in order to repudiate the shrill nationalism of both the Ceauşescu era and the early 1990s. For example:

> According to the Romanian laws, adopted after 1989, the minorities are entitled to pursue their interests, exercise their rights and preserve their cultural identity.
>
> (National Tourism Authority, undated b, p. 2)

Highlighting historical and cultural ties with Western Europe

Coupled with its efforts to present itself as a 'new' and *post*-socialist country which shares the political, economic and social values of the EU, Romania, like other countries in the region, has also been seeking to highlight (and reaffirm) long-standing historical and cultural ties with Western Europe (Morgan and Pritchard, 1998). This is another way in which Romania has sought to demonstrate its 'European-ness' but it is also an element of the post-socialist rewriting of history (Verdery, 1999). In seeking to excise the socialist era from the country's historical narrative Romania (like other countries in the region) has sought to turn back the clock and resume the course of economic and political development of the pre-socialist era (a period when Romania was much more integrated into the political and economic life of Western Europe).

As such, Romania's tourist promotion has stressed a long shared history with the Western and Central parts of Europe. For example, there are insistent references to the Roman origins of the country. One brochure declaims: 'The very name "Romania" reminds us that ancient Rome exercised a decisive influence on this country' (Ministry of Tourism, undated a, p. 3). Similarly: '. . . the ancient Roman inheritance that gave the country its name and its Latin characteristics. Even the climate of south west Romania is Mediterranean' (Ministry of Tourism, undated c, p. 2). The Romanians are also presented as being a Latin people:

> This Latin ancestry is apparent in all sorts of ways today, not least in the warm, outgoing temperament of the people . . . it is an ancestry

which has miraculously survived a thousand years of barbarian and other invasions in the Dark Ages.

(Ministry of Tourism, undated c, p. 3)

There are also prominent references to settlements around the country that played an important role within the Roman Empire (such as the spa resort of Băile Herculane and the coastal city/resort of Constanța) (Fig. 20.1).

At first sight this emphasis on Roman and Latin origins may not seem unexpected since most countries in some way present their national history within their tourist promotion. However, the emphasis on Roman/Latin origins represents a significant departure from the way in which Ceaușescu sought to define Romanian national identity. In accordance with the import-ance attached to native and indigenous – rather than European – values, Ceaușescu sought to downplay (or even deny) the Roman origins of the Romanians. Instead, greater priority was attached to the Dacian ancestry of the Romanians (the Dacians were the pre-Roman inhabitants of what is now Romania) (Verdery, 1991; Boia, 2001). The renewed emphasis on Roman origins after 1989 parallels Romania's efforts to present itself once again as a European country by asserting a common inheritance with much of the rest of Europe. Similarly, by highlighting their Latin origins and temperament, the Romanians themselves are presented as sharing characteristics with their Latin 'cousins' of Western Europe (the French, Italians, Portuguese and Spanish, all of whom are members of the EU).

Another way in which Romania has asserted its long-standing links with Western and Central Europe is through stressing con-tinuity with European architectural styles. For example, one brochure states:

A kaleidoscope of architectural styles – Baroque, Renaissance, Neoclassical, Romanesque, Art Nouveau, Rococo . . . You would be forgiven for believing we are describing the attractions of a tour of Europe, but we are referring to the great cultural wealth encapsulated in just one country – Romania.
(National Tourism Authority, undated a, p. 20)

The shared inheritance with European architecture is also apparent with references to

Saxon architecture in Transylvania. This theme is developed most fully in the presentation of Bucharest, where the congruence with French architectural styles is repeatedly stressed. For example:

the city developed into an acknowledged European centre of culture and good living. . .French architects, who had contributed so much to its [Bucharest's] style, its tree-lined boulevards and elegant fin de siecle architec-ture in the 19th century, again added grace to its buildings. An Arc de Triomphe was erected in 1935 . . . Boulevard cafes proliferated . . . Bucharest remains a Garden City, leafy and pleasant, architecturally eclectic with pavement cafes open in the warm summer, and boating on the lakes.
(Ministry of Tourism, undated d, p. 2)

There are also repeated efforts to draw parallels between Bucharest and Paris. These take the inter-war period as their inspiration when the French influence in Bucharest was such that the city was known by some in the West as the 'Paris of the East' or the 'Little Paris'. Although, the 'Little Paris' may have been more myth than reality (Boia, 2001) it is a myth that is frequently evoked by Romania's tourist promotional materials. For example:

the city developed into an acknowledged European centre of culture and good living, earning it the nickname the 'Little Paris'.
(Ministry of Tourism, undated d, p. 2)

Bucharest used to be called the 'Little Paris', and with good reason.
(Ministry of Tourism, undated a, p. 3)

Bucharest was acquiring the Belle Epoque architecture and intellectual vibrancy that made it the 'Little Paris'.
(Ministry of Tourism, undated c, p. 2)

Although there is little in Bucharest today that recalls Paris, the 'Little Paris' epithet is ideal material to enable Romania to present itself as sharing a common heritage with Western Europe. As Morgan and Pritchard (1998) argue, this is a strategy that attempts to mediate and legitimize the unfamiliar by positioning it along-side the familiar: the presentation of Haapsalu in Estonia as the 'Venice of the Baltics' has a similar intent.

The stress on historical ties with Western Europe (particularly France) is also apparent in

Table 20.1. Romania: content analysis of images (*N* = 109) in two brochures.

Primary category	No. of images	%	Secondary category	No. of images	%
Buildings or townscapes	42	38.5	Modern (post-war)	7	6.4
			19th century/*Fin de siècle*	14	12.8
			Medieval – monasteries and churches	10	9.2
			Medieval – other	11	10.1
Rural lifestyles and traditions	20	18.3	People in traditional costume	11	10.1
			Folk art	6	5.5
			Other	3	2.8
Landscape/scenery	20	18.3	Countryside	3	2.8
			Mountains	4	3.7
			Coast/Beach/Delta	9	8.3
			Urban parks/lakes	4	3.7
Recreation and leisure	20	18.3	Land-based (including spas)	16	14.7
			Water-based	4	3.7
Wildlife and nature	5	4.6		5	4.6
Other	2	1.8		2	1.8

Source: author's original research.

the imagery used to promote Romania. Table 20.1 presents the results of a content analysis (Pritchard and Morgan, 1995; Finn *et al.*, 2000) of two 'general' English-language brochures (Ministry of Tourism, undated a; National Tourism Authority, undated a) produced in the mid- to late 1990s for the English-speaking market.

The table indicates that the largest category of images is that featuring buildings or townscapes and, within this category, images of 19th century and *fin de siècle* buildings (many in French styles or designed by French architects) are dominant. Images featuring churches or monasteries are also prominent. After four decades of official atheism (even if the Church was not actively suppressed during the socialist period) Romania is eager to reassert its Christian traditions as another means to emphasize shared values and a common history with the rest of Europe.

However, the evocation of Romania's historical and cultural links with the rest of Europe is partial and selective: in particular, the promotional materials produced in 1994/95 make almost no mention of Hapsburg influences in Transylvania. Yet Transylvania was under Hungarian rule until 1918 and the architecture of many of its towns displays obvious AustroHungarian influences. Instead, Transylvania is presented solely in terms of Romanian cultural traditions. This mirrors Romania's long-established wariness of Hungary (particularly the fear among many Romanians of Hungarian irredentist claims on Transylvania, something which was fully exploited in the early and mid-1990s by nationalist politicians) and a reluctance to acknowledge Hungarian influences in Transylvania.

Promotion of rural lifestyles and traditions

A further theme that is prominently highlighted in Romania's tourist promotion is the country's rural culture, lifestyles and traditions. Indeed, there are many leaflets dedicated to the rural traditions of the various regions of Romania. Visitors are invited to 'experience for yourselves one of Europe's best kept secrets – the Romanian village' (National Tourism Authority, undated a, p. 18) and to encounter 'the most important, living, folk culture to be found anywhere in Europe'. (Ministry of Tourism, undated c, p. 4). Moreover, the authenticity of

Romania's rural traditions is stressed. For example:

> You can watch folk festivals in Transylvania that are genuine expressions of local culture, not merely staged for visitors. . .One of many extraordinary aspects of this country is its vibrant rural culture, which for decades the outside world heard little about. . . Wherever you go in Transylvania you will discover rural traditions that are a real part of everyday life . . . Few other parts of Europe have preserved so distinctive a rural culture.
>
> (Ministry of Tourism, undated a, pp. 3, 15)

A similar emphasis is apparent in the images used in promotional materials. As Table 20.1 indicates, almost 20% of brochure images feature rural traditions and lifestyles, with people in traditional costumes being the largest sub-category (10.1% of all images). This focus on rural heritage is not something particular to the post-socialist period: the promotion of rural tourism (particularly for domestic tourists) was a characteristic of the socialist era throughout Central and Eastern Europe (Hall, 1998). Neither is the priority currently accorded to rural traditions unique to Romania, since most of the formerly socialist countries of this region have stressed similar themes, with their promotional materials making prominent references to people dressed in traditional costumes (Morgan and Pritchard, 1998).

On one hand, the prominence given to rural heritage and traditions in Romania's officially-sponsored tourist imagery appears paradoxical given the country's concern to present itself as a new, invigorated and forward-looking country with ambitions for EU accession. The focus on the rural (and particularly lifestyles which have largely disappeared from much of Western Europe) highlights the ways in which Romania is 'different' and (in rural areas at least) less developed than the West. In effect, Romania is presenting itself as a pre-modern 'other'. This is certainly not unique to Romania: through an emphasis on the rural many other peripheral areas of Europe similarly construct themselves in this way (O'Connor, 1993). However, in the case of Romania the strategy to highlight the pre-modern rural potentially undermines EU

aspirations by contributing to Balkanist ways of seeing the country as marginal and underdeveloped. That said, the rural lifestyles that Romania is so vigorously promoting are themselves likely to change substantially as a result of the agricultural restructuring which will inevitably follow EU accession.

Romania's motives for placing so much emphasis on its rural heritage are both pragmatic and ideological. On one hand, while there are many other European destinations offering beach and skiing tourism, the rural is one of Romania's unique attributes as a destination. Rural tourism enables Romania to project itself as the 'exotic' and 'authentic' within Europe, by projecting the pastoral idyll to Western tourists seeking rural traditions and lifestyles that no longer exist in their own countries (Morgan and Pritchard, 1998). In a more down to earth sense, rural tourism enables Romania to play to its strengths without exposing the weaknesses of the tourist infrastructure inherited from the socialist period (Roberts, 1996). At a time when the state showed little concern for tourism (so that Black Sea, mountain and spa resorts remained in state ownership and experienced prolonged underinvestment), the development of rural tourism has been led by the private sector, and coordinated and regulated by various non-governmental organizations.

However, there are also ideological reasons for promoting rural tourism. Within Romania the rural environment is an important symbol of identity and there is a long history (generally, although not exclusively, among more nationalist commentators) of idealizing the Romanian peasant and rural life more generally. As such, the prominence given to the rural within tourist promotion reflects its importance for national identity (although Western tourists may not necessarily recognize this). However, there is also a specifically postsocialist dimension: the importance attached to rural lifestyles is a means of asserting and promoting values and traditions which pre-date Communist Party rule and which have survived (relatively unscathed) Ceauşescu's attempts to bring about a radical restructuring of the rural environment. Giving priority to the rural – and more generally presenting Romania as a new country with old traditions (Morgan and

Pritchard, 1998) – is another component of the attempt to erase the socialist period from national memory and affirm the country's post-socialist status.

Conclusion

Tourism promotion is as much a political as an economic activity and Romania, like many other countries, illustrates the ways in which tourist promotional materials are intended to present and affirm national identity. Since the country decided in the mid-1990s to adopt a more integrationist foreign policy and embrace the values and agenda of the EU, it has engaged in a concerted (and successful) campaign to present itself as a stable democratic country and a serious contender for membership of both the EU and NATO. However, given the long-term under-performance of Romanian tourism there are few people from Western Europe with first hand experience of the country. As a result, Romania is viewed in terms of predominantly negative stereotypes (such as orphans, instability and, at least in Britain, asylum seekers) within the long-established Balkanist discourse that constructs the country as not 'fully' European. Hence, Romania has recognized the need to reposition and 're-image' itself in order to convince Western public opinion that it can be a credible partner within Euro-Atlantic integration processes.

Tourism promotion has been one element of this strategy and as this chapter has discussed, in addition to presenting Romania's abundant attractions for tourism, such promotion has been circumscribed by an imperative to demonstrate the country's post-socialist and European credentials. As such, various themes are emphasized within the language and imagery of tourist promotional materials. These include an emphatic rejection of totalitarianism and the construction of a 'new' Romania, commitment to the same political and economic values as the Western European countries, and an insistence on historical and cultural links with Western and Central Europe which were only temporarily disrupted by state socialism. The priority given to rural culture and lifestyles, although seemingly antithetical to efforts to present Romania as a modern European country, is a further way of emphasizing a heritage which pre-dates state socialism. This is something that Romania shares with the other formerly socialist countries of the region, many of which are now EU members.

During the campaign for the parliamentary elections in November 2004 (and following the European Commission report that recognized Romania to be a functioning market economy) the country's politicians declared that the prolonged 'transition period' had finally come to an end. While Romania is expected to join the EU in January 2007 the impacts for tourism in the country are less easy to predict. One government source suggested that the most immediate effect would be the migration of skilled tourism workers to other EU countries in search of higher wages. On a more positive note, Romanian tourism is likely to benefit from the country's accession to the EU (and eventually the adoption of a common currency). This is likely to be expressed in a number of ways: through greater foreign investment, increased business tourism, and, in the longer term, increased arrivals from other EU countries, particularly for post-mass and niche forms of tourism for which the country has so much to offer. Nevertheless, while Romania has succeeded in closing accession negotiations with the EU, the country is still regarded with uncertainty by much of Western public opinion. As such, tourism promotion in the short to medium term will have a continuing role in legitimizing Romania's place within the Union.

Acknowledgements

I would like to thank a senior Romanian civil servant (who wished to remain anonymous) for a stimulating discussion on the current state of Romanian tourism, and David Phinnemore for his comments on an earlier draft of this chapter.

Note

[1] These data were obtained from a former employee of the National Tourist Office (*Oficiul Naţional de Turism*).

References

Andrei, C. (2004) Creşte ponderea turismului în PIB. *România Liberă,* 18 November, p. 4.

Anon (1995) O rază de sperantă pentru turismul românesc. *Adevărul,* 2 June, p. 5.

Anon (2005) Bugetul de promovare turistică în 2005, jumătate faţă de anul trecut. *Adevărul,* 25 February, p. 7.

Ateljevic, I. and Doorne, S. (2002) Representing New Zealand: tourism imagery and ideology. *Annals of Tourism Research* 29, 648–667.

Boia, L. (2001) *History and Myth in Romanian Consciousness.* Budapest: Central European University Press (first published in Romanian in 1997).

CNS (Comisia Naţională pentru Statistică) (1995) *Anuarul Turistic al României 1995.* Bucharest: CNS.

CNS (Comisia Naţională pentru Statistică) (1997) *Turismul în România 1997.* Bucharest: CNS.

CNS (Comisia Naţională pentru Statistică) (1998) *Turismul României: Breviar Statistic.* Bucharest: CNS.

Deletant, D. (1991) Rewriting the past: trends in contemporary Romanian historiography. *Ethnic and Racial Studies* 14, 64–86.

Dumbrăveanu, D. (2001) The challenge of privatisation: the tourist accommodation industry in transition. In: Light, D. and Phinnemore, D. (eds) *Post-Communist Romania: Coming to Terms with Transition.* Basingstoke, UK: Palgrave, pp. 207–223.

Dumbrăveanu, D. (2004) *Strategia de Ecoturism a României: Cadru Theoretic de Dezvoltare.* Bucharest: Autoritatea Naţională pentru Turism.

Finn, A., Elliott-White, M. and Walton, M. (2000) *Tourism and Leisure Research Methods: Data Collection, Analysis and Interpretation.* Harlow, UK: Longman.

Florian, M. (1994) Progamul PHARE pentru turism. *Revista Română de Turism* 1(1–2), 34–41.

Gallagher, T. (1995) *Romania after Ceauşescu.* Edinburgh: Edinburgh University Press.

Gallagher, T. (2001) Nationalism and Romanian political culture in the 1990s. In: Light, D. and Phinnemore, D. (eds) *Post-Communist Romania: Coming to Terms with Transition.* Basingstoke, UK: Palgrave, pp. 104–124.

Gavrilescu, C. (1973) Turismul internaţional – activitate economică de mare eficientă. In: Barbu, G. (ed.) *Turismul, Ramură a Economiei Nationale.* Bucharest: Editura pentru Turism, pp. 61–74.

Hall, D.R. (1991) Evolutionary patterns of tourism development in Eastern Europe and the Soviet Union. In: Hall, D.R. (ed.) *Tourism and Economic Development in Eastern Europe and the Soviet Union.* London: Belhaven, pp. 79–115.

Hall, D.R. (1995) Tourism change in Central and Eastern Europe. In: Montanari, A. and Williams, A.M. (eds) *European Tourism: Regions, Spaces and Restructuring.* Chichester, UK: John Wiley & Sons, pp. 221–244.

Hall, D. (1998) Tourism development and sustainability issues in Central and South-eastern Europe. *Tourism Management* 19, 423–431.

Hall, D. (1999) Destination branding, niche marketing and national image projection in Central and Eastern Europe. *Journal of Vacation Marketing* 5, 227–237.

Hall, D. (2002a) Branding and national identity: the case of Central and Eastern Europe. In: Morgan, N., Pritchard, A. and Pride, R. (eds) *Destination Branding: Creating the Unique Destination Proposition.* Oxford: Butterworth Heinemann, pp. 87–103.

Hall, D. (2002b) Brand development, tourism and national identity: the re-imaging of former Yugoslavia. *Brand Management* 9, 323–334.

Hughes, H. and Allen, D. (2005) Cultural tourism in Central and Eastern Europe: the views of 'induced image formation agents'. *Tourism Management* 26, 173–183.

INS (Institutul Naţional de Statistică) (2003a) *Anuarul Statistic al României 2003 (serii de timp 1990–2002).* Bucharest: INS (CD Rom).

INS (Institutul Naţional de Statistică) (2003b) *Turismul Internaţional al României în Semestrul I 2003.* Bucharest: INS.

INS (Institutul Naţional de Statistică) (2004a) *Turismul României: Breviar Statistic.* Bucharest: INS.

INS (Institutul Naţional de Statistică) (2004b) *Turismul Internaţional al României în Semestrul I 2004.* Bucharest: INS.

INS (Institutul Naţional de Statistică) (2005a) *Turismul României: Breviar Statistic.* Bucharest: INS.

INS (Institutul Naţional de Statistică) (2005b) *Turismul Internaţional al României în Anul 2004.* Bucharest: INS.

Light, D. (2001) Facing the future: tourism and identity-building in post-socialist Romania, *Political Geography* 20, 1053–1074.

Light, D. and Dumbrăveanu, D. (1999) Romanian tourism in the post-communist period. *Annals of Tourism Research* 26, 898–927.

Ministry of Tourism (undated a) *Romania: Come as a Tourist, Leave as a Friend.* Bucharest: Ministry of Tourism.

Ministry of Tourism (undated b) *The Black Sea: Romania's Riviera.* Bucharest: Ministry of Tourism.

Ministry of Tourism (undated c) *A Rich and Inspiring Cultural Heritage.* Bucharest: Ministry of Tourism.

Ministry of Tourism (undated d) *Bucharest.* Bucharest: Ministry of Tourism.

Morgan, N. and Pritchard, A (1998) *Tourism, Promotion and Power: Creating Images, Creating Identities.* Chichester, UK: John Wiley & Sons.

National Tourism Authority (undated a) *Romania: a Close Encounter.* Bucharest: National Tourism Authority.

National Tourism Authority (undated b) *Romania: Discover the Mystery.* Bucharest: National Tourism Authority.

O'Connor, B. (1993) Myths and mirrors: tourist images and national identity. In: O'Connor, B. and Cronin, M. (eds) *Tourism in Ireland: a Critical Analysis.* Cork: Cork University Press, pp. 68–85.

Phinnemore, D. (2001) Romania and Euro-Atlantic integration since 1989: a decade of frustration. In: Light, D. and Phinnemore, D. (eds) *Post-Communist Romania: Coming to Terms with Transition.* Basingstoke, UK: Palgrave, pp. 245–269.

Pritchard, A. (2000) Ways of seeing 'them' and 'us': tourism representation, race and identity. In: Robinson, M., Long, P., Evans, N., Sharply, R. and Swarbrooke, J. (eds) *Expressions of Culture, Identity and Meaning in Tourism.* Sunderland, UK: Business Education Publishers, pp. 245–262.

Pritchard, A. and Morgan, N. (1995) Evaluating vacation destination brochure images: the case of local authorities in Wales. *Journal of Vacation Marketing* 2(1), 23–38.

Pritchard, A. and Morgan, N. (2001) Culture, identity and tourism representation: marketing Cymru or Wales? *Tourism Management* 22, 167–179.

Roberts, L. (1996) Barriers to the development of rural tourism in the Bran area of Transylvania. In: Robinson, M., Evans, N.and Callaghan, P.M. (eds) *Tourism and Culture: Image, Identity and Marketing.* Sunderland, UK: Business Education Publishers, pp. 185–197.

Smith, A. (2001) The transition to a market economy in Romania and the competitiveness of exports. In: Light, D. and Phinnemore, D. (eds) *Post-Communist Romania: Coming to Terms with Transition.* Basingstoke, UK: Palgrave, pp. 127–149.

Todorova, M. (1997) *Imagining the Balkans.* New York: Oxford University Press.

Turnock, D. (1977) Rumania and the geography of tourism. *Geoforum* 8, 51–56.

Verdery, K. (1991) *National Ideology under Socialism: Identity and Cultural Politics in Ceaușescu's Romania.* Berkeley CA: University of California Press.

Verdery, K. (1999) *The Political Life of Dead Bodies: Reburial and Post-Socialist Change.* New York: Columbia University Press.

21 Turkey: EU Membership Implications for Sustainable Tourism Development

Cevat Tosun, John Fletcher and Alan Fyall

Introduction

Approaches to tourism development in Turkey have undergone an evolutionary process reflecting changes in political, economic, cultural and developmental spheres of policy (Tosun, 2005). While tourism was seen as a purely economic growth strategy during the 1960s and 1970s, it was also a political, diplomatic and socio-cultural tool to project a more positive image on the international stage and to ease ideological clashes among the young (Tosun and Jenkins, 1996; Tosun and Fyall, 2005).

To achieve the above goals of tourism the military-led government in 1982 enacted the *Tourism Encouragement Law* No. 2634 to provide generous monetary, fiscal and other incentives to tourism entrepreneurs (Tosun, 1999). Consequently, Turkey experienced a rapid growth of mass tourism in terms of volume and value during the 1980s and 1990s. This is reflected in Turkey's current standing in the global tourism market within the top 15 and top nine international tourist destinations in terms of arrivals and receipts respectively (WTO, 2005a, 2005b). However, this rapid growth of mass tourism development has also ushered in a number of potentially serious developmental problems that appear to threaten not only the sustainable development of tourism, but wider issues of sustainability because of the negative 'spill-over' effects of the tourism industry into other sectors and environments. Although public authorities, private sector representatives and non-governmental organizations (NGOs) have recognized, to some extent, the challenges of sustainable tourism development, necessary strategies and policy measurements have not yet been put in place to confront them.

It is assumed that the continuing enlargement of, and Turkey's eventual accession to the EU, will have several implications for the tourism industry in Turkey. While EU enlargement, in conjunction with global changes in the international tourism market and consumer preferences, may bring about new opportunities, it may also bring with it some negative consequences. It is thus the main objective of this chapter to examine tourism development in Turkey in the context of EU enlargement and accession and to offer policy recommendations and strategies to respond to the challenges and opportunities likely to accrue from such processes.

In view of the above, the structure of this chapter is as follows. The first two sections discuss the importance of tourism to the Turkish economy and the country's principal tourism resources and attractions by region. The third section provides a brief account of the likely impacts both of EU enlargement and of Turkey's accession on Turkey's tourism industry. The chapter then provides some preliminary policy recommendations and strategies for achieving better forms of tourism development within the context of EU regulation and conditions, and changing international tourism market trends. Finally, the chapter offers some concluding thoughts for the implementation of policy, recommendations and strategies.

The Contribution of International Tourism to the Turkish Economy

While international tourism arrivals in Turkey totalled just 200,000 in 1963, their number rose to 1.6m in 1983, 6.5m in 1993 and to 14.0m in 2003. Similar growth trends also took place in bed capacity and revenues from tourism. The latter rose from US$7.7m to US$13.2bn during this period. Meanwhile, bed capacity and the number of lodging establishments increased from 28,354 and 292 respectively in 1970 to 404,500 and 2036 in 2003 (Ministry of Culture and Tourism, 2004a, 2004b). The share of international tourism receipts in export earnings and GDP was 2.1% and 0.1% respectively in 1963, gradually increasing to 28.2% and 5.5% by 2003 (Ministry of Culture and Tourism, 2004a, 2004b).

The tourism industry has generated significant employment opportunities for Turkey's large number of young unemployed people. Registered employment in the tourism sector exceeds one million, or 5.5% of registered total employment. It is estimated that the Turkish tourism industry will generate around three million jobs

by 2010. The latest 5-year development plan anticipates that international tourism will play an increasing role in the Turkish economy. The Minister of Culture and Tourism foresees that by 2010 international tourist arrivals and receipts will increase to 30m visitors and US$30bn respectively, while bed capacity will reach one million (Mumcu, 2004).

Turkey's Principal Tourism Attractions and Resources

Turkey, covering approximately 780,000 km², and with a 8000 km coastline extending along the Black Sea, the Sea of Marmara, the Aegean Sea, and the Mediterranean Sea, has a unique position connecting Europe and Asia, geographically as well as ecologically (see Fig. 21.1). The flora and fauna of Anatolia and Thrace have a rich biodiversity (Adaman and Arsel, 2005, p. 3). The heritage of Turkey's geographical and geopolitical position embracing important civilizations, from Ancient Hitites, Greek, Persian, Helenistic, Roman, Early Christianity, Early Islam, Seljcuks, and Ottoman have served as significant tourist attractions (see Table 21.1). However, the role of these core factors including cultural heritage, natural endowments and built facilities in the spatial distribution of tourism development have not been well-considered (Tosun et al., 2003). Although the full implications of this issue are beyond this chapter, their

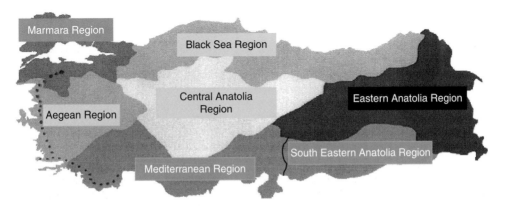

Fig. 21.1. Turkey: location map of regions. Key: The dotted line shows the coastal strip declared as the priority region for the concentration of both public and private investment. Source: Derived from data in Duzgunoglu and Karabulut (1999) cited in Tosun, Timothy and Ozturk (2003).

Table 21.1. Turkey: regional endowments of main tourism attractions and resources.

Regions	Living culture	Natural	Historical heritage	Built facilities
Aegean	Dominantly Western-oriented Authentic local rural Turkish bath	Sun-sea-sand (Garlic beach, ladies beach, etc.) Pamukkale Travertines Rivers (Hermos, Caicus, etc.) National Parks (Dilek, Davutlar, etc.)	Ancient cities (Laodicea Ad Lycum, Hierapolis, Pergamum, Ephesus (Artemision), Troy, Priene, Miletus, Herakleia, Philadelphia, etc.), ancient churches (Laodicea, the Virgin Mary House, Temple of Ascepion, Euromos, etc.) Archaeology Museum, Underwater Archaeology Museum Castle of St Peter Ottoman Mosques	Well-developed infra-super structure: rich shopping opportunities, accommodations for every budget, bars, restaurants, discos
Black Sea	Dominantly regional Authentic local rural Turkish bath	Kackar Mountains, Forest Relatively unpopular beaches Wildlife Highland pastures	Sumela Monastery Ottoman Mosques	Moderate infra-super structure
Central Anatolia	Western and regional culture equally exist in cities Authentic local rural Turkish bath	Mount Erciyas (Argaeus) Fairy Chimneys River valleys (surrounded by ancient churches) National Parks Sunny summer	Ancient underground cities (Derinkuyu & Kaymakli) Various ancient rock churches Mosques Various museums (Anatolian, Civilizations, Mevlana, Goreme and Zelve Outdoor, etc.)	Well-developed infra-super structure: rich shopping opportunities, accommodations for every budget, bars, restaurants, discos
Eastern Anatolia	Dominantly regional Authentic local rural Turkish bath	Sunny summer Mount Ararat – Turkey's highest mountain Van Lake Wildlife	Ottoman's and Seljuk's mosques, and Georgian's churches Ishak Pasa Place	Moderate infra-super structure

Region			
Marmara	Dominantly Western Authentic local rural Turkish bath	Sun-sea-sand Mountains (Uludag, Ida, etc.) The Dardanelles Bird Paradise National Park, etc. Wildlife	Hippodrome Egyptian Obelisk Serpentine & Constantine Column Blue Mosque Hagia Sophia Ottoman Palaces Various museums: The Gallipoli Campaign, Troy (relics of Trojan War), Assos, etc.	Well-developed infra-super structure: rich shopping opportunities, accommodations for every budget, bars, restaurants, discos
Mediter-ranean	Dominantly Western Authentic local rural Turkish bath	Sun-sea-sand Rivers (Melas, Cestrus, Eurymedon, Duden) Caves (Damlatas, Hell & Paradise) Highland pastures	Ancient cities (Phaselis, Perge, Side, Myra, etc.) Churches (St Nicholas, St Pierre, etc.) Mosques Ancient theatres (Aspendus, etc.) Various museums	Well-developed infra-super structure: rich shopping opportunities, accommodations for every budget, bars, restaurants, discos
South East Anatolia	Dominantly regional Authentic local rural Turkish bath	Sunny summer Dramatic sunset–sunrise Mount Nemrut Religious Fishery Lake	Hasan Keyf The religious monuments in Ahlat Akdamar Church The monasteries of Deyrul Zafaran and Morgabriel	Moderate infra-super structure

Source: derived from Yenen, 1997; Ministry of Culture and Tourism, 2005; Yale *et al.*, 2005; and the lead author's personal observations.

role in tourism development will be discussed indirectly in relation to the principal tourism attractions and resources in Turkey (see Table 21.1).

Turkey's natural tourism attractions can be classified under four sub-headings.

Sun-sea-sand

This includes the mass tourism attractions which are to be found on Turkey's western and southern coasts. While the hot, dry Mediterranean climate on the western and southern coasts along with long sandy beaches has helped Turkey become one of the most popular '3S' tourist destinations, it also provides opportunities for various water sports, yachting and golf (see Fig. 21.1).

Geological formations

These include two spectacular attractions: Pamukkale Travertines and Fairy Chimneys of Cappadocia. While the Pamukkale Travertines – giant steps of limestone deposits – are located in the Aegean region, the Fairy Chimneys are situated in Central Anatolia. Both of these natural spectacular formations are listed as UNESCO World Heritage Sites and attract large numbers of tourists and tourism investment in their locality (Tosun, 1998; Yuksel *et al.*, 1999).

Flora and fauna

These include a considerable diversity, and generate special interest tourism including ornithology, hunting and endemic plant picking (Adaman and Arsel, 2005; Ministry of Culture and Tourism, 2005).

Adventure environments

Turkey has a wide range of mountains, rivers, lakes, caves and caverns, and highland pastures. Each has potential to be utilized for a range of adventure activities, including rafting, underwater diving, mountaineering, winter sports and spelunking (caving). Tourists can enjoy water sports such as diving and water skiing in the Mediterranean or Aegean Sea, and during the same visit they can take part in winter sports in Central or Eastern Anatolia.

Culturally, Anatolia (Asian Turkey, historically known as 'Asia Minor') has acted as the crossroads of many civilizations throughout history, from palaeolithic onwards, through to Greek, Persian, Roman, early Christian, early Islamic, Ottoman, and the Republic of Turkey (Yenen, 1997; Ministry of Culture and Tourism, 2005; Yale *et al.*, 2005). For living culture, Turkey contains considerable diversity among its regions. However, as a consequence of elite oriented modernization efforts (see Keyman, 2005), impacts of technological change and globalization, industrialization, urbanization, and tourist–host interactions (see Tosun, 2002), a significant part of traditional Turkish society has changed and moved towards a Western lifestyle. None the less, rural Turkey has managed to preserve its unique cultural characteristics. These include a hybrid rural culture reflecting a mix of Turkish, Greek and Bulgarian orientation in the Aegean region. Authentic *Yoruk Koyleri* (Nomad Villages) can be found in the inner part of the Mediterranean region, while in the Eastern and South-eastern Anatolia regions, a mixture of Turkish, Arabic and Persian cultures can be found.

Tourism infrastructure is well developed in the Aegean, Mediterranean and Marmara regions, and less so in the relatively less developed regions such as the interior of the Black Sea region, Central Anatolia, Eastern and South-eastern Anatolia. Tourism accommodation, cuisine, entertainment, and retail facilities are well-developed in the tourism regions whose boundaries were determined by the Tourism Encouragement Law in 1982. Most of these are on the western and southern coasts. Due to the generous fiscal, financial and bureaucratic incentives given to the tourism industry during 1980s and early 1990s the coastal part of Turkey has experienced a rapid growth in terms of supply capacity and tourism demand (Sezer and Harrison, 1994; Tosun 1999). In this regard,

> a pronounced spatial dichotomy has evolved in Turkish tourism between a privileged space along the coast and an underprivileged space in the interior of the country.
>
> (Göymen, 2000, p. 1030)

The implication of this is that although tourism development taking place in the more developed regions has made a considerable contribution to the country's GNP, it has also magnified the developmental problems of Turkey by inducing regional disparities and class inequities (Seckelmann, 2002; Tosun et al., 2003).

It is reported that while the Aegean, Marmara and Mediterranean regions, as relatively developed areas, received on average 77.8% of the tourism credits and 78.7% of the bed capacity supported by tourism incentives between 1985 and 2000, the Black Sea and Central, South-east and East Anatolia, as relatively less-developed areas, obtained only 22.1% of the tourism credits and attracted only 21.3% of the bed capacity developed in the same period. However, this appeared to change dramatically in 2001. For example, while East and South-east Anatolia received 33% and 30% respectively of the tourism credits given as tourism incentives, the Aegean and Marmara regions obtained only 3% and 1% of this credit (Turkiye Kalkinma Bankasi, 1990, 2002) (Table 21.2). The relevant international tourist figures support the above figures. For example, 91% of Turkey's international tourists visited the most developed regions, and 96% of the nights spent by foreign visitors in 1997 and 2000 were in these regions (Table 21.3). Moreover, 84% of licensed beds in tourism operations and 86% of investment in providing licensed beds in tourism establishments are in the Marmara, Aegean and Mediterranean regions – the most developed parts of Turkey (Ministry of Tourism, 1993; 2001b). The comprehensive spatial shift in investment between 2000 and 2001 probably reflects the recognition of an excess capacity of tourism supply in the relatively developed regions.

EU Enlargement and Tourism Development Patterns in Turkey

While enlargement of the EU and Turkey's accession to it will have various implications for and impacts on Turkish tourism development patterns, Turkey's membership of the EU will equally have influences on tourism within the EU.

Implication of EU enlargement for tourism development in Turkey

Enlargement of the EU brings with it opportunities and pitfalls for sustainable development in general and sustainable tourism development in particular. The acceptance of the euro as a single currency, considerable reduction in entry formalities, guaranteed consumer rights by a single European law might motivate European people to visit primarily countries within the EU. EU enlargement to the eastern Mediterranean and CEE may have negative implications for the Turkish tourism industry, particularly in the short term, such that the rate of increase in potential and actual tourist demand for Turkey may decrease in relative terms. However, when the tourism profiles of the new accession countries are examined, none of them offer an equivalent substitute for the Turkish tourism product. Although Cyprus and Malta can offer similar coastal tourism opportunities to Turkey, their small size limits their capacity and their impact.

For the eight new members from the former Communist bloc, cultural heritage, ecotourism, and other 'niches' can be developed as a unique attraction of those countries, which may have some negative implications for Turkish tourism demand. Yet Turkey's cultural heritage is notably different from the rest of Europe. Further, as the EU provides subsidies and more regional assistance, the new accession countries will become more affluent, such that demand from those countries for Turkish tourism is likely to increase in the long term. Clearly, much depends on the tourism policies and marketing strategies of Turkey to secure some of the potential tourism demand of the new EU.

Impacts of Turkey's accession to the EU on tourism development in Turkey

Turkey's accession to the EU will have various positive impacts on political, social, cultural and economic development of the country. Of course, not only will Turkey benefit from this membership, but the EU will gain as well (Birand, 2004a). However, it is beyond the scope of this chapter to consider wider impacts of Turkey's accession to the EU on the EU and Turkey. Thus, the scope will be limited to discussing

Table 21.2. Turkey: credit given as incentives to tourism investment by region, 1985–2001.

Regions	1985		1986		1987		1988		1989		1990		2000		2001		Average	
	a %	b %	a %	b %	a %	b %	a %	b %	a %	b %	a %	b %	a %	b %	a %	b %	a %	b %
Aegean	13.45	20.15	14.17	25.18	41.25	40.41	27.90	39.74	43.00	51.34	25.8	–	93	82	3	4	32.99	37.50
Black Sea	0.86	2.29	4.31	4.72	2.09	2.16	0.71	1.04	2.28	1.72	4.3	–	3	6	12	7	3.99	3.56
Central Anatolia	11.88	9.19	32.05	12.66	2.93	5.68	3.39	7.01	6.53	7.86	5.7	–	0	0	1	1	7.94	6.20
East Anatolia	0.08	–	0.10	0.71	0.46	1.25	0.30	0.78	2.58	1.93	0.31	–	4	12	33	29	5.10	6.52
Mediterranean	64.70	52.49	35.26	40.47	42.22	37.50	35.85	36.91	35.20	30.05	43.3	–	0	0	20	30	33.40	32.48
Marmara	7.41	14.21	13.71	14.66	10.48	11.56	31.35	13.52	9.70	6.14	20.46	–	0	0	1	1	11.76	8.77
South-east Anatolia	1.62	1.67	0.40	1.60	0.57	1.44	0.50	1.00	0.71	0.96	0.07	–	0	0	30	28	4.20	4.95
Total	100	100	100	100	100	100	100	100	100	100	100	–	100	100	100	100	100	100

a = amount of credit given ; b = number of beds.
Source: Tosun *et al.*, 2003.

Table 21.3. Turkey: international tourist arrivals and overnight stays by region, 1997 and 2000.

Regions	1997			2000		
	Arrivals (and %)	Nights spent (and %)	Average length of stay (nights)	Arrivals (and %)	Nights spent (and %)	Average length of stay (nights)
Aegean	2,530,900 (27)	11,077,200 (31)	4.38	1,569,376 (0.24)	6,788,307 (25)	4.3
Black Sea	114,206 (1)	160,708 (0.4)	1.41	131,038 (6)	161,336 (3)	1.2
Central Anatolia	735,440 (8)	1,404,036 (4)	1.91	492,765 (12)	937,620 (7)	1.9
Eastern Anatolia	63,360 (0.7)	88,379 (0.2)	1.39	34,868 (2)	55,072 (1)	1.6
Marmara	3,332,782 (36)	7,175,868 (20)	2.15	2,017,619 (27)	4,419,277 (18)	2.2
Mediterranean	2,649,613 (28)	16,233,604 (45)	6.13	2,537,798 (26)	16,119,574 (45)	6.4
South-east Anatolia	16,898 (0.2)	27,401 (0.08)	1.62	20,612 (3)	401,120 (1)	1.4
Grand Total	9,443,199 (100)	36,167,196 (100)	2.71	6,804,076 (100)	28,510,906 (100)	

Sources: Ministry of Tourism, 2001a, 2001b.

impacts of Turkey's accession to the EU membership on tourism development and vice versa. These impacts are considered below.

Political stability, EU membership and Turkish tourism development

Political instability has been one of the biggest problems for the emergence of a modern Turkish State since the 1960s. Turkey wasted many years because of political inconsistency that has prevented emergence of a strong government essential for taking the necessary measures required for sustainable (tourism) development (Tosun, 2001). It has been argued that during the 1990s few structural reforms could take place owing to political instability (Tosun and Timothy, 2001, p. 356). Three hard and one soft military coups in the last 45 years may imply that civilian governments have not had enough time and security to take comprehensive, integrative and systematic long-term measures for moving towards sustainable development. The average length of term of office for governments in power has been less than two years. As argued by Okumus and Karamustafa (2006), between 1963 and 1996, 34 tourism ministers were appointed, with an average length of stay in office of just 1.6 years.

Not surprisingly, the historical position of the Turkish State with respect to both sustainable development generally and tourism development in particular has been inconsistent. While political instability has not provided sufficient time for successive governments to establish a development agenda for the nation, it has also encouraged conditions feeding corruption, clientelism and wide-spread favouritism, which have emerged as more challenging obstacles to sustainable democratic development. Birand (2004b) argues that through accession to the EU, Turkey's multi-party secular and democratic political life and the republican system can be secured, and that the continuous efforts to protect the secular system would no longer be necessary. Based upon the above discussion, it may be argued that Turkey's acceptance as a full member of the EU would offer a permanent assurance for multi-party liberal democracy and political stability, which is *sine qua non* for sustainable tourism development (see Kösebalaban, 2002; Birand, 2004b). Clearly, a

secured political, cultural, social and economic stability would provide for tourism authorities and all stakeholders the context for stronger motivation, improved ability, and a wider vision to move towards more sustainable forms of tourism development.

Increased foreign investment

The stability that EU accession should bring will encourage foreign investment (Oguzlu, 2004, p. 99). For example, Fiat and Mercedes Benz have recently applied to bring their regional headquarters and plants to Turkey following the government's decision to let foreign nationals set up business there. In the past, multi-national companies have operated hotels and other tourism facilities based on management contracts rather than involving fixed investment in the tourism industry in Turkey (S. Kusluvan, 1994, unpublished PhD thesis; Tosun, 1998). To a large extent, this is a result of the lack of political and economic stability in the country. Having established such stability, the Turkish tourism industry may attract a large amount of foreign investment because of low cost factors of production such as labour, land and other investment requirements. Foreign investment would bring not only capital, but know-how, invaluable management and operational experience, and new marketing opportunities. These can increase the quality of tourism products to render Turkey a more attractive and competitive international tourist destination.

Improvement in the perceived image of Turkey as a tourist destination

To complement quality improvements there is a need for reinvigorated image promotion (Eclipse, 2003, p. 1; Tosun *et al.*, 2005). Turkey has made considerable progress in the area of human rights and overall democratization processes so as to fulfil the so-called Copenhagen criteria (Anon, 2004; Kanli, 2004; Phillips, 2004). Having obtained EU membership, somewhat paradoxically, Turkey's ambiguous image of being neither European nor Asian should change, while its role of being a bridge between East and West, and between the Muslim and Christian worlds may be strengthened.

Hitherto, there has been a close relationship between the country's 'organic' image and the tourism destination image. For example, international tourism demand for Turkey in 2003 decreased unexpectedly due to the War in Iraq, although the country's coastal resorts are geographically far removed from the areas of conflict in the neighbouring country. Turkey's accession to the EU can assist developing the perception of Turkey as a more secure, safe and responsible destination, while also helping to remove historical prejudices prevailing in the mind of Western societies (e.g. Kanli, 2004; Paris, 2004; Tosun and Temizkan, 2004).

Benefiting from accumulated experience of the EU

It will be easier for Turkey to share accumulated experience and expertise of the EU in the area of tourism planning, management and marketing when Turkey becomes a full member of the EU. As the EU has helped Spain, Greece and Italy utilize tourism as an instrument to reduce regional developmental inequalities, it could encourage the Turkish authorities to plan, manage and develop tourism in such a way as to achieve more balanced development outcomes and assist progress towards sustainable forms of tourism.

It is claimed that the country has failed to use its educated human resources effectively and efficiently in the tourism industry because of widespread nepotism, lack of objective criteria and the absence of equal opportunities. Thus, many students who studied at Western universities supported with public money have either not returned to Turkey or have only stayed for a short time because of dissatisfaction with the mismanagement of human resources in the public sector (Tosun, 2000, 2001). EU accession would be expected to reduce nepotism and create an environment for equal opportunities in employment and promotion. This would enable Turkey to deploy human resources in a more effective and efficient manner and reduce the costly brain drain currently suffered (although, potentially, it could exacerbate the outflow of educated labour in the shorter term). Theoretically at least, Turkey would benefit not only from the EU's experience in tourism management, but also from her own educated and experienced citizens hitherto living abroad.

Improvement in product quality

Establishment of greater political stability, increased foreign investment, and the sharing of accumulated experience and expertise should result in an overall improvement in product quality. As a requirement of EU membership, Turkey will need to enact new rules and take measures to produce goods and services consistent with EU standards. When Turkey increases the quality of tourism products to attain EU standards, costs of production will increase as well, creating new challenges.

Internationally, the numbers of tourists with special needs (through age and various forms of disablement) are increasing (CEC, 2003, p. 6). To respond to the needs of these growing markets, Turkey will need to restructure tourism facilities both to increase the satisfaction levels of such tourists and to increase the country's long-term competitiveness.

Other new market opportunities

Turkey has hitherto targeted Western European low- and middle-income groups, largely through the direction provided by international tour operators. With the improvement in quality of tourism supply, her organic image as a country and induced image as a destination, Turkey should have a capability to reach higher income groups in the international tourism market. Collaboration and cooperation should be pursued with neighbouring Greece, particularly in destination marketing growth strategies such as market penetration, market development, product development and product diversification strategies. Although there are currently political, diplomatic and financial barriers to this (Tosun et al., 2005), despite the public polemics, Turkey's EU accession bid has already brought both countries closer in terms of diplomatic and political relationships. As a reflection of this, a bilateral agreement in the field of tourism was signed in 2000:

> The Parties, in order to stimulate the tourist flows from third countries into their countries, shall encourage bilateral cooperation between the representatives of the tourism sectors of

both countries including the coordination of their activities within the Black Sea Economic Cooperation (BSEC) . . . The Parties shall facilitate tourist traffic between their countries in accordance with their respective laws and regulations and without prejudice to their international obligations and will encourage the cooperation between enterprises and organizations operating in the field of tourism. In this context, mutual visits, meetings and seminars between entities operating in the field of tourism shall be encouraged and organized.

(Turkish Ministry of Foreign Affairs, 2000: Articles 2 and 9)

European Union accession will encourage Turkish tourism stakeholders to cooperate with their partners in the EU, from whatever country. It can be idealized that Turkey and Greece could promote themselves as a single destination to tourists for whom travelling to only one country in Europe and/or the Middle East is not a desirable option. While this kind of cooperation might increase the attractiveness of both countries to overseas travellers and their bargaining power against foreign tour operators (Timothy, 2002), establishing facilities in their common borderlands may increase demand from a wide range of markets. Such cooperation in tourism is required across Europe to encourage macro-level rationalization of resource use and sustainability (not least in Cyprus – see Chapters 16 and 18).

Turkey's movement towards EU membership has encouraged many EU citizens, most of them retired, to settle on a temporary or permanent basis in the country's coastal zones. By 2004, 11,000 foreigners had bought holiday homes; 4900 of these foreigners from Germany, Sweden, Norwegian, Finland, Denmark and Northern Ireland settled in Alanya (Turizm Gazetesi, 2004a). As is the case for many mass tourism destinations, seasonality is one of the biggest problems for the tourism industry in Turkey (Tosun, 1999). However, the burden of seasonality and its spill-over affect appear to be lessened in some local mass-tourism destination such as Alanya, Fethiye and Anamur due to the fact that retired people from EU countries tend to spend their winters in coastal hotels, while some have settled permanently (Turizm Gazetesi, 2004b). This appears to help utilize over-capacity and to attract and retain employees (see CEC, 2003).

Strategies for Sustainable Tourism Development in a 'Europeanized' Turkey

If Turkey does not take measures and establish strategies for its own tourism development by taking into account global trends in the international tourism market, its competitiveness and sustainability will be compromised. Possible strategies and policy recommendations for sustainable tourism development in Turkey will now be considered.

Product differentiation for sustainable tourism development

Existing tourism development requirements, as represented by Tourism Encouragement Law No. 2636, were designed and put into effect in 1980 by the military-led government without taking into account environmental, social and developmental impacts of tourism. At that time the main objectives of tourism were to generate desperately needed foreign currency and establish political credibility for the government (Tosun and Jenkins, 1996). Thus, the government gave priority to large-scale mass tourism investment projects to meet its short-term policy objectives (Tosun *et al.*, 2003).

The myopic policy objectives of the 1980s and 1990s, in tandem with the encouragement of international tour operators, saturated the carrying capacity of coastal regions (Tosun and Fyall, 2005). Table 21.3 indicates that in 2000, 83% of Turkey's international tourists visited the coastal regions, and 91% of the nights spent by foreign visitors were in these regions, down from 92% and 96% respectively in 1997. Given the problems associated with coastal mass tourism development and the implications of Turkey's EU accession for its own tourism, this suggests that product differentiation is a major requirement for a structurally and spatially more balanced tourism development. There appear to be several areas where diversification of the tourism product can take place.

Cultural and heritage tourism, ecotourism, faith tourism, event tourism, rural tourism, spa and health tourism, sport tourism and winter tourism are among the range of activities and attractions for which Turkey has considerable supply potential (see Table 21.1). As an example, cultural tourism will be considered here both because it appears to have the greatest potential in terms of supply and demand, and because cultural tourism can be seen to be a more complex phenomenon than other potential forms of tourism development.

Cultural tourism

With its historic and cultural heritage, diverse lifestyle, food and people, Turkey demonstrates enormous potential for cultural tourism. Given the considerable cultural differences with its main competitors in the Mediterranean basin, Turkey has a unique opportunity to meet cultural and coastal oriented tourism demand simultaneously, through balanced, integrated destination marketing strategies and regional collaboration. Accession to the EU may activate a large potential demand for cultural tourism, and thus Turkey needs to prepare itself for this. Cultural heritage can be employed to assist the move towards sustainable tourism development in a number of ways:

- A comprehensive inventory of cultural heritage resources should be made.
- Strict measures should be taken to protect cultural heritage.
- Human resource planning should be in place to develop and manage cultural heritage as a tourism product. A comprehensive training programme should be designed and implemented for those working in such areas of cultural heritage as museums, historic buildings and historic sites.
- With local community participation, the scope and context of cultural events and values should be determined for promoting cultural tourism products. There should be no compromising of cultural authenticity for the sake of short-term economic benefits.
- Tour guides should be trained to present cultural heritage, but given the diverse range of civilizations and their cultural heritages found in Turkey (see Table 21.1), a careful specialization programme for tour guides may be necessary. In this regard, it may be argued that tour guides should be encouraged to specialize in the cultural

heritage of certain regions in the country. This may lead tour guides to be more knowledgeable and experienced in a few regions of the country where certain cultural and historical heritage exist. Eventually, such specialization of tour guides will result in a higher level of tourist satisfaction from guided tours.

- Facility and environmental planning for cultural tourism should be pursued.

Changing demographic structures and lifestyles suggest that the value of non-traditional forms of tourism, particularly related to natural and cultural heritage, will increase gradually (Klein, 2001, p. 1; CEC, 2003).

The need for a new destination image

Two elements require change: the image of a cheap mass tourism destination solely visited by downmarket sun-, sea-, sand- and sex-oriented tourists, and the pejorative historical construction of 'Turk', 'Turkish' and the 'other Europe' held in the West (e.g. Aktan, 2004; Kanli, 2004; Paris, 2004). In cooperation with appropriate ministries, including that for foreign affairs, tourism authorities need to promote Turkey as a bridge between civilizations and cultures. While the existence of diverse cultural heritage built by different civilizations, and meeting points of Muslim and Christian civilization are emphasized, peace, security, safety, stability, modernity and high standards of facilities provided for tourist and community should be promoted in the establishment of a new destination image for Turkey. However, appropriate wider political and economic circumstances are needed to establish a suitable environment for this.

Restructuring the public administration of tourism

Local governments in Turkey lack power and financial resources to respond to public and tourists needs effectively (Tosun, 1998). The structure of local government reflects bureaucratic and fiscal concerns of central government rather than acting as a source of local democratic participation (Tosun, 2006). Therefore, without meaningful devolution in public administration, it may not be possible for local authorities to respond to the needs of tourists and local people simultaneously in a satisfactory manner. Although the current government has recognized the need for restructuring public administration systems and has prepared new legislation to give them more power, the enactment of this has been delayed by strong political opposition.

Without empowering local governments in an appropriate manner, it may not be possible for local authorities to deal effectively with environmental, social and economic impacts of tourism. Municipalities have difficulty in serving foreign tourists, second-home owners and their permanent residents simultaneously because their budgets are based on the number of permanent residents, excluding second-home owners and tourists (Suyolcu, 1980). When large numbers of tourists and second-home owners come and visit popular local tourist destinations during peak season, the service demands on these local municipalities goes beyond their capacities. Consequently, undesirable environmental, social, cultural and economic impacts result.

Need for greater environmental protection

Turkish Mediterranean, Aegean and Marmara coastal tourism destinations have suffered from the unplanned ribbon development of hotels and second homes, and tourist pollution from the careless discarding of packaging and food waste (Tosun, 1998, 2001). Tourism development has also disrupted the ecological balance of flora and fauna – for example, hotels and second homes being built on the sites of olive and citrus groves and displacing the livelihoods of many agricultural workers (Tosun and Fyall, 2005). Owing to the loss of fertile agricultural lands, former workers in the agricultural sector have been economically forced to work as cheap labour for hotel construction or have low-paid seasonal and relatively lower status jobs in the tourism industry. Tourist developments on beaches coupled with lighting and noise from tourist facilities have disrupted the natural life-cycle movements of sea turtles along a small part of the Mediterranean Sea (Morrison and Selman, 1991; Türkozan, 2000; Tosun, 2001).

Increased waste residues from tourism facilities coupled with the failure to install appropriate sewage disposal systems have caused pollution of underground and surface water (Kocasoy, 1989; Tosun, 2001). Even some World Heritage Sites such as the Pamukkale Travertines and the Fairy Chimneys of Goreme have been damaged by rapid, unplanned and mismanaged tourism growth (Tosun and Fyall, 2005). For example, it is reported that some hotels and motels have utilized the thermal water as their hot water source for swimming pools and baths. Such an excessive misuse of the thermal water that keeps the Travertines fresh has changed their ecological balance (Tosun, 2001; Yuksel *et al.*,1999). Moreover,

> Some open fissures are being filled by domestic waste from adjacent municipalities, hotels and motels. Surface waters collecting in these fissures will wash pollutants into the main thermal-water reservoir. This will bring two major problems. Firstly, the polluted thermal waters will precipitate unclean travertine of unsightly appearance and, secondly and more importantly, the polluted thermal waters will pose a threat to human health where they continue to be used supplying baths, swimming pools . . .
> (Altunel and Hancock, 1994, p. 129)

Concentration of too many visitors in time and space, and careless attitudes and activities of visitors towards the fragile fairy chimneys and rock-churches has also brought some irreversible damage (Tosun, 1998).

In order to give priority to environmental concerns in tourism development, the design and implementation of training programmes for environmental awareness is vital. These should target appropriate local authority employees, private sector representatives and members of NGOs. Appropriate information and interpretation should be published and provided for tourists to inform them about the fragile nature of the country's historic and natural assets.

It is strongly recommended that Turkey should draw lessons from the European experience in the area of management and protection of heritage sites and the natural environment. In this regard, it is believed that accession to the EU will make it easier for Turkey to share European experience and utilize its expertise in the area of overall environmental protection.

The need to move towards societal-oriented destination marketing

Until the late 1980s, Turkey followed a production-oriented marketing approach whose main objective was to build sufficient physical capacity including hotels, restaurants and tourist transport, such as car hire facilities. By the mid-1990s a product-oriented marketing approach had been adopted to raise the quality of tourism products, but it was undertaken without seeking knowledge of the real needs of customers in the target tourism markets. The resulting five-star hotels and other luxury physical facilities have thus not been appropriate to satisfy adequately tourists' needs.

Although there have been some moves towards market and societal-oriented marketing management philosophies, in practice their principles and strategies have not been implemented (Tosun and Fyall, 2004). If progress towards sustainable tourism development is to be achieved, societal-oriented destination marketing strategies need to be adopted that seek to establish a balance between environmental protection, enhanced societal well-being, and long-term customer satisfaction and destination profitability.

Conclusion

This chapter has considered the implications of Turkey's accession to the EU and of EU enlargement of the EU for Turkish tourism development. It has dealt with a number of unknown interrelated and interdependent variables that have and will have various implications for and impacts on tourism development both in Turkey and in the EU. Thus, some parts of the arguments raised in this chapter may be speculative in nature. Notwithstanding, it is possible to draw some general conclusions as well as making policy recommendations for sustainable tourism development in Turkey in the era of New Europe.

First, Turkish authorities should recognize that the preservation of floral and faunal diversity, maintaining cultural authenticity, considering community well-being, avoiding architectural pollution alongside coastal zones, and protecting cultural and natural heritage are a prerequisite for ensuring quality of tourism supply, remaining as a competitive tourist destination and providing a high quality tourist experience in the long term. But such basic principles of sustainable tourism development may not be implemented in Turkey because there is an insufficient capacity to overcome clientelistic relationships between decision-makers and the business elite in the tourism industry that operates at the cost of environmental degradation and societal well-being (Tosun, 2001, 2005). In this context, it is strongly believed that Turkey's accession to the EU will accelerate the emergence of a more democratic developmental state and strong NGOs that are necessary to scrutinize and enforce rigorously the implementation of sustainable (tourism) development principles.

Second, while experience of developed democratic countries suggests that for efficiency and effectiveness of public services, sufficient political, legal and financial power should be given to local authorities, Turkish development experience reveals that an over-centralization of the public administration system has actually accelerated socio-cultural and environmental problems. Management of every single communal issue by state bodies in Ankara has been proved to be not only ineffective and inefficient, but also undesirable. Similarly, the over-centralized nature of tourism administration is unrepresentative and unable to innovate and adapt to new global conditions and market demands (Tosun, 2006). Thus, a reorganization and restructuring of public administration in Turkey appears to be an urgent requirement in order to give more power to local governments, to enable local people and NGOs to participate in the tourism development process, and to empower NGOs in participatory (tourism) development decision-making. Local governments cannot provide high quality services and deal effectively with environmental problems without having appropriate legal and financial authority.

Third, although Turkey has a rich potential for non-mass forms of tourism development such as ecotourism, cultural and rural tourism, mass coastal tourism was deliberately developed to contribute to the short-term economic objectives of successive governments during the 1980s and 1990s. Various negative impacts of this uncontrolled, unplanned and mismanaged tourism development, strongly driven by powerful business interests and international tour operators, have revealed coastal tourism destinations to be exceeding their carrying capacity, to be architecturally polluted, and to be losing their competitiveness in the international market. If Turkey wants the tourism industry to continue to contribute to her economy by generating employment for her increasing unemployed young population and foreign currency earnings desperately needed for the finance of industrialization, a balanced product diversification strategy should be adopted.

The following steps are recommended:

- different steering committees involving relevant experts from a wide range of interests should be established to plan, develop and manage relevant forms of tourism and design operational strategies for sustainable development;
- local communities should be encouraged to participate in the development process including key decision-making processes;
- while the steering committees in collaboration with local people prepare plans and strategies to develop 'niche' tourism, careful market segmentation for each form of tourism should be made – for example, the requirements and profile of demand for sport tourism will be different to those of religious tourism;
- new forms of tourism should be developed within an incremental tourism planning approach. Past experience of coastal tourism development has shown that rapid development is difficult to control and manage. Thus, necessary measures should be taken to prevent further rapid tourism growth in environmentally and socially fragile destinations. Encouraging small-scale investment and identifying an anticipated threshold for each local destination may be used as a policy instrument for incremental tourism development.

Turkey's accession to, and the further enlargement of, the EU present opportunities and pitfalls for both the Turkish and European tourism industries. It appears that the profile of tourism demand generated in the EU is tending to change towards 'alternative' forms including cultural and heritage tourism. By taking into account new trends in the international tourism market and impacts of global change, Turkish decision-makers should pursue a careful evolutionary development approach to tourism policy, destination marketing, environmental planning, and the public administration of tourism in order to best utilize opportunities emerging from EU accession processes.

Finally, it is evident that tourism seems to have widened the developmental gaps between regions in Turkey and elsewhere in many countries. For example, studies in many developing countries in the Mediterranean basin, such as the former Yugoslavia, Turkey, Egypt, Tunisia, Morocco and Algeria, suggest that tourism has been playing a significant role in industrialization and economic growth at the cost of regional, class, and inter-/intra-generation inequality since the 1970s (Allcock, 1986; Lea, 1988; Poirier, 2001; Tosun, 2001; Var and Imam, 2001). Polarization of tourism investment in the relatively developed regions of these countries may be partly explained by comparative advantage theory and the endowments accruing from that. In this context, Turkey's western regions have experienced more growth because they are better endowed with mass tourism resources (Tosun *et al.*, 2003, p. 150). However, wider factors, such as political-social stability, interest of power groups, and preferences of central governments and international tour operators may also have played an important role in the regional allocation of tourism investment. For example, Tosun *et al.* (2003, p. 157) argue that

> the political dimension of regional tourism development should also be considered. . . . the political and social unrest ushered in by the Kurdish Workers Party's (PKK) violence and terror activities have discouraged local, national and international investors from investing in the east and south-east regions of Turkey.

Consequently, an unplanned spatial dichotomy has evolved in Turkish tourism between a privileged space in the relatively developed regions along the coast and an underprivileged space in relatively less developed regions in the interior of the country.

Lessons from a number of countries suggest that unless special measures are taken, tourism may magnify development gaps between regions. However, it is not the tourism itself widening such gaps. Political preferences of central governments, factor endowments of regions, preferences of tourists in the international market and regional social-political stability together direct tourism investment towards certain regions in a country. In this context, it should be kept in mind that unless relatively undeveloped regions in a country are made attractive through various financial, fiscal and other possible means, any potential of the tourism industry may not be able to be used as a tool to decrease regionally imbalanced development.

References

Adaman, F. and Arsel, M. (2005) Introduction. In: Adaman, F. and Arsel, M. (eds) *Environmentalism in Turkey: Between Democracy and Development*. Aldershot, UK: Ashgate, pp. 1–11.

Aktan, G. (2004) Opinion: becoming aware of the EU truth? *Turkish Daily News*, 4 October. Available at: http://www.turkishdailynews.com/old_editions/10_04_04/gunduz.htm

Allcock, J.B. (1986) Yugoslavia's tourism trade: pot of gold or pig in a poke. *Annals of Tourism Research* 14, 565–588.

Altunel, E. and Hancock, P.L. (1994) Pollution of the Pamukkale travertine as a consequence of urbanisation: what future for a unique natural Turkish monument? In: *Turkiye Jeoloji Kurultayi 1994 Bildiri Ozleri, Cevre Jeolojisi Oturumu*. Izmir: Dokuz Eylul Universitesi, pp. 4–7.

Anon (2004) To Brussels, on a wing and prayer; Turkey and the European Union. *The Economist*, 9 October, p. 39.

Birand, M.A. (2004a) EU will gain much from Turkey's membership. *Turkish Daily News*, 31 July. Available at: http://www.turkishdailynews.com/old_editions/07_31_04/birand.htm

Birand, M.A. (2004b) The reasons why Turkey should access to the EU. *Turkish Daily News*, 2 August. Available at: http://www.turkishdailynews.com/old_editions/08_02_04/birand.htm

CEC (Commission of the European Communities) (2003) Basic orientations for the sustainability of European tourism. Brussels: CEC. Available at: http://europa.eu.int/comm/enterprise/services/tourism/consultation/

Duzgunoglu, E. and Karabulut, E. (1999) *Development of Turkish Tourism: Past and Present*. Istanbul: TURSAB, Association of Turkish Travel Agencies.

Eclipse (2003) *Destination Image Evaluation (Part 1)*. Madrid: Moonlight Travel Marketing. Available at: http://www.moonshine.es/ECLIPSE/E9.pdf

Göymen, K. (2000). Tourism and governance in Turkey. *Annals of Tourism Research* 27(4), 1025–1048.

Kanli, Y. (2004) Viewpoint: time to concentrate on image building in EU. *Turkish Daily News*, 29 September. Available at: http://www.turkishdailynews.com/old_editions/09_29_04/yusuf.htm

Keyman, E.F. (2005) Modernity, democracy, and civil society. In: Adaman, F. and Arsel, M. (eds) *Environmentalism in Turkey: Between Democracy and Development*. Aldershot, UK: Ashgate, pp. 35–52.

Klein, R. (2001) Public policies and cultural tourism. In: *The 1st Conference on Cultural Tourism-EU Activities*. Fira de Barcelona, Spain, 29–31 March. Available at: http://europa.eu.int/comm/enterprise/services/tourism/tourism-publications/documents/barcelona30-03-2001.pdf

Kocasoy, G. (1989) The relationship between coastal tourism, sea pollution and public health: a case study from Turkey. *Environmentalist* 9(4), 245–251.

Kösebalaban, H. (2002) Turkey's EU membership: a clash of security culture. *Middle East Policy* 9(2), 130–147.

Lea, J. (1988) *Tourism and Development in the Third World*. London: Routledge.

Ministry of Culture and Tourism (2004a) *Tourism Accommodation Statistics*. Ankara: Ministry of Tourism.

Ministry of Culture and Tourism (2004b) *Tourism Statistics*. Ankara: Ministry of Tourism.

Ministry of Culture and Tourism (2005) *Tourism Activities*. Ankara: Ministry of Tourism. Available at: http://www.turizm.gov.tr/EN/BelgeGoster.aspx?17A16AE30572D3136407999D5EC

Ministry of Tourism (1993) *Bulletin of Tourism Statistics*. Ankara: Ministry of Tourism.

Ministry of Tourism (2001a) *Bulletin of Tourism Statistics 2000*. Ankara: Ministry of Tourism.

Ministry of Tourism (2001b) *Bulletin of Accommodation Statistics 2000*. Ankara: Ministry of Tourism.

Morrison, P. and Selman, P. (1991) Tourism and the environment: a case study from Turkey. *Environmentalist* 11(2), 113–129.

Mumcu, E. (2004) *Türkiye'nin 2010 Turizm Vizyonu ve II. Hamle Dönemi Konulu Basin Toplantisi* (press meeting on the 2010 Tourism Vision of Turkey and the Second Initiation Period). Available at: http://www.kultur.gov.tr/portal/turizm_tr.asp?BELGENO=49979

Oguzlu, T.H. (2004) Changing dynamics of Turkey's US and EU relationships. *Middle East Policy* 11(1), 98–105.

Okumus, F. and Karamustafa, K. (2006) Impact of an economic crisis: evidence from Turkey. *Annals of Tourism Research* 32(4), 942–961.

Paris, L.H. (2004) Letter page: we need Turkey in Europe. *Turkish Daily News*, 25 September. Available at: http://www.turkishdailynews.com/old_editions/09_25_04/letter.htm

Phillips, D.L. (2004) Turkey's dream of accession. *Foreign Affairs* 83(5), 86–91.

Poirier, R.A. (2001) The political economy of tourism in Algeria. In: Apostolopoulos, Y., Loukissas, P. and Leontidou, L. (eds) *Mediterranean Tourism: Facets of Socioeconomic Development and Cultural Change.* London: Routledge, pp. 211–225.

Seckelmann, A. (2002) Domestic tourism: a chance for regional development in Turkey? *Tourism Management* 23, 85–92.

Sezer, H. and Harrison, A. (1994) Tourism in Greece and Turkey: An economic view for planners. In: Seaton, A.V. (ed.) *Tourism: the State of the Art.* Chichester, UK: John Wiley & Sons, pp. 74–83.

Suyolcu, L. (1980) Foreword. In: Kemal, S. and Kartal, O.C. (eds) *Kiyi Kentlermizin Temel Sorunlari: Kusadasi Sempozyumu Bildirileri, 1979.* [Basic Problems of the Cities on the Coast]. Ankara.

Timothy, D.J. (2002) Tourism in borderlands: competition, complementary, and cross-frontier cooperation. In: Krakover, S. and Gradus, Y. (eds) *Tourism in Frontier Regions.* Baltimore MD: Lexington Books, pp. 233–258.

Tosun, C. (1998) Roots of unsustainable tourism development at the local level: the case of Urgup in Turkey. *Tourism Management* 19(6), 595–610.

Tosun, C. (1999) An analysis of contributions of international inbound tourism to the Turkish economy. *Tourism Economics* 5(3), 217–250.

Tosun, C. (2000) Limits to community participation in the tourism development process in developing countries. *Tourism Management* 21(6), 613–633.

Tosun, C. (2001) Challenges of sustainable tourism development in the developing world: the case of Turkey. *Tourism Management* 22(3), 285–299.

Tosun, C. (2002) Host perceptions of tourism impacts: A comparative study. *Annals of Tourism Research* 28(4), 231–253.

Tosun, C. (2005) Stages in emergence of participatory tourism development process in developing countries. *Geoforum* 36(3), 333–352.

Tosun, C. (2006) Expected level of community participation in the tourism development process. *Tourism Management* 27(1), 493–504.

Tosun, C. and Fyall, A. (2004) An evaluation of the marketing orientation of 4 and 5 star hotels. In: *EuroCHRIE Congress 2004 November 3–7, Global Issues and Trends in the Hospitality and Tourism Industries, Congress Proceedings.* Ankara: Bilkent University CD-ROM, pp. 74–83.

Tosun, C. and Fyall, A. (2005) Making tourism sustainable: prospects and pitfalls. In: Adaman, F. and Arsel, M. (eds) *Environmentalism in Turkey: Between Democracy and Development.* Aldershot, UK: Ashgate, pp. 249–262.

Tosun, C. and Jenkins, C.L. (1996) The need for regional planning approaches to tourism development: the case of Turkey. *Tourism Management* 17(7), 519–531.

Tosun, C. and Temizkan, R. (2004) Türkiye'nin ülke imaji oluşumunda turist rehberlerinin rolü [The role of tourist guide on establishing country image of Turkey]. *I. Balikesir Ulusal Turizm Kongresi Kitapcigi* [Conference Proceedings: The First Balikesir National Tourism Conference, 15–16 April]. Balikesir, Turkey: Balikesir Universitesi, pp. 345–365.

Tosun, C. and Timothy, D.J. (2001) Defects in planning approaches to tourism development developing countries: the case of Turkey. *International Journal of Contemporary Hospitality Management* 13(7), 352–359.

Tosun, C., Timothy, D.J. and Öztürk, Y. (2003) Tourism growth, national development and regional inequality in Turkey. *Journal of Sustainable Tourism* 11(2-3), 133–161.

Tosun, C., Timothy, D.J., Parpairis, A. and MacDonald, D. (2005) Cross-border co-operation in tourism marketing for sustainable tourism development: the case of Greece and Turkey. *Journal of Travel and Tourism Marketing* 18(1), 5–23.

Turizm Gazetesi (2004a) Alanya'da gecen yil 670 yabanci ev aldi (Foreigners bought houses in Alanya). *Turizm Gazetesi*, 7 May. Available at: http://www.turizmgazetesi.com/news.arsiv2id=3251

Turizm Gazetesi (2004b) Alanya'da doluluk orani yuzde 56 [Occupancy rate is 56% in Alanya]. *Turizm Gazetesi*, 13 November. Available at: http://www.turizmgazetesi.com/news.arsiv2id=2576

Turkish Ministry of Foreign Affairs (2000) *Agreement Between the Republic of Turkey and the Hellenic Republic on Cooperation in the Field of Tourism*. Ankara: Ministry of Foreign Affairs.

Turkiye Kalkinma Bankasi (1990) *Turizm El Kitabi (Tourism Handbook)*. Ankara: Turkiye Kalikinma Bankasi.

Turkiye Kalkinma Bankasi (2002) *Turizm El Kitabi (Tourism Handbook)*. Ankara: Turkiye Kalikinma Bankasi.

Türkozan, O. (2000) Reproductive Ecology of the Loggerhead Turtle, *Caretta Caretta*, on Fethiye and Kixilot Beaches, Turkey. *Chelonian Conservation and Biology* 3(4), 686–692.

Var, T. and Imam, K.Z. (2001) Tourism in Egypt: history, policies, and the state. In: Apostolopoulos, Y. Loukissas, P. and Leontidou, L. (eds) *Mediterranean Tourism: Facets of Socioeconomic Development and Cultural Change*. London: Routledge, pp. 181–196.

WTO (World Tourism Organisation) (2005a) *Tourism Highlights, Edition 2004*. Madrid: WTO.

WTO (World Tourism Organisation) (2005b) *Tourism Market Trends in Europe, Edition 2004*. Madrid: WTO.

Yale, P., Carillet, J.B., Maxwell, V. and Raphael, M. (2005) *Turkey*. London: Lonely Planet.

Yenen, S. (1997) *Turkish Odyssey*. Istanbul: Serif Yenen. Available at: http://www.turkishodyssey.com/turkey/history/history.htm

Yuksel, F., Bramwell, B. and Yuksel, A. (1999) Stakeholder interviews and tourism planning at Pamukkale, Turkey. *Tourism Management* 20, 351–360.

22 Croatia in the New Europe: Culture Versus Conformity

Irena Ateljevic and Sanda Čorak

Introduction

When speaking of the implications for Croatian tourism of the enlargement of the European Union (EU), one important aspect needs to be stressed in comparison to other Central and Eastern Europe countries (CEECs). Croatia, as a former republic of the Socialist Federal Republic of Yugoslavia (SFRJ), was not part of the Soviet bloc. Notably, up to the end of the 1980s, Yugoslavia was generating more hard currency tourism income than the rest of CEE; Croatia generated the lion's share of this. It was predominantly Western tourists who travelled to the Adriatic coast freely without any visa requirements, whilst people from CEE had to go through difficult paperwork in their own country. They could only travel on business and package tours organized by their companies and often with the goal of socialist 'ideologically sound' holidays. Milan Kundera writes in many of his books (e.g. Kundera, 2002) about Czech(oslovakian) dissidents who used their travel to Yugoslavia to escape to the West.

From the early 1960s, Yugoslavia developed 'market socialism', where federal devolution and private sector expansion was allowed, particularly in the area of tourism. Questions of interregional flows and the overall restructuring of both tourism production and consumption in CEE (e.g. Hall and Danta, 2000; Coles and Hall, 2005) take on a different dimension

when speaking from the experience of a non-aligned country that experienced freedom of mobility during much of the Cold War era (e.g. Allcock, 1991).

Within this context, the chapter addresses the most critical issues and implications of EU enlargement for Croatian tourism over the next decade. First, the Yugoslav wars of succession in the 1990s, also coincided with an apparent early decline stage of tourism development based on the traditional '3S' market. With consumers seeking cultural and more active experiences (e.g. Morgan and Pritchard, 2000), the concentration of simple sun and sea consumption could not sustain continuous tourism growth. Equally, local and global forces have created pressures for restructuring and repositioning of the Croatian tourism product at destination and national levels.

Conflict speeded the emergence of Croatia as a newly independent state, but it also severely damaged the tourism industry (Ivanić and Radnić, 1996) and demanded a re-imaging away from pejorative notions of 'Balkan-ness' (Hall and Danta, 1996; Todorova, 1997), to create a clear and positive national brand (Hall, 2002). Paradoxically, the opening of political borders and the end of conflict in and around Croatia saw new emerging tourist flows from CEE in the mid-1990s providing a short-term fix which, in conjunction with transitional political and economic complexities, postponed much-needed marketing, product and spatial diversification (Hall, 2003).

Aims and Objectives: from the Economic to the Cultural

Against this backdrop, the aim of the chapter is twofold. First, it will present an overview of tourism development in Croatia in the local context of post-conflict recovery and the regional context of new Europe. Building on Hall's (2003) work on rejuvenation and diversification of tourism in the Eastern Adriatic, we will provide a brief historical background with the particular focus on the last few years. Second, we respond to the urge made by Coles and Hall (2005, pp. 53–54) to 'go beyond the rhetoric and hyperbole of sweeping generalisations made by (EU) tourism industry spokespersons', to provide an insider/cultural perspective by Croatian authors. Hall (2002, 2003, 2004) has raised this point elsewhere, pointing to the CEE's economic transition literature which dominantly stresses political and economic factors whilst social, cultural and psychological conditions remain overshadowed.

Therefore, the first part of the chapter will give a structuralist account of likely and future tourism development. The second part will deconstruct the economic (mostly statistical) generalizations in an attempt to unravel the complexity of culture and values that shape tourism processes 'on the ground'. Facing the prospect of joining the EU in 2007, which basically requires conformity to EU governance and economic and social reorganizations, the issue of local values, traditions, attitudes and practices is critical. Our articulation of the cultural is necessarily founded on a reflexive understanding of insider perspectives. We argue that growing up in the early stages of the Croatian tourism boom in the 1970s, and subsequently making tourism the choice for our academic careers, provide a useful historical and ethnographic position from which to comment on what lies behind contemporary change.

We draw on our similar but distinctive life experiences. Irena Ateljevic was born in a small Adriatic fishing/tourist village and spent her first 27 years 'breathing and living' tourism in Croatia, and since then has lived and worked abroad as a tourism academic in the 'West'. By contrast, Sanda Čorak is currently the Director of the Institute for Tourism, which as a governmental research institution, constantly needs to maintain a balance between the academic agenda and research for tourism industry and policy needs. Working in the Institute for the last 20 years, and being at the interface between various tourism stakeholders within the private and public sectors, she has a rich experience of observing dynamics of tourism processes in Croatia.

Tourism Development in Croatia: a Historical Background

The origins of Croatian tourism can be traced back to the 19th century when a few popular seaside/health resorts, such as Opatija and Hvar were hosting the European aristocracy of the time. After World War II, the coast became popular as a holiday destination for the domestic population of Yugoslavia. Because of a shortage of formal accommodation facilities, the local population started to be involved heavily in tourism, renting their own rooms, apartments and houses to tourists. Statistical data were first collected by the Central Bureau of Statistics in 1960 with 10 million overnights recorded (see Fig. 22.1) (Weber, 1998). The initial domestic demand was followed by the rapid growth of international tourism in the late 1960s and early 1970s as a result of three key factors:

- Yugoslavia fully opened its borders to tourists from Western Europe;
- the state began supporting tourism development by giving very favourable loans for major hotel investment which became 'socially owned' enterprises; and
- the accessibility of the Adriatic coast and islands was improved by building new roads, notably the Adriatic Highway, and improving ferry links.

When tourism brought prosperity to coastal Croatia, it slowed down the depopulation (mostly economic emigration to Western Europe and the USA) that had characterized much of maritime Yugoslavia and particularly the islands (Weber et al., 2001). Being part of

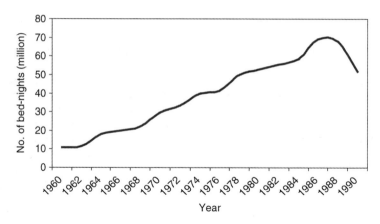

Fig. 22.1. Croatia: growth in registered bed-nights, 1960–1990. Source: Weber, 1998, p. 42.

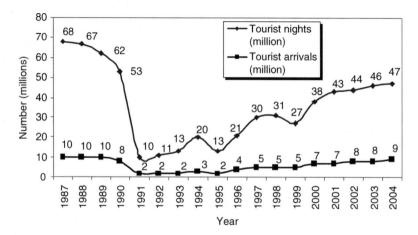

Fig. 22.2. Croatia: measures of tourism development, 1987–2004. Source: Institut za Turizam, 2005.

the traditional '3S' market booming in Western Europe in the 1970s, tourism development in coastal areas of former Yugoslavia (Slovenia, Croatia and Montenegro) continuously grew. This reached its zenith in the late-1980s when it was claimed to be one of the world's top ten international destinations (Pearce, 1991, p. 224). With 1777 km of mainland coastline and 1185 islands, Croatia hosted over 80% of the overall tourist turnover of the former Yugoslavia (see Hall, 2003), registering 68m nights and 10m tourists in 1988, the peak year of what had been continuous tourism growth for 30 years (see Figs 22.1 and 22.2).

Extreme regional concentration was found on the Adriatic coast (mainland and islands),

especially of foreign tourism. In 1988, 96% of all Croatian accommodation capacities, 93% of all overnight stays and 97% of all foreign overnight stays were concentrated on this littoral (RZzS, 1989). While the coast had a tourism intensity (overnight stays per 100 inhabitants) of 4089 in 1988, the figure amounted to an average of just 122 in interior counties (Jordan, 2000).

Croatia's attractions were thus summer recreation and bathing at the sea combined with relatively low prices. Visitors were mainly families for whom Western Mediterranean holidays were too expensive (Studienkreis für Tourismus Starnberg, 1989). Per tourist spend was much lower in Croatia than in Spain or Italy (Jordan, 2000) and the nature of this market and its motivations resulted in short seasons. In 1988, 59% of all overnight stays in Croatia were concentrated in July and August (61% at the coast), 81% (84%) between June and September, and 91% (93%) May to October (RZzS, 1989).

The interior and major part of Croatia – about two-thirds by area and population – has been barely exploited for tourism purposes. Urban and cultural attractions exist mainly in and around Zagreb, but also in the baroque Varaždin, in Karlovac as a former centre of the military border, Samobor, Osijek and Vinkovci, as well as a rural popular culture in those regions less affected by depopulation such as Slavonia and North Croatia. A range of spas, for example, at Varaždinske Toplice and Krapinske Toplice, complement natural phenomena such as the waterfalls of the 16 Plitvice lakes, karst phenomena in the Dinaric zone such as caves, and in the Pannonian basin the large floodplain woods of the Lonjsko polje and the Kopački rit with their wealth of birdlife. However, it has proved difficult to diffuse tourism into rural areas, not least because of poor infrastructure. Inadequate rural roads are especially damaging to this type of tourism, since many potential tourists are travelling by car. Most other facilities are also usually absent, from high-quality accommodation to designated walking paths, hiking trails, bicycle lanes, attractive inns, park benches, shops and evening entertainment (Jordan, 2000).

Yugoslavia had broken from the Soviet bloc in 1948, and later employed its political independence to introduce 'market socialism' based on worker 'self-management' of 'socially owned' enterprises. Agriculture was predominantly privately managed and small-scale, private sector development elsewhere was endorsed, particularly in tourism. Given the nature of demand, the tourism industry has been structured primarily around the accommodation sector. There have been two main categories of accommodation. The first is large, publicly owned hotels catering to group bookings and representing 32% of the overall accommodation capacity with average of 300 beds per facility (Hitrec, 2000). The second is small-scale, family-run home-stay rentals, often on a room-by-room basis.

This latter sector has been a dynamic area of entrepreneurship with the emergence of purpose-built tourist flats, apartments, and bungalows, constructed from the proceeds of families renting their own residential space. These facilities have been aligned with upgraded modern standards of hygiene and technical specifications, catering to the perceived needs of Western consumers. As the state did not provide incentives or strategic direction for small-scale businesses, but primarily concentrated on bigger hotel investments in selected areas of strategic importance, such as Dubrovnik (Vukonic, 2005), the locally based developments were organic and often chaotic. The local entrepreneurial spirit is reflective of the socio-cultural context we discuss in the last part of the chapter.

Another group of significant entrepreneurs were returning 'guest-workers' from Germany, many of whom perceived tourism on the Adriatic coast as a lucrative business opportunity to capitalize on their contacts and experiences acquired working abroad. These individuals either built tourist businesses on their own land inherited from parents (Vukonic, 2005) or acquired land from local landowners, which then provided further capital impetus for locals to invest in their properties and tourism businesses (Pearce, 1991, p. 229). The significance of small-scale, local involvement in tourism is illustrated in the fact that by 1987, private accommodation providers together with campsites comprised two-thirds of the overall accommodation capacity in Croatia (Institut za Turizam, 2005). The dual structure of the accommodation sector was built around two major market segments: package groups, and independent travellers exemplified by the 'young automobile society' (Gosar, 1999, p. 67).

Supplementing the accommodation sector has been a plethora of cafes and restaurants, mostly small-scale and under private ownership, displaying the second most dynamic domain of local tourism entrepreneurship. As a consequence of tourism development, several parallel processes were noticed and one of them was abandonment of the traditional economic activities of agriculture and fishing. Tourism became almost a monoculture for many destinations along the coast, with fishing boats used for (mostly day) tours during summer months. The Adriatic coastline and the islands became dependent on the tourism economy, and this was reflected in landscapes of increasingly large private houses with restaurants and private rooms. The supply dominance of small tourism firms challenged the assumption that '3S' mass tourism facilitated only large-scale projects that displaced local communities.

The first decline after 30 years of continuous growth was registered in 1989 (from 68m nights in 1988, down to 62m), signalling difficult times to come (Radnić and Ivanić, 1999). Weber (1998, p. 40) argued that the development cycle of the Croatian tourism product from 1960 to 1990 was 'almost a textbook example of trends in a life cycle curve'. A homogeneous market (seasonal, summer tourism and uniformity of motives for visiting) and product (seaside passive recreation at favourable prices), formed the ingredients for the occurrence and identification of stagnation and decline. This conclusion was further strengthened by the notion of declining value for money, tour operator withdrawals, and uncoordinated promotion (Weber, 1998).

From Crisis to New Horizons?

The impact of conflict from 1991 to 1995 and the subsequent Bosnian and Kosovo crises, significantly reduced international tourist demand to Croatia to around 10m nights and 2m visitors in 1992 (see Fig. 22.2). The newly independent state of Croatia faced many challenges and losses.

The authorities took energetic steps to renovate tourism, which they regarded as the highest economic priority alongside agriculture, and as the potential motor of the Croatian economy (Jordan, 2000). The Ministry of Tourism, Chamber of Commerce, and the Croatian Centre of Tourism developed top-down approaches for subsidiary and regional structures, initiated a profound reform of legislation and tried to internationalize management training. The Ministry and the Institute of Tourism in Zagreb produced 'Development Strategies of Croatian Tourism' (Ministarstvo Turizma and Institut za Turizam, 1993), and the Austrian consultants Horwath provided a tourism master plan, co-financed by the Austrian government (Horwarth Consulting and Institut za Turizam, 1993). These documents proposed: a holistic renewal and protection of all tourist attractions;

the development of a new tourism identity; quality upgrading and removal of the image of mass and low-budget tourism; an updating of the sun/sea product; priority for projects with benefits for the resident population; creation of regional identities; inclusion of cultural identity; and to present Croatia as a 'green' country with large protected areas, clean coastal waters and without overcrowded beaches (Jordan, 2000). Unfortunately, the early implementation of these strategies was not successful (e.g. Dragičević et al., 1998).

Radnić and Ivanić (1999) estimated the loss from unrealized tourism consumption during the conflicts at a minimum of US$14bn (1998 rates), excluding the physical damage to accommodation facilities. Recovery began slowly in 1997 and 1998 recorded 31.2m overnight stays (Institut za Turizam, 2005). By 2004, figures of 8.6m tourists and 46.7m overnight stays suggest that Croatia was on the road to recovery (see Fig. 22.2).

In this process of crisis and subsequent recovery, the changing structure of international tourism markets paints an interesting picture (Table 22.1). Early tourist growth was experienced from CEE, particularly the Czech Republic, Hungary and Poland. Indeed, Czechs, who have a tradition of spending vacations on the Croatian coast going back to the late 19th century, and who did not neglect it during the Communist era, notably helped to fill the gaps created by the absence of Western tourists in the most critical years of Croatian tourism (Jordan, 2000). In 1994 they accounted for the largest number of foreign overnight stays (DZzS, 1995).

Subsequent diversification of markets has not necessarily helped the repositioning of the Croatian tourism product, as current demand reflects characteristics typically associated with early stages of the Western consumption of the '3S' product in the 1960s and 1970s (Smeral, 1993). It is also interesting to observe that the most significant growth occurred in the early post-conflict years. In the desperation to attract any form of tourist income, Croatia reduced prices significantly in the mid-1990s and turned to what was perceived to be the inexperienced and lower end of the market (Weber, 1998). Yet, Table 22.2 suggests that the more recent years have shown a trend of declining visits from

Table 22.1. Croatia: leading international tourist markets, 1987–2004.

Generating markets	% share in bed nights					
	1987	1989	1994	1997	2001	2004
Germany	29.1	28.3	19.4	21.9	25.2	25.7
Italy	7.1	9.5	11.5	13.5	12.1	12.4
Slovenia	11.5	11.3	13.3	15.1	13.5	12.0
Czech Republic	2.8	2.3	21.2	16.9	13.0	10.0
Austria	7.7	7.2	15.5	11.5	9.1	8.2
Hungary	1.2	1.4	5.8	3.1	4.1	4.9
Netherlands	3.8	5.1	1.8	2.5	2.8	4.0
Poland	1.0	0.6	0.9	2.8	6.6	3.0
France	1.8	1.7	0.9	0.4	0.6	2.9
Slovakia	1.4	1.2	2.7	4.5	3.5	2.6
Great Britain	7.9	8.2	0.7	1.3	1.4	2.3
Bosnia and Herzegovina	6.5	6.5	1.6	2.0	2.1	1.8
Russian Federation	0.3	0.4	0.6	0.5	1.1	1.5
Sweden	0.9	0.9	0.2	0.2	0.4	1.1
Belgium	1.1	1.6	0.8	0.9	0.9	1.1
Other European countries	14.7	12.6	2.1	1.9	2.5	4.8
Other non-European countries	1.3	1.3	1.2	1.0	1.2	1.7

Source: Institut za Turizam, 2005.

Table 22.2. Croatia: regional distribution of tourist nights, 1987–2004.[a]

County (Županije)	% share of total tourist nights					
	1987	1989	1994	1997	2001	2004
Istarska	32.0	32.0	51.1	40.5	37.5	35.0
Primorsko-goranska	21.3	22.2	31.5	27.0	23.6	21.4
Splitsko-dalmatinska	16.3	16.4	5.7	11.6	14.0	14.7
Zadarska	7.0	6.8	1.0	5.9	7.7	9.3
Dubrovačko-neretvanska	10.4	10.1	2.3	5.4	7.2	8.3
Šibensko-kninska	4.9	4.7	0.6	3.3	4.8	5.3
Ličko-senjska	2.1	2.1	1.0	1.6	1.8	2.3
The total % of tourist nights in Adriatic regions	93.9	94.2	93.2	95.5	96.7	96.3
The total % of tourist nights in continental counties	6.1	5.8	6.8	4.5	3.3	3.7
Total	100.0	100.0	100.0	100.0	100.0	100.0

[a]Nautical tourism data not included.
Source: Adapted from Institut za Turizam, 2005.

CEE and slow but steady growth from the traditional Western markets of Germany and Italy.

The accommodation sector as the main area of tourism entrepreneurship has continued the trend of pre-conflict times. While the major hotel capacity remained more or less the same in the 1987–2004 period, small-scale enterprises increased their share and in

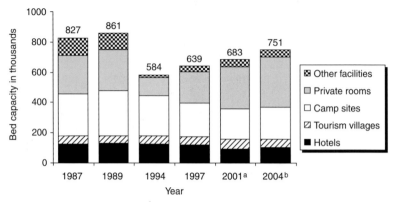

^{a}Capacity of marinas not included. ^{b}Categorization according to international standards.

Fig. 22.3. Croatia: structure of the accommodation sector, 1987–2004. Source: Institut za Turizam, 2005.

2004 represented 73% of the overall accommodation capacity (Institut za Turizam, 2005) (Fig. 22.3).

The re-emergence of tourism has been facilitated by central government rhetoric aimed at transforming the concept of Croatia through the development of a layer of 'value-added' attractions and infrastructure. This layer is based on the 'stimulation and acceleration of privatisation process with general emphasis on the development of entrepreneurship, particularly in the area of the so-called economy of small scale' (Ministry of Tourism 1997, p. 14). Reflecting this initiative, the Ministry of Tourism published *Guidelines for Entrepreneurs in Tourism*, in 1999 in conjunction with the state budget to secure funding for promoting tourism amongst small and medium-sized enterprises. Changes to the structure of tourism administration have been aligned with broader policy initiatives facilitating economic transition within the European Union's *Agenda 2000* supporting SMEs in candidate countries. As such it is argued that tourism entrepreneurs at the micro level have a strategic role in the macro-integration of Croatia as a developed Western-allied nation (Dulcic, 2000).

Product and Spatial Diversification

Croatia is politically divided into 21 counties, so-called Županija; 14 continental and seven coastal counties (Fig. 22.4). Within stated global and EU aspirations towards sustainability, Hall (2003, 2004) speaks about the need in Croatia for product and spatial diversification away from the coast into various forms of rural and cultural tourism development. Table 22.2 shows that out of 21 Croatian counties, seven Adriatic-based regions continuously comprise an average of 94% of all tourist nights (Institut za Turizam, 2005). Thus, it could be concluded that tourist flows remain concentrated on coastal-based tourist consumption.

However, the spatial distribution of tourist flows cannot portray the full detailed story. In the last few years there have been some significant infrastructural, policy and industry developments that suggest the mid-2010s will see a turning point in Croatian tourism. There are several reasons for this.

First, various associations and groups of 'special-interest tourism' have emerged for the first time at the national level. The Croatian Chamber of Economy has been the main leader in the process, facilitating public and private relationships between the central government and the tourism industry, forming associations in a number of sub-sectors:

- private family-based accommodation providers (home-stays);
- health and well-being tourism;
- rural family-based tourism (agriturismo);
- cultural tourism;
- adventure tourism;
- hotels and restaurants;

Fig. 22.4. Croatia: the 21 administration counties. Source: University of Zagreb and CARNet, 2004.

- travel agencies;
- nautical tourism (comprising four different groups of marinas, charters, cruisers and boat trip operators, plus scuba diving).

The concept of associations is designed to create public–private alliances and the Chamber of Economy plays an important facilitating role. It has designated (central and regional) offices with a range of responsibilities related to the regulation and organization of each specific sub-sector and their industry linkages with other groups and players (e.g. international tour operators), to coordinate specific events and projects, to build a database of resources and product development opportunities, and to

promote groups at various trade shows. Rural tourism growth has been particularly impressive, as the number of rural tourism businesses has grown from less than 100 in 1999 to 251 in 2003 (Croatian Chamber of Economy, 2005).

The group of adventure tourism operators, founded in 2004, soon registered more than 100 members involved in the provision of such activities as rafting, surfing, kayaking, trekking, horse riding, paragliding, climbing, paintball, mountain biking, jeep safaris and team building. Such product diversification does not necessarily suggest spatial diversification, as the leaders of these developments tend to be located in the coastal areas. For example, two Adriatic-based, and traditionally the most successful, counties of Istria and Dubrovacka-Neretvanska together comprise more than half of all registered rural tourism projects.

Alongside small-scale tourism entrepreneurship, many large public–private projects are in development. Targeting the top end of the market, luxury hotels, resorts, wellness centres and golf courses have been developing through joint ownership between central and local government. For example, for the Brijuni Riviera project in Istria, with €5bn investment and potential of creating 5000 new jobs, the central government is investing 67% of the capital and the local county of Istarska the remaining 33%. The project will include, in addition to the renovation of three existing hotels, luxurious villas, polo fields and golf courses, the building of two new hotels, a new golf course and a wellness centre (Pesut, 2005). Another example is Park Prevlaka, on the border with Montenegro, which already has a centre for adventure tourism (team building, free climbing, kayaking, paintball and cycling) and has major plans to be developed in partnership between the central government and local county of Dubrovacko-Neretvanska. One billion euros are being invested in a hotel resort with 2000 beds, wellness facilities, a conference centre, a marina with the capacity for 300 yachts, a retailing area and luxurious auto-camp with the capacity for 1000 visitors, and the restoration of a 19th century castle into a museum, night club, wine cellar and luxurious restaurant (Pesut, 2005). Many public–private partnership 'green field projects', are planned for central Dalmatia.

In terms of general infrastructure, the major investment has been made in the construction of highways connecting the main centres of Zagreb, Rijeka, Split, Zadar, and Sibenik. The most significant of these is the Zagreb–Split highway, with a total length of 375.7 km (completed in June 2005) which has significantly improved traditionally difficult road access to central Dalmatia as a gateway for travel to the Dalmatian islands. Dubrovnik remains relatively isolated by road (there is an international airport) whereby a car journey from Zagreb can take up to 8 hours. Other tourism investments for 2005 are shown in Table 22.3.

The changing industry structure reflects recent policy development whereby the Office for the Strategic Development of Croatia has launched the strategic vision for Croatia in the 21st century with the central emphasis on tourism, identifying specific objectives for Croatian tourism to 2010 (USRH, 2002). The overall rhetoric of the vision is based on principles of sustainability where tourism will serve as an agent of economic and social development in peripheral regions whereby the preservation of natural and cultural resources is conditional for achieving the long-term sustainability of Croatian tourism. The document promotes product and spatial diversification, but with a particular emphasis given to rural tourism development to alleviate problems of peripheral regions, especially depopulation.

Changing policies have been translated into national marketing and branding by the Croatian Tourist Board, which has changed its previous slogan of 'Small country for a great holiday to the Mediterranean – as it once was', which is meant to connote authenticity, atmosphere, rurality and nature, with no 'artificial' additives (N. Bulic, 2002, personal communications). The projection is thus the image of an implicitly pre-mass package culture and environment. Whereas under the general heading 'About Croatia', the Adriatic Sea, heritage and cuisine are still dominantly promoted, the 'Tourism plus' link lists the diversity of various activities, such as horse riding, cycling, diving, pilgrim tourism, health tourism, kayaking, rafting and adventure racing. The significant tourist investment made by the central government (as clearly shown in Table 22.3) represents a different trend from the post-Communist reduction of the role of the state elsewhere in CEE (Light, 2000; Hall, 2004).

Culture Versus Conformity

In our previous two sections we presented the overview of tourism development in Croatia from the 1960s to today. The economic indicators based on quantitative figures of tourist flows and investments reveal a number of structural changes at national, regional and product level. At this point we want to return to our cultural perspective to deconstruct structural and de-personalized accounts and draw on our 'intimate' experience of Croatian tourism through our personal and professional lives.

Table 22.3. Croatia: estimated value of major tourism and infrastructural investments (to be) made in 18 counties in 2005.

County (Županije)	€m	The nature of investments (the greatest share)
Istarska	191.3	Private sector (upgrade of existing hotels and resorts, new small-scale entrepreneurship in coastal and rural forms of tourism)
Primorsko-goranska	135.5	Private sector (hotels; conference and wellness facilities)
Dubrovačko-neretvanska	95.6	Private and public sector (luxurious hotels; public mega projects of historical and adventure-based products)
Zadarska	11.8	Private and public sector (upgrade of existing hotel facilities; infrastructure: heritage signposting, roads; beaches; promenades, etc.)
Splitsko-dalmatinska	35.5	Private and public sector (upgrade of existing accommodation facilities; infrastructure)
Šibensko-kninska	9.9	Public sector (infrastructure: heritage signposting, roads, ferry links, harbour)
Ličko-senjska	3.7	Private and public sector (new hotels; skiing facilities; revival of historical sites to become tourist attractions, e.g. the only watermill in the country)
Grad Zagreb[a]	N/A	Diversification of existing hotels and first thematic hotel in the country (Movie hotel)
Karlovacka Zupanija	0.3	Public sector (tourism infrastructure; cycling routes; tourism marketing); the region had major hotel investment in 2 new hotels in 2004
Sisacko-Moslavacka	0.7	Public sector (tourism infrastructure: 250 km of cycling route; revival of traditional Moslavian houses turned into accommodation facilities)
Krapinsko-zagorska	1.3	Public sector (upgrade of existing and new health/wellness resorts)
Varazdinska I Medjimurska	6.5	Public sector (500 km of cycling routes and health resort/wellness resort)
Osjecko-Baranjska I Vukovarsko-Srijemska[b]	N/A	Public and private sector (new and upgrade of existing hotels in Osijek; re-build of 4-star hotel Lav in Vukovar; conference centres, small-scale rural tourism projects, stopover in Vukovar for Dunav cruises; Dunav beach on the border with Serbia)

[a]Grad Zagreb had major investment in hotels and facilities between 2000–2004.
[b]The value of investments is not given; rural tourism projects are cited as family-based, eco-projects focused on gastronomy.
Source: Pesut, 2005.

Irena Ateljevic was born in a small fishing village which experienced a tourist boom in the early 1970s. By the mid-1980s the local population of around 1700 people 'hosted' tourist flows of up to 10,000 in the peak season months of July and August (Ateljevic and Doorne, 2003). Irena worked in tourism from the age of 13, which involved paid work in local cafes and visitor information centres, as well as

unpaid work at the family 'homestay tourist operation', helping her mother and grand-mother. Her university study was supported by seasonal work over the summer. Being a Croat married to a Serb at the time of the conflict between Croats and Serbs, this pushed her even further from her village: all the way to New Zealand. For her PhD she interviewed numerous tourists and particularly younger visitors from Western Europe who revealed in the course of conversations that they had visited Croatia (or what they would often refer to as former Yugoslavia) with their parents and now were searching for more 'exotic' places far away from home (Ateljevic, 1998, unpublished PhD thesis).

In contrast, Sanda Čorak was born in the capital of Zagreb and her early involvement (since the age of 2) was on the consumption side in the form of summer family holidays. Typically, and in the tradition which continues to the present day, the urban population of Zagreb (the capital city) travelled to the coast for their annual 2-week summer holiday, either staying in their own second holiday homes or in private accommodation. Throughout her life, Sanda has spent her summer holidays on the coast and islands, first with her parents and then with her own family. Her research career began with the Institute for Tourism 20 years ago. The position of observing and researching tourism phenomenon for almost two decades created many frustrations which prompted her to become more actively involved in shaping and influencing the future of Croatian tourism. In 2001, she established the Zagreb School of Management – Tourism Studies, to pass her enthusiasm and knowledge to new generations.

In our reflections, while acknowledging regional cultural differences at many different levels (north/south, coast/interior, islands/coast, urban/rural) we have identified a number of interconnected social elements which have underpinned local entrepreneurial spirit and the dominance of small-scale businesses. These relate to:

- the patriarchal society and the inter-generational nature of businesses, gender and family;
- black-market practice, informal economy and local resourcefulness; and
- local politics, personal economies and social networks.

In a country with strong historical ties with the Roman Catholic church, where today 90% of the population claims to be Catholic (Statisticki Ured Hrvatske, 2003), it is not surprising that family values are deeply embedded in society. The consistency of local ownership and the intergenerational nature of tourism businesses are very much a reflection of the traditional practice of financially supporting children and assuming a nurturing responsibility for them throughout one's life. The flourishing businesses, particularly in the accommodation sector, originate from the fact that most parents build houses on two or three storeys expecting their grown-up children to remain living in their family home where they can look after their grandchildren and then the younger generation takes care of parents when they grow old. So, separate living space the rest of the year becomes apartments for renting which usually requires the extended family to 'squeeze' into a common living space over the summer months.

Close family relationships also reflect a deep-seated suspicion and mistrust of socialist state institutions and banks, to the extent that the extended family has become the main source of financial, social and emotional support.

The legacy of being part of a ('market') socialist state for 45 years and the frequent shifting of political boundaries undermined local trust in the public sector, particularly with respect to benefits received from collective taxation. The socialist system of public ownership, which ensured the absence of individual accountability, provided political protectionism and privileges and eroded any sense of public good. As a result, many small, family-run businesses traditionally have chosen to distance themselves from formal taxation, either by remaining unregistered or disguising income by not registering all guests.

In this context, coupled with the lack of regulation of the small-scale tourism sector, many local businesses flourished in the absence of strict tax control, enabling locals to generate capital over a short period of time. The extent to which tourism sustained the local economy is illustrated in the fact that many families in coastal areas generated sufficient tourism income over the 2 months of peak summer business to sustain themselves for the rest of the year (additionally supported by fishing and their own subsistence agriculture). Furthermore, the savings accumulated over two decades of the tourism 'golden age' (1970s and 1980s) were so significant that they helped people to 'survive' the war years and the cessation of tourism in the early 1990s.

In an intensely patriarchal society, where the birth of a son is always to be celebrated, issues of gender and tourism in the Balkans are yet to be fully explored. Family businesses and properties are inherited down the male line: when women marry it is generally expected that they will move into their husbands' houses. In such a living space the extended family makes rules and creates certain expectations of what is the proper behaviour of 'a good wife, mother and daughter-in-law'.

In a masculine culture where many domesticated responsibilities are considered to be beneath male dignity, activities such as making beds and cooking for guests are traditionally regarded as a 'natural' extension of women's domestic role. In contrast, their husbands maintain financial control and the male role generally involves the broader orientation of the business based around male social networks, and any technical and maintenance requirements.

As well as local and personal politics the structure of the industry and economy is very much enmeshed in the wider dynamics of party politics. During the socialist era membership of the Communist Party would secure power for individuals and, similarly, the significance of the Nationalist Party during the 1990s prevailed. It should be noted that despite the oscillations of politics, the relationships and often the roles of individuals within political structures have remained relatively consistent. The widespread practice of *mito* (*baksheesh*) represents a transparent form of 'taxation' involving favours and preferential treatment not only for services, but for all facets of social, political and economic interactions, such as securing a job or a child-care place. These forms of exchange are based on personal economies and social networks, usually formed around extended family relations, geographic and ethnic connections. The social skills and resourcefulness required for economic survival in this environment are a key characteristic of the cultural context of entrepreneurship, and is not only apparent in political dealings but prevail in most managerial and operational activities. The nature of current product diversification in tourism, for example, reflects socio-cultural resourcefulness, since local entrepreneurs generally remain unconvinced about the value of state assistance and support. In this context, increasingly rigorous government regulation, privatization and the shift towards EU and the Western systems of free trade, taxation, formalized relationships and transparency are widely perceived as a potential threat, an economic 'other'.

Conclusion

The description and interpretation of Croatian tourism and its entrepreneurial characteristics over the last 45 years reveals a complex web of structural and social/agency elements, which condition and shape the nature of the industry. On the basis of the descriptive account of economic indicators in the first part we could easily conclude that EU regulations and the conformity necessary for accessing the enlarged European Community are bringing positive changes to Croatian tourism. Emerging product and spatial diversification suggest that Croatia is at the turning point of its tourism development. Yet, we also illustrate the role of local culture as the principle regulator of the economic, which simultaneously reveals elements and practices in which the cultural manifests as materialization of the economic (see Crang and Malbon, 1996). The cultural context described here through the use of insider perspectives reveals a rationality through which social structures, politics and economy are maintained and advanced despite the last decade of political instability, upheaval and war. Horvat (1999) identifies the Croatian entrepreneurial culture as suffering from post-war stress, yet it is still grounded in traditional values and orientations to family and community networks. She suggests that culturally specific attitudes to work and lifestyle provide stability, while at the same time providing initiative and motivation for entrepreneurs at the local level. So, when speaking about the implications of the potential access of Croatia to the EU it becomes clear that political and socio-cultural elements represent key ingredients which can explain the speculations of how well (or not) Croatia will conform to the 'EU embrace'. The fact that the delivery of the claimed war criminal General Gotovina (locally a hero) to the Hague tribunal jeopardized inauguration of EU accession negotiations, derives from an intricate geo-political history entangled with issues of tradition and identity.

We have tried to reflect how social and cultural identity has been perpetuated in its traditional form. One of the most persistent characteristics of the cultural environment remains the nature of gender division in terms of work roles and attitudes, which act to reaffirm patriarchal and social relations. It is these cultural attributes closely associated with place, landscape and its people, which simultaneously form the principle elements of the tourism product.

Despite decades of change with respect to national and regional affiliations at the political level, the persistence of tourism and its representation has provided a continuity of local and regional identity. Yet critical issues of gender, ethnicity and family relations as sources of power structures and dominant ideologies in Southeastern Europe remain to be fully explored.

References

Allcock, J.B. (1991) Yugloslavia. In: Hall, D.R. (ed.) *Tourism and Economic Development in Eastern Europe and the Soviet Union*. London: Belhaven Press, pp. 236–258.

Ateljevic, I. and Doorne, S. (2003) Unpacking the local: a cultural analysis of tourism entrepreneurship in Murter, Croatia. *Tourism Geographies* 5(2), 123–150.

Coles, T. and Hall, D. (2005) Tourism and European Union enlargement. Plus ça change? *International Journal of Tourism Research* 7(2), 51–61.

Crang, P. and Malbon, B. (1996) Consuming geographies: a review essay. *Transactions of the Institute of British Geographers* 21(4), 704–711.

Croatian Chamber of Economy (2005) *Croatian Chamber of Economy*. Zagreb: Croatian Chamber of Economy. Available at: http://www.hgk.biznet.hr

Croatian Tourist Board (2005) *Lonely Planet*. Zagreb: Croatian Tourist Board. Available at: http://www.croatia.hr/misc/LonelyPlanet.aspx

Dragiečvić, M., Čižmar, S. and Poljanec-Borič, S. (1998) Contribution to the development strategy of Croatian tourism. *Turizam* 46(5–6), 243–253.

Dulcic, A. (2000) Croatian tourism, transition and global development processes. *Turizam* 48(2), 175–187.

DZzS (Državni Zavod za Statistiku) (ed.) (1995) *Promet Turista u Primorskim Gradovima i Općinama 1994*. Zagreb: DZzS.

Gosar, A. (1999) Reconsidering tourism strategy as a consequence of the disintegration of Yugoslavia – the case of Slovenia. *Turizam* 47(1), 67–73.

Hall, D. (2002) Branding and national identity: the case of Central and Eastern Europe. In: Morgan, N., Pritchard, A. and Pride, R. (eds) *Destination Branding: Creating the Unique Destination Proposition*. Oxford: Butterworth-Heinemann, pp. 87–105.

Hall, D. (2003) Rejuvenation, diversification and imagery: sustainability conflicts for tourism policy in the Eastern Adriatic. *Journal of Sustainable Tourism* 11(2/3), 280–294.

Hall, D. (2004) Rural tourism development in Southeastern Europe: transition and the search for sustainability. *International Journal of Tourism Research* 6, 165–176.

Hall, D. and Danta, D. (eds) (1996) *Reconstructing the Balkans*. Chichester: John Wiley & Sons.

Hall, D. and Danta, D. (eds) (2000) *Europe Goes East: EU Enlargement, Diversity and Uncertainty*. London: The Stationery Office.

Hitrec, T. (2000) Small and medium-sized enterprises in the hospitality industry: some European trends and Croatian experiences. *Tourism* 48(1), 5–12.

Horvat, B. (1999) The role of culture during the period of recovery and the development of tourism. *Turizam* 47(1), 55–60.

Horwath Consulting and Institut za Turizam Zagreb (eds) (1993) *Glavni Turistički Plan Hrvatske*. Zagreb: Horwath Consulting.

Institut za Turizam (2005) *TOMAS – Stavovi i Potrošnja Turista u Hrvatskoj*. Zagreb: Institut za Turizam.

Ivanić, N. and Radnić, A. (1996) The war's indirect damage to tourism in Croatia. *Turizam* 44(1–2).

Jordan, P. (2000) Restructuring Croatia's coastal resorts: change, sustainable development and the incorporation of rural hinterlands. *Journal of Sustainable Tourism* 8(6), 525–539.

Kundera, M. (2002) *Ignorance*. London: Faber and Faber.

Light, D. (2000). An unwanted past: contemporary tourism and the heritage of communism in Romania. *International Journal of Heritage Studies* 6(2), 145–160.

Ministarstvo Turizma and Institut za Turizam (eds) (1993) *Razvojna Strategija Hrvatskog Turizma.* Zagreb: Ministarstvo Turizma and Institut za Turizam.

Ministry of Tourism (1997) *Tourism: Guide for Investors and Business Partners.* Zagreb: Ministry of Tourism, Republic of Croatia.

Morgan, N. J. and Pritchard, A. (2000) *Advertising in Tourism and Leisure.* Oxford: Butterworth–Heinemann.

Pearce, D. (1991) Challenge and change in East European tourism: a Yugoslav example. In: Sinclair, M.T. and Stabler, M.J. (eds) *The Tourism Industry: an International Analysis.* Wallingford, UK: CAB International, pp. 223–240.

Pesut, M. (2005) Investicije u turizmu po zupanijama. *Restaurant and Hotel Strucni Magazin za Ugostiteljstvo i Turizam*, broj 3, svibanj/lipanj.

Radnić, A. and Ivanić, N. (1999) War and tourism in Croatia – consequences and the road to recovery. *Turizam* 47(1), 43–54.

RZzS (Republićki Zavod za Statistiku) (ed.) (1989) *Promet Turista u Primorskim Općinama 1988.* Zagreb: RZzS.

Smeral, E. (1993) Emerging Eastern European markets. *Tourism Management* 14(4), 411–418.

Studienkreis für Tourismus Starnberg (ed.) (1989) *Das Image Jugoslawiens als Reiseland – Eine Motiv- und Meinungspsyschologische Untersuchung.* Starnberg: Studienkreis für Tourismus.

Todorova, M. (1997) *Imagining the Balkans.* Oxford: Oxford University Press.

University of Zagreb and CARNet (2004) *Facts About Croatia.* Zagreb: University of Zagreb Department of Telecommunications and CARNet. Available at: http://www.hr/hrvatska/counties.hr.html

USRH (Ured za Strategiju Razvitka Hrvatske) (2002) *Hrvatska u 21 Stoljecu.* Zagreb: USRH.

Vukonic, B. (2005) *Povijest Hrvatskog Turizma.* Zagreb: Prometej.

Weber (1998) Life cycle of Croatian tourism product: what have we learned from the past? In: Zins, A. (ed.) *Europäische Tourismus- und Freizeitforschung, 28 October 1998.* Vienna: Institut für Tourismus und Freizeitwirtschaft, pp. 37–51.

Weber, S., Horak, S. and Mikacic, V. (2001) Tourism Development in the Croatian Adriatic Islands. In: Ioannides, D., Apostolopoulos, Y. and Sönmez, S. (eds) *Mediterranean Islands and Sustainable Tourism Development.* London: Continuum, pp. 171–192.

Part VI

Conclusions

23 Summary and Conclusions

Melanie Smith and Derek Hall

This book has aimed to provide an overview of the tourism implications of accession for the EU's most recent member states, those countries that still wish to join, and those that are directly or indirectly affected by EU enlargement. One of the key conclusions that emerges, not suprisingly, is that it is difficult to generalize about the impacts of EU accession on the countries in question. Impacts are varied and more research is required to ascertain the extent to which accession has had a *direct* impact on tourism development. In the case of the CEE8 in particular, EU accession has followed a process of complex political and social transition. It is therefore sometimes difficult to separate the impacts of this 'new' process from the ongoing implications of the 'old'. Indeed, a central issue that applies to most tourism impact studies is the degree to which the consequences of tourism development processes can be distinguished from those of wider change agents of development, restructuring, modernization and globalization.

The diversity of the countries included in this book manifests itself in their political structures, their policy frameworks, the priority that tourism is accorded, their economic situation, and their social and cultural differences. The rationale for including a country-by-country analysis was to demonstrate this diversity while highlighting key factors that are pertinent to all EU members, newly acceded and otherwise.

The overview chapters and section introductions served as a means of highlighting some of the geographical, historical, political and social similarities between certain groups of countries (i.e. The Baltic States, East Central Europe, the Mediterranean islands of Malta and Cyprus, and those countries seeking accession). Many countries clearly feel a certain affinity to each other, and this may be expressed in terms of economic and political binding agents, such as that of the Visegrad Group (see Chapters 1 and 8). They are often bound by common legacies of occupation, colonization or oppression, and subsequent liberation, as well as by culture and environment. Indeed, the EU will have fulfilled one of its original objectives if the common affinities and historical antagonisms shared by member countries are expressed no more belligerently than on the front-stage provided by the annual Eurovision Song Contest, which has become notable for apparent mutual voting allegiances among neighbouring countries and historic allies (BBC News Online, 2004).

While the book has not claimed to be comprehensive in its coverage, it has aimed to provide the reader with an introductory understanding of some of the most significant issues relating to tourism in the new Europe. These include the policies and structures of the new EU (Anastasiadou, Chapter 2); the social and cultural complexities of unification and expansion (Smith and Hall, Chapter 3); the global

©CAB International 2006. *Tourism in the New Europe: the Challenges and Opportunities of EU Enlargement* (eds D. Hall, M. Smith and B. Marciszewska)

impacts of EU enlargement (Hall, Chapter 4); and the educational and training implications (Richards, Chapter 5). The regional overviews aimed to contextualize the individual country chapters further (Jordan, Chapter 6; Komppula and colleagues, Chapter 12; Alipour and Hall, Chapter 16; and Hall and Smith for Section 5). Within this framework, individual country authors were then asked to provide an overview of contemporary developments in tourism in their respective countries, emphasizing in particular the extent to which accession or aspirations towards accession have been influential. The remainder of this chapter therefore offers a summary of some of the key issues raised, while addressing issues relating to the future direction of the EU, tourism, education, and research.

It is unfortunate that tourism is still accorded such a relatively low priority in EU policy-making and funding (as noted in Chapters 1, 2 and 4). The European Commission's Tourism Unit (part of Directorate-General Enterprise) aims to undertake projects in such fields as sustainable tourism, networking, regulation and skills development, but support is still woefully inadequate. Personal attendance at one of the Unit's annual European Tourism Forums demonstrated only too clearly the vagaries of EU tourism policy and research. It is therefore unsurprising that many countries endeavour to undertake their own policy-making, planning and research for tourism independently of EU frameworks. Indeed, it is clear from some of the chapters in this book (e.g. Chapter 3) that many countries are starting to question their involvement in the EU project at all (e.g. rejection of the Constitution, and fears about the euro).

Nevertheless, it appears that change might be forthcoming if the words of the EU Commissioner for Enterprise and Industry are to be believed. He stated that tourism had been identified as one of three key sectors where sustainable growth and job creation were anticipated:

> Tourism is a sector that needs more political attention . . . Tourism has a huge potential in Europe that is not fully exploited, in particular after the EU enlargement.
>
> (HOTREC, 2005)

It also seems to be the case overall that most countries (especially the newer accession countries) consider the benefits of EU accession to far outweigh the disadvantages. As a summary, accession to the EU can create a number of important benefits for countries. These include:

- increased liberalization and competition leading to greater productivity and growth;
- employment creation and new opportunities for migrant workers;
- harmonization of legislation;
- increased business investment opportunities;
- freedom of movement for EU citizens;
- access to EU funds;
- opportunities to join the euro and stabilize currencies;
- ongoing liberalization of civil aviation and the consequent growth of the low-cost airline sector;
- ease of cross-border trading;
- educational mobility, new skills development and training programmes;
- guidelines for nature and heritage conservation;
- rising standards of living and quality of life; and
- image enhancement.

Nevertheless, it should not be implied that EU accession is some kind of panacea, or that EU accession processes are necessarily the most appropriate. Indeed, Smith (2000) has argued that negotiation of 'framework agreements' for the wider post-Cold War European order has both exposed contradictions in the EU's performance, and raised questions about its capacity to shape the 'new Europe' in the face of conflict in South-eastern Europe, social unrest in some of its founding members, and rejection of its proposed constitution (see also Graham and Hart, 1999).

Most accession countries are aware that the symbolic implications of EU accession are more significant than economic or financial ones. Regional aid from Brussels is notoriously miserly. As *The Economist* (2004) has suggested, 'it is what EU membership inspires – political stability, economic openness, fiscal rectitude – not what it provides that counts'. However, access *can* be created for funds and grants that can benefit tourism development, but as noted in Chapter 1, funds are not specifically allocated for tourism, therefore countries have to couch their bids in such terms that give priority to other issues, such as regional development or social regeneration (Coles and Hall, 2005). Such funding programmes include INTERREG (cross-border projects), LEADER (for boosting rural economies), URBAN (for regenerating cities and creating social benefits), EQUAL (for human resources development), and PHARE (assisting pre-accession requirements). Most of the countries discussed in this book have benefited significantly from structural and cohesion funds.

However, it is clear that the benefits of accession are uneven both within and between new member states. Although cheap labour is an attractive feature of many accession countries, it is noticeable that income levels are often not commensurate with the cost of living and the rising prices of consumer goods and services. There are still fears that accession countries (particularly in Central and Eastern Europe) continue to act as a playground for rich, foreign investors with little or no knowledge of local markets, culture or language. Opportunities for travel on low-cost airlines also appear to be biased in favour of Western generating countries, given income differentials. Consequently, (particularly leisure) travel *from* many of the new accession states is often severely limited.

One positive benefit of EU membership that is mentioned by many of the authors is the enhancement of destination image or brand value. Tourist perceptions of safety and quality are of considerable importance, especially as we are led to believe that the world has become a more insecure place within which to travel. It should also be noted that many EU citizens (up to 75%) never travel beyond the EU (European Commission, 2003). A further positive impact is that accession countries are bound by legislation regarding the protection of natural and cultural heritage. The Common Agricultural Policy, in urgent need of reform, may also help to support many of the new accession countries in the short term. However, EU membership has also created extra pressure on those countries to modernize and address important issues of health and safety, often an expensive process. Overall, adoption of the principles of the *Acquis Communautaire* is important in the harmonization of legislation and of regulation in such key

areas as mobility, transport, law, justice, environment, health, culture and education. Its benchmarking role in relation to assessing accession eligibility was, at the time of writing, proving to be critical for the applications of Turkey and Croatia in relation to human rights issues.

Freedom of movement for new EU citizens is creating wider opportunities (despite the cost differentials). These include new educational, cultural and work opportunities, as well as possibilities of visiting friends and relatives more easily. However, a disadvantage for the VFR market is that new visa requirements for non-EU countries have created barriers to cross-border travel for ethnic groups now straddling EU external borders. Such impositions have also adversely affected cross-border petty-trading and shopping tourism (e.g. see Chapter 8). It is difficult to say whether this will increase or decrease the degree of illegal trafficking in border regions.

One of the most positive aspects of accession, as noted by Richards in Chapter 5, is that a degree of commonality and consistency in the European education and qualifications system has led to opportunities for mobility and exchange, access to international curricula and languages, as well as increasing specialization in tourism education. Nevertheless, there is still a need to develop closer links to the tourism industry and further develop vocational training to improve career opportunities. Indeed, one of the biggest problems that continues to affect the coherent development of tourism in the EU is the seemingly unbridgeable gap between academic institutions offering tourism courses, and the apparent needs of the tourism industry. Tourism professionals still view academics with some suspicion, and academics often seem incapable of communicating their often excellent research and consultancy skills to the industry (and not least to EU tourism policy-makers). The major objectives of ATLAS (the Association for Tourism and Leisure Education), founded by Greg Richards in 1991, are likely to play a pivotal role in the future development of European tourism education and research, and in the establishment of relationships between tourism industry representatives, EU policy-makers and tourism academics.

Overall, destinations in the new accession countries currently stand to benefit considerably from tourism. The WTO (2003) notes that Europe is losing its market share as the world's largest receiving region. Although this trend began before 1999, one reason for its continuation is that euro-zone countries have suffered considerable price increases in recent years, which has had a negative impact on tourism. As well as the relatively low value of the US dollar (and thus other currencies pegged against it), and the continued overall vigorous growth of the Pacific rim, a further factor is that many established European destinations have reached saturation point. The role of the accession countries in creating unique and innovative products – an argument voiced at least a decade and a half ago (Hall, 1991) – may therefore be pivotal to the continued growth of tourism in Europe, especially as prices are still relatively competitive. Although infrastructural limitations and service quality problems continue to constrain otherwise healthy tourism growth rates, the apparent popularity of up-market hotels has increased considerably in the eight CEE accession countries. One explanation put forward is that just because travellers fly with budget airlines, they do not necessarily stay in budget accommodation, but indeed may spend the money saved on travel to upgrade their accommodation quality (EU Business, 2005). The impact of budget airlines on many of the new accession countries has clearly been significant in assisting an almost exponential growth in the number of arrivals at several airports, the impacts of which are being extended to secondary regions and towns.

Rural tourism in particular is seen as being a potentially lucrative sector for the CEE8. In the Mediterranean, Malta and Cyprus have been seeking to diversify into village tourism for some time, to gain added value from combining elements of the natural, rural environment and cultural heritage. Indeed, cultural tourism continues to be a growth market in accession countries, even as the post-transition fascination with communist heritage wanes. Many countries are turning their attention towards even more lucrative markets, such as:

- business tourism – only really a possiblity for destinations with good access, infrastructure and quality facilities and services;

- skiing tourism – where accession countries can compete in terms of novelty value and relatively low cost; and
- health and spa tourism – a long tradition for many countries, especially in ECE.

The development and promotion of more intangible aspects of culture and heritage (e.g. relating to indigenous communities and ethnic minorities) is also a potential growth sector, but the political implications of such decisions often still need to be addressed.

Indeed, in social and cultural terms, the creation of a unified Europe has been more problematic than political or economic integration. The restructuring of Europe after 1989 has been a complex process. Clearly, the comprehensive reorientation of political economies, coupled, in the case of the Baltic States, Czech and Slovak republics and Slovenia, with a new-found independence, is bringing long-term benefits that are being further enhanced by EU accession, despite short-term tensions in some cases. Indeed, some of the more intangible aspects of identity still need to be addressed. A decade and a half ago, many countries were keen to extricate themselves from particular political blocs and structures and to create their own sense of nationhood. In some cases, this has exacerbated nationalism and problems for ethnic minorities and migrant workers in such countries. In others, it has led to a degree of uncertainty and anxiety amongst (particularly older) citizens, who have been unsure how to embrace fully a sense of democracy and to perceive benefits deriving from a capitalist economy. Uncertainty of identity has sometimes created confusion about how to deal with legacies from the past and displaced symbols of hegemony and oppression. Even the creation of a unique destination image in terms of marketing and promotion has been a challenging process for some countries that were under-developed (or, somewhat paradoxically, over-urbanized), and which conveyed a negative image, or more commonly, no specific image at all (at least to potential international visitors steeped in Cold War perceptions).

Culturally, there have always been dilemmas within the European context about how far to celebrate and promote a common

European heritage, or even to identify what that means. In many ways, it has been easier for politicians and policy-makers to focus on selling the benefits of economic and political unification than to try to engage citizens in complex debates about social or cultural unity. It is no coincidence that many countries and regions have asserted their autonomy all the more strongly at a time when there is perceived pressure to further affiliate themselves to an apparently homogenizing supranational bloc. Fears about globalization and a concomitant trivialization of cultures, has led to excessive protectionism or even violent protest. Region-alism is also still a strong underlying movement in Europe (e.g. Rodriguez Pose and Gill, 2003). Many of the tensions about economic and political inequality and social and cultural identity originate from regions trying to assert autonomy or claiming the need for greater support. It is clear that tourism can act as a powerful tool for regional development, the diversification of economies, and the projection of regional imagery, but it cannot solve political and social problems directly.

As noted earlier, it is interesting that the most resistance to EU enlargement seems to be emerging within the older members of the EU. Fears of expansion are particularly pronounced in such founding countries as Germany and France. Germany in particular fears a repeat of the economic consequences of the reunification process, whereby eastern Länder became a heavy burden on the state's exchequer. In 2004, some EU15 countries imposed work permits in order to restrict the number of migrant workers from new accession countries. It has become a media cliché that the French rejected the EU Constitution in 2005 because they had been overwhelmed by Polish plumbers:

> The fear of the Polish plumber became
> a symbol, a symbol of a danger for France
> and a symbol of the possibility to make a
> social criticism of the constitution project.
> The constitution became a symbol of the EU
> enlargement and the Polish plumber
> the symbol of the social danger of cheap
> labour against the French social model.
> (Radio National, 2005)

Leonard (2005) notes that the actual number of migrant workers was much lower than expected, even in countries where there were fewer restrictions (e.g. Britain, Ireland and Sweden) (see also Coles and Hall, 2005). Germany and France have been grappling with problems of unemployment, and the 2005 riots in France demonstrated clearly the political, social and economic disenchantment of the population. By contrast, the British needed to fill gaps in the labour market, in such areas as construction, semi-skilled manual work and health-care provision.

Of course, many Western companies are more than happy to exploit the cheap labour that exists in CEE and elsewhere, and residents from neighbouring countries have always benefited from cheap, cross-border shopping. It should also be remembered that many of the countries and their inhabitants who are now complaining about enlargement think nothing of colonizing other countries' coastlines as tourists and buying up second homes, pricing local residents out of their own market. The very countries whose citizens are now being rejected as migrant workers ironically tend to be those countries that are proving to be the most attractive to Western investors and tourists.

Concern continues over problems of persistent racism against ethnic minorities, in both old and new EU members states, where right-wing nationalism has emerged in the former as a reaction to perceived levels of in-migration, and in the latter as a reaction to years of Communist oppression (or even as a continuation of some of the more fascistic tendencies of its mentality). Although some anti-Islamic expression has been stimulated by a series of terrorist attacks across Europe and elsewhere, much of the tension is historical and unfortunately deep-seated. For example, anti-semitism is well-documented in Poland (e.g. Kimel, 1996), and prejudice against Roma people continues in Hungary, Slovakia and elsewhere (e.g. Hancock, 1994). The election of the conservative new President in Poland (2005) also resulted in demonstrations by gays and lesbians against homophobia (Ireland, 2005).

Although some countries seeking accession have been criticized over their human rights or war crimes records, it would be of increasing pertinence for all EU members to closely examine their own policies of tolerance, inclusiveness and integration. As indicated in Chapter 1, an economic survey in 1999 found the then pre-accession states more suitable for EU membership than two or three of the incumbent EU15. The same might equally apply in the field of social and cultural development today.

Social unrest clearly has profound implications for tourism. Not only does it create a temporary situation of insecurity and fear, which can deter visitation across a wide geographical area, it can severely damage the long-term image of countries and regions. Research has shown that the most productive, economically prosperous and creative cities are those with high levels of tolerance and inclusion regardless of colour, ethnicity, class, gender, ablement or sexual orientation (e.g. Pritchard and Morgan, 2000; Florida, 2002). In addition, it is often the case that minority groups, as distinct 'communities', can and have provided some of the most exciting new developments in tourism (e.g. Caribbean Carnivals, Asian *Mela* Festivals, China Towns, 'ethnoscapes', gay quarters) (e.g. Richards and Hall, 2000). In fact, many such developments are integral to the regeneration of former industrial cities, a process that is becoming widespread in Europe and is vital to the future of many destinations (Smith, 2006).

The debate continues on where the (political, psychological, social and cultural) borders of Europe are and should be. European Union membership may be viewed by outsiders as something of a cosy club, despite extensive enlargement. The EU is often perceived as rather inward-looking, self-serving and overly protectionist. Political and economic frameworks can facilitate tourism development, but it is arguably the social, cultural and environmental policies that ultimately shape the future of a healthier, happier and more integrated Europe. These are still under-prioritized. None the less, notwithstanding its ongoing difficulties, the EU project is one of the most progressive, democratic and exciting initiatives in the world today. Most member states can only benefit from their involvement, and tourism is an integral part of Europeanization. This book has represented an opportunity to contribute to this process and to the exchange of ideas, not least through the medium of the ATLAS networking organization, and we end by identifying key themes for carrying forward debate, both inside and outside the ATLAS framework (Box 23.1).

Box 23.1.   Key themes for further debate.

- The importance of continuity as well as change.
- The problem of distinguising the impacts of tourism from other change processes.
- The ongoing role and impacts of low-cost airlines.
- A continuing element of uncertainty concerning the 2004 accession (particularly relating to Cyprus).
- The uncertainty of future enlargement.
- The significance of continuing Balkan instability linked to future enlargement.
- The tourism significance of the EU's relationship with other supranational organizations such as NATO.
- The relatively miserly attitude within the institutions of the EU towards tourism, despite its important economic and integrating role in Europe.
- The interrelationships between different mobilities – tourism, migration, cross-border petty trading and shopping, retirement and second homes – being influenced by the nature and role of transport and transport infrastructures, and the role of internal and external borders.
- Tourism and citizenship, and the nature, role and appropriateness of European identity.
- The interrelationships between tourism, education and culture (and implicitly mobility).
- The likely geographical consolidation of the EU in the Mediterranean and Black Sea regions and the emphasis this will bring to the important continuing role of mass tourism.
- Climate change and the possibility of future constraints on fossil fuel-dependent travel.

References

BBC News Online (2004) Ukraine celebrates Eurovision win. *BBC News Online*, 16 May. Available at: http://news.bbc.co.uk/2/hi/entertainment/3715907.stm

Coles, T. and Hall, D. (2005) Tourism and European Union enlargement. Plus ça change? *International Journal of Tourism Research* 7(2), 51–61.

EU Business (2005) Luxury hotels cash in on tourism boom in new EU countries. *EU Business,* 21 June. Available at: http://www.eubusiness.com/East_Europe/050622041934.nndypr28

European Commission (2003) *Tourism and the European Union.* Brussels: European Commission. Available at: http://europa.eu.int/comm/enterprise/services/tourism/tourismeu.htm#future

Florida, R. (2002) *The Rise of the Creative Class.* New York: Basic Books.

Graham, B. and Hart, M. (1999) Cohesion and diversity in the European Union: irreconcilable forces? *Regional Studies* 33(3), 259–268.

Hall, D.R. (ed.) (1991) *Tourism and Economic Development in Eastern Europe and the Soviet Union.* London: Belhaven Press.

Hancock, I. (1994) *The Consequences of Anti-Gipsy* [sic] *Racism in Europe.* Warsaw: Joint Seminar on Roma (Gypsies) in Europe, September 20–23. Available at: http://www.usm.maine.edu/~bcj/issues/two/hancock_text.html

HOTREC (2005) *Commissioner Verheugen: Tourism Among EU Commission's Top Priorities.* Brussels: HOTREC press release, 18 February. Available at: http://www.hotrec.org/Press%20Release%20Meeting%20Verheugen-18.02.05-EN.pdf

Ireland, D. (2005) Gay Eurosocialists organize alliance, demonstration for Polish gays in Paris. *Direland,* 31 October. Available at: http://direland.typepad.com/direland/2005/10/demonstration_f.html

Kimel, A. (1996) The Jews and the Poles. *Online-Holocaust-Magazine* December. Available at: http://www.kimel.net/jewpol.html

Leonard, D. (2005) *How Many Polish Plumbers?* London: Foreign Policy Centre. Available at: http://fpc.org.uk/topics/europe

Pritchard, A. and Morgan, N. (2000) Constructing tourism landscapes – gender, sexuality and space. *Tourism Geographies* 2(2), 115–139.

Radio National (2005) The Europeans: 150 Polish plumbers. *Radio National,* 19 June. Available at: http://www.abc.net.au/rn/talks/europe/stories/s1392882.htm

Richards, G. and Hall, D. (eds) (2000) *Tourism and Sustainable Community Development.* London: Routledge.

Rodriguez Pose, A. and Gill, N. (2003) The global trend towards devolution and its implications. *Environment and Planning C* 21(3), 333–351.

Smith, M. (2000) Negotiating new Europes: the roles of the European Union. *Journal of European Public Policy* 17(5), 806–822.

Smith, M.K. (ed.) (2006) *Tourism, Culture and Regeneration.* Wallingford, UK: CAB International.

WTO (World Tourism Organization) (2003) *Performance and Trends of International Tourism in Europe.* Warsaw: VI CEI Summit: Economic Tourism, 19–20 November.

Index